Not For Tourists Guide to
NEW YORK CITY

T0191293

Not For Tourists, Inc

Skyhorse Publishing

designed by:
Not For Tourists, Inc
NFT_{TM}—Not For Tourists_{TM} Guide to New York City

Printed in China
Print ISBN: 978-1-5107-8103-0
Ebook ISBN: 978-1-5107-8104-7
ISSN 2162-6103
Copyright © 2024 by Not For Tourists, Inc.
26th Edition

Every effort has been made to ensure that the information in this book is as up-to-date as possible at press time. However, many details are liable to change—as we have learned. Not For Tourists cannot accept responsibility for any consequences arising from the use of this book.

Not For Tourists does not solicit individuals, organizations, or businesses for listings inclusion in our guides, nor do we accept payment for inclusion into the editorial portion of our book.

Visit our website at www.skyhorsepublishing.com.

Please follow our publisher Tony Lyons on Instagram @tonylyonsisuncertain.

10 9 8 7 6 5 4 3 2 1

"New York is the concentrate of art and commerce and sport and religion and entertainment and finance, bringing to a single compact arena the gladiator, the evangelist, the promoter, the actor, the trader and the merchant." —E. B. White

Dear NFT User:

We released our first book, the NFT Guide to Manhattan, in May, 2000, after two grueling years of research and development in which we pounded the pavement so hard that our feet still hurt. Looking back on those heady first days it's hard to fathom that over two decades later, we'd be working on our twenty-sixth edition of the guide. That's 26—a number so high copy editors cry when they see it written out.

But even after 26 editions, it always warms each of our cold, crusty, curmudgeonly hearts when we come across someone on the street consulting their little black book. Whether you're navigating your way through this "concrete jungle where dreams are made of" (as Alicia Keys once sang) using our specially formulated maps that at least one optometrist has ensured us is at least 30 percent less strain-inducing than it once was, or just quietly taking in the full force of our collective genius as we distill the best bar on the block down to a haiku-like three- to ten-word blurb, trust us, we always feel a flush of pride when we see people out in public reading a NFT guide.

That's because like the best house-cured meat along Arthur Avenue, the finest crust on a Staten Island pizza pie, or the most transcendent Brooklyn ice cream, this little black guide is, at its core, an artisanal product. With NFT, the blurbs and recs you get are all house made, never processed, even via some faceless algorithm—because, let's face it, our servers could never handle it anyway. Like your favorite low-key boutique, NFT is carefully curated to offer you the best of what a neighborhood has to offer. And if a trendy, stinky, or otherwise unfun place isn't worth your or anyone else's time, we feel free to exclude it, because at NFT we pride ourselves on not only being "well edited" but actually "best edited."

Anyway, as we like to say, wrap your furry paws around this superior guide of all things New York City and get ready to scout the holes in the wall so holey the Department of Buildings should have long since shut them down, bars so divey you'll need a scuba tank to get there, and shops so indispensable they're worth three subway transfers even after you move to another borough. So if you're new to us, welcome! And if you're coming back, thanks for continuing to trust us enough to show us around in public…

Table of Contents

Map 1 • **Financial District**

1 **2**

Murray St

Robert F Wagner Sr

Greenwich St

W Broadway

Park Pl

City Hall Park

Frankfort St **BROOKLYN BRIDGE**

Pace University

Spruce St

3

Peck Slip

Bridge Café

PAGE 280

Park Row

2

Vesey St

Barclay St Place

**Park
Place**
2 3

St Paul's
Chapel & Cemetery

Theatre Alley

Nassau St

Beekman St

Gold St

South Bridge
Resdential
Tower

Pearl St

South St Seaport
Historical District

Water St

Front St

Beekman St

World Trade
Center

2

World
Trade
Center

PAGE 288

Church St

Dey St

Cortlandt
Street

A C

Fulton Street-
Broadway
Nassau

J Z

2 3

Fulton St

John St

Ryders Alley

Cliff St

Fulton St

Building Slip

E

4 5

World Trade Center

R W

Memorial & Museum

Cortlandt
Street

Liberty
Plaza

American
Stock
Exchange

Maiden Lane

Platt St

Pearl St

John St

Battery
Park
City

Albany St

Liberty St

Thames St

Zuccotti Park

Equitable
Building

Liberty Pl

The Federal
Reserve Bank

Legion Memorial Sq

Liberty St

Fletcher St

Trinity Church

Canyon of
Heroes

Chase
Plaza

Cedar St

American
International
Building

Maiden Ln

PAGE 250

Cedar St

Bankers
Trust
Company
Building

The First
JP Morgan
Bank

Pine St

Pine St

Water St

Wall St

R W

Greenwich St

Trinity Pl

Rector Street

Federal
Hall

40 Wall Street

Wall St

Front St

**Rector
Street**

1

Wall Street

4 5

Broadway

New
York
Stock
Exchange

**Broad
Street**

J Z

Wall Street

2 3

Exchange Pl

**20 Exchange
Place**

William St

Pier 13

West Side Hwy

Exchange Alley

Edgar St

Broad St

**Delmonico's
Building**

India House

Gouverneur Ln

Pier 11

VEHICULAR
TRAFFIC
PROHIBITED

Morris St

**Cunard
Building**

Beaver St

S William St

Stone St

Old Slip

Old Slip

Pier 9

Morris St

**Charging
Bull**

Marketfield St

**Standard Oil
Building**

Stone St

FOR Dr

Alexander Hamilton U.S. Custom House

Bowling Green

Whitehall St

Bridge St

Water St

Vietnam
Veterans
Plaza

Heliport Auth

Battery Pl

**Bowling
Green**

4 5

Battery Park Plaza

Broad St

Moore St

New York
Plaza

Pier A

State St

Peter Minuit Pl

**Ferry to
Ellis Island**

Battery
Park

Hugh L. Carey Tunnel

Battery Park Underpass

1

**South
Ferry**

R W

**Whitehall
Street**

**Battery Maritime
Building**

**Staten Island
Ferry Terminal**

Battery
Park

Hudson River

East River

| 1/4 mile | .25 km |

Neighborhood Overview

Map 1

This is where it all began. Site of the original Dutch settlement on Manhattan Island, the Financial District contains more historical markers than any other part of the city. If you're looking for a place to start, check out **St. Paul's Chapel and Cemetery**, which dates back to 1766, **Trinity Church**, whose spire was once the tallest point in Manhattan, and **Federal Hall**, site of the first capitol of the United States. You can also head to Battery Park to take the **ferry** to the Statue of Liberty, and, far more interestingly, to Ellis Island where you can explore the history of immigration in the United States.

That's just the beginning. The importance of New York as a financial and commercial center is evident on practically every street. To take it in, check out, in no particular order, the **New York Stock Exchange**, the NYSE American (formerly known as the **American Stock Exchange**), the **Federal Reserve Bank**, the first **JP Morgan Bank** (still visibly scarred from a bombing in 1920), John D. Rockefeller's **Standard Oil Building**, and the **Alexander Hamilton US Custom House** (now the National Museum of the American Indian). The architecture of the chocolate brown federal-style **India House** and stunning maritime-themed interior of the **Cunard Building** both represent distinct eras of New York's commercial past. Rivaling Grand Central and Brooklyn Bridge as Manhattan's most gorgeous gateway, the **Battery Maritime Building** is the departure point for the summer ferry to Governor's Island, where you can stroll around fortifications built during the Revolutionary War. Last but not least, the **Charging Bull** statue at **Bowling Green**, initially installed as a piece of guerrilla art, has become the ultimate symbol for New York's financial strength, and beloved by photo-snapping tourists from all over the world.

Financial growth led to the creation of the modern skyscraper, and many famous examples soar above these streets. Notable buildings include **40 Wall Street** (now known as the "Trump Building"), art-deco gems **20 Exchange Place** and the **American International Building**, the massive **Equitable Building**, and the **Bankers Trust Company Building**. Of course, the most famous structure is the one that's missing—the World Trade Center Towers, which were destroyed by a terrorist attack on September 11, 2001. That said, the **World Trade Center** has been reborn in an inspiring if slightly schizophrenic monument to both its tragic past and hopeful future. Two mammoth pools mark the footprint of the original towers and the gut-wrenching **National September 11 Memorial & Museum** literally digs deep to tell the definitive story of that day and commemorate those lives lost. Looking up, One World Trade Center, the city's (and Western Hemisphere's) tallest skyscraper, towers over the site. The 1,776-foot-high landmark restored Lower Manhattan's visual and psychic balance; now it is one of many landmarks on the site, towering over the Oculus, a shopping and transit hub designed by Spanish architect Santiago Calatrava to resemble a dove flying free from a child's hands.

When you're ready for a break from all that history and architecture, take in some people watching at **Zuccotti Park** (onetime hub for the Occupy Wall Street protest) or reflect in the relative peace and quiet of the **Vietnam Veterans Plaza**. The best way to chill out might be by simply grabbing a beer on board the free **Staten Island Ferry** and checking out the awesome views of New York Harbor commuters get to enjoy every day. The tourists will all be at **South Street Seaport**, which might be best avoided unless you like crowded cobblestoned shopping malls. As far as kicking back in quaint downtown is concerned, Stone Street and Front Street are perfect spots to grab a bite and a drink after a day of wandering around. We'll see you there!

It ain't the village by any stretch, but Front Street has some good options like **Harry's Café & Steak** and **Fresh Salt**. Old stalwarts like the **The Paris Cafe** capture the history of the area. The semi-secret Blue Bar at **India House** is a NFT favorite—you can thank us later.

Financial District

O Landmarks

- **20 Exchange Place** •
  20 Exchange Pl [William St]
  Cool facade with bronze depictions of various
  modes of transport.
- **40 Wall St** • 40 Wall St [William St]
  Tallest building in the world for a day in 1930.
  Oh and Trump owns it.
- **70 Pine Street** • 70 Pine St [Pearl St]
  Great Art Deco skyscraper.
- **8 Spruce Street** • 8 Spruce St [William St]
  76-story Gehry masterpiece overlooking the
  Brooklyn Bridge. Sublime.
- **Alexander Hamilton U.S. Custom House** •
  1 Bowling Green [State St]
  Stately Cass Gilbert building; check out the
  oval staircases.
- **American Stock Exchange** •
  86 Trinity Pl [Thames St]
  212-608-7888
  New York's other stock exchange.
- **Bankers Trust Company Building** •
  14 Wall St [Nassau St]
  More neck-craning excitement from the NYC
  skyline!
- **Battery Maritime Building** •
  10 South St [Broad St]
  Ready-to-be-converted riverfront building.
- **Bowling Green** • Broadway & State St
  Watch the tourists take pics of the bull. New
  York's first park.
- **Canyon of Heroes** •
  Broadway b/n Bowling Green & City Hall Park
  Markers in the sidewalk remember those
  honored with a ticker tape parade.
- **Charging Bull** • Bowling Green Park
  Rub his cojones for luck.
- **Cunard Building** • 25 Broadway [Morris St]
  Former Cunard headquarters, former post
  office, currently a locked building with great
  ceiling mosaics.
- **Delmonico's** • 56 Beaver St [S William St]
  212-381-1237
  Once the site of THE restaurant in New York.
- **Equitable Building** • 120 Broadway [Cedar St]
  (212) 490-0666
  Its massiveness gave momentum to zoning
  laws for skyscraper
- **Federal Hall** • 26 Wall St [Broad St]
  212-825-6990
  Where George the First was inaugurated.

- **Federal Reserve Bank of New York** •
  33 Liberty St [William St]
  212-720-5000
  Where *Die Hard 3* took place.
- **Ferry to Ellis Island** • Pier A & Battery Park
  The main building features beautiful domed
  ceilings and Guastavino tiled arches.
- **The First JP Morgan Bank** •
  23 Wall St [Broad St]
  Still visibly scarred from an anarchist bombing
  in 1920.
- **National September 11 Memorial &
  Museum** • 180 Greenwich St
  212-312-8800
  Awe-inspiring tribute to those lost,
  surrounded by rebirth.
- **New York Stock Exchange** •
  11 Wall St
  212-656-3000
  Where *Wall Street* took place.
- **The Oculus** • Greenwich St [Dey St]
  212-284-9982
  Yes, it's a shopping mall, but it's the most
  beautiful one ever made.
- **One World Trade Center** • Vesey St [West St]
  At 1,776 feet, the tallest building in the
  Western Hemisphere.
- **South Street Seaport** • 12 Fulton St [South St]
  212-732-8257
  Mall with historic ships as backdrop.
- **St. Paul's Chapel & Cemetery** •
  Broadway & Fulton St
  212-602-0800
  Old-time NYC church and cemetery.
- **Standard Oil Building** •
  26 Broadway [Morris St]
  Sweeping wall of a building overlooking
  Bowling Green.
- **Staten Island Ferry** • 4 Whitehall St [Stone St]
  Grab a tall boy on board and enjoy the view.
- **Vietnam Veterans Memorial Plaza** •
  55 Water St [Coenties Slip]
  212-471-9496
  A nice quiet spot to contemplate our faded
  dreams of empire.
- **World Trade Center** • Church St & Vesey St
  Inspiring (if schizophrenic) monument to
  tragic past and hopeful future.
- **Zuccotti Park** • Trinity Pl & Cedar St
  Birthplace of Occupy Wall Street, ca. 2011.

Our Stone Street favorite is **Adrienne's Pizzabar**. You can eat cheaply at **Sophie's** and greasy spoon **Pearl Diner** while you wait for financial success and a table at **Mark Joseph**.

🍎 Farmers Markets
- **Bowling Green Greenmarket** •
  Broadway & Battery Pl
  212-788-7900
  Tues & Thurs 8 am–5 pm, year-round.
- **Oculus Greenmarket** • Fulton St & Church St.
  Tues 8 am–5 pm, June 6–Oct 24

🍸 Nightlife
- **The Dead Rabbit** • 30 Water St [Broad St]
  917-540-5228
  Fancy cocktails in an old-timey, Irish-American atmosphere.
- **Fresh Salt** • 146 Beekman St [Front St]
  212-962-0053
  Where architects go for happy hour.
- **Harry's Cafe & Steak** • 1 Hanover Sq [Pearl St]
  212-785-9200
  The vintage French wine flows like a river. Or at least it used to.

- **Jeremy's Ale House** • 228 Front St [Peck Slip]
  212-964-3537
  Weekend nights are at your own risk.
- **Killarney Rose** • 127 Pearl St [Hanover St]
  212-422-1486
  Irish pub where you can pregame for the Staten Island Ferry.
- **Liquid Assets** • 55 Church St [Fulton St]
  212-693-2001
  Plush seating and soft lighting.
- **Paris Café** • 119 South St [Peck Slip]
  646-846-6270
  Good, historic bar but used to be better. Best very late.
- **Ulysses Folk House** • 95 Pearl St [Hanover Sq]
  212-482-0400
  Slightly hipper downtown bar.
- **White Horse Tavern** •
  25 Bridge St [Whitehall St]
  212-668-9046
  Downtown dive. Not to be confused with the one in the West Village.

🍴Restaurants

• **Adrienne's Pizzabar** •
54 Stone St [S William St]
212-248-3838 • $$
Delectable rectangular pies from a NYC pizza master.

• **The Capital Grille** • 120 Broadway [Pine St]
212-374-1811 • $$$$$
High-end chain perfect for someone else's expense account.

• **Cowgirl Sea-Horse** • 259 Front St [Dover St]
212-608-7873 • $$
Surf shack serving up home "beach baskets."

• **Delmonico's** • 56 Beaver St [S William St]
212-381-1237 • $$$$
Classic NYC spot. Since 1837.

• **Dig Inn Seasonal Market** •
80 Pine St [Pearl St]
212-785-1110 • $
Excellent farm-fresh meat and veggie buffet, surprisingly inexpensive.

• **Dorlan's Tavern** • 213 Front St [Beekman St]
212-779-2222 • $$$
At least ten raw oyster options. We're there.

• **Eataly NYC Downtown** • 101 Liberty St [Church St] 212-897-2895 • $$$
Bustling WTC version of Batali/Bastianich brainchild.

• **El Luchador** • 87 South St [John St]
917-409-3033 • $$
Great taqueria w/ outdoor seating.

• **Felice 15** • 15 Gold St [Platt St]
212-785-5950 • $$$
Nice contemporary Italian with good appetizers.

• **Grotto Pizzeria** • 69 New St [Beaver St]
212-809-6990 • $$
More quick, tasty Italian. Less nudity than that other grotto.

• **Harry's Cafe & Steak** • 1 Hanover Sq [Pearl St]
212-785-9200 • $$$$
When the market is flush so is Harry.

• **Luke's Lobster** • 26 S William St [Broad St]
212-747-1700 • $$
Fresh-from-the sea lobster rolls, without sticker shock.

• **Mark Joseph Steakhouse** •
261 Water St [Peck Slip]
212-277-0020 • $$$$
Luger's wannabe: damn close, actually, and they take plastic.

• **Melt Shop** • 111 Fulton St [Dutch St]
646-741-7910 • $$
"Shop" tots and fried chicken grilled cheese sandwiches. Ah.

• **Neapolitan Express** • 40 Wall St [Williams St]
646-918-6169 • $$
Mission-driven pizza; 900-degree ovens with zero emissions.

• **Nobu** • 195 Broadway
212-219-0500 • $$$$$
Designer Japanese. When we have 100 titles, we'll go here.

Gourmet market **Jubilee** keeps Financial District dwellers fed. **Nobu** has top-shelf sushi. Pick up some wine from **Pasanella**.

- **Paris Café** • 119 South St [Peck Slip]
  646-846-6270 • $$$
  Good burgers and seafood, a bit pricey though.
- **Pearl Diner** • 212 Pearl St [Platt St]
  212-344-6620 • $
  Greasy spoon hidden among the skyscrapers.
- **Sophie's Cuban** • 76 Fulton St [Gold St]
  212-608-6769 • $$
  Great cheap Cuban/Caribbean.
- **Suteishi** • 24 Peck Slip [Front St]
  212-766-2344 • $$$
  Hip seaport sushi. Get the Orange/Red Dragon split.
- **Trinity Place** • 115 Broadway [Cedar St]
  212-964-0939 • $$$$
  Good drinks and American-Irish cuisine in bank vault space.
- **Ulysses Folk House** • 95 Pearl St [Hanover Sq]
  212-482-0400 • $$$
  Highlight: the buffet spread.
- **Underdog** • 55 Stone St [Mill Ln]
  917-409-0251 • $$
  Pub grub, craft beer, and a dog-friendly patio.
- **Wall Street Bath & Spa** • 88 Fulton St [Gold St]
  212-766-8600 • $$
  Pre- and post- rub and tub grub.

🛍 Shopping

- **Alex's Shoe Repair** • 123 Fulton St [Dutch St]
  646-559-6713
  When your sole needs fixin'.
- **Bowne & Co Stationers** •
  211 Water St [Beekman St]
  646-315-4478
  Old fashioned presses make prints, maps & cards.
- **Dick's Cut Rate Hardware** • 9 Gold St [Platt St]
  212-425-1070
  Not a sex shop.
- **Jubilee Marketplace** • 99 John St [Cliff St]
  212-233-0808
  Godsend for Financial District dwellers.
- **La Petite Cave** • 83 Maiden Ln [Liberty St]
  212-514-9817
  Friendly owner with well curated wine selection.
- **Pasanella and Son Vintners** •
  115 South St [Peck Slip]
  212-233-8383
  Great wine shop. Movies screenings in the back tasting room!
- **xCubicle** • 40 Wall St [William St]
  917-809-6227
  Game system and smartphone repair.

Map 2 · TriBeCa

Dominick St
Broome St
Broome St
6
Holland Tunnel
5
Watts St
Fleming Smith Warehouse
Desbrosses St
New York Telephone Company Building
Washington St
Vestry St
PAGE 262
Laight St
Thompson St
West Broadway
Wooster St
Greene St
Mercer St
Grand St
Canal Street
1
Canal Street
A C E
1 York Street
Canal St
3
Ped Bridge
St. John's Ln
Varick St
Avenue of the Americas
Lispenard St
Canal Street
N R J
Q 6 Z
Hubert St
Collister St
Hudson St
Greenwich St
Hudson Sq
Ericsson Pl
North Moore St
American Thread Building
Walker St
Beach St
Ghostbusters Firehouse
White St
The Dream House
Franklin St
Hudson River
Pier 25
West St
Borough of Manhattan Community College
9A
Franklin Street
1
Powell Building
New York Law School
56 Leonard
Leonard St
Textile Building
Broadway
Harrison St
Harrison Street Row Houses
Jay St
Staple St
Duane Park
Duane St
Worth St
No. 8 Thomas Street
Thomas St
Trimble Pl
Church St
Duane St
Reade St
Tribeca Bridge
Washington Market Park
Chambers St
Cary Building
Chambers Street
Chambers St
Chambers St
Warren St
Park Pl
Ball Fields
Murray St
Chambers Street
1 2 3
Warren St
Chambers Street
A C
City Hall
R W
City Hall Park
North End Ave
River Ter
PAGE 250
Battery Park City
Park Pl
Park Place
2 3
Barclay St
7 WTC
1
World Trade Center
E
Park Row
Civic Center

| 1/4 mile | .25 km |

Neighborhood Overview

Map 2

Thinking of moving to Tribeca? Well, then, congratulations—you've clearly made your first $10 million! And, if you already live there…well, you're not reading a guidebook anyway… but maybe your assistant is. As for the rest of us, we'll just have to be content with walking around the neighborhood and choosing which fabulous converted loft building we'd live in when WE make our first $10 million. Such is life in one of New York's prime neighborhoods—minutes away from downtown, the West Village, Soho, and Chinatown, decent subway access, a few minutes' walk to either the Battery Park City promenade or Hudson River Park, excellent restaurants, a few killer bars—if you can afford it, of course.

But even if you can't, there's no question that walking around is our favorite pastime in the Triangle Below Canal Street (Canal Street being the north side of the triangle, Broadway being the east side of the triangle, and the West Side Highway being the west side of the triangle). On your walk, you'll pass one of the city's oldest parks (**Washington Market Park**), some ancient row houses (the **Harrison Street Row Houses**) and our favorite Tribeca landmark, the **Ghostbusters Firehouse** (you'll know it when you see it, trust us). A great starting point for seeing Tribeca is its nexus, lovely little **Duane Park**. It's a quaint little triangle surrounded on all sides by gorgeous factory buildings converted into lofts you'd give an arm and a leg to live in.

As for the buildings themselves, there are several worth noting, including Henry J. Hardenbergh's **Textile Building**, Carrère and Hastings' **Powell Building**, Ralph Walker's massive **New York Telephone Company Building**, the rounded front of the **American Thread Building**, the Venetian mash-up of **No. 8 Thomas Street**, cast-iron gem the **Cary Building**, and, the "pièce de résistance," Stephen Decatur Smith's **Fleming Smith Warehouse** on Washington Street.

Although most of the new construction (especially along Broadway) fits into the boring/puerile category, one of the newer buildings to check out is Enrique Norten's postmodern **One York Street**; his insertion of a glass tower in the middle of two 19th-century buildings is pretty cool. **New York Law School's** new building at 185 West Broadway shines brightly at night as its law students burn the candle at both ends. Meanwhile, Herzog & de Meuron's **56 Leonard** project set records for residential sales.

Unfortunately, we just don't get to Tribeca as much at night any more, as two of its most interesting cultural hotspots—the Knitting Factory and Roulette—have long since moved on. However, one of the coolest long-running sound and light installations in the world is here, at 275 Church Street, just steps from the swanky **Roxy Hotel**. La Monte Young and Marian Zazeela's **Dream House** is a special place to chill out and get in touch with your inner being in the midst of all this residential poshness.

Nightlife is quieter here than in other neighborhoods, but upscale drinks can be found at **Roxy**, and **Nancy Whiskey** and **Puffy's** are classic dives. Old school hangout **Walker's** is a New York classic and should not be missed; otherwise, check out the **Flea Theatre**'s calendar or wait for the **Tribeca Film Festival**.

Map 2

8 9 10
5 6 7
2 3 4
1

TriBeCa

O Landmarks

- **56 Leonard** • 56 Leonard St [Church St]
  212-965-1500
  Knee-buckling 60-story glass Jenga palace.
- **American Thread Building** •
  260 W Broadway [Beach St]
  212-966-0886
  Check out cool rounded front; watch out for
  tunnel traffic.
- **Cary Building** • 105 Chambers St [Church St]
  Cast-iron goodness on Chambers. We like it.
- **Dream House** • 275 Church St [White St]
  917-603-9715
  Cool sound + light installation by La Monte
  Young and Marian Zazeela. Closed during
  summer.
- **Duane Park** • Duane St & Hudson St
  One of the nicest spots in all of New York.
- **Fleming Smith Warehouse** •
  451 Washington St [Watts St]
  TriBeCa's most sublimely beautiful structure.
  Believe it.
- **Ghostbusters Firehouse** •
  14 N Moore St [Varick St]
  Are you the gatekeeper?
- **Harrison Street Row Houses** •
  Harrison St & Greenwich St
  Nice collection of preserved Federalist
  architecture.
- **New York Law School** •
  185 W Broadway [Leonard St]
  212-431-2100
  New York Law's new main building burns
  brightly on cold TriBeCa nights.
- **New York Telephone Company Building** •
  140 West St [Vestry St]
  Massive Art Deco gem still looms over
  now-fashionable TriBeCa.
- **No. 8 Thomas Street** •
  8 Thomas St [Broadway]
  Bizarre Venetian townhouse in the middle of
  downtown. Really.
- **Powell Building** • 105 Hudson St [Franklin St]
  Carrere & Hastings gem.
- **Textile Building** • 66 Leonard St [Church St]
  Henry J. Hardenbergh goodness in TriBeCa.
- **Washington Market Park** •
  199 Chambers St
  One of the city's oldest marketplaces.

Coffee

- **Kaffe 1668 South** • 275 Greenwich St [Murray St]
  212-693-3750
  Excellent coffee in a really cool space.
- **La Colombe Torrefaction** •
  319 Church St [Lipsenard St]
  212-343-1515
  New York's first outpost of top-notch Philly
  roasters.
- **Le Pain Quotidien** •
  81 W Broadway [Warren St]
  646-652-8186
  Excellent coffee and pastries. Thanks Belgium.
- **Square Diner** • 33 Leonard St [W Broadway]
  212-925-7188
  Old-school diner coffee.

Farmers Markets

- **Tribeca Greenmarket** •
  Greenwich St b/n Chambers & Duane
  Wed & Sat 8 am–2 pm year-round.

Nightlife is quieter here than in other neighborhoods, but upscale drinks can be found at **Roxy Hotel** and **Smith & Mills** and **Nancy Whiskey** and **Puffy's** are classic dives. Make sure to also check out the **Flea Theatre**'s calendar or time your visit with the **Tribeca Film Festival**.

 Nightlife

- **Anotheroom** • 249 W Broadway [N Moore St]
  212-226-1418
  Cosy, cute, and narrow.
- **Brandy Library** • 25 N Moore St [W Broadway]
  212-226-5545
  Refined but cozy with lots of free tasting events.
- **Kenn's Broome Street Bar** •
  363 W Broadway [Broome St]
  212-925-2086
  Real low-key for this part of town.
- **Macao** • 311 Church St [Walker St]
  212-431-8642
  Expensive but exquisite cocktails inspired by 1930s Chinese opium dens.
- **Nancy Whiskey Pub** •
  1 Lispenard St [W Broadway]
  212-226-9943
  Good dive. As if there were any other kind.
- **Puffy's Tavern** • 81 Hudson St [Harrison St]
  212-227-3912
  Suits, old timers, and hipsters. Top TriBeCa watering hole.

- **Smith & Mills** • 71 N Moore St [Greenwich St]
  646-858-1433
  Upscale cool cocktails. Limited seating.
- **Soho Grand Hotel** •
  310 W Broadway [Canal St]
  212-965-3000
  Swank sophistication.
- **Terroir** • 24 Harrison St [Greenwich St]
  212-625-9463
  Happening wine bar with funky list and tasty eats.
- **Toad Hall** • 57 Grand St [W Broadway]
  212-431-8145
  Laid back vibe with SoHo locals.
- **The Roxy Hotel** • 2 6th Ave [White St]
  212-519-6600
  Posh drinks in an uber-cool space; service is another matter.
- **Walker's** • 16 N Moore St [W Broadway]
  212-941-0142
  Where old and new Tribeca neighbors mix.

Map 2

8 9 10
5 6 7
2 3 4
1

TriBeCa

Restaurants

- **American Cut** • 363 Greenwich St [Franklin St]
212-226-4736 • $$$$$
Forgione + steak = a perfect pairing.
- **Benares** • 45 Murray St [Church St]
212-766-4900 • $$$
Decent Indian option, very good naan.
- **Blue Smoke** • 255 Vesey St
212-889-2005 • $$$$
Finger lickin' BBQ, Danny Meyer style (with downstairs jazz club).
- **Bubby's** • 120 Hudson St [N Moore St]
212-219-0666 • $$
Great atmosphere — good home-style eats and homemade pies.
- **Cafe Clementine** •
227 West Broadway [White St]
212-965-9900 • $$
Fresh, satisfying soups, salads, and sandwiches in a tiny space.
- **Edward's** • 136 W Broadway [Duane St]
212-233-6436 • $$
Middle-of-the-road, kid's menu, mostly locals, sometimes great.
- **Estancia 460** • 460 Greenwich St [Watts St]
212-431-5093 • $$
Louche Argentines and brilliant french toast. Formerly Sosa Borella.

- **Félix** • 340 W Broadway [Grand St]
212-431-0021 • $$$
Buzzing Brazilian with French overtones, see and be seen.
- **Gotan** • 130 Franklin St [Varick St]
212-431-5200 • $$
Serious sandwiches, serious espresso, settle in for some mood lighting.
- **Grandaisy Bakery** •
250 W Broadway [Beach St]
212-334-9435 •
Breads and pizzas by the one and only.
- **The Greek** • 452 Washington St [Desbrosses St]
646-476-3941 • $$$$
Bang-on Greek miles from Astoria.
- **Jungsik** • 2 Harrison St [Hudson St]
212-219-0900 • $$$$
White tablecloth multi-star Korean.
- **Khe-Yo** • 157 Duane St [W Broadway]
212-587-1089 • $$
Laotian goodness for the TriBeCa set
Reasonable prices.

If you've got cash, Tribeca's got you covered. **Odeon** has the cool factor **Locanda Verde** has killer pasta. Otherwise, we go for the far-above-average pub grub at **Walker's**.

• **Locanda Verde** •
377 Greenwich St [N Moore St]
212-925-3797 • $$$$
Top-shelf Italian in ever-hip TriBeCa.

• **Lupe's East LA Kitchen** •
110 Ave of the Americas [Watts St]
212-966-1326 • $
Tex-Mex. Quaint. Eat here.

• **Marc Forgione** • 134 Reade St [Hudson St]
212-941-9401 • $$$$$
Top-end TriBeCa perfection. Go. If you can.

• **The Odeon** • 145 W Broadway [Thomas St]
212-233-0507 • $$$$
We can't agree about this one, so go and make your own decision.

• **Square Diner** • 33 Leonard St [W Broadway]
212-925-7188 • $
Classic neighborhood diner.

• **Thalassa** • 179 Franklin St [Hudson St]
212-941-7661 • $$$
Greek. But it's cheaper and better in Astoria.

• **Tribeca Grill** • 375 Greenwich St [Franklin St]
212-941-3900 • $$$$$
Are you looking at me?

• **Viet Café** • 345 Greenwich St [Jay St]
212-431-5888 • $$$
Glossy out of a magazine.

• **Walker's** • 16 N Moore St [W Broadway]
212-941-0142 • $$
Surprisingly good food for a pub!

• **Zutto** • 77 Hudson St [Harrison St]
212-233-3287 • $$$
Neighborhood Japanese.

Map 2

8 9 10
5 6 7
2 3 4
1

TriBeCa

Shopping

- **Babesta Cribz** • 56 Warren St [W Broadway]
  646-290-5508
  Stuff for hipster babies and their parents.
- **Balloon Saloon** • 133 W Broadway [Duane St]
  212-227-3838
  We love the name.
- **Boffi Soho** • 31 Greene St [Grand St]
  212-431-8282
  High-end kitchen and bath design.
- **Duane Park Patisserie** •
  179 Duane St [Staple St]
  212-274-8447
  Yummy!

- **Grandaisy Bakery** •
  250 W Broadway [Beach St]
  212-334-9435
  Breads and pizzas by the one and only.
- **Issey Miyake** • 119 Hudson St [N Moore St]
  212-226-0100
  Flagship store of this designer.
- **Korin** • 57 Warren St [W Broadway]
  212-587-7021
  Supplier to Japanese chefs and restaurants.
- **Let There Be Neon** • 38 White St [Church St]
  212-226-4883
  Neon gallery and store.
- **MarieBelle's Fine Treats & Chocolates** •
  484 Broome St [Wooster St]
  212-925-6999
  Top NYC chocolatier. Killer hot chocolate.
- **The Mysterious Bookshop** • 58 Warren St [W Broadway]
  212-587-1011
  Specialty—mystery books.

Hit up **Grandaisy Bakery** and **Duane Park Patisserie** for baked goods and **MarieBelle** for chocolate. We like **Selima Optique** for cool specs, and **Korin** for cutlery.

- **Oliver Peoples** • 366 W Broadway [Watts St]
  212-925-5400
  Look as good as you see, and vice-versa.
- **Selima Optique** • 59 Wooster St [Broome St]
  212-343-9490
  Funky eyewear for the vintage inclined.
- **SoHo Art Materials** • 3 Wooster St [Crosby St]
  212-431-3938
  A painter's candy store.
- **Tribeca Wine Merchants** •
  40 Hudson St [Duane St]
  212-393-1400
  High quality for a high rollers neighborhood.
- **Urban Archaeology** •
  158 Franklin St [W Broadway]
  212-371-4646
  Retro fixtures.

- **What Goes Around Comes Around** •
  351 W Broadway [Broome St]
  212-343-1225
  LARGE, excellent collection of men's, women's, and children's vintage.
- **Whole Foods** • 270 Greenwich St [Murray St]
  212-349-6555
  Tribeca natural market outpost means strollers and celebrities.
- **Zucker's Bagels and Smoked Fish** •
  143 Chambers St [W Broadway]
  212-608-5844
  Damn good, fresh, hand-rolled bagels and hearty schmears.

Map 3 • **City Hall / Chinatown**

Neighborhood Overview

Chinatown. Home of the NFT offices from 1998 until 2010, we truly have a love-hate relationship with this neighborhood. On one hand you have one of the highest concentrations of great (and cheap!) food in all of New York, one of the city's most interesting and diverse parks in **Columbus Park**, lots of history, and a daytime hustle-and-bustle that is probably only matched by midtown Manhattan.

On the other hand…there is almost no nightlife, and peace and quiet is, of course, nonexistent during daylight hours. But hey—if you want peace and quiet, what are you doing in the middle of New York City anyway?

Our advice is to just get in there and mix it up with the locals, many of whom live in the huge **Confucius Plaza** complex at the base of the Manhattan Bridge. And mixing it up is something that New Yorkers have been doing in this area for hundreds of years, starting with the incredibly dangerous "Five Points" area north of Collect Pond (the setting for Scorcese's seething *Gangs of New York*). Both the Five Points and Collect Pond are gone (the area itself is now **Columbus Park**), but little **Doyers Street** (aka "Bloody Angle") was the scene of gang wars for over 50 years.

Today, though, you can stroll around like the most clueless tourist and have absolutely no problems at all—gang wars have been replaced with street and shop commerce, from the tourist vendors of Mott Street to the **produce market** in the shadow of the Manhattan Bridge, with Canal Street's wall of tourists and locals connecting the two. The mass of humanity is sometimes overwhelming.

Fortunately, there are some cool places to try and hide away for a few moments, including the **Eastern States Buddhist Temple** and Maya Lin's new **Museum of Chinese in America**. The best "living museum," however, is without a doubt **Columbus Park**, which has an incredible range of activities—from early-morning tai chi to afternoon mah-jongg—happening within its borders throughout the day. In summer, a stop at classic **Chinatown Ice Cream Factory** will also cool your jets momentarily.

Columbus Park also serves as the northeast border of the City Hall area. There are several standout examples of civic architecture, including **City Hall** itself, the **Tweed Courthouse**, the **US Courthouse**, the condo-ized **Woolworth Building**, the sublime **Hall of Records/Surrogate Court** building, and, one of our favorite buildings in all of New York, McKim, Mead, & White's masterful **Municipal Building**, complete with a wedding-cake top and the Brooklyn Bridge stop of the 4-5-6 trains underneath.

From the Municipal Building, a walk over the **Brooklyn Bridge** is almost a *de rigueur* activity; if you'd rather stay in Manhattan, though, check out the **African Burial Ground** or watch police procedurals being filmed from **Foley Square**. Or head back east a bit to discover another bit of New York City history, an ancient **Jewish Burial Ground** on St. James Place.

No matter what you do here don't forget to EAT. It's worth the traffic, the crowds, and the lines. Believe it.

Map 3

8	9	10
5	6	7
2	**3**	4
	1	

City Hall / Chinatown

O Landmarks

- **87 Lafayette St** • 87 Lafayette St [White St]
Ex-firehouse designed in Chateau style by
Napoleon LeBrun.
- **African Burial Ground** •
290 Broadway [Duane St]
212-238-4367
Colonial burial ground for 20,000+
African-American slaves.
- **Brooklyn Bridge** • Chambers St & Centre St
The granddaddy of them all. Walking toward
Manhattan at sunset is as good as it gets.
- **Centre Marketplace** • Centre St & Broome St
Another great street we can't afford to live on.
- **Chatham Towers** • 170 Park Row [Worth St]
1960s poured-concrete apartment buildings
overlooking Chatham Square. Nice windows.
- **Chinatown Fair** • 8 Mott St [Bowery]
212-964-1001
Sneak out of the office to play Ms. Pac Man
here.
- **Chinatown Ice Cream Factory** •
65 Bayard St [Mott St]
212-608-4170
The best ice cream (ginger, black sesame,
mango, red bean, et al.), ever.
- **Chinatown Visitors Kiosk** •
Walker St & Baxter St
Good meeting point. Just look out for the
dragon.
- **City Hall** • 260 Broadway [Park Pl]
212-639-9675
Built in 1811, the diminutive seat of
government.
- **Columbus Park Playground** •
67 Mulberry St [Bayard St]
212-639-9675
Former Five Points hub now operates as prime
Chinatown hangout.
- **Confucius Plaza** • Bowery & Division St
Confucius say: live here!
- **Criminal Courthouse** •
100 Centre St [Leonard St]
646-386-4511
Imposing.
- **Doyers Street (Bloody Angle)** •
Doyers St [Chatham Sq]
Rare curvy street in Manhattan; film scouts
love it.

- **Eldridge Street Synagogue** • 12 Eldridge St
[Division St]
212-219-0302
The first large-scale building by Eastern Euro
immigrants in NY.
- **Foley Square** • Worth St & Centre St
Now with bizarre black obelisk. Guiliani hated
it.
- **Lighting District** • Bowery [Broome]
Light up your life with products from these
fine purveyors…
- **Municipal Building** • Chambers St & Park Row
Wonderful McKim, Mead & White masterpiece.
- **Museum of Chinese in America** •
215 Centre St [Howard St]
212-619-4785
Beautiful new home designed by Maya Lin.
- **Not For Tourists** • 2 E Broadway [Chatham Sq]
NFT headquarters from 1998 to 2010.
- **Old New York Life Insurance Company** •
346 Broadway [Leonard St]
Great narrow McKim, Mead & White with
hand-wound clock and cool internal stairwells.
- **Old Police Headquarters** •
240 Centre St [Grand St]
A beautiful building in the center of the not so
beautiful Little Italy/Chinatown area.
- **Shearith Israel Cemetery** •
55 St James Pl [Oliver St]
Oldest Jewish cemetery in New York.
- **Super-Cool Cast Iron** • Crosby St & Grand St
We want to live on the top floor of this
building.
- **Surrogate's Courthouse** •
31 Chambers St [Elk St]
Great lobby and zodiac-themed mosaics.
- **Thurgood Marshall US Courthouse** •
40 Centre St [Pearl St]
Cass Gilbert masterpiece from 1935.
- **Tweed Courthouse** •
52 Chambers St [Broadway]
Great interior dome, but will we ever see it?
- **Woolworth Building** • 233 Broadway [Park Pl]
A Cass Gilbert classic. Stunning lobby.

Think Kansas is boring at night? You haven't been to Chinatown at 10 pm on a Monday.

Coffee

- **Ferrara Café** • 195 Grand St [Mulberry St]
212-226-6150
The best of the Little Italy cafés.
- **Kung Fu Tea** • 234 Canal St [Centre St]
212-966-2786
Milky bubble tea for your afternoon sugar shot.
- **Saturdays Surf** • 31 Crosby St [Grand St]
347-449-1668
Small espresso bar with laid-back surfer vibe.

Farmers Markets

- **City Hall Park Greenmarket** •
Broadway at Chambers St
Tues & Fri 8 am–3 pm, year-round.

Nightlife

- **Apotheke** • 9 Doyers St [Bowery]
212-406-0400
Flaming expensive Euro-cocktails in a (supposedly) former opium den.
- **Capitale** • 130 Bowery [Grand St]
212-334-5500
Formerly the Bowery Savings Bank. Cool space.
- **Experimental Intermedia** •
224 Centre St [Grand St]
212-431-6430
Experimental art/performance art shows involving a variety of artistic media.

Map 3

8 9 10
5 6 7
2 **3** 4
1

City Hall / Chinatown

Restaurants

- **Banh Mi Saigon** • 198 Grand St [Mulberry St]
212-941-1541 • $
The best Vietnamese sandwiches. Ever.
- **Big Wong King** • 67 Mott St [Bayard St]
212-964-0540 • $
If you're gonna be a king, that's the kind of
king to be.
- **Billy's Bakery** • 75 Franklin St [Broadway]
212-647-9958 • $
Yummiest treats this side of homemade.
- **Bo Ky** • 80 Bayard St [Mott St]
212-406-2292 • $
Chinese/Vietnamese hybrid. Killer soups.
- **Breakroom** • 83 Baxter St [White St]
212-227-2802 • $$
If you need a burger or a taco in Chinatown,
this is the place.
- **Buddha Bodai** • 5 Mott St [Worth St]
212-566-8388 • $$
Veg heads dig this place.
- **Chee Cheong Fun Food Cart** •
159 Hester St • $
Try a pork steamed rice roll ("chee cheong
fun") for breakfast.
- **Deluxe Green Bo** • 66 Bayard St [Mott St]
212-625-2359 • $
Amazing Shanghainese. Nice alternative to
Joe's.
- **Despana** • 408 Broome St [Centre St]
212-219-5050 • $
Excellent Spanish take-out/gourmet grocery,
complete w/ bull.
- **Dim Sum Go Go** • 5 E Broadway [Catherine St]
212-732-0797 • $$
New, hip, inventive dim sum; essentially,
post-modern Chinese.

- **Ferrara Café** • 195 Grand St [Mulberry St]
212-226-6150 • $
Classic Little Italy patisserie.
- **Fried Dumpling** • 106 Mosco St [Mulberry St]
212-693-1060 • $
Five for a buck.
- **Golden Unicorn** •
18 E Broadway [Catherine St]
212-941-0911 • $$
Dim sum—great for medium-sized groups.
- **Great NY Noodletown** •
28 Bowery [Bayard St]
212-349-0923 • $
Cheap Chinese soups and BBQ and deep-fried
squid. At 2 am.
- **Jing Fong Restaurant** •
202 Centre St
212-964-5256 • $$
Large dim sum house.
- **Joe's Shanghai** • 46 Bowery St [Bowery]
212-233-8888 • $
Soup dumpling nirvana. Worth the wait.
- **La Mela Ristorante** •
167 Mulberry St [Grand St]
212-431-9493 • $$$
Family-style Italian dining.

City Hall / Chinatown

First stop: the crab soup dumplings at **Joe's Shanghai**. On from there, dim sum at **Dim Sum Go Go** or Malaysian at **Nyonya**. Too much Asian? Head to SoHo gem **Despaña** for Spanish sandwiches.

• **Luna Pizza** • 225 Park Row [Pearl St]
212-385-8118 • $
Go for the grandma pie.
•**May Wah Fast Food** • 190 Hester St [Baxter St]
212-925-6428 • $
Linoleum floors, fluorescent lights, and an amazing pork chop over rice.
• **Mei Lai Wah Bakery** •
64 Bayard St [Elizabeth St]
212-966-7866 • $
Sweet pastries, savory buns, tea, and noodles.
• **Nha Trang** • 87 Baxter St [White St]
212-233-5948 • $$
Excellent Vietnamese. Pho beef satee is good.
• **Nyonya** • 199 Grand St [Mulberry St]
212-334-3669 • $$
Malaysian when you're sick of Chinese.
• **OK 218 Restaurant** •
218 Grand St [Elizabeth St]
212-226-8039 • $
Perfect name for this average Chinese spot.
• **Pho Pasteur** • 85 Baxter St [White St]
212-608-3656 • $
Excellent soup. Pho sure.
• **Piacere** • 351 Broome St [Elizabeth St]
212-219-4080 • $$$
Decent 'za, especially for Little Italy. Go figure.
• **Ping's** • 22 Mott St [Mosco St]
212-602-9988 • $$
Eclectic Asian seafood. And we mean "eclectic."

• **Shanghai 21** •
21 Mott St [Mosco St]
212-766-6311 • $$
You can't have too many soup dumplings or scallion pancakes.
• **West New Malaysia** • 69 Bayard St [Mott St]
212-964-0284 • $$
A hidden gem that's literally hidden. Try the specials.

Map 3

City Hall / Chinatown

8 9 10
5 6 7
2 **3** 4
1

- **Smile To Go** • 22 Howard St [Crosby St]
646-863-3893 • $
Deliciously fresh veggies, small sandwiches, and baked goods, tiny space.
- **Sofia's of Little Italy** •
143 Mulberry St [Grand St]
212-219-9799 • $$$
A cut above the other tourist traps around here.
- **Super Taste** • 26 Eldridge St [Canal St]
646-283-0999 • $
Beginners: Try the spicy beef noodle soup.
- **Tasty Hand-Pulled Noodles Inc.** •
1 Doyers St [Bowery]
212-791-1817 • $
Stop by for a bowl on your post office run.
- **Vegetarian Dim Sum House** •
24 Pell St [Mott St]
212-577-7176 • $$
Cheap lunches for those who don't eat animals. Tip: Snow pea dumplings.
- **Wah Fung** • 79 Chrystie St [Hester St]
212-925-5175 • $
Succulent BBQ pig for stunningly cheap prices.
- **Wo Hop** • 17 Mott St [Mosco St]
212-962-8617 • $
Chinatown mainstay. Best when drunk.

🛍 Shopping

- **Bangkok Center Grocery** •
104 Mosco St [Mulberry St]
212-349-1979
Curries, fish sauce, and other Thai products.
- **Chinatown Fair** • 8 Mott St
212-964-1001
Long-standing video game arcade.
- **Chinatown Ice Cream Factory** •
65 Bayard St [Mott St]
212-608-4170
Take home a quart of mango. Oddest flavors in NYC.
- **Civil Service Book Shop** •
34 Carmine St
212-226-9506
Specialty—civil services.
- **Clic** • 255 Centre St [Broome St]
212-966-2766
Art books and an art gallery.
- **CT Food Market** •
250 Grand St [Chrystie St]
212-274-0990
Cantonese market with fresh fish and veggies.
- **Di Palo Fine Foods** • 200 Grand St [Mott St]
212-226-1033
Delicacies from across Italy. Excellent cheese.
- **Downtown Music Gallery** •
13 Monroe St [Catherine St]
212-473-0043
Independent labels and artists.
- **Fay Da Bakery** • 83 Mott St [Canal St]
212-791-3884
Chinese pastry and boba like nobody's business.

Don't do much shopping along tourist trap Canal Street, unless you're in the market for poorly made knockoffs whose proceeds probably help fund all manner of badness. Do hit **Harney & Sons** for a cup of tea, **Di Palo Fine Foods** for Italian imports, and **K & M Camera** for shutterbug stuff.

• **Forsyth Outdoor Produce Market** •
26 Forsyth Ave
Cheapest veggies and fruit in Manhattan.
Long lines.

• **Fountain Pen Hospital** •
10 Warren St [Broadway]
212-964-0580
They don't take Medicaid.

• **Harney & Sons** • 433 Broome St [Crosby St]
212-933-4853
Awe-inspiring tea selection. Sampling
encouraged.

• **K & M Camera** • 54 Orchard St [White St]
212-523-0954
Good all-around camera store; open
Saturdays!

• **Lendy Electric** • 176 Grand St [Baxter St]
212-431-3698
Great bastion of the electrical supply world.

• **Madewell** • 486 Broadway [Broome St]
212-226-6954
Always-packed, casually cool J.Crew offshoot.

• **Muji Soho** • 455 Broadway [Grand St]
212-334-2002
Why is Japanese design so functional and
cute?

• **CityStore** • 1 Centre St [Chambers St]
212-386-0007
Great NYC books and schwag you can't get
anywhere else.

• **New York Mart** • 128 Mott St [Grand St]
212-680-0178
Solid Chinatown grocery, lots of produce, roast
duck to-go.

• **No 6** • 8 Centre Market Pl [Grand St]
212-226-5759
Notable selection of carefully selected original
American and European vintage.

• **Piemonte Ravioli** • 190 Grand St [Mulberry St]
718-429-1972
Old-school and homemade.

• **Sun's Organic Tea Shop** •
79 Bayard St [Mott St]
212-566-3260
Inexpensive loose leaf teas, knowledgeable
staff.

• **Yunhong Chopsticks Shop** •
50 Mott St [Bayard St]
212-233-0288
Super-cute chopstick shop in C-town.

Map 4 · **Lower East Side**

1

2

E 3rd St

E 2nd St

Lilian
Wald
Houses

E 1st St

E Houston St

7

Hamilton
Fish
Park

Katz's Delicatessen

Angel Orensanz
Theatre

Stanton St

Attorney St

Sheriff St

Columbia St

Masaryk
Towers

Baruch
Dr

Baruch
Houses

Samuel Gompers
Houses

Baruch
Houses

A

Blue Condo

Delancey Street
Essex Street

Essex Street Market

Rivington St

Clinton St

Ridge St

Attorney St

Pitt St

Willett St

Sheriff St

Williamsburg Bridge

East River
Houses

East
River
Park

Delancey St

Lower East Side
Tenement
Museum

Suffolk St

Broome St

Norfolk St

Hillman
Houses

Abraham Kazan St

Columbia St

Cannon St

Lewis St

Bialystoker
Synagogue

Hillman
Houses

Grand St

Samuel
Dickstein
Plz

Vladeck
Houses

Forsyth St

Allen St

Orchard St

Eldridge St

Seward
Park
Houses

Seward Park Houses

Jackson St

Corlears
Hook
Park

Hester Street Fair

WH
Seward
Park

East Broadway

Montgomery St

Gouverneur St

Water St

Canal St

East
Broadway

Jefferson St

Henry St

Madison St

Gouverneur
Hospital
(old building)

E Gouverneur Slip

Division St

La Guardia
Houses

Marginal St

Pier 43

3

Forsyth St

Pike St

Catherine St

Monroe St

Market St

Water St

Rutgers St

Rutgers
Houses

Cherry St

W Gouverneur Slip

FDR Dr

Pier 42

East River

B

Knicker-
bocker
Village

Manhattan Bridge

Gov
Alfred E Smith
Houses

Robert F Wagner Sr Pl

30

Marshall St

John St

Plymouth St

Jay St

Water St

Front St

BROOKLYN

1/4 mile

.25 km

Neighborhood Overview

Now characterized by bars and nightclubs and the high-heeled, cologne-drenched crowds that flock to them, the Lower East Side has traditionally been known as the epicenter of immigrant cultures. At one time the term "Lower East Side" applied to what's now called the East Village as well, but starting in the latter part of the 20th century, the two neighborhoods have commonly been referred to separately, with Houston Street as the dividing line. While the Lower East Side has the grittier reputation, with its sprawl of housing projects along the East River, and shared border with Chinatown on the southern and western edges, gentrification is quickly sweeping across the landscape; one of the more obvious signs is the incongruous **Blue Condo** rising above Norfolk Street.

Of all the groups who settled here, the area is perhaps most known for its Jewish roots, and traces can still be found if you look hard enough. A number of historic synagogues still stand, including **Bialystoker Synagogue** on Willett Street, and the **Angel Orensanz Foundation**, which has been converted into an art gallery and performance space. The venerable **Katz's Delicatessen** on Houston Street is an obvious starting point for any culinary tour, and if you still have room after all that pastrami, head to **Russ & Daughters** for bagels, smoked fish, and old world appetizing. If a light snack is what you're after, **Kossar's Bialys** is still one of the best deals in town. Once your belly is full, walk along the tenement buildings and clothing stores along Orchard Street until you reach the **Tenement Museum**. There you can tour restored apartments of actual people who lived in the area long ago, and thank your lucky stars that at least you don't share your tiny studio with a half dozen relatives.

The overlapping of Jewish, Puerto Rican, and Chinese cultures, as well as the changes wrought by the neighborhood's rising attractiveness to developers make any walking tour fascinating. Along Clinton Street, old school Latino businesses stand side-by-side with cutting-edge eateries. On Broome Street, pungent Chinese vegetable markets encounter pricey boutiques. Art center **ABC No Rio**, which grew out of downtown's squatter movement and punk rock scene is located a couple blocks from the swanky **Hotel on Rivington**. You get the picture.

When you're done with history, you can always do some more eating. Check out the stalls at **Essex Street Market**—established in the 1930s to replace the pushcarts that once clogged these streets—for gourmet groceries, meats, and produce. If you're passing by on a Saturday, **Hester Street Fair** will give you a taste of the city's booming foodie scene with its many artisanal delights. And then there's the infamous nightlife, a slice of party heaven (or hell) clustered around Orchard, Clinton, Ludlow, Rivington, and Stanton Streets. **Mercury Lounge** is one of our favorite venues, and there's always something going on at **Arlene's Grocery**. This is best attempted on a week night, of course. Don't say we didn't warn you.

Ready for a night out on the Lower East Side? Chug some PBRs at **Welcome to the Johnsons** then head to **Arlene's Grocery** for live music. Or check out burlesque at **Nurse Bettie**, then get cozy on a couch at **The Back Room**. Go!

O Landmarks

- **Angel Orensanz Foundation for the Arts** •
172 Norfolk St [Stanton St]
212-253-0452
Performance space in ex-synagogue. Amazing.
- **Bialystoker Synagogue** •
7 Bialystoker Pl [Grand St]
212-475-0165
The oldest building in NY to currently house a
synagogue. Once a stop on the Underground
Railroad.
- **Blue Condo** • 105 Norfolk St [Delancey St]
Bernard Tschumi's odd masterpiece.
- **East River Park** • East River Park at Broome St
The park the FDR Drive built.
- **Gouverneur Hospital** •
621 Water St [Gouverneur St]
One of the oldest hospital buildings in the
world.
- **Katz's Delicatessen** •
205 E Houston St [Ludlow St]
212-254-2246
Classic New York pastrami; I'll have what she's
having!
- **Tenement Museum** •
103 Orchard St [Broome St]
877-975-3786
Great illustration of turn-of-the-century (20th,
that is) life.

Coffee

- **Caffe Vita** • 124 Ludlow St [Rivington St]
212-260-8482
Seattle coffee ballers' first outpost east of the
Mississippi.
- **Kopitiam** • 151 E Broadway
646-609-3785
The Malaysian-style white coffee garners raves.
- **Ludlow Coffee Supply** • 176 Ludlow St
[Houston St]
917-472-7632
Quality coffee, above-average food, and a
barber component.
- **Roasting Plant** • 81 Orchard St [Broome St]
212-775-7755
Custom-ground coffee. Theatrical.

Farmers Markets

- **Hester Street Fair** • 18 Fulton St
Fancy street grub and artisanal boutiques
every Thursday–Sunday, Nov 30–Mar 31.
- **Lower East Side Youthmarket** •
Grand Ave b/n Pitt St & Abraham Pl
Thursdays, July–Nov, 8 am–3 pm.

Nightlife

- **169 Bar** • 169 E Broadway [Rutgers St]
516-986-7938
Sometimes good, sometimes not.
- **Arlene's Grocery** • 95 Stanton St [Ludlow St]
212-358-1633
Cheap live tunes.
- **Bacaro** • 136 Division St [Ludlow St]
212-941-5060
Wine and pretty snacks from Venice.
- **The Back Room** • 102 Norfolk St [Delancey St]
212-228-5098
The secret room is behind a bookcase.

Lower East Side

Ready for a night out on the Lower East Side? Chug some PBRs at **Welcome to the Johnsons** then head to **Arlene's Grocery** for live music. Or check out burlesque at **Nurse Bettie**, then get cozy on a couch at **The Back Room**. Go!

- **Chloe 81** • 81 Ludlow St [Broome St]
212-677-0067
Another secret bar you won't get into.
- **Clandestino** • 35 Canal St [Ludlow St]
212-475-5505
Inviting bar off the beaten track.
- **Clockwork Bar** • 21 Essex St [Hester St]
212-677-4545
Much needed punk rock dive in an increasingly chic nabe.
- **The Delancey** • 168 Delancey St [Clinton St]
212-254-9920
Overrated, but the roof is cool if you can get up there.
- **Donnybrook** • 35 Clinton St [Stanton St]
212-228-7733
Upscale yet rustic pub for the professional crowd.
- **Eastwood** • 200 Clinton St [Clinton St]
212-233-0124
Drinks and eclectic grub + brunch.
- **JIA at Hotel Rivington** •
105 Rivington St [Ludlow St]
212-796-8040
Groovy baby.
- **Local 138** • 181 Orchard St
212-477-0280
Great happy hour. No douchebags most of the time.
- **The Magician** • 118 Rivington St [Essex St]
212-673-7851
Hipster haven. The NFT cartographer loves it.
- **Mercury Lounge** • 217 E Houston St [Essex St]
212-260-4700
Rock venue with occasional top-notch acts.

- **Mr. Purple** • 180 Orchard St [Stanton St]
212-237-1790
Crafty cocktails and a stunning 15th floor view of Manhattan.
- **Nurse Bettie** • 106 Norfolk St [Rivington St]
212-477-7515
Cozy cocktails and burlesque. Recommended on weeknights.
- **Parkside Lounge** •
317 E Houston St [Attorney St]
212-673-6270
Good basic bar, live acts in the back.
- **Pianos** • 158 Ludlow St [Stanton St]
212-505-3733
Painful scene with decent live tunes.
- **Set L.E.S.** • 127 Ludlow St [Rivington St]
929-505-3163
Drinks with above-average gastropub grub.
- **The Skinny** • 174 Orchard St [Stanton St]
212-228-3668
Shimmy through sweating crowds in this appropriately named dive bar.
- **The Slipper Room** • 167 Orchard St [Stanton St]
212-253-7246
Striptease for the arty crowd.
- **The Ten Bells** • 247 Broome St [Ludlow St]
212-228-4450
Organic wine bar with candlelit Euro-vibe. Nice!
- **Verlaine** • 110 Rivington St [Essex St]
212-614-2494
Mellow, French-Vietnamese motif with deceptively sweet cocktails.
- **Welcome to the Johnsons** •
123 Rivington St [Essex St]
Great decor, but too crowded mostly.

Map 4

Lower East Side

8 9 10
5 6 7
2 3 4
1

🍽 Restaurants

- **Bacaro** • 136 Division St [Ludlow St]
  212-941-5060 • $$
  Venetian snack bar.
- **Barrio Chino** • 253 Broome St [Orchard St]
  212-228-6710 • $$
  Started as a tequila bar, but now more of a
  restaurant.
- **Cafe Katja** • 79 Orchard St [Broome St]
  212-219-9545 • $$$
  The LES Euro zone welcomes Austria into the
  fold.
- **Cheeky Sandwiches** • 35 Orchard St [Hester St]
  646-504-8132 • $
  New Orleans po' boys dressed. The real deal.
- **Clinton Street Baking Co.** •
  4 Clinton St [E Houston St]
  646-602-6263 • $$
  Homemade buttermilk everything. LES laid
  back. Top 5 bacon.
- **Congee Village** • 100 Allen St [Delancey St]
  212-941-1818 • $$
  Porridge never tasted so good.
- **Creperie** • 135 Ludlow St [Rivington St]
  212-979-5521 • $
  A hole-in-the-wall that serves sweet and
  savory crepes.
- **Dimes** • 49 Canal St [Orchard St]
  212-925-1300 • $$$
  California-to-table cuisine; young creative
  vibe.

- **Dirt Candy** • 86 Allen St [Broome St]
  212-228-7732 • $$$
  Haute-vegetarian that's fun for all.
- **Dirty French** • 180 Ludlow St [E Houston St]
  212-254-3000 • $$$$
  Hip French inside the hipper-than-thou
  Ludlow Hotel.
- **Eastwood** • 200 Clinton St
  212-233-0124 • $$$
  Fish 'n chips, Scotch eggs, and, of course, kale.
- **El Castillo de Jagua** •
  113 Rivington St [Essex St]
  212-982-6412 • $
  Great cheap Dominican.
- **Essex** • 124 Rivington St
  212-533-9616 • $$$
  Great space, OK food.
- **Grey Lady** • 77 Delancey St [Allen St]
  646-580-5239 • $$$
  Oysters, noshes and goodness for pre-Bowery
  Ballroom sustenance.
- **il laboratorio del gelato** •
  188 Ludlow St [E Houston St]
  212-343-9922 • $
  Mind-bogglingly incredible artisanal gelato.

Lower East Side

Sliders at **Set L.E.S.** and brunch at **Clinton Street Baking Co.** keep 'em lined up, but if you're with a group, just get a big table at **Congee Village**. We love **Kossar's Bialys** for a quick bite, and **Shopsin's** when we just need some good old fashioned mac n' cheese pancakes.

• **Katz's Delicatessen** •
205 E Houston St [Ludlow St]
212-254-2246 • $$
Classic New York pastrami; I'll have what she's having!

• **Kossar's Bialys** • 367 Grand St [Essex St]
212-473-4810 • $
Where NFT gets their morning bialys and bagels.

• **La Contenta** • 102 Norfolk St [Delancey St]
212-432-4180 • $$$
We're contented with the fish tacos and margaritas, gracias.

• **LES Enfants de Boheme** •
177 Henry St [Jefferson St]
646-476-4843 • $$$
French goodness deep in the heart of the LES.

• **Nakamura** • 172 Delancey St [Attorney St]
212-614-1810 • $$
Internationally renowned ramen.

• **Pig and Khao** • 68 Clinton St [Rivington St]
212-920-4485 • $$$$
Filipino fusion that's all good—short rib, pork belly, chicharron, ahhh.

• **Russ & Daughters Cafe** •
127 Orchard St [Rivington St]
212-475-4881 • $$$
Cheery café serving up fish noshes from popular retail store.

• **Set L.E.S.** • 127 Ludlow St [Rivington St]
929-505-3163 • $$$
Go for the sliders and the clams casino…and drinks, of course.

• **Shopsin's** • 88 Essex St [Rivington St]
917-907-4506 • $
Kenny's back! Get your Blisters on My Sisters in the Essex St Market.

• **Souvlaki GR** • 116 Stanton St [Essex St]
212-777-0116 • $$
Perfect Greek sandwiches to transport you away to the islands.

• **Sticky Rice** • 85 Orchard St [Broome St]
212-274-8208 • $$
Thai treats, Asian BBQ, BYOB, and Wi-Fi?!

• **Sweet Chick** • 178 Ludlow St [Houston St]
646-657-0217 • $$$
Your basic chicken 'n waffle hangover solution.

• **Wildair** • 142 Orchard St [Rivington St]
646-964-5624 • $$$
Cozy wine bar with inventive dishes.

Map 4

8 9 10
5 6 7
2 3 4
1

Lower East Side

Shopping

- **Babeland** • 94 Rivington St [Ludlow St]
  212-375-1701
  Sex toys without the creepy vibe.
- **Dah Bike Shop** • 134 Division St [Ludlow St]
  212-925-0155
  BMX experts. Totally rad!
- **Doughnut Plant** • 379 Grand St [Norfolk St]
  212-505-3700
  Great, weird, recommended.
- **Economy Candy** • 108 Rivington St [Essex St]
  212-254-1531
  Floor-to-ceiling candy madness.
- **Edith Machinist** •
  104 Rivington St [Ludlow St]
  212-979-9992
  Where to buy your vintage boots and bags.
- **Erin McKenna's Babycakes NYC** •
  248 Broome St [Ludlow St]
  855-462-2292
  Awfully good vegan, gluten-free pastries, and
  cupcake tops!
- **Essex Street Market** •
  88 Essex St [Rivington St]
  Classic public market with a great combo of
  old-school and fresh-faced vendors.

- **Frank's Bike Shop** • 533 Grand St [Jackson St]
  212-533-6332
  Sales, repairs, and rentals.
- **il laboratorio del gelato** •
  188 Ludlow St [E Houston St]
  212-343-9922
  Mind-bogglingly incredible artisanal gelato.
- **Joy's Flower Pot** • 40 Hester St [Essex St]
  917-663-6388
  Flowers, succulents, cacti, air plants, and
  too-cute terrariums.
- **Kossar's Bialys** • 367 Grand St [Essex St]
  212-473-4810
  Oldest bialy bakery in the US. The absolute
  sh**.
- **Labor Skate Shop** • 46 Canal St [Orchard St]
  646-351-6792
  Hip skate kids roll on in to hang and pick up a
  cool board.
- **Moishe's Bakery** • 504 Grand St [E Broadway]
  212-673-5832
  Best babka, challah, hamantaschen, and
  rugalach.
- **Moscot** • 94 Orchard St [Delancey St]
  212-477-3796
  Glasses like your grandfather used to wear.

Lower East Side

We buy our groceries at **Essex Street Market**, and uhhh…just browse at **Babeland**. **Economy Candy** has everything, and if you're hungry, hit **Cheeky Sandwiches**, and **Doughnut Plant**.

- **Petee's Pie** • 61 Delancey St [Allen St]
  646-494-3630
  Pie engineers with "best of" pedigree.
- **Roni-Sue's Chocolates** •
  148 Forsyth St [Rivington St]
  212-677-1216
  Chocolate-covered bacon and other sweets
  sold from inside Essex Market.
- **Russ & Daughters** •
  179 E Houston St [Orchard St]
  212-475-4880
  Fab Jewish soul food—lox, herring, sable, etc
- **September Wines & Spirits** •
  100 Stanton St [Ludlow St]
  212-388-0770
  Wines from a varity of family-operated
  vineyards. Free tastings!
- **Zarin Fabrics** • 72 Allen St
  212-925-6112
  Major destination in the fabric district.

Map 4

Map 5 · **West Village**

W 16th St

1

2

W 15th St

Old Homestead

W 14th St

A C E
14th Street

8th Avenue

L

14th Street

1 2 3
14th Street

PATH
14th St

14th
Street

F M

The Standard Hotel

Ninth Ave

6th Avenue

L

PAGE
260

Little W 12th St

W 13th St

The High Line

Gansevoort St

Greenwich Ave

W 12th St

Whitney Museum
of American Art

Horatio St

Washington St

Jane St

Abingdon
Sq

W 11th St

Eighth Ave

Waverly Pl

Patchin Place

W 10th St

PATH
9th St

W 12th St

Bethune St

4th St

W 9th St

A

Seventh Ave S

Westbeth Artists
Housing

Bank St

W 11th St

Bleecker St

Stonewall
Inn

W 8th St

White Horse
Tavern

Christopher Street
Sheridan Square

Sheridan
Sq

Waverly

A C E
B D F M

Perry St

Washington Pl

Charles St

Avenue of the Americas (Sixth Ave)

Bob Dylan's
One-Time Apt.

W 4th St

W 10th St

Greenwich Ave

Jones St

Cornelia St

The Cage

Christopher St

West Side Hwy

PATH
Christopher
St

Grove St

Commerce St

W 3rd St

Minetta Ln

PAGE
262

Barrow St

Bedford St

Carmine St

Bleecker St

Hudson
River
Park

6

9A

Morton St

St Luke's

Dominick St

W Houston St

Hudson
River

Leroy St

James J
Walker
Park

1

Downing St

Houston
Street

W Houston St

Clarkson St

Washington St

King St

Varick St

Charlton St

Greenwich St

Hudson St

MacDougal St

Sullivan St

B

Spring
Street

C E

Vandam St

Spring St

Spring St

Dominick St

The Ear Inn

Renwick St

Broome St

Broome St

Watts St

Grand St

2

Holland Tunnel

Canal St

1/4 mile

.25 km

Neighborhood Overview

Map 5

8 9 10
5 6 7
2 3 4
1

Ah, the West Village. This is the idyllic neighborhood of Jane Jacobs, the district of odd-angled streets designed to disorient grid-seasoned New Yorkers. Bordered by collegiate Greenwich Village to the east, millionaire stronghold Tribeca to the South, and factory-turned-gallery heaven Chelsea to the North, this neighborhood has quaint beauty, a thriving restaurant scene, and top-notch shopping, making it the ultimate address for the very, very rich. But its draw goes deeper than finding the boots or the cheeseburger that will change your life, because of all the famous artists, musicians, and writers who once lived, worked, drank, strolled, and starved here.

To catch a glimpse of more Bohemian times, head to the **White Horse Tavern** (1880), which has the dubious honor of being the place where Dylan Thomas drank himself to death. You can see where Edgar Allen Poe was treated at **Northern Dispensary** (1831), and visit Bob Dylan's old apartment at **161 West 4th Street**. Charming, gated **Patchin Place** (1849) was once home to writers Theodore Dreiser, e.e. Cummings, and Djuna Barnes. Thelonious Monk, Miles Davis, and every other jazz great under the sun played at **Village Vanguard** (1935). Poet Edna St. Vincent Millay helped found **Cherry Lane Theater** (1924), which remains the oldest continuously operating off-Broadway theater. Absent is Gertrude Vanderbilt Whitney's Studio Club on West 8th Street, which moved uptown in the 1950s. In 2015 the **Whitney Museum of American Art** returned to its West Village roots with a new building at Washington and Gansevoort Streets right next to the High Line.

The atmosphere of artistic creativity and non-conformity that permeated this neighborhood in the early 20th century (and still does, to some extent) gave rise to the gay rights movement, sparked by the 1969 riots at the **Stonewall Inn**. The West Village has also been the scene of vehement preservation efforts. **The Ear Inn** (1817), one of the oldest bars in Manhattan, was an early example of the New York City Landmarks Preservation Commission acting to protect a historic building. The **Jefferson Market Courthouse** (1877), now part of the New York Public Library, was also saved by the outcry of the community when faced with demolition. Since 1969 much of the area has been preserved as a historic district that runs from 14th Street to West 4th or St. Luke's Place, and from Washington St. to University Place.

Despite all that architectural preservation, perhaps no area has seen as dramatic change in recent years as the blocks between 14th, Gansevoort, and Hudson Streets, also known as the Meatpacking District. The slaughterhouses, meat markets, and sex workers have been displaced by highest of high-end shops, nightclubs, and glittering hotels, paving the way for a different kind of meat market entirely. The Standard Hotel, one of the most visible signs of the area's resurgence, straddles **The High Line**, converted from a railway to a green public space that runs all the way up to 34th Street. It's worth a stroll, if only to remind yourself that you're (literally) above all the luxury below. Continue your walk along ever-popular **Hudson River Park**, before hitting one of the West Village's fine bars and restaurants and having more fun than you can afford.

Along Sixth Avenue at West 4th Street is **The Cage**, one of the city's most heralded outdoor basketball courts. The level of play is high and the competition intense; not your typical neighborhood pick-up game, several NBA players learned their chops here. When you've worked up an appetite watching from the sidelines, hit up the **Old Homestead**, New York's oldest steakhouse; the only thing better than the wood paneling and leather banquettes is that nifty retro neon out front.

Map 5

8 9 10
5 6 7
2 3 4
1

West Village

O Landmarks

- **Bob Dylan's One-Time Apartment** •
161 W 4th St [Cornelia St]
Bob Dylan lived here in the '60s.
- **The Cage (Basketball Court)** •
6th Ave & W 4th St
Where everybody's got game…
- **The Ear Inn** • 326 Spring St [Greenwich St]
212-226-9060
Second-oldest bar in New York; great space.
- **The High Line** •
Gansevoort to 34th St b/n 10th & 11th Ave
212-500-6035
Stunning elevated park; a testament to human creativity.
- **Hudson River Park** • Battery Pl to 59th St
212-627-2020
Bicycle and walking paths; tennis, batting cages, dog runs!
- **Jefferson Market** • 425 6th Ave [W 10th St]
212-243-4334
Now a library.
- **Old Homestead Steakhouse** •
56 9th Ave [W 14th St]
212-242-9040
Said to be NY's oldest steakhouse, circa 1868.
- **Patchin Place** •
W 10th St b/n 6th Ave & Greenwich Ave
Tiny gated enclave, once home to E.E. Cummings.
- **The Standard** • 848 Washington St [W 12th St]
212-645-4646
Hip Meatpacking District hotel straddling the High Line.
- **The Stonewall Inn** •
53 Christopher St [7th Ave S]
212-488-2705
Uprising here in 1969 launched the gay rights movement.
- **Westbeth Artists Housing** •
55 Bethune St [Washington St]
212-691-1500
Cool multifunctional arts center.
- **White Horse Tavern** •
567 Hudson St [W 11th St]
212-989-3956
Another old, cool bar. Dylan Thomas drank here (too much).
- **Whitney Museum of American Art** •
99 Gansevoort St [10th Ave]
212-570-3600
Always has something to talk about, like the controversial Biennial.

Coffee

- **Joe the Art of Coffee** • 141 Waverly Pl [Gay St]
212-924-6750
Excellent espresso.
- **Partners Coffee** • 44 Charles St [7th Ave S]
917-675-7668 Australian artisanal coffee powerhouse.

Farmers Markets

- **Abingdon Square Greenmarket** •
W 12th St & Hudson St
Sat 8 am–2 pm, year-round.

Nightlife

- **Art Bar** • 52 8th Ave [W 4th St]
212-727-0244
Great spaces, cool crowd.
- **Arthur's Tavern** • 57 Grove St [Bleecker St]
212-414-4314
Featuring great jazz and blues since 1937.
- **Automatic Slims** • 733 Washington St [Bank St]
212-645-8660
LOUD. Yes, that loud.
- **Barrow's Pub** • 463 Hudson St [Barrow St]
212-741-9349
Low-key, old man bar.
- **Blind Tiger Ale House** •
281 Bleecker St [Jones St]
212-462-4682
Beer heaven. Good food. Good vibe.
- **Boom Boom Room** •
848 Washington St [W 13th St]
212-645-4646
Chic beautiful things drink at the top of the Standard Hotel.
- **Brass Monkey** • 55 Little W 12th St [10th Ave]
917-765-6746
Lots of beers, big wood tables, low light, and multiple levels.

West Village

Map 5

So many bars, so little time. The **Ear Inn** and **White Horse Tavern** are classics while **Employees Only** and **Little Branch** have speakeasy cocktails covered. Check out live jazz at **Village Vanguard**, world music at **SOB's**, cabaret at **Marie's Crisis** and **The Duplex**, and movies at **IFC** or revival house **Film Forum**.

- **City Winery** • 25 11th Ave [15th St]
  646-751-6033
  Adult yupsters sip pinot while David Byrne plays a live set.
- **Cubbyhole** • 281 W 12th St [W 4th St]
  212-243-9041
  Homey atmosphere and friendly crowd at this lesbian bar mainstay.
- **The Duplex** • 61 Christopher St [7th Ave S]
  212-255-5438
  Everything's still fun.
- **The Ear Inn** • 326 Spring St [Greenwich St]
  212-226-9060
  Second oldest bar in NYC. A great place.
- **Employees Only** • 510 Hudson St [W 10th St]
  212-242-3021
  Classy cocktails for big bucks.
- **Fiddlesticks Pub & Grill** •
  56 Greenwich Ave [Perry St]
  212-463-0516
  Good Irish fare, depressing environs.
- **The Four-Faced Liar** • 165 W 4th St [Cornelia St]
  212-206-8959
  A spirited neighborhood bar with wonderfully friendly bartenders.
- **Henrietta Hudson** • 438 Hudson St [Morton St]
  212-924-3347
  Good lesbian vibe.
- **Hudson Bar and Books** •
  636 Hudson St [Horatio St]
  212-229-2642
  Like *Cheers* for a hipper, more sophisticated crowd.

- **Johnny's Bar** • 90 Greenwich Ave [W 12th St]
  212-741-5279
  Occassional celeb sightings at this popular dive.
- **Kettle of Fish** • 59 Christopher St [7th Ave S]
  212-414-2278
  Cozy couches and darts.
- **Little Branch** • 20 7th Ave S [W 12th St]
  212-929-4360
  Clever cocktails in an intimate, cavernous setting.
- **Marie's Crisis** • 59 Grove St [7th Ave S]
  646-470-6040
  Showtunes only! And no, Billy Joel doesn't count.
- **Off The Wagon** • 109 MacDougal St [Minetta Ln]
  212-533-4487
  College bar at it's finest. If that's possblie.
- **The Other Room** • 143 Perry St [Washington St]
  212-645-9758
  Surprisingly decent beer selection with great, low-key vibe.
- **Pieces** • 8 Christopher St [Gay St]
  212-929-9291
  Favorite local gay dive, newly renovated, cheap drinks.
- **Plunge** • 18 9th Ave [W 13th St]
  212-660-6736
  The Gansevoort's rooftop bar for pretty people.
- **Smalls Jazz Club** • 183 W 10th St [W 4th St]
  Classic New York jazz scene; all night for $20.
- **SOB's** • 204 Varick St [W Houston St]
  212-243-4940
  World music venue with salsa lessons on Mondays.
- **Soho Cigar Bar** • 32 Watts St [Sullivan St]
  212-941-1781
  Smoker-friendly lounge.
- **Standard Biergarten** •
  848 Washington St [W 13th St]
  212-645-4100
  Gallons of beer, pretzels, and partying young ones.

Map 5

West Village

8 9 10
5 6 7
2 3 4
1

- **The Stonewall Inn** •
  53 Christopher St [7th Ave S]
  212-488-2705
  From the L to the GB and T, this is where it all
  began.
- **Paul's Casablanca** • 305 Spring St [Renwick St]
  212-620-5220
  A sexy Moroccan hot spot or an ode to Pier 1
  Imports?
- **Turks & Frogs** • 323 W 11th St [Greenwich St]
  212-691-8875
  Wine bar off the beaten track.
- **Village Vanguard** • 178 7th Ave S [Perry St]
  212-255-4037
  Classic NYC jazz venue. Not to be missed.
- **Vin Sur Vingt** • 192 7th Ave S
  212-924-4442
  Bold wine choices and French small plates in a
  cozy space.
- **Vol de Nuit** • 148 W 4th St [6th Ave]
  212-982-3388
  Belgian beers, cool vibe.
- **White Horse Tavern** •
  567 Hudson St [W 11th St]
  212-989-3956
  Another NYC classic.
- **Wilfie and Nell** • 228 W 4th St [W 10th St]
  212-242-2990
  Cool space, good food; too bad someone told
  the i-bankers.
- **Wogie's** • 39 Greenwich Ave [Charles St]
  212-229-2171
  Philly-caliber cheesesteaks & 700-level Phans.

🍴 Restaurants

- **A Salt & Battery** • 112 Greenwich Ave [Jane St]
  212-691-2713 • $$
  If you can eat it, they can fry it.
- **Agave** • 140 7th Ave S [Charles St]
  212-989-2100 • $$$
  Surprisingly good Southwest-Mex.
- **Alice** • 126 W 13th St [Ave of the Americas]
  212-691-4886 • $$$$
  Romantic Italian loyal to the regular customers.
- **Bar Six** • 502 6th Ave [W 13th St]
  212-691-1363 • $$$
  Pretty much a perfect French bistro.
- **Black Tap** • 529 Broome St [Sullivan St]
  917-639-3089 • $$
  Soho burger spot with the buzzy milkshakes.
- **Bleeker Street Pizza** • 69 7th Ave S [Bleeker St]
  212-924-4466 • $
  A couple pepperonis above the average
  grab-a-slice pizza place.
- **Bobo** • 181 W 10th St [7th Ave]
  212-488-2626 • $$$$
  Hip eats, if you can find the unmarked basement
  entrance.
- **Bonsignour** • 35 Jane St [8th Ave]
  212-229-9700 • $$
  Over-priced but tasty café, celeb-sighting likely.

Taïm has some of the best falafel on the planet, and for a cheap breakfast that even celebs appreciate, La Bonbonnière can't be beat. Impress dates by locating the unmarked basement door of Bobo. Try EN Brasserie for Japanese izakaya and Numero 28 Pizzeria for pizza.

• **Bubby's** •
120 Hudson St
212-219-0666
Comfort food masters' West Village outpost.
• **Buvette** • 42 Grove St [Bleecker St]
212-255-3590 • $$$
French all the way, grâce à Dieu.
• **Café Altro Paradiso** • 234 Spring St [6th Ave]
646-952-0828 • $$$$
Fancified basic Italian in stylish setting.
• **Café Cluny** • 284 W 12th St [W 4th St]
212-255-6900 • $$$$
The Odeon's younger cousin in the West Village, also French.
• **Caliente Cab Co** • 61 7th Ave S [Bleecker St]
212-243-8517 • $$
Cheesy spot the kids would probably like.
• **Casa la Femme** • 140 Charles St [Washington St]
212-505-0005 • $$$$
A Fantastic Culinary Experience on the West Village.
• **Charlie Bird** • 5 King St [6th Ave]
212-235-7133 • $$ $$
Italo-comfort cuisine/paean to NYC.
• **Coppelia** • 207 W 14th St [7th Ave]
212-858-5001 • $$
Fancy-ish diner with a Cuban twist. Always open.
• **Corner Bistro** • 331 W 4th St [Jane St]
212-242-9502 • $
Top NYC burgers. Perfect at 3 am.

• **Cowgirl** • 519 Hudson St [W 10th St]
212-633-1133 • $$
Good chicken fried steak.
• **Deb's Catering** • 3 Madison St
212-964-1300 • $
Get cheap but interesting food for lunch from their "salad bar."
• **Decoy** • 529 Hudson St [Charles St]
212-691-9700 • $$$$
If they're elevating Peking duck why is the place subterranean?
• **Employees Only** • 510 Hudson St [W 10th St]
212-242-3021 • $$$$
Deco-decorated eatery with a damn good bar.
• **EN Japanese Brasserie** •
435 Hudson St [Leroy St]
212-647-9196 • $$$$
Amazing izakaya not to be missed.
• **Extra Virgin** • 259 West 4th St [Perry St]
212-691-9359 • $$$$
Brunch, dinner, and a little bit of everything. Pure New York.
• **Fiddlesticks Pub & Grill** •
56 Greenwich Ave [Perry St]
212-257-0630 • $$
This pub's authentic Irish fare is nothing to fiddle around with.

Map 5

8 9 10
5 6 7
2 3 4
1

West Village

- **Gottino** • 52 Greenwich Ave [Perry St]
212-633-2590 • $$$
The Italian small plate trend fulfills its potential here.
- **Hector's** • 44 Little W 12th St [Washington St]
212-206-7592 • $$
Unfancy burgers under the fancy High Line.
- **Houseman** • 508 Greenwich St [Spring St]
212-641-0654 • $$$
Rustic, elegant, ever-changing menus in Hudson Square.
- **I Sodi** • 314 Bleecker St [Grove St]
646-675-8672 • $$$
Tuscan through and through.
- **Jeffrey's Grocery** •
172 Waverly Pl [Christopher St]
$$$
All-day affair with emphasis on oysters.
- **Joe's Pizza** • 7 Carmine St [Bleecker St]
212-366-1182 • $
Excellent slices.
- **John's Pizzeria** • 278 Bleecker St [Jones St]
212-243-1680 • $$
Quintessential NY pizza.
- **Joseph Leonard** • 170 Waverly Pl [Grove St]
$$$
Top-notch NYC dining experience. Worth the splurge and wait.
- **La Bonbonniere** • 28 8th Ave [Jane St]
212-741-9266 • $
Best cheap breakfast in the city.

- **La Nacional** • 239 W 14th St [8th Ave]
917-388-2888 • $$$
Hidden Spanish social club serving traditional tapas.
- **La Sirene** • 558 Broome St [Varick St]
212-925-3061 • $$$
Gourmet French that's BYOB? We're in heaven.
- **Le Gigot** • 18 Cornelia St [Bleecker St]
212-627-3737 • $$$$
Classic cuisine Française, complete with Parisian price tag.
- **Little Owl** • 90 Bedford St [Barrow St]
212-741-4695 • $$$$
Fun, intimate bistro.
- **Malatesta Trattoria** •
649 Washington St [Christopher St]
212-741-1207 • $$
Authentic Italiano in cozy surroundings—e delizioso gnocchi!
- **Mah Ze Dahr** • 28 Greenwich Ave [Charles St]
212-498-9810
Deluxe baked goods with a neighborhood vibe.
- **Mary's Fish Camp** • 64 Charles St [W 4th St]
646-486-2185 • $$$
Amy Sedaris used to wait tables here for fun. Killer food!
- **Mighty Quinn's** • 75 Greenwich Ave [11th St]
646-524-7889 • $$$
Highly regarded "Texalina" hybrid barbecue mini-chain.
- **Moustache** • 90 Bedford St [Grove St]
212-229-2220 • $$
Excellent sit-down falafel.
- **Numero 28** • 28 Carmine St [Bleecker St]
212-463-9653 • $$
Finally, real Napoli pizza for reasonable prices.
- **Old Homestead Steakhouse** •
56 9th Ave [W 14th St]
212-242-9040 • $$$$$
Said to be NY's oldest steakhouse, circa 1868.

Map 5

- **One If By Land, TIBS** • 17 Barrow St [Bleecker St]
212-255-8649 • $$$$$
Exudes romance.
- **Palma** • 28 Cornelia St [W 4th St]
212-691-2223 • $$
Italian restaurant with cooks who have Italian accents.
- **Perry Street** • 176 Perry St [Washington St]
212-352-1900 • $$$$$
Satisfyingly simplified New French from Jean-Georges Vongerichten.
- **Piccolo Angolo** • 621 Hudson St [Jane St]
212-229-9177 • $$
The lobster cannelloni is famous. The service is colorful.
- **Pinto** • 117 W 10th St
212-366-5455 • $$
Fun, fusion-y Thai; good takeout option.
- **RedFarm** • 529 Hudson St [Charles St]
212-792-9700 • $$$
Farm-fresh dim sum. Home of the Pac Man dumpling.

- **Rosemary's** • 18 Greenwich Ave [W 10th St]
212-647-1818 • $$$
Greenmarket Italian from a garden (with chickens!) on the roof.
- **Sanpanino** • 494 Hudson St [Christopher St]
212-645-7228 • $
Mouthwatering Italian sandwiches. We love #14.
- **Slowly Shirley** • 121 W 10th St [Greenwich Ave]
212-243-2827
Subterranean mixological excellence from NYC cocktail veterans.
- **Snack Taverna** • 63 Bedford St [Morton St]
212-929-3499 • $$$
Greek for hipsters. More upscale than its sister restaurant on Thompson.
- **Taim** • 222 Waverly Pl [Perry St]
212-691-1287 • $$
Gourmet falafel with mind-blowing housemade sauces.
- **Tartine** • 253 W 11th St [W 4th St]
212-229-2611 • $$$
BYOB + Solid French = NFT pick.

Map 5
8 9 10
5 6 7
2 3 4
1
West Village

• **Tea & Sympathy** •
108 Greenwich Ave [W 13th St]
212-989-9735 • $$$
Eccentric English. Cult favorite.
• **Two Boots** • 101 7th Ave
646-863-2668 • $
Cajun pizza.
• **Via Carota** • 51 Grove St [7th Ave S]
212-255-1962 • $$$$
All-day Tuscan cuisine, done to perfection.
• **Wallsé** • 344 W 11th St [Washington St]
212-352-2300 • $$$$
Top-notch Austrian cuisine keeps the West
Villagers coming back.
• **Waverly Diner** •
385 Ave of the Americas [Waverly Pl]
212-675-3181 • $$
Great old-school diner with classy waiters.
• **The Waverly Inn** • 16 Bank St [Waverly Pl]
917-828-1154 • $$$$
Hip, café-cum-speakeasy. Good luck getting in.

🛍 Shopping

• **Alexander McQueen** •
747 Madison Ave [E 65th St]
212-645-1797
Brit bad boy designs.
• **C.O. Bigelow Chemists** • 414 6th Ave [W 9th St]
212-533-2700
Classic village pharmacy. Do try and patronize it.
• **Casa Magazines** • 22 8th Ave [W 12th St]
212-645-1197
Seemingly every magazine ever, among the last
of its kind.
• **Citarella** • 424 6th Ave [W 9th St]
212-874-0383
Wealthy foodies love this place.
• **The End of History** • 548 Hudson St [Perry St]
212-647-7598
Very cool shop specializing in antique glass.
• **Faicco's Italian Specialties** •
260 Bleecker St [Cornelia St]
212-243-1974
Proscuitto bread, homemade sausage, huge
heros, pork heaven.

West Village

Foodies, hit **Murray's Cheese**, **Myers of Keswick**, **Ottomanelli & Sons**, **Citarella**, **Faiccos**, and **Murray's Bagels**. Sip java at **Joe The Art of Coffee**, browse for books at **Three Lives & Company**, or go ahead and blow your bonus at **Té Company**, **Alexander McQueen**, and **Stella McCartney**.

- **Health & Harmony** • 470 Hudson St [Barrow St]
212-691-3036
Small health food store with good selection and decent prices.
- **The Leather Man** •
111 Christopher St [Bedford St]
212-243-5339
No, you won't look like James Dean. But it'll help.
- **Murray's Bagels** • 500 6th Ave [W 13th St]
212-462-2830
Classic New York–style bagels.
- **Murray's Cheese** • 254 Bleecker St [Leroy St]
212-243-3289
We love cheese, and so does Murray's.
- **Music Inn** • 169 W 4th St [Jones St]
212-243-5715
Bursting with beautiful drums & stringed world instruments, they do repairs.
- **Myers of Keswick** • 634 Hudson St [Horatio St]
212-691-4194
Killer English sausages, pasties, etc. And "Bounty!"

- **O. Ottomanelli & Sons** •
285 Bleecker St [Jones St]
212-675-4217
High quality meats and the friendliest butchers in town.
- **Stella McCartney** • 112 Greene St [Prince St]
212-255-1556
Hip, animal-friendly fashion.
- **Suprema Provisions** • 305 Bleecker St
[7th Ave S] 646-964-4994
Super-shmancy gourmet Italian food market and wine bar/small plate powerhouse.
- **Té Company** • 163 W 10th St [7th Ave S]
929-335-3168
High-end tea store.
- **Three Lives & Company** •
238 W 10th St [Waverly Pl]
212-741-2069
Classic Village bookshop. Thank God.
- **Waterfront Bike Shop** •
391 West St [Christopher St]
212-414-2453
Sales, service, repairs, and rentals.

Map 6 • **Washington Sq / NYU / NoHo / SoHo**

Neighborhood Overview

Map 6

8 9 10
5 6 7
2 3 4
1

Simply put, this is still the center of the universe. It all radiates from the corner of Broadway and Houston, which serves as the intersection for four of New York City's most exciting neighborhoods: Greenwich Village, Soho, NoHo, and NoLITa. While the area is far from bucolic—green space is limited to a few patches of grass in **Washington Square Park**—it has everything one could possibly want in terms of culture. Architecture, art galleries, movie theaters, live music, shopping, restaurants, old New York, new New York, and every other kind of New York are all here for the taking. If you're new to the city and ready to dive in and explore, start here.

One of this area's highlights is the sheer number of buildings from every period of New York City's development. Just walk the streets and you'll traverse over two hundred years of architectural history. Start with the somewhat-hidden former stables at **Washington Mews** for a taste of 18th-century New York. Other ancient (for New York) buildings include **St. Marks Church in-the-Bowery** (1799), **Colonnade Row** (1830s), the **Old Merchant's House** (1832), **Grace Church** (1846) and the **Cooper Union Building** (1859). The stunning white terra cotta exterior of Louis Sullivan's **Bayard-Condict Building** (1899), and Ernest Flagg's **Great Jones Fire House** (1899) and **Little Singer Building** (1904) hearken back to New York at the turn of the 20th century. In the early 20th century Daniel Burnham (**Wanamaker's**, 1904/1907) and Henry J Hardenbergh (**376 Lafayette St**, 1888, and the **Con Edison Building**, 1914) added their contributions to the area. Our ultimate favorite is the little-known **DeVinne Press Building** (1885) by Babb, Cook & Willard (and not just because **Astor Wines** is there). Starting in the 21st century, modern (or should we say postmodern?) architecture has run rampant along the Bowery, transforming the once derelict district. Notable examples include Thom Mayne's **Cooper Union New Academic Building** (2009), Kazuyo Sejima and Ryue Nishizawa's brilliant **New Museum of Contemporary Art** (2007), and Herzog & de Mauron's bizarre **40 Bond** (2007).

Unlike these buildings, some historical places of interest seem hidden in plain sight. Our favorite of these is the lovely **New York City Marble Cemetery**, tucked away on Second Street between The Bowery and Second Avenue. NYU's **Brown (formerly Asch) Building** was the site of the horrific Triangle Shirtwaist Fire, while **18 West 11th Street** was the site of the Weathermen explosion. A plaque at the **Mark Twain House** on West 4th Street commemorates his time as a Greenwich Villager. And, while you can't rock out at **CBGB** anymore, you can still visit the site (now a John Varvatos store), right around the corner from where Joey Ramone lived on East 2nd Street, also known as **Joey Ramone Place**.

Just as there's no shortage of history, the cultural options here can make your head spin. A few of our favorites include the **Salmagundi Club** for art, the Astor Center for food and cooking events, and **Anthology Film Archives** for experimental film. The **Bowery Ballroom** is one of the best venues in NYC to catch up-and-coming musical acts. Browsing **The Strand**'s 18 miles of books is a must.

For all the history and culture here, signs of the area's down-and-out heyday in the 1970s and 1980s are few and far between. **Milano's** still serves up divey goodness, as it's been doing since the 1800s. Skate punks still hang out at **The Alamo** (give it a spin), even though fancy glass towers rise around it. You can still get your punk rock and goth gear at **Trash & Vaudeville**. Much of the rest of St. Mark's Place between Second and Third Avenues now resembles a cross between a strip mall and Little Tokyo, which stretches along 9th Street as well. If you're ready for a break from all this excitement, grab some ramen, then explore the sake list at **Decibel** while feeling like you've left the Village far behind.

Map 6

8 9 10
5 6 7
2 3 4
1

Washington Sq / NYU / NoHo / SoHo

○ Landmarks

- **376 Lafayette St** •
376 Lafayette St [Great Jones St]
Henry Hardenbergh's NoHo masterpiece, circa 1888.
- **40 Bond** • 40 Bond St [Bowery]
Uber-futuristic condo projects by Herzog & de Meuron et al.
- **The Alamo (The Cube)** • 4th Ave & Astor Pl
Give it a spin sometime.
- **Bayard-Condict Building** •
65 Bleecker St [Crosby St]
Louis Sullivan's only New York building.
- **Brown Building of Science** •
23-29 Washington Pl [Greene St]
Site of the Triangle Shirtwaist Fire.
- **Colonnade Row** • 428 Lafayette St [Astor Pl]
Remains of a very different era.
- **Con Edison Building** • 145 E 14th St [Irving Pl]
Cool top.
- **Cooper Union** • 30 Cooper Sq [Bowery]
212-353-4100
Great brownstone-covered building.
- **Cooper Union New Academic Building** •
41 Cooper Sq [E 6th St]
Supercool, futuristic, and eco-friendly architecture.
- **DeVinne Press Building** •
399 Lafayette St [E 4th St]
Killer 1885 brick-and-glass masterpiece by Babb, Cook & Willard.
- **Former location of CBGB & OMFUG** •
315 Bowery [Bleecker St]
Now houses high-end retail. Ew.
- **Great Jones Firehouse** •
Bowery & Great Jones St
The coolest firehouse in NYC.
- **Joey Ramone Place** • Bowery & E 2nd St
It's Joey Ramone's place. Period.
- **Little Singer Building** •
561 Broadway [Prince St]
A fine building by Ernest Flagg.
- **Mark Twain House** • 14 W 10th St [5th Ave]
Mark Twain lived here. It's also NYC's most haunted portal.
- **The Merchant's House Museum** •
29 E 4th St [Lafayette St]
212-777-1089
The merchant is now dead.

- **New Museum** • 235 Bowery [Prince St]
212-219-1222
Brilliant white stacked cubes houses contemporary art and killer bookstore. Yah.
- **The New School** • 66 W 12th St [5th Ave]
212-229-5600
Legendary progressive university located in and around Greenwich Village.
- **New York City Marble Cemetery** •
41½ 2nd Ave
917-780-2893
Cool, but generally closed. But you can still see in.
- **New York University** •
70 Washington Sq S [LaGuardia Pl]
212-998-1212
One of the city's largest private employers.
- **Salmagundi Club** • 47 5th Ave [E 12th St]
212-255-7740
Cool building.
- **Site of the Weathermen Explosion** •
18 W 11th St [5th Ave]
Townhouse where the Weathermen's plans to destroy Columbia's library went awry.
- **St. Mark's Church In The Bowery** •
131 E 10th St [3rd Ave]
212-674-6377
Old church with lots of community ties.
- **Union Square Clock/Metronome** •
52 E 14th St [Broadway]
Get lost in time while looking South in Union Square.
- **University Settlement** •
184 Eldridge St [Rivington St]
212-674-9120
Providing a haven for lower east siders of all ages since 1886.
- **Wanamaker's** • E 8th St & Broadway
Former classiest department store in the city is now a Wegman's grocery store.
- **Washington Mews** •
University Pl (entrance) [5th Ave]
Where horses and servants used to live. Now coveted NYU space.
- **Washington Square Park** •
W 4th St & Washington Square W
From Potter's field to counterculture mecca and everything in between.

For better or worse, this area is why New York is called the city that never sleeps. For dives, we like **Scratcher**, **Milano's**, and **Blue & Gold**. For cocktails, check out **Mayamezcal**. Catch a reading at **KGB**, an indie film at **Angelika Film Center**, or live music at **Joe's Pub** or **Le Poisson Rouge** or **Bowery Ballroom**. We guarantee you won't be bored.

Map 6

Coffee

- **Café Gitane** • 242 Mott St [Prince St]
  646-870-0087
  Worth the wait. Delicious food, beautiful people.
- **Caffe Reggio** • 119 MacDougal St [W 3rd St]
  212-475-9557
  A New York classic. Check out the custom coffee cups.
- **Coffee Project New York** •
  239 E 5th St [2nd Ave]
  212-228-7888
  Home of the deconstructed latte.
- **Ground Support Cafe** •
  399 W Broadway [Spring St]
  212-219-8722
  Serving up the almighty coffee from Intelligentsia.
- **Joe The Art of Coffee** • 9 E 13th St [5th Ave]
  212-924-3300
  Joe really knows his joe. Collegiate coffee house. NYU hangout.
- **Hi Collar** • 231 E 9th St
  212-777-7018
  Japanese coffee shop by day/sake bar by night.

- **La Colombe Torrefaction** •
  400 Lafayette St [E 4th St]
  212-677-5834
  Philly's Stumptown expands toward the East Village.
- **La Colombe Torrefaction** •
  270 Lafayette St [Prince St]
  212-625-1717
  Philly's Stumptown.
- **Mudspot** • 307 E 9th St [2nd Ave]
  212-228-9074
  The Mudtruck's stationary shop.
- **Porto Rico Importing Co.** •
  40 St Marks Pl [2nd Ave]
  212-533-1982
  Beans by the barrel full.
- **Think Coffee** • 248 Mercer St [W 3rd St]
  212-228-6226
- **Third Rail Coffee** • 240 Sullivan St
  646-580-1240
  Quality coffee and baked goods.

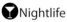
Nightlife

• **8th Street Wine Cellar** •
28 W 8th St [MacDougal St]
212-260-9463
Classy and calm. Luckily NYU kids don't drink wine.
• **Amelie Wine Bar** • 22 W 8th St [Macdougal St]
212-533-2962
French wine bar with delish foie gras, escargot, etc. Bon ap'!
• **Amsterdam Billiards Club** •
110 E 11th St [4th Ave]
212-995-0333
Expensive and more posh than most pool halls.
• **Attaboy** • 134 Eldridge St [Delancey St]
Milk & Honey torchbearers carry on mixological tradition.
• **Bar Goto** • 245 Eldridge St [Houston St]
Crafted cocktails and Japanese bar comfort food.
• **Bar Next Door** • 129 MacDougal St [W 3rd St]
917-639-3236
For serious jazz enthusiasts with a penchant for wine and crispy pizza.
• **Bar Veloce** • 175 2nd Ave [E 11th St]
646-684-3174
Sip grappa on a first date. Also in Chelsea.
• **Beauty Bar** • 231 E 14th St [3rd Ave]
212-539-1389
Just a little off the top, dahling?
• **Blue & Gold Tavern** • 79 E 7th St [1st Ave]
212-777-1006
Another fine East Village dive.

• **Blue Note** • 131 W 3rd St [MacDougal St]
212-475-8592
Classic jazz venue. Pricey.
• **Boiler Room** • 86 E 4th St [2nd Ave]
212-529-2100
Longtime comfortable, welcoming, no-nonsense gay dive.
• **Botanica Bar** • 47 E Houston St [Mulberry St]
212-343-7251
Good bar, but we still miss the Knitting Factory.
• **Bowery Ballroom** • 6 Delancey St [Bowery]
212-260-4700
Great space that attracts great bands.
• **The Box** • 189 Chrystie St [Rivington St]
212-982-9301
Burlesque and bottle service for the filthy rich.
• **Burp Castle** • 41 E 7th St [2nd Ave]
212-982-4576
Belgian ales and hushed voices.
• **Carroll Place** • 157 Bleecker St [Thompson St]
212-260-1700
Multi-level brunch, dinner, wine bar, live music destination.
• **The Cock** • 93 2nd Ave [5th Ave]
In spot formerly known as The Hole; so there's that.
• **Comedy Cellar** •
117 MacDougal St [Minetta Ln]
212-254-3480
Big names make surprise appearances.
• **Corkbuzz** • 13 E 13th St [5th Ave]
646-873-6071
Outstanding wine selection in a classy setting.
• **Fanelli's Cafe** • 94 Prince St [Mercer St]
212-226-9412
Old-time SoHo haunt. Nice tiles.
• **The Fat Black Pussycat** •
130 W 3rd St [MacDougal St]
212-533-4790
Average rock venue.

Washington Sq / NYU / NoHo / SoHo

Map 6

McSorley's Old Ale House has been in operation 1854, and has a great old-school barroom atmosphere; weekend nights are insane. For a great beer selection, seek out Peculier Pub in Greenwich Village or if you're on the other side of Broadway Burp Castle, which is great for Belgian beer and quiet conversation.

- **Home Sweet Home** •
  131 Chrystie St [Broome St]
  646-389-4544
  Non-descript taxidermy hang out.
- **The Immigrant** • 341 E 9th St [1st Ave]
  646-308-1724
  Wine and snacks in a sexy tenement.
- **Jadis Wine Bar** • 42 Rivington St [Eldridge St]
  212-254-1675
  Perfect date spot for poor NFT employees.
- **Joe's Pub** • 425 Lafayette St [Astor Pl]
  212-967-7555
  Excellent range of acts in intimate space.
- **KGB Bar** • 85 E 4th St [2nd Ave]
  347-441-4481
  Former CP HQ. Meet your comrades. Readings, too.
- **Le Poisson Rouge** •
  158 Bleecker St [Sullivan St]
  212-505-3474
  Seductive and strangely fun eclectic live music.
- **Lobby Bar** • 335 Bowery [E 2nd St]
  212-505-9100
  Great spot for a night cap.
- **Loreley Beer Garden** • 7 Rivington St [Bowery]
  212-253-7077
  Tons of beer, individual pitchers optional.
- **Marshall Stack** • 66 Rivington St [Allen St]
  212-228-4667
  Winner for best bar that seemed like it would be awful.
- **Mayamezcal** • 304 E 6th St [2nd Ave]
  212-253-5888
  Tequila and mezcal den with awesome old Mexico decor.
- **McSorley's Old Ale House** •
  15 E 7th St [3rd Ave]
  212-473-9148
  Lights or darks?
- **Milano's** • 51 E Houston St [Mott St]
  212-226-8844
  Grungy, narrow, awesome, narrow, grungy.
- **Mother Ruin** • 18 Spring St [Elizabeth St]
  212-219-0942
  Handcrafted cocktails and small plates.
- **Peasant** • 194 Elizabeth St [Spring St]
  212-965-9511
  For ambience, head down to the dark cave o' wine.
- **Peculier Pub** • 145 Bleecker St [LaGuardia Pl]
  212-353-1327
  Large beer selection. NYU hangout.
- **Proletariat** • 21 E 7th St [3rd Ave]
  833-328-4588
  Beer library/deep dive into the brewing arts.
- **Reservoir** • 70 University Pl [E 10th St]
  212-475-0770
  Surprisingly good food, lots of sports.
- **Rockwood Music Hall** •
  196 Allen St [E Houston St]
  212-477-4155
  Live music nightly.
- **Sake Bar Decibel** • 240 E 9th St [2nd Ave]
  212-979-2733
  Hip, underground sake bar.

- **Scratcher** • 209 E 5th St [Bowery]
212-477-0030
Low-key port for you and your Guinness.
- **Sly Fox** • 140 2nd Ave [St Marks Pl]
212 – 614-3283
Bring your own space heater.
- **Spring Street Lounge** •
48 Spring St [Mulberry St]
All-ESPN-watchin' post-college moochers.
- **Standings** • 43 E 7th St [2nd Ave]
212-420-0671
Hardest working (and smallest) sports bar in New York.
- **Sweet & Vicious** • 5 Spring St [Bowery]
212-334-7915
Great outdoor space.
- **Swift Hibernian Lounge** •
34 E 4th St [Bowery]
212-260-3600
Irish bar that tries harder than most.
- **Terra Blues** • 149 Bleecker St [Thompson St]
212-777-7776
Live blues. If you're into that.
- **Tom & Jerry's** • 288 Elizabeth St [E Houston St]
646-869-0345
Low key and friendly place for a drink.
- **The Uncommons** •
230 Thompson St [W 3rd St]
646-543-9215
Board game cafe in former Village Chess spot.
- **Von** • 3 Bleecker St [Bowery]
212-473-3039
Great vibe. Great bar.
- **Webster Hall** • 125 E 11th St [4th Ave]
Feel the music through the floor.

🍴 Restaurants

- **12 Chairs** • 56 MacDougal St [King St]
212-254-8640 • $
Rough around the edges. Fantabulous blintzes and pierogies.
- **ACME** • 9 Great Jones St [Lafayette St]
212-203-2121 • $$$$
Nordic hotspot for the chic and loaded.
- **Alidoro** • 105 Sullivan St [Prince St]
212-334-5179 • $$
High-end Italian sandwiches.
- **Alta** • 64 W 10th St [Ave of the Americas]
212-505-7777 • $$$
Unique tapas. Good date place.
- **Amelie Wine Bar** • 22 W 8th St [Macdougal St]
212-533-2962 • $$$
French wine bar with delish foie gras, escargot, etc. Bon ap'!
- **Misirizzi** • 36 E 4th St [Bowery]
212-375-0100 • $$$$
Quaint, lovely Italian place with excellent service.
- **Artichoke Basille's Pizza** •
321 E 14th St [2nd Ave]
212-228-2004 • $$
Stand in line for amazing Sicilian slices.
- **Artichoke Basille's Pizza** •
111 MacDougal St [Minetta Ln]
646-278-6100 • $$
Gut-busting artichoke slices.
- **Arturo's** • 106 W Houston St [Thompson St]
212-677-3820 • $$
Classic NYC pizza joint with live jazz. NFT favorite.
- **Aurora Soho** • 510 Broome St [Watts St]
212-334-9020 • $$$
Hip Williamsburg Italian opens on the big island.
- **Awash** • 338 E 6th St [2nd Ave]
212-982-9589 • $$
Ethiopian. It's ok to eat with your hands.
- **B&H Dairy** • 127 2nd Ave [St Mark's Pl]
212-505-8065 • $
Eat mushroom barley soup and homemade challah at the counter.

It's probably unfair for one neighborhood to claim all the glory, but this one's tops for restaurants too, from wallet-busting upscale (**Babbo** and **Strip House**), to awesome street carts (**NY Dosas** in Washington Square Park). We like **Frank** for Italian. Out late? **Veselka** and **Blue Ribbon** have your back.

- **Babbo** • 110 Waverly Pl [MacDougal St]
  212-777-0303 • $$$$
  Super Mario: Go for the pasta tasting menu.
- **Balthazar** • 80 Spring St [Crosby St]
  212-965-1414 • $$$$$
  Simultaneously pretentious and amazing.
- **Bar Primi** • 325 Bowery [E 2nd St]
  212-220-9100 • $$$$
  Pasta-forward Italian with daily specials.
- **Ben's Pizza** • 123 MacDougal St [W 3rd St]
  212-677-0976 • $
  Top NYC slices; unusual cheese taste.
- **Blue Hill** • 75 Washington Pl [MacDougal St]
  212-539-1776 • $$$$$
  Wonderful food in an unexpected location.
- **Blue Ribbon Brasserie** •
  97 Sullivan St [Spring St]
  212-274-0404 • $$$$$
  Open 'til 4am. Everything's great.
- **Blue Ribbon Sushi** • 119 Sullivan St [Prince St]
  212-343-0404 • $$$$$
  Great sushi.
- **Bowery Meat Company** • 9 E 1st St [Bowery]
  212-460-5255 • $$$$
  Young creative steakhouse treatment, meat ecumenical.
- **Café Gitane** • 242 Mott St [Prince St]
  646-870-0087 • $$
  Can be busy, but worth the wait. Delicious food, beautiful people.

- **Café Habana** • 17 Prince St [Elizabeth St]
  212-625-2001 • $$
  Grilled corn + beautiful staff = amazing Cuban joint.
- **Calexico Carne Asada** • Prince St & Wooster St
  $
  Taco truck run by hipsters. Tasty!
- **Carroll Place** • 157 Bleecker St [Thompson St]
  212-260-1700 • $$$
  Brunch. And wood-fired rosemary wings. And brunch. Again.
- **Cha-An Japanese Tea House** •
  230 E 9th St [Stuyvesant St]
  212-228-8030 • $$
  Japanese tea ceremonies Fridays and Sundays. Must reserve.
- **ChikaLicious** • 203 E 10th St [2nd Ave]
  212-995-9511 • $$
  Dessert for dinner? We vote yes.
- **Claudette** • 24 5th Ave [9th St]
  212-868-2424 • $$$$
  Seasonal Provençal comfort cuisine.
- **Cocoron** • 16 Delancey St
  212-477-1212 • $$$
  Soba for you, me, and the jerk talking on his cell phone.
- **Cocoron Market** • 61 Delancey St
  212-925-5220 • $$$
  Cocoron's inventive soup-curry hybrid sister restaurant.
- **Cones** • 272 Bleecker St [Morton St]
  212-414-1795 • $
  Putting butterfat to use in flavors you never imagined.

Map 6

8 9 10
5 **6** 7
2 3 4
1

Washington Sq / NYU / NoHo / SoHo

- **Cozy Soup 'n' Burger** •
  739 Broadway [Astor Pl]
  212-477-5566 • $
  Big cheap greasy burgers; i.e., Heaven.
- **Cuba** • 222 Thompson St [W 3rd St]
  212-420-7878 • $$
  Authentic Cuban, bar, live music, etc.
- **Dos Toros Taqueria** • 137 4th Ave [E 13th St]
  212-677-7300 • $
  Solid Mission-style burritos.
- **Downtown Bakery** • 69 1st Ave [E 4th St]
  212-254-1757 • $
  Authentic hole-in-the-wall Mexican. Awesome
  breakfast sandwiches.
- **Duane Park** • 308 Bowery [Hudson St]
  212-732-5555 • $$$$$
  Underrated New American.
- **Epistrophy** • 200 Mott St [Spring St]
  212-966-0904 • $$
  Genuine Italian coffee spot with light dishes
  and heavenly pasta.
- **Estela** • 47 E Houston St [Mulberry St]
  212-219-7693 • $$$
  Shareable diverting/diverse dishes and great
  wine program.
- **Famous Ben's Pizza** •
  177 Spring St [Thompson St]
  212-966-4494 • $
  Good slice pizza.
- **Frank** • 88 2nd Ave [E 5th St]
  212-420-0202 • $$
  Good food, great breakfast.
- **Freemans** • Freeman Alley [Rivington St]
  212-420-0012 • $$$
  Taxidermy-filled hideaway with fab cocktails
  and delicious, rustic fare.

- **Gotham Bar & Grill** • 12 E 12th St [5th Ave]
  212-380-8660 • $$$$$
  Excellent New American—one of the best.
- **Il Buco** • 47 Bond St [Bowery]
  212-533-1932 • $$$$$
  Lovely Italian food. Great wines by the glass.
  Uber-hip scene.
- **Il Mulino** • 86 W 3rd St [Thompson St]
  212-673-3783 • $$$$
  Fine Italian dining at fine Italian dining prices.
- **Indochine** • 430 Lafayette St [Astor Pl]
  212-505-5111 • $$$
  You can do better.
- **Jane** • 100 W Houston St [Thompson St]
  212-254-7000 • $$$$
  Good all-around; perfect location for pre-post
  Angelica movie.
- **Japonica** • 90 University Pl [E 12th St]
  212-243-7752 • $$$
  Madonna went here once.
- **John's of 12th Street** • 302 E 12th St [2nd Ave]
  212-475-9531 • $$
  Classic Italian. Get the rollatini.

Map 6

There is no shortage of top-notch pizza around these parts. **Lombardi's** was the first pizzeria in the US, and still puts its coal oven to good use. For great pizza along with live jazz, check out **Arturo's** on Houston Street. And you can get great slices at **Artichoke Basille's Pizza**.

- **Kenka** • 25 St Marks Pl [2nd Ave]
  212-254-6363 • $
  Step into rural Japan for a dirt cheap feast of traditional grub. Don't expect sushi.
- **La Esquina** • 114 Kenmare St [Cleveland Pl]
  646-613-7100 • $
  Taqueria trifecta: taco stand, corner cantina, and secret subterranean abode.
- **Little Poland** • 200 2nd Ave [E 12th St]
  212-777-9728 • $$
  Best breakfast special in the city.
- **Lombardi's** • 32 Spring St [Mott St]
  212-941-7994 • $$$
  Said to be the first pizzeria in the US, circa 1905.
- **Love Mama** • 174 2nd Ave [11th St]
  212-254-5370 • $$$
  Viet-Thai-Malay mashup goodness.
- **Lucien** • 14 E 1st Ave
  212-260-6481 • $$$
  Solid brasserie, small and cozy.
- **Maman** • 211 West Broadway [Franklin St]
  646-882-8682 • $$$
  High-end all-day café channeling the South of France.
- **Manousheh** • 193 Bleecker St [Macdougal St]
  347-971-5778 • $
  Lebanese-style flatbreads for the win.
- **Max Brenner Chocolate by the Bald Man** •
  841 Broadway [E 13th St]
  646-467-8803 • $$
  For tourists who like chocolate for dinner.

- **Mighty Quinn's** • 103 2nd Ave [E 7th St]
  212-677-3733 • $$
  Wood smoked meats with a Texas and Carolina twang.
- **Momofuku Noodle Bar** •
  171 1st Ave [E 10th St]
  212-777-7773 • $$$$
  The launchpad of a culinary empire.
- **Motorino** • 349 E 12th St [1st Ave]
  212-777-2644 •
  Excellent pies via Napoli via Brooklyn.
- **Nomad** • 78 2nd Ave [E 4th St]
  212-253-5410 • $$
  Funky North African food and funkier atmoshere.
- **NY Dosas** • Washington Sq S at Thompson St
  917-710-2092 • $
  Cheap and yummy Indian lunch cart.
- **Olive's** • 191 Prince St [Wooster St]
  212-941-0111 • $
  Killer soups/sandwiches. A top take-out option.

- **Parm** • 248 Mulberry St [Prince St]
  212-993-7189 • $$
  Chicken, eggplant, and meatball hero heaven
  is only an hour wait away.
- **Paul's Da Burger Joint** •
  131 2nd Ave [St Marks Pl]
  212-529-3033 • $
  Burger heaven.
- **Pasquale Jones** • 187 Mulberry St
  917-453-0339 • $$$
  Pizza-pasta-farm-to-table haute comfort
  cuisine.
- **Pepe Rosso** • 168 Sullivan St [W Houston St]
  212-677-4555 • $
  Italy on a budget. Fast.
- **Rai Rai Ken** • 218 E 10th St [2nd Ave]
  212-995-2877 • $
  Tiny and tasty ramen shop.
- **Raoul's** • 180 Prince St [Sullivan St]
  212-966-3518 • $$$$
  A Soho institution. You may like the steak frites
  more than your date.
- **Red Bamboo Soul Café** •
  140 W 4th St [Ave of the Americas]
  212-260-1212 • $$
  Vegetarian soul food. Killer lunch special.
- **Rice to Riches** • 37 Spring St [Mott St]
  212-274-0008 • $$
  24 kinds of rice pudding in a bright fishbowl.

- **Ruby's** • 219 Mulberry St [Spring St]
  212-925-5755 • $$
  Down under delights for the downtown scene.
- **S'mac** • 197 1st Ave
  212-358-7912 • $$
  Classic comfort cuisine achieves more cheesy
  goodness.
- **Sadelle's** • 463 West Broadway [Houston St]
  212-254-3000 • $$$$
  Jewish deli by day/fancy candlelit Eastern
  European by night.
- **Saigon Shack** •
  114 MacDougal St [Bleecker St]
  212-228-0588 • $$
  Modern Vietnamese on a NYU-friendly budget.
- **Senza Gluten** • 206 Sullivan St [Bleecker St]
  212-475-7775 • $$$
  Elegantly crafted gluten-free Italian (!).
- **Shuko** • 47 E 12th St [Broadway]
  212-228-6088 • $$$$$
  Stylish, scrumptious, 'spensive sushi tasting
  menus.

This 'hood is definitely over-represented when it comes to general buzz. **Sadelle's** is an all-day joint elevating traditional deli food, and Veselka will have you dreaming of pierogies and borscht for weeks.

- **Soba-ya** • 229 E 9th St [3rd Ave]
  212-533-6966 • $$$
  Japanese noodle perfection to the highest level.
- **Spice Thai** • 39 E 13th St [University Pl]
  212-982-3758 • $$
  Trendy Thai. Always packed.
- **Strip House** • 13 E 12th St [5th Ave]
  212-328-0000 • $$$$$
  Super downtown steakhouse. NFT favorite.
- **Taj Restaurant** • 310 E 6th St [2nd Ave]
  212-505-8056 • $$
  Rich sauces, fresh naan, and live music half underground.
- **Ukrainian East Village Restaurant** •
  140 2nd Ave [E 9th St]
  212-614-3283 • $
  Pierogies, borscht, blintzes, goulash. Comfort food.
- **Upstate Craft Beer & Oyster Bar** • 95 1st Ave [6th St]
  646-791-5400 • $$$
  Curated fresh seafood, craft beer, and oysters.
- **Veselka** • 144 2nd Ave [E 9th St]
  212-228-9682 • $
  Pierogies absorb beer. At 4 am that's all you need to know.

- **Vic's** • 31 Great Jones St [Lafayette St]
  212-253-5700 • $$$$
  Italo-New American comfort food.
- **Yakitori Taisho** • 9 St Marks Pl [3rd Ave]
  212-673-1300 • $
  Skewered chicken and pan-fried noodles washed down with Asahi.

🛍 Shopping

- **Alabaster Bookshop** • 122 4th Ave [E 12th St]
  212-982-3550
  Quintessential overstuffed used book shop.
- **Apple Store (SoHo)** •
  103 Prince St [Greene St]
  212-226-3126
  Don't come looking for produce.
- **Astor Wines & Spirits** •
  399 Lafayette St [E 4th St]
  212-674-7500
  NFT fav. The king of all NYC liquor stores.
- **Balenciaga** • 148 Mercer St [Prince St]
  212-226-2052
  Gorgeous, super high-end clothes and accessories.
- **Bfold** • 224 E 13th St [3rd Ave]
  212-529-7247
  Folding bikes.
- **Bicycle Habitat** • 228 7th Ave
  212-206-6949
  Full-time mechanics and sales, too.
- **Black Seed** • 170 Elizabeth St [Spring St]
  332-900-3090
  For your Montreal bagel fix; let the debate begin.

- **Bonnie Slotnick Cookbooks** •
28 E 2nd St [2nd Ave]
212-989-8962
Specializing in cookbooks; great out-of-print finds.
- **Chess Forum** • 219 Thompson St [W 3rd St]
212-475-2369
Ornate, themed, and traditional chess sets, play 'til midnight.
- **Coclico** • 275 Mott St [E Houston St]
212-965-5462
Women's shoes made from eco-friendly leather and other materials.
- **Dashwood Books** • 33 Bond St [Lafayette Ave]
212-387-8520
Photography.
- **Dominique Ansel Bakery** •
189 Spring St [Sullivan St]
212-219-2773
Home of the Cronut.
- **Dual Specialty Store** • 91 1st Ave [E 6th St]
212-979-6045
Indian grocery store stocked with every spice imaginable.
- **Forbidden Planet** • 832 Broadway [E 13th St]
212-473-1576
Let your inner sci-fi/fantasy nerd run wild.
- **Global Table** • 107 Sullivan St [Spring St]
212-431-5839
Quietly elegant tableware.

- **John Derian** • 6 E 2nd St [Bowery]
212-677-3917
Whimsical découpage plates and curios for the home.
- **Kiehl's** • 109 3rd Ave [E 13th St]
212-677-3171
Great creams, lotions, and unguents; laughably good service.
- **Laduree Soho** • 398 West Broadway [Spring St] 646-392-7868
International macaron experts.
- **McNally Jackson** • 52 Prince St [Mulberry St]
212-274-1160
General Interest books.
- **MoMA Design Store** • 81 Spring St [Crosby St]
646-613-1367
Cutting-edge, minimalist, ergonomic, offbeat, and funky everything.

Sample lotions at **Kiehl's**, and browse for housewares at **John Derian**, designer shoes at **Coclico**, trendy threads at **Odin**, books at **The Strand**, old prints at **Pageant Print Shop**, and cool gifts at **MoMA Design Store**. The selections at **Astor Wines & Spirits** remind us why we live here.

- **NYC Velo** • 66 2nd Ave [E 4th St]
212-253-7771
This shop has a special place in our heart.
Good clothing!
- **Pageant Print Shop** • 69 E 4th St [2nd Ave]
212-674-5296
Just prints, really. But really great prints.
- **Pino's Prime Meats** •
149 Sullivan St [Prince St]
212-475-8134
Old-world Italian butcher. Pino's tips are priceless.
- **Prada** • 575 Broadway [Prince St]
212-334-8888
Rem Koolhaas-designed store that you can only afford to look at.
- **Raffetto's** • 144 W Houston St [MacDougal St]
212-777-1261
Take-home Italian foods. Ravioli like mamma used to make.
- **REI** • 303 Lafayette St [E Houston St]
212-680-1938
Outdoor gear superstore in the Puck Building.
- **Stereo Exchange** •
857 Broadway [Bleecker St]
212-505-1111
Just-under-obscenely-priced audiophile equipment. Good for male depression.
- **Strand Book Store** • 828 Broadway [E 12th St]
212-473-1452
Used mecca; world's messiest and best bookstore.
- **Sullivan Street Tea & Spice Company** •
208 Sullivan St [Bleecker St]
212-387-8702
Worldly herbs, spices, salts, and teas.
- **Sunrise Mart** • 494 Broome St [W Broadway]
212-219-0033
Japanese specialties and an affordable lunch counter in back.

- **Tokio 7** • 83 E 7th St [1st Ave]
212-353-8443
Designer consignment. Great for lucky finds.
- **Trader Joe's** • 142 E 14th St [Irving Pl]
212-529-4612
Legendary bargain food chain with legendary long lines.
- **Uniqlo** • 546 Broadway [Spring St]
877-486-4756
Cashmere, cashmere, and more cashmere—in every color!
- **Warby Parker** •
121 Greene St [Prince St]
646-568-3720
Where everyone shops for their $95 retro eyeglasses.
- **Whole Foods** • 4 Union Sq E [University Pl]
212-673-5388
Always natural. Always crowded. Tons of NYU kids.
- **Whole Foods** • 95 E Houston St [2nd Ave]
212-420-1320
Beautiful produce for beautiful people.
Surprisingly uncrowded.

Map 7 · East Village

1 **2**

JOHN MURPHY PARK

Stuyvesant Town

E 16th St

E 15th St

East River

10

1st Avenue

E 14th St

A

444

L

E 13th St

Avenue A

E 12th St

Russian and Turkish Baths

E 11th St

Avenue B

E 10th St

General Slocum Monument

Charlie Parker House

E 9th St

Avenue C

Szold Pl

Jacob Riis Houses

Ped Bridge

First Ave

Tompkins Square Park

Avenue D

E 8th St

PAGE 256

St Marks Pl

St Brigid Roman Catholic Church

E 7th St

Jacob Riis Houses

FDR Dr

East River Park

6

Pyramid Club

Joe Strummer Mural

E 6th St

6BC Botanical Garden

E 5th St

Ped Bridge

Village View Houses

E 4th St

Lillian Wald Houses

E 3rd St

Nuyorican Poet's Café

E 2nd St

E Houston St

4

E 1st St

Hamilton Fish Park

Baruch Houses

Second Ave

F

Stanton St

Essex St

Norfolk St

Suffolk St

Clinton St

Attorney St

Ridge St

Pitt St

Columbia St

Masaryk Towers

Mangin Pl

Rivington St

Samuel Gompers Houses

Chrystie St

Forsyth St

Eldridge St

Allen St

Orchard St

Delancey Street Essex Street

F **J Z M**

Delancey St

Williamsburg Bridge

Willet St

Lewis St

Broome St

| 1/4 mile | .25 km |

Neighborhood Overview

It's no longer the city's Bohemia—we hear that's somewhere in Philly. But if you're dead-set on staying in Manhattan, the East Village might be downtown's most livable neighborhood. Blame that on all the well-worn tenements and their (relatively) affordable small studios and "junior" one-bedrooms, some of them rent stabilized. In these apartments dwell old timers, NYU kids, and everyone in between, making for awesome people watching, day or night. A stroll through **Tompkins Square Park** on any warm weekend pretty much sums it up. Cute pooches and their oh-so-hip owners convene at the dog run while bongo drums echo over near Avenue B. Little kids shriek at the playground while crusty punks and gritty old men occupy the benches on the Southwestern side. Just a typical slice of life in the East Village, and a sweet life it is if you can swing the rent.

Before the crowds young professionals lived here, and before the artists, musicians, and squatters that preceded them, this area was home to waves of German, Irish, Italian, Jewish, Ukrainian, and Polish immigrants. A few historical sites remain from those times. One of our favorites is **Saint Brigid's Church** (1848), which was built by Irish immigrants. The church was saved from the developer's cudgel in just the nick of time, and restored thanks to a generous anonymous donor, the whole episode a miracle befitting the Roman Catholic church's namesake. Another holdout, **Russian and Turkish Baths** (1892) still offers old-world platza treatments. One more significant marker from the neighborhood's past is the **General Slocum Monument**, which commemorates the tragic sinking of the General Slocum steamship on the East River in 1904. The deadliest single disaster in the city's history until 9/11, over 1,000 lives were lost, mainly German women and children from a neighborhood church that chartered the boat for a day trip to Long Island.

In the 1960s, Puerto Rican immigrants flooded into Alphabet City, another name for the blocks between Avenue A and Avenue D. Avenue C, also known as Loisaida Avenue, retains some of this character today, even while bars and restaurants catering to more recent arrivals open shop. The loveliest aspects of this area are the many community gardens, planted on once-blighted lots and maintained by volunteers. We particularly like the always-tranquil **6BC Botanical Garden** on 6th Street between Avenue B and Avenue C. The best times to visit are Saturday and Sunday afternoons from May through October.

The term "East Village" came into use in the 1960s, when artists, musicians, writers, performers, intellectuals, and political radicals flocked to the neighborhood. A hugely influential art scene sprang up from the 1960s through the 1980s, but unfortunately, many of those galleries and performance spaces fell victim to skyrocketing rents in the 1990s and early 2000s. A few institutions have survived, though—you can still catch a poetry slam at the **Nuyorican Poet's Café**, or dance the night away like it's still 1984 at **The Pyramid Club**. One of our favorite summer events, the Charlie Parker Jazz Festival, takes place in **Tompkins Square Park**, right across the street from the **Charlie Parker House**. When you visit the park be sure to pass by the **Joe Strummer Mural**, a neighborhood landmark honoring one of the icons of punk rock. For live rock n' roll (or any kind of music scene), you're better off heading to the Lower East Side. But if you've come for the awesome bars, restaurants, and shopping that make this the neighborhood you'll never want to leave, read on.

61

Map 7

8 9 10
5 6 7
2 3 4
1

East Village

O Landmarks

- **6BC Botanical Garden** •
  624 E 6th St [Avenue C]
  Early Alphabet City community garden, now
  permanent park.
- **Charlie Parker Residence** •
  151 Avenue B [E 10th St]
  The Bird lived here. Great festival every
  summer in Tompkins Square.
- **General Slocum Monument** •
  Tompkins Sq Park [Avenue A]
  Memorial to one of the worst disasters in NYC
  history.
- **International Bar** • 102 1st Ave [E 7th St]
  212-777-1643
  RIP…but wait! It's back from the dead!
- **Joe Strummer Mural** •
  132 Avenue A [E 7th St]
  Ha, you think it's funny…turning rebellion into
  money?
- **Nuyorican Poets Café** •
  236 E 3rd St [Avenue C]
  212-780-9386
  Where mediocre poets die of humiliation.
- **Russian and Turkish Baths** •
  268 E 10th St [1st Ave]
  212-674-9250
  Sweat away all your urban stress.
- **St. Brigid Roman Catholic Church** •
  119 Avenue B [E 8th St]
  Historic Irish church spared demolition, still
  standing on Tompkins Square.
- **Tompkins Square Park** • E 10th St
  212-639-9675
  Home to many.

Coffee

- **Abraco** • 81 E 7th St [1st Ave]
  646-398-7835
  Sip an amazing espresso by the window.
- **Ninth Street Espresso** •
  700 E 9th St [Avenue C]
  212-358-9225
  Absolutely fantastic coffee drinks. Cool
  Portland vibe.

Farmers Markets

- **Tompkins Square Greenmarket** •
  Ave A & E 7th St
  Sun 9 am–4 pm, year-round.

Dive bars are an East Village specialty, and some of the finest specimens in the city are right here: try **Lucy's**, **7B**, and **International Bar**. This hood rules for cocktails too: check out **Summit Bar** or **Maiden Lane** if you can't bear the wait at **Death and Company**. **Drop Off Service** has our favorite happy hour this side of the East River. Cheers!

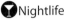 Nightlife

- **11th Street Bar** • 510 E 11th St [Avenue A]
212-982-3929
Darts, Irish, excellent.
- **2A** • 25 Avenue A [E 2nd St]
212-505-2466
Great upstairs space.
- **7B (Horseshoe Bar)** • 108 Avenue B [E 7th St]
212-677-6742
Godfather II shot here. What can be bad?
- **Ace Bar** • 531 E 5th St [Ave A]
212-979-8476
Darts, pinball, pool, and even skee-ball!
- **Alphabet City Beer Co.** • 96 Ave C [6th St]
646-422-7103
Tons of rotating craft beers on tap; great to-go offerings.
- **Amor y Amargo** • 95 Avenue A
833-328-4588
Closet bitters bar.
- **B Side** • 204 Ave B [13th St]
646-559-4710
Jukebox, games, and shot-and-a-beer specials.
- **Blind Barber** • 339 E 10th St [Ave B]
212-228-2123
Consider how many licenses they need; the mind simply reels.
- **Bua** • 122 St Marks Pl [1st Ave]
212-979-6276
Neighborhood bar during the week, mobs of pretty people on the weekend.
- **Cherry Tavern** • 441 E 6th St [1st Ave]
212-777-1448
Get the Tijuana Special.
- **d.b.a.** • 41 1st Ave [E 2nd St]
212-475-5097
Awesome beer list and outdoor patio. NFT fave.
- **Death and Company** •
433 E 6th St [Avenue A]
212-388-0882
Classy cocktails served Prohibition style. No password required.

- **Doc Holliday's** • 141 Ave A [9th St]
212-979-0312
Longtime dive in it through thick and thin; respect.
- **Drop Off Service** • 211 Avenue A [E 13th St]
212-260-2914
Awesome half-off everything happy hour 'til 8 pm.
- **Josie's Bar** • 520 E 6th St [Ave A]
646-590-0044
Pleasantly woody tavern trending toward dive (not a bad thing).
- **Karma Lounge** • 51 1st Ave [E 3rd St]
212-677-3160
Hookah lounge; party like it's 2002; make Bloomberg weep.
- **Lucy's** • 135 Avenue A [St Marks Pl]
212-673-3824
Classic dive. Say hi to Lucy.
- **Maiden Lane** • 162 Avenue B [E 10th St]
646-755-8911
Cozy high-top tables and muscular cocktails.
- **Mama's Bar** • 34 Avenue B [E 3rd St]
212-777-5729
Laid-back respite from the Avenue B craziness, with food from Mama's next door.
- **Mona's** • 224 Avenue B [E 13th St]
212-353-3780
Depressing. Recommended.

Map 7

8 9 10
5 6 7
2 3 4
1

East Village

- **Niagra** • 112 Avenue A [E 7th St]
212-420-9517
Neighborhood rocker watering hole.
- **Nublu** • 62 Ave C [E 5th St]
646-546-5206
Sexy lounge with world music, nice ambience,
and outdoor porch.
- **Nuyorican Poets Café** •
236 E 3rd St [Avenue C]
212-780-9386
Where mediocre poets die of humiliation.
- **Otto's Shrunken Head** •
538 E 14th St [Avenue A]
212-228-2240
Not your grandma's tiki bar.
- **PDT** • 113 St Marks Pl [Avenue A]
212-614-0386
Enter through a phone booth in a hot dog
joint. No joke.
- **The Phoenix** • 447 E 13th St [1st Ave]
212-477-9979
Gay dive bar with great jukebox.
- **Planet Rose** • 219 Avenue A [E 13th St]
212-353-9500
Karaokeeeeee.
- **Sophie's** • 507 E 5th St [Avenue A]
212-228-5680
More crowded counterpart to Joe's.
- **St Dymphnas** • 117 Avenue A
646-776-4865
Homey Irish drinks and food.

- **The Summit Bar** • 133 Avenue C [E 8th St]
347-465-7911
Clean classic cocktails.
- **Ten Degrees Bar** • 121 St Marks Pl [1st Ave]
516-400-4147
Cozy wine bar with live jazz on Wednesdays.
- **The Wayland** • 700 E 9th St [Ave C]
212-777-7022
Tiny bar, small snacks, lovely cocktails.
- **WCOU Radio (Tile Bar)** • 115 1st Ave [7th St]
212-206-0381
East Village survivor. Low key and great.

🍴 Restaurants

- **Big Arc Chicken** • 233 1st Ave [E 14th St]
212-477-0091 • $
Cheap Middle Eastern food complete with
Arabic TV.
- **Bobwhite Counter** • 94 Ave C [6th St]
646-760-7786 • $$$
Three words: Fried Chicken Supper.
- **The Brindle Room** • 277 E 10th St [Ave A]
646-590-0274 • $$$
Gastropublicly comfortable cuisine with
sought-after burgers.
- **Buenos Aires** • 513 E 6th St [Ave A]
212-228-2775 • $
Superior Argentine food: steaks, wine, friendly
atmosphere.

East Village

Residents here are spoiled rotten when it comes to food. Just head to 7th Street between First and A: burgers at **The Brindle Room**, pizza at **Gruppo**, and delicious Greek fare at **Pylos**. **7A**'s always open.

- **Café Mogador** • 101 St Marks Pl [1st Ave]
  212-677-2226 • $$
  Perfect place for hummus and a latte.
- **Caravan of Dreams** • 405 E 6th St [1st Ave]
  212-254-1613 • $
  Organic vegan cuisine.
- **Crif Dogs** • 113 St Marks Pl [Ave A]
  646-922-8524 • $
  Kick-ass wieners.
- **Dumpling Man** • 100 St Marks Pl [1st Ave]
  212-505-2121 • $
  Constantly rotating dumpling roster; good but not great.
- **Gruppo** • 98 Ave B [E 11th St]
  212-995-2100 • $$
  Pizza and pasta in a casual setting.
- **Hearth** • 403 E 12th St [1st Ave]
  646-602-1300 • $$$
  Rich, feast-like farm-to-table Italian.
- **Il Posto Accanto** • 190 E 2nd St [Ave B]
  212-228-3562 • $$$
  Tiny, rustic Italian enoteca.

- **Kafana** • 116 Ave C [7th St]
  212-353-8000 • $$$
  Serbian sausages and spirits for sunny Sundays.
- **Lavagna** • 545 E 5th St [Ave A]
  212-979-1005 • $$$
  We hear it's great….
- **Lil' Frankie's Pizza** • 19 1st Ave [E 1st St]
  212-420-4900 • $$
  Cheap, good pizzas and Italian.
- **Mala Project** • 122 1st Ave [7th St]
  212-353-8880 • $$
  Dry pot Sichuan spiciness; handsome, authentic, and welcoming.
- **Milon** • 93 1st Ave [E 6th St]
  212-228-4896 • $
  Cheap Indian. Unbelievable decor.

Map 7

- **Noreetuh** • 128 1st Ave [St Marks Pl]
646-892-3050 • $$$
Modern Hawaiian cuisine.
- **Panna II Indian Restaurant** •
93 1st Ave [E 6th St]
212-598-4610 • $
Another psycho-decor Indian. Whatever.
- **Pardon My French** • 103 Ave B [E 7th St]
212-358-9683 • $$$
Great French spread. Nice music a plus.
- **Poco** • 33 Ave B [E 3rd St]
212-228-4461 • $$$
Warning: Home of the all-u-can drink $20
brunch.
- **Punjabi Grocery & Deli** • 114 E 1st St [1st Ave]
212-533-3356 • $
Deli, grocery, and cabbie-worthy Indian eats.•
Pylos • 128 E 7th St [Ave A]
212-473-0220 • $$
Delicious Greek, cool hanging-pot ceiling.
- **Ray's Candy Store** • 113 Avenue A [E 7th St]
212-505-7609 • $
Avenue A's Belgian fries-and-ice cream
institution.
- **Royale** • 157 Loisaida Ave [E 10th St]
212-254-6600 • $$
Perfect burgers with stellar fixin's, and a deal
to boot.
- **Sigiri** • 91 1st Ave [E 6th St]
212-614-9333 • $$
Excellent BYOB Sri Lankan above a great beer
shop.
- **St Dymphna's** • 117 Avenue A [1st Ave]
646-776-4865 • $
A great Irish pub doesn't need shamrocks.

- **Supper** • 156 E 2nd St [Ave A]
212-477-7600 • $$$
Spaghetti con limone is yummy. Great brunch.
Otherworldly atmosphere.
- **Takahachi** • 85 Ave A [E 6th St]
212-505-6524 • $$$
Super-good Japanese and sushi. A mainstay.
- **Tuome** • 536 E 5th St [Ave B]
646-833-7811 • $$$$
Farm-to-table New American; we recommend
the "Pig Out" for two.
- **Westville East** • 173 Ave A [E 11th St]
212-677-2033 • $$
Trendy organic belly timber served with a
fresh market flair.
- **Xe May** • 96 St Marks Pl [1st Ave]
212-388-1688 • $
Killer bánh mì served with a smile.
- **Yuca Bar** • 111 Ave A [E 7th St]
212-982-9533 • $$$
Amazing Latin-style brunch, less amazing
Latin-style dinner.

We can't decide if we like **Abraço** or **Ninth Street Espresso** better—we'll take both! Browse used tomes at **Mast Books**, and jewelry at **The Shape of Lies**. Cute boutiques? 9th Street between First and Second. Late-night bodega taco fix? **Zaragoza**.

🛍 Shopping

- **11th Street Flea Market** • 1st Ave & E 11th St
  Stuff you didn't even know you needed!
- **Black Seed** • 176 1st Ave [11th St]
  646-859-2289
  For your Montreal bagel fix; let the debate begin.
- **East Village Books** • 99 St Marks Pl [1st Ave]
  212-477-8647
  Messy pile of used stuff.
- **East Village Wines** • 138 1st Ave [St Marks Pl]
  212-677-7070
  Classic EV liquor store. With booze!
- **Enchantments** • 165 Avenue B
  212-228-4394
  Witchy apothecary, custom carved candles, and all things occult.
- **Exit 9** • 51 Avenue A [E 3rd St]
  212-228-0145
  Always fun and changeable hipster gifts. First place to sell NFT!
- **Fly Dove NYC** • 197 E 7th St [Avenue B]
  212-300-4370
  Women's clothing boutique.
- **Gringer & Sons** • 29 1st Ave [E 2nd St]
  212-475-0600
  Kitchen appliances for every price range.

- **Mast Books** • 72 Avenue A [E 4th St]
  646-370-1114
  Small but excellent selection.
- **Mr. Throwback** • 437 E 9th St [Avenue A]
  917-261-7834
  Vintage NBA jerseys, Starter jackets, Nintendo, and toys for dudes.
- **L Train Vintage** • 204 1st Ave [E 13th St]
  212-228-5201
  Cheap vintage basics for patient sifters.
- **Ray's Candy Store** • 113 Avenue A [E 7th St]
  212-505-7609
  Avenue A's Belgian fries-and-ice cream institution.
- **Saifee Hardware & Garden** •
  114 1st Ave [E 7th St]
  212-979-6396
  Classic East Village hardware store. It has everything.
- **The Shape of Lies** • 127 E 7th St [Avenue A]
  212-533-5920
  Vintage and locally-made jewelry.
- **Sunny and Annie's** • 94 Ave B [6th St]
  212-677-3131
  This bodega's PHO Real sandwich is worth the wait.
- **Zaragoza Mexican Deli and Grocery** •
  215 Avenue A [E 13th St]
  212-780-9204
  Bodega with burritos.

Map 8 · Chelsea

Lincoln Tunnel
← to NJ

Hudson River Park

Jacob K Javits Convention Center
PAGE 264

W 40th St
W 39th St
W 38th St
W 37th St
W 36th St
W 35th St

A C E
34th Street Penn Station

7 34th Street ←

W 34th St
W 33rd St
W 31st St

High Line Elevated Railroad

James A. Farley Post Office

Penn Station MS

W 30th St
W 29th St
W 28th St

Chelsea Park

9

Hudson River Park
PAGE 262

Starrett-Lehigh Building ←
W 27th St ←

Penn Station South Houses

The Frying Pan

9A

W 26th St
W 25th St
W 24th St

C E
23rd Street

Hudson River

Chelsea Waterside Park

W 23rd St
W 22nd St
W 21st St
W 20th St

Chelsea Piers
PAGE 328

The High Line
PAGE 260

W 19th St
W 18th St

General Theological Seminary

IAC Building ←

W 17th St

Hudson River Park

W 16th St

The Maritime Hotel

Chelsea Market

W 15th St

5

A C E
14th Street

8th Ave

L

W 14th St ←

| 1/4 mile | .25 km |

Neighborhood Overview

Map 8

Located due south of Midtown's gazillion office buildings and due north of the West Village and the Financial District, Chelsea is a magnet for the young, the beautiful, and the wealthy. A polished mix of quaint, restored townhouses and sparkling new condos in the sky combine to create a unique and appealing neighborhood that deftly handles the transition from downtown to Midtown. With the opening of the long-awaited **High Line** in 2009, luxury marched west towards the river, with multiple shiny new buildings clustered around the new ribbon of green that cuts through the heart of the neighborhood.

While the neighborhood is diverse and welcoming to all, it would be dishonest to pretend that it isn't best known as the epicenter of all things gay. A substantial, muscle-bound gay population spawned the term "Chelsea boy," used either derisively or admiringly depending on one's taste. Several of the city's best LGBTQ bars, book stores, and social service organizations are located within the borders of this neighborhood. And while the gyms aren't exclusively gay, they know who their best and most loyal customers are.

But the charms of Chelsea are many and unmistakable: a thriving, inclusive nightlife with something for everyone, great dining for almost any budget, and great shopping for…middle budgets and upwards (though the odd deal can certainly be found tucked into a side street or a more modest storefront on one of the avenues). On top of that, there are ample opportunities for recreation here— aside from the aforementioned High Line, there's the Hudson River Park (which, unsurprisingly, is alongside the body of water bearing the same name), massive sports complex Chelsea Piers, brilliant **Chelsea Market**, with its wonderfully diverse food vendors, and the safety-first, divided bike lanes on 8th and 9th Avenues.

The architecture of the neighborhood is some of New York's most noteworthy. Frank Gehry's translucent, iceberg/schooner hybrid **IAC Building** is regrettably too short to be seen from vantage points that aren't near its location at the intersection of 18th Street and the West Side Highway. But it's a leading candidate for coolest building in Chelsea and one of the loveliest, most unique buildings erected in Manhattan in recent years. A few blocks away lies the gorgeous, Neo-Gothic campus of the **General Theological Seminary**, the oldest Episcopal theological school. Just north of there, the historic **London Terrace** luxury apartment complex fills an entire city block. Up a few blocks more, the **Starrett-Lehigh Building** is an art deco freight warehouse and factory that now houses several high-profile media and fashion companies.

Farther uptown, on 8th Avenue between 31st and 33rd Streets, the **James A. Farley Post Office** stands in proud, marble magnificence across the street from the grotesquely ugly Madison Square Garden (the unworthy replacement for the demolished Penn Station). A couple blocks west of there is the **Javits Center**, the biggest exhibition hall in the city and another architectural lowlight. As a New Yorker, the best reason you'll ever have for going there is a comic con or an industry expo—the latter being preferable because there's likely to be free food or booze.

Instead of heading up into the 30s, take a walk through west Chelsea in the 20s and you'll find yourself in one of the great visual art districts of the world. Over 300 galleries show the newest work of the best artists working today. Despite the occasional dud, you have a better-than-even chance of encountering exhilarating, high-quality work. Now and then, you might even find something you can afford to buy!

Add in some of the best people-watching in the city, and you'll know why so many other New Yorkers choose to pay a small fortune every month to live in a shoebox here.

The Kitchen's list of performances over the years is legendary, and rock shows still happen at the **Hammerstein** and **Highline** Ballrooms. Various LGBTQ subcultures have their home bars here: **Gym** (hunks!) and **The Eagle** (leather-daddies and cubs) are two of the best.

Map 8

14 15
11 12 13
8 9 10
5 6 7

O Landmarks

- **100 Eleventh Avenue** •
  100 11th Ave [W 19th St]
  Jean Nouvel's West Side condo/window frame depot.
- **Chelsea Market** • 75 9th Ave [W 16th St]
  212-652-2111
  Foodies flock here. So should you.
- **Chelsea Piers** • W 23rd St & Hudson River Park
  212-336-6666
  28-acre waterfront sports mecca.
- **Frying Pan** • 207 12th Ave
  212-989-6363
  Old ship makes for amazing party digs.
- **General Theological Seminary** •
  440 W 21st St [9th Ave]
  212-243-5150
  Oldest seminary of the Episcopal Church; nice campus.
- **IAC Building** • 555 W 18th St [West Side Hwy]
  Gehry finally comes to NYC. And kicks ass.
- **Jacob K. Javits Convention Center** •
  429 11th Ave
  212-216-2000
  Glass-sheathed behemoth hosting various and sundry cons.
- **James A. Farley Post Office** •
  421 8th Ave [W 31st St]
  800-275-8777
  Another McKim, Mead & White masterpiece. Slated to become Moynihan Station.
- **The Maritime Hotel** • 363 W 16th St [9th Ave]
  212-242-4300
  Ahoy! Porthole office building now uber-cool hotel.
- **Starrett-Lehigh Building** •
  601 W 26th St [11th Ave]
  One of the coolest factories/warehouses ever built.

☕ Coffee

- **Billy's Bakery** • 184 9th Ave [W 21st St]
  212-647-9406
  Mindblowingly good cakes to go with your coffee.
- **Joe The Art of Coffee** •
  405 W 23rd St [9th Ave]
  212-206-0669
  Joe really knows his joe.

🍸 Nightlife

- **Billymark's West** • 332 9th Ave [W 29th St]
  646-590-2999
  Down and dirty dive.
- **Death Ave Brewing Company** •
  315 10th Ave [28th St]
  212-695-8080
  Good space, beer, cocktails, and Greek-inspired grub.
- **The Distinguished Wakamba Cocktail Lounge** • 543 8th Ave [W 37th St]
  Plastic palm trees and provocatively-clad barmaids.
- **The Eagle** • 554 W 28th St [11th Ave]
  646-473-1866
  Get your leather on (or off).
- **Gallow Green** • 542 W 27th St [11th Ave]
  212-904-1880
  Lush rooftop garden, crisp cocktails, and a macabre train car.
- **Gym Sports Bar** • 167 8th Ave [W 19th St]
  212-337-2439
  Where the boys go to watch the game…and each other.

Grand Sichuan is one of our favorite spots for Chinese food in all of New York. Across the street, check out **Ovest Pizzoteca**'s stellar pizzas. Got a bonus? Indulge at **Buddakan** or **Porteno**. For diner food, there's always the **Skylight**.

- **Hammerstein Ballroom** •
  311 W 34th St [8th Ave]
  212-695-6600
  Lofty rock venue.
- **The Kitchen** • 512 W 19th St [10th Ave]
  212-255-5793
  The kind of place Jesse Helms would have hated.
- **The Molly Wee Pub** • 402 8th Ave [W 30th St]
  212-967-2627
  You may just need a pint after a trip to Penn Station.
- **Westside Tavern** • 360 W 23rd St [9th Ave]
  212-366-3738
  Local mixture.

🍴Restaurants

- **Artichoke Basille's Pizza** •
  114 10th Ave [17th St]
  212-792-9200 • $$
  Perfect pies under the High Line, open till pretty late, too.
- **Bottino** • 246 10th Ave [W 24th St]
  212-206-6766 • $$$
  Good, clean Italian. A good post-gallery spot.
- **Buddakan** • 75 9th Ave [W 16th St]
  212-989-6699 • $$$$$
  NYC branch of Stephen Starr's insanely popular Philadelphia behemoth.

- **Cookshop** • 156 10th Ave [W 20th St]
  212-924-4440 • $
  Loft-like, local ingredient-focused eatery.
- **Cull & Pistol** • 75 9th Ave [15th St]
  646-568-1223 • $$$$
  Sit-down oysters and shellfish inside Chelsea Market.
- **Death Ave Brewing Company** •
  315 10th Ave [28th St]
  212-695-8080 • $$$
  Your very basic pub grub, but it's necessary.
- **Dickson's Farmstand Meats** •
  75 9th Ave [W 15th St]
  212-242-2630 • $
  Great sandwiches at lunch time like sloppy joe and meatball.

Map 8

Map 8

Chelsea

14 15
11 12 13
8 9 10
5 6 7

- **Friedman's Lunch** • 75 9th Ave [W 16th St]
212-929-7100 • $
Super-delish brunch/lunch spot inside
bustling Chelsea Market.
- **Grand Sichuan** • 229 9th Ave [W 24th St]
212-620-5200 • $$
Some of the best Chinese in NYC.
Recommended.
- **Le Grainne Cafe** • 183 9th Ave [21st St]
646-486-3000 • $$$
All-day cute French brunch/lunch/dinner w/
savory crepes.
- **Los Tacos No.1** • 75 9th Ave [9th Ave]
212-246-0343 • $
Chelsea Market's yummy taco option.
- **Ovest Pizzoteca** • 513 W 27th St [10th Ave]
212-967-4392 • $$$
Decent 'za under the High Line.
- **Pepe Giallo** • 195 10th Ave [W 25th St]
212-242-6055 • $$
Takeout Italian.
- **Pomodoro** • 518 9th Ave [W 39th St]
212-239-7019 • $$
Takes "fast food" Italian to the next level;
superb foccacia.

- **Porteno Restaurant** • 299 10th Ave [27th St]
212-695-9694 • $$$$
Modern Argentine; above and beyond steak
and red wine.
- **Salinas** • 136 9th Ave [19th St]
212-776-1990 • $$$$
Good Spanish w/ a nice back garden.
- **Sergimmo Salumeria** •
456 9th Ave [W 35th St]
212-967-4212 • $
Serious sandwiches stuffed with
mouthwatering Italian meats.
- **Skylight Diner** • 402 W 34th St [9th Ave]
212-244-0395 • $
24-hour diner. If you must.
- **Sullivan Street Bakery** •
236 9th Ave [W 24th St]
212-929-5900 • $
Artisan breads, foodie approved. NFT
approved. God approved.
- **Tia Pol** • 205 10th Ave [W 22nd St]
212-675-8805 • $$
Very good, very popular (crowded) tapas joint.
- **Tick Tock Diner** • 481 8th Ave [W 34th St]
212-268-8444 • $
Midtown outpost of "Eat Heavy" Clifton, NJ
roadside diner.
- **Txikito** • 240 9th Ave [W 24th St]
212-242-4730 • $$$
Unique gourmet Basque cooking.

Chelsea

Map 8

B&H Photo remains a go-to electronics store (closed Saturdays) and Printed Matter's selection of artists' books is probably the best in the world. For food, simply hit brilliant Chelsea Market to get Italian imports (Buon Italia), wine (Chelsea Wine Vault), ice cream (L'Arte del Gelato), fish (The Lobster Place), and bread (Amy's Bread).

🛍 Shopping

- **192 Books** • 192 10th Ave [W 21st St]
  212-255-4022
  Reads like a library—with a premium on art books and literature.
- **Amy's Bread** • 75 9th Ave [W 15th St]
  212-462-4338
  Perfect breads.
- **Aperture Bookstore** •
  548 W 28th St
  212-505-5555
  We love Aperture. Say hi to us.
- **Apple Store (Chelsea)** •
  401 W 14th St [9th Ave]
  212-444-3400
  Less crowded than the other locations.
- **Artists & Fleas** • 88 10th Ave
  917-488-0044
  Market for quirky jewelry, accessories, vintage, housewares.
- **B&H Photo** • 420 9th Ave [W 33rd St]
  212-615-8820
  Where everyone in North America buys their cameras and film. Closed Saturdays.
- **Billy's Bakery** • 184 9th Ave [W 21st St]
  212-647-9406
  Yummiest treats this side of homemade.
- **Buon Italia** • 75 9th Ave [W 16th St]
  212-633-9090
  Italian import mecca—get the 24-month prosciutto.
- **Chelsea Market Baskets** •
  75 9th Ave [W 16th St]
  212-727-1111
  Gift baskets for all occasions.

- **Chelsea Wine Vault** • 75 9th Ave [W 16th St]
  212-462-4244
  Excellent shop inside the Chelsea Market.
- **City Bicycles** • 307 W 38th St [Eighth Ave]
  212-563-3373
  Sales and rentals.
- **Enoch's Bike Shop** • 480 10th Ave [37th St]
  212-582-0620
  Sales, rentals and repairs.
- **Esposito's Pork Store** •
  500 9th Ave
  212-279-3298
  Authentic 1890 butcher shop.
- **Fat Witch Bakery** • 75 9th Ave [W 16th St]
  212-807-1335
  Excellent chocolate brownies.
- **L'Arte del Gelato** • 75 9th Ave [W 16th St]
  212-366-0570
  Gelato to make you sing an aria. Or just pig out.
- **The Lobster Place** • 75 9th Ave [W 16th St]
  212-255-5672
  Fresh fish and Maine lobster, if you can afford it.
- **Milk & Hops** • 166 9th Ave [20th St]
  212-989-1999
  Great craft beer selection and artisanal cheeses.
- **Printed Matter** • 231 11th Ave
  212-925-0325
  Astounding selection of artist's books; highly recommended.
- **Saxelby Cheesemongers** •
  Chelsea Market: 75 9th Ave
  646-892-3077
  All-American and artisinal.

Map 9 • **Flatiron / Lower Midtown**

1

2

W 39th St

W 38th St

W 37th St

W 36th St

VEHICULAR TRAFFIC PROHIBITED

Morgan Library

De Lamar Mansion

W 35th St

Herald Square

Macy's

B D F M
N Q R W

34th Street Herald Square

Empire State Building

PAGE 258

A

34th Street Penn Station

A C E

1 2 3
34th Street Penn Station

33rd Street

6

PATH
33rd St

W 33rd St

PAGE 336

J A Farley Post Office

Madison Square Garden

Penn Station

PAGE 317

W 32nd St

Koreatown

W 31st St Garment District

W 30th St

W 29th St

Flower District

1
28th Street

Tin Pan Alley

10 ▶

28th Street

6

R W

28th Street

Seventh Ave (Fashion Ave)

Eighth Ave

Park Ave S

Sixth Ave (Ave of the Americas)

W 28th St

W 27th St

W 26th St

New York Life Insurance Company

Madison Ave

Broadway

Croisic Building

Madison Sq Plz

New York State Appellate Court

6

8 ◀

W 25th St

W 24th St

Stern Brothers' Dry Goods Store

Madison Square Park

B

R W
23rd Street

23rd Street

Metropolitan Life Insurance Company

W 23rd St

C E

23rd Street

Chelsea Hotel

1

PATH
23rd St

23rd Street

F M

Flatiron Building

W 22nd St

W 21st St

Hugh O'Neill's Dry Goods Store

Theodore Roosevelt Birthplace

W 20th St

Broadway Lord & Taylor

The "Palace of Trade"

W 19th St

Arnold Constable's Dry Good Store

Old Town Bar

1
18th Street

Siegel-Cooper Department Store

W 18th St

W 17th St

W 16th St

Union Square

A C E L
8th Avenue
14th Street

W 15th St

5 ▼

PATH
14th St
6th Avenue

N Q R W
4 5 6 7

14th Street

L

PAGE 284

6 ▼

1/4 mile

.25 km

14th Street

1 2 3

14th Street-Union Square

14th Street

F M

Neighborhood Overview

Map 9

The amazing variety of people, places and things that typifies New York cannot be better experienced than in this area. Containing some of the most tourist-heavy areas—the **Empire State Building** and **Macy's** at Herald Square—you will also find the hip, expensive, and fabulously exclusive communities of Gramercy (to the east) and Chelsea (to the west). Flatiron is also the home to the lesser-known "Silicon Alley," after the many start-ups in the area. In this incredibly diverse and unassuming neighborhood you will see moms pushing strollers, and wealthy elderly women walking their perfectly groomed pups.

One of the most obvious draws of the area is the impressive architecture. You certainly can't miss the amazing sight of the towering **Empire State Building** or the aptly-named **Flatiron Building**. But also not to miss is the less-obvious **Chelsea Hotel**, a favorite of many musicians and artists from Bob Dylan to Sid Vicious (and, more recently, a luxury hotel). Early 20th century additions to the area include the **MetLife Tower**, the **New York Life Building**, and the **New York State Appellate Court**, all of which are ranged on the east side of **Madison Square Park**. Equally impressive are the myriad number of current and former cast-iron department store buildings that make up the historic "Ladies' Mile" area, including the **Arnold Constable Dry Goods Store**, the **Broadway Lord & Taylor**, the **Croisic Building**, the **Hugh O'Neill Dry Goods Store**, the **Stern Brothers' Dry Goods Store**, and, our all-time favorite, the **Siegel-Cooper Department Store**. We can't help but mention that this area was also the scene of one of the greatest crimes *against* architecture—namely, the destruction of McKim, Mead & White's original Penn Station in 1963.

Venture to the **Garment District** and you will be surrounded by the shops and people that helped make New York City the fashion leader of the world in the late 1800's and early 1900's. The nearby **Flower District** was once several blocks filled with lush greenery of every variety. By the 2010s however, high rent and massive competition squeezed most retailers out, and it's now less than a block in size and can easily be missed. Luckily **Koreatown** is still going strong on 32nd Street (between Fifth and Broadway). Stroll through here on a Friday night to find the restaurants and bars packed to the brim.

Look down as you walk on 28th Street between Fifth Avenue and Broadway and you will see a plaque in the sidewalk dedicated to **Tin Pan Alley**. If you're a music buff you'll want to take in the historical significance of this area, dated back to 1885 when a group of songwriters and music publishers got together to lobby for copyright laws.

For a piece of Presidential history, visit the **Birthplace of Theodore Roosevelt**. A recreated version of the brownstone President Roosevelt was born in on October 27th, 1858 now serves as a museum dedicated to the 26th President.

Finding a small patch of fresh green grass in Manhattan is almost as challenging as finding a parking spot, but in this area you have not one, but two parks. **Madison Square Park** is a beautifully manicured park where you can be sure to catch hundreds of sunbathers on any summer Saturday. It is also home to the long lines of the original **Shake Shack**, where you will still be treated to one of the best hamburgers of all-time. Farther south, **Union Square** is one of the more famous parks in Manhattan, having had several historic rallies and riots as well as being a main subway hub; it is busier than most parks. If you can squeeze yourself into a spot on one of the overflowing park benches, you'll be treated to some entertaining people watching. It's also worth noting for the dog lovers out there, that both of these parks have sizable dog parks.

Map 9

Flatiron / Lower Midtown

O Landmarks

- **The "Palace of Trade"** • 885 Broadway [E 19th St]
  The mansard roof to end all mansard roofs.
- **Croisic Building** • 220 5th Ave [E 26th St]
  Just another outstanding NYC building. Circa 1912.
- **De Lamar Mansion** • 233 Madison Ave [E 37th St] Dutch sea captain's mansion now inhabited by Polish diplomats.
- **Empire State Building** • 20 W 29th St 212-736-3100. View unlike any other (except maybe Top of the Rock).
- **Flatiron Building** • 175 5th Ave [W 22nd St]
  A lesson for all architects: design for the actual space.
- **Flower District** • W 28th St b/n 6th & 7th Aves
  Lots of flowers by day, lots of nothing by night.
- **Garment District** • 34th to 40th St b/n 6th to 9th Ave.
  Clothing racks by day, nothing by night. Gritty, grimy.
- **Hotel Chelsea** • 222 W 23rd St [7th Ave]
  The scene of many, many crimes.
- **Hugh O'Neill's Dry Goods Store** • 655 6th Ave [W 20th St].
  Brilliant cast-iron from Mortimer Merritt.
- **Koreatown** • W 32nd St b/n Broadway & 5th Ave
  Korean restaurants, bars, and shops. Bustling on the weekends.
- **Lord & Taylor Building** • 901 Broadway [E 20th St]
  Incredible detail on former Lord & Taylor outlet.
- **Macy's** • 151 W 34th St [7th Ave] 212-695-4400
  13 floors of wall-to-wall tourists! Sound like fun?
- **Madison Square Garden** • 4 Penn Plaza [W 31st St] 212-465-6000
  MSG's one thing in Chinatown; in Midtown it's something different.
- **Madison Square Park** • 11 Madison Ave 212-520-7600. One of the most underrated parks in the city. Lots of great weird sculpture.
- **Metropolitan Life Insurance Co** • 1 Madison Ave [E 23rd St]
  Cool top, recently refurbished.
- **The Morgan Library & Museum** • 225 Madison Ave [E 37th St] 212-685-0008
  See cool stuff the dead rich dude collected.
- **New York Life Insurance Company** • 51 Madison Ave [E 26th St]
  The gold roof? Your insurance premiums at work.
- **New York State Appellate Court** • Madison Ave & E 25th St
  Insanely ornate 1899 courthouse; where new lawyers get sworn in.
- **Old Town Bar** • 45 E 18th St [Broadway] 212-529-6732. Classic NY pub housed in former speak-easy.
- **Penn Station** • 8th Ave & W 32nd St
  Well, the old one was a landmark, anyway…
- **Siegel-Cooper Co. Department Store** • 616 6th Ave [W 18th St]
  Beaux-Arts retail madness.
- **Stern Brothers' Dry Goods Store** • 32 W 23rd St [6th Ave]
  Awesome ornate cast-iron; now houses Home Depot. Whatever.
- **Theodore Roosevelt Birthplace** • 28 E 20th St [Broadway] 212-260-1616. Recreation of childhood home of only president born in NYC.
- **Tin Pan Alley** • W 28th St b/n 6th Ave & Broadway
  Where American popular music climbed out of the crib.
- **Union Square** • E 14th St & University Pl
  Famous park for protests and rallies. Now bordered by chain stores.

Coffee

- **Culture Espresso** • 72 W 38th St [6th Ave] 212-302-0200
  Amazing coffee right near Bryant Park.
- **Gregorys Coffee** • 874 6th Ave [W 31st St] 877-231-7619
  Take a break from Macy's or Koreatown with a latte.
- **Stumptown Coffee** • 18 W 29th St [Broadway] 855-711-3385
  The real deal straight outta Portland.

Flatiron / Lower Midtown

Whether you prefer celebrity sighting at **Raines Law Room**, dress-code mandatory joints like **230 Fifth**, or classic NYC watering holes like **Old Town Bar** and **Peter McManus**, you have options.

Farmers Markets

- **Union Square Greenmarket** •
  E 17th St & Broadway
  NYC's best greenmarket.
  Mon, Wed, Fri & Sat 8 am–6 pm, year-round.

Nightlife

- **230 Fifth** • 230 5th Ave [E 26th St]
  212-725-4300
  Dress code and overpriced drinks. Best view of NYC makes it worthwhile.
- **Ace Hotel Lobby Bar** • 20 W 29th St [Broadway]
  212-679-2222
  Amazing cocktails in an amazing space.
- **Barracuda** • 275 W 22nd St [8th Ave]
  212-645-8613
  Neighborhood fave, low-key gay bar.
- **Birreria** • 200 5th Ave [W 23rd St]
  212-937-8910
  Retractable-roof beer garden atop Eataly.
- **Gotham Comedy Club** • 208 W 23rd St [7th Ave]. 212-367-9000
  In a new, shiny location.•
- **Jazz Gallery** • 1160 Broadway [W 27th St]
  Not-for-profit jazz venue.

- **Lillie's** • 13 E 17th St [5th Ave]
  212-337-1970
  Perfect for anyone with an Irish-Victorian fetish.
- **The Lookup Rooftop Bar** • 45 W 35th St [6th Ave] 212-279-3535
  Fresh air + beer 14 floors above Manhattan.
- **Old Town Bar** • 45 E 18th St [Broadway]
  212-529-6732
  Excellent old-NY pub.
- **Park Bar** • 15 E 15th St [Fifth Ave]
  212-367-9085
  Good date spot; small enough to encourage a little conversation.
- **Peter McManus** • 152 7th Ave [W 19th St]
  917-261-5504
  Refreshingly basic. Gorgeous old phone booths.
- **The Raines Law Room** • 24 E 39th St
  Cocktails worth your time. And money.
- **Society Billiards + Bar** • 10 E 21st St [5th Ave]
  212-420-1000
  Well-appointed, classy pool hall.
- **Stout** • 133 W 33rd St [7th Ave]
  212-629-6191
  Huge Midtown pub.
- **Taj Lounge** • 48 W 21st St [5th Ave]
  212-620-3033
  Indian lux lounge. Lots of private events.
- **Tir Na Nog** • 254 W 31st St
  212-630-0249
  Penn Station hangout.
- **Triple Crown Restaurant & Ale House** •
  330 7th Ave [W 29th St]
  212-736-1575
  Typical Midtown bar. Expensive, insipid. But, hey, we hear the bartenders are nice.

Map 9

Flatiron / Lower Midtown

🍴 Restaurants

- **ABC Kitchen** • 35 E 18th St [Broadway]
212-475-5829 • $$$$
Fancy farm-to-table. In a carpet store.
- **Alidoro** • 18 E 39th St [Madison Ave]
646-692-4330 • $$
High-end Italian sandwiches.
- **Basta Pasta** • 37 W 17th St [5th Ave]
212-366-0888 • $$$$
Pac-rim Italian. Hmmm.
- **BCD Tofu House** • 5 W 32nd St [5th Ave]
212-967-1900 • $$$
California-based Korean tofu chain.
- **Blaggard's Pub** • 8 W 38th St [5th Ave]
212-382-2611 • $$
Smells like last night's vomit. Overpriced, awful service.
- **BonChon Chicken** • 325 5th Ave [33rd St]
212-686-8282 • $$
Fast-casual Korean fried chicken powerhouse.
- **BonChon Chicken** • 207 W 38th St [7th Ave]
212-221-3339 • $$
Times Square location of Korean fried chicken powerhouse.
- **Boqueria** • 53 W 19th St [6th Ave]
212-255-4160 • $$$
Cheese stuffed dates wrapped in bacon? We're there.
- **Burger & Lobster** • 39 W 19th St [6th Ave]
646-833-7532 • $$$
London-based burger-lobster joint; menu boiled down to essentials.

- **BXL Zoute** • 50 W 22nd St [6th Ave]
646-692-9282 • $$$
Belgian cuisine with requisite beer-mussels specials.
- **Cafeteria** • 119 7th Ave [W 17th St]
212-414-1717 • $$$
Comfort food, open all night.
- **Chick-fil-A** • 1000 6th Ave [W 37th St]
212-704-9920 • $
Legendary fried chicken sandwiches; closed Sunday.
- **Cho Dang Gol** • 55 W 35th St [6th Ave]
212-695-8222 • $$$
There's usually a line for good reason at this homey Korean.
- **Chop't** • 24 E 17th St [Union Square W]
646-336-5523 • $
Salads for office drones.
- **The Clocktower** • 5 Madison Ave [E 24th St]
212-413-4300 • $$$$
Superstar-filled roster brings Britishy elegance to sleek hotel restaurant.
- **Cosme** • 35 E 21st St [Broadway]
212-913-9659 • $$$$
Locally sourced haute Mexican from one of Mexico's top chefs.
- **Craft** • 43 E 19th St [Broadway]
212-780-0880 • $$$$$
Outstanding. A top-end place worth the $$$$.
- **Don's Bogam** • 17 E 32nd St [Madison Ave]
212-683-2200 • $$$
Korean BBQ heaven.
- **Eataly** • 200 5th Ave [W 23rd St]
212-229-2560 • $$$$
Try to get a seat somewhere. Go ahead, we dare you.

Map 9

Impress a date with the size of your wallet at **Gramercy Tavern**, **Eleven Madison Park** and NFT-fave **Craft**, or impress them with your wit and conversation over tapas at **Boqueria**.

- **Eleven Madison Park** • 11 Madison Ave [E 24th St] • 212-889-0905 • $$$$$
  Where the elite meet to greet.
- **Elmo** • 156 7th Ave [W 19th St]
  212-337-8000 • $$
  Lounge downstairs, dine upstairs at this swanky Chelsea venue.
- **Evergreen Shanghai Restaurant** • 10 E 38th St [5th Ave] • 212-448-1199 • $
  Their scallion pancakes are worth the wait, and they know it.
- **Giorgio's of Gramercy** • 27 E 21st St [Broadway] • 212-477-0007 • $$$$$
  Cozy Italian.
- **Go! Go! Curry!** • 273 W 38th St [8th Ave]
  212-730-5555 • $$
  Japanese deep fried fast food.
- **Gramercy Tavern** • 42 E 20th St [Broadway]
  212-477-0777 • $$$$$
  Expensive, but good, New American.
- **Hanbat** • 53 W 35th St [6th Ave]
  212-629-5588 • $$
  The Bi Bim Bab is amazing. Open all night!
- **Hangawi** • 12 E 32nd St [5th Ave]
  212-213-0077 • $$$$
  Serene, top-end vegetarian Korean.
- **Her Name Is Han** • 17 E 31st St [Madison Ave]
  212-779-9990 • $$$
  Korean soul food for homesick students, and the rest of us.
- **Hill Country** • 30 W 26th St [Broadway]
  212-255-4544 • $$$
  Good ol' Texas 'cue; go for the wet brisket.
- **ilili** • 236 5th Ave [W 27th St]
  212-683-2929 • $$$
  Hearty Lebanese food in a fancy setting.
- **Johny's Luncheonette** • 124 W 25th St [6th Ave] • 212-243-6230 • $
  Sit at the counter and get an egg and cheese on a roll.
- **Kunjip** • 32 W 32nd St [Broadway]
  212-564-8238 • $$
  The best Korean food in Manhattan; try the bo saam!
- **Lan Sheng** • 128 W 36th St
  212-575-8899 • $$
  Szechuan fare that once earned a Michelinstar.
- **Le Zie** • 172 7th Ave [W 20th St]
  212-206-8686 • $$$
  Venetian. That means it's Italian.
- **The Liberty** • 29 W 35th St [5th Ave]
  212-967-4000 • $$$
  New American tavern with not a statue in sight.
- **Marta** • 29 E 29th St [Madison Ave]
  212-651-3800 • $$$
  Wood-fired pizzas and Italian seasonal entrees.
- **Mendy's Kosher Deli** • 441 Park Ave
  212-576-1010 • $$
  Pastrami, matzoh ball soup, and knishes.
- **Momoya** • 185 7th Ave [W 21 St]
  212-989-4466 • $$
  Nice selection of unique sushi.
- **Mr. Broadway** • 209 W 38th St [7th Ave]
  212-921-2152 • $$
  Deli standards, Middle Eastern and Kosher Chinese.
- **New Wonjo** • 23 W 32nd St [Broadway]
  212-695-5815 • $$$
  Can you ever have enough 24/7 Korean BBQ restaurants?
- **Nuchas Empanadas** •
  97 W 32nd St [Broadway] • 212-912-0035 • $
  Flawless, juicy Argentine turnovers from a kiosk and truck.

Map 9

11 12 13
8 **9** 10
5 6 7
2 3 4

Flatiron / Lower Midtown

- **Periyali** • 35 W 20th St [5th Ave]
  212-463-7890 • $$$$
  Upscale Greek. Pretty damned great.
- **Ravagh** • 173 Madison Ave [Madison Ave]
  212-696-0300 • $
  All your kebab needs.
- **Rosa Mexicano** • 9 E 18th St [5th Ave]
  212-533-3350 • $$$
  Union Square outpost of Manhattan Mexi
  chain.
- **Shake Shack** • 11 Madison Ave [E 23rd St]
  212-889-6600 • $
  Enjoy homemade shakes 'n burgers in the
  park. On a 2-hour line.
- **Socarrat** • 259 W 19th St [8th Ave]
  212-462-1000 • $$$
  Authentic paella feast, sit next to the
  Spaniards at the communal table.
- **Soju Haus** • 315 5th Ave [E 32nd St]
  212-213-2177 • $$$
  Wash down Korean food with namesake
  booze.
- **Tarallucci E Vino** • 15 E 18th St [5th Ave]
  212-228-5400 • $$
  Espresso in the morning, wine after work.
  Delicious and versatile.
- **Tocqueville** • 1 E 15th St [5th Ave]
  212-647-1515 • $$$$$
  Lovely everything—and you can actually hear
  each other speak!

- **Toledo** • 6 E 36th St [5th Ave]
  212-696-5036 • $$$$
  Classy Spanish.
- **Triple Crown Restaurant & Ale House** •
  330 7th Ave [W 29th St] • 212-736-1575 • $$
  Pub grub that will make you shrug.
- **Woorijip** • 12 W 32nd St [5th Ave]
  212-244-1115 • $
  Cheap Korean buffet, hot and cold, great
  variety.
- **Zero Otto Nove Trattoria** •
  15 W 21st St [5th Ave] • 212-242-0899 • $$$
  Arthur Avenue pizza import; highly
  recommended.

Shopping

- **30th Street Guitars** • 234 W 27th St
  212-868-2660
  Ax heaven. Seriously.
- **ABC Carpet & Home** •
  888 Broadway [E 19th St]
  212-473-3000
  A NYC institution for chic, even exotic, home
  decor and design.
- **Abracadabra** • 19 W 21st St [5th Ave]
  212-627-5194
  Magic, masks, costumes—presto!
- **Academy Records** • 12 W 18th St [5th Ave]
  212-242-3000
  Top jazz/classical mecca.
- **Adorama** • 42 W 18th St [5th Ave]
  212-741-0063
  Good camera alternative to B&H. Still closed
  Saturdays, though.
- **Ariston Flowers** • 110 W 17th St [6th Ave]
  212-929-4226
  Excellent florist with orchids as well.

Flatiron / Lower Midtown

Map 9

Need sporting goods? **Paragon** is the paragon of sporting goods stores. Food heaven is found at **Eataly**—just bring your credit card. **30th Street Guitars** and **Rogue Music** will rock your world.

- **Barnes & Noble** • 33 E 17th St [Broadway]
212-253-0810
Chain bookstore.
- **Books of Wonder** • 42 W 17th St [5th Ave]
212-989-3270
Top NYC children's bookstore, always has signed copies around too.
- **Bottlerocket Wine & Spirit** •
5 W 19th St [5th Ave]
212-929-2323
Free tastings every Thursday, Friday, and Saturday!
- **Breads Bakery** • 18 E 16th St [Union Square W] 212-633-2253
Artisanal bakers and babka specialists.
- **The Container Store** • 629 6th Ave [W 19th St]
212-366-4200
Organize your closet…and your life!
- **Design Within Reach** •
903 Broadway [E 20th St]
212-477-1155
"Within reach" is relative, but the stuff is definitely cool.
- **Eataly** • 200 5th Ave [W 23rd St]
212-229-2560
Over the top (in a good way) Italian culinary superstore.
- **Fishs Eddy** • 889 Broadway [E 19th St]
212-420-9020
Bizarre dishes to complete your cool abode.
- **Jazz Record Center** • 236 W 26th St
212-675-4480
All that jazz!
- **M&J Trimmings** • 1008 6th Ave [W 38th St]
212-391-6200
For your DIY sewing projects.
- **Macy's** • 151 W 34th St [7th Ave]
212-695-4400
Love the wooden escalators.
- **Muji Chelsea** • 16 W 19th St [5th Ave]
212-414-9024
Beautiful Japanese aesthetic applied to daily living.

- **NYC Racquet Sports** • 157 W 35th St [7th Ave]
212-695-5353
Serious tennis supplies.
- **Paragon Sporting Goods** •
867 Broadway [E 18th St]
800-961-3030
Top NYC sporting goods store, plus tennis permits!
- **Rogue Music** • 220 W 30th St [7th Ave]
212-629-3708
Used equipment you probably still can't afford.
- **Sound by Singer** • 242 W 27th St [8th Ave]
212-924-8600
High end audio and video. And we mean "high-end."
- **Spokesman Cycles** • 49 W 36th St [6th Ave]
646-590-0386
Sales, service, repairs, and rentals.
- **Tannen's Magic** • 45 W 34th St [6th Ave]
212-929-4500
Serving both professional and amateur magicians since 1925.
- **Trader Joe's** • 675 6th Ave [W 21st St]
212-255-2106
Staple groceries and fun snacks in private label packaging.
- **Whole Foods** • 250 7th Ave [W 24th St]
212-924-5969
Healthy shopping of the gayborhood.

Map 10 · **Murray Hill / Gramercy**

1
2

13

E 39th St

Second Ave

Tunnel Approach St

E 38th St

Tunnel Exit St

E 37th St

Queens Midtown Tunnel

● The Corinthian

E 36th St

E 35th St

St. Vartan
Park ○

Sniffen Court
Sniffen Ct

A

✉

E 34th St

E 33rd St

33rd Street
6

E 32nd St

Kips Bay
Plaza

✚
NYU
Medical
Center

East
River

E 31st St

First Ave

Park Ave S

Lexington Ave

Second Ave

Third Ave

E 30th St

E 29th St

Curry Hill

E 28th St

28th Street
6

Broadway Aly

E 27th St

E 26th St

69th
Armory

Bellevue
Hospital
Center

✚

E 25th St

Baruch
College

E 24th St

Vet Adm
Medical
Center

Waterside
Plaza

E 23rd St

23rd Street
6

Protestant Welfare
Agencies Building

Mayor James
Harper Residence

✚

Asser Levy Pl

Marina &
Skyport

FDR Dr

Marginal St

National
Arts Club

Gramercy
Park

E 22nd St

E 21st St

Baruch Field ○

Peter Cooper Village

B

The Players ○

E 20th St

Augustus St.
Gaudens Playground ○

Irving Pl

E 19th St

Pete's
Tavern ○

E 18th St

Tammany Hall/
Union Sq Theater

E 17th St

✚

Stuyvesant
Town

Avenue C

Friends Meeting
House

E 16th St

16th St ○

E 16th St

Union Sq

PAGE
284

4 5 6 L

N R Q W

E 16th St

Rutherford Pl

Stuyvesant
Square

Nathan D Perlman Pl

E 15th St

E 15th St

14th Street-
Union Square ○

6

L

3rd Avenue

L

1st Avenue

7

| 1/4 mile | .25 km |

Neighborhood Overview

Map 10

The Murray Hill/Gramercy area of New York is one of New York's largest studies in contrast. On one hand, there are massive housing and hospital complexes that take up several city blocks; on the other hand, there are narrow alleys and small, gated parks of unparalleled beauty. Add it all together and we get (ho-hum) just another brilliant slice of New York.

Murray Hill's contrast, for instance, can be found by checking out lovely little **Sniffen Court**, one's of Manhattan's finest residential alleys, and then walking south to teeming **Kips Bay Plaza**, a set of two parallel housing towers designed by I.M. Pei. Or by watching kids play in **St. Vartan's Park**, then walking south on First Avenue to gaze at the humongous **NYU** and **Bellevue** Medical Centers (by which time, the "hill" portion of Murray Hill has evaporated). For the hill itself, head to Park Avenue and Lexington Avenue in the upper 30s—from there, you can get a sense of why this area is so-named (our unofficial guess is that Park Avenue and 38th Street is about the highest point in these parts). Then walk the side streets in the East Thirties to see some really prime real estate, as well as consulates, hotels, and lots of other stuff you likely can't afford.

Moving south from Murray Hill, the neighborhood changes rather dramatically in the East 20s. You first encounter "**Curry Hill**" on Lexington Avenue in the upper 20s, a fantastic strip of Indian restaurants and groceries. Two large landmarks, one old and one new, punctuate the southern end of this strip—the looming brickwork of the **69th Armory**, now home to many special events throughout the year, and then **Baruch College**'s postmodern main building just south of there (architects like to call this type of building a "vertical campus;" what that means is a 15-minute wait for an elevator between classes). Baruch is joined in this area by two other schools of note, the **School of Visual Arts** and NYU's **Dental School**, both on East 23rd Street.

The area changes again south of 23rd Street, becoming one of New York's loveliest residential neighborhoods, Gramercy Park. The **Gramercy Park** itself is gated, controlled and accessed by those who actually live around it. For the rest of us, we'll just need to be content with looking in at the park through its wrought-iron gates and staring at incredible period architecture facing the park. Our favorite three examples of this architecture are the **Mayor James Harper Residence** on the west side of the park, and the **Players** and **National Arts** Clubs on the southwestern side of the park. Then stroll down hidden Irving Place, a six-block long stretch of restaurants and nightlife options which dead-ends at 14th Street. Classic watering hole **Pete's Tavern**, where writer O. Henry drank, is a must-stop on this walk.

But the aforementioned contrast is still alive and kicking down here, because a few blocks to the east of warm, intimate Gramercy are the hulking **Stuyvesant Town** and Peter Cooper Village housing complexes, which together comprise over 11,000 residential units. Controversy has marked these two huge complexes for the past decades, as longtime owner MetLife spurned a (lower) offer from a tenant's group to buy the complex, instead selling to Tishman Speyer for $5.4 billion in 2006. It was the largest single sale of American property, and then, thanks to a deflated housing market, the largest property fiasco in American history (since Tishman had to turn over the property to its creditors to avoid bankruptcy). For us: no thanks, we'll stick with our Brooklyn walk-ups, and just visit.

Irish pubs abound in this neighborhood, and all of them (**Failte, Molly's, Paddy Reilly's**) have their devotees. We prefer the live music venue **Irving Plaza**, and (of course!) classic watering hole **Pete's Tavern**.

Map 10

14 15
11 12 13
8 9 10
5 6 7

Murray Hill / Gramercy

O Landmarks

- **69th Armory** • 68 Lexington Ave [E 26th St]
  Event space, historic landmark, hookers at night.
- **Baruch College** • 55 Lexington Ave [E 25th St]
  646-312-1000
  Baruch's "vertical campus;" very cool unless you need an elevator quickly.
- **Curry Hill** • Lexington Ave & E 28th St
  Eat your way down Lexington in the 20s!
- **Gramercy Park** • E 20th St & Irving Pl
  New York's only keyed park. This is where the revolution will doubtlessly start.
- **Kips Bay Plaza** • 1st Ave & E 30th St
  I. M. Pei does the superblock, 1960s-style. A tad brutalist.
- **Mayor James Harper Residence** •
  4 Gramercy Park W [E 21st St]
  Cool wrought-iron madness from 1846.
- **MeetingHouse of the Religious Society of Friends** • 15 Rutherford Pl [E 16th St]
  212-673-5750
  Quaker meeting house from 1861. No guns, please.
- **The National Arts Club** •
  15 Gramercy Park S [E 20th St]
  212-475-3424
  One of two beautiful buildings on Gramercy Park South.
- **Pete's Tavern** • 129 E 18th St [Irving Pl]
  212-473-7676
  Where O. Henry hung out. And so should you, at least once.
- **The Players** • 16 Gramercy Park S [E 20th St]
  212-475-6116
  The other cool building on Gramercy Park South.
- **Protestant Welfare Agencies Building** •
  281 Park Ave S [E 22nd St]
  Looming Gothic structure circa 1894. Worth a look.
- **Sniffen Court** • 3rd Ave & E 36th St
  Great little space.
- **St. Vartan Park** • 1st Ave & E 35th St
  Murray Hill kid/playground nexus.
- **Stuyvesant Town** • 1st Ave & E 20th St
  Would you really want to live here? Really?

Coffee

- **Franchia** • 12 Park Ave [E 35th St]
  212-213-1001
  Modern Korean tea and treats.
- **Irving Farm Coffee Roasters** •
  71 Irving Pl [E 19th St]
  212-206-0707
  Brilliant coffee.
- **Lady Mendl's Tea Salon** •
  56 Irving Pl [E 17th St]
  212-533-4600
  It's tea time for the ladies of Manhattan.

Farmers Markets

- **Stuyvesant Town Greenmarket** •
  14th Street Loop & Avenue A
  Sun 9:30 am–4 pm, May–Dec

Murray Hill / Gramercy

Map 10

Irish pubs abound in this neighborhood, and all of them (**Failte, Molly's, Paddy Reilly's**) have their devotees. We prefer the live music venue **Irving Plaza** and (of course!) classic watering hole **Pete's Tavern**.

🅨 Nightlife

- **Bar Jamon** • 125 E 17th St [Irving Pl]
212-253-2773
Pig out at this wine bar.
- **Failte Irish Whiskey Bar** •
531 2nd Ave [E 29th St]
212-725-9440
Sip Guiness by the fire. Shoot a round of pool.
A favorite of Irish Ex-pats.
- **Gramercy Theater** •
127 E 23rd St [Lexington Ave]
212-614-6932
Music venue.
- **Irving Plaza** • 17 Irving Pl [E 15th St]
212-777-6817
Staple rock venue.
- **Molly's** • 287 3rd Ave [E 22nd St]
212-889-3361
Great Irish pub with a fireplace.

- **New York Comedy Club** •
241 E 24th St [3rd Ave]
212-696-5233
…and the bartender asks, "where did you get that?"
- **Paddy Reilly's Music Bar** •
519 2nd Ave [E 29th St]
212-686-1210
Sunday night means pints of Guinness and live Irish fiddlin'.
- **Pete's Tavern** • 129 E 18th St [Irving Pl]
212-473-7676
Where O. Henry hung out. And so should you, at least once.
- **Plug Uglies** • 256 3rd Ave [E 20th St]
212-780-1944
Full length shuffle board table!
- **Rolf's** • 281 3rd Ave [E 22nd St]
212-477-4750
December holiday visit is a must for some German bier.
- **Ted's Corner Tavern** • 523 3rd Ave [E 35th St]
212-689-2676
Ted sure has good taste in craft beer. Plus Mediterranean food.

Map 10

14 15
11 12 13
8 9 **10**
5 6 7

Murray Hill / Gramercy

Restaurants

- **2nd Avenue Deli** •
  162 E 33rd St [Lexington Ave]
  212-689-9000 • $$
  Reborn in a new location. Miracles do happen.
- **Anjappar Chettinad** •
  116 Lexington Ave [E 28th St]
  917-540-5287 • $$$
  Southern Indian food from a global chain. And
  a full bar.
- **Bar Jamon** • 125 E 17th St [Irving Pl]
  212-253-2773 • $
  Pig out at this wine bar.
- **Chote Nawab** • 115 Lexington Ave [E 28th St]
  212-679-4603 • $$$
  Nice Indian restaurant with lots of seafood
  options.
- **Coppola's** • 378 3rd Ave [E 27th St]
  212-679-0070 • $$
  Neighborhood Italian.
- **El Parador Café** • 325 E 34th St [2nd Ave]
  212-679-6812 • $$$
  NY's oldest and friendliest Mexican.
- **El Pote** • 718 2nd Ave [E 39th St]
  212-889-6680 • $$$
  Spanish food in all its classic, old-school
  glory.
- **Franchia** • 12 Park Ave [E 35th St]
  212-213-1001 • $$
  Modern Korean tea and treats.
- **Friend of a Farmer** • 77 Irving Pl [E 19th St]
  212-477-2188 • $$$
  Chic country-cooking.

- **Gemini Diner** • 641 2nd Ave [E 35th St]
  212-532-2143 • $$
  Open 24 hours. Diner.
- **Haandi** • 113 Lexington Ave [E 28th St]
  212-685-5200 • $$
  Stellar Pakistani grilled meats.
- **Irving Farm Coffee Roasters** •
  71 Irving Pl [E 19th St]
  212-206-0707 • $
  Good coffee, great treats, superior service.
- **Jackson Hole** • 521 3rd Ave [E 35th St]
  212-679-3264 • $$
  Extremely large burgers. A post-drinkfest
  must.
- **Joe Jr** • 167 3rd Ave [E 16th St]
  212-473-5150 • $
  Great diner atmosphere, fairly decent diner
  food.
- **L'Express** • 249 Park Ave S [E 20th St]
  212-254-5858 • $$
  Always-open French diner.
- **Le Parisien Bistrot** • 163 E 33rd St [3rd Ave]
  212-889-5489 • $$$
  Classic French bistro fare.

Murray Hill / Gramercy

Everyone has their Curry Hill favorite; ours is vegetarian dosa house **Pongal**. **Riverpark** spiffs up an underserved corner of Kips Bay. The sleeper pick here is **Turkish Kitchen**, our favorite Turkish in all of New York.

- **Mexico Lindo** • 459 2nd Ave [E 26th St]
  212-679-3665 • $$$
  Famous Mexican food.
- **Murray Hill Diner** •
  222 Lexington Ave [E 33rd St]
  212-686-6667 • $$
  Last of a vanishing breed. Simple Greek food and greasy classics.
- **Novita** • 102 E 22nd St [Park Ave S]
  212-677-2222 • $$$$
  Sophisticated Italian without the pretension.
- **Penelope** • 159 Lexington Ave [E 30th St]
  212-481-3800 • $$
  Gingham décor but oh, what a menu!
- **Pete's Tavern** • 129 E 18th St [Irving Pl]
  212-473-7676 • $$$$
  Good pub food, especially after/while drinking!
- **Pongal** • 110 Lexington Ave [E 28th St]
  212-696-9458 • $$
  Possibly NY's best vegetarian Indian. Sada dosa...mmmm.
- **Posto** • 310 2nd Ave [E 18th St]
  212-716-1200 • $$
  Savory thin-crust pizza, salads.
- **Riverpark** • 450 E 29th St [1st Ave]
  212-706-4131 • $$$$$
  Seasonal cuisine in an underserved corner of Kips Bay.
- **Sam's Place** • 132 E 39th St [Lexington Ave]
  212-599-6360 • $$$
  Hidden old-school Italian haunt

- **Saravana Bhavan** •
  81 Lexington Ave [E 26th St]
  212-684-7755 • $$
  All about the dosas at this multi-national Indian vegetarian spot.
- **Sarge's Deli** • 548 3rd Ave [E 37th St]
  212-679-0442 • $$
  24-hour-a-day pastrami, convenient to GCT.
- **Turkish Kitchen** • 386 3rd Ave [E 28th St]
  212-679-6633 • $$$
  Excellent Turkish, great décor, brilliant bread. NFT pick!
- **Union Square Café** • 101 E 19th St
  212-243-4020 • $$$$$
  Second location of first restaurant of Danny Meyer's empire.
- **Upland** • 345 Park Ave S [E 26th St]
  212-686-1006 • $$$$
  If San Bernandino County were on the Tyrrhenian Sea.
- **Vatan** • 409 3rd Ave [E 29th St]
  212-689-5666 • $$$
  All-you-can-eat vegetarian Indian feast.
- **Vezzo** • 178 Lexington Ave [E 31st St]
  212-839-8300 • $$
  From the owners of Gruppo and Posto. Delizioso.
- **The Water Club** • FDR Drive & 30th St
  212-683-3333 • $$$$
  Romantic, good brunch on the East River.
- **Yama** • 122 E 17th St [Irving Pl]
  212-475-0969 • $$$
  Sushi deluxe.

Map 10

14 15
11 12 13
8 9 **10**
5 6 7

Murray Hill / Gramercy

 Shopping

- **City Opera Thrift Shop •**
  222 E 23rd St [3rd Ave]
  212-684-5344
  They always have something or other.
- **Dover Street Market •**
  160 Lexington Ave [30th St]
  646-837-7750
  Multi-floor multi-brand orgy of fashion.
- **Foods of India** • 121 Lexington Ave [E 28th St]
  212-679-4444
  Huge selection including harder to find spices.
- **Housing Works Thrift Shop •**
  157 E 23rd St [Lexington Ave]
  929-314-2149
  Our favorite thrift store.

- **Kalustyan's** • 123 Lexington Ave [E 28th St]
  212-685-3451
  International spice and specialty food market
  dating back to 1944.
- **La Delice Pastry Shop •**
  372 3rd Ave [E 27th St]
  212-532-4409
  Delectable pastries, buttery croissants, layer
  cakes.

Murray Hill / Gramercy

Map 10

The constantly changing **Dover Street Market** is a boffo orgy of high-end designers. Hit **Lamazou** cheese shop to go along with pastries from **La Delice**. Indian shops **Foods of India** and **Kalustyan's** are always worth a look—and will have any cheese you could ever need and **Nuthouse Hardware** is New York's only 24-hour hardware store, with power tool rentals. Cool.

- **Ligne Roset** • 250 Park Ave S [E 20th St]
  212-375-1036
  Modern, sleek furniture. Only for people with very good jobs.
- **Max Nass** • 118 E 28th St [Lexington Ave]
  212-679-8154
  Vintage jewelry, repairs, restringing, and restoration.
- **Nemo Tile Company** • 48 E 21st St [Broadway]
  212-505-0009
  Good tile shop for small projects.
- **Nuthouse Hardware** • 202 E 29th St [3rd Ave]
  212-545-1447
  Open 24-hours; equipment rentals, too.

- **Vintage Thrift Shop** • 286 3rd Ave [E 22nd St]
  212-871-0777
  Vintage clothes you can actually afford.

Map 11 · Hell's Kitchen

Time Warner Center

PAGE 266

Columbus Circle

59th Street Columbus Circle

Dewitt Clinton Park

Daily Show Studio

Hudson River

Hudson River Park

West Side Hwy

PAGE 262

Henry Hudson PKWY

Eleventh Ave

Tenth Ave

Ninth Ave

Eighth Ave

50th Street

Associated Musicians of Greater New York

Intrepid Sea, Air and Space Museum

Restaurant Row

Broadway Dance Center

Theatre Row

42nd Street Port Authority Bus Terminal

Port Authority Bus Terminal

PAGE 320

Lincoln Tunnel

The Annex/ Hell's Kitchen Flea Market

Dyer Ave

Jacob K Javits Convention Center

PAGE 264

| 1/4 mile | .25 km |

W 60th St
W 59th St
W 58th St
W 57th St
W 56th St
W 55th St
W 54th St
W 53rd St
W 52nd St
W 51st St
W 50th St
W 49th St
W 48th St
W 47th St
W 46th St
W 45th St
W 44th St
W 43rd St
W 42nd St
W 41st St
W 40th St
W 39th St
W 38th St
W 37th St

Neighborhood Overview

Map 11

Named for the squalor its early immigrant tenements epitomized, the scruffy patch of bodega-infused real estate between Broadway and that unlikely landing strip known as the Hudson is home to intimate theaters, niche restaurants and—along with a rising tide of gentrification—an army of toy dogs likely to stage a coup one day. The neighborhood is also characterized by an abundance of things too big and ugly to put anywhere else in Manhattan: car dealerships, cell phone towers, cruise liners, the Port Authority, and stables for those hansom cab horses, the last of which accounts for certain odors and the distinct clip-clop of every rush hour.

It's also farther west than most subways venture, harshly industrial-looking and often beset by Lincoln Tunnel traffic or gale-force nautical winds. Yes, Hell's Kitchen may seem like the edge of the civilized world, and the panoramic view of New Jersey does little to dampen this grungy impression. Yet most locals come to cherish the mellow vibe and dearth of McDonald's locations that come with living just outside Manhattan's hyperkinetic and tourist-infested core. And as for the out-of-towners—well, they only get as far in as Ninth Avenue before their legs get tired.

Hell's Kitchen may be close to Central Park, but why fight the crowds? Instead explore **Hudson River Park**, an elegantly sculpted swath of greenery running along the coast of the island. Its linearity makes for ideal bikers and joggers, but the idle will find plenty of lovely spots to spread a picnic blanket and watch lunatics paddle by in kayaks. **Dewitt Clinton Park** always has an entertaining game going on its baseball/soccer/everything field; it also boasts two popular dog runs for the bonding of canines and their owners alike. Community gardens have sprung up there and close by, thanks to green-thumbed volunteers from the area.

Two essential elements to absorb: one you find on stage, and the other you find on the end of a fork—usually in that order. The former is available at one of the countless off- and off-off-Broadway theatres lying around—you know, the type that isn't showing something along the lines of "A Musical Loosely Cobbled Together From A String Of #1 Hit Singles"? **Theatre Row** is, as the name suggests, a lineup of such venues featuring, ahem, riskier fare—though perhaps not as scandalous as the peepshows that once littered that stretch of 42nd Street. Satirical mainstay **The Daily Show** also tapes around here, if you're looking for entertainment that's as free as it is hilarious. Head up to **Restaurant Row** on 46th to sample one of the cozy eateries and candlelit nightlife nooks that cater to audiences after the curtain falls. Almost every sub-genre of food is accounted for, and authenticity is rampant—don't be surprised to find actual French people eating at a French bistro!

Mom-and-pop places have proved resilient—everything from artisanal bread to custom-made paints can be found in tiny stores run by devoted experts. You might even see an old-school coffee shop without so much as a name on a sign out front. The usual gridlock is traded for a bazaar of vintage clothing, jewelry and collectibles, most priced a bit cheaper than they were before these particular vendors moved from a Chelsea location known as The Annex.

Map 11

Hell's Kitchen

O Landmarks

- **Broadway Dance Center** • 322 W 45th St [Broadway]
  212-582-9304
  The place for tap lessons.
- **Daily Show Studio** • 733 11th Ave [W 52nd St]
  Home of our favorite TV show. Thank you Jon Stewart.
- **Dewitt Clinton Park** • 11th Ave & W 52nd St
  Where the neighborhood mutts meet to sniff butts.
- **Intrepid Sea, Air and Space Museum** •
  Pier 86, W 46th St
  212-245-0072
  Holy crap! An aircraft carrier in the middle of the Hudson River!
- **Port Authority Bus Terminal** •
  625 8th Ave [W 41st St]
  212-564-8484
  Add an "S" and you've got a sporting goods chain.
- **Restaurant Row** • 8th Ave & W 46th St
  Mingle with tourists during pre-theater dinners.
- **Theatre Row** • W 42nd St b/n 9th & Dyer Aves
  Cluster of off-Broadway theatres including Playwrights Horizons.

Farmers Markets

- **57th Street Greenmarket** •
  10th Ave & W 57th St
  Wed and Sat 8am–3pm, Jun–Nov.

Land of contrast: Reservations are essential at **Bar Centrale**, with its speakeasy vibe and classic cocktails—and then there's an utter dive like **Rudy's Bar & Grill**, which serves each beer with a free hot dog. Elsewhere, you've got a decadent club-style concert venue **Terminal 5**.

 Nightlife

- **Bar Centrale** • 324 W 46th St [8th Ave]
  212-581-3130
  Make reservations to see Broadway stars relaxing after the show.
- **Birdland** • 315 W 44th St [8th Ave]
  212-581-3080
  Top-notch jazz.
- **Blue Ruin** • 538 9th Ave [W 40th St]
  917-346-7043
  Pressed tin ceiling and lots of booze.
- **Don't Tell Mama** • 343 W 46th St [8th Ave]
  212-757-0788
  Good cabaret space.
- **Flaming Saddles** • 793 9th Ave [W 53rd St]
  212-713-0481
  Country-western, gay, bartenders dance on the bar, lots of cuties.
- **Gossip Bar & Restaurant** •
  733 9th Ave [W 50th St]
  212-265-2720
  Amazing staff, great selection, comfortable atmosphere
- **Harbor NYC Rooftop** • 621 W 46th St [11th Ave]
  212-944-0458
  Rooftop space with nice views.
- **Industry** • 355 W 52nd St [9th Ave]
  646-476-2747
  Large space with great decor, hot bartenders; come with friends.
- **Laurie Beechman Theatre** •
  407 W 42nd St [9th Ave]
  212-695-6909
  Intimate basement cabaret with fabulous drag shows.
- **The Ritz** • 369 W 46th St [9th Ave]
  212-333-4177
  Three floors, two patios, no cover.
- **Rudy's Bar & Grill** • 627 9th Ave [W 44th St]
  646-707-0890
  Classic Hell's Kitchen. Recommended.
- **Swing 46** • 349 W 46th St [9th Ave]
  212-262-9554
  Good place for a drink before a show.
- **The Tank** • 312 W 36th St
  212-563-6269
  Major destination for experimental music.
- **Terminal 5** • 610 W 56th St [11th Ave]
  212-582-6600
  Ex-club space now used for mid-level indie bands.
- **Valhalla** • 815 9th Ave [W 54th St]
  212-757-2747
  Warm, wooden watering hole with staggering beer selection.

Map 11

Hell's Kitchen

Restaurants

- **2 Bros Pizza** • 542 9th Ave [W 40th St]
  212-695-2642 • $
  Decent pizza for the price.
- **5 Napkin Burger** • 630 9th Ave [W 45th St]
  212-757-2277 • $$
  Pricey burgers.
- **99 Cents Fresh Pizza** • 1723 Broadway [W 41st St]
  212-245-2155 •
  Yeah it's cheap, but watch out for the crazies.
- **Ariana Afghan Kebab** •
  787 9th Ave [W 52nd St]
  212-262-2323 • $
  Afghan. Always go for the lamb.
- **Arriba Arriba Mexican Restaurant** •
  762 9th Ave [W 51st St]
  212-489-0810 • $$
  Sangria and large Mexican lunch for $7 bucks.
- **Bar Masa** • 10 Columbus Cir [Broadway]
  212-823-9800 • $$$$
  Brilliant and expensive. But still a lot cheaper than Masa.
- **Burrito Box** • 885 9th Ave [W 57th St]
  212-489-6889 • $
  Cheap and tasty Mexican with killer guac.
- **Chipotle** • 620 9th Ave [W 44th St]
  212-247-3275 • $
  Cheap, fast, Mex-American goodness in mall-like setting.
- **Churrascaria Plataforma** •
  316 W 49th St [8th Ave]
  212-245-0505 • $$$$
  Brazilian Feast! Don't eat all day…then come here.

- **Danji** • 346 W 52nd St [9th Ave]
  212-586-2880 • $$$
  Gourmet Korean small plates with a twist.
- **Don Giovanni Ristorante** •
  358 W 44th St [9th Ave]
  212-581-4939 • $$
  One of the better cheap pies in the city.
- **El Centro** • 824 9th Ave [W 54th St]
  917-409-1171 • $
  Open late for those sudden south-of-the-border cravings.
- **Empanada Mama** • 763 9th Ave [W 51st St]
  212-698-9008 • $
  No one fries them better.
- **Gossip Bar & Restaurant** •
  733 9th Ave [W 50th St]
  212-265-2720 • $$
  Irish fare, amazing staff, guilty-pleasure menu, awesome bar.
- **Guantanamera** • 939 8th Ave [W 56th St]
  212-262-5354 • $$$
  Tasty Cuban. Great for lunch.

Hell's Kitchen

Map 11

14 15
11 12 13
8 9 10
5 6 7

The breadth and depth of deliciousness is staggering here. Guantanamera has live music some nights and delicious Cuban eats every night. Middle Eastern lovers get their fix at **Hummus Kitchen**.

- **Hummus Kitchen** • 768 9th Ave [W 51st St]
212-333-3009 • $$
Hummus so good they named a kitchen after it.
- **Ippudo** • 321 W 51st St [8th Ave]
212-974-2500 • $$
Famous ramen with less wait than the downtown location.
- **Joe Allen** • 326 W 46th St [8th Ave]
212-581-6464 • $$$
De rigueur stargazing, open late.
- **Luckys Famous Burgers** •
370 W 52nd St [9th Ave]
(212) 247-6717 • $
Minimalist, messily-devoured takeout burgers.
- **Marseille** • 630 9th Ave [W 44th St]
212-333-2323 • $$$$
True to the name, an expatriate's delight.
- **Nizza** • 630 9th Ave [W 45th St]
212-956-1800 • $$
Share some fantastic antipasti: socca, tapenade, focaccette, and more.
- **Orso** • 322 W 46th St [8th Ave]
212-489-7212 • $$$$
Popular busy Italian.
- **Per Se** • 10 Columbus Cir [W 58th St]
212-823-9335 • $$$$$
Divine…but you practically have to sell a kidney to afford it.
- **Pio Pio** • 604 10th Ave [W 44th St]
212-459-2929 • $$
Excellent Peruvian in great setting, especially the ceviche and chicken.
- **Pure Thai Cookhouse** • 766 9th Ave [51st St]
212-581-0999 • $$
Tasty, affordable Thai in a classy little dining room.

- **Shake Shack** • 691 8th Ave [W 44th St]
646-435-0135 • $$
Danny Meyer's pitch-perfect burger joint.
- **Totto Ramen** • 464 W 51st St [9th Ave]
646-596-9056 • $$
Incredible ramen, just be prepared to line up.
- **Turkish Cuisine** • 631 9th Ave [W 44th St]
212-397-9650 • $$
Turkish food, in case you were wondering. It's always good.
- **ViceVersa** • 325 W 51st St [8th Ave]
212-399-9291 • $$$$
Creative yet accessible Italian cuisine with a cool, sleek vibe.
- **Whole Foods** • 10 Columbus Cir [8th Ave]
212-823-9600 • $
By far the cheapest eats in Time Warner Center. Euros love it.

Map 11

14 | 15
11 | 12 | 13
8 | 9 | 10
5 | 6 | 7

Shopping

- **10th Avenue Wines & Liquors** •
  812 10th Ave [W 54th St]
  212-245-6700
  Boozehound specials and tastings.
- **Amish Market** • 731 9th Ave [W 50th St]
  212-245-2360
  Good prepared foods, unfortunately not
  delivered via horse and buggy.
- **Amy's Bread** • 672 9th Ave [W 47th St]
  212-977-2670
  Providing the heavenly smells that wake up
  Hell's Kitchen.

- **Coco and Toto** • 730 11th Ave [W 52nd St]
  212-956-5822
  Adorable pet boutique grooms, walks, and
  babysits beloved furballs.
- **Delphinium Home** • 353 W 47th St [9th Ave]
  212-333-7732
  For the "too lazy to make my own card" set.
- **Epstein's Paint Center** •
  562 W 52nd St [W 52nd St]
  212-265-3960
  Honest advice, top quality from century-old
  shop.
- **Happy Feet** • 754 10th Ave [W 51st St]
  212-757-8400
  Reliable deals on all imaginable pet supplies.

Hell's Kitchen

Map 11

14 15
11 12 13
8 9 10
5 6 7

Amish Market is the top-end supermarket; Ninth Avenue International is amazing for Greek groceries. Sullivan Street Bakery makes bundles of heaven disguised as bread. Delphinium is the store where you can buy a non-Hallmark card.

- **Janovic** • 766 10th Ave
212-245-3241
Top NYC paint store. Shades/blinds too.
- **Liberty Bicycles** • 846 9th Ave [W 55th St]
212-757-2418
This bike shop totally rocks.
- **Little Pie Company** • 424 W 43rd St [9th Ave]
212-736-4780
A homemade dessert equals happiness.
- **Ninth Avenue International Grocery** •
543 9th Ave [W 40th St]
212-279-1000
Mediterranean/Greek specialty store.
- **Ninth Avenue Vintner** •
669 9th Ave [W 46th St]
212-664-9463
Good suggestions from the staff.
- **Pan Aqua Diving** • 460 W 43rd St [10th Ave]
212-736-3483
SCUBA equipment and courses.

- **Poseidon Greek Bakery** •
629 9th Ave [W 44th St]
212-757-6173
Old-school Greek delicacies like spanakopita.
- **Sea Breeze Fish Market** •
541 9th Ave [W 40th St]
212-563-7537
Bargains on fresh seafood.
- **Sullivan Street Bakery** •
533 W 47th St [11th Ave]
212-265-5580
Artisan breads, foodie approved. NFT approved. God approved.
- **Tumi** • 10 Columbus Cir [8th Ave]
212-823-9390
When your luggage gets lost and insurance is paying.
- **Whole Foods** • 10 Columbus Cir [8th Ave]
212-823-9600
"Whole Paycheck" everywhere except NYC, where it beats Food Emporium.

Map 12 • Midtown

Neighborhood Overview

Welcome to the heart of everything—clogged arteries and all. An utter tourist hell to some, Midtown may also be where you slave away in an antiseptic glass tower for more than half your waking day. But while many avoid the area altogether, **Times Square** and its side streets possess ample virtues. If you can tolerate the slow walkers, group photos, and incessant invitations to comedy shows, you'll be rewarded with some of New York's finest art and most impressive architecture, the brightest lights this side of Tokyo, world-famous hotels and cathedrals, a pair of iconic animal statues, and of course a little animal known as Broadway.

Topping our Midtown list is **The Museum of Modern Art**. Yes, it's pricey and gets packed on the weekend, but the art will blow your mind and the sculpture garden is divine. Bargain tip: it's free on Friday evenings. If you still enjoy the smell and feel of real-live books, the main branch of the **New York Public Library** (guarded by the famous lion statues *Patience* and *Fortitude*) is spectacular. Inside, visit The Map Room and The Rose Main Reading Room, one of the most beautiful spaces in the world to get lost in a book. Right outside, you can bask on the lawn of beautiful **Bryant Park**, stare up at the sky, and transcend the chaos of the city. At least until a pigeon poops on you or a swarm of moviegoers tramples your mellow.

For a dose of glamour and history, stop in at the **Algonquin Hotel**, where famous writers, entertainers, and socialites used to cavort and carouse in the 1920s. To see how the ultra-rich used to (and still) live, pop into the gorgeous **Plaza Hotel**. If you have a small fortune lying around unused, we hear the Edwardian Suite is quite suitable. Gaze at the exquisite, 1908 facade of the **Alwyn Court Apartments** and decide if you would rather live behind those walls or just look at them like a fine sculpture.

Times Square is the dominion of tourists, but it's worth walking around in late at night when they're back in their hotels, so you can check out the cool pedestrian plaza where the street used to be (though we kind of miss the comfy lawn chairs from the first summer they tried it). One of the area's greatest assets is, of course, the Broadway theatre scene. If you need cheap tickets to a play or musical, weave through the crowds to the **TKTS** booth. After braving the line, grab a seat on the actually-really-awesome bleachers that climb over the booth like a staircase. The real gems, though, can be found on the periphery of the square, including the striking **New York Times Building**, and the rare tourist-free bar, **Jimmy's Corner**.

Midtown is home to oodles of thrilling architecture. Arguably, the most exciting is the **Hearst Tower**, a stunning masterpiece blending old and new, and the first "green" skyscraper in New York. Sprouting through the roof of the original 1928 building is an angular tower built with recycled steel, completed in 2006. Duck into the lobby to check out the one-of-a-kind water sculpture. Other architectural highlights include **Carnegie Hall**, **St. Patrick's Cathedral**, **St. Thomas Church**, **Villard House**, **Rockefeller Center**, **One Bryant Park**, and the **American Radiator Building**. And finally, don't miss the trippy **Austrian Cultural Forum**, which hosts a number of events open to the public.

For a change of pace, check out **Little Brazil**'s small strip of restaurants, bars (some with live music), and shops. Or go north a block to the famous **Diamond District**, which appeared in the 1940s when Orthodox Jews transplanted here from war-torn Europe. Finally, stare up at **The Debt Clock** and ponder how this nation's permanent structural deficit will likely bankrupt your theoretical grandchildren. You may decide you need a drink after seeing how the debt-to-GDP ratio creeps inexorably ever upward; on second thought, make that a double.

Map 12

Midtown

14 15
11 **12** 13
8 9 10
5 6 7

○ Landmarks

- **30 Rockefeller Plaza** •
30 Rockefeller Plaza [W 51st St]
Tallest building at Rock Center;
RCA = GE = Comcast.
- **Algonquin Hotel** • 59 W 44th St [6th Ave]
212-840-6800
Where snark was invented.
- **Alwyn Court Apartments** •
180 W 58th St [7th Ave]
212-581-4940
100-year-old apartment building with
awesomely detailed exterior.
- **American Radiator Building** •
40 W 40th St [6th Ave]
Massive gold-and-black Art Deco gem looms
over Bryant Park.
- **Bryant Park** • 6th Ave & W 42nd St
Summer movies, winter ice-skating, hook-ups
year-round.
- **Carnegie Hall** • 881 7th Ave [W 57th St]
212-247-7800
Stock up on free cough drops in the lobby.
- **The Debt Clock** • 6th Ave & W 44th St
How much the US has borrowed—pennies,
really.
- **Diamond District** •
W 47th St b/n 5th & 6th Ave
Big rocks abound! Center of the world's
diamond industry.
- **Hearst Tower** • 300 W 57th St [8th Ave]
It's green! It's mean! It's fit to be seen!
- **Little Brazil** • W 46th St b/n 5th & 6th Ave
Small stretch of Brazilian businesses. Gisele
not included.
- **Museum of Modern Art (MoMA)** •
11 W 53rd St [5th Ave]
212-708-9400
Is there anything these Rockefellers don't do?
- **New York Public Library** •
5th Ave & W 42nd St
917-275-6975
Wonderful Beaux-Arts building with stunning
reading room.
- **New York Times Building** •
8th Ave & W 40th St
Renzo Piano's impressive new home for The
Gray Lady.
- **One Bryant Park** • 1111 6th Ave [W 42nd St]
212-257-6600
Sleek, elegant, and environmentally friendly.

- **The Plaza Hotel** • 768 5th Ave [W 58th St]
212-759-3000
Now anyone can be Eloise with her own Plaza
condo.
- **Rockefeller Center** •
45 Rockefeller Plaza [W 49th St]
212-588-8601
Sculpture, ice skating, and a mall!
- **St. Patrick's Cathedral** • 5th Ave & E 51st St
212-753-2261
NYC's classic cathedral.
- **Times Square** • 7th Ave & W 42nd St
It looks even cooler than it does on TV!
- **TKTS** • Broadway & W 47th St
Get cheap Broadway tix underneath the cool
looking stairs.
- **Villard House** • 457 Madison Ave [E 51st St]
Killer brownstone palazzos by holy fathers
McKim, Mead & White.
- **Ziegfeld Ballroom** • 141 W 54th St [6th Ave]
212-268-9400
Glorious 1969 movie palace-turned-event
space.

Coffee

- **Blue Bottle Coffee** •
1 Rockefeller Ctr [5th Ave]
Cult coffee that's more lab than shop.
- **Blue Bottle Coffee** •
54 W 40th St [6th Ave]
Bryant Park outpost of cult coffee masters.
- **Zibetto** • 1385 6th Ave [W 56th St]
646-707-0505
A real Italian espresso bar. Un caffe, per favore!

Midtown

Grab a cocktail at the elegant and laid-back **Faces & Names**, or belly up to the bar at **Jimmy's Corner** for a beer and a shot. Bowl some frames at, uh, **Frames** in Port Authority or the nearby **Bowlero**. Other options: **Iridium** for jazz, **King Cole** for class, or escape it all on the patio of **Bookmarks**.

Nightlife

- **Blue Bar** • 59 W 44th St [6th Ave]
212-840-6800
If you're in the mood for a Harvey Wallbanger.
- **Bookmarks** • 299 Madison Ave [E 41st St]
212-204-5498
Escape the Midtown ruckus at this nifty rooftop bar.
- **Bowlero** • 222 W 44th St [7th Ave]
212-680-0012
Huge portions of pub grub & flat-screen TV sports in a stadium-themed eatery inside Bowlmor Lanes.
- **The Carnegie Club** • 156 W 56th St [7th Ave]
212-957-9676
Drink your 50-year-old cognac with your 22-year-old date.
- **Dave & Busters** • 234 W 42nd St [6th Ave]
646-495-2015
Another dateless Friday night.
- **Faces & Names** • 159 W 54th St [7th Ave]
212-586-9311
Fabulous staff, elegant vibe, superb bar and very good food.
- **Flute** • 205 W 54th St [7th Ave]
212-265-5169
Munch on strawberries and cream with your bubbly.
- **Frames** •550 9th Ave [40th St]
212-268-6909
Bowling alley with cocktails and dancing.
- **Iridium Jazz Club** •
1650 Broadway [W 51st St]
212-582-2121
Good mainstream jazz venue. Pricey.

- **Jimmy's Corner** • 140 W 44th St [Broadway]
212-221-9510
This cozy joint is the best bar around here, trust us.
- **Judge Roy Bean Public House** •
38 W 56th St [5th Ave]
212-262-8300
When you need a craft beer in Midtown.
- **King Cole Bar** • 2 E 55th St [5th Ave]
212-753-4500
Drink a red snapper and admire the gorgeous mural.
- **R Lounge** • 714 7th Ave [W 48th St]
212-261-5114
Sip cocktails with (gulp) tourists and take in the fine view.
- **Royalton Hotel** • 44 W 44th St [5th Ave]
212-869-4400
Starck + Schrager = cool.
- **The Rum House** • 228 W 47th St [Broadway]
646-490-6924
Dive smell gone, but fun still remains.
- **Russian Vodka Room** •
265 W 52nd St [8th Ave]
212-307-5835
Russian molls and cranberry vodka. Awesome.
- **Sardi's** • 234 W 44th St [7th Ave]
212-221-8440
Absorb the sacred DNA at the upstairs bar.
- **View Lounge** • 1535 Broadway [W 46th St]
212-704-8900
Down a drink on the 48th floor, then get out.
- **Whiskey Trader** • 71 W 55th St [6th Ave]
212-582-2223
Awesome lounge/sports bar hybrid with good drink specials.

Map 12

Map 12

Midtown

14 15
11 12 13
8 9 10
5 6 7

🍴 Restaurants

- **Akdeniz** • 19 W 46th St [5th Ave]
212-575-2307 • $$
Turkish oasis in Midtown.
- **Angelo's Pizza** • 1697 Broadway [W 53rd St]
212-245-8811 • $$
For total tourist pizza, it ain't half bad.
- **Applejack Diner** • 230 W 55th St [Broadway]
212-586-6075 •
Endless cup of coffee.
- **BG** • 754 5th Ave [W 57th St]
212-872-8977 • $$$$$
Another reason to spend the whole day at
Bergdorf's.
- **Blue Fin** • 1567 Broadway [W 47th St]
212-918-1400 • $$$
Sleek, stylish seafood & sushi spot in the W
Hotel.
- **Burger Joint** • 119 W 56th St [6th Ave]
212-708-7414 • $
Fancy hotel lobby leads to unexpected burger
dive. Awesome.

- **Cafe Zaiya** • 1073 6th Ave
212-764-6785 • $$
Japanese food court that's cheap and fast.
- **Carmine's** • 200 W 44th St [7th Ave]
212-221-3800 • $$
Pre-theater Italian standby with ungodly
portions.
- **Cosmic Diner** • 888 8th Ave [W 53rd St]
212-333-5888 • $
Great food, large portions, they do take out.
- **Estiatorio Milos** • 125 W 55th St [6th Ave]
212-245-7400 • $$$$
Fancified Greek food for people with expense
accounts.
- **Faces & Names** • 159 W 54th St [7th Ave]
212-586-9311 • $$
Fabulous staff, elegant vibe, superb bar, and
very good food.
- **Gabriel Kreuther** • 41 W 42nd St [6th Ave]
212-257-5826 • $$$$$
Danny Meyer alum's Alsatian-inflected
four-star dining experience.
- **Haru** • 229 W 43rd St [7th Ave]
212-398-9810 • $$$$
Excellent mid-range Japanese. Loud, good.
- **Indian Accent** • 123 W 56th St [6th Ave]
212-842-8070 • $$$$
Elegant, high-end Indian cuisine; nary a steam
table in sight.
- **John's Pizzeria** • 260 W 44th St [8th Ave]
212-391-7560 • $$
A tad touristy, but fantastic pizza and a great
space.

14 | 15
11 | 12 | 13
8 | 9 | 10
5 | 6 | 7

There's something for every taste in this area. Greasy burgers tucked inside a fancy hotel at **Burger Joint**, cheap Cuban sandwiches at Margon, street food at the halal cart at **53rd & 6th**. For high-end experiences, savor the French-American fare at **The Modern** or the seafood at **Le Bernardin**.

- **La Bonne Soupe** • 48 W 55th St [5th Ave]
  212-586-7650 • $$
  Ooh la la, the best salad dressing accompanies my soupe a l'oignon.
- **Le Bernardin** • 155 W 51st St [7th Ave]
  212-554-1515 • $$$$$
  Top NYC seafood.
- **Mangia** • 50 W 57th St [6th Ave]
  212 582-5882 • $
  Caterers with a café.
- **Margon** • 136 W 46th St [7th Ave]
  212-354-5013 • $
  Great Cuban sandwiches but the coffee is the real hit.
- **The Modern** • 9 W 53rd St [5th Ave]
  212-333-1220 • $$$$
  With gnocchi to die for, spend a lot and then STILL splurge on dessert.
- **Nobu 57** • 40 W 57th St [5th Ave]
  212-757-3000 • $$$$$
  Uptown branch of wildly popular and renowned downtown sushi joints.
- **Obica Mozzarella Bar** •
  590 Madison Ave [E 57th St]
  212-355-2217 • $$
  A strange but tasty concept.
- **Oceana** • 120 W 49th St [6th Ave]
  212-759-5941 • $$$$$
  Le Bernadin Jr.
- **The Palm Restaurant** •
  250 W 50th St [8th Ave]
  212-333-7256 • $$$$
  Upscale but friendly, everything is delicious and staff is superb.
- **Petrossian** • 911 7th Ave [7th Ave]
  212-245-2217 • $$$$$
  The decor's not updated, but the fare is FINE.
- **Pret a Manger** • 1350 6th Ave [W 54th St]
  646-609-3360 • $
  British sandwich chain.
- **Redeye Grill** • 890 7th Ave [W 56th St]
  212-541-9000 • $$$
  Sprawling and diverse.
- **Robert** • 2 Columbus Cir [W 58th St]
  212-299-7730 • $$$$$
  Posh dining atop the Museum of Arts & Design. Someone take us, please?
- **Russian Samovar** • 256 W 52nd St [8th Ave]
  212-757-0168 • $$$
  Classic Russian food and flavored vodkas.
- **The Russian Tea Room** •
  150 W 57th St [7th Ave]
  212-581-7100 • $$$$$
  Exquisite Russian dining experience & New York icon.
- **Tina's Cuban Cuisine** • 23 W 56th St [5th Ave]
  212-315-4313 • $$
  Straight up classics like rice, beans, roast pork and plantains.
- **Toloache** • 251 W 50th St [8th Ave]
  212-581-1818 • $$$
  Designer Mexican in Midtown.
- **Virgil's Real BBQ** • 152 W 44th St [6th Ave]
  212-921-9494 • $$$
  It's real. Hush puppies and CFS to die for.

Map 12

14 15
11 **12** 13
8 9 10
5 6 7

Midtown

Shopping

- **Apple Store (Fifth Avenue)** •
767 5th Ave [E 59th St]
212-336-1440
Giant glass shrine houses all things Apple.
- **Bergdorf Goodman** • 754 5th Ave [W 57th St]
212-753-7300
Hands down—the best windows in the
business.
- **Burberry** • 9 E 57th St [5th Ave]
212-407-7100
Signature "beige plaid" purveyor.
- **Chanel** • 15 E 57th St [5th Ave]
212-355-5050
Official outfitter of "ladies who lunch."

- **Ermenegildo Zegna** • 4 W 57th St
212-421-4488
A truly stylish and classic Italian designer.
- **Forever 21** • 1540 Broadway [W 45th St]
212-302-0594
Open til 1 am, lifesaver during late-night
wardrobe emergencies.
- **MoMA Design and Book Store** •
11 W 53rd St [5th Ave]
212-708-9700
Cutting-edge, minimalist, ergonomic, offbeat,
and funky everything.
- **Muji Times Square** • 620 8th Ave [W 40th St]
212-382-2300
Like a Japanese IKEA, but cooler and without
meatballs.

Midtown

Map 12

Midtown is home to one of the great world shopping districts. Legendary retailers like **Bergdorf Goodman** and **Saks Fifth Avenue** are majestic retail palaces, while numerous boutiques and flagships for individual brands jostle for position. For unique finds, check out **MoMA Design Store** or **Muji**, and stock up on spirits at **Park Avenue Liquor** or **Oak and Steel**.

• **Oak and Steel Fine Wines & Spirits** •
1776 Broadway [W 57th St]
212-262-7702
Excellent selection, very knowledgeable staff.

• **Park Avenue Liquor Shop** •
270 Madison Ave [E 41st St]
212-685-2442
Amazing selection of scotch. Makes us wish we had more $$$.

• **Petrossian Boutique** •
911 7th Ave [W 58th St]
212-245-2217
Caviar and other delectables. Bring the Gold Card.

• **Roberto's Winds** • 149 W 46th St [6th Ave]
212-391-1315
Saxophones, horns, clarinets, and flutes. If it blows, bring it here.

• **Saks Fifth Avenue** • 611 5th Ave [E 49th St]
212-753-4000
Fifth Avenue mainstay with lovely holiday windows and bathrooms.

• **Steinway & Sons** • 1133 Ave of the Americas
212-246-1100
Cheap knockoff pianos. Just kidding.

• **The Store at Museum of Arts and Design** •
2 Columbus Cir [8th Ave]
212-299-7777
Not your average museum store.

• **Sunrise Mart** • 12 E 41st St [5th Ave]
646-380-9280
Pick up a bento box, lunch special or Japanese groceries.

• **Tiffany & Co.** • 610 5th Ave
212-331-3312
Grande dame of the little blue box.

• **Uniqlo** • 666 5th Ave [W 52nd St]
877-486-4756
Japanese t-shirts and more—in every color!

Map 13 • **Midtown East**

E 61st St

ROOSEVELT ISLAND TRAMWAY

Lexington
Avenue/
59th Street

E 60th St

Queensboro Bridge

15

N R W

E 59th St

59th Street

Roosevelt
Island Tram

E 58th St

Sutton
Place

4 5 6

E 57th St

A

E 56th St

Central
Synagogue

E 55th St

Sutton
Place

Citicorp
Center

E 54th St

The Lever
House

E M

E 53rd St

Lexington Ave
53rd Street

51st Street

6

E 52nd St

Seagram Building

The Seven
Year Itch

12

St. Bartholomew's
Church

General
Electric
Building

E 51st St

E 50th St

Waldorf
Astoria

E 49th St

General D
MacArthur Plaza

E 48th St

East
River

E 47th St

Dag
Hammarskjold
Plaza

Peace
Garden

E 46th St

PAGE
318

Grand
Central
Terminal

E 45th St

United
Nations

E 44th St (Archbishop Fulton J Sheen Pl)

PAGE
286

B

E 43rd St

Grand Central
42nd Street

Chrysler
Building

E 42nd St

Queens Midtown Tunnel

4 5 6

Daily News
Building

Tudor
City

7 S

Chanin
Building

To Queens

E 41st St

495

Robert
Moses
Playground

E 40th St

E 39th St

10

E 38th St

| 1/4 mile | .25 km |

Neighborhood Overview

Map 13

No matter how angry, late, or tired we are from dealing with the overwhelming crowds in this part of town, one glance up at Grand Central Terminal with the Chrysler Building looming in the background never fails to give us a burst of energy and a shot of civic pride. Welcome to Midtown East, which has a major personality disorder—in a good way. It's got the tranquility of elegant Sutton Place and Tudor City, the rowdy nightlife along Second Avenue, the commuter bustle of Grand Central, the international crowd around the UN, and legendary architecture bursting from every corner.

The hub of this neighborhood—and arguably the city—is **Grand Central Terminal**. One of the busiest train stations in the world, this gorgeous building also houses many hidden surprises under its vaunted ceiling. Start in the main concourse where you'll see a magnificent clock above the information booth. This spot is what New Yorkers mean when they say, "Meet me at the clock." Some of these meet ups turn into dates at the deluxe and hard-to-find cocktail lounge **Campbell Apartment**. Others wisely opt for a trip into the world of old-school New York dining at the highly recommended **Oyster Bar**. Ask to sit in the Saloon for a real treat. Shopping options abound here with lots of cool shops (books, MTA souvenirs, etc.) and the best food shopping in Midtown at **Grand Central Market**.

You may have heard of a little organization called the **United Nations**. It's housed in an iconic glass building perched on the edge of the East River. We highly recommend the public tour where you get to see the General Assembly, an amazing art collection, and international diplomats scurrying about.

Architecture nerds rave and worship at Mies van der Rohe's **Seagram Building**, argue over the value of Phillip Johnson's **Lipstick Building**, and contemplate the public art underneath **The Lever House**. One of the city's most unique places of worship is the **Central Synagogue** with vivid Moorish details. Stroll by at night for an otherworldly experience. **St. Bart's** on Park Avenue is gorgeous in a more traditional way, while the **Chrysler Building**, **Chanin Building**, and **General Electric Building** (570 Lexington) are worshiped for their Art Deco brilliance.

If you want a break from all the tall buildings, check out the **Seven Year Itch** subway grate where Marilyn Monroe's dress blows up for all the world to see. Head way east to walk down **Sutton Place** to see where lots of exclusive New Yorkers take up residence. Or stroll around Tudor City and marvel at the handsome Neo-Gothic apartments that diplomats and divas call home. It's a nice way to unwind and enjoy this unique urban enclave without having to drop $2.7 gazillion on a condo.

Not many budget drinking options around here (except **Blarney Stone**), so go highbrow at **Campbell Apartment** inside Grand Central or **World Bar** inside the Trump Tower. If you like to drink with the suits after work, **PJ Clarke's** is your spot.

Map 13

Midtown East

○ Landmarks

• **Chanin Building** •
122 E 42nd St [Lexington Ave]
Not the Chrysler, but still a way-cool Art Deco masterpiece.
• **Chrysler Building** •
405 Lexington Ave [E 42nd St]
212-682-3070
The stuff of Art Deco dreams. Wish the Cloud Club was still there.
• **Citicorp Center** •
153 E 53rd St [Lexington Ave]
How does it stand up?
• **Daily News Building** •
220 E 42nd St [2nd Ave]
Great Caesar's ghost! An Art Deco gem.
• **General Electric Building** •
570 Lexington Ave [51st St]
Ornate 50-story Art Deco-Gothic tower.
• **Grand Central Terminal** •
89 E 42nd St [Park Ave]
212-340-2583
Another Beaux-Arts masterpiece. Ceiling, staircases, tiles, clock, Oyster Bar, all great.
• **The Lever House** • 390 Park Ave [E 54th St]
Great example of modernism, but even better, it's so fresh and so clean!
• **Lipstick Building** • 885 3rd Ave [E 53rd St]
Philip Johnson does New York, deliriously (well).
• **Seagram Building** • 375 Park Ave [E 53rd St]
Or, "how to be a modernist in 3 easy steps!"
• **The Seven Year Itch** •
E 52nd St & Lexington Ave
Marilyn Monroe's lucky subway grate.
• **St. Bartholomew's Church** •
325 Park Ave [E 51st St]
212-378-0222
Brilliant Byzantine-style church with great dome, performances, etc.
• **Sutton Place** • Sutton Pl b/n E 57th & E 59th St
Quiet, exclusive little lane for the rich and sometimes famous.
• **Tudor City** • Tudor City Place [E 42nd St]
3000 apartments in "American" Tudor style. Hmmmm.
• **United Nations** • 405 E 42nd St [1st Ave]
212-963-4475
NYC is the capital of the planet. Just sayin'.
• **Waldorf Astoria** • 301 Park Ave [E 49th St]
212-355-3000
Great hotel, undergoing a partial condo conversion and renovation.

Coffee

• **Ground Central** • 155 E 52nd St [3rd Ave]
646-609-3982
Hip coffee shop in Midtown? How times have changed.
• **Ground Central** • 800 2nd Ave [E 43rd St]
646-861-0015
Pour-overs and boxes to go; open weekends, too.
• **Joe The Art of Coffee** •
44 Grand Central Terminal [Park Ave]
212-924-7400
Located in the Graybar passage off Lexington Ave.

Farmers Markets

• **Dag Hammarskjold Plaza Greenmarket** •
E 47th St & 2nd Ave
Wed 8 am–3 pm, year-round.

The Oyster Bar should be on any New Yorker's list of must eats. **Aquavit**'s Scandinavian Sunday buffet brunch is as amazing as it is expensive. **Sakagura** is a great option for Japanese and sake, while **Sushi Yasada** has the best raw fish in the city. For a classic NYC burger, P.J. **Clarke's** is a good bet.

Nightlife

- **The Campbell Apartment** •
15 Vanderbilt Ave [E 42nd St]
917-209-3440
Awesome space, awesomely snooty!
- **Lips** • 227 E 56th St [3rd Ave]
212-675-7710
Drag shows, bitchy bingo, fierce lip syncing, good campy fun.
- **P.J. Clarke's** • 915 3rd Ave [E 55th St]
212-317-1616
Old-timey midtown pub with burgers, beers, and bankers.
- **Sofia Wine Bar & Cafe** •
242 E 50th St [2nd Ave]
212-888-8660
Italian wine bar, plus food goodies…
- **The World Bar** •
845 United Nations Plaza [E 46th St]
212-935-9361
Expensive, classy hideaway for diplomats and Derek Jeter.

Restaurants

- **99 Cents Fresh Pizza** • 151 E 43rd St [3rd Ave]
212-922-0257 • $
Fresh slice of pizza for 99 cents. Deal of the century.
- **Aquavit** • 65 E 55th St [Park Ave]
212-307-7311 • $$$$$
Stellar dining experience: top-drawer Scandinavian.
- **Aretsky's Patroon** • 160 E 46th St [3rd Ave]
212-883-7373 • $$$$$
An oasis of civility.
- **Chola** • 232 E 58th St [2nd Ave]
212-688-4619 • $$$$
Pricey south Indian cuisine.
- **Cipriani Dolci** • 89 E 42nd St [Park Ave]
212-973-0999 • $$$
Eat with people richer than you on the West Balcony of Grand Central.
- **Cipriani Le Specialità** •
120 E 42nd St [Park Ave]
212-557-5088 • $$$
Fancy, ya know.
- **Comfort Diner** • 214 E 45th St [3rd Ave]
212-867-4555 • $$
A hearty breakfast is served.
- **Docks Oyster Bar** • 633 3rd Ave [E 40th St]
212-986-8080 • $$$$
Great seafood, good atmosphere.
- **Ess-A-Bagel** • 831 3rd Ave [E 51st St]
212-980-1010 • $
Bagels with attitude.

Map 13

14 15
11 12 **13**
8 9 10
5 6 7

Midtown East

- **Grand Central Oyster Bar** •
89 E 42nd St [Park Ave]
212-490-6650 • $$$
Classic New York seafood joint. Go for the Saloon.
- **The Grill** • 99 E 52nd St [Park Ave]
212-254-3000 • $$$$$
Designer everything. Even the cotton candy.
- **Hide-Chan Ramen** • 248 E 52nd St [2nd Ave]
212-813-1800 • $$
This broth is porktastic.
- **Le Relais De Venise L'Entrecote** •
155 E 54th St [Lexington Ave]
212-758-3989 • $$$
Good steak frites and salad via Paris.
- **Little Collins** • 570 Lexington Ave [E 51st St]
917-463-3388 • $$
Excellent coffee shop with Aussie accents.
- **Momosan** • 342 Lexington Ave [40th St]
646-201-5529 • $$$
Iron Chef-caliber ramen in sleek Midtown digs.
- **Mr Chow** • 324 E 57th St [2nd Ave]
212-751-9030 • $$$
Decades-old upscale Chinese joint focusing on Beijing cuisine (duck!).
- **New York Luncheonette** •
135 E 50th St [Lexington Ave]
212-838-0165 • $$
Diner where Obama lunched with Bloomberg.

- **P.J. Clarke's** • 915 3rd Ave [E 55th St]
212-317-1616 • $$$
Pub grub. A fine burger.
- **Pershing Square** • 90 E 42nd St [Park Ave]
212-286-9600 • $$$$
Excellent food and awesome space.
- **Sakagura** • 211 E 43rd St [3rd Ave]
212-953-7253 • $$$
Midtowners are very happy to have this excellent izakaya.
- **Shun Lee Palace** •
155 E 55th St [Lexington Ave]
212-371-8844 • $$$$$
Top-end Chinese.
- **Sidecar at PJ Clarke's** • 205 E 55th St [3rd Ave]
212-317-2044 • $$$$$
P. J. Clarke's quieter, more refined restaurant sibling.
- **Smith & Wollensky** • 797 3rd Ave [E 49th St]
212-753-1530 • $$$$$
Don't order the fish.
- **Soba Totto** • 211 E 43rd St [3rd Ave]
212-377-8947 • $$$
Dig into noodles next to Japanese office workers. Top lunch deals.
- **Sparks Steak House** • 210 E 46th St [3rd Ave]
212-687-4855 • $$$$$
If you can't go to Luger's.
- **Sushi Yasuda** • 204 E 43rd St [3rd Ave]
212-972-1001 • $$$$
Best sushi in NYC. Let the debate begin…

Midtown East

14	15
11	12	**13**
8	9	10
5	6	7

Map 13

The New York Transit Museum Gallery Annex and Store has fun gift ideas. **Sherry-Lehmann** has a ridiculous selection of fancy booze you can't afford. And there's a **Home Depot** in a basement on 59th Street? That's just plain weird.

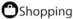

Shopping

- **Amish Market** • 240 E 45th St [3rd Ave]
212-370-1761
Lots prepared foods. Do they deliver by horse and buggy?
- **Apple Store (Grand Central)** •
45 Grand Central Terminal
212-284-1800
Because Grand Central needs more people.
- **Architects & Designers Building** •
150 E 58th St [Lexington Ave]
212-644-2766
Over 200,000 sq. ft. of commercial and residential furnishings. Wow.
- **Beer Table** • Grand Central Terminal
[42nd St] 212-922-0008
Great craft beer to go, conveniently located in GCT
- **Buttercup Bake Shop** •
973 2nd Ave [E 52nd St]
212-350-4144
Move over Magnolia. Buttercup's all grown up.
- **Conrad's Bike Shop** •
25 Tudor City Pl [E 42nd St]
212-697-6966
Good Euro bikes. Sweet logo.
- **Crush Wine & Spirits** •
153 E 57th St [Lexington Ave]
212-980-9463
Stock up on booze to survive the walk through Midtown.
- **Grand Central Market** •
89 E 42nd St [Park Ave]
212-808-5227
Pick up fixings for a gourmet dinner before jumping on the train.
- **Home Depot** • 980 3rd Ave [E 59th St]
212-888-1512
Mega home improvement chain comes to the city.
- **Ideal Cheese** • 942 1st Ave [E 52nd St]
212-688-7579
All cheese is ideal.
- **Innovative Audio Video** •
150 E 58th St [Lexington Ave]
212-634-4444
Quality music systems and home theaters.
- **New York Transit Museum
Gallery Annex & Store** • Grand Central
Terminal, Main Concourse [E 42nd St]
212-878-0106
Specialty—NYC/transit books.
- **Sherry-Lehmann Wine & Spirits** •
505 Park Ave [E 59th St]
212-838-7500
Wines and spirits for the connoisseur.
- **United Nations Bookshop** •
1st Ave & E 42nd St
212-963-7680
The UN's college bookstore: official reports, tchotchkes and T-shirts.
- **Urbanspace Vanderbilt** •
230 Park Ave [45th St]
646-747-0810
The ultimate foodie court.
- **Whole Foods** • 226 E 57th St [3rd Ave]
646-497-1222
"Whole Paycheck" but great, fresh food.
- **Yankees Clubhouse Shop** •
110 E 59th St [Park Ave]
212-758-7844
Any Yankee fan's paradise.

Map 14 • **Upper West Side (Lower)**

Neighborhood Overview

Away from the bustle of midtown and downtown Manhattan, the lower part of the Upper West Side offers a decidedly different, slower pace. But by no means does this neighborhood feel sleepy. Sandwiched between two parks, this neighborhood offers great food, museums, dive bars, and beautiful Art Deco architecture, not to mention the cultural meccas of Lincoln Center and the American Museum of Natural History, all of which remind you that New York is a livable city after all.

Many of the buildings that line the streets of the Upper West Side are landmarks. **The Ansonia** (built between 1899 and 1904) was originally a hotel and is now an exclusive apartment building. It has had many famous residents including Babe Ruth and Theodore Dreiser. **The Dakota** (built from 1880-1884) is best known for being the home of John Lennon and Yoko Ono, and the place where Lennon was killed at the entrance to the building. **The Dorilton** (built in 1902), **The Majestic** (built in 1894), and **The San Remo** (completed in 1931) all attest to bygone days of elaborate building construction.

Green space surrounds this neighborhood. To the east lies Central Park, but most locals head west to the gorgeous Riverside Park. It is filled with beautiful flower gardens, wonderful playgrounds, and some great spots to sit down and relax by the water. For those looking for something more active, a path runs along the Hudson River, perfect for jogging and biking. **The Boat Basin at 79th Street** is the only facility in the city that allows year-round residency in boats. It is also used as a launch site for kayaks, canoes, and sailboats, which you can rent in the summer.

Like a city unto itself, **The American Museum of Natural History** is one of the largest museums in the world. Founded in 1869, the museum contains 25 interconnected buildings with lots of famous permanent exhibits (anthropological collections, rooms on human biology and evolution, a life-sized model blue whale, and the world's largest sapphire, to name a few). Be sure to check out the always popular **Hayden Planetarium** and its spectacular space show—it's a great spot to experience the wonders of the universe—and of course the collection of dinosaur fossils that tantalize visitors of all ages. Just south of AMNH is **The New-York Historical Society** which has a fabulous collection documenting the history of New York and the United States. Some highlights include many of James Audubon's watercolors, paintings from the Hudson River School, and materials from the Civil War and Reconstruction.

When Upper West Siders tire from museums, they join the rest of the city's cultural elite at **Lincoln Center**, probably the most famous arts and culture center in the world. Home of the Film Society of Lincoln Center, Jazz at Lincoln Center, the Lincoln Center Theater, the Metropolitan Opera, the City Opera, the City Ballet, and the New York Philharmonic, as well as Juilliard, the School of American Ballet, and the Library for the Performing Arts, this place is just bursting with artistic brilliance.

Map 14

18 19 20
16   17
14   15
11 12 13

Upper W...

O Landmarks

- **American Museum of Natural History** •
  Central Park W & W 79th St
  212-769-5100
  Includes an outstanding planetarium and lots
  and lots of stuffed animals.
- **The Ansonia** • 2109 Broadway [W 73rd St]
  212-787-7707
  Truly unique residence on Broadway.
- **The Apthorp** • 2201 Broadway [W 78th St]
  212-787-7707
  Huge, city-block-spanning condos complete
  with inner courtyard.
- **The Dakota** • W 72nd St & Central Park W
  Classic Central Park West apartment building,
  designed by Henry J Hardenbergh.
- **The Dorilton** • Broadway & W 71st St
  Understated it ain't. But damn, it's pretty.
- **Hotel Des Artistes** •
  1 W 67th St [Central Park W]
  212-362-6700
  $4,000,000 artist studios on CPW. Nice one.
- **Lincoln Center** •
  70 Lincoln Center Plaza [W 62nd St]
  212-875-5456
  A rich and wonderful complex. Highly
  recommended—movies, theater, music, opera.
- **The Majestic** • 115 Central Park W [W 71st St]
  Great brick by Chanin.
- **MLK Sculpture** •
  122 Amsterdam Ave [W 65th St]
  Massive brutalist-but-cool square monument
  to MLK.
- **New-York Historical Society** •
  170 Central Park W [W 77th St]
  212-873-3400
  Oldest museum in New York City.
- **Rotunda at 79th St Boat Basin** •
  W 79th St [Riverside Dr]
  212-496-2105
  Rotunda, arcade, arches, and boats.
- **The San Remo** • Central Park West & W 74th St
  Emery Roth's contribution to the Upper West
  Side skyline.
- **West End Collegiate Church** •
  368 West End Ave [W 77th St]
  212-787-1566
  Dutch/Flemish goodness from Robert Gibson,
  circa 1892.

O Coffee

- **Irving Farm Coffee Roasters** •
  224 W 79th St [Broadway]
  212-206-0707
  Kalita brew bar, reclaimed wood, medium on
  the hipster scale.
- **Joe The Art of Coffee** •
  514 Columbus Ave [W 85th St]
  212-875-0100
  Joe really knows his joe.
- **Le Pain Quotidien** • 60 W 65th St [Lincoln Sq]
  212-721-4001
  Excellent coffee and pastries. Thanks Belgium.
- **Plowshare Coffee** • 2730 Broadway [105th St]
  212-222-0280
  Sustainable Rockland County artisan roasters.

O Farmers Markets

- **79th Street Greenmarket** •
  Columbus Ave & W 79th St
  Sun, 9 am–4 pm, year-round.
- **Tucker Square Greenmarket** •
  W 66th St & Columbus Ave
  Thurs and Sat, 8 am–3 pm, year-round.

For a night of culture, go to Lincoln Center or see a concert at the **Beacon Theater**. For drunken revelries and beer pong, hit **Jake's Dilemma**. Was that out loud? We meant to say, With a selection of wine for everyone, seek out **Bin 71**. And Harry and Sally set up their best friends at **Cafe Luxembourg**.

Nightlife

- **Beacon Theater** • 2124 Broadway [W 74th St]
212-465-6225
Former movie palace with beautiful neo-Grecian interior.
- **Bin 71** • 237 Columbus Ave [W 71st St]
212-362-5446
Sip wine with 30-something Upper West Siders.
- **Blondies Sports Bar** •
212 W 79th St [Amsterdam Ave]
212-362-3311
Want to catch a game? Any game? Come here.
- **Café Luxembourg** •
200 W 70th St [Amsterdam Ave]
212-873-7411
Hey, is that Tom Hanks over there?
- **The Dead Poet** •
450 Amsterdam Ave [W 82nd St]
212-595-5670
Good Irish feel. No secret society that we know of.
- **Dive 75** • 101 W 75th St [Columbus Ave]
212-362-7518
The quintessential dive bar with the friendliest staff around.
- **Dublin House** • 225 W 79th St [Broadway]
212-874-9528
Great dingy Irish pub. Recommended.
- **Fred's** • 476 Amsterdam Ave [W 83rd St]
212-579-3076
Sort of old-school. Sort of fun.

- **George Keeley** •
485 Amsterdam Ave [W 83rd St]
212-873-0251
A rotation of good draft beers and all the sports you need.
- **Hi Life Bar & Grill** •
477 Amsterdam Ave [W 83rd St]
212-787-7199
Not a bad option for this part of town.
- **Jake's Dilemma** •
430 Amsterdam Ave [W 81st St]
212-580-0556
Drink beer and pretend you're still in college.
- **Malachy's Donegal Inn** •
103 W 72nd St [Columbus Ave]
212-874-4268
Friendly Irish dive keeping it real on the Upper West Side.
- **Prohibition** • 503 Columbus Ave [W 84th St]
212-579-3100
Cool space, music, people, etc. Sometimes.
- **Stand-Up NY** • 236 W 78th St [Broadway]
212-595-0850
The frog replies, "Brooklyn—they're a dime a dozen out there!"

Map 14

Upper West Side (Lower)

18	19	20
16		17
14		15
11	12	13

Restaurants

- **Amber Restaurant** •
  103 W 70th St [Columbus Ave]
  212-799-8122 • $$
  Multiple asian cuisines, all decent. Fast service.
  Comfortable seating.
- **Bar Boulud** • 1900 Broadway [W 63rd St]
  212-595-0303 • $$$
  Before the opera, stop in for the fabulous
  charcuterie plate.
- **Blondies** • 212 W 79th St [Amsterdam Ave]
  212-362-3311 • $$
  Pair wings with a salad to save your arteries.

- **Bustan** • 487 Amsterdam Ave [W 84th St]
  212-595-5050 • $$$
  Modern Middle Eastern with a multicultural
  spin.
- **Café Lalo** • 201 W 83rd St [Amsterdam Ave]
  212-496-6031 • $$
  Packed dessert and coffee destination.
- **Café Luxembourg** •
  200 W 70th St [Amsterdam Ave]
  212-873-7411 • $$$$$
  Top-end bistro. Anyone know what
  Luxembourgian cuisine is?
- **Celeste** • 502 Amsterdam Ave [W 84th St]
  212-874-4559 • $$
  Cheap and tasty homemade pastas. A true
  gem.
- **Chirping Chicken** •
  355 Amsterdam Ave [W 77th St]
  212-787-6631 • $
  Grilled birds done right. No chirping.
- **Fairway Café** • 2131 Broadway [W 74th St]
  212-712-1570 • $$$
  When it's all too much.

Upper West Side (Lower)

Map 14

For Daniel Boulud's take on seasonal French cuisine, check out **Bar Boulud** and its charcuterie bar. But if breaking the bank isn't the agenda, check out **Nice Matin** for the best French food around. Meanwhile, sushi snobs don't even have to leave the neighborhood with **Gari** close by.

• **Freddie & Pepper's Pizza** •
303 Amsterdam Ave [W 74th St]
212-799-2378 • $
Thin crust pizza. Has been around forever.

• **French Roast** • 2340 Broadway [W 85th St]
212-799-1533 • $$
Good croque-monsieur.

• **Gari Columbus** •
370 Columbus Ave [W 78th St]
212-362-4816 • $$$$$
Why UWS sushi snobs no longer have to take the cross-town bus.

• **Good Enough to Eat** •
520 Columbus Ave
212-496-0163 • $$
Good brunch but Sunday line starts early.

• **Gray's Papaya** • 2090 Broadway [W 71st St]
212-799-0243 • $
Open 24 hours. An institution.

• **Han Dynasty** • 215 W 85th St [Broadway]
212-858-9060 • $$$
Spicy Szechuan. Dan dan noodles, anyone?

• **Jacob's Pickles** •
509 Amsterdam Ave [W 84th St]
212-470-5566 • $$
Upmarket Southern-style menu and booze, and yes, plenty of pickles.

• **Land Thai Kitchen** •
450 Amsterdam Ave [W 82nd St]
212-501-8121 • $$
Standard Thai.

• **The Milling Room** •
446 Columbus Ave [82nd St]
212-595-0380 • $$$
Fancy tavern food.

• **Nice Matin** • 201 W 79th St [Amsterdam Ave]
212-873-6423 • $$$
Traditional French food staple with outdoor seating.

• **Nougatine** • 1 Central Park W [Columbus Cir]
212-299-3900 • $$$$$
Brilliant $24.07 prix fixe lunch!

• **Parm** • 235 Columbus Ave [W 71st St]
212-776-4921 • $$
Mini-chain frying up righteous namesake sandwiches.

• **Patsy's Pizza** • 61 W 74 St [Columbus Ave]
212-579-3000 • $$
Small city chain. Excellent thin-crust pizza. Fresh ingredients.

• **Pier i Cafe** • 500 W 70th St [West Side Hwy]
212-362-4450 • $$
In season, sip a beer, munch a burger, and take in that view.

• **RedFarm** • 2170 Broadway [W 77th St]
212-724-9700 • $$$
Creative, farm-fresh dim sum. Home of the Pac Man dumpling.

• **Rosa Mexicano** •
61 Columbus Ave [W 62nd St]
212-977-7700 • $$$$
Inventive Mexican. Great guac.

Map 14

Upper West Side (Lower)

- **Salumeria Rosi Parmacotto** •
283 Amsterdam Ave [W 73rd St]
212-877-4800 • $$
Eatery doubles as excellent salami shop.
- **Santa Fe** • 73 W 71st St [Columbus Ave]
212-724-0822 • $$$
Calm Southwest.
- **Sarabeth's** • 423 Amsterdam Ave [W 80th St]
212-496-6280 • $$
Brunch, brunch, and brunch.
- **Schaller's Stube** • 1652 2nd Ave (E 86th St)
646-726-4355 • $
Sausage counter from the German meat
market next door.
- **Shake Shack** • 366 Columbus Ave [W 77th St]
646-747-8770 • $$
Now you can get your Shack Burger
year-round.
- **Sushi Yasaka** • 251 W 72nd St [West End Ave]
212-496-8460 • $$
Assorted Japanese with tons of rolls. Try the
mini omakase.
- **Tessa** • 349 Amsterdam Ave [77th St]
212-390-1974 • $$$$
Exposed brick and steel French-Italian-
Mediterranean tavern.

🛍 Shopping

- **67 Wine** • 179 Columbus Ave [W 68th St]
212-724-6767
Top-notch selection and helpful staff. Lots of
tastings.
- **Bloomingdale's Outlet** •
2085 Broadway [W 72nd St]
212-634-3190
Multi-floor outlet version of the classic
department store.
- **Citarella** • 2135 Broadway [W 75th St]
212-874-0383
Expensive but delicious breads, meats,
cheeses, and pastries.
- **Eddie's Bicycles** •
490 Amsterdam Ave [W 83rd St]
212-580-2011
Plus rentals.
- **Fairway Market** • 2131 Broadway [W 74th St]
212-595-1888
Top-notch supermarket, but always packed.

Upper West Side (Lower)

Zabar's (cheeses, fish, coffee, free samples) and **Fairway** (fresh produce, breads, dry goods, total chaos) are within blocks of each other. To pair some wine with that fine food, we like **67 Wine & Spirits**. And everyone can find something to wear at the uptown **Bloomingdale's Outlet**.

Map 14

- **GreenFlea Market** •
Columbus Ave & W 77th St
212-239-3025
Fantastic craft and antique market with local vendors. Sundays only.
- **Jonathan Adler** •
304 Columbus Ave [W 74th St]
212-787-0017
Funky, fun housewares.
- **Levain Bakery** • 351 Amsterdam Ave [77th St]
917-464-3782
Mega-cookie purveyors' expanded domicile.
- **Patagonia** • 426 Columbus Ave [W 81st St]
917-441-0011
Eco-conscious store selling fleece for your adventurous subway ride.

- **Strings and Other Things** •
1995 Broadway [W 68th St]
212-362-0857
Petite and lovely shop for violin, viola, and cello.
- **Toga Bikes** • 110 West End Ave [W 65th St]
212-799-9625
NYC's oldest bike shop.
- **Town Shop** • 2270 Broadway [W 82nd St]
212-595-6600
Where experts will fit you for the perfect bra.
- **Westsider Records** •
233 W 72nd St [Broadway]
212-874-1588
Cool record store. You'll find some interesting stuff.
- **Zabar's** • 2245 Broadway [W 80th St]
212-787-2000
Manhattan supermarket legend. NFT's favorite.

119

Map 15 · Upper East Side (Lower)

Map 15 · Upper East Side (Lower)

2nd Avenue/
86th Street

E 86th St

86th Street
4 5 6

E 85th St
The
Jeffersons
High-rise
Zion St Marks Evangelical
Lutheran Church
E 84th St

Carl
Schurz
Park

17

E 83rd St

E 82nd St

Metropolitan
Museum
of Art
PAGE
378

Frank E. Campbell
Funeral Chapel
Parisian-style
Chimneys

E 81st St

E 80th St

East End Ave

A

New York
Society
Library

E 79th St

E 78th St

PAGE
252

77th Street
6

E 77th St

E 76th St

John
Jay
Park

Bemelmans Bar

E 75th St

E 74th St

Fifth Ave

Madison Ave

Park Ave

Lexington Ave

Third Ave

Second Ave

First Ave

York Ave

E 73rd St

E 72nd St

2nd Avenue/
72nd Street

Q

Bobby Wagner Walk

Central
Park

Breakfast at Tiffany's
Apartment Building

E 71st St

Weill
Medical
College
(Cornell)

Frick
Collection
Asia
Society
The Explorers
Club

E 70th St

E 69th St

B

68th Street
Hunter College
6
Park East
Synagouge

E 68th St

E 67th St

Memorial
Sloan Kettering
Cancer Center

The Lotos
Club
The Manhattan House

E 66th St

Rockefeller
University

Temple
Emanu-El
Bernie Madoff
Apartment

E 65th St

E 64th St

Lexington Avenue
63rd Street
F

E 63rd St

Foot Bridge

East
River

E 62nd St

Mount Vernon
Hotel Museum
and Garden

The Metropolitan
Club

E 61st St

Roosevelt Island Tramway

N R W
5th Avenue/
59th Street

E 60th St

Lexington
Avenue/
59th Street
N R W

13

59th Street

4 5 6

Roosevelt
Island Tram

Queensboro Bridge
To Queens →

1/4 mile
.25 km

Neighborhood Overview

Map 15

You know the reputation of the Upper East Side: Snooty, fancy, and rich. But while this historical neighborhood is home to some of the oldest wealth in New York, it's home to a lot more: On the weekends, especially in the warm days, check out everyone in their flip flops and sunglasses (designer, please) heading to the most green space in Manhattan, Central Park. If you're not sunbathing or throwing a Frisbee, check out some of the most famous museums in the world, lively restaurants, shopping, and brunch—oh you must be a lady/gentleman who brunches if you wander up here. Old or young, this neighborhood is changing—and especially in the summer, sans a trip to the Hamptons, there is no better place to be.

Long before **Bernie Madoff** and multiple generations of Gossip Girls made this neighborhood infamous, the fabulously wealthy started settling into the Upper East Side over a century ago. As a result, there are beautiful high rises up and down Park Avenue. Fifth Avenue is the home of what was dubbed "Millionaires Row" at the turn of the 19th century—the Carnegies, the Vanderbilts, the Astors, and their friends all walked the streets lined with glorious mansions, now known as Museum Mile. For a different sort of landmark head up to 85th for **The Jeffersons High Rise**…you know, that "dee-luxe apartment in the sky" from the classic TV show. Or walk by where Holly Golightly frolicked at the **Breakfast at Tiffany's Apartment**.

There are many historical sites to check out in the neighborhood, even if it's changed a bit since the Gilded Age (and you won't recognize much from the HBO show by that name). Check out the **New York Society Library**, which moved to its current location on 79th Street from University Place in 1937. **Temple Emanu-El** on 65th Street is one of the oldest temples in New York City—it was founded as a result of the second wave of immigration of Jews to America. Established in 1845, the reform congregation moved to its current location in 1927, where it welcomes Jews whose families have been going for generations and those who just moved to the city.

Want to stop and see a couple of exhibits? How about some of the most famous museums in the world? **The Frick Collection**, housed in the 1914 mansion of industrialist Henry Clark Frick, includes works by Rembrandt, Degas, Goya, and many more of the art world's best-known names. (Visitor's tip: "Pay what you wish" admission every Sunday between 11 am and 1 pm.) For a look into the art of worlds past, head over to **The Met**, which houses, oh, over two million pieces and can take days to see it all. One last stop? **The Asia Society and Museum**, which houses an impressive art collection and performing arts program.

If you love classic New York entertainment (and have a giant wad of cash), this your neighborhood. Step inside the Carlyle Hotel to find **Bemelmans Bar**, named for the Austrian-born artist who created Madeline children's books. It's a lovely place to stop for a drink and hear some piano during happy hour. Right next door is **Café Carlyle** which attracts big stars to its intimate, cabaret-style stage.

Map 15

Upper East Side (Lower)

O Landmarks

- **Asia Society** • 725 Park Ave [E 70th St]
  212-288-6400
  Small-scale modernism.
- **Bemelmans Bar** • 35 E 76th St [Madison Ave]
  212-744-1600
  Features lovely mural by creator of Madeline books, Ludwig Bemelmans.
- **Bernie Madoff Apartment** •
  133 E 64th St [Park Ave]
  Madoff lived here, before he went to The Big House.
- **Breakfast at Tiffany's Apartment** •
  169 E 71st St [Lexington Ave]
  Where Holly Golightly and "Fred" lived in *Breakfast at Tiffany's*.
- **The Explorers Club** • 46 E 70th St [Park Ave]
  212-628-8383
  Indiana Joneses of the world hang out here. Some events open to the public.
- **Frank E. Campbell Funeral Chapel** •
  1076 Madison Ave [E 81st St]
  212-288-3500
  Undertaker to the famously deceased like Lennon and Joan Crawford.
- **The Frick Collection** • 1 E 70th St [5th Ave]
  212-288-0700
  Lots of furniture.
- **The Jeffersons High-Rise** •
  185 E 85th St [3rd Ave]
  We're movin' on up...to a dee-luxe apartment in the sky-hi.
- **The Lotos Club** • 5 E 66th St [5th Ave]
  212-737-7100
  Twain loved this private literary club. NFT is still waiting for an invite.
- **The Manhattan House** •
  200 E 66th St [3rd Ave]
  Seminal UES "white-brick" building.
- **Metropolitan Club of New York** • 1 E 60th St [5th Ave]
  212-838-7400
  1894 millionaire's clubhouse built by McKim, Mead & White.
- **Metropolitan Museum of Art** •
  1000 5th Ave [E 81st St]
  212-535-7710
  The mother of all art musuems. Check out: temple, roof garden, Clyfford Still room, baseball cards.
- **Mount Vernon Hotel Museum and Garden** •
  421 E 61st St [1st Ave]
  212-838-6878
  Nice old building.

- **New York Society Library** •
  53 E 79th St [Madison Ave]
  212-288-6900
  A subscription library that predates the public library (1754!).
- **Parisian-Style Chimneys** •
  E 80th St & Park Ave
  A touch of Paris on the UES.
- **Park East Synagogue** •
  163 E 67th St [3rd Ave]
  212-737-6900
  1890 Moorish-Jewish asymmetrical brilliance from Schneider & Herter.
- **Roosevelt Island Tram** • E 59th St & 2nd Ave
  As featured in *Spider Man*.
- **The Sherry-Netherland Hotel** •
  781 5th Ave [E 59th St]
  212-355-2800
  Super-cool spired tower and super-stuffy hotel.
- **Zion-St Mark's Evangelical Lutheran Church** •
  339 E 84th St [2nd Ave]
  212-288-0600
  Last "Germantown" church (see the General Slocum memorials inside).

☕ Coffee

- **Le Pain Quotidien** • 1270 1st Ave [E 68th St]
  212-988-5001
  Excellent coffee and pastries. Thanks Belgium.
- **Le Pain Quotidien** •
  861 Lexington Ave [E 64th St]
  646-762-2209
  Excellent coffee. Excellent pastries. Thanks Belgium.
- **Le Pain Quotidien** •
  1131 Madison Ave [E 84th St]
  212-327-4900
  Excellent coffee. Excellent pastries. Thanks Belgium.

Upper East Side (Lower)

For a down and out dive (translation: our kind of bar) ride the **Subway Inn** or go old country Irish whiskey tasting at **Donohues**. For a little more class grab the perfect glass of wine at **Uva**. For even more class, no old money Upper East Side evening is complete without a visit to **Bemelmans Bar**.

- **Oslo** • 422 E 75th St [1st Ave]
718-782-0332
Coffee with attention to detail.
- **Via Quadronno** • 25 E 73rd St [Madison Ave]
212-650-9880
Straight up Italian espresso from Milan.
- **Viand** • 673 Madison Ave [E 61st St]
212-751-6622
Old-school diner complete with long counter.

Farmers Markets

- **82nd Street / St. Stephen's Greenmarket** •
E 82nd St & York Ave
Sat, 9 am–3 pm, year-round.

Nightlife

- **Bailey's Corner Pub** •
1607 York Ave [E 85th St]
212-650-1341
Friendly Irish local. Watch the game or play darts.
- **Bemelmans Bar** • 35 E 76th St [Madison Ave]
212-744-1600
When NFT actually has money, we drink here. Classic UES vibe.
- **Brandy's Piano Bar** • 235 E 84th St [3rd Ave]
212-744-4949
Good ol' rollicking time.
- **Café Carlyle** • 35 E 76th St [Madison Ave]
212-744-1600
Classic cabaret venue where Woody plays. Hellishly expensive.
- **Caledonia Scottish Pub** •
1609 2nd Ave [E 83rd St]
212-734-4300
Put on your kilt to sip Scotch and nibble on haggis.

- **Club Macanudo** • 26 E 63rd St [Madison Ave]
212-752-8200
A perfect environment for smokers (and non-smokers).
- **Comic Strip Live** • 1568 2nd Ave [E 81st St]
212-861-9386
A rabbi walks into a bar with a frog on his shoulder…
- **Donohue's Steak House** •
845 Lexington Ave [E 64th St]
212-744-0938
Old-school Irish. Sit at the bar and drink whiskey.
- **Dorrian's** • 1616 2nd Ave [E 84th St]
212-772-6660
Pop your collar for the last beer of the night here.
- **Finnegan's Wake** • 1361 1st Ave [E 73rd St]
212-737-3664
Standard Irish pub. Therefore, pretty good.
- **Hungarian House** • 213 E 82nd St [3rd Ave]
212-249-9360
Party Hungarian-style. Lots of special events.
- **Iggy's** • 1452 2nd Ave [E 75th St]
212-327-3043
Super-friendly bartenders help cue up the cheesy karaoke action.
- **The Jeffrey** • 311 E 60th St [2nd Ave]
212-355-2337
Tons of craft beer, truffle potato chips and giant TVs.
- **Jones Wood Foundry** • 401 E 76th St [1st Ave]
212-249-2700
Chill with the European expats and cheer on their favorite 'football' squads.

Map 15

Upper East Side (Lower)

- **The Penrose** • 1590 2nd Ave [83rd St]
  212-203-2751
  Tasty cocktails & pub grub with a touch of class.
- **Ryan's Daughter** • 350 E 85th St [2nd Ave]
  212-628-2613
  Free chips!
- **The Stumble Inn** • 1454 2nd Ave [E 76th St]
  212-650-0561
  Thanks to the amazing specials, expect to stumble out.
- **Subway Inn** • 1140 2nd Ave [E 60th St]
  212-758-0900
  Sad, bad, glare, worn-out, ugh. Totally great.
- **Trinity Pub** • 299 E 84th St [2nd Ave]
  212-327-4450
  Low on the UES meathead scale. Thank goodness!

🍴Restaurants

- **Agora Turkish** • 1565 2nd Ave [E 80th St]
  212-717-1220 • $$
  BYO family-run Turkish with big flavors and a small price.
- **Alice's Tea Cup Chapter II** •
  156 E 64th St [Lexington Ave]
  212-486-9200 • $$
  Eat brunch or take tea in a fairy tale setting.
- **Andre's Cafe** • 1631 2nd Ave [E 85th St]
  212-327-1105 • $$
  Low-key Hungarian savories (goulash) and sweets (strudel).
- **Antonucci** • 170 E 81st St [3rd Ave]
  212-570-5100 • $$$$$
  Pleasant Italian spot on quiet block for dining al fresco.

- **Atlantic Grill** • 50 W 65th St
  212-362-7800 • $$$$$
  Seafood galore. Old money loves this place.
- **Barking Dog** • 1678 3rd Ave
  212-831-1800 • $$
  Bring Fido along for brunch.
- **Beach Cafe** • 1326 2nd Ave [E 70th St]
  212-988-7299 • $$
  Comfort food for brunch, dinner easy as a beach here.
- **Burger One** • 1150 Lexington Ave [W 80th St]
  212-737-0095 • $
  Pint-sized counter with burgers, fries, and tacos (of course).
- **Calexico** • 1491 2nd Ave [E 78th St]
  347-967-5955 • $$
  Wonderful, welcoming Tex-Mex or Cali-Mex, as the case may be.
- **Canyon Road** • 1470 1st Ave [E 77th St]
  212-734-1600 • $$$
  Southwest haven.

Upper East Side (Lower)

Map 15

JG Melon's burger is one of the best reasons to go above 14th Street. For an old-time favorite, try **Lexington Candy Shop**. Get your seafood any way you like it at **Atlantic Grill** or grab a lobster roll from **Luke's Lobster**.

- **Daniel** • 60 E 65th St [Park Ave]
  212-288-0033 • $$$$$
  Overrated $150+ meal.
- **The East Pole** • 133 E 65th St [Lexington Ave]
  212-249-2222 • $$$$
  Sort of like a four-star British tavern, if you can imagine that.
- **EAT** • 1064 Madison Ave [E 81st St]
  212-772-0022 • $$$
  Great brunch spot—part of the Eli Zabar empire.
- **Eat Here Now** • 839 Lexington Ave [E 64th St]
  212-751-0724 • $$
  Clean, classic diner. Fast, friendly service.
- **EJ's Luncheonette** • 1271 3rd Ave [E 73rd St]
  212-472-0600 • $$
  Homey mini-chain diner.
- **Elio's** • 1621 2nd Ave [E 84th St]
  212-772-2242 • $$$$$
  UES Italian where schmoozing with the "who's-who" goes down.
- **Flex Mussels** • 1431 3rd Ave
  212-717-7772 • $$$
  23 flavors—try the Abbey or Spaniard.
- **Heidelberg** • 1648 2nd Ave [E 86th St]
  212-628-2332 • $$$
  Dirndls and lederhosen serving colossal beers and sausage platters.
- **Heidi's House** • 308 E 78th St [2nd Ave]
  212-249-0069 • $$
  Cozy comfort food in a happy place.
- **Hummus Kitchen** • 1613 2nd Ave [E 84th St]
  212-988-0090 • $$
  Hummus so good they named a Kitchen after it.
- **Indian Tandoor Oven** •
  175 E 83rd St [3rd Ave]
  212-628-3000 • $$
  Delectable Indian specialties in cozy, color-draped surroundings.

- **Jackson Hole** • 232 E 64th St [3rd Ave]
  212-371-7187 • $$
  Extremely large burgers from this mini-chain.
- **Jacques Brasserie** • 206 E 85th St [3rd Ave]
  212-327-2272 • $$$$
  UES spot for tasty moules frites and Stella on tap.
- **JG Melon** • 1291 3rd Ave [E 73rd St]
  212-744-0585 • $$
  Top NYC burgers. Always crowded.
- **JoJo** • 160 E 64th St [Lexington Ave]
  212-223-5656 • $$$$
  Charming French bistro.
- **Kings' Carriage House** •
  251 E 82nd St [2nd Ave]
  212-734-5490 • $$$$$
  Romantic fine dining in a charming, old carriage house.
- **Le Pain Quotidien** •
  861 Lexington Ave [E 64th St]
  646-762-2209 • $$
  Great breads. Communal Table. Euro vibe.
- **Le Pain Quotidien** •
  1131 Madison Ave [E 84th St]
  861-2544 • $$
  Great breads. Communal Table. Euro vibe.
- **Lexington Candy Shop** •
  1226 Lexington Ave [E 83rd St]
  212-288-0057 • $
  Charming old-timey soda shop with twirly stools.
- **Luke's Lobster** • 242 E 81st St [2nd Ave]
  212-249-4241 • $$
  Fresh-from-the sea lobster rolls, without sticker shock.

Map 15

Upper East Side (Lower)

- **Maya** • 1191 1st Ave [E 65th St]
212-585-1818 • $$$$
Top-drawer Mexican.
- **Mei Jin Ramen** • 1574 2nd Ave [E 82nd St]
212-327-2800 • $$
Hard-to-find beef ramen with sweet lunch specials.
- **Nica Trattoria** • 354 E 84th St [1st Ave]
212-472-5040 • $$$
Cash-only Italian with great food and lots of rules.
- **Orsay** • 1057 Lexington Ave [E 75th St]
212-517-6400 • $$$$$
Upscale brasserie popular with "about-town" uptowners.
- **Pastrami Queen** •
1125 Lexington Ave [E 78th St]
212-734-1500 • $$
Meats worthy of their royal names.
- **Poke** • 343 E 85th St [2nd Ave]
212-249-0569 • $$
Good sushi. BYO Sake.
- **Serafina** • 33 E 61st St [Madison Ave]
212-702-9898 • $$
Pretty decent pizza and pasta.
- **Serendipity 3** • 225 E 60th St [3rd Ave]
212-838-3531 • $$
Home of the legendary "Frrrozen Hot Chocolate."
- **Sette Mezzo** • 969 Lexington Ave [E 70th St]
212-472-0400 • $$$$$
Oprah's fave.

- **Sushi of Gari** • 402 E 78th St [1st Ave]
212-517-5340 • $$$$$
Sure to please even the snootiest sushi snobs.
- **Tony Dragonas Cart** •
Madison Ave & E 62nd St
917-299-1550 • $
Street meat goes Greek.
- **Up Thai** • 1411 2nd Ave [E 74th St]
212-256-1199 • $$$
Thai classics on a higher level. And cocktails!
- **Uva** • 1486 2nd Ave [E 77th St]
212-472-4552 • $
Come for the wine list, food optional.
- **Via Quadronno** • 25 E 73rd St [Madison Ave]
212-650-9880 • $$
This paninoteca is the cheapest lunch option around.
- **Viand** • 673 Madison Ave [E 61st St]
212-751-6622 • $$
Basic diner.

🛍 Shopping

- **Agata & Valentina** • 1505 1st Ave [E 79th St]
212-452-0690
Great gourmet market that will suck your wallet dry.
- **Agent Provocateur** •
675 Madison Ave [E 61st St]
212-840-2436
Super fabulous, slightly hardcore lingerie, get your credit cards ready.

Although pricey, **Eli's** is one of the best places to buy food in the city, and **Fairway** is another great option for UES victuals. For unique wine breads try **Orwasher's**.

- **Bicycles NYC** • 1400 3rd Ave [E 79th St]
  212-794-2929
  Since 1977; convenient to Central Park.
- **Bloomingdale's** • 1000 3rd Ave [E 60th St]
  212-705-2000
  Where your mother disappears when she's in town.
- **Butterfield Market** •
  1114 Lexington Ave [E 78th St]
  212-758-2800
  UES gourmet grocer circa 1915.
- **Creel & Gow** • 131 E 70th St [Lexington Ave]
  212-327-4281
  Super fancy, arty things for rich people in a former stable.
- **Eli's Market** • 1415 3rd Ave [E 80th St]
  212-717-8100
  Blissful gourmet shopping experience. Just bring $$$.
- **Fairway Market** • 240 E 86th St [2nd Ave]
  718-569-4511
  So big. So good. So New York.
- **Garnet Wines & Liquors** •
  929 Lexington Ave [E 69th St]
  212-772-3211
  Huge selection for people with money.
- **In Vino Veritas** • 1375 1st Ave [E 73rd St]
  212-288-0100
  These bros know their wine.
- **Laduree** • 864 Madison Ave [70th St]
  646-558-3157
  International macaron specialists.

- **Modern State** • 1243 3rd Ave [E 72nd St]
  212-879-8076
  Longstanding party supply store with costumes, piñatas, and kid stuff.
- **Orwashers** • 308 E 78th St [2nd Ave]
  212-288-6569
  Handmade wine breads. Best challah on the east side.
- **Park East Kosher** •1733 1st Ave
  212-737-9800
  Meats and smoked fish. It's all good, and it's all kosher.
- **Sprinkles** • 780 Lexington Ave [E 61st St]
  212-207-8375
  Cupcakes and cookies.
- **Two Little Red Hens** •
  1652 2nd Ave [E 86th St]
  212-452-0476
  Lovely cases of cakes and pies flanked by kitschy hen memorabilia.
- **Ursus Books and Prints** •
  50 E 78th St
  212-772-8787
  Rare titles and first-rate art books.

Map 16 · **Upper West Side (Upper)**

Neighborhood Overview

Map 16

Close to Columbia University, this neighborhood is home to much of New York's liberal intelligentsia. But the neighborhood is far from snobby. Mixed in with the college professors, theater directors, doctors, and lawyers are many families with young children, and twenty-somethings, all of whom enjoy the slower pace of life and physical beauty of Manhattan's Upper West Side.

This neighborhood is one of the greenest spaces in New York. Situated between Riverside and Central Park, there are many places to run, bike, or sit in the shade of a tree. There are few tourist attractions in this part of Central Park, but the natural beauty of the park and its recreational spaces are abundant. You can enter the reservoir from this end of the park, and enjoy a scenic view while running 1.6 miles around a dirt path. Walking west from Central Park to Riverside Park, peek into **Pomander Walk**, a tiny, pedestrian-only street of little houses. In Riverside Park, take the time to explore the many famous monuments. After 9/11, neighborhood residents gathered at the **Fireman's Memorial** to commemorate those that were lost. The statue of **Joan of Arc** sits within an island on Riverside Drive that is maintained by neighborhood residents. Dedicated on Memorial Day in 1902 and modeled after a Corinthian temple, the **Soldiers and Sailors Monument** commemorates those who served during the Civil War. If you're just looking for some place to sit and read, **Straus Park**, a small green island between West End and Broadway, offers a quiet spot to rest amid the bustle of the street.

For a neighborhood so far from the bustling theater hub of Times Square and Museum Mile, the Upper West Side offers its fair share of cultural entertainment. **Symphony Space** is a multidisciplinary arts center. There is always a reading or concert on the main stage, and the **Leonard Nimoy Thalia** next door is always showing a classic movie. Symphony Space also occasionally hosts free marathon concerts, and is known for its fun "Wall To Wall" series. Come early to get a seat and stay as long as you want. For jazz, check out **Smoke**; many well-known musicians perform. They also have excellent food. **The Underground Lounge** hosts decent comedy nights and also occasionally has live music. The West Side Arts Coalition sponsors visual arts exhibitions at the **Broadway Mall Community Center** in a renovated Beaux-Arts building in the middle of Broadway. **El Taller Latino Americano** has live music, salsa dancing, and an occasional film, as well as Spanish classes, all very affordable.

When you're ready to eat, wait in line for bagels and lox at Barney Greengrass, or enjoy the rice and beans at either Flor de Mayo or El Malecon. Dine on awesome Mexican at Taqueri Y Fonda and rich Indian at Manhattan Valley. For cheap drinks, check out **Broadway Dive**. For a good LGBTQ spot, head to **Suite**.

Map 16

18	19	20
16		17
14		15
11	12	13

Upper West Side (Upper)

O Landmarks

- **Broadway Mall Community Center** •
  W 96th St & Broadway
  Beaux-Arts home of The West Side Arts
  Coalition.
- **Firemen's Memorial** •
  W 100th St & Riverside Dr
  Memorial to fallen fire fighters.
- **Joan of Arc Memorial** •
  Riverside Dr & W 93rd St
  Impressive statue erected in 1915.
- **New York Language Center** • 2710 Broadway
  [W 104th St]
  212-678-5800
  Vibrant cultural hub for Latino art, music, and
  dance.
- **Pomander Walk** • 261 W 94th St [Broadway]
  Great little hideaway.
- **Riverside Park** •
  Hudson River b/n 59th & 155th St
  212-870-3070
  330 acres of Olmsted/Moses parkland along
  the Hudson River.
- **Schinasi Mansion** •
  351 Riverside Dr [W 107th St]
  My name is Elmer J. Fudd, I own a mansion…
- **Soldiers and Sailors Monument** •
  W 89th St & Riverside Dr
  It's been seen in *Law & Order*, along with
  everything else in New York.
- **Straus Park** • Broadway & W 106th St
  Green respite just off the craziness of
  Broadway.

Coffee

- **Silver Moon Bakery** •
  2740 Broadway [W 105th St]
  212-866-4717
  Delicious morning coffee and croissant.

O Farmers Markets

- **97th Street Greenmarket** •
  Columbus Ave & W 97th St
  Fri 8 am–2 pm, year-round.

Y Nightlife

- **Broadway Dive** • 2662 Broadway [W 101st St]
  212-865-2662
  How's that for a name?
- **Buceo 95** • 201 W 95th St [Amsterdam Ave]
  212-662-7010
  Surprisingly affordable wine bar with delicious
  tapas.
- **Cleopatra's Needle** •
  2485 Broadway [W 92nd St]
  212-769-6969
  Solid middle eastern food and solid live jazz
  performances.
- **Dive Bar** • 732 Amsterdam Ave [W 96th St]
  212-749-4358
  That's "dive" as in "deep"; Columbia hangout.
- **Lion's Head Tavern** •
  995 Amsterdam Ave [W 109th St]
  212-866-1030
  Sports bar where locals and Columbia
  students drink cheaply.
- **Smoke** • 2751 Broadway [W 106th St]
  212-864-6662
  Local jazz hangout. Sunday nights are fun.
- **Suite** • 992 Amsterdam Ave [W 109th St]
  212-222-4600
  Karaoke on Thursdays. Rare gay bar in the
  neighborhood.
- **Tap A Keg** • 2731 Broadway [W 104th St]
  212-749-1734
  Cheap beer and pool tables!

Upper West Side (Upper)

Map 16

On the go? Swing by **Roti Roll** for Indian treats, **Absolute Bagels** for freshness right out of the oven, and pastry rivaling what you'd find in Paris at **Silver Moon Bakery**.

🍴Restaurants

- **Awash** • 947 Amsterdam Ave [W 106th St]
212-961-1416 • $$
Tasty Ethiopian.
- **Barney Greengrass** •
541 Amsterdam Ave [W 86th St]
212-724-4707 • $$$
Sturgeon and eggs make the perfect NYC b-fast.
- **Bella Luna** • 574 Columbus Ave [W 88th St]
212-877-2267 • $$$
Old fashion Italian with live jazz Tuesdays.
- **Carmine's** • 2450 Broadway [W 91st St]
212-362-2200 • $$$
Large-portion Italian.
- **City Diner** • 2441 Broadway [W 90th St]
212-877-2720 • $$
Neighborhood joint.
- **Crepes on Columbus** •
990 Columbus Ave [W 109th St]
212-222-0259 • $$
Savory & sweet crepes in abundance.
- **Edgar's Café** •
650 Amsterdam Ave [W 92nd St]
212-595-6261 • $$
Salads, desserts, and atmosphere.
- **El Malecon** • 764 Amsterdam Ave [W 97th St]
212-864-5648 • $
Roast chicken and a con leche.

- **Flor de Mayo** • 484 Amsterdam Ave
212-787-3388 • $$
Cuban-Chinese-Chicken-Chow.
- **Gennaro** • 665 Amsterdam Ave [W 92nd St]
212-665-5348 • $$$
Crowded Italian.
- **Giovanni's** • 1011 Columbus Ave [W 109th St]
212-663-7000 • $$
Pretty good slice.
- **Kouzan** • 685 Amsterdam Ave [W 93rd St]
212-280-8099 • $$
Upscale Japanese dining with a pseudo nightclub-like atmosphere.
- **Malaysia Grill** • 224 W 104th St [Broadway]
212-579-1333 • $$
Inexpensive Malaysian pleasure.
- **Manhattan Valley** • 2636 Broadway
[W 100th St]
212-222-9222 • $$$
Locals rave about this Indian food but it costs.
- **Metro Diner** • 2641 Broadway [W 100th St]
212-866-0800 • $$
Get in line for weekend brunch.

Map 16

18	19	20
16		17
14		15
11	12	13

- **Momofuku Milk Bar** •
  561 Columbus Ave [W 87th St]
  212-256-0586 • $$
  A dessert-lover's delight (try the cake truffles!).
- **Noche Mexicana** •
  842 Amsterdam Ave [W 102nd St]
  212-662-6900 • $$
  Certainly more authentic than Blockheads up the street.
- **Pio Pio Salon** •
  702 Amsterdam Ave [W 94th St]
  212-665-3000 • $$
  Tasty rotisserie chicken with all the fixins. Thanks Peru!
- **Roti Roll Bombay Frankie** •
  994 Amsterdam Ave [W 109th St]
  212-666-1500 • $
  Hole-in-the-wall rotis to soak up alcohol.

- **Saiguette** • 935 Columbus Ave [W 106th St]
  212-866-8886 • $
  Damn good Vietnamese including scrumptious banh mi sandwiches.
- **Silver Moon Bakery & Cafe** •
  2740 Broadway [W 105th St.]
  212-866-4717 • $$
  Cakes, tarts, cookies, pastries.
- **Talia's Steakhouse** •
  668 Amsterdam Ave [W 93rd St]
  212-580-3770 • $$$$
  Your basic everyday kosher steakhouse.
- **Taqueria Y Fonda** •
  968 Amsterdam Ave [W 108th St]
  212-531-0383 • $$
  Amazing Mexican dive. Columbia kids love this place.
- **Thai Market** •
  960 Amsterdam Ave [W 107th St]
  212-280-4575 • $$
  Another favorite Thai among locals.

Upper West Side (Upper)

Map 16

Looking for a nice bottle of wine to bring to dinner? Try **Whole Foods Wine**, which is the first branch of the upscale grocery store to have one. **Barzini's** has nice fresh produce as does **Garden of Eden**. For smoked fish and prepared foods try **The Kosher Marketplace**. **Schatzie's** is the best butcher around.

Shopping

- **Absolute Bagels** •
2788 Broadway [W 108th St]
212-932-2052
Amazing. Home of the hard-to-find pumpernickel raisin.
- **Barzini's** • 2451 Broadway [W 91st St]
212-874-4992
Huge selection of cheeses. Fresh bread and produce.
- **Ben & Jerry's** • 2722 Broadway [W 104th St]
212-866-6237
Hippie treat trifecta: Cherry Garcia, Phish Food, and Half Baked.
- **Champion Bicycles** •
896 Amsterdam Ave [W 104th St]
212-662-2690
Well priced, good guys.
- **Garden of Eden** •
2780 Broadway [W 107th St]
212-222-7300
Produce is pretty good here.
- **Gotham Wines And Liquors** •
2517 Broadway [W 94th St]
212-932-0990
Friendly neighborhood favorite.
- **Gothic Cabinet Craft** •
2652 Broadway [W 101st St]
212-678-4368
Real wood furniture. Made in Queens!
- **Health Nuts** • 2611 Broadway [W 99th St]
212-678-0054
Standard health food store.
- **Innovation Bike Shop** •
105 W 106th St [Columbus Ave]
212-678-7130
Sales, service, rentals, and accessories.
- **Janovic** • 2625 Broadway [W 102nd St]
212-531-2300
Top NYC paint store.
- **The Kosher Marketplace** •
2442 Broadway [W 90th St]
212-580-6378
For all of your Kosher needs.

- **Mani Marketplace** •
697 Columbus Ave [W 94th St]
212-662-4392
Fantastic little grocery with jazz on the sound system.
- **Mitchell's Wine & Liquor Store** •
200 W 86th St [Amsterdam Ave]
212-874-2255
Worth a trip just for the gorgeous neon sign.
- **Mugi Pottery** •
993 Amsterdam Ave [W 109th St]
212-866-6202
Handcrafted pottery. Like in the movie *Ghost*.
- **Murray's Sturgeon Shop** •
2429 Broadway [W 90th St]
212-724-2650
UWS comfort food: rugelah, knishes, and, lots of sturgeon.
- **New Westlane Wines & Liquor** •
689 Columbus Ave [W 93rd St]
212-678-4908
Behind the bullet proof glass is a pretty good selection.
- **New York Flowers & Plant Shed** •
723 Amsterdam Ave [96th St]
212-662-4400
Makes you wish you had more (or any) garden space.
- **Schatzie The Butcher** •
2665 Broadway
212-410-1555
Butcher with good prime meat and poultry.
- **Soccer Post** •
250 W 86th St [Broadway]
646-661-3951
Great selection of soccer apparel and accessories.
- **Whole Foods** • 808 Columbus Ave [W 97th St]
212-222-6160
Finally. Good fresh food north of 96th Street.
- **Whole Foods Wine** •
808 Columbus Ave [W 100th St]
212-222-6160
Featuring lots of NY State wines.

Map 17 · **Upper East Side / East Harlem**

Duke Ellington Circle

110th Street

E 111th St
E 110th St
E 109th St
E 108th St
E 107th St

20

1199 Plaza

Randa Island

Graffiti Wall of Fame

Museo del Barrio

Julia de Borgos Cultural Center

E 106th St
E 105th St
E 104th St

Wilson Houses

Museum of the City of New York

103rd Street

George Washington Houses

E 103rd St
E 102nd St
E 101st St

East River House

Foot Bridge

PAGE
252

Central Park

Carver Houses

George Washington Houses

E 100th St
E 99th St

Wa Isla

St Nicholas Russian Orthodox Cathedral

E 98th St

George Washington Houses

Islamic Cultural Center

96th Street

E 97th St

E 96th St

Harlem River

Q
96th street

E 95th St
E 94th St
E 93rd St

Jewish Museum

92nd Street Y

E 92nd St
E 91st St

Stanley Isaacs Houses

Old Municipal Asphalt Plant

Cooper-Hewitt Museum

E 90th St
E 89th St

Guggenheim Museum

E 88th St
E 87th St

86th Street

Papaya King

4 5 6

York Ave

Gracie Mans

Henderson Place

Carl Schurz Park

15

E 86th St
Schaller & Weber

Q
2nd Avenue/ 86th Street

East End Ave

E 85th St

Fifth Ave
Madison Ave
Park Ave
Lexington Ave
Third Ave
Second Ave
First Ave

1/4 mile   .25 km

Neighborhood Overview

Map 17

18 19 20
16 17
14 15
11 12 13

Whew, finally a break from the chaos. This part of the Upper East Side is a place for families, young, old, Black, white, Latino, rich, poor—it just depends what block you stumble upon. Head above 96th Street for some of the best Mexican food on the planet, or head west to Central Park, where you'll find kids and adults playing soccer, softball, and football. Get some culture at the neighborhood's museums, get some knowledge at a lecture at the **92nd Street Y**, but most importantly, get ready to be somewhere where people can actually live, work, and shop. Nothing hip or cool here, this is just a good old-fashioned New York neighborhood.

Much of this part of the Upper East Side is known as Carnegie Hill, named for the Carnegie Mansion on 91st and Fifth Avenue (it's now the **Cooper-Hewitt Design Museum**). **Gracie Mansion**, the charming Federal-style mansion in Carl Schurz Park, dates to 1799 and has served as the official residence of New York City mayors since the days of Fiorello La Guardia. **Henderson Place**, built in 1881 for families of "moderate means" was designed by the architectures of Lamb and Rich and with 24 units still remaining, serves as an example of original middle-class living in the Big Apple.

Ever think a Soviet battle could take place on American soil? The **Russian Orthodox Cathedral of St. Nicholas** was the site of a power struggle between czarist and Soviet Russians after its founding in 1902. Finally conflict-free, it is an amazing sight to see. **Asphalt Green**, an old municipal asphalt plant, now houses sports fields; the source of much controversy, some called it the ugliest thing they'd ever seen, but MoMA hailed it as a masterpiece of functional design. Head over to 91st Street and decide for yourself. Both visitors and native New Yorkers will learn something new at **The Museum of the City of New York**, with its vast collection of over 1.5 million objects and images telling the story of the city's past.

The Jewish Museum features works by Chagall, a video and film archive, and traveling exhibits that are always worth a peek. Head up to 104th Street and down to the Caribbean at **Museo del Barrio**, where you can find an excellent collection of Latin American art. Elsewhere, **The Guggenheim** not only houses Picasso, Chagall, Mondrian, and Kandinsky but is also a piece of art itself, with Frank Lloyd Wright's influence seen on the swirling staircase that guides visitors through. One of the best ways to see the Guggenheim is at Art After Dark, where visitors can tour the museum and enjoy some cocktails and music along the way. Before you leave, check the schedule at the **92nd Street Y**, which frequently hosts boldface-name speakers. And the **Graffiti Wall of Fame** at 106th and Park (yes, that 106 & Park for those BET fans out there) is an awesome collection of street art at its best.

There are plenty of beer-filled sports bars, or stop for a cozy drink at **Auction House**, or even the mixology of **The Guthrie Inn**.

Map 17 — Upper East Side / East Harlem

Landmarks

- **92nd Street Y** •
  1395 Lexington Ave [E 92nd St]
  212-415-5500
  Community hub for film, theater, and interesting lectures.
- **Asphalt Green** • E 90th St & East End Ave
  212-369-8890
  Industrial architecture turned sports facility.
- **Cooper-Hewitt National Design Museum** • 2 E 91st St [5th Ave]
  212-849-8400
  Great design shows; run by the Smithsonian.
- **El Museo del Barrio** •
  1230 5th Ave [E 104th St]
  212-831-7272
  NYC's only Latino museum.
- **Gracie Mansion** • E End Ave & 88th St
  212-570-4751
  Our own Buckingham Palace, right above the FDR drive.
- **Graffiti Wall of Fame** • E 106th St & Park Ave
  This street art will blow you away.
- **Guggenheim Museum** •
  1071 5th Ave [E 88th St]
  212-423-3500
  Wright's only building in NYC, but it's one of the best.
- **Henderson Place** • E End Ave & E 86th St
  Charming Queen Anne-style apartment houses circa 1881–82.
- **Islamic Cultural Center** •
  1711 3rd Ave [E 96th St]
  212-722-5234
  Enormous and extraordinary mosque. Bustling on Fridays.
- **The Jewish Museum** •
  1109 5th Ave [E 92nd St]
  212-423-3200
  Over 28,000 artifacts of Jewish culture and history.
- **Julia de Burgos Latino Cultural Center** •
  1680 Lexington Ave [E 105th St]
  212-233-8955
  Artistic and community hub of East Harlem.

- **Museum of the City of New York** •
  1220 5th Ave [E 103rd St]
  212-534-1672
  Fascinating exhibitions on life in the big city.
- **Schaller & Weber** • 1654 2nd Ave [E 86th St]
  212-879-3047
  A relic of old Yorkville with great German meats.
- **St. Nicholas Russian Orthodox Cathedral** •
  15 E 97th St [5th Ave]
  This UES cathedral, built in 1902, remains the center of Russian Orthodoxy in the US.

Coffee

- **Gracie's Diner** • 352 E 86th St [2nd Ave]
  212-737-8505
  Old-school diner. Open 24 hrs.

Farmers Markets

- **92nd St Greenmarket** • 1st Ave & E 92nd St
  Sun 9 am–4 pm June–Nov.
- **Harvest Home East Harlem Farmers Market** •
  8 W 126th St
  212-828-3361
  Thu 8 am–4pm, Jul–Nov.
- **Mount Sinai Greenmarket** •
  Madison Ave & E 99th St
  Wed 8 am–3 pm June–Nov.

Nightlife

- **Auction House** • 300 E 89th St [2nd Ave]
  212-427-4458
  Stylish lounge…or at least stylish for the Upper East Side.
- **Biddy's Pub** • 301 E 91st St [2nd Ave]
  917-870-5626
  Skip the pretension, grab the beer at this small neighborhood spot.
- **The District** • 1679 3rd Ave [E 94th St]
  212-289-2005
  Upscale pub for the grown up frat boys.

Don't miss the the bar food at **Earl's Beer & Cheese**, *cemitas* sandwiches at **Cafe Ollin**, and Alsatian at **Cafe D'Alsace**. Between paydays, head over to **Shake Shack**.

- **Earl's Beer & Cheese** •
  1259 Park Ave [E 97th St]
  212-289-1581
  Best beer selection for miles. And awesome food.
- **East End Bar and Grill** •
  1672 1st Ave [E 87th St]
  212-348-3783
  Mellow Irish hang out.
- **The Guthrie Inn** • 1259 Park Ave [E 97th St]
  646-907-0169
  Amazing cocktails from a well-known mixologist.
- **The Lexington Social** •
  1634 Lexington Ave [E 104th St]
  646-820-1033
  Good happy hour and tapas.
- **Phil Hughes** • 1682 1st Ave [E 88th St]
  646-467-1468
  An honest-to-god dive bar on the UES.
- **Reif's Tavern** • 302 E 92nd St [2nd Ave]
  212-426-0519
  Dive-o-rama since 1942.
- **Third Avenue Ale House** •
  1644 3rd Ave [E 92nd St]
  646-559-9131
  New school pub food and beer brunches.

🍴 Restaurants

- **Barking Dog** • 1678 3rd Ave [E 94th St]
  212-831-1800 • $$
  Woof woof. This food ain't too bad.
- **Burritos Y Mas** • 1571 Lexington Ave
  [E 101st St]• $
  646-918-7478
  Tiny spot, big burritos, from steak to seitan.

- **Café D'Alsace** • 1703 2nd Ave [E 88th St]
  212-722-5133 • $$$$
  Chic Alsatian bistro with an actual beer sommelier.
- **Cafe Ollin** • 339 E 108th St [1st Ave]
  212-828-3644 • $
  Tiny Mexican hole cranking out awesome cemitas and more.
- **Cafe Sabarsky** • 1048 5th Ave [E 86th St]
  212-288-0665 • $$$
  Beautiful wood-paneled surroundings for sipping Viennese coffee.
- **Delizia 92 Ristorante & Pizza** •
  1762 2nd Ave [E 92nd St]
  212-996-3720 • $$
  Great, if slightly overpriced, NYC pizza and pasta.
- **El Caribeno** • 1675 Lexington Ave [E 105th St]
  212-831-3906 • $$
  Dominican hang out for roast chicken and pork.
- **El Paso Taqueria** • 64 E 97th St [Park Ave]
  212-996-1739 • $$
  Finally, real Mexican food at incredibly good prices.
- **Gracie's Diner** • 352 E 86th St [2nd Ave]
  212-737-8505 • $$
  Diner that's open all night.

Map 17

18 19 20
16 17
14 15
11 12 13

Upper East Side / East Harlem

- **La Isla Restaurant** • 1883 3rd Ave [E 104th St]
212-534-0002 • $
Locals get take-out from this Puerto Rican diner.
- **Mansion Restaurant** •
1634 York Ave [E 87th St]
212-535-8888 • $
Don't be scared of anything on this diner's massive menu.
- **Maz Mezcal** • 316 E 86th St [2nd Ave]
212-472-1599 • $$
Decent Mexican in a soulless area, good salsa.
- **Midnight Express Diner** • 1715 2nd Ave [E 89th St]
212-860-2320 • $
Fine for breakfast, downright amazing for 3 am food.
- **Naruto Ramen** • 1596 3rd Ave [E 90th St]
212-289-7803 • $$
Sip Japanese soup at the cramped counter.
- **Nick's Restaurant & Pizzeria** •
1814 2nd Ave [E 94th St]
212-987-5700 • $$$
Piping hot, thin-crust, brick oven pizza (and pasta).
- **Noglu** • 1266 Madison Ave [E 91st St]
646-895-9798 • $$$
Upscale gluten-free French import.

- **Pinocchio Ristorante** •
300 E 92nd St
212-828-5810 • $$$$$
Itty bitty sleeper Italian with rave reviews and loyal fans.
- **Pio Pio** • 1746 1st Ave [E 91st St]
212-426-5800 • $$
The Matador chicken combo will feed the whole family.
- **Russ & Daughters at the Jewish Museum** •
1109 5th Ave 92nd St
212-475-4880 ext. 3 • $$$
Lower East Side lox masters' cafe inside the Jewish Museum.
- **Sabor A Mexico** • 1744 1st Ave [E 90th St]
212-289-8675 • $$
Small, home-cooked, cheap, and delicious.
- **Schaller's Stube** • 1652 2nd Ave [E 86th St]
646-726-4355 • $$
Sausage counter from the German meat market next door.
- **Sfoglia** • 1402 Lexington Ave [E 92nd St]
212-831-1402 • $$$
Exquisite and experimental Italian by 92nd Street Y.
- **Shake Shack** • 154 E 86th St [Lexington Ave]
646-237-5035 • $
Finally, something good on 86th Street.
- **Table d'Hote** • 44 E 92nd St [Madison Ave]
212-348-8125 • $$$$
Cozy French vibe. Good Prix Fixe.
- **White Castle** • 351 E 103rd St [1st Ave]
212-876-6737 • $
One of four in Manhattan.

Feed your mind at **The Corner Bookstore**. For German treats and meats, **Schaller & Weber** is the place. **Mister Wright** knows his wine and booze.

🛍 Shopping

- **Blacker & Kooby Stationers** •
1390 Lexington Ave [E 92nd St]
212-369-8308
Good selection of stationery, pens, and art supplies.
- **Cooper-Hewitt National Design Museum Shop** • 2 E 91st St [5th Ave]
212-849-8400
Cool design stuff.
- **Corner Bookstore** •
1313 Madison Ave [E 93rd St]
212-831-3554
Tiny, old-school shop. Great selection.
- **Housing Works Thrift Shop** •
1730 2nd Ave [E 90th St]
212-722-8306
Uptown outpost of our favorite thrift shop.
- **Kitchen Arts & Letters** •
1435 Lexington Ave [E 93rd St]
212-876-5550
Fine selection of food and wine books.
- **La Tropezienne Bakery** •
2131 1st Ave [E 110th St]
212-860-5324
Excellent French bakery in El Barrio.

- **Mister Wright Fine Wines & Spirits** •
1593 3rd Ave [E 90th St]
212-722-4564
Good liquor store with huge selection and tastings.
- **Museum of the City of New York** •
1220 5th Ave [E 103rd St]
212-534-1672
Great NYC-focused gift shop.
- **Schaller & Weber** • 1654 2nd Ave [E 86th St]
212-879-3047
A relic of old Yorkville with countless German meats.
- **Trek Bicycle** • 1690 2nd Ave [E 87th St]
212-722-2201
Service, repair, and rentals.
- **Vinyl Wine** • 1491 Lexington Ave [E 96th St]
646-370-4100
Excellent hand-picked selection. And a record player.

Map 18 · **Columbia / Morningside Heights** Ⓝ

12th Ave

21

Marginal St

W 135th St

W 134th St

W 133rd St

135th
Street
B C

9

Old Broadway

Riverside Dr

W 132nd St

W 131st St

600

W 130th St

City
College

Convent Ave

St Nicholas Park

St Clair Pl

Manhattan-
ville
Houses

Convent Hill

A

Riverside Dr E

W 129th St

W 125th Street

Tiemann Pl

Old Broadway

W 126th St

W 128th St

1

W 125th St

W 127th St

19▶

Riverside Dr W

General
Grant
Houses

La Salle St

W 125th St

W 124th St

St Nicholas Ave

Hudson
River

Grant's
Tomb

Morningside
Houses

General
Grant
Houses

Broadway

W 123rd St

Claremont Ave

W 122nd St

Amsterdam Ave

W 121st St

Morningside Ave

Manhattan Ave

125th
Street
A C
B D

W 120th St

PAGE
274

Riverside
Park

Barnard College

Pupin
Hall

W 119th St

Frederick Douglass Blvd

PAGE
254

W 118th St

Columbia
University

Morningside Dr

W 117th St

B

W 116th St

Henry Hudson Pkwy

116th Street
Columbia
University

1

W 116th St

116th
Street
B C

W 115th St

W 114th St

W 113th St

Morningside
Park

W 112th St

Cathedral
of St John
the Divine

9A

Riverside Dr

W 111th St

Cathedral
Parkway 110th St

1

Cathedral
Parkway
110th St
B C

16

W 110th St (Cathedral Pkwy)

Central
Park

1/4 mile   .25 km

Neighborhood Overview

Map 18

Squeezed between the Upper West Side and Harlem, Columbia and Morningside Heights have had a symbiotic relationship with ups and downs. In truth, any institution with a multi-billion-dollar endowment (and we're talking multi-multi-billion-dollar here) is going to get to call the shots, but like every other behemoth institution of learning in an urban environment understands, the delicate dance takes constant maintenance. For your purposes, 116th Street between Broadway and Amsterdam is the main entrance of the gorgeous main campus of Columbia. A stroll through here is almost edifying—or at the very least a pleasant escape from the chaotic city around. Just watch out for the freshmen rushing to and from class.

Until the late 19th century, Morningside Heights was mostly undeveloped farmland. In 1895, **Columbia University** moved from Midtown Manhattan to 116th and Broadway, the site of a former insane asylum, and the rest is history. Over time the university was perceived as a Gibraltar of culture within a barren, dangerous part of town; that psychodrama played out in the notorious 1968 campus protests, ostensibly over plans to build a gym in Morningside Park but really over just about everything as the world around seemed to implode. Tensions eased over time, especially after Morningside Heights rents began to skyrocket in the '90s, but Morningside Park still serves as the dividing line between Columbia and basically everything else.

But speaking of "seeing light" (or whatever Columbia's "In lumine Tuo videbimus lumen" motto refers to; our Latin basically sucks), there's also the **Cathedral of St. John the Divine**, the world's largest Anglican church and sixth largest church in the world. An awe-inspiring display of architecture and that something else that makes people want to build stuff very high into the air, the cathedral is a beacon for procrastinators everywhere; although it dates back to the 19th century, the thing is still unfinished. The church has three distinct phases of construction that are immediately visible as you gaze up at the Gothic masterwork. The grounds are just as fun; look for the resident peacocks and sculptor Greg Wyatt's 40-foot-high *Peace Fountain* that goofs on tried-and-true allegorical representations of good and evil.

Meanwhile, there's an old corny joke that should hip you to who is actually buried in **Grant's Tomb**—or not, since it's really a mausoleum for the head of the Union Army and the 18th President of the United States (along with the 19th First Lady). The final resting place of Ulysses S. Grant, who spent the last part of his life in New York City working on a memoir, is actually a national memorial under the supervision of the National Park Service. Don't miss the asinine mosaic tile benches around the perimeter, someone's screwy idea of a "fun" public art project from the late 1960s.

Right across the street from Grant's Tomb is **Riverside Church**, an interdenominational house of worship with longstanding ties to the city's Black community. Martin Luther King, Jr., Nelson Mandela, and Kofi Annan have all given notable speeches at the church; Dr. King most famously denounced the Vietnam war here. The Gothic architecture is modeled after the cathedral in Chartres, France and the 392-foot-high tower—one of Upper Manhattan's most notable landmarks—is unusual in that it's actually functional, with 24 floors worth of programming space.

Neighborhood nightlife mostly consists of grad students avoiding dissertations in beer bars (**1020 Bar**) and undergrads avoiding papers with heavier drinking (**The Heights Bar & Grill**). Columbia will regularly bring in world-class operas at the **Miller Theater**.

Map 18

Columbia / Morningside Heights

O Landmarks

- **Cathedral Church of St. John the Divine** •
  1047 Amsterdam Ave [W 112th St]
  212-316-7540
  Our favorite cathedral. Completely unfinished
  and usually in disarray, just the way we like it.
- **Columbia University** •
  2960 Broadway [W 116th St]
  212-854-1754
  A nice little sanctuary amid the roiling masses.
- **Grant's Tomb** • W 122nd St & Riverside Dr
  646-670-7251
  A totally underrated experience, interesting,
  great grounds.
- **Pupin Hall** • 550 W 120th St [Broadway]
  Original site of the Manhattan Project.

Coffee

- **Cafe Amrita** • 301 W 110th St [Central Park W]
  212-222-0683
  Study (or update your blog) while you
  caffeinate.
- **Hungarian Pastry Shop** •
  1030 Amsterdam Ave [W 111th St]
  212-866-4230
  Professors and grad students love to read here.
- **Joe Coffee** •
  550 W 120th St [Broadway]
  212-924-7400
  Third-wave Joe mini-chain Columbia campus
  outpost.
- **Oren's Daily Roast** •
  2882 Broadway [W 112th St]
  212-749-8779
  Hip staff pours superior java at local
  mini-chain.
- **Toast** • 3157 Broadway [La Salle St]
  212-662-1144
  Good coffee starting at 11 am.

O Farmers Markets

- **Columbia Greenmarket** •
  Broadway & W 114th St
  Sun & Thurs 8 am–4 pm, year-round.
- **Morningside Park Farmers Market** •
  Manhattan Ave & W 110th St
  914-923-4837
  Sat, 9 am–2 pm, year-round.

Columbia / Morningside Heights

The Columbia kids have many long-standing quick favorites such as the giant slices of **Koronet Pizza**. For something more relaxed, try Ethiopian at **Massawa** or the dangerously delicious meat emporium of **Dinosaur BBQ**. Italian lovers get their fix at cozy **Max SoHa** and the wonderful **Pisticci**.

Nightlife

- **1020 Bar** • 1020 Amsterdam Ave [W 110th St]
  212-531-3468
  Columbia dive with super cheap beer.
- **Alfred Lerner Hall** • 2920 Broadway [W 114th St]
  212-854-9067
  Columbia student union features coffee, conventions, and wacky parties.
- **Cafe Amrita** • 301 W 110th St [Central Park W]
  212-222-0683
  Caffeinated Columbia students, snacks, wine, beer.
- **Cotton Club** • 656 W 125th St [St Clair Pl]
  212-663-7980
  Good, fun, swingin' uptown joint.
- **The Heights Bar & Grill** •
  2867 Broadway [W 111th St]
  212-866-7035
  Hang out on the rooftop with Columbia students.

Map 18
Columbia / Morningside Heights

18 19 20
16 17
14 15
11 12 13

Restaurants

• **Community Food and Juice** •
2893 Broadway [W 113th St]
212-665-2800 • $$$
Columbia foodies dig this place. And so should
you.

• **Dinosaur Bar-B-Que** •
700 W 125th St [Broadway]
212-694-1777 • $$$
Not just for Syracuse fans.

• **The Heights Bar & Grill** •
2867 Broadway [W 111th St]
212-866-7035 • $$
Columbia students can't drink all the time so
they eat here.

• **Hungarian Pastry Shop** •
1030 Amsterdam Ave [W 111th St]
212-866-4230 • $
Exactly what it is—and excellent.

• **Jin Ramen** • 3183 Broadway [Tiemann Pl]
646-559-2862 • $$
Kickin' ramen for Columbia crowd to slurp on.

• **Koronet Pizza** • 2848 Broadway [W 111th St]
212-222-1566 • $
Just one slice. Really. That's all you'll need.

• **Le Monde** • 2885 Broadway [W 112th St]
212-531-3939 • $$
French bistro pub with a nice bar.

• **Massawa** • 1239 Amsterdam Ave [W 121st St]
212-663-0505 • $$
Neighborhood Ethiopian joint.

• **Max Soha** • 1274 Amsterdam Ave [W 123rd St]
212-531-2221 • $$
The Italian genius of Max, uptown.

• **Miss Mamie's Spoonbread Too** •
366 W 110th St [Manhattan Ave]
212-865-6744 • $$
Soul food spectacular.

• **Pisticci** • 125 La Salle St [Broadway]
212-932-3500 • $$
Wonderful, friendly Italian. A true gem.

• **Subsconscious** •
1213 Amsterdam Ave [W 120th St]
212-864-2720 • $
Lunch deli with quality usually reserved for
Midtown.

• **Symposium** •
544 W 113th St [Amsterdam Ave]
212-865-1011 • $$
Traditional underground (literally) Greek fare.

• **Toast** • 3157 Broadway [La Salle St]
212-662-1144 • $$
Great diverse café menu.

• **Tom's Restaurant** •
2880 Broadway [W 112th St]
212-864-6137 • $
Yes. This is the Seinfeld diner. Can we go now?

• **V&T Pizzeria** •
1024 Amsterdam Ave [W 110th St]
212-663-1708 • $
Columbia pizza and pasta. Family friendly if
you're into that.

Columbia / Morningside Heights

Map 18

Book Culture is a world-class academic bookstore. Grab coffee on the go at **Oren's** or sit and talk Nietzsche at **Hungarian Pastry Shop**. Groceries and free samples at the 24-hour **Westside Market**. And then you have a world-class neighborhood wine store in **Vino Fino**.

Shopping

• **Appletree Market** •
1225 Amsterdam Ave [W 120th St]
212-865-8840
One of the better grocery options for Columbia kids.

• **Book Culture** •
536 W 112th St [Amsterdam Ave]
212-865-1588
Excellent bookstore servicing Columbia/ Barnard students.

• **Book Culture** • 2915 Broadway [W 114th St]
646-403-3000
Offshoot of the original location that Columbia students love.

• **C-Town** • 560 W 125th St [Old Broadway]
212-662-2388
No-frills market way cheaper than your local bodega.

• **Clinton Supply Co.** •
1256 Amsterdam Ave [W 122nd St]
212-222-8245
Random hardware stuff for your new dorm or apartment.

• **Franklin & Lennon Paint Co.** •
537 W 125th St [Broadway]
212-864-2460
Long-standing outlet with biggest selection of paint and supplies.

• **Hartley Pharmacy** •
1219 Amsterdam Ave [W 120th St]
212-749-8480
Mom-and-pop pharmacy with staff that knows you personally.

• **Mondel Chocolates** •
2913 Broadway [W 114th St]
212-864-2111
Mom-and-pop candy shop with great chocolates.

• **Samad's Gourmet** •
2867 Broadway [W 111th St]
212-749-7555
Hard to find Middle Eastern and world delicacies.

• **Sea & Sea Fish Market** •
310 St Nicholas Ave [W 125th St]
646-476-5569
Fish and more fish. They'll fry it up for you!

• **University Hardware** •
2906 Broadway [W 113th St]
212-882-2798
Where the smart kids get their hammers.

• **Vino Fino** •
1252 Amsterdam Ave [W 122nd St]
212-222-0388
Lots of tastings and friendly owners.

• **Westside Market** •
2840 Broadway [W 110th St]
212-222-3367
Bordering on gourmet shopping for Columbia U.

Map 19 · **Harlem (Lower)**

City College

St Nicholas Park

135th Street
B C

W 135th Street
135th Street
Harlem YMCA
Speakers' Corner
22
Lenox Terrace
W 134th Street
W 133rd Street
W 132nd Street
W 131st Street
W 130th Street
W 129th Street
W 128th Street
W 127th Street

St Nicholas Houses

A

18

Alhambra Theatre and Ballroom

Langston Hughes Place

Sylvia's

Apollo Theater

W 126th Street

125th Street
A C
B D

W 125th Street

125th Street
2 3

W 124th Street
W 123rd Street
W 122nd Street
W 121st Street
W 120th Street
W 119th Street
W 118th Street
W 117th Street
W 116th Street

Mt Morris Pk W

Marcus Garvey Park

Harlem Fire Watchtower

20

Morningside Park

Manhattan Ave

Frederick Douglass Blvd

St Nicholas Ave

Adam Clayton Powell Jr Blvd (Seventh Ave)

Lenox Ave (Malcolm X Blvd)

Fifth Ave

Madison Ave

116th Street
B C

116th Street
2 3

W 115th Street
W 114th Street
W 113th Street
W 112th Street
W 111th Street

Martin Luther King Jr Towers

Cathedral Parkway
110th Street
B C

W 110th St (Central Park N)

Central Park North
110th Street
2 3

Central Park

Duke Ellington Circle

PAGE 252

1/4 mile

.25 km

Neighborhood Overview

Map 19

Harlem is a thriving neighborhood in every sense of the word—great community spirit, great street life, great architecture, great arts and culture…pretty much great everything. The lifeline of this neighborhood is 125th Street, a thoroughfare known for the **Apollo Theater**, a zillion stores, and players strutting their stuff.

That said, Harlem has been evolving for some time now—brownstones sell for millions and condos have replaced most of the row-houses with shattered windows and planked doors. Bill Clinton made national headlines when he found some reasonably priced office space up on 125th Street; he still maintains the Clinton Foundation office there. But the nabe retains a sense of gritty pride. 125th Street is packed with vendors selling everything from fur vests to coco helado. A random TV in the wall next door to the Apollo plays Soul Train on repeat. Storefront churches fill Sunday mornings with Gospel ballads. Just journey uptown to check it out.

Over the years, a mind-boggling number of writers, artists, and civil rights leaders made names for themselves in Harlem, and the community is proud of its past. At the northeast corner of Central Park, a statue of jazz great **Duke Ellington** sitting at his piano welcomes you to the neighborhood. Dedicated in 1997, this memorial was surprisingly the first to be dedicated to an African American in New York City. Within the Morris Historical District lies **Marcus Garvey Park**, renamed for the famous black nationalist leader in 1973. If you're into literary history, visit Langston Hughes Place, the street where the poet lived; look for the ivy-covered building halfway down the block. Then check out his first residence at the still-operating **Harlem YMCA**. The facilities became an oasis for black visitors and artists during the Harlem Renaissance, when many of New York's hotels, theaters, and restaurants were segregated. The list of short-term residents is impressive, with Hughes, Ralph Ellison, Claude McKay, and James Baldwin all once calling the 135th Street location home.

Food, music, and entertainment happily collide in Harlem. The **Apollo Theater** is easily the area's most notable landmark, with everyone from Ella Fitzgerald to the Jackson Five kicking off their careers on that stage. The Amateur Night show has been running since 1934 and still happens most Wednesdays—just prepare for a line. Even more musical greats—Billie Holiday, Bessie Smith—haunted the **Alhambra Theatre and Ballroom**. If it had been around, we like to think they all would have chowed at **Sylvia's**, a soul food institution that has dished out piping hot fried chicken, waffles, and mashed potatoes since 1962.

Dive bars, underground jazz, and live music spectacles mesh for a diverse scene. Catch a show at the landmark **Apollo Theater** (Harlem residents, bring proof of address for a discount); sip fancy cocktails at **67 Orange Street**; or watch indie movies (many about Harlem) at **Maysles Cinema**, part of the documentary film center founded by filmmaker Albert Maysles.

Map 19

Harlem (Lower)

O Landmarks

- **Alhambra Ballroom** •
2116 Adam Clayton Powell Blvd [W 121st St]
917-965-2104
Last Harlem dance hall.
- **Apollo Theater** •
253 W 125th St [Frederick Douglass Blvd]
212-531-5300
The one and the only.
- **Duke Ellington Circle** •
5th Ave & Central Park N
Nice monument to a jazz great.
- **Harlem Fire Watchtower** •
Marcus Garvey Park
It's tall.
- **Harlem YMCA** • 180 W 135th St [7th Ave]
212-912-2100
Sidney Poitier, James Earl Jones, and Eartha
Kitt have performed in this Y's "Little Theatre."
- **Langston Hughes Place** •
20 E 127th St [5th Ave]
212-534-5992
Where the prolific poet lived and worked
1947–1967.
- **Marcus Garvey Park** •
E 120th St & Madison Ave
Appealingly mountainous park.
- **Speaker's Corner** • Lenox Ave & W 135th St
Famous soapbox for civil rights leaders,
including Marcus Garvey.
- **Sylvia's** • 328 Malcolm X Blvd [W 127th St]
212-996-0660
This restaurant is worth the trip.

Coffee

- **Starbucks** • 83 W 125th St [Lenox Ave]
917-492-2454
Use the bathroom. Then head to the closest
indie shop.

Farmers Markets

- **Harlem State Office
Building Farmers' Market** •
163 W 125th St [Adam Clayton Powell Jr Blvd]
917-515-8046
Tues 10 am–7 pm & Sat 8 am–4 pm, Jul–Nov.

Harlem dining is increasingly global and Marcus Samuelsson's **Red Rooster** has brought a lot of foot traffic to 125th Street, but don't stop there. Kick off the morning at **Il Caffe Latte** with steaming lattes and breakfast wraps. Settle in at **Patisserie des Ambassades** for French-Senegalese entrees. And head to **Amy Ruth's** or **Sylvia's** when home-style cooking beckons.

Nightlife

- **67 Orange Street** •
  2082 Frederick Douglass Blvd [W 113th St]
  212-662-2030
  Classy cocktail bar with speakeasy style.
- **Apollo Theater** •
  253 W 125th St [Frederick Douglass Blvd]
  212-531-5300
  The one and the only.
- **Ginny's Supper Club** •
  310 Lenox Ave [W 126th St]
  212-421-3821
  Hopping jazz club under Red Rooster.
- **Harlem Tavern** •
  2153 Frederick Douglass Blvd [W 116th St]
  212-866-4500
  Hybrid duties: Beer garden, sport bar, and pub food.
- **Just Lorraine's Place** •
  2247 Adam Clayton Powell Jr Blvd [W 132nd St]
  212-234-0720
  Friendly watering hole that locals love.
- **Shrine** •
  2271 Adam Clayton Powell Jr Blvd [W 134th St]
  212-690-7807
  Drink for cheap while Harlem and Columbia bands play.
- **W XYZ Bar** •
  2296 Frederick Douglass Blvd [W 124th St]
  212-749-4000
  Drinkin' and mixin' inside the Harlem Aloft Hotel.

Restaurants

- **Africa Kine Restaurant** •
  2267 7th Ave [133rd St]
  212-666-9400 • $$
  Highly regarded Senegalese restaurant.
- **Amy Ruth's** • 113 W 116th St [Lenox Ave]
  212-280-8779 • $$
  Soul food, incredible fried chicken.
- **Boulevard Bistro** •
  2149 Frederick Douglass Blvd
  212-678-6200 • $$$
  Modern Southern food for modern Harlem.
- **The Cecil** •
  210 W 118th St [Adam Clayton Powell Jr Blvd]
  212-866-1262 • $$$$
  Upscale mash up of modern Asian fare and soul food.
- **Corner Social** • 321 Lenox Ave [W 126th St]
  212-510-8552 • $$$
  A solid backup when the Rooster is packed across the street.
- **Harlem BBQ** •
  2367 Frederick Douglass Blvd [W 127th St]
  212-222-1922 • $$
  Football-sized frozen cocktails and entire $6 chickens-to-go.

Map 19

Harlem (Lower)

- **Harlem Shake** • 100 W 124th St [Lenox Ave]
212-222-8300 • $$
Shakes and burger joint with throwback look.
- **Il Caffe Latte** •
189 Malcolm X Blvd [W 119th St]
212-222-2241 • $
Fresh sandwiches, massive $3 lattes and a
stellar Latin wrap.
- **Jacob Restaurant** •
373 Malcolm X Blvd [W 129th St]
212-866-3663 • $
Soul food and salad by the pound for cheap.
- **Le Baobab** • 120 W 116th St [Lenox Ave]
212-864-4700 • $
Satisfying Senegalese complete with TV in
French.
- **Lido** •
2168 Frederick Douglass Blvd [W 117th St]
646-490-8575 • $$$
Sophisticated Northern Italian with requisite
exposed brick atmosphere.
- **LoLo's Seafood Shack** •
303 W 116th St [Frederick Douglass Blvd]
646-649-3356 • $$
Spicy Caribbean steampots and fritters in a
ramshackle backyard.
- **Manna's** •
2353 Frederick Douglass Blvd [W 125th St]
212-749-9084 • $$
Pile a buffet plate with everything from oxtail
to collard greens.
- **Melba's** •
300 W 114th St [Frederick Douglass Blvd]
212-864-7777 • $$$
Upscale soul food.
- **Minton's** •
206 W 118th St [Adam Clayton Powell Jr Blvd] •
$$$$
The famous jazz club reborn with haute-soul
food.

- **Patisserie Des Ambassades** •
2200 Frederick Douglass Blvd [W 119th St]
212-666-0078 • $
Great breakfast pastries. Senegalese food too.
- **Red Rooster** •
310 Lenox Ave
212-792-9001 • $$$
The latest uptown craze from chef star Marcus
Samuelsson.
- **Shrine** •
2271 Adam Clayton Powell Jr Blvd [W 134th St]
212-690-7807 • $$
Atmosphere first, foodstuffs second. Local
bands play.
- **Sylvia's** • 328 Malcolm X Blvd [W 127th St]
212-996-0660 • $$$
An institution. Not overrated.

Shopping

- **467 Lenox Liquors** •
467 Lenox Ave [W 133rd St]
212-234-7722
Standard liquor store, sans bullet-proof glass.
- **Adja Khady Food** •
243 W 116th St [Frederick Douglass]
212-933-0374
Friendly West African culinary supplies and
community hang out.

Harlem (Lower)

Map 19

With everything from **Champs** to **M.A.C. Makeup**, 125th Street anchors Harlem shopping. **H&M** stocks the same trendy threads as everywhere else, without the long lines. Street vendors fill any other gaps. Everything you want is here, guaranteed. And don't forget to check out the open-air **Malcolm Shabazz Harlem Market**.

- **B.O.R.N. Boutique** •
  52 W 125th St [Malcolm X Blvd]
  718-986-5373
  Upscale vintage for stylish Harlemites.
- **The Brownstone** •
  24 E 125th St [Madison Ave]
  212-996-7980
  Clothing boutique featuring local designers.
- **Champs** • 208 W 125th St [7th Ave]
  212-280-0296
  Sports, street shoes, and wear. For losers too.
- **Grandma's Place** • 84 W 120th St [Lenox Ave]
  212-360-6776
  Harlem toy store. Your grandkid will probably
  love it.
- **H&M** • 125 W 125th St [Lenox Ave]
  855-466-7467
  Sort-of-hip, disposable fashion.
- **Hats by Bunn** • 2283 7th Ave [W 134th St]
  212-694-3590
  Cool caps.
- **Jimmy Jazz** •
  239 W 125th St [Frederick Douglass Blvd]
  212-663-2827
  Urban designers with a range of sizes.

- **Levain Bakery** •
  2167 Frederick Douglass Blvd [117th St]
  917-464-3789
  Bodacious, weighty super-mega cookies.
- **MAC** • 202 W 125th St [7th Ave]
  212-665-0676
  Beauty products in many colors and shades.
- **Malcolm Shabazz Harlem Market** •
  52 W 116th St [Lenox Ave]
  212-987-8131
  An open-air market for all your daishiki needs.
- **Settepani** • 196 Lenox Ave [W 120th St]
  917-492-4806
  Lovely baked goods.
- **Trunk Show Consignment** •
  275 W 113th St [8th Ave]
  212-662-0009
  Cool designer fashions recycled, but just bring
  a fat wad of cash.
- **United Hardware** •
  2160 Frederick Douglass Blvd [W 117th St]
  212-666-7778
  Good for basic tools; that's about all.

Map 20 · El Barrio / East Harlem

Neighborhood Overview

El Barrio, also known as Spanish Harlem or East Harlem (just don't call it "SpaHa"), is a neighborhood that is alive with history and culture—Puerto Rican, African American, Mexican, Italian, Dominican, and increasingly Asian…it's really one of the most diverse neighborhoods in the city. It's not uncommon to find people playing congas on the street or riding tricked-out bicycles with Puerto Rican tunes blasting. You can feel a real sense of community in the bodegas and on the streets as residents chat up their neighbors and warmly greet one another with "Papi" or "Mami." In the summer locals crowd into **Thomas Jefferson Park** and the abundant community gardens provide locals with the perfect chill out spots. Exploring this neighborhood is highly recommended.

But it's not all pretty. East Harlem has been through some tough times to say the least. And unfortunately, to a lot of New Yorkers, it is still a place to avoid. **Keith Haring's "Crack is Wack" Mural** is a symbol of the urban decay in the 1970s and '80s when drugs, poverty, and violence ravaged the neighborhood. Burnt-out buildings were the norm and social problems skyrocketed. Today concrete housing projects dominate the landscape (some very unique like **Taino Towers**), but crime is way down and rents are way up.

In recent years the neighborhood has rapidly changed with new condos sprouting up everywhere (some even with doormen), a growing Mexican population moving in (check out 116th Street between Second and Third for amazing food and groceries), and even a touch of suburbia with the gigantic **Costco** that opened in 2009.

Before the Puerto Rican migration, Italians used to call East Harlem home. In the 1930s there were tens of thousands of immigrants from Southern Italy living here. The Italian legacy has not entirely disappeared. Remnants include the gorgeous **Church of Our Lady of Mount Carmel** (the first Italian church in New York), the **Virgen del Carmen Shrine**, and restaurants like **Rao's** and **Patsy's Pizza**.

Underneath the Metro-North viaduct is another remnant of the old neighborhood, the historic public market **La Marqueta**. Established by Mayor La Guardia in 1936, this place was the hub of shopping activity for decades with over 500 vendors. Now it only has a few businesses left selling Puerto Rican delicacies like bacalao. But it is slowly being revived by the city with new vendors selling everything from baked goods to garden supplies. In the meantime, locals pack the public plaza between 115th & 116th Street on Saturdays in the summer for live music and dancing.

To see the neighborhood in full party mode, head here for the second weekend in June when the Puerto Rican Day Parade is in full swing. On Sunday the parade strolls down Fifth Avenue, but on Saturday, Third Avenue and 116th Street come alive for a full-on Puerto Rican party—live music, barbecues on the sidewalk, and lots of Nuyorican pride.

Map 20

18 19 20
16 17
14 15
11 12 13

El Barrio / East Harlem

O Landmarks

- **Church of Our Lady of Mt Carmel** •
  448 E 116th St [Pleasant Ave]
  212-534-0681
  The first Italian parish in NYC.
- **Danny's Club & Fashion** • 1st Ave & E 114th St
  Funky neighborhood fashion shop going
  strong for 30+ years.
- **Harlem Courthouse** •
  170 E 121st St [Lexington Ave]
  One of the most impressive buildings in
  Manhattan.
- **Keith Haring "Crack is Wack" Mural** •
  2nd Ave & E 127th St
  Keith was right.
- **La Marqueta** • 1590 Park Ave [E 115th St]
  212-534-4900
  This public market used to be bustling; not so
  much anymore.
- **Religious Street Shrine: Virgen del Carmen** •
  240 E 117th St
  Shrine built by Italians in memory of soldiers
  who died in WW II.
- **Taino Towers** • 3rd Ave & E 123rd St
  Unique low-income housing development
  opened in 1979.
- **Thomas Jefferson Park** •
  2180 1st Ave [E 112th St]
  212-639-9675
  Green space with a giant pool and bbqs in the
  summer.

Coffee

- **Love Cafe** • 283 Pleasant Ave [E 115th St]
  212-369-6916
  Super friendly indie shop almost too good to
  be true.

El Barrio / East Harlem

Map 20

Patsy's pizza really is the "original" New York thin-crust pizza. The slices are the best in NYC. Unless you know the Mayor, Rao's is another New York restaurant you'll never see the inside of. 116th Street is a budget culinary wonderland. Try Taco Mix or El Nuevo Caridad.

Farmers Markets

- **La Marqueta** • 1590 Park Ave & E 115th St
212-534-4900
Tue–Sun, year-round

Nightlife

- **Amor Cubano** • 2018 3rd Ave [E 111th St]
212-996-1220
The house band always has this place grooving.

21 22
18 19 20
16   17
14   15
11 12 13

Map 20

El Barrio / East Harlem

Restaurants

- **A Taste of Seafood** •
  2530 Frederick Douglas Blvd
  212-866-0275 • $
  Fried fish sandwiches on white bread. Lord,
  have mercy!
- **Amor Cubano** • 2018 3rd Ave [E 111th St]
  212-996-1220 • $$
  Good Cuban food. Great live music.
- **Charlie's Place** •
  1960 Madison Ave [E 125th St]
  212-410-0277 • $$
  Harlem's first sushi bar.
- **Cuchifritos** • 168 E 116th St [Lexington Ave]
  212-876-4846 • $
  Puerto Rican fried treats.
- **El Nuevo Caridad** • 2257 2nd Ave [E 116th St]
  212-860-8187 • $
  Dominican baseball stars approve of this
  chicken.
- **Makana** • 2245 1st Ave [E 115th St]
  212-996-3534 • $$
  A great little Hawaiian-Japanese BBQ takes
  Manhattan.

- **Patsy's Pizzeria** • 2287 1st Ave [E 118th St]
  212-534-9783 • $$
  The original thin-crust pizza. Best take-out
  slices in NY.
- **Pee Dee Steakhouse** •
  2006 3rd Ave [E 110th St]
  212-996-3300 • $
  Grilled meats for cheap.
- **Polash** • 2179 3rd Ave [E 119th St]
  212-410-0276 • $$
  Surprisingly solid uptown Indian Restaurant.
- **Quesadillas Doña Maty** •
  228 E 116th St [2nd Ave]
  917-261-4278 • $
  Friendly Mexican joint grilling quesadillas on
  the sidewalk.
- **Rao's** • 455 E 114th St [1st Ave]
  212-722-6709 • $$$$$
  An Italian institution, but you'll never get in.
- **Ricardo Steak House** •
  2145 2nd Ave [E 110th St]
  212-289-5895 • $$
  Steak, bar, outside patio with upscale vibe and
  valet parking.
- **Taco Mix** • 234 E 116 St [3rd Ave]
  212-289-2963 • $
  The best tacos in El Barrio. Go for the al pastor.

Casablanca Meat Market is always packed, and for good reason with excellent homemade sausages. For do-it-yourself projects **The Demolition Depot** is a gold mine (but where do they get this stuff?). There's even a touch of suburbia in East Harlem with **Costco.**

🛍 Shopping

- **Capri Bakery** • 186 E 116th St [3rd Ave]
  212-410-1876
  Spanish El Barrio bakery.
- **Casablanca Meat Market** •
  125 E 110th St [Park Ave]
  212-534-7350
  The line out the door every Saturday says it all.
- **Costco** • 517 E 117 St [Pleasant Ave]
  212-896-5875
  Giving Long Islanders another reason to drive into the city.
- **The Demolition Depot** •
  159–161 E 126th St
  212-860-1138
  Amazing selection of architectural salvage.
- **Don Paco Lopez Panaderia** •
  2129 3rd Ave [E 116th St]
  212-876-0700
  Mexican bakery famous for Three Kings Day cake.
- **Eagle Tile & Home Centers** •
  2250 2nd Ave [E 115th St]
  212-423-0333
  Update the tile in your kitchen or bathroom.
- **Heavy Metal Bike Shop** • 2016 3rd Ave [E 110th St]
  646-952-4930
  Pedal to the metal for repairs and parts.
- **La Marqueta** • 1590 Park Ave [E 115th St]
  212-534-4900
  Puerto Rican food stalls, baked goods, and a huge garden center.
- **Lore Decorators** • 213 E 120th St
  212-534-1025
  Well Known by Madison Avenue clientele, Reupholster your sidewalk/dumpster chair.
- **Mi Mexico Lindo Bakery** •
  2267 2nd Ave [E 116th St]
  212-996-5223
  Grab a tray at this old-school bakery.
- **Raices Dominican Cigars** •
  2250 1st Ave [E 116th St]
  212-410-6824
  Hand-rolled cigars. With a smoking room!
- **Raskin Carpets** • 2143 3rd Ave [E 122nd St]
  212-369-1100
  Long time East Harlem store has Santa at Xmas.
- **V&M American Outlet** •
  1950 3rd Ave [E 121st St]
  212-423-1066
  Everything for your apartment
- **V.I.M.** • 2239 3rd Ave [E 122nd St]
  212-369-5033
  Street wear—jeans, sneakers, tops—for all.
- **Young Fish Market** • 2004 3rd Ave [E 110th St]
  646-476-4443
  Get it fresh or fried.

Map 21 · **Manhattanville / Hamilton Heights**

Neighborhood Overview

Map 21

Hamilton Heights doesn't quite feel like Manhattan. Wedged between the Hudson River to the west and St. Nicholas Park to the east, this neighborhood of hilly parks, museums, and beautiful old brownstones offers a pleasant respite from the concrete and steel of the rest of the island. Columbia University's continuing expansion threatens to throw gentrification into double-time, but even in the face of rising rents, Alexander Hamilton's former country estate retains almost a bucolic feel.

Counting landmark buildings in Hamilton Heights is like keeping track of nuns in Rome. The number is staggering, but none are as striking as **City College**'s white and brick Neo-Gothic buildings; turrets, towers, and gargoyles practically litter the historic campus. For classic New York, mosey up to the **Hamilton Heights Historic District**, just north of City College, where stunning homes line the streets where Alexander Hamilton's original home sat; **Hamilton Grange National Memorial** has since been moved to nearby St. Nicholas Park. The **James Bailey House**, the home of P.T. Barnum's partner James Bailey, is one of the coolest residences in all of Manhattan, and probably the only one built on a circus fortune. For crazy concrete church design, nothing beats the **Church of the Crucifixion**.

Sure, the authorities built Riverbank State Park to appease residents after the city dumped a sewage plant along the river, but it's a great neighborhood resource and includes a roller skating rink, running track, and a soccer field. Skip the gym fees, and swim laps at the nice indoor pool. The **Trinity Cemetery Graveyard of Heroes** feels almost otherworldly, with lovely rolling paths that feel out of place in Upper Manhattan. Several Astors, Charles Dickens' son, and John James Audubon are all buried here, as is three-term mayor Ed Koch. St. Nicholas Park is worth a visit just for its spacious lawns, but don't miss Hamilton Grange. The National Park Service restored the building after moving it to the park in 2009.

In a city where museums charge in excess of $30 just to elbow strangers for a glimpse of a Botticelli, the **Hispanic Society of America** Museum and Library is miraculous. Admission is free to the museum and reference library, which showcases the arts and cultures of Spain, Portugal, and Latin America. Browse the society's prints, paintings and artifacts, but linger in **Audubon Terrace**. The square-city block plot was named for the famous naturalist, John James Audubon, who once farmed in Washington Heights. The land became a cultural center in 1904 and also houses the **American Academy of Arts and Letters**. Years of neglect left the terrace looking drab, but a a recent glass structure addition linking the Academy of Arts and Letters and the Hispanic Society signals a welcome rejuvenation.

Harlem Public serves up good food and great drinks and is a welcome addition to a somewhat sparse nightlife scene.

Meander up Broadway for your pick of taquerias and Dominican eats. **Picante** boasts some of the nabe's best sit-down Mexican. Cheap Middle Eastern can be found at **Queen Sheeba**. **Trufa** provides a bistro option.

⚪ Landmarks

- **American Academy of Arts & Letters** •
  633 W 155th St [Riverside Dr]
  212-368-5900
  New glass structure links it to the Hispanic
  Society.
- **Audubon Terrace** • Broadway & W 155th St
  Pleasant, if lonely, Beaux Arts complex. What's
  it doing here?
- **Bailey House** • 10 St Nicholas Pl [W 150th St]
  Romanesque revival mansion from PT
  Barnum's partner James Bailey.
- **City College** • 160 Convent Ave [W 130th St]
  212-650-7000
  Peaceful gothic campus.
- **The Episcopal Church Of The Crucifixion** •
  459 W 149th St [Convent Ave]
  212-281-0900
  Whacked-out concrete church by Costas
  Machlouzarides, circa 1967.
- **Hamilton Grange National Memorial** •
  414 W 141st St [St Nicholas Ave]
  Alexander Hamilton's house, twice relocated
  and now facing the wrong way. Damn those
  Jeffersonians!
- **Hamilton Heights Historic District** •
  W 140th & W 145th St b/n Amsterdam &
  St Nicholas Ave
  192 houses, apartments, and churches on the
  National Registry of Historic Places. Who
  knew?
- **Hispanic Society Museum** •
  613 W 155th St [Broadway]
  212-926-2234
  Free museum (Tues–Sat) with Spanish
  masterpieces.
- **Trinity Church Cemetery Graveyard of
  Heroes** • 3699 Broadway [W 153rd St]
  Hilly, almost countryish cemetery.

☕ Coffee

- **Café One** • 1619 Amsterdam Ave [W 139th St]
  212-690-0060
  Free wifi, quality pastries, and reliable java.
- **The Chipped Cup** • 3610 Broadway [149th St]
  212-368-8881
  Fair trade, third wave, and fancy pastries.
- **Manhattanville Coffee** •
  142 Edgecombe Ave [142nd St]
  646-781-9900
  Quality cups and small bites.

🍏 Farmers Markets

- **Grass Roots Farmers Market** •
  Edgecombe Ave & W 145th St
  212-996-1514
  Sat 9 am–4 pm, Jul–Nov.

🌙 Nightlife

- **Harlem Public** • 3612 Broadway [W 149th St]
  212-939-9404
  Good food, good drinks, exciting addition to
  neighborhood.

Manhattanville / Hamilton Heights

Check out **V.I.M.** for duds and kicks; when someone says they're the best jeans and sneaker store in America, you should probably pay attention.

🍴Restaurants

• **Blue Corn Mexican Restaurant** •
1969 Amsterdam Ave [W 157th St]
212-283-7752 • $
One of the best in a parade of taquerias.

• **Ecuatoriana Restaurant** •
1685 Amsterdam Ave [W 143rd St]
212-491-4626 • $$
Legit Ecuadorian fare, sans guinea pig.

• **Famous Fish Market** •
684 St Nicholas Ave [W 145th St]
212-491-8323 • $
Deep fried and from the sea.

• **Jimbo's Hamburger Palace** •
528 W 145th St [Amsterdam Ave]
212-926-0338 • $
Cheap, fast, easy burgers.

• **Oso** • 1618 Amsterdam Ave [140th St]
646-858-3139 • $$$
Stylish Mexican.

• **Picante** • 3424 Broadway [W 139th St]
212-234-6479 • $$
Arguably Manhattanville's best Mexican, plus affordable margs.

• **Queen Sheeba** •
317 W 141st St [Frederick Douglass Blvd]
212-862-6149 • $
Cafeteria-style Middle Eastern that's friendly on the wallet.

• **Subsconcious** •
1213 Amsterdam Ave [W 140th St]
212-864-2720 • $
Standard sandwiches and full blown salad bar.

• **Trufa** • 3431 Broadway [W 140th St]
646-522-4142 • $$
Bistro featuring pastas and New American entrees.

🛍Shopping

• **Foot Locker** • 3549 Broadway [W 146th St]
212-491-0927
Get your sneakers from a fake referee.

• **Junior Bicycle Shop** •
1826 Amsterdam Ave [W 150th St]
212-690-6511
Repairs.

• **Sister's Uptown Bookstore and Cultural Center** • 1942 Amsterdam Ave [W 156th St]
212-862-3680
Books and events celebrating black women, amazing staff.

• **Unity Liquors** •
704 St Nicholas Ave [W 146th St]
212-491-7821
Right by the subway, where all liquor stores should be.

• **V.I.M.** • 508 W 145th St [Amsterdam Ave]
212-491-1143
Street wear—jeans, sneakers, tops—for all.

Neighborhood Overview

Map 22

25
24
23
22
18 19 20
16 17

At first glance, upper Harlem lacks character. Generic buffets and 99-cent stores line Lenox, one of the nabe's anchor streets. 145th Street sprawls with suburban gas stations and an entrance to the 145th Street Bridge. High rises dot the uptown skyline. But this 20-block triangle sandwiched between St. Nicholas to the west and the Harlem River to the east is the lifeline of Black culture in New York. Everyone from starving artists to self-made millionaires have called upper Harlem home, and a visit to the **Schomburg Center for Research** reveals the neighborhood's significant impact. Not surprisingly, gentrification is a sensitive point of controversy. But for now, the culture remains intact. Old churches maintain a sense of community. Heavenly food attracts locals and tourists. Historic districts preserve the look and feel. Upper Harlem has it all—you just have to dig a little.

Start at 135th Street and Lenox, or "Speaker's Corner," an intersection where back in the day anyone shouted their concerns and critiques of current events. Most famously, Marcus Garvey presented his views on race at this corner. The Harlem Hellfighters, an all-black military unit that fought in World War I and World War II, housed their headquarters at the imposing **369th Regiment Armory**. The building still operates as a sustainment brigade, but an obelisk outside honors the soldiers. Long before the Hellfighters, Ethiopian traders protested segregation policies by founding the **Abyssinian Baptist Church** in 1808. After 203 years, the congregation only moved once, in 1923, to its striking Neo-Gothic building.

The Rockefeller family built the **Dunbar Houses** in 1926 to provide affordable housing in Harlem. The complex attracted writers, artists, musicians, and poets, including W.E.B. DuBois, the first African-American to graduate from Harvard. Similarly ambitious residents moved in to the **St. Nicholas Historic District**. Sometimes called "Strivers' Row," Stanford White designed the houses, where many upwardly mobile residents lived. Note the original "Walk your Horses" signs (there aren't any carriage rides in the neighborhood).

Rucker Park is home to famously intense pickup games. Kareem Abdul-Jabbar, Kobe Bryant, and hundreds of exceedingly talented locals have dribbled on these courts. Swing by to try your hand or just enjoy the show. The **Schomburg Center** focuses on preserving the history of people of African descent worldwide. The center's dizzying array of artifacts, prints, images and manuscripts includes more than 100,000 items. The **Countee Cullen Regional Branch Library** also has an excellent African American reference section; at the turn of the century, Madame C.J. Walker lived at this same address—the "richest woman in Harlem" earned her fortune by selling hair care products specifically for Black women.

There isn't a lot of nightlife above 135th Street but stalwart **Londel's Supper Club** has classic jazz on Fridays and Saturdays with no cover.

The parade of routine delis on Lenox hides some of Manhattan's tastiest eats. Do not miss **Charles' Country Pan Fried Chicken** to chow down on mindblowing hot birds.

Map 22

Harlem (Upper)

o Landmarks

- **The 369th Regiment Armory** •
  2366 5th Ave [W 142nd St]
  Home of the Harlem Hellfighters.
- **Abyssinian Baptist Church** •
  132 Odell Clark Pl [Lenox Ave]
  212-862-7474
  NY's oldest black congregation.
- **The Dunbar Houses** •
  W 149th St & Frederick Douglass Blvd
  Historic, multi-family apartment buildings
  from the 1920s.
- **Holcombe Rucker Park** •
  Frederick Douglass Blvd & W 155th St
  Famous basketball court that birthed the likes
  of Kareem Abdul-Jabbar and more.
- **St. Nicholas Historic District** •
  202 W 138th St [7th Ave]
  Beautiful neo-Georgian townhouses.

Coffee

- **Dunkin' Donuts** • 110 W 145th St [Lenox Ave]
  212-234-3440
  Decent coffee served in gigantic cups.
- **Dunkin' Donuts** •
  2103 Frederick Douglass Blvd [W 145th St]
  212-280-6414
  Decent coffee served in gigantic cups.
- **Manhattanville Coffee** •
  142 Edgecombe Ave [W 142nd St]
  646-781-9900
  Independent coffee shop with great baked
  goods.
- **Starbucks** •
  356 W 145th St [Frederick Douglass Blvd]
  212-281-0056
  One of the few coffee spots around here.

Farmers Markets

- **Harlem Hospital Market** •
  W 137th St & Lenox Ave
  Fri 8 am–4 pm, June–Nov.

Map 22

Make My Cake has sugary cupcakes, cheesecakes and regular cakes.

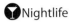

Nightlife

- **Harlem Nights** •
2361 7th Ave [138th St]
646-820-4603
Handsome, crafty bar with much live music.
- **Londel's** •
2620 Frederick Douglass Blvd [W 140th St]
212-234-6114
Great live music on Friday & Saturdays.

Restaurants

- **Grini's Grill** • 100 W 143rd St [Lenox Ave]
212-694-6274 • $
This "tapas bar" actually serves heaping plates
of meat and rice.
- **Londel's** •
2620 Frederick Douglass Blvd [W 140th St]
212-234-6114 • $$$
Good Southern with live music on the
weekend.
- **Mama Tina's Pizza** •
2649 Frederick Douglass Blvd [W 141st St]
212-368-2820 • $
Decent pizza for late-night pangs.

Shopping

- **Baskin-Robbins** •
110 W 145th St
212-234-3440
Do they still have 31 flavors?
- **Make My Cake** •
2380 7th Ave [W 139th St]
212-234-2344
Freshly baked cakes from a Southern family
recipe.
- **The Schomburg Shop** •
515 Malcolm X Blvd [W 135th St]
212-491-2206
Shop specializing in Black history and culture.

Map 23 · **Washington Heights**

Neighborhood Overview

Map 23

Washington Heights is a veritable United Nations of immigrant stories. Irish settlers moved up north in the 1900s. After World War I, European Jews called this hilly stretch of Manhattan home. Now, the 'hood swings to an undeniable merengue beat. The largely Dominican sliver of northern Manhattan probably claims more authenticity than any Punta Cana all-inclusive. Street vendors whip up delectable chimichurris, a sort of Dominican hamburger. Broadway houses a seemingly limitless number of chicken-and-rice eateries. English almost feels like a second language. As with all of Manhattan, this swath of delis and pollerias sees change around every corner. Students and young adults searching for cheap rent keep hiking uptown, and higher end eateries are breaking into the restaurant scene. It looks like everyone knows that all you have to do is take the A train even farther than Harlem.

Some of Manhattan's most storied buildings live far uptown, and The Heights are no exception. Most notable is the **Morris-Jumel Mansion**, a hilltop home that looks like it belongs in *Gone With the Wind*, not Gotham. British Colonel Roger Morris built the abode in 1765, but George Washington famously stationed his headquarters here in the fall of 1776. After the Revolutionary War, Morris left the estate, which stretched up from Harlem. If that's not impressive enough, note that Washington also took John Adams, Thomas Jefferson, and John Quincy Adams to dine there in 1790. The museum is open for visits, but beware: There have been rumors of hauntings. For a less ghostly architecture tour, check out the two-block historic district of **Sylvan Terrace**. This stretch of wooden row-houses line the skinny street leading up to the mansion. Although the turn-of-the-century homes underwent a few incarnations—from wooden to faux brick to stucco—they are now largely restored to their original facades. Another turn of the century creation, the **New York Armory**, had a similar rebirth. The armory first served as a training center for the National Guard in 1909. It rose to fame as a center for track and field competitions until the 1980s, when it became a homeless shelter. Now, the armory has been restored and functions as a track and field center.

This skinny expanse of Manhattan boasts some of the country's top transportation accomplishments. Construction began in 1948 for the **Cross-Bronx Expressway**, one of the country's first highways to forge through such a densely populated urban area; suffice it to say, "first" does not necessary mean "best." Heading west into Fort Lee, NJ, the **George Washington Bridge** is the only 14-lane suspension crossing in the country. Hikers, bikers, and skaters can skip the pricey tolls and enjoy views of Palisades Interstate Park in New Jersey. The best part about the bridge: **The Little Red Lighthouse** that rests underneath. The charmingly out-of-place tower only operated between 1921 and 1948, but it earned fame from the 1942 children's book *The Little Red Lighthouse and the Great Gray Bridge*, by Hildegarde Swift and Lynd Ward.

Duck into **Le Chéile** for a pint. When the live music itch strikes, the grand **United Palace** hosts a bevy of artists.

Map 23

Washington Heights

O Landmarks

- **The Armory** •
  216 Fort Washington Ave [W 169th St]
  212-923-1803
  World class running facility houses Track &
  Field Hall of Fame.
- **Cross Bronx Expressway** •
  Cross Bronx Expressway [Ittner Pl]
  Worst. Highway. Ever.
- **George Washington Bridge** •
  W 178th St [Henry Hudson Pkwy]
  Try to see it when it's lit up. Drive down from
  Riverdale on the Henry Hudson at night and
  you'll understand.
- **George Washington Bridge Bus Station** •
  4211 Broadway [178th St]
  973-275-5555
  Nervi's bus masterpiece connecting
  Washington Heights with the world.
- **High Bridge Water Tower** • Highbridge Park
  Defunct but cool water tower; tours inside are
  worth the hassle.
- **The Little Red Lighthouse** •
  Fort Washington Park [W 178th St]
  Enter from 181st Street. It's there, really!
- **Morris-Jumel Mansion** •
  65 Jumel Terrace [W 162nd St]
  212-923-8008
  The oldest building in New York, at least until
  someone changes it again.
- **Sylvan Terrace** •
  b/n Jumel Ter & St Nicholas Ave
  The most un-Manhattanlike place in all the
  world.
- **United Palace Theater** •
  4140 Broadway [W 175th St]
  212-568-6700
  Movie theater, then church, now live
  performance venue. Gorgeous inside.

Coffee

- **Starbucks** •
  803 W 181st St [Ft Washington Ave]
  212-927-4272
  Fuel up and take a break from 181st.

Hit up **Malecon** for unsurpassed roast chicken. When variety beckons **Sushi Yu** dishes up a tasty alternative and **Saggio** is a pleasant Italian trattoria. And good luck choosing from the massive **Hudson View** menu (though we're sorry to report that there is not much of a view).

Farmers Markets

• **175th Street Greenmarket** •
Broadway & W 175th St
Thurs, 8 am–4 pm, June–Nov.

Nightlife

• **Le Chéile** • 839 W 181st St [Cabrini Blvd]
212-740-3111
Nice-looking Irish bar with good beer & food.

Map 23

Washington Heights

25
24
23
21 22
18 19 20
16 17

🍴Restaurants

- **181 Cabrini** • 854 W 181st St [Cabrini Blvd]
  212-923-2233 • $$
  Seasonal American bistro.
- **Aqua Marina** • 4060 Broadway [W 171st St]
  212-928-0070 • $
  OK Uptown Italian.
- **Carrot Top Pastries** •
  3931 Broadway [W 165th St]
  212-927-4800 • $
  Baked goods and coffee too!
- **Dallas BBQ** • 3956 Broadway [W 166th St]
  212-568-3700 • $$
  When you can't get to Virgil's.
- **El Conde** • 4139 Broadway [W 175th St]
  212-781-3231 • $$$
  Big slabs of MEAT.
- **Flaco's Pizza** • 3876 Broadway [W 162nd St]
  212-923-3733 • $
  Chowing on this cheap, delish pizza won't
  keep you flaco.

- **GG Gourmet Deli** •
  603 W 168th St [Broadway]
  $
  Standard deli fare, with a large doctor
  clientele.
- **Hudson View Restaurant** •
  770 W 181st St [Fort Washington Ave]
  212-781-0303 • $$
  Ch- ch- ch- choices.
- **Malecon** • 4141 Broadway [W 175th St]
  212-927-3812 • $
  Fabulous roast chicken.
- **Manolo Tapas** • 4165 Broadway [W 176th St]
  212-923-9100 • $$$
  Uptown portal to Spain with rustic cuisine and
  ambiance.
- **Saggio Restaurant** •
  827 W 181st St [Cabrini Blvd]
  212-795-3080 • $$$
  Every good neighborhood needs a solid Italian
  trattoria.
- **Sushi Yu II** • 825 W 181st St [Pinehurst Ave]
  212-781-5255 • $
  Raw fish for when you need to take a plantain
  break.

Washington Heights

Broadway's chaos anchors this nabe's shopping options. Stroll the street for a mind-boggling number of hardware stores, check out oodles of vendors at **La Plaza de las Americas**. Find a decent selection of wine and liquor at **Columbia Wine**. For a taste of Russia, check out **Moscow on the Hudson**. It's all here.

Shopping

- **3841 Hardware** • 3875 Broadway [W 160th St]
646-912-9249
No name required at this classic, Broadway tool supply shop.
- **Baskin-Robbins** •
728 W 181st St [Colonel Robert Magaw Pl]
212-765-0101
31 flavors and other frozen treats.
- **Carrot Top Pastries** •
3931 Broadway [W 165th St]
212-927-4800
Top carrot cake, muffins, chocolate cake, rugalach, and more.
- **The Children's Place** •
600 W 181st St [St Nicholas Ave]
212-923-7244
Cute clothes for little ones.
- **Columbia Wine** • 4038 Broadway [169th St]
212-543-2633
Well-appointed, non-plexiglass wine & liquor store.
- **Fort Washington Bakery & Deli** •
808 W 181st St [Fort Washington Ave]
212-795-1891
Damn good looking cookies.
- **La Bella Nails & Spa** •
4117 Broadway [W 169th St]
212-927-2023
Time for that bi-weekly pedicure.

- **La Plaza de Las Americas** •
Broadway & W 175th St
Outdoor street vendor market.
- **Moscow on the Hudson** •
801 W 181st St [Fort Washington Ave]
212-740-7397
Comrades, this place is Russian culinary heaven.
- **Nunez Hardware** •
2800 3rd Ave
718-665-8380
Scavenge for tools at this old-school, stocked-to-bursting shop.
- **Spoiled Brats** • 4 Bennett Ave [W 181st St]
212-543-2202
Because your pet can never have enough toys.
- **Total Beauty Supplies** •
650 W 181st St [Wadsworth Ave]
212-923-6139
Bad hair days are over.
- **Vargas Liquor Store** •
114 Audubon Ave [W 171st St]
212-781-5195
Convenient for paper-bag-drinking in Highbridge Park, if that's your thing.
- **Victor's Bike Repair** •
4125 Broadway [174th St]
212-740-5137
Sales, service, repairs, and rentals.

Map 23

Map 24 • **Fort George / Fort Tryon**

Riverside Dr

Dyckman Street

Dyckman St

Post Ave

W 205th St

W 204th St

Ninth Ave

W 203rd St

Tenth Ave

W 202nd St

Dyckman Houses

W 201st St

Academy St

Thayer St

Dongan Pl

Arden St

Sherman Ave

Sickles St

Margaret Corbin Dr

The Cloisters

1 Dyckman Street

Ellwood St

Nagle Ave

The Cloisters

Broadway

W 196th St

Bogardus Pl

Hillside Ave

Peter Jay Sharp Boathouse

Ft George Ave

Fort Tryon Park

Ft George Hill

High Bridge Park

Margaret Corbin Plaza

9

W 193rd St

W 192nd St

Fairview Ave

Wadsworth Ter

W 193rd St

W 192nd St

1 191st Street

W 191st St

190th Street

W 190th St

Fort Washington Ave

Broadway

Gorman Park

W 190th St

Bennett Ave

W 189th St

Audubon Ave

Amsterdam Ave

Cabrini Blvd

Overlook Ter

W 188th St

W 187th St

W 187th St

Wash. Ter

High Bridge Park

Chittenden Ave

Pinehurst Ave

W 186th St

Broadway

W 185th St

W 186th St

Wadsworth Ave

W 185th St

St Nicholas Ave

Yeshiva University

Bennett Park

W 183rd St

Col R Magaw Pl

W 184th St

W 183rd St

W 182nd St

Laurel Hill Ter

23

1 181st St

181st Street

W 181st St

W 180th St

Washington Bridge

Plaza Lafayette

Henry Hudson Pkwy

9A

Hudson River

Harlem River

Harlem River Dr

A

B

25

1/4 mile   .25 km

Neighborhood Overview

Map 24

The Fort George/Fort Tryon area is also known locally as Hudson Heights, mostly for the benefit of realtors showing off this area's huge upside (literally!). Fort George is the name of the last fort of its kind, built in 1776 at the intersection of Audubon Avenue and 192nd Street. The area is diverse: The neighborhoods surrounding Fort Tryon Park and Yeshiva University are predominantly Jewish, while east of Broadway tends to be more Latin and Caribbean. The streets are some of the steepest on the island, and provide pleasant views (and a lower-body workout). Residents appreciate the quiet streets and better values and best of all, the commute to Lower Manhattan is just a half-hour.

Built in 1935 by Frederick Law Olmsted, Jr. (the son of one of the master architects behind both Central and Prospect Parks) on land donated to the city by John D. Rockefeller, **Fort Tryon Park** is the 67-acre chunk of green high up on the bluff above the Hudson River. From here, the Hudson is stunning; the pristine Palisades on the New Jersey side of the river were also made possible by Rockefeller philanthropy, in an effort to protect the view for future generations. In 1995 Bette Midler's New York Restoration Project assisted on a much-needed renovation of the park. If you are feeling cultural, pay a visit to **The Cloisters**. The complex, an extension of the Metropolitan Museum of Art, is a fully formed Medieval wonderland, with elements from four French cloisters, stained-glass windows, tapestries, and gardens. Don't miss the Medieval Festival that takes place every year in Fort Tryon Park when reenactors reimagine life in the Middle Ages. Warderere!

Down at the edge of the Harlem River stands the **Peter Jay Sharp Boathouse**. The first new community boathouse in New York City in years, it opened in 2004 and offers rowing lessons to members of the community. To reach the boathouse go to Tenth Avenue and Dyckman and walk south on the Lillian Goldman Walkway. Just before you get there, you'll pass by the restored Swindler Cove Park, a nice spot to stare at ducks or contemplate the river. If you decide to continue south on the walkway, the only way out is through the bridge that connects to 155th Street in Harlem.

On the campus of Yeshiva University, the unusual **Zysman Hall** was designed by Charles B. Meyers and blends Art-Deco and Moorish styles. Today, the building is home to Yeshiva's High School for Boys. If you feel the need to stock up on kosher goodies, now is the time. Cross the street for a full selection of delis, restaurants, and bodegas that carry them.

There isn't a ginormous selection of bars but don't leave the neighborhood just yet. **The Monkey Room** is ideal for game nights or late-night drinks. For a good neighborhood spot, try **Locksmith Wine Bar**.

Find great Indian cuisine at **Kismat**. Enjoy a real Caribbean meal at **La Casa Del Mofongo** or go Venezuelan at **Cachapas Y Mas**. The Mexican food can't be beat at **Tacos El Paisa**. For perfect falafel make your way to **Golan Heights**.

Map 24

Fort George / Fort Tryon

O Landmarks

- **The Cloisters** •
  99 Margaret Corbin Dr [Ft Tryon Pl]
  212-923-3700
  The Met's storehouse of medieval art. Great
  herb garden, nice views.
- **Fort Tryon Park** •
  W 181st St & Hudson River Greenway
  A totally beautiful and scenic park on New
  York's north edge.
- **Peter Jay Sharp Boathouse** •
  Swindler Cove Park
  See the West Bronx by boat.
- **Yeshiva University Zysman Hall** •
  2540 Amsterdam Ave [W 186th St]
  Interesting Byzantine-style building.

Coffee

- **Cafe Buunni** • 213 Pinehurst Ave [W 187th St]
  212-568-8700
  Espresso drinks and Ethiopian foods.
- **Dunkin' Donuts** •
  1599 St Nicholas Ave [W 190th St]
  212-568-1039
  Decent coffee served in gigantic Styrofoam
  cups.

Nightlife

- **Locksmith Wine & Burger Bar** •
  4463 Broadway [W 192nd St]
  212-304-9463
  Friendly spot to grab a glass of wine or beer.
- **Monkey Room** •
  589 Fort Washington Ave [W 187th St]
  212-543-9888
  Tiny like a capuchin.

Restaurants

- **809 Bar & Grill** • 112 Dyckman St [Nagle Ave]
  212-304-3800 • $$$
  Dominican grilled meat-a-thon.
- **Cachapas Y Mas** • 107 Dyckman St [Post Ave]
  212-304-2224 • $
  Fried Latin tastiness in corn and meat form.
- **Golan Heights** •
  2553 Amsterdam Ave [W 187th St]
  212-795-7842 • $
  Tasty Israeli falafel and shawarma. Popular for
  lunch.
- **Kismat** •
  603 Fort Washington Ave [W 187th St]
  212-795-8633 • $$
  Throw your taste buds a surprise party.
- **La Casa Del Mofongo** •
  1447 St Nicholas Ave [W 182nd St]
  212-740-1200 • $$
  The obvious: have the mofongo.
- **Tacos El Paisa** •
  1548 St Nicholas Ave [W 188th St]
  917-521-0972 • $
  Fantastic hole-in-the-wall Mexican.

Fort George / Fort Tryon

Get gourmet edibles at **Frank's Market** or enjoy a rhyme by buying wine from **Vines on Pine**.

Shopping

- **Apex Supply Co.** •
4580 Broadway [W 196th St]
212-304-0808
Where eggshell is considered a color.
- **Associated Supermarkets** •
592 Fort Washington Ave [W 187th St]
212-543-0721
No-frills market way cheaper than your local bodega.
- **Century Hardware** •
4309 Broadway [W 184th St]
212-927-9000
Experts in nuts and bolts.
- **The Cloisters Museum Store** •
99 Margaret Corbin Dr [Fort Tryon Park]
212-650-2277
Dark Age trinkets.

- **Foot Locker** • 140 Dyckman St [Sherman Ave]
212-544-8613
No lockers. But lots of sneakers.
- **Frank's Gourmet Market** •
807 W 187th St [Fort Washington Ave]
212-795-2929
Gourmet meats, cheeses, and groceries. A neighborhood institution.
- **NHS Hardware** •
1539 St Nicholas Ave [W 187th St]
212-927-3549
Get into the DIY spirit.
- **Vines on Pine** •
814 W 187th St [Pinehurst Ave]
212-923-0584
One-of-a-kind selections.

Map 25 • **Inwood**

THE BRONX
PAGE 242

Hudson River

Edsall Ave

Knolls Cres

Bodley Ave

Adrian Ave

W 225th St

Harlem River

Broadway Bridge

Henry Hudson Bridge

Urban Ecology Center

Baker Field

W 220th St

W 219th St

W 218th St

Broadway

Ninth Ave

Gaelic Field

W 218th St

Seaman Ave

Indian Rd

Park Ter W

Park Ter E

W 217th St

Inwood Hill Park

W 215th St

W 215th St Steps

215th Street

W 214th St

W 213th St

Isham Park

W 212th St

Emerson Playground

Homers Run

W 211th St

Emerson St

Inwood 207th Street

Subway Yards

Dyckman Farmhouse Museum

Broadway

Cooper St

Seaman Ave

W 207th St

Vermilyea Ave

Sherman Ave

Isham St

W 208th St

University Heights Brid

W 207th St

207th Street

Beak St

Payson Ave

W 204th St

Post Ave

W 206th St

Cumming St

Academy St

W 205th St

W 204th St

Tenth Ave

Ninth Ave

W 203rd St

Dyckman Street

W 202nd St

Tubby Hook

Henshaw St

Seaman Ave

Riverside Drive

Dyckman St

W 201st St

Academy St

Exterior St

Margaret Corbin Dr

The Cloisters

Dongan Pl

Nagle Ave

Dyckman Houses

Thayer St

Arden St

Hillside Ave

Dyckman Street

Sherman Creek

High Bridge Park

Henry Hudson Pkwy

Seamus Meadow

Overlook Meadow

1/4 mile   .25 km

Neighborhood Overview

Located on the northernmost tip of the island, the hilly neighborhood of Inwood has something for everyone. And at a moment when there are so few places left in Manhattan where you can get affordable housing and fit all your belongings in something bigger than a shoebox, the 'hood is a solid alternative for those considering abandoning the island for one of the outer boroughs.

West of Broadway offers views, pathways, quiet streets, and artsy cafés. Parking is tricky, but possible—worst-case scenario is parking in one of the many lots around the area, which are still an affordable option. Rents west of Broadway can be higher because of the aforementioned perks and because it's right next to Inwood Hill Park, which is arguably the best neighborhood resource. The grass might be greener on this side of Broadway, but the predominantly Dominican area east of Broadway has even cheaper housing alternatives. That, and you'll find the air is filled with free *bachata*, especially during the summer.

Speaking of **Inwood Hill Park**, its 160 acres of greenspace stretch along the Hudson from Dyckman Street to the northern tip of the island. The park is home to last remaining natural forest in Manhattan, affording one the opportunity to brag about hiking through real woods without leaving the city. Take your kids (or nephews or nieces) to **Emerson Playground** on a sunny day, let your dog play with its kinfolk at **Homer's Run** or use one of several outdoor tennis courts. The **Inwood Greenmarket** happens rain or shine Saturdays at the foot of Inwood Hill Park.

That little house on the hill at 204th Street that looks out of place among the low-slung apartment buildings along Broadway is the **Dyckman Farmhouse** (c. 1784). Originally part of several hundred acres of farmland owned by a family with roots stretching back to New York's Dutch beginnings, today it's a stark visual reminder of just how much the city has evolved. On weekends say hello (or *hola*) to the seniors sitting on the benches by the farmhouse's garden.

The **Henry Hudson Bridge** connects Manhattan and The Bronx via a two-level, seven-lane structure. With thousands of vehicles crossing back and forth each day, drivers and passengers can take a minute to admire the lavish engineering efforts, views of the Hudson River, and the Harlem Ship Canal below. And speaking of channels, channel your inner Rocky by climbing the **West 215th Steps**. All 111 of them (yep, we counted). On the way up note Park Terrace East to see a few rare species: Actual houses with driveways.

Well, if you refuse to take the 1 or A trains south for more exciting options, **Inwood Local** has many brews on tap and a fun neighborhood feel.

Get brunch at **Garden Cafe**. Go calorie crazy at **Elsa La Reina del Chicharron** with the best pork rinds in town. Sushi lovers go to **Mama Sushi** and Italian aficionados go to **Il Sole**. Practice your Spanish at **Mamajuana Cafe** and be artsy at **Inwood Farm**.

Map 25

25
24
23
21 22
18 19 20

Inwood

O Landmarks

- **Dyckman Farmhouse Museum** •
4881 Broadway [W 204th St]
212-304-9422
Oldest farmhouse in Manhattan, now restored
as a museum.
- **Emerson Playground** •
Seaman Ave & Isham St
Kids (and adults) love playing around on the
iron wolf.
- **Henry Hudson Bridge** • Henry Hudson Pkwy
Affords a nice view from the Inwood Hill Park
side.
- **Homer's Run** • Isham St [W 211th St]
Where dogs par-tay.
- **Inwood Hill Park** • Dyckman St & Payson Ave
The last natural forest and salt marsh in
Manhattan!
- **West 215th Street Steps** •
W 215th St & Park Terrace E
Elevation of sidewalk requires steps. Now get a
move on it!

Coffee

- **Beans & Vines** • 4799 Broadway [Academy St]
646-360-3570
Cozy coffee shop and wine bar serving food.
- **Dunkin' Donuts** •
4942 Broadway [W 207th St]
212-544-0453
Decent coffee served in gigantic Styrofoam
cups.
- **Inwood Farm** • 600 W 218th St [Indian Rd]
212-884-2111
Friendly neighborhood café.

Farmers Markets

- **Inwood Greenmarket** •
Seaman Ave & Isham St
Sat 8 am–3 pm, year-round.

Nightlife

- **Inwood Local** • 4957 Broadway [W 207th St]
212-544-8900
Beer garden, wine bar, and sports pub with a
side of tasty grub.
- **Post Billiards Café** • 154 Post Ave [W 207th St]
212-569-1840
When you need to shoot pool way way
uptown.

Shopping isn't exactly Inwood's forte but **El Nuevo Azteca** does have a huge selection of Mexican foods.

🍴 Restaurants

- **Capitol Restaurant** •
  4933 Broadway [W 207th St]
  212-942-5090 • $
  Nice neighborhood diner.
- **El Lina** • 500 W 207th St [10th Ave]
  212-567-5031 • $
  Satisfying though tiny Dominican diner.
- **Elsa La Reina Del Chicharron** •
  4840 Broadway [W 204th St]
  212-304-1070 • $
  It's worth the coronary bypass.
- **Garden Café** • 4961 Broadway [Isham St]
  212-544-9480 • $$
  Homestyle brunch for less than 10 bucks.
- **Grandpa's Brick Oven Pizza** •
  4973 Broadway [Isham St]
  212-304-1185 • $
  Personal brick oven pies and catering.
- **Guadalupe** • 597 W 207th St [Broadway]
  212-304-1083 • $$
  High class Mexican.
- **Il Sole** • 233 Dyckman St [Seaman Ave]
  212-544-0406 • $$
  Neighborhood Italian.
- **Junior's Tacos** • 253 Sherman Ave [Isham St]
  212-942-7202 • $
  Low budget, high taste.
- **Mamasushi** • 237 Dyckman St [Broadway]
  212-567-2450 • $
  As good as uptown sushi gets.
- **Mamajuana Cafe** •
  247 Dyckman St [Seaman Ave]
  212-304-0140 • $$$
  Tasty Nuevo Latino cuisine.
- **Papasito** • 223 Dyckman St [Broadway]
  212-544-0001 • $$
  Margaritas, music, and Mexican food.
- **Pizza Haven** • 4942 Broadway [W 207th St]
  212-569-3720 • $
  They bring-a the pizza.
- **Yummy Thai** • 4959 Broadway [Isham St]
  917-529-0811 • $$
  Affordable and reliable, especially for take-out and delivery.

🛍 Shopping

- **El Nuevo Azteca** • 3861 10th Ave [W 206th St]
  212-567-6028
  For the Mexican junkfood junky.
- **Inwood Paint & Hardware** •
  165 Sherman Ave [W 204th St]
  212-569-6002
  High security locks and more.
- **Portes Cigars** • 5009 Broadway [W 214th St]
  212-544-9623
  Fresh out of the hand cigars.
- **Richie's Cleaners and Tailors** •
  4915 Broadway [W 204th St]
  212-304-0289
  Trust the R. man.
- **Tread Bike Shop** •
  250 Dyckman St [Broadway]
  212-544-7055
  Where to fix your bike after riding through Inwood Hill Park.
- **V.I.M.** • 565 W 207th St [Vermilyea Ave]
  212-942-7478
  Street wear—jeans, sneakers, tops—for all.

Map 26 · **Astoria**

Neighborhood Overview

Despite the influx of young people, Astoria holds onto its diversity tooth and nail, and thank goodness. North Africans on Steinway Street, Greeks and Italians in northern Astoria, Brazilians and Bangladeshis in the south and east, and Croatians, Serbians, Bosnians, Mexicans, Japanese, and so many others (including an expanding LGBTQ community and seemingly most of New York's young standup comics) call this neighborhood home.

Astoria is roughly split in two parts. The blocks south of the Grand Central tend to be filled with low-slung, well-appointed apartment buildings, providing tons of decent rentals within 20 minutes from Midtown. 30th Avenue in particular is packed with great restaurants and nightlife. There are more single- and two-family homes on the other side of the Grand Central, which gives that part of Astoria more of a neighborhood feel. Ditmars Boulevard is the main street north of the Grand Central, and its storefronts are filling in as a secondary destination for great restaurants. You'll find that many retail establishments have branches both north and south of the Grand Central.

Before the subway's arrival in 1917, Astoria was made up of several small communities, including Ravenswood, Dutch Kills, Steinway, and Old Astoria Village. Among the many ornate neighborhood houses of worship are the **Astoria Center of Israel**, founded in 1925 and recently added to the National and State Registers of Historic Places, and **Saint Demetrios Cathedral**, spiritual center of the Greek Orthodox community.

With its reasonable rents and proximity to Manhattan, Astoria, and Western Queens in general, has a thriving arts scene. Movies have been made here since the days of silent films, and the revitalized **Kaufman Astoria Studios** is the city's main film and TV studio complex. Just down the street from Kaufman Astoria is the **Museum of the Moving Image**, which recently underwent a major expansion, resulting in a sleek new building by architect Thomas Leeser. Sculpture buffs should also check out the **Noguchi Museum**. Just across the street is the **Socrates Sculpture Park**, located on the East River waterfront, open year-round with rotating contemporary outdoor exhibits plus international film screenings in the summer.

Not many green spaces exist in Astoria, but the neighborhood is blessed with **Astoria Park** and its massive WPA-era Olympic-sized pool, one of 11 such pools that were opened across the city in 1936. It hosted the Olympic swimming trials that summer for the U.S. swim and diving teams. Although the city no longer allows diving boards in parks, Astoria Park's diving pool and its intriguing towers are slated to become part of an outdoor venue. The park also has many (underutilized!) tennis courts and a large running track, along with great views of Manhattan and the Robert F. Kennedy Bridge and the Hell Gate Bridge, the approaches for both of which cross through the park. Elsewhere, the vest-pocket **Athens Square Park** is a nod to Astoria's Greek roots, and features a mini-amphitheater and a sculpture donated by the mayor of Athens.

Map 26

26

27

Astoria

O Landmarks

- **Astoria Center of Israel** • 27-35 Crescent St
  718-278-2680
  Beautiful Louis Pierre Rigal murals grace the
  sanctuary.
- **Astoria Park and Pool** • 19th St & 23rd Dr
  718-626-8620
  60 acres of waterfront parkland and an
  awesome pool.
- **Athens Square** • 30th Ave & 30th St
  You'll love it as much as the kids.
- **Kaufman Astoria Studios** • 34-12 36th St
  718-392-5600
  US's largest studio outside of LA, and just as
  historic.
- **Museum of the Moving Image** •
  36-01 35th Ave
  718-777-6800
  Fantastic interactive film/TV museum, with
  screenings of classic films.
- **The Noguchi Museum** • 9-01 33rd Rd
  718-204-7088
  Noguchi's converted factory studio with
  representative works and beautiful garden.
- **Saint Demetrios Cathedral** • 30-11 30th Dr
  718-728-1718
  The main Greek Orthodox church in Astoria.
- **Socrates Sculpture Park** • 32-01 Vernon Blvd
  718-956-1819
  Cool, gritty sculpture park with events and
  films.

Coffee

- **Astoria Coffee** • 30-04 30th St
  347-619-3915
  Sleek, friendly café with ecumenical roasting
  approach.
- **OK Cafe** • 22-04 33rd St
  718-440-8789
  Cozy artisanal coffee shop on the way to the
  train.
- **The Queen's Room** • 36-02 Ditmars Blvd
  347-987-3994
  Part of the first wave of Astoria's third-wave
  coffee shops.

Farmers Markets

- **Ditmars Park Farmstand** • 22–55 Ditmars Park
  212-788-7476
  Sat, July–Nov, 9:30 am–2 pm.

Nightlife

- **Albatross Bar** • 36-19 24th Ave
  718-204-9707
  Gay dive bar with a raucous karaoke night
- **Astoria Tavern** • 33-16 23rd Ave
  347-813-4954
  Platonic ideal of Astoria Irish bar.

There's something for everyone, from Irish bars like **Cronin & Phelan** and the **Irish Rover** to artisanal cocktails at **Sweet Afton**. SingleCut has a great taproom. **The Sparrow** is a go-to north of the Grand Central, and the **Bohemian Hall & Beer Garden** is always a jam-packed summertime favorite.

- **Bohemian Hall & Beer Garden** •
29-19 24th Ave
718-274-4925
Over 100 years old; room for 500 in the garden.
- **The Bonnie** • 29-12 23rd Ave
718-274-2105
Heady cocktail lounge/gastropub from folks behind Sweet Afton.
- **Cronin & Phelan** • 38-14 Broadway
718-545-8999
Open mic, live music, and karaoke! Irish you'd buy me another ale.
- **Daly's Pub** • 31-86 31st St
718-606-2561
Another Irish pub, but featuring live music from local artists.
- **Diamond Dogs** • 34-04 31st Ave
929-522-0061
Rotating craft cocktails by way of Bowie.
- **DiWine** • 41-15 31st Ave
718-777-1355
Another Astoria wine bar, another bad pun.
- **Gilbey's** • 32-01 Broadway
718-545-8567
The local yokels and cheap brews will have you saying, "Gib me's another beer."
- **Icon** • 31-84 33rd St
917-832-6364
Gay bar/lounge with mixed crowd.
- **Irish Rover** • 37-18 28th Ave
718-278-9372
A well-loved hangout with live music, quiz nights, and Irish sports.
- **Judy & Punch** • 34-08 30th Ave
718-626-3101
Friendly mixological spot also featuring many craft beers on tap.

- **The Let Love Inn** • 27-20 23rd Ave
718-777-5683
Good cocktails and no TVs from folks behind Sparrow.
- **Q.E.D.** • 27-16 23rd Ave
347-451-3873
Safe space for comedy, crafting, and game nights.
- **The Quays** • 45-02 30th Ave
718-204-8435
Guinness, live music, and about that dart league…
- **Sekend Sun** • 32-11 Broadway
917-745-0745
Smart cocktails from people who own Williamsburg's ba'sik.
- **Sissy McGinty's** • 25-67 Steinway St
718-545-4286
Typical Irish pub, nuff' said.
- **The Sparrow Tavern** • 24-01 29th St
718-606-2260
A hipster outpost from the folks who brought us Tupelo.
- **Sunswick 35/35** • 35-02 35th St
718-752-0620
Convenient to Museum of the Moving Image; dozens of beers on tap.
- **Sweet Afton** • 30-09 34th St
718-777-2570
Salvaged wood, comfort food, fancy drinks. Sweet.

Map 26

Astoria

🍴Restaurants

- **Agnanti Meze** • 19-06 Ditmars Blvd
  718-545-4554 • $$
  Wonderful Greek/Cypriot cuisine just across
  from Astoria Park.
- **Aliada** • 29-19 Broadway
  718-932-2240 • $$
  Excellent Cypriot with deservedly famous
  lamb chops.
- **Bareburger** • 33-21 31st Ave
  718-777-7011 • $$
  Organic burgers and sides. Try the elk or bison!
- **Basil Brick Oven Pizza** • 28-17 Astoria Blvd
  718-204-1205 • $$
  Elegant ingredients and great crust.
- **BZ Grill** • 27-02 Astoria Blvd
  718-932-7858 • $$
  Fantastic gyros, kebabs, and souvlaki.
- **Cevabdzinica Sarajevo** • 37-18 34th Ave
  718-752-9528 • $$
  Bosnian diner grub.
- **Christos Steak House** • 41-08 23rd Ave
  718-777-8400 • $$$$$
  Excellent Greek-inflected steakhouse.
- **Crave Astoria** • 28-55 36th St
  718-726-4976 • $$
  Greek stoner food that will please the entire
  family.
- **De Mole II** • 42-20 30th Ave
  718-771-1655 • $$$
  Fresh Mexican in bistro setting after Sunnyside
  original.
- **Djerdan Burek** • 34-04 31st Ave
  718-721-2694 • $$
  Bureks and other Eastern European delights.
- **Elias Corner** • 24-02 31st St
  718-932-1510 • $$
  No menu, just pick your fish from the counter.
- **Enthaice** • 33-20 31st Ave
  718-932-1111 • $$
  Haute-Thai cuisine & cocktails; forgive the
  word play.
- **Favela** • 33-18 28th Ave
  718-545-8250 • $$$
  Hearty Brazilian food. Think meat, and piles
  of it.
- **Gregory's 26 Corner Taverna** •
  26-02 23rd Ave
  718-777-5511 • $$$
  Highly recommended low-key Greek taverna.
- **HinoMaru Ramen** • 33-18 Ditmars Blvd
  718-777-0228 • $$
  Authenticated ramen shop on Ditmars;
  "kaedama" gets you more!
- **Il Bambino** • 34-08 31st Ave
  718-626-0087 • $
  Paninis, tapas, and other light Italian/
  Mediterranean grub.
- **JJ's** • 37-05 31st Ave
  718-626-8888 • $$
  Sushi-French fusion.
- **Jujube Tree** • 35-02 30th Ave
  718-545-1888 • $$
  Vegan Asian fusion with fun fake meat.
- **Kabab Café** • 25-12 Steinway St
  718-728-9858 • $$
  Haute Egyptian cooked to order by friendly
  chef-owner, Ali.
- **Koliba Restaurant** • 31-11 23rd Ave
  718-626-0430 • $$$
  Nice Czech option north of the Grand Central.
- **Kondo** • 29-13 Broadway
  347-617-1236 • $$$$
  Japanese that transcends the tempura-
  California roll industrial complex.
- **Los Amigos Mexican Restaurant** •
  32-73 31st St
  718-726-8708 • $$
  Cheap, reliable, easy-going Mexican joint with
  generous portions.
- **Loukoumi** • 45-07 Ditmars Blvd
  718-626-3200 • $$$
  Excellent Greek taverna off the beaten path
  down Ditmars.

Sure, there are plenty of Greek restaurants (**Agnanti** and **Taverna Kyclades** are local faves), but why stop there? Visit **Vesta** for good, cheap Italian food and wine, **Djerdan** for Bosnia's best, and **Favela** for a taste of Rio. **Tufino** has some of the best pizza in the city, minus the waits.

- **Mar's** • 34-21 34th Ave
  718-685-2480 • $$$
  Oysters + good cocktails.
- **Max Bratwurst und Bier** • 47-02 30th Ave
  718-777-1635 • $$
  German-style beer hall/sports bar.
- **Milkflower** • 34-12 31st Ave
  718-204-1300 • $$
  Reclaimed wood-fired pizza.
- **Mokja** • 35-19 Broadway
  718-721-0654 • $$$
  Stylish all-purpose Korean.
- **Mombar** • 25-22 Steinway St
  718-726-2356 • $$
  Egyptian by Kabab Café Ali's brother in a
  beautiful setting.
- **Ovelia** • 34-01 30th Ave
  718-721-7217 • $$$
  Not your yiayia's tzatziki, or her brunch.
- **Petey's Burger** • 30-17 30th Ave
  718-267-6300 • $
  It's like an In-N-Out cover band; fills a need.
- **The Pomeroy** • 36-12 Ditmars Blvd
  718-721-1579 • $$$
  Haute-fried food with carefully crafted
  cocktails.
- **Pye Boat Noodle** • 35-13 Broadway
  718-685-2329 • $$
  Thai beyond the usual pad thai staples.

- **Rizzo's Pizza** • 30-13 Steinway St
  718-721-9862 • $
  Yummy thin-crust square pies.
- **Sabry's Seafood** • 24-25 Steinway St
  718-721-9010 • $$
  Great Egyptian seafood.
- **Sanford's** • 30-13 Broadway
  718-932-9569 • $$
  Family diner remodeled and spiffed up by
  the kids.
- **Seva Indian Cuisine** • 34-11 34th St
  718-626-4440 • $$
  Go-to Indian in a neighborhood without many
  South Asian options.
- **The Shady Lady** • 34-19 30th Ave
  718-440-9081 • $$$
  Inspired and slightly off-key bistro you want
  to root for.
- **Snowdonia** • 32-01 35th Ave
  347-730-5783 • $$$
  Gastropub open late.
- **Stamatis** • 29-09 23rd Ave
  718-932-8596 • $$$
  Basic Astoria Greek, octopus and other grilled
  fish recommended.
- **SugarFreak** • 37–11 30th Ave
  718-606-1900 • $$$
  Authenticated Lousiana/Cajunesque cuisine
  on 30th Ave restaurant row.
- **Taverna Kyclades** • 36-01 Ditmars Blvd
  718-545-8666 • $$-$$$
  Consistent, homey Greek seafood; worth
  the wait.

Map 26

17
26
27

Astoria

• **Telly's Taverna** • 28-13 23rd Ave
718-728-9056 • $$
Creative specials and bang-up Greek classics.
• **The Thirsty Koala** • 35-12 Ditmars Blvd
718-626-5430 •
You may have to Google "eschalot"; not so for
"kangaroo."
• **Trattoria L'Incontro** • 21-76 31st St
718-721-3532 • $$$$$
One of the city's best Italian restaurants.
Seriously.
• **Tufino Pizzeria** • 36-08 Ditmars Blvd
718-278-4800 • $$
Big-boy, big-time Neopolitan from a custom-
built oven.
• **Vesta** • 21-02 30th Ave
718-545-5550 • $$$
Italian heaven in Greek haven.
• **Vite Vinosteria** • 31-05 34th St
718-278-8483 • $$$
Great Italian wine and food from Manhattan
restaurant veterans.
• **Watawa** • 33-10 Ditmars Blvd
718-545-9596 • $$$
Best-of-Ditmars destination sushi.
• **Yaar Indian Restaurant** • 22-55 31st St
718-721-0205 • $$
Solid Indian cuisine from folks behind Seva.

🛍 Shopping

• **Adega Wine & Spirits** • 31-25 Ditmars Blvd
718-545-2525
Nicely curated and well-appointed liquor
store.
• **Astoria Bier and Cheese** • 34-14 Broadway
718-545-5588
The Craft cheesemonger and beermonger
Astoria's been waiting for.
• **Astoria Bookshop** • 31-29 31st St
718-278-2665
Curated selection and community events.

• **Astoria Park Wine & Spirits** • 28-07 24th Ave
718-606-1142
Curated selection with good prices;
convenient to Astoria Park.
• **Astoria Wine & Spirits** • 34-12 Broadway
718-545-9463
New wine store, featuring frequent tastings.
• **Bike Stop** • 37-19 28th Ave
718-278-2453
Bike store on north end of Astoria.
• **Brass Owl** • 36-19 Ditmars Blvd
347-848-0905
Stylish boutique selling shoes, jewelry and
gifts.
• **Brooklyn Bagel & Coffee Company** •
35-05 Broadway
718-204-0141
Forgive the geographic confusion and enjoy
the wacky cream cheeses.
• **Brooklyn Bagel & Coffee Company** •
35-09 Ditmars Blvd
718-932-8280
The neighborhood's best bagels.
• **Brooklyn Bagel & Coffee Company** •
36-14 30th Ave
718-777-1121
Also good coffee, fresh OJ, and signature
sandwiches.
• **Butcher Bar** • 37-10 30th Ave
718-606-8140
Organic, natural butcher with barbecue to eat
in or take home.
• **Ditmars Thrift Shop** • 31-20 Ditmars Blvd
718-545-2529
Awesome cheap finds for clothing, winter
coats, and housewares.
• **Euro Market** • 30-42 31st St
718-545-5569
Best of Eurofoods.

Map 26

Titan Foods, Parrot Coffee, and EuroMarket offer the best of Europe, and Family Market has everything Japanese, including bento boxes. Astoria Bier and Cheese fills a craft beer and cheese niche. Find that special vintage clothing item at Loveday 31 and reward yourself with sweets from La Guli or Martha's.

- **Family Market** • 29-15 Broadway
  718-956-7925
  Japanese convenience store, and resource center for the neighborhood Japanese.
- **Fresh Start** • 29-13 23rd Ave
  718-204-7868
  Organic/natural market for most of your needs, plus prepared foods.
- **Grand Wine & Liquor** • 30-05 31st St
  718-728-2520
  One of the best in the borough, crazy international offerings.
- **International Meat Market** • 36-12 30th Ave
  718-626-6656
  The Citarella of Astoria.
- **La Guli Pastry Shop** • 29-15 Ditmars Blvd
  718-728-5612
  Old-school Italian pastry shop. A neighborhood institution.
- **Lockwood Shop** • 32-15 33rd St
  718-626-6030
  Lifestyle shop run by Astoria boosters; good events and extras.
- **Loveday 31 Vintage** • 33-06 31st Ave
  718-728-4057
  Hip new and vintage clothes.
- **Martha's Country Bakery** •
  36-21 Ditmars Blvd
  718-545-9737
  Best pound cake around, and everything else is good too.
- **Mediterranean Foods** • 22-78 35th St
  718-728-0266
  Great spot for Mediterranean-imported groceries.
- **New York City Bagel & Coffee House** •
  29-08 23rd Ave
  718-728-9500
  With a nice emphasis on good coffee drinks.
- **Omega Wines & Spirits** • 23-18 31st St
  718-726-0056
  Great selection of Greek wines.

- **Parrot Coffee** • 31-12 Ditmars Blvd
  718-545-7920
  Gourmet European food, mostly Eastern Europe, plus fresh roasted coffee.
- **Rosario's Deli** • 22-55 31st St
  718-728-2920
  Italian specialty foods, great sandwiches, and pizza, too.
- **Rose & Joe's Italian Bakery** • 22-40 31st St
  718-721-9422
  Fresh cannolis made to order.
- **Sal, Kris, and Charlie Deli** • 33-12 23rd Ave
  718-278-9240
  They don't call them the "sandwich kings of Astoria" for nothing.
- **Silver Age Comics** • 22-55 31st St
  718-721-9691
  Comics.
- **SingleCut Beersmiths** • 19-33 37th St
  718-606-0788
  Queens' first brewery in decades; visit tap room for growlers.
- **Titan Foods** • 25-56 31st St
  718-626-7771
  The Zabar's of Astoria.
- **Tony's Bicycles** • 35-01 23rd Ave
  718-278-3355
  Bike store north of the Grand Central.
- **Trade Fair** • 30-08 30th Ave
  718-728-9484
  Phenomenal selection of international foods; best Trade Fair around.
- **Triboro Beverage** • 45 Astoria Blvd S
  718-278-0620
  Probably the best beer selection in the city.
- **United Brothers Fruit Markets** •
  32-24 30th Ave
  718-932-9876
  Great 24-hour fruit/vegetable market.

Map 27 · **Long Island City**

Ⓝ

Broadway

N W
Broadway

M R

33rd Ave
33rd Rd
14th Pl
13th St
12th St
11th Pl
23rd St
33rd Rd
33rd Ave

34th Ave

Steinway St
34th St
42nd St
43rd St

▲
26

35th Ave

36th Avenue
N W

36th Ave

21st St
12th St
11th St
13th St
24th St
28th St
29th St
30th St
Crescent St
31st St
32nd St
33rd St
34th St
35th St
36th St
37th St
38th St

Northern Blvd

37th Ave

M R
36th Street
25a

Green Space
9th St
10th St
11th St
12th St
38th Ave

NY Design Center
Crescent St
Old DB Pl
37th Ave

Fisher Landau
Center for Art
39th Ave
N W

39th St

A

39th Ave

40th Ave
Vernon Blvd

40th Rd

Honeywell St

43

21 Street
Queensbridge
14th St
F
41st Ave

23rd St
Fardom Gallery
N W 7
Queensboro
Plaza

Hunter St

Queens
Plaza

41st Rd
Queens Plz E
Queens Plz N
Crescent St

The
Work
Space
West St
Queens Plaza
E M R

Queens Blvd

Queensboro Bridge
Silvercup
Studios
22nd St
42nd Rd

Orchard St
Queens St

33rd Avenue
7
Thomson Av

36th St
35th Pl

Taxi
Depot
9th St
10th St
43rd Ave
43rd Rd

Long Island
City Art Center
24th St
Sculpture
Center
Dutchkills St
Purves St
G

Van Dam St
31st Pl
32nd Pl
33rd St
34th St

44th Dr
Local Project
E M
23rd Street -
Ely Avenue

Long Island City
Court Square

Citicorp Building
Long Island City
Courthouse

Hunter's Point Historic District
45 Rd Courthouse Sq
45th Ave
7 Space Womb
Court Sq

Pearson St

Gale Ave

B

11th St
PS 1
21st
Street
Jackson Ave
NY Center for
Media Arts
5 Pointz/
Crane Street
Studios
Pearson St

Austell Pl
36th St

Davis Ct

Hunters Point Ave

Long Island Expy

LIC
Community
Boathouse
46th Ave
46th Rd

Skillman Ave
49th Ave

Pepsi
Cola Sign
47th Ave
47th Rd
The
Chocolate
Factory
7

Hunters
Point
Avenue
7

50th Ave
51st Ave
Borden Ave

Fresh
Direct

Starr Ave
Review Ave

Dutch
Kill

Gantry Plaza
State Park
48th Ave

Vernon Boulevard-
Jackson Avenue
New York
Irish Center

▼
28

Hunters
Point
South Park
11th St
50th Ave
51st Ave

Queens Midtown Tunnel

53rd Ave
Pulaski Bridge

| 1/4 mile | .25 km |

Neighborhood Overview

Map 27

27

13

28

Long Island City has some excellent waterfront features, but it's also one of Queens' most developed, Manhattanish neighborhoods, plus when the 7 train is acting up, it turns a 5-minute ride between boroughs into a commuting nightmare. LIC's technical boundaries stretch from Newtown Creek to the south to roughly 34th Avenue to the north, bordering Astoria, but LIC has two distinct areas separated by Queens Plaza.

South of Queens Plaza beyond the **Citigroup Building**, which until recently was the only large tower in the area, Beaux-arts **Long Island City Courthouse** and **Hunter's Point Historic District** lies gentrified Hunter's Point, which has grown rapidly thanks to rezoning that allowed Battery Park City-like high rises along the waterfront. The young professional influx brought new stores and restaurants to Vernon Boulevard. Sushi, that leading gentrifying indicator, shows the evolution: until relatively recently Hunter's Point had no sushi at all, but today there are several sushi joints, not to mention a handful of comfort food spots and even a full-time comedy club. Even the **New York Irish Center** arrived, providing a community center for the city's Irish diaspora. **Gantry Plaza State Park** along the waterfront is hands-down the best view of Manhattan anywhere, and it has grown along with the neighborhood; all the way up to Anable Basin near 46th Avenue. South of Gantry Plaza State Park the city has started work on Hunters Point South, a project that will bring thousands of middle-income units to the waterfront. The city-owned **Hunters Point South Park** completes the ribbon of waterfront open space along the East River; the park offers the requisite panoramic Midtown skyline vista along with well-maintained recreational facilities and a lovely concession attached to the water taxi dock. Also along the waterfront is the **LIC Community Boathouse**, which heralds the triumphant reuse of the city's waterways; just keep your kayak out of Newtown Creek until the EPA is finished there.

The area around Queens Plaza has seen much new development. Expensive condos with great Manhattan views now surround Queensboro Plaza, the first stop in Queens for the N and Q trains and a transfer point for the 7 train out to Flushing. Also north of Queens Plaza lies the vestigial Dutch Kills neighborhood, which looks much like Astoria (so much so that you are forgiven in advance for simply referring to it as Astoria), and Queensbridge Houses, one of the largest public housing projects in the nation. Onetime home to artists like Marley Marl's Juice Crew and Nas, Queensbridge is to hip-hop as Addisleigh Park is to jazz. Linked to Midtown via one or two stops, the area between 37th and 41st Avenues north of Queens Plaza has seen a (literal) rise in mid-range hotels slowly squeezing out light industry while providing an inexpensive and convenient option for visitors. Meanwhile, the area south of Queens Plaza is filling up quickly with luxury condos and rentals. The Citigroup Building is looking a lot less lonely these days.

Light industry sprang up in LIC after the Queensboro Bridge (or 59th Street Bridge, depending on your point of view) opened in 1909 and thrived until the middle of the century, though parts of the area are currently designated an Industrial Business Zone by the city. The iconic **Pepsi-Cola Sign** along the waterfront is a vestige of LIC's industrial past best suited for all Beekman Place to see. Many of LIC's industrial buildings were repurposed for studio space in the 1970s and 1980s, giving the neighborhood its artistic reputation that survives today. **MoMA PS1**, housed in a historic school building, dates to 1976. Other museums and galleries followed, including the **Noguchi Museum** (1985) and **SculptureCenter** (2001). Smaller galleries, performance spaces, and collectives such as **Flux Factory**, **Local Project**, and **The Chocolate Factory** thrive even as real estate prices have risen.

Long Island City is about location, location, location — both in terms of real estate and as a hub of New York City's film and television industry. **Silvercup Studios** uses the former Silvercup Bakery building along the East River, and what was once a sleepy industrial area best suited for taxi companies is now clogged with film crews for on-location shoots. The two are combined at **Taxi Depot**, whose vintage cabs parked out front are not for hacks but rather film crews needing props.

Hit **Anable Basin Sailing Bar & Grill** for outdoor waterfront drinks or indulge in mixology at **Dutch Kills**. Join the locals at **LIC Bar** and **Dominie's Hoek**.

Map 27

Long Island City

O Landmarks

- **The Chocolate Factory** • 38-33 24th St
718-482-7069
Performance space for experimental theater.
- **Citicorp Building** • 1 Court Sq
This 48-story structure is the tallest New York
building outside of Manhattan.
- **Gantry Plaza State Park** • 4-9 47th Road
718-786-6385
Waterfront park and piers with breathtaking
skyline views.
- **Green Space** • 37-24 24th St
718-956-3037
Dance company sublets professional rehearsal
space sublets to artists.
- **Hunters Point Historic District** •
21st St & 45th Ave
Well-preserved homes from LIC's first heyday
in the late 1800s.
- **Hunters Point South Park** •
Center Blvd & 50th Ave
10 acres of prime parkland along the East
River.
- **LIC Art Center** • 44-02 23rd St
Theaters, galleries, and studios in former LIC
factory building.
- **LIC Community Boathouse** • 46-01 5th St
Launch kayaks from here, explore the
waterfront like never before.
- **Long Island City Courthouse** •
25-10 Court Sq
718-520-3909
Built in 1876 and rebuilt in 1904, an
architectural gem.
- **MoMA PS1** • 22-25 Jackson Ave
718-784-2086
MoMA's contemporary art space, w/ dance
parties every summer Saturday.

- **New York Irish Center** • 10-40 Jackson Ave
718-482-0909
Bingo nights for the tri-state Irish community.
- **Pepsi-Cola Sign** • 47th Ave & Center Blvd
Iconic sign atop the Pepsi Bottling Company
building saved here.
- **Queensbridge Park** • Vernon Blvd & 41st Ave
Park for the people under the Queensboro
Bridge.
- **SculptureCenter** • 44-19 Purves St
718-361-1750
An artist-run nonprofit and gallery supporting
experimental sculpture since 1928.
- **Silvercup Studios** • 42-22 22nd St
718-906-2000
Former bakery is now a busy film and
television studio.
- **Taxi Depot** • 24-50 47th St
718-784-4737
Check out the vintage cabs parked out in
front.

🍴 Coffee

- **Sweetleaf** • 10-93 Jackson Ave
917-832-6726
Stumptown coffee and tasty homemade
sweets.

🕐 Farmers Markets

- **Socrates Sculpture Park Greenmarket** •
3205 Vernon Blvd
718-956-1819
May–Oct, 10 am–2 pm.

Map 27

Standbys like **Manducatis** and **Tournesol** all chug along. **Casa Enrique**'s offerings are inspired by the cuisine of the Mexican state of Chiapas, and **John Brown Smokehouse** is the current neighborhood go-to for barbecue.

Nightlife

- **Anable Basin Sailing Bar & Grill** • 4-40 44th Dr
718-433-9269
Outdoor spot along East River with direct view of Midtown.
- **The Baroness** • 47-18 Vernon Blvd
718-255-1336
High-concept wine and beer joint close to Queens Plaza.
- **Domaine Bar a Vins** • 50-04 Vernon Blvd
718-784-2350
Great new wine bar from the people who brought you Tournesol, with oysters to boot.
- **Dominie's Hoek** • 48-17 Vernon Blvd
718-706-6531
No-frills bar with backyard patio and live music.

- **Dutch Kills** • 27-24 Jackson Ave
718-383-2724
Old time saloon decor and a classic cocktail menu.
- **LIC Bar** • 45-58 Vernon Blvd
718-786-5400
Vintage New York saloon with serene backyard BBQ patio and photo booth.
- **Penthouse 808 at the Ravel Hotel** •
8-08 Queens Plaza S
718-289-6118
Former hotsheet now swank hotel, still under the Queensboro Bridge though.
- **PJ Leahy's** • 50-02 Vernon Blvd
718-472-5131
Sports bar. Aka WP Dick Whistle's and HB Hanratty's.
- **Veronica's Bar** • 34-04 36th Ave
718-255-1886
Formerly old-school, with new ownership…

Restaurants

- **Arepas Cafe** • 33-07 36th Ave
  718-937-3835 • $$
  Sabor Venezolano!
- **Blend** • 47-04 Vernon Blvd
  718-729-2800 • $$
  Sleek Cuban-fusion spot.
- **Cafe Henri** • 10-10 50th Ave
  718-729-5794 • $$
  Low-key French bistro.
- **Cafe Ole** • 38-09 36th Ave
  718-349-7777 • $$$
  Spanish, paella, etc. sprucing up 36th Avenue.
- **Cafe Triskell** • 33-04 36th Ave
  718-472-0612 • $$
  Cash-only French-style bistro on 36th Avenue.
- **Casa Enrique** • 5-48 49th Ave
  347-448-6040 • $$$
  Mexican cuisine from Chiapas via Bar Henry folks.
- **Chela & Garnacha** • 33-09 36th Ave
  917-832-6876 • $$
  Charming brick-and-mortar outpost of Mexico Blvd food truck.
- **Court Square Diner** • 45-30 23rd St
  718-392-1222 • $
  Reliable grub available 24 hours.

- **Cyclo** • 5-51 47th Ave
  718-786-8309 • $$
  Vietnamese pho and banh mi from the folks behind Tuk Tuk.
- **John Brown Smokehouse** • 27-20 40th Ave
  347-617-1120 • $$
  Kansas City-style barbecue just off the E train.
- **M. Wells Steakhouse** • 43-15 Crescent St
  718-786-9060 • $$$$
  More boffo dishes from strange animal parts at this hipster meat palace.
- **Manducatis** • 13-27 Jackson Ave
  718-720-4602 • $$$
  Classic Italian cuisine expertly prepared; a beloved neighborhood institution.
- **Manetta's** • 10-76 Jackson Ave
  718-786-6171 • $$
  Above-average brick oven pizza and good house-made pastas.

Long Island City

Map 27

Get your custom-built axe at **Sadowsky Guitars**. Go to **Hunter's Point Wines & Spirits** for a carefully curated selection and great guidance. Quality and prices are both elevated at **Foodcellar**, which is the cost of doing business here. And **Just Things** is a quirky amalgamation of thrift, junk, and antique store that we hope never ever leaves.

- **Petey's Burger** • 46-46 Vernon Blvd
  718-937-4040 • $
  It's like an In-N-Out cover band; fills a need.
- **Shi** • 47-20 Center Blvd
  347-242-2448 • $$
  The view is LIC. The decor is Soho. The diners are Murray Hill.
- **Skinny's Cantina** • 47-05 Center Blvd
  718-729-8300 • $$$
  Upscale Mexican comfort food.
- **Tournesol** • 50-12 Vernon Blvd
  718-472-4355 • $$$
  Cozy French bistro, a neighborhood gem.
- **Tuk Tuk** • 49-06 Vernon Blvd
  718-472-5598 • $$
  Hip space. Good Thai food.

🛍 Shopping

- **Artbook @ MoMA PS1** • 22-25 Jackson Ave
  718-433-1088
  Fabulous selection of art books.
- **Astoria Seafood** • 37-10 33rd St
  718-392-2680
  Top-notch seafood in unsuspecting location.
- **Blue Streak Wine & Spirits** • 4720 Center Blvd
  718-706-9463
  Wine and booze from around the globe.
- **Court Square Wine & Spirits** •
  24-20 Jackson Ave
  718-707-9911
  Excellent selection and prices.
- **Duane Reade** • 47-02 5th St
  718-472-3600
  Good for toilet paper, nail polish remover, and Us Weekly.
- **Foodcellar & Co. Market** • 4-85 47th Rd
  718-606-9786
  Like Whole Foods, but not.

- **Hunter's Point Wines & Spirits** •
  47-07 Vernon Blvd
  718-472-9463
  Trust the owner to recommend great wines from $5 to $50. Also a well-edited liquor selection.
- **Just Things** • 47-28 Vernon Blvd
  718-786-3675
  Quirky amalgamation of thrift store, junk store, and antique store.
- **Matted** • 46-36 Vernon Blvd
  718-786-8660
  Picture framing plus an assortment of artsy tchotckes.
- **Rio Bonito Market** • 32-15 36th Ave
  718-706-7272
  Brazilian-focused specialty store.
- **Sadowsky Guitars** • 21-07 41st Ave
  718-433-1990
  Custom-made guitars and basses since 1979.
- **Spokesman Cycles** • 49-04 Vernon Blvd
  718-433-0450
  Great bike store on Vernon Blvd.
- **Vernon Blvd Pharmacy** • 48-15 Vernon Blvd
  718-361-7390
  Local pharmacy gives you the attention the chains don't.
- **Vernon Wine & Liquor** • 50-06 Vernon Blvd
  718-784-5096
  Use when you need cheap prosecco for the party.

Map 28 · Greenpoint

Map 28 · Greenpoint

N

1   2

44th Rd
44th Ave
45th Ave
45th Rd
Pearson St
Davis St
Crane St
47th Ave
47th Rd
46th Ave
46th Rd
48th Ave
21st St
Arch St
Austell Pl
Pearson Pl
Davis Ct
Skillman Ave
Dutch Kills
45th Ave
Hunters Point Ave
28th St
29th St
30th St
30th Pl
31st St
Van Dam St
Gale Ave
32nd Ave
33rd St
35th St
36th St
37th St
Vernon Blvd
Jackson Ave

21st Street
G

Hunters Point Avenue
7

50th Ave
51st Ave
2nd St
25th St

Long Island Exwy **495**
Bradley Ave
Star Ave
Review Ave

Vernon Blvd-Jackson Avenue
7

Borden Ave
Pulaski Bridge

Greenpoint Avenue

Calvary Cemetery

Queens Midtown Tunnel

Newtown Creek

27

Newtown Creek Nature Walk

Paidge Ave
Ash St
Box St
Clay St
Dupont St
Eagle St
Freeman St
Green St
Huron St
India St
Java St
Kent St
Calyer St
Kingsland Ave
Kingsland Ave
Monitor St
North Henry St
Russell St
Humboldt St
Moultrie St
Norman Ave
Jewel St
Diamond St
Newell St
Manhattan Ave
McGuinness Blvd
Franklin St
West St
Commercial St
Provost St

John Smolenski Funeral Home

Newtown Creek Sewage Treatment Plant

Newtown Creek Sewage

Greenpoint Avenue

Morgan Ave
Sutton St
Nassau Ave
Moore St

Monsignor McGolrick Park

Greenpoint Avenue
G

Saint Anthony of Padua Church

Greenpoint Historic District

Milton St
Noble St
Oak St
Clifford Pl
Guernsey St
Lorimer St
Leonard St
Eckford St
Driggs Ave

Transmitter Park

American Playground

Banker St
Dobbin St
Banker St
Norman Ave

Nassau Avenue
G

McGuinness Blvd S
Graham Ave
Manhattan Ave
Russell St
Bayard Ave
Leonard Ave
Newton St

Greenpoint Piers

Quay St
Gem St
N 15th St
N 14th St
N 13th St

29

Nassau Ave
Lorimer St

McCarren Park

East River

N 12th St
N 11th St
N 10th St
Kent Ave
Wythe Ave
Barry St
Bedford Ave
Driggs Ave
Union Ave
Guernsey St
Bayard St
N 9th St
N 8th St
110
Leonard St
Richardson St
Frost St
210
260
Withers St
Richardson St
Skillman Ave

Brooklyn Queens Exwy **278**

1/4 mile	.25 km

Neighborhood Overview

Map 28

The northernmost neighborhood in Brooklyn, Greenpoint has multiple personality disorder. It's strongly Polish (hence the mouth-watering bakeries and butcher shops) and solidly trendy. As the name suggests, parts are indeed green, but it's also home to one of America's filthiest waterways.

As longtime hub for shipping and manufacturing, Greenpoint sits at the nexus of Newtown Creek and the East River. Newtown Creek is infamous for the 1950 oil spill more than twice the size of Exxon Valdez; now an EPA Superfund site, remediation will continue for years. On a brighter note, Newtown Creek's quarter-mile **Nature Walk** is a valiant attempt to spruce things up, and the tree-lined **Greenpoint Historical District** (originally home to local industrial workers) is still in excellent shape. Greenpoint is also the proud owner of the verdant oasis known as **McGolrick Park**. Manhattan Avenue Park (at the northern dead-end of that thoroughfare) is a well-kept, tiny gem with several cool sculptures. Also check out the impressive **Eagle Street Rooftop Farm**; support their efforts by buying fresh greens (give your regards to the rabbits and chickens). And **Transmitter Park**, the former home of WNYC's radio towers at the end of Greenpoint Avenue, is a rare spot of green along the waterfront; head to the end of the zig-zagging pier for a respite from the heat of the city—it's like ten degrees cooler out in the middle of the East River.

Manhattan Avenue is the neighborhood's main artery (buses and the G train run along it). Mass is held at the stunning **Saint Anthony of Padua Church** and your everyday needs are met along the way—fruit & vegetable stands, restaurants, bars and the like. Franklin Street is a relaxing antidote to the grimy bustle of Manhattan Avenue, with galleries, boutiques and various high-concept entities. East of McGuinness Boulevard you'll find various cheap bars, liquor stores, restaurants, Polish bakeries, and a few real, respectable coffee shops, including Hannah Horvath's employers, **Café Grumpy**.

One exciting aspect of Greenpoint (though not for locals with cars) is the frequent number of movie and television productions filmed here. It's close to Manhattan and Long Island City (where a number of studios are based) and can stand in for a green, industrial, or cozy neighborhood setting. *Flight of the Conchords* shot their French song video in McGolrick Park. *30 Rock* filmed in front of a dollar store on Manhattan Avenue. Recent productions have included *Blue Bloods*, *Date Night*, *Boardwalk Empire*, and *Girls*. If you keep your ears open at a bar, you may even hear someone who worked on a shoot giving the lowdown on which star is a bitch or which guy played the diva and spent the entire shoot moaning about a recent breakup. Ah, New York.

Pencil Factory and **Black Rabbit** are excellent standbys on Greenpoint Avenue and NFT staffers can be found at the **Palace Cafe**.

Map 28

Greenpoint

O Landmarks

- **Greenpoint Historic District** •
  Oak St & Guernsey St
  Charming rowhouses that were built for
  workers of early merchants.
- **Newtown Creek Nature Walk** •
  Provost St & Paidge Ave
  Great views of the sewage plant!
- **Newtown Creek Wastewater
  Treatment Plant** •
  Greenpoint Ave & Provost St
  Take a moment to contemplate all of the
  famous and beautiful peoples' crap floating
  around in here.
- **Saint Anthony of Padua Church** •
  862 Manhattan Ave [Milton St]
  718-383-3339
  Beautiful church sticking out like a healthy
  thumb on congested avenue.
- **Transmitter Park** •
  West St b/n Kent St & Greenpoint Ave
  Greenpoint's waterfront park; former home of
  WNYC transmitter towers.

Coffee

- **Ashbox** • 1154 Manhattan Ave [Ash St]
  718-389-3222
  Cool shop on the very north tip of Greenpoint.
- **Café Grumpy** •
  193 Meserole Ave [Diamond St]
  718-349-7623
  The finest coffee house in Brooklyn now has its
  own roastery.
- **Café Riviera** • 830 Manhattan Ave [Noble St]
  718-383-8450
  Delicious baked-goods and such.
- **Crema BK** • 182 Driggs Ave [Diamond St]
  347-457-5363
  Cold-brewed in Brooklyn.

- **Uro Café** • 277 Driggs Ave [Leonard St]
  718-599-1230
  Best espresso south of Greenpoint Ave.
- **Van Leeuwen Ice Cream** •
  620 Manhattan Ave [Nassau Ave]
  347-987-4774
  Excellent coffee to go with your coffee ice
  cream.
- **Variety Coffee & Tea** •
  142 Driggs Ave [Russell St]
  718-383-2326
  Nice coffee shop with views of McGolrick Park.

Farmers Markets

- **Eagle Street Rooftop Farm** •
  44 Eagle St [West St]
  Sunday, 1 pm–4pm during growing season.

Nightlife

- **Achilles Heel** • 180 West St [Green St]
  347-987-3666
  Worn, hip local bar way over by the docks.
- **Black Rabbit** • 91 Greenpoint Ave [Franklin St]
  718-349-1595
  Fantastic fireplace, delicious mini-burgers.
  Trivia night is packed.
- **Greenpoint Beer & Ale Co.** •
  1150 Manhattan Ave
  347-725-3061
  Excellent brewed-on-site beer with German
  food as a bonus. Great space, too.

Map 28

A Greenpoint visit must include a meal at a cheap and hearty Polish restaurant, like **Christina's**. Afterwards, get a Polish pastry at **Café Riviera** or have some caffeine at **Cafe Grumpy**.

- **Good Room** • 98 Meserole Ave [Manhattan Ave]
  718-349-2373
  Lowkey spot with live music, dance parties, and good vibes.
- **Mary's Bar** •
  134 Kingsland Ave [Beadel St]
  718-599-0128
  LGBTQ Irish pub.
- **The Palace** • 206 Nassau Ave [Russell St]
  718-383-3476
  Heavy jukebox, pub grub, and stiff drinks.
- **Pencil Factory Bar** •
  142 Franklin St [Greenpoint Ave]
  718-609-5858
  Great beer; great vibe. Perfectly understated.
- **Spritzenhaus** • 33 Nassau Ave [Dobbin St]
  347-987-4632
  Predictably packed beer garden in Greenpoint.
- **Torst** • 615 Manhattan Ave [Nassau Ave]
  718-389-6034
  Not just a beer bar, a fancy beer bar with Danish accents.
- **Warsaw** • 261 Driggs Ave [Eckford St]
  929-441-3114
  Brooklyn's best concert venue.

🍴 Restaurants

- **Acapulco Deli & Restaurant** •
  1116 Manhattan Ave [Clay St]
  718-349-8429 • $
  Authentic Mexican includes homemade chips and telenovelas at full volume.
- **Amarin Café** •
  617 Manhattan Ave [Nassau Ave]
  718-349-2788 • $
  Good, cheap Thai food.
- **Amber Steak House** •
  119 Nassau Ave [Eckford St]
  718-389-3757 • $$$$
  Porterhouse for two and Crestor to go.
- **Ashbox** • 1154 Manhattan Ave [Ash St]
  718-389-3222 • $
  Japanese-influenced café fare at the mouth of Newton Creek.
- **Boon Thai** • 681 Manhattan Ave [Norman Ave]
  718-349-8215 • $$
  Terrific Thai; try the curry noodles.
- **Calexico** •
  645 Manhattan Ave [Bedford Ave]
  347-763-2129 • $
  The tasty Mexi food truck settles down in Greenpoint.
- **Christina's** • 853 Manhattan Ave [Noble St]
  718-383-4382 • $
  Traditional Polish food, cheap breakfasts!
- **Greenpoint Beer & Ale Co.** •
  1150 Manhattan Ave
  347-725-3061 • $$
  Craft brewery with killer German plates—schnitzel, roast, etc.

Map 28

Greenpoint

- **El Born** • 651 Manhattan Ave [Nassau Ave]
347-844-9295 • $$$
Spanish/tapas with some nice surprises.
- **Esme** • 999 Manhattan Ave [Huron St]
347-689-3071 • $$$
Just love, no squalor. Or, capaccio & cocktails.
- **Five Leaves** • 18 Bedford Ave [Nassau Ave]
718-383-5345 • $$$
Heath Ledger's post-mortem restaurant is cooler than you.
- **Fornino** • 849 Manhattan Ave [Noble St]
718-389-5300 • $$
Brick oven 'za wedged in between Polish food heaven.
- **Glasserie** • 95 Commercial St [Manhattan Ave]
718-389-0640 • $$$
Light-filled Mediterranean with luscious side dishes.
- **God Bless Deli** •
818 Manhattan Ave [Calyer St]
718-349-1828 • $
The only 24-hour joint in the 'hood. Cheap sandwiches and burgers.
- **Greenpoint Fish & Lobster Co.** •
114 Nassau Ave [Eckford St]
718-313-1913 • $$$
Fresh oysters, cold Narragansetts, and a hot 'nabe spot.
- **Karczma** •
136 Greenpoint Ave [Manhattan Ave]
718-349-1744 • $$
Homestyle Polish, rightly popular among locals, rustic interior.
- **Kestane Kebab** • 208 Franklin St [Eckford St]
718-349-8601 • $
Refuel your party tank around the clock for cheap.
- **Kyoto Sushi** • 161 Nassau Ave [Diamond St]
718-383-8882 • $$
Best sushi in Greenpoint; dine in for the sake and after-dinner Dum Dums.

- **Lobster Joint** • 1073 Manhattan Ave [Eagle St]
718-389-8990 • $$$
What the world needs: more lobster rolls. And bloody marys.
- **Manhattan Three Decker** •
695 Manhattan Ave [Norman Ave]
718-389-6664 • $$
Greek and American fare.
- **Paulie Gee's** • 60 Greenpoint Ave [West St]
347-987-3747 • $$
Top brick-oven 'za right by the river. Nice.
- **Peter Pan Doughnuts** •
727 Manhattan Ave [Norman Ave]
718-389-3676 • $
Polish girls in smocks serving tasty donuts.
- **Raizes** • 139 Nassau Ave [McGuinness Blvd]
718-389-0088 • $$$
Portuguese meat-on-a-stick with some surprises.
- **Sapporo Ichiban** •
622 Manhattan Ave [Nassau Ave]
718-389-9712 • $$
Fresh sushi, friendly service.

Shop **Eastern District** for that which is artisanal and Brooklyn-based. **Charlotte Patisserie** has baked goods and **Word**'s is an English-language independent bookstore.

🛍 Shopping

- **Alter Men** • 140 Franklin St [Greenpoint Ave]
718-349-0203
Nice selection of vintage and hard-to-find labels.
- **Bellocq Tea Atelier** • 104 West St [Kent St]
800-495-5416
Exquisite tea sold per ounce, look hard for the sign.
- **Brooklyn Craft Company** •
165 Greenpoint Ave [Franklin St]
646-201-4049
Girly DIY classes to while away the crafternoon…
- **Brouwerij Lane** •
78 Greenpoint Ave [Franklin St]
347-529-6133
For beer junkies. Global bottles or pour-your-own growlers.
- **Charlotte Patisserie** •
596 Manhattan Ave [Driggs Ave]
718-383-8313
Polish-run dessert and coffee shop, delicious French-style pastries.
- **Cracovia Liquors** • 150 Nassau Ave [Newell St]
718-383-2010
Easiest place to spot a bum in Greenpoint. Open late.
- **Dandelion Wine** • 153 Franklin St [Java St]
347-689-4563
Knowledgeable staff and frequent wine tastings—double win!
- **Eastern District** •
1053 Manhattan Ave [Freeman St]
718-349-1432
Cheese and beer shop with tons of Brooklyn brands.
- **Ovenly** • 31 Greenpoint Ave [West St]
888-899-2213
Growing bakery serving sweet and salty treats.
- **Pentatonic Guitars & Music** •
139 Franklin St [Java St]
718-930-4650
Guitars, basses, ukuleles, banjos, mandolins, gear, and repairs.
- **Pop's Popular Clothing** •
7 Franklin St [Meserole Ave]
718-349-7677
Work clothes & boots for blue-collar authenticity.
- **The Thing** • 1001 Manhattan Ave [Huron St]
718-349-8234
Unusual second-hand store offers thousands of used LPs.
- **WORD** • 126 Franklin St [Milton St]
718-383-0096
Literary fiction, non-fiction, and kids' books.

Map 29 · **Williamsburg**

Ⓝ

Clifford Pl
Noble St
Oak St
Calyer St
Quay St
Banker St
Dobbin St
Guernsey St
Lorimer St
Nassau
Leonard St
McGuinness Blvd S
Meeker Ave
Kingsland Ave
Newel St
Dupont St
Banker St
Norman Ave
Eckford St
Leonard St
Graham Ave
Monitor St
Manhattan Ave
Ebcebue St
Woodpoint Rd
Green St

Ⓖ **Nassau Avenue**

28 ▲

N 15th St
N 14th St
N 13th St
N 12th St
N 11th St
N 10th St
N 9th St

Bushwick Inlet

Brooklyn Brewery

Bushwick Inlet Park

Ⓐ

East River State Park

N 8th St
N 7th St
N 6th St
N 5th St
N 4th St
N 3rd St

Kent Ave

Bedford Ave

Wythe Ave

Berry St

Nassau Ave

McCarren Park

McCarren Pool

Manhattan Ave

Union Ave

Bayard St

Richardson St

Frost St

Withers St

Jackson St

Skillman Ave

Conselyea St

Frost St

Humboldt St

Graham Ave

Ⓛ Graham Avenue

Leonard St

Brooklyn Queens Expwy

Lorimer St

Metropolitan Avenue Ⓛ

Lorimer Street ✉

Ainslie St

Devoe St

Metropolitan Ave

Ⓖ

Ⓛ **Bedford Avenue**
Ⓛ **Bedford Avenue L Station**

Driggs Ave

Roebling St

Havemeyer St

Powers St

Grand St Ⓛ

Union Ave

Mauger St

Manhattan Ave

City Reliquary

Metropolitan Ave

Metropolitan Ave

Fillmore Pl

Hope St

278

Hope St

Ten Eyck St

Stagg St

Scholes St

Meserole St

Montrose Ave Ⓖ

Ⓑroad

Grand Ferry

N 1st St

Grand St

Hope St

Grand St

Borinquen Pl

Marcy Ave

Rodney St

S 1st St

S 2nd St

S 3rd St

S 4th St

S 5th St

Keap St

Hewes St

Grand Ferry Park

S 1st St

S 2nd St

S 3rd St

Washington Plaza

Williamsburg Bridge

✉

Hewes Street Ⓙ Ⓜ

Broadway

Marcy Avenue

Ⓙ Ⓜ Ⓩ

Harrison Ave

Ⓐ

Ⓑ

East River

S 6th St

Broadway

Bedford Ave

Driggs Ave

Roebling St

S 8th St

S 9th St

S 10th St

S 11th St

Division Ave

Marcy Ave

Penn St

Rutledge St

Heyward St

Lee Ave

Hooper St

Wallabout St

Flushing Ave

Bedford Ave

Skillman Ave

Myrtle Ave

Middleton St

Lynch St

Williamsburg Bridge

Williamsburg St W

Williamsburg St E

Williamsburg Bridge

Dunham Pl

Wythe Ave

Berry St

Bedford Ave

Rush St

Morton St

Conselyea St

Taylor St

Wilson St

Ross St

Wythe Ave

Kent Ave

Bedford Ave

Franklin St

30 ▼

31 ▼

Wallabou Channel

Navy Yard

1/4 mile   .25 km

Neighborhood Overview

Map 29

You've probably already made up your mind about Williamsburg, but let's be honest, there is always something that brings you back. But a handful of blocks around Bedford and North 7th have enough excellent restaurants, unique shops, live music, bowling alleys, enviable parks, real bookstores, and *record stores* for God's sake to make the rest of us schmos salivate at what our own neighborhoods can't possibly offer. Which is when you find yourself squeezing onto the L or the B62 with everyone else who knows the same to be true.

The hulking steel towers of the **Williamsburg Bridge** (1903), long before the L came to be, connected the working class neighborhoods of Brooklyn with jobs in Manhattan. Before the bridge there was the Grand Street Ferry, which departed from the end of Grand Street. That spot is now taken up by the scrappy and pleasant **Grand Ferry Park**, which was one of the few parcels of waterfront open to the public during the area's industrial heyday.

The East River of today bears the fruit of Bloomberg-era rezoning in the form of gleaming high-rise rentals and condos and a manicured waterfront. **East River State Park**, reclaimed from the weeds and still slightly rustic around the edges, is a sunny, sometimes a little too sunny, spot along the river. On summer weekends, the park hosts all manner of fairs and events. Even after the tents and tables are gone, however, East River State Park is definitely worth a weekly trip; the picnic tables at the river's edge are one of the best spots in Brooklyn to gawk at that gorgeous skyline and a killer sunset. A few blocks away is **Brooklyn Brewery**. Brooklyn branded long before Brooklyn was a brand, only a small portion of its beer is actually brewed on site (the bottles, for example, come from Utica), though this spiritual home has anchored Williamsburg's identity since the late 1990s.

Just down the street from Brooklyn Brewery at the northern end of Williamsburg sits **McCarren Park**, with its 35 acres of ball fields, dog runs, and gardens where residents of every stripe convene when the sun is out. Although not the nicest looking park in the city, or even the neighborhood, there's an anarchic spirit to the park that's hard to resist, from the infantilizing children's games being played by aging cool hunters to the pick-up softball, basketball, and soccer on dirt patches and concrete fields to the steady stream of low-key craft-film-food-music events that fill up the weekend docket during the summer; it's a park that is well used and not fussed over, unlike some of the bigger, newer, "nicer" parks. **McCarren Pool**, shuttered for decades, reopened as an actual pool and recreation center in 2012, and as such is a state-of-the-art year-round facility.

Stretching south from McCarren Park is Bedford Avenue, Williamsburg's main thoroughfare, full of shops, bars, boutiques, and activity. The **Bedford Avenue L station** at North 7th Street functions as a sort of epicenter. Williamsburg's excesses ease the farther south and east you move from here. Along Metropolitan Avenue to the south is **City Reliquary**, a clever little (literally little) museum filled with New York City artifacts and historical tidbits, and a great way to connect with pre-gentrified Williamsburg. The south side of Williamsburg, especially south of Broadway, where stately **Peter Luger** has served steak since 1887, is one of the city's largest and most established Hasidic neighborhoods.

Map 29

Williamsburg

O Landmarks

- **Bedford L Train Station** •
  Bedford St & N 7th St
  Williamsburg's epicenter.
- **Brooklyn Brewery** • 79 N 11th St [Wythe Ave]
  718-486-7422
  Connect with your beer by witnessing its birth;
  free samples also encourage closeness.
- **City Reliquary** •
  370 Metropolitan Ave [Havemeyer St]
  718-782-4842
  Artifacts from New York's vast and rich history.
- **East River State Park** • Kent Ave & N 9th St
  Swath of waterfront greenspace, Williamsburg
  style.
- **Grand Ferry Park** • Grand St & River St
  Ferry is gone. Park remains.
- **McCarren Park** • Bedford Ave & N 12th St
  212-639-9675
  Hipsters, Poles, and athletes unite!
- **McCarren Park Pool** • Lorimer St & Bayard St
  718-218-2380
  Massive WPA-era pool and recreation center.
- **Williamsburg Bridge** • Driggs St & S 5th St
  Bridge of the chosen people—Jews and well-
  off hipsters.

Coffee

- **Black Brick** • 300 Bedford Ave [S 1st St]
  718-384-0075
  Cool exposed-brick-and-distressed-wood
  coffee hangout.
- **Devocion** • 69 Grand St [Wythe Ave]
  718-285-6180
  Williamsburg via Colombia; emphasis on
  sourcing and fair trade.
- **Momofuku Milk Bar** •
  382 Metropolitan Ave [Havemeyer St]
  347-799-2732
  Coffee and a bunch of other weird stuff.
- **Oslo** • 133 Roebling St [N 4th St]
  718-782-0332
  Flagship store; coffee with attention to detail.
- **Partners Coffee** • 125 N 6th St [Berry St]
  347-586-0063
  Australian artisanal coffee powerhouse's first
  US shop.

Head to **Spuyten-Duyvil** or **Radegast** for beers, **The Richardson** for a proper cocktail, or **Barcade** for 8-bit goodness.

Farmers Markets

• **Greenpoint/McCarren Park Greenmarket** •
Union Ave & N 12th St [Driggs Ave]
Saturday, 8 am–3 pm, year-round.

Nightlife

• **Alligator Lounge** •
600 Metropolitan Ave [Lorimer St]
718-599-4440
Ignore the decor, and enjoy the free brick oven pizza with your beer.

• **Ba'sik** • 323 Graham Ave [Devoe St]
347-889-7597
Awesome cocktails this far East? Don't tell them over in 11249.

• **Bar Blondeau at Wythe Hotel** •
80 Wythe Ave [N 11th St]
718-460-8006
Ridiculous city views (in a good way) for a chicster crowd.

• **Barcade** • 388 Union Ave [Powers St]
718-302-6464
Paradise for '80s console champions and craft-beer guzzlers.

• **Berry Park** • 4 Berry St [N 14th St]
718-782-2829
Williamsburg's best rooftop: great beer and plenty of skyline.

• **Charleston** • 174 Bedford Ave [N 7th St]
718-599-9599
Still going.

• **Clem's** • 264 Grand St [Roebling St]
718-387-9617
Classic narrow bar + drink specials = a neighborhood staple.

• **D.O.C.** • 83 N 7th St [Wythe Ave]
718-963-1925
All-Italian wine list with upscale finger food.

• **Duff's Brooklyn** • 168 Marcy Ave [Broadway]
718-599-2092
Heavy metal basement dive in the J train shadow.

• **East River Bar** • 97 S 6th St [Berry St]
718-302-0511
Fun interior, patio, and live music.

Map 29

Williamsburg

- **The Gibson** • 108 Bedford Ave [N 11th St]
  718-387-6296
  Quiet, classy Williamsburg bar.
- **Hotel Delmano** • 82 Berry St [N 9th St]
  718-387-1945
  Classic cocktails. Great date spot.
- **Iona** • 180 Grand St [Bedford Ave]
  718-384-5008
  Plenty of choices on tap.
- **Jr. and Son** •
  575 Metropolitan Ave [Lorimer St]
  917-499-3248
  Unabashedly hipster free.
- **The Levee** • 212 Berry St [Metropolitan Ave]
  718-218-8787
  Formerly Cokies, now a laid-back vibe with
  free cheese balls.
- **Maison Premiere** •
  298 Bedford Ave [Grand St]
  347-889-5710
  Cocktails and oysters, New Orleans-style.
- **Music Hall of Williamsburg** •
  66 N 6th St [Kent Ave]
  718-486-5400
  Brooklyn's Bowery Ballroom; national acts.
- **Nitehawk Cinema** •
  136 Metropolitan Ave [Berry St]
  646-963-9288
  Dinner, cocktails, and craft beer while you
  watch indie flicks.

- **Pete's Candy Store** •
  709 Lorimer St [Richardson St]
  718-302-3770
  Live music, trivia nights, awesome back room,
  and Scrabble.
- **Radegast Hall & Biergarten** •
  113 N 3rd St [Berry St]
  718-963-3973
  German beer hall with retractable roof. Only in
  Williamsburg.
- **The Richardson** •
  451 Graham Ave [Richardson St]
  718-389-0839
  Proper cocktails and small plates served in the
  BQE's shadow.
- **Spuyten Duyvil** •
  359 Metropolitan Ave [Havemeyer St]
  718-963-4140
  Join the Belgian beer cult.
- **Turkey's Nest Tavern** •
  94 Bedford Ave [N 12th St]
  718-384-9774
  Best dive in Williamsburg.
- **Union Pool** • 484 Union Ave [Skillman Ave]
  718-609-0484
  Good starting point—or finishing point.
- **The Woods** • 48 S 4th St [Wythe Ave]
  Spacious non-hipster bar plus burgers, bacon,
  and tacos in back.
- **Wythe Hotel** • 80 Wythe Ave [N 11th St]
  718-460-8000
  Home to rooftop bar The Ides, and hip
  restaurant Reynard.

Don't miss the dressed-up American spots: **Walter Foods** and the more casual **DuMont**. Carnivores must pay respects to **Fette Sau** and **Peter Luger**.

Restaurants

- **Anna Maria Pizza** • 179 Bedford Ave [N 7th St]
718-599-4550 • $
A must after late-night drinking.
- **Aurora** • 70 Grand St [Wythe Ave]
718-388-5100 • $$$
Warm, friendly rustic Italian. Just about perfect.
- **Baci & Abbracci** • 204 Grand St [Driggs Ave]
718-599-6599 • $$
Old-world Italian in a modern setting.
- **Bakeri** • 150 Wythe Ave [N 8th St]
718-388-8037 • $$
Adorably Amish decor and hipster vibe. Excellent baked goods.
- **Bamonte's** • 32 Withers St [Union Ave]
718-384-8831 • $$$
Historic Italian joint; mediocre food but a great space.
- **Baoburg** • 614 Manhattan Ave
718-349-0011 • $$$
Delicious fusion, wings to die for.
- **Bozu** • 296 Grand St [Havemeyer St]
718-384-7770 • $$
Amazing Japanese tapas and sushi bombs.
- **Cerveceria Havemeyer** •
149 Havemeyer St [S 2nd St]
718-599-5799 • $$
Delish Mex and you know, those drinks that start with "M."
- **The Commodore** •
366 Metropolitan Ave [Havemeyer]
718-218-7632 • $
Southern hipster cuisine. Good and cheap.
- **Da Francesco** • 442 Graham Ave [Frost St]
718-349-1627 • $$
Family-style restaurant with Northern and Southern Italian dishes.
- **DeStefano's Steak House** •
593 Lorimer St
718-384-2836 • $$$$
Fun old school steakhouse.
- **Diner** • 85 Broadway [Berry St]
718-486-3077 • $$
Amazing simple food like you've never tasted—never disappoints.
- **Dokebi** • 199 Grand St [Driggs Ave]
718-782-1424 • $$$
Cook your own Korean BBQ with tabletop hibachis.
- **DuMont Burger** • 314 Bedford Ave [S 1st St]
718-384-6127 • $$
The mini burger is even better proportioned than the original.

Map 29

Williamsburg

• **Fette Sau** •
354 Metropolitan Ave [Roebling St]
718-963-3404 • $$
Enjoy pounds of meat and casks of beer in a
former auto-body repair shop.

• **Juliette** • 135 N 5th St [Bedford Ave]
718-388-9222 • $$
Northside bistro with rooftop deck.

• **La Locanda** • 432 Graham Ave [Withers St]
718-349-7800 • $$
Fried calamari, chicken parm, and so forth.

• **La Superior** • 295 Berry St [S 2nd St]
718-388-5988 • $$
Authentic Mexican street food.

• **Lilia** • 567 Union Ave [N 10th St]
718-576-3095 • $$$
Sunny upscale Italian in repurposed auto
body shop.

• **Llama Inn** • 50 Withers St [Meeker Ave]
718-387-3434 • $$$
Elegant Peruvian, undoing ceviche/roasted
chicken tropes.

• **Mable's Smokehouse & Banquet Hall** •
44 Berry St [N 12th St]
718-218-6655 • $$
Totally decent BBQ in hipster ambiance
(babies at the bar!).

• **Marlow & Sons** • 81 Broadway [Berry St]
718-384-1441 • $$$
Oysters and beer, old timey-like—go for
Happy Hour.

• **Meadowsweet** • 149 Broadway [Bedford Ave]
347-889-5042 • $$$$
Postmodern American in the old Dressler
space. Nice.

• **Mexico 2000** • 369 Broadway [Keap St]
718-407-0109 • $
Inner-bodega taco counter replete with
Mexican soap operas.

Williamsburg

Map 29

Llama Inn highlights Peruvian food's true culinary qualities, and features the sort of haute deliciousness you might find in Miraflores.

- **Okonomi** • 150 Ainslie St [Lorimer St]
  929-295-0480 • $$$
  Photo-worthy bite-sized Japanese, with brekkie…
- **Peter Luger Steak House** •
  178 Broadway [Driggs Ave]
  718-387-7400 • $$$$$
  Best steak, potatoes, and spinach in this solar system.
- **Pies 'N' Thighs** • 166 S 4th St [Driggs]
  347-529-6090 • $$
  Comfortable, Southern-style where the chicken biscuits reign supreme.
- **Reunion** • 544 Union Ave [Frost St]
  718-599-3670 • $$
  Two shakshukas and then back to bed for us.
- **Sal's Pizzeria** • 544 Lorimer St [Devoe St]
  718-388-6838 • $$
  Calzones, slices, heroes, and pastas.
- **Santa Salsa** • 234 Starr St [Richardson St]
  347-365-2710 • $$
  Venezuelan hot dogs, parillas, and more.

- **Sea** • 114 N 6th St [Berry St]
  718-384-8850 • $$
  Outshines its Manhattan counterpart.
- **St Anselm** •
  355 Metropolitan Ave [Havemeyer St]
  718-384-5054 • $$$
  We have no reservations about this sizzling steak spot.
- **Sweetwater** • 105 N 6th St [Berry St]
  718-963-0608 • $$
  Just a cozy bar with nice bistro food.
- **Tabare** • 221 S 1st St [Roebling]
  347-335-0187 • $$
  Authentic Uruguayan food serving delicious family recipes.
- **Taj Kabab & Curry** • 568 Grand St [Lorimer St]
  718-782-1722 • $$
  Cheap takeout and delivery.
- **Teddy's Bar and Grill** • 96 Berry St [N 8th St]
  718-384-9787 • $
  Best bar food ever. Hipster and Polish locals unite.
- **Traif** • 229 S 4th St [Havemeyer St]
  347-844-9578 • $$$
  Small plates brilliance under the Williamsburg Bridge. Go.

Map 29

Williamsburg

28
5
7
29
4
30
31

Shopping

- **10 Ft. Single by Stella Dallas** •
  285 N 6th St [Meeker Ave]
  718-486-9487
  Dress up like you're in *Dazed & Confused 2*.
- **Academy Records Annex** •
  85 Oak St [Franklin St]
  718-218-8200
  Bins and bins of new and used LPs.
- **Amarcord Vintage Fashion** •
  223 Bedford Ave [N 4th St]
  718-963-4001
  Well-edited vintage goodies, many pieces
  direct from Europe.
- **Artists & Fleas** • 70 N 7th St [Wythe Ave]
  917-488-4203
  Market for quirky jewelry, accessories, vintage,
  housewares.
- **Beer Street** • 413 Graham Ave [Withers St]
  347-294-0495
  Rotating taps, growlers, bottles, & more at
  Williamsburg's craft beer store.
- **BQE Wine & Liquors** •
  504 Meeker Ave [Humboldt St]
  718-389-3833
  Good selection, cheap.

- **Brooklyn Winery** • 213 N 8th St [Driggs Ave]
  347-763-1506
  Craft your own barrel of wine from crushing
  the grapes to bottling.
- **Buffalo Exchange** • 504 Driggs Ave [N 9th St]
  718-384-6901
  Recycled clothing chain's first NYC store.
- **Catbird** • 219 Bedford Ave [N 5th St]
  718-599-3457
  Unique clothing and jewelry from up-and-
  coming designers.
- **Crest True Value Hardware** •
  558 Metropolitan Ave [Lorimer St]
  718-388-9521
  Arty hardware store, believe it or not.
- **Desert Island** •
  540 Metropolitan Ave [Union Ave]
  718-388-5087
  Comics, visual arts books, zines, and
  consignment finds.
- **Earwax Records** • 167 N 9th St [Bedford Ave]
  718-486-3771
  Record store with all the indie classics.
- **Emily's Pork Store** •
  426 Graham Ave [Withers St]
  718-383-7216
  Broccoli rabe sausage is their specialty.

Williamsburg

Map 29

Buffalo Exchange requires some stamina, but it's worth it; **Amarcord**'s nicely edited vintage selection is the antidote. Vinyl collectors geek out within blocks of the Bedford stop at **Academy** and **Earwax**. **Marlow & Daughters**'s locally sourced, quality (i.e., expensive) meat is paired with helpful advice.

• **KCDC Skateshop** • 80 N 3rd St
718-387-9006
Shop and gallery featuring locally designed gear.
• **Marlow & Daughters** • 95 Broadway [Berry St]
718-388-5700
Gorgeous (yes, expensive) cuts for the discerning carnivore.
• **Monk Vintage** • 500 Driggs Ave [N 9th St]
718-384-6665
Young and fun selection of vintage clothes, shoes, accessories.
• **The Natural Wine Company** •
211 N 11th St [Roebling St]
718-388-8423
Smart staff and excellent selection of sustainably produced, tasty wines.
• **Open Air Modern** •
489 Lorimer St [Nassau Ave]
718-383-6465
Old and rare books and furniture.

• **Savino's Quality Pasta** •
111 Conselyea St [Manhattan Ave]
718-388-2038
Homemade ravioli.
• **Smorgasburg** • N 7th St & Kent Ave
Massive Saturday food fest. Sunglasses mandatory.
• **Spoonbill & Sugartown** •
218 Bedford Ave [N 5th St]
718-387-7322
Art, architecture, design, philosophy, and literature. New and used.
• **Treehouse** • 430 Graham Ave [Frost St]
718-482-8733
Quirky, one-of-a-kind clothing and jewelry.
• **Uva Wines & Spirits** •
237 Bedford Ave [N 5th St]
718-963-3939
The staff knows and loves their small, meticulous selection.

Map 30 · **Brooklyn Heights/DUMBO/Downtown**

East River

Navy Yard Basin

Cherry St

FDR Dr

A

Manhattan Bridge

DUMBO

Navy Yard

Marshall St

John St

Little St Perry Plz

Plymouth St

Water St

Front St

York St

Gold St

Sands St

Navy St

Vinegar Hill

VINEGAR HILL

Jetsons Building

York Street
Ⓕ

Nassau St

Commodore J Barry Park

Brooklyn Queens Expwy

N Portland Ave

N Oxford St

Flushin

Cumberla

31▶

Brooklyn Bridge

York St

Old Fulton St

Brooklyn Ice Cream Factory

Cadman Plz W

Prospect St

High St

Pearl St

Concord St

Abel St

278

Raymond Ingersoll Houses

Myrtle Ave

University Towers Housing

Auburn N

Long Isl Univers

Brooklyn Bridge Park

Vine St

Poplar St

Middagh St

Cranberry St

Chapel Pl

Cathedral Pl

Laughlin

Ⓐ Ⓒ High Street

Cadman Plaza

Orange St

BROOKLYN HEIGHTS

Pineapple St

NYC Technical College

Polytechnic

Flatbush Avenue Ext

Myrtle Ave

Clark St

Clark Street
❷❸

Cadman Plz E

Tillary St

Adams St

Johnson St

Lawrence St

Bridge St

Duffield St

MetroTech Center

Willoughby

Fleet St

Fleet Pl

Ⓑ Ⓠ Ⓡ

DeKalb Avenue

Junio

Brooklyn Heights Promenade

College Pl

Love Ln

Hicks St

Willow St

Ⓐ Ⓒ
Ⓕ Ⓡ Jay Street MetroTech

Jay St

Bridge St

Gold St

Ashland Pl

Hanson Pl

Rockwell Pl

Fulton St

B

Brooklyn Historical Society

Court Street
Ⓡ

Borough Hall

Fulton St

Fulton St Mall

N Fulton St

Hanover

S

Montague St

Montague Ter

Pierrepont St

Pierrepont Pl

Remsen St

Hunts Ln

Joralemon St

Brooklyn Borough Hall

Borough Hall
❷❸
❹❺

Clinton St

Brooklyn Tabernacle

New York Transit Museum

Boerum Pl

Hoyt Street
❷❸

Hoyt-Schermerhorn
Ⓐ Ⓒ Ⓖ

Schermerhorn St

Atlantic Ave

Livingston St

State

278

Columbia Pl

Henry St

Sidney Pl

Grace Ct

Garden Pl

Aitken Pl

State St

Willow Pl

Clinton St

Pacific St

Dean St

Bergen St

Congress St

Amity St

Pacific St

Smith St

Ⓕ Ⓖ
Bergen Street

Bergen St

Wyckoff St

Court St

Furman St

Atlantic Ave

1/4 mile   **.25 km**

32▼

Neighborhood Overview

Map 30

Three 'nabes for the price of one! Or is that three 'nabes for the price of ten? Yes, Brooklyn Heights really is that expensive, but there's a reason: it's one of the most sublimely beautiful neighborhoods in all of New York, with jaw-dropping city views along the **Brooklyn Heights Promenade**, two friendly retail strips on Montague and Henry Streets, views of the iconic **Brooklyn Bridge**, and perhaps the city's best stock of brownstones and clapboard homes, especially around the "fruit street" area of Orange, Cranberry, and Pineapple, but even heading all the way south along Henry and Hicks Streets until the neighborhood ends at busy Atlantic Avenue.

By the time one hits Court Street heading east from Brooklyn Heights, however, you can chuck the sublime right out the window. The borough's central nervous system, Downtown Brooklyn, features several courthouses (you'll learn your way around when Kings County jury duty calls), **Brooklyn Borough Hall**, **Metrotech Center** (encompassing the **New York City College of Technology**, a large Marriott hotel, **Polytechnic Institute of New York University**, Brooklyn Law School, the **Fulton Street Mall**, jam-packed daily with lunchtime shoppers, and finally, a warren of subways that can take you to any other point in New York City. Speaking of which, don't miss the **New York Transit Museum**, a fascinating look at how our underground web of trains came to be—and not just for aficionados.

DUMBO ("Down Under the Manhattan Bridge Overpass," the acronym appropriated from Walt Disney since the late 1970s), the third neighborhood in this trilogy, has followed the warehouse-turned-artist-studio-turned-expensive-condo route. Like Brooklyn Heights, DUMBO features killer views of downtown Manhattan, just closer to the waterfront. Retail in DUMBO, will be forever limited, and many shops close early (by New York standards). As DUMBO truly only has one subway stop (the York Street F), it can get a little desolate, especially late at night. And while this all sounds like a quiet, idyllic little neighborhood, there's only one problem: the *constant* rumble of the B, D, N, and Q trains overhead on the **Manhattan Bridge**. Thank goodness for double-pane windows.

For true peace and quiet, you'd have to head east about five blocks from DUMBO to check out one of our favorite micro-neighborhoods, **Vinegar Hill**. Literally only three blocks wide and two blocks long, Vinegar Hill is bordered by a power plant to the north, the **Navy Yard** to the east, the Farragut Houses to the south, and DUMBO to the west. Inside its cobblestoned streets are a vestige of 19th-century Navy housing and an ex-retail strip along Hudson Street.

And then there's **Brooklyn Bridge Park**, stretching 1.3 miles along the East River waterfront from Atlantic Avenue to the south all the way past Manhattan Bridge to the north. Comprising six repurposed shipping piers, the former Empire-Fulton Ferry State Park, two Civil War-era historic buildings, and various city-owned open spaces along the waterfront, the 85-acre site combines active and passive recreation with the stunning backdrop of the Brooklyn and Manhattan Bridges, Lower Manhattan, and the New York Harbor beyond.

By 8 p.m., teeming Downtown Brooklyn is a ghost town; you'll either need to head north to DUMBO or west to the Heights to wet your whistle. In DUMBO check out a performance at brilliant **St. Ann's Warehouse**.

⭕ Landmarks

- **Brooklyn Borough Hall •**
  209 Joralemon St [Cadman Plz W]
  718-802-3700
  Built in the 1840s, this Greek Revival landmark
  was once employed as the official City Hall of
  Brooklyn.
- **Brooklyn Bridge •** Adams St & East River
  If you haven't walked over it at least twice yet,
  you're not cool.
- **Brooklyn Bridge Park •**
  Old Fulton St & Furman St
  718-222-9939
  Waterfront park with stellar views and many
  active recreational amenities.
- **Brooklyn Heights Promenade •**
  Montague St & Pierrepont Pl
  The best place to really see Manhattan. It's the
  view that's in all the movies.
- **Brooklyn Historical Society •**
  128 Pierrepont St [Clinton St]
  718-222-4111
  Want to really learn about Brooklyn? Go here.
- **Brooklyn Ice Cream Factory •**
  14 Old Fulton St
  718-522-5211
  Expensive, old-fashioned ice cream beneath
  the bridge.
- **The Brooklyn Tabernacle •**
  17 Smith St [Livingston St]
  718-290-2000
  Home of the award-winning Brooklyn
  Tabernacle Choir.
- **Fulton Street Mall •** Fulton St & Flatbush Ave
  The shopping experience, Brooklyn style. Hot
  sneakers can be had for a song.
- **Jetsons Building •** 110 York St [Jay St]
  View this sculptural roof from the Manhattan
  Bridge at night when it's lit with colored lights.
- **Junior's Restaurant •**
  386 Flatbush Avenue Ext [DeKalb Ave]
  718-852-5257
  For the only cheesecake worth its curds and
  whey.

- **Manhattan Bridge •**
  Flatbush Avenue Ext & Nassau St
  Connecting Brooklyn to that other borough.
- **MetroTech Center •**
  16-acre commercial/governmental/
  educational/cultural entity in Downtown
  Brooklyn.
- **New York Transit Museum •**
  99 Schermerhorn [Boerum St]
  718-694-1600
  Ride vintage subway cars through formerly
  abandoned tunnels? Yes, please!
- **Vinegar Hill •** Water St & Hudson Ave
  NYC's coolest micro-neighborhood. Promise.

Coffee

- **Absolute Coffee •** 327 Atlantic Ave [Hoyt St]
  718-522-0969
  Absolutely perfect for an Atlantic Ave. pit stop.
- **Almondine Bakery •** 85 Water St [Main St]
  718-797-5026
  Grab a cup and check out the view.
- **Two For the Pot •** 200 Clinton St [Atlantic Ave]
  718-855-8173
  Coffee, tea, and British imports as well.

🍎 Farmers Markets

- **Brooklyn Borough Hall Greenmarket •**
  Court St & Montague St
  Tue and Sat, 8 am–3 pm, year-round.

Map 30

Our favorite places here are mostly in the "special occasion" category due to price: game-oriented old-school **Henry's End** and the superb **Vinegar Hill House**. Otherwise, get great pizza at **Juliana's**, grab fast food on **Fulton Street Mall**, or hit classic **Junior's** for hangover food.

Nightlife

- **68 Jay Street Bar** • 68 Jay St [Front St]
718-260-8207
Arty local bar.
- **Grand Army** • 336 State St [Hoyt St]
718-643-1503
Cocktails and oysters, do we need anything else really?
- **Henry Street Ale House** •
62 Henry St [Cranberry St]
718-522-4801
Cozy, dark space with good selections on tap.
- **Le Boudoir** • 135 Atlantic Ave [Hoyt St]
347-227-8337
Marie Antoinette-themed cocktail lounge underneath Chez Moi.
- **O'Keefe's Bar & Grill** •
62 Court St [Livingston St]
718-855-8751
Sports bar (large Mets following). Surprisingly decent food.
- **St Ann's Warehouse** • 45 Water St
718-254-8779
Be careful not to cut yourself on the edginess.

Restaurants

- **AlMar** • 111 Front St [Washington St]
718-855-5288 • $$$
Cavernous, friendly, communal-table Italian in DUMBO. Go to hang.
- **Bijan's** • 81 Hoyt St [Atlantic Ave]
718-855-5574 • $$$
Lamb burgers and rosemary chicken. It's good.
- **Chef's Table at Brooklyn Fare** •
200 Schermerhorn St [Hoyt St]
718-243-0050 • $$$$$
When you get a seat, give it to us.
- **Chez Moi** • 135 Atlantic Ave [Henry St]
347-227-8337 • $$$$
Even more French on Atlantic Avenue. We love it.

- **Colonie** • 127 Atlantic Ave [Henry St]
718-855-7500 • $$$$
Hip to be square. Oysters, cocktails, and much more.
- **Dellarocco's of Brooklyn** •
214 Hicks St [Montague St]
718-858-1010 • $$
Perfectly good brick oven tucked away on Hicks. Nice.
- **Fascati Pizza** • 80 Henry St [Orange St]
718-237-1278 • $
Excellent slice pizza.
- **Grimaldi's** • 1 Front St [Cadman Plaza W]
718-858-4300 • $
Excellent, respected, arguably among the best NYC pizza joints.
- **Henry's End** • 72 Henry St [Cranberry St]
718-834-1776 • $$$
Inventive, game-oriented menu.

- **Iron Chef House** • 92 Clark St [Monroe Pl]
718-858-8517 • $$
Dependable sushi and cozy atmosphere.
- **Juliana's Pizza** • 19 Old Fulton St [Front St]
718-596-6700 • $$
Patsy makes his triumphant return to original
Grimaldi's space.
- **Junior's Restaurant** •
386 Flatbush Avenue Ext [DeKalb Ave]
718-852-5257 • $
American with huge portions. Cheesecake.
- **Lantern Thai** • 101 Montague St [Hicks St]
718-237-2594 • $$
Mediocre Thai. The Montague curse.
- **Luzzo's BK** • 145 Atlantic Ave [Henry St]
718-855-6400 • $$$
East Village Italian pizza masters say hello to
Brooklyn.
- **Miso** • 40 Main St [Front St]
718-858-8388 • $$$
Japanese fusion cuisine.
- **Noodle Pudding** • 38 Henry St [Middagh St]
718-625-3737 • $$
Northern Italian fare.
- **Park Plaza Restaurant** •
220 Cadman Plaza W [Clark St]
718-596-5900 • $
NFT-approved neighborhood diner.

- **The River Café** • 1 Water St [Old Fulton St]
718-522-5200 • $$$$$
Great view, but overrated.
- **Shake Shack** • 409 Fulton St [Boerum Pl]
718-307-7590 • $
The empire comes to Brooklyn.
- **Shake Shack** • 2 Water St [Old Fulton St]
347-435-2676 • $$
Danny Meyer's burgers, conveniently located
near Brooklyn Bridge Park.
- **Superfine** • 126 Front St [Pearl St]
718-243-9005 • $$
Mediterranean-inspired menu, bi-level bar,
local art and music. NFT pick.
- **Sushi Gallery** • 71 Clark St [Henry St]
718-222-0308 • $$
Sushi Express, reasonable prices.
- **Vinegar Hill House** •
72 Hudson Ave [Water St]
718-522-1018 • $$$
Excellent wood fired meats and veggies
served in old-timey setting.

Need something, anything, quick and cheap? The **Fulton Street Mall** area is your answer, with a **Macy's** and tons of discount shops. In DUMBO, you can get great books at **powerHouse**, chocolate at **Jacques Torres**, and cupcakes at **One Girl Cookies**. In the Heights, browse women's clothing at **Tango** on Montague.

Shopping

- **Barnes & Noble** • 194 Atlantic Ave [Court St]
  718-473-3667
  Chain bookstore.
- **Bridge Fresh** • 68 Jay St [Water St]
  718-488-1993
  Organic grocer.
- **Brooklyn Historical Society** •
  128 Pierrepont St [Clinton St]
  718-222-4111
  Fun gift shop with all manner of Brooklyn-themed merch.
- **Brooklyn Ice Cream Factory** •
  14 Old Fulton St [Water St]
  718-522-5211
  Get your ice cream fix on the Brooklyn waterfront.
- **Housing Works Thrift Shop** •
  150 Montague St [Henry St]
  347-644-2269
  Our favorite thrift store.
- **Jacques Torres Chocolate** •
  66 Water St [Main St]
  718-875-1269
  The Platonic ideal of chocolate.
- **Lassen & Hennigs** •
  114 Montague St [Henry St]
  718-875-6272
  Specialty foods and deli.

- **Macy's** • 422 Fulton St [Hoyt St]
  718-875-7200
  Less crazed than Herald Square by about 1700%.
- **Montague Wine & Spirits** •
  78 Montague St [Hicks St]
  718-254-9422
  Consistently good wine store in Brooklyn Heights.
- **One Girl Cookies** • 33 Main St [Water St]
  212-675-4996
  Delicious treats via Cobble Hill.
- **Peas & Pickles** • 55 Washington St [Front St]
  718-488-8336
  DUMBO's first grocery.
- **powerHouse Arena** • 28 Adams St [Water St]
  718-666-3049
  Art-focused books and event space.
- **Recycle-A-Bicycle** • 858 Fulton St
  718-858-2972
  Bikes to the ceiling.
- **Super Runners Shop** • 123 Court St [State St]
  718-858-8550
  Running sneaks and the like.
- **Tango** • 145 Montague St [Henry St]
  718-625-7518
  Jodie loves the clothes here. 'Nuff said.
- **Waterfront Wines & Spirits** •
  360 Furman St [Joralemon St]
  718-246-5101
  Well curated selection; stop before visiting friends for dinner.
- **West Elm** • 2 Main St
  718-243-0149
  Cool home decor at reasonable prices.

Map 31 · **Fort Greene / Clinton Hill**

Ⓝ

1

2

Division Ave
Bedford Ave
Williamsburg St W
Williamsburg St E
Lee Ave

S 11th St
Taylor St
Wilson St
Ross St

Wythe Pl

Wythe Ave

Kent Ave

Hewes St
Penn St
Rutledge St
Lynch St
Middleton St

Heyward St

Flushing
Avenue

Hopkins St
Ellery St
Park Ave
M L K Jr Pl

Marcy
Houses

Myrtle-
Willoughby
Avenue Ⓖ

29

Wallabout St

Flushing Ave

Nostrand Ave
Marcy Ave
Stockton St

A

Navy
Yard

Steiner
Studios

Brooklyn
Navy Yard

Williamsburg
Place

Little Nassau St
Park Ave
Franklin Ave
Taaffe Pl
Classon Ave
Steuben St

Stanwix St
Sanford St
Walworth St
Bedford Ave
Stillman St
Myrtle Ave

Vernon Ave
Willoughby Ave

Spencer St

Pulaski

**CLINTON
HILL**

DeKalb Ave Ⓖ
Bedford-
Nostrand
Avenue

Flushing Ave

Brooklyn Queens Expressway

130

Com J
Berry
Park

N Oxford St
N Portland Ave
N Elliott Pl
Washington Ave
Carlton Ave
Vanderbilt Ave
Clermont Ave
Adelphi St
Hall St

Waverly Ave
Grand Ave
Emerson Pl
Ryerson St
Steuben St

Pratt
Institute

The
Quadrangles

Lafayette
Gardens

Classon
Avenue Ⓖ

Clifton Pl
Greene Ave
Lexington Ave
Franklin Ave

Quincy St
Gates Ave

Broken
Angel

Monroe St

**FORT
GREENE**

Walt Whitman
Houses

Carlton Ave

St Joseph's
College

Brooklyn
Masonic
Temple

Clinton-Washington
Avenue Ⓖ

Cambridge Pl
Grand Ave
Saint James Pl
Downing St
Irving Pl

Putnam Ave

Navy St
Ashland Pl

Fort
Greene
Park

N Elliott Walk
Auburn Pl
S Oxford St

Lafayette Ave

Washington Ave
Waverly Ave
Clinton Ave
Vanderbilt Ave
Cumberland St

S Portland Ave
S Elliott Pl
S Oxford St

Lafayette Ave Presbyterian Church

Fulton St Ⓒ

Clinton-
Washington
Avenue

Jefferson Pl

B

Ⓑ Ⓡ Ⓠ
DeKalb
Avenue

Fleet St

DeKalb Ave

Fort Greene Pl
S Elliott Pl

Ⓖ Fulton Street

Fulton St Ⓒ

Nevins
Street
ⒶⒸ

Fulton
St Mall
Livingston St

Brooklyn
Academy
of Music

Lafayette Avenue Ⓒ

Elm Pl

ⒶⒸ
④⑤

Ashland Pl

Williamsburgh
Savings Bank
Building

Hanson Pl

Long Island
Railroad Station

Atlantic Ave

Pacific St

Dean St

Bergen St

Washington Ave

Schermerhorn St

Ⓓ Ⓝ Ⓡ

Harrison Pl

State St
Atlantic Ave

Pacific Street

3rd Ave
4th Ave

Atlantic Avenue
②③④⑤⑥ Ⓠ

33

Bergen St
Saint Marks Ave

Underhill Ave

Pacific St

Dean St

Bergen St

Wyckoff St
Warren St

Nevins St

Saint Marks Ave

Quisenbury Pl

Flatbush Avenue Ext

Prospect Pl

Park Pl

Butler Pl

Sterling Pl

1/4 mile   .25 km

Neighborhood Overview

Map 31

Fort Greene could be the perfect outer borough neighborhood: the population is diverse, it's close to Manhattan, it's got a stellar park, tons of restaurants, a farmer's market, the hippest swap meet on the planet, beautiful tree-and brownstone-lined streets, historic buildings, subway and LIRR access, and a world-class performing arts center. Unfortunately, many people already know this, so rents are increasingly high, but the area still retains a homey, community vibe.

Fort Greene's landmarks run the gamut from religious to cultural to economic to civic to military. Check out the Underground Railroad murals at the **Lafayette Avenue Presbyterian Church**. In addition to templing Masons, the **Brooklyn Masonic Temple** also hosts indie concerts. The **Brooklyn Academy of Music** (BAM) has two live performance spaces, movie theaters, a café (which hosts free shows), plus the "Next Wave" festival of dance, opera, music, and theater. (Also, the Mark Morris Dance Center is just down the block.) The **Williamsburgh Savings Bank Building** is one of the tallest structures in Brooklyn and has now been converted to condos. The **Brooklyn Navy Yard** now houses businesses as well as **Steiner Studios**. Shoppers and those who need the soul-sucking DMV flock to the hulking, commercial **Atlantic Terminal Mall**, which sits above a massive **Long Island Railroad Station**.

On weekends, hilly **Fort Greene Park** is rollicking with a **farmer's market**, playgrounds, cricket, soccer, and local community groups. Just a few blocks away, **Brooklyn Flea** is a major shopping (and eating!) destination, complete with tons of Etsy-type crafts, vendors, and enough food to fill up a year's worth of blog entries.

But that's only half the story, because Fort Greene's "sister" neighborhood, Clinton Hill, has a lot going for it, namely a proximity to the amenities of Fort Greene with fewer crowds. Clinton Hill hosts bucolic **St. Joseph's College** and the **Pratt Institute**, whose grounds are home to both sculpture art and a **Power Plant**. Several historic churches also dot the Clinton Hill landscape, which is filled with beautiful brownstones as well as some massive single-family homes on Washington Street.

Clinton Hill is home to an African community that has set up a number of restaurants and shops in the neighborhood, and it's also home to a whole row of artist's studios on Lexington Avenue. And film shoots—that peculiar New York City metric of neighborhood self-worth—are a regular occurrence in Clinton Hill.

Brooklyn Public House and **Alibi** are great places to grab a drink before or after a movie at **BAM Rose Cinemas** or a performance at the **Masonic Hall**.

Map 31

Fort Greene / Clinton Hill

O Landmarks

- **Brooklyn Academy of Music (BAM)** •
  30 Lafayette Ave [Ashland Pl]
  718-636-4100
  America's oldest continuously operating
  performing arts center. Never dull.
- **Brooklyn Masonic Temple** •
  317 Clermont Ave [Lafayette Ave]
  347-721-6706
  Its vestrymen have included Robert E. Lee and
  Thomas J. (Stonewall) Jackson.
- **Brooklyn Navy Yard** •
  Flushing Ave & Clinton Ave
  718-907-5900
  Nation's first navy yard employed 70,000
  people during WWII. Today, it houses a diverse
  range of businesses.
- **Fort Greene Park** •
  Willoughby Ave & Washington Park
  212-639-9675
  Liquor store proximity is a plus on a warm
  afternoon when you visit this welcome chunk
  of green.
- **Lafayette Avenue Presbyterian Church** •
  85 S Oxford St [Lafayette Ave]
  718-625-7515
  Nationally known church with performing
  arts; former Underground Railroad stop.
- **Long Island Rail Road Atlantic Terminal** •
  Flatbush Ave & Hanson Pl
  718-217-5477
  A low red-brick building hosting more than 20
  million passengers annually. A total craphole.
- **Pratt Institute Steam Turbine Power Plant** •
  200 Willoughby Ave [Hall St]
  This authentic steam generator gets fired up
  a few times a year to impress the parents. Cool.
- **Prison Ship Martyrs' Monument** •
  Fort Greene Park
  Crypt holds remains of thousands of
  Revolutionary War-era prisoners.
- **Steiner Studios** •
  15 Washington Ave [Flushing Ave]
  718-858-1600
  Film studio in the Brooklyn Navy Yard.
- **Williamsburgh Savings Bank Building** •
  1 Hanson Pl [Ashland Pl]
  When you're lost, a sight for sore eyes.

Coffee

- **Bittersweet** • 180 Dekalb Ave [Carlton Ave]
  718-852-2556
  Line-out-the-door coffee on weekend
  mornings.
- **Greene Grape Annex** •
  767 Fulton St [S Portland Ave]
  718-233-2700
  Bright, busy, super-quiet, with alcohol, too.
- **Hungry Ghost** • 781 Fulton St [S Oxford St]
  718-797-3595
  Perfect coffee and a few fun noshes.
- **Marcy & Myrtle Cafe** •
  574 Marcy Ave [Myrtle Ave]
  917-662-0727
  Small coffee shop with pastries and a cool
  design.

Farmers Markets

- **Fort Greene Park Greenmarket** •
  Dekalb Ave & Washington Park
  Saturday, 8 am–3 pm, year-round, southeast
  corner of park.

Fort Greene / Clinton Hill

It's all here, folks: Italian (**Locanda**), French (**Chez Oskar**), tapas (**Olea**), hip (**No. 7**), Middle Eastern (**Black Iris**), Mexican (**Castro's**), and a reliable greasy spoon diner (**Mike's Coffee Shop**). Full yet?

🍸 Nightlife

- **The Alibi** • 242 Dekalb Ave [Vanderbilt Ave]
  Real deal neighborhood bar.
- **Bar Olivino** • 905 Fulton St [Vanderbilt Ave]
  718-857-7952
  Companion wine bar to Olivino Wines.
- **Brooklyn Masonic Temple** •
  317 Clermont Ave [Lafayette Ave]
  347-721-6706
  Masons + Indie Rock = smiles all around.
- **Brooklyn Public House** •
  247 Dekalb Ave [Vanderbilt Ave]
  347-227-8976
  Lots of beers, with food, open 'till 2 am.
  Perfect.
- **Der Schwarze Kolner** •
  710 Fulton St [S Oxford St]
  347-841-4495
  German beer hall, w/ food. Ft. Greene now
  almost perfect.
- **Dick & Jane's Bar** •
  266 Adelphi St [Dekalb Ave]
  347-739-1027
  A very, very cool speakeasy hidden behind
  four garage doors. Sssshhhh…
- **The Emerson** • 561 Myrtle Ave [Emerson Pl]
  347-763-1310
  Good pub for Pratt students and locals.
- **Rustik Tavern** • 471 Dekalb Ave [Kent Ave]
  347-406-9700
  Neighborhood tap draws cozy clientele.

🍴 Restaurants

- **Baron's** • 564 Dekalb Ave [Spencer Ct]
  718-230-7100 • $$$
  Burgers, cocktails, and perfect brunchtime
  breakfast sandwiches.
- **Bati** • 747 Fulton St [S Portland Ave]
  718-797-9696 • $$
  Friendly (aren't they all?) Ft. Greene Ethiopian.
  Good pre-BAM option.
- **Black Iris** • 228 Dekalb Ave [Clermont Ave]
  718-852-9800 • $$
  Middle Eastern; good lamb, okay chicken,
  excellent Zataar bread.
- **Castro's** • 511 Myrtle Ave [Grand Ave]
  718-398-1459 • $$
  Burritos delivered con cervesas, if you like.
- **Chez Oskar** • 310 Malcolm X Boulevard [Adelphi St]
  718-852-6250 • $$$
  French cuisine in a good neighborhood bistro.
- **Choice Market** •
  318 Lafayette Ave [Grand Ave]
  718-230-5234 • $
  Excellent sandwiches, baked goods, burgers,
  etc. served w/ maddening slowness.
- **Colonia Verde** • 219 Dekalb Ave [Adelphi St]
  347-689-4287 • $$$$
  Latin American flavors and 3 great dining
  spaces. Nice.

Map 31

Map 31

Fort Greene / Clinton Hill

- **Emily** • 919 Fulton St [Clinton Ave]
  347-844-9588 • $$$
  Delicious pizza, and, well, who cares about
  anything else?
- **Il Porto** • 37 Washington Ave [Flushing Ave]
  718-624-0954 • $$
  Cute Italian/pizzeria in front of the Navy Yard.
- **Locanda Vini & Olii** •
  129 Gates Ave [Cambridge Pl]
  718-622-9202 • $$$$$
  Rustic but pricey neighborhood Italian.
  Marvelous decor.

- **Mekelburg's** • 293 Grand Ave [Clifton Pl]
  718-399-2337 • $$$
  Great craft beers and nice little bites to go
  along with 'em.
- **Mike's Coffee Shop** •
  328 Dekalb Ave [St James Pl]
  718-857-1462 • $
  Classic diner option.
- **Olea** • 171 Lafayette Ave [Adelphi St]
  718-643-7003 • $$
  Friendly, buzzing neighborhood tapas/
  Mediterranean. Get the bronzino.
- **Putnam's Pub & Cooker** •
  419 Myrtle Ave [Clinton Ave]
  347-799-2382 • $$$
  Buzzing bar, oysters, burgers, mussels, two
  levels, outdoor seating…we love it.
- **Roman's** • 243 Dekalb Ave [Vanderbilt Ave]
  718-622-5300 • $$$
  Postmodern Italian buzzes in Fort Greene.
  Recommended.

Fort Greene / Clinton Hill

Map 31

Hit **Greene Grape Provisions** for gourmet groceries to go with that nice bottle of wine from **Olivino**, **Gnarly Vines**, or **Thirst**. Pick up books at **Greenlight Books**, mid-century antiques at **Yu Interiors**, and everything else at **Target**. Watch for the occasional artsy bazaar outside of BAM.

- **Speedy Romeo** • 376 Classon Ave [Greene St]
  646-542-1848 • $$
  Bizzarro pizzas, good grilled meats, and a killer Caesar salad.
- **Walter's** • 166 Dekalb Ave [Cumberland St]
  718-488-7800 • $$$
  Hip oysters, meats, and fish steps from Ft. Greene Park.
- **Zaytoons** • 594 Vanderbilt Ave
  718-230-3200 • $$
  Above-average Middle Eastern's second outpost. Get the chicken.

Shopping

- **Atlantic Terminal Mall** •
  Atlantic Ave & Flatbush Ave
  718-834-3400
  And then there's Target.
- **Bicycle Station** • 171 Park Ave [Adelphi St]
  718-638-0300
  Laid-back store convenient to points east and west.
- **Blick Art Materials** •
  536 Myrtle Ave [Grand Ave]
  718-789-0308
  Cavernous art store servicing Pratt students & local artists.
- **Gnarly Vines** • 350 Myrtle Ave [Carlton Ave]
  718-797-3183
  Cool Myrtle wine merchant.

- **Green in BKLYN** •
  432 Myrtle Ave [Clinton Ave]
  718-855-4383
  One-stop shop to help you live an eco-friendly lifestyle.
- **The Greene Grape** •
  765 Fulton St [S Oxford St]
  718-797-9463
  Ft. Greene wine nexus.
- **Greene Grape Provisions** •
  767 Fulton St [S Portland Ave]
  718-233-2700
  Excellent gourmet meat-cheese-fish trifecta.
- **Greenlight Bookstore** •
  686 Fulton St [S Portland Ave]
  718-246-0200
  Ft. Greene's best bookstore.
- **Olivino Wines** • 905 Fulton St [Clinton Ave]
  718-857-7952
  Micro-sized wine shop.
- **Out of the Closet** •
  475 Atlantic Ave [Nevins St]
  718-637-2955
  Thrift shop with clothing, furniture, pharmacy, and free HIV testing.
- **Target** • 139 Flatbush Ave [Atlantic Ave]
  718-290-1109
  The everything store. Seriously.
- **Thirst Wine Merchants** •
  11 Greene Ave
  347-762-5628
  Brilliant wine and alcohol selection, plus bar.
- **Yu Interiors** • 15 Greene Ave [Cumberland St]
  718-237-5878
  Modern furniture, bags, and candles.

221

Map 32 · **BoCoCa / Red Hook**

COBBLE
HILL

BOERUM
HILL

Grace Ct
Aitken Pl
Schermerhorn
Hoyt-
Schermerhorn
30
State St
Atlantic Ave
Atlantic Ave
Pacific St
Dean St
Bergen St
St Marks
Warren St
Baltic St
Butler St
Douglass
Degraw
Sackett

Pacific St
Amity St
Warren St
Bergen
Street
Wyckoff St

Congress St
Warren St
Warren St
Baltic St
Butler St
Gowanus
Housing
Douglass St
Degraw St
Sackett St
Union St
President St

Kane St
Warren Pl
Warren St
Irving St
Henry St
Clinton St
Tompkins Pl
Strong Pl
Sedgwick St
Degraw St
Union St
President St
Carroll St
Carroll
Street
Carroll St
1st St Basin

Hamilton Ave
Hugh L. Carey Tunnel
278
1st Pl
2nd Pl
3rd Pl
4th Pl

CARROLL
GARDENS

33
1st St
2nd St
3rd St
4th St
4th St Basin

Summit St
Woodhull St
Rapelye
Bowne St
Hamilton Ave
Coles St
Seabring St
Commerce St
Delevan St
Verona St
Visitation Pl

Luquer St
Nelson St
Huntington St
W 9th St
Mill St
Dennett Pl
Huntington St

5th St Basin
6th St
7th St Basin
8th St
Second Ave

G F
Smith-
9th Street
W 9th St
Garnet St
10th St
11th St Basin
Gowanus
Canal
Gowanus Expy
Hamilton

Pioneer St
King St
Sullivan St

Red Hook
Park

Red Hook
Housing

Columbia St
Henry St
Clinton St
Court St
Centre St
Bush St
Lorraine St
Creamer St

Gowanus Canal

11th St
12th St
13th St
14th St
15th St

Wolcott St
RED
HOOK
Dikeman St
Coffey St
Van Dyke St
Brooklyn Clay
Retort and Fire
Brick Building
Beard St

Creamer St
Bay St
Sigourney St
Otsego St
Halleck St

Red Hook
Recreational
Area

Red Hook
Ballfields
Sigourney St
Halleck St
Percival St

16th

Reed St
Cool
House
Beard
Street
Pier

Red Hook
Grain Terminal

Bryant St
Court St

20th St

Henry St Basin

A

B

| 1/4 mile | .25 km |

Neighborhood Overview

Map 32

Sorry for the "BoCoCa" thing, but we just can't fit "Boerum Hill / Cobble Hill / Carroll Gardens" along with "Red Hook" on the header bar. Crusty oldtimers will say "I remember when this area was just called 'South Brooklyn.'" Well, Mr. Crusty Oldtimer, this is what happens when neighborhoods age, become economically stable, and are ravaged by hungry real estate agents.

Cobble Hill is like the bastard child of Brooklyn Heights—waterfront without the Promenade, nice-but-not-stunning brownstones, and slightly less convenient subway access. That said, Cobble Hill's dining, shopping, and nightlife are far and away superior to the Heights. Plus, it has one of the quaintest small parks in all of New York—if you've ever seen **Cobble Hill Park** right after a snowfall, you'll know what we're talking about.

Boerum Hill, immortalized in Jonathan Lethem's *The Fortress of Solitude*, has an unusual floor plan in that it's much wider east-west than north-south; Boerum Hill extends east all the way to 4th Avenue, and encompasses more retail along the Atlantic Avenue corridor, as well as Smith Street's northern half. Boerum Hill has come a long way, as evidenced by Smith Street's high commercial rents (say goodbye to porn video, furniture rental, and dollar stores) and the ongoing renovation of many brownstones.

The image of Carroll Gardens is of hard-working immigrant Italian families tending to wide brownstones with those unusual garden frontages. Now many of these owners are either condo-izing or selling outright to Manhattanites who flock to Carroll Gardens for its schools, amenities, a 20-minute subway ride to Manhattan, and huge retail options on lower Court and Smith Streets. There are still old-school Italian shops and eateries that hold their own against the influx of hip restaurants on lower Court Street and the design shops of Smith Street. Somewhere east of Carroll Gardens lies/flows the **Gowanus Canal**, the notorious gonorrhea-breeding waterway/polluted vestigial nightmare that is home to various and sundry household refuse and alleged mafia dumping ground. All that aside, things are looking up for this low-lying stretch of "South Brooklyn," what with new remediation technologies and even a Whole Foods on 3rd Avenue.

And then there's Red Hook. Isolated, peppered with derelict industrial sites (re: the **Red Hook Grain Terminal**), and lacking high-quality housing, Red Hook still draws folks to the other side of the BQE. Even with the closest subway stop over a mile away, **IKEA** has chosen to make Red Hook its Brooklyn home. Elsewhere, the vibrant sports-and-food-stall scene at the **Red Hook Ball Fields** during summer is not to be missed, and did we mention the view of New York Bay from **Louis J Valentino Park**? It rocks.

Map 32

BoCoCa / Red Hook

O Landmarks

- **Beard Street Pier** • Van Brunt St & Reed St
  Historic 19th century warehouses, now a
  cluster of shops and offices.
- **Brooklyn Clay Retort and Fire Brick Works** •
  76 Van Dyke St [Richards St]
  Red Hook's first official Landmark building
  dates to the mid-19th century.
- **Cobble Hill Park** • Clinton St & Verandah Pl
  One of the cutest parks in all of New York.
- **Cool House** • 26 Reed St [Van Brunt St]
  One of the coolest single-family dwellings in
  the city.
- **Gowanus Canal** • Smith St & 9th St
  Brooklyn's answer to the Seine.
- **Louis Valentino Jr Park and Pier** •
  Coffey St & Ferris St
  Escape gentrification-industrial complex with
  perfect view Statue of Liberty.
- **Red Hook Ball Fields** • Clinton St & Bay St
  Watch futbol and eat Central American street
  food every Saturday from spring through fall.
- **Red Hook Grain Terminal** •
  Columbia St & Halleck St
  Visit this abandoned grain elevator just to
  wonder what it's doing there.
- **Warren Place** • Warren Pl [Warren St]
  Public housing from the 1870s.

Coffee

- **The Black Flamingo** •
  168 Borinquen Pl
  201-515-5719
  Hippest spot in the 'hook for java.
- **Black Gold** • 461 Court St [Luquer St]
  347-227-8227
  Coffee, records, antiques, baked goods. All
  they're missing is cheese.
- **Blue Bottle Coffee** • 85 Dean St [Smith St]
  510-661-3510
  Bay Area masters with the long lines for pour
  overs.
- **D'Amico Foods** • 309 Court St [Degraw St]
  718-875-5403
  The neighborhood spot for fresh beans.
- **Henry's Local** • 570 Henry St [1st Pl]
  Very chill, quiet cafe with baked goods.
- **Konditori** • 114 Smith St [Pacific St]
  347-721-3738
  Cozy/packed mini-chain of Swedish
  coffeehouses.

Farmers Markets

- **Carroll Gardens** • Smith St & Carroll St
  Sunday, 8 am–2 pm, year-round.

Each of the 'nabes here has their stalwarts. In Boerum Hill, it's classic **Brooklyn Inn** or the jukebox at **The Boat**. Cobble Hill has several great places on Atlantic (**Floyd**, **Montero's**), or stick with old-time cocktails at **Henry Public**. In Carroll Gardens, it's **Gowanus Yacht Club** in summer and **Brooklyn Social** in winter, and in Red Hook, check out the classic dive **Sunny's**.

Nightlife

- **Abilene** • 442 Court St [3rd Pl]
  718-522-6900
  Cozy and unpretentious. Drink specials galore.
- **Bar Great Harry** • 280 Smith St [Sackett St]
  347-457-5650
  Great draft beer section.
- **Black Mountain Wine House** •
  415 Union St [Hoyt St]
  718-522-4340
  Try the Lebanese wine!
- **Boat Bar** • 175 Smith St [Wyckoff St]
  718-254-0607
  Dank, dark, and friendly. Nice tunes to boot.
- **Botanica** • 220 Conover St [Coffey St]
  718-304-2227
  Classy looking joint.
- **The Brazen Head** • 228 Atlantic Ave [Court St]
  718-488-0430
  Cask ale, mixed crowd.
- **The Brooklyn Inn** • 148 Hoyt St [Bergen St]
  718-522-2525
  When you're feeling nostalgic.
- **Brooklyn Social** • 335 Smith St [Carroll St]
  718-858-7758
  Old boy's lounge revamped. Cocktails still the same. NFT Pick.
- **Clover Club** • 210 Smith St [Baltic St]
  718-855-7939
  Charming den of cocktails and conversation.
- **Floyd** • 131 Atlantic Ave [Henry St]
  718-858-5810
  Indoor bocce ball court!

- **Gowanus Yacht Club** •
  323 Smith St [President St]
  718-246-1321
  Dogs, burgers, and beer. Love it.
- **Henry Public** • 329 Henry St [Atlantic Ave]
  718-852-8630
  From those that brought us Brooklyn Social.
- **Hollow Nickel** • 494 Atlantic Ave [Nevins St]
  347-236-3417
  Fried pickles, BLTs, and burgers for the Barclays crowd.
- **Jalopy Tavern** •
  317 Columbia St [Hamilton Ave]
  718-797-3246
  Live music from rockabilly to out jazz; banjos in the window.
- **Montero's Bar and Grill** •
  73 Atlantic Ave [Hicks St]
  646-729-4129
  A taste of what things used to be like.
- **Other Half Brewing** •
  195 Centre St [Hamilton Ave]
  212-564-6065
  Elegant/bold brews sold in cans or from tasting room.
- **Sunny's** • 253 Conover St [Reed St]
  718-625-8211
  No longer pay-what-you-wish, but still cheap and good.

Map 32

BoCoCa / Red Hook

🍴Restaurants

- **Alma** • 187 Columbia St [Degraw St]
718-422-7500 • $$$
Top NYC Mexican with great views of lower Manhattan.
- **Avlee** • 349 Smith St [Carroll St]
718-855-5125 • $$$
Good Greek that you don't have to schlep to Astoria for.
- **Bacchus** • 409 Atlantic Ave [Bond St]
718-852-1572 • $$$
Low key neighborhood Frenchy bistro.
- **Bar Bruno** • 520 Henry St [Union St]
347-763-0850 • $$$
Mexican gastropub just off the main drag in Carroll Gardens.
- **Bar Tabac** • 128 Smith St [Dean St]
718-923-0918 • $$$
Open late; fabulous frites, burgers, et al.
- **Bedouin Tent** • 405 Atlantic Ave [Bond St]
718-852-5555 • $
Two words: lamb sandwich. No, four: best lamb sandwich ever.
- **Brooklyn Crab** • 24 Reed St [Van Brunt St]
718-643-2722 • $$$$
3 floors of delish seafood with a view of New York Bay. We love it, except for weekends.
- **Brooklyn Farmacy & Soda Fountain** •
513 Henry St [Sackett St]
718-522-6260 • $
A blast from the past. Homemade sodas and shakes.

- **Buddy's Burrito & Taco Bar** •
260 Court St [Baltic St]
718-488-8695 • $
Fast, cheap, and out-of-control huge burritos.
- **Buttermilk Channel** •
524 Court St [Huntington St]
718-852-8490 • $$$
Oysters, sausages, fried chicken, waffles, burgers, ahhh.
- **Café Luluc** • 214 Smith St [Butler St]
718-625-3815 • $$$
Friendly French bistro.
- **Chocolate Room** • 269 Court St [Douglass St]
718-246-2600 • $
Guess what's here?
- **Court Street Grocers** •
485 Court St [Nelson St]
833-533-3200 • $$
Killer breakfast sandwiches and yes! Taylor Pork Roll.
- **DeFonte's Sandwich Shop** •
379 Columbia St [Luquer St]
718-625-8052 • $
Crazy-ass Italian hero shop.

BoCoCa / Red Hook

Map 32

There's more good food here than in some entire states, trust us, from brick-oven goodness at **Lucali** (we're still waiting for a table), loud Thai at **Joya**, fried chicken at **Buttermilk Channel**, seasonal Italian at **Frankies 457**, Middle Eastern haven **Bedouin Tent**, late-night French at **Bar Tabac**, or rooftop Mexican at **Alma**.

- **Fatoosh** • 330 Hicks St [Atlantic Ave]
  718-243-0500 • $
  Nicely priced Middle Eastern Food.
- **Ferdinando's Focacceria** •
  151 Union St [Hicks St]
  718-855-1545 • $
  Sicilian specialties you won't find anywhere else! Get the panelle special.
- **Fragole Ristorante** • 394 Court St [Carroll St]
  718-522-7133 • $$
  Fresh and cozy Italian. An absolute gem.
- **Frankie's 457** • 457 Court St [Luquer St]
  718-403-0033 • $$
  Fantastic meatballs. Cool space. Killer brunch.
- **French Louie** • 320 Atlantic Ave [Smith St]
  718-935-1200 • $$$
  Friendly French on Atlantic. More is better.
- **The Good Fork** • 391 Van Brunt St [Coffey St]
  718-643-6636 • $$$
  Yep. It's good. VERY good.
- **Hanco's** • 134 Smith St [Dean St]
  718-858-6818 • $
  Bánh mi for people who won't trek to Sunset Park.
- **Hibino** • 333 Henry St [Pacific St]
  718-260-8052 • $$
  Highly regarded Cobble Hill sushi.
- **Hometown Bar-B-Que** •
  454 Van Brunt St [Reed St]
  347-294-4644 • $$
  Grab some 'cue while the significant other shops for groceries at Fairway.
- **Joya Thai** • 215 Court St [Warren St]
  718-222-3484 • $$
  Excellent, inexpensive, but super-noisy Thai.
- **Ki Sushi** • 122 Smith St [Dean St]
  718-935-0575 • $$
  Affordable sushi in sleek surroundings; Michelin-starred.
- **Layla Jones** • 214 Court St [Warren St]
  718-624-2361 • $
  The best pizza delivery in the hood.
- **Le Petit Café** • 502 Court St [Nelson St]
  718-596-7060 • $$
  Good bistro food—check out the garden.
- **Libertador** • 404 Henry St [Baltic St]
  347-689-3122 • $$$
  Mixed grill for two and call us in the morning.
- **Lucali** • 575 Henry St [Carroll St]
  718-858-4086 • $$
  One man makes every perfect pizza by hand. Be prepared to wait.
- **Mazzat** • 208 Columbia St [Sackett St]
  718-852-1652 • $$
  Donut-style falafel will make you a believer.
- **Mile End** • 97 Hoyt St [Atlantic Ave]
  718-852-7510 • $$
  Jewish deli, Montreal-style. Two words: smoked meat.
- **Petite Crevette** • 144 Union St [Hicks St]
  718-855-2632 • $$$
  Tucked-away French hard by the BQE.
- **Pizza Moto** • 338 Hamilton Ave [Clinton St]
  718-834-6686 • $$$
  Artisanal pizza made in a 100-year-old-plus oven.

Map 32

BoCoCa / Red Hook

30
31
32
33
Prospe

- **Rucola** • 190 Dean St [Bond St]
718-576-3209 • $$$
Rustic neighborhood Northern Italian. Just a great vibe.
- **Sottocasa Pizzeria** •
298 Atlantic Ave [Smith St]
718-852-8758 • $$
Top pizza on Atlantic, with great Italian beer selection.
- **Tripoli** • 156 Atlantic Ave [Clinton St]
718-596-5800 • $$
A Lebanese standby since 1973 is great for a party, with meze platters and BYOB.
- **Yemen Café** • 176 Atlantic Ave [Clinton St]
718-834-9533 • $
More good Yemeni food, because you can never have too much lamb.

🛍 Shopping

- **Article&** • 198 Smith St [Baltic St]
718-852-3620
Designer duds and accessories. Who needs the LES?
- **Baked** • 359 Van Brunt St [Dikeman St]
718-222-0345
Death by dessert.
- **Bien Cuit** • 120 Smith St [Pacific St]
718-852-0200
Stand-out breads and pastries.
- **Botanica El Phoenix** •
224 Columbia St [Union St]
718-422-0300
Santeria accessories, religious candles, icons, books.
- **Caputo's Fine Foods** • 460 Court St [3rd Pl]
718-855-8852
Italian gourmet specialties. The real deal.
- **City Foundry** • 369 Atlantic Ave [Hoyt St]
718-923-1786
If you can afford it your place will be in a magazine.
- **Clayworks on Columbia** •
195 Columbia St [Degraw St]
718-858-9256
Unique, practical pottery and classes for all levels.

BoCoCa / Red Hook

Map 32

You can find anything on Atlantic, Smith, or Court Streets, especially food: **Sahadi's**, **Staubitz**, **D'Amico's**, **Caputo's**, **Fish Tales**, and **Smith & Vine** are all great. Treat yourself at **Article & Clayworks on Columbia**'s housewares are made by local artists, **GRDN** has lush plants, **Idlewild Books** is the spot for travel books.

- **D'Amico Foods** • 309 Court St [Degraw St]
  718-875-5403
  The best coffee in the 'hood, if not the city.
- **Erie Basin** • 388 Van Brunt St [Dikeman St]
  718-554-6147
  Jewelry and stuff from the 19th and early 20th century.
- **Eva Gentry Consignment** •
  371 Atlantic Ave [Hoyt St]
  718-522-3522
  Fashionista consignment emporium.
- **Exit 9** • 127 Smith St [Dean St]
  718-422-7720
  Quirky gifts.
- **Fish Tales** • 191 Court St [Wyckoff St]
  718-246-1346
  The place for expensive, but fresh, fish.
- **Gowanus Nursery** • 9 Carroll St [Van Brunt St]
  917-716-8713
  Make your garden happen in a not-so-green 'hood.
- **GRDN** • 103 Hoyt St [Pacific St]
  718-797-3628
  Great store…if you're lucky enough to have a garden.
- **Hard Soul Boutique** •
  418 Atlantic Ave [Bond St]
  718-625-2838
  Fierce jewelry, recording studio founded by Strafe ("Set It Off").
- **Heights Chateau Wines** •
  123 Atlantic Ave [Henry St]
  718-330-0963
  Consistently good store straddling Brooklyn Heights & Cobble Hill.

- **Idlewild Books** • 249 Warren St [Court St]
  Extensive foreign-language offerings and language classes.
- **IKEA** • 1 Beard St [Otsego St]
  718-246-4532
  Everything you need for your 312-sq ft apt.
- **Malko Karkanni Bros.** •
  174 Atlantic Ave [Clinton St]
  718-834-0845
  Cashew Baklava makes you believe again.
- **Mazzola Bakery** • 529 Henry St
  718-643-1719
  Top bakery in CG. Get the lard bread.
- **One Girl Cookies** • 68 Dean St [Smith St]
  212-675-4996
  Custom cookies in Cobble Hill.
- **Red Hook Lobster Pound** •
  284 Van Brunt St [Visitation Pl]
  718-858-7650
  Mmmmm…fresh gorgeous lobsters.
- **Sahadi's** • 187 Atlantic Ave [Court St]
  718-624-4550
  Totally brilliant Middle Eastern supermarket—olives, cheese, bread, etc.
- **Smith & Vine** • 317 Smith St [Douglass St]
  718-243-2864
  If NFT owned a liquor store, this would be it.
- **Staubitz Market** • 222 Court St [Baltic St]
  718-624-0014
  Top NYC butcher.
- **Trader Joe's** • 130 Court St [Court St]
  718-246-8460
  The line moves pretty fast, really.

Park Slope is an easy target. Power moms use their strollers as battering rams, stylish dads use the hippest bars and bistros as daycare centers, and the children, *the children*, they are born into this vicious cycle. But you know what? The Slope isn't just a haven for wealthy breeders and toiling serfs at the **Park Slope Food Co-op**. It's also got some amazing restaurants and shops, incredible brownstones, and the only park in the city that truly rivals Central Park.

The park they're referring to at the top of the slope is **Prospect Park**, Frederick Law Olmsted and Calvert Vaux's Brooklyn masterpiece. The ultimate design was executed piecemeal in the 1860s and 1870s, delayed in part by the Civil War. People, not all of whom from Brooklyn, claim that Prospect Park was the quintessence of Olmsted and Vaux park design, eclipsing a certain little vestpocket nicety that stretches for 50-some-odd blocks in the middle of Manhattan island. Whatever the one-upmanship, the man-made landscape is a pretty nice amenity to have in your backyard. Its charms include its historic bridges and walks, the largest swath of forest in the borough, remarkable summer concerts, a zoo, and last but certainly not least, the rare opportunity to grill in a city park. The Beaux-Arts arch and neoclassical columns around **Grand Army Plaza** were added toward the end of the 19th century. Across from Grand Army Plaza is the fantastic main branch of the **Brooklyn Public Library**.

Park Slope is nineteenth-century brownstone architecture at its best. The rows of houses all have distinct touches on their stoops and facades; idyllic and photo ready. It seems every other block has a soaring limestone church, lending skyline of regal steeples. But that brings us to the modern side: The number of cool shops, restaurants, and bars on 5th Avenue, 7th Avenue, and Flatbush Avenue is simply astounding. (If you look at these three streets on a map, it forms Pi, which clearly means something.) There is so much retail on these streets that you'd think there wouldn't be room for any more, but the action has spread to 4th Avenue and now even 3rd Avenue, near the appalling **Gowanus Canal**, now an EPA Superfund site thanks to decades of factory sediment, coal-tar, heavy metals, paint, sewage, and waste-fed algae.

And the wave of development is expanding ever outward. The world-class **Barclays Center** arena, home court of the Brooklyn Nets and New York Liberty, is a destination for music and basketball fans alike. Sports arenas aside, Vanderbilt and Washington Avenues in Prospect Heights have been bustling commercial strips for years now.

O Landmarks

• **Bailey Fountain** •
Grand Army Plaza [Flatbush Ave]
With sculpted figures of Neptune, Triton and
attendants (some said to represent Wisdom
and Felicity), the power eminating from this
fountain could supply the Justice League.

• **Barclays Center** •
620 Atlantic Ave [Flatbush Ave]
917-618-6100
World-class arena in the heart of Brooklyn.

• **Brooklyn Museum** •
200 Eastern Pkwy [Washington Ave]
718-638-5000
Breathtakingly beautiful building, excellent
collection.

• **Brooklyn Public Library** •
10 Grand Army Plaza [Grand Ave]
718-230-2100
Fabulous Art Deco temple to knowledge.

• **The Co-Cathedral of St. Joseph** •
856 Pacific St [Underhill Ave]
718-638-1071
Check out this stunning just-renovated interior
of this 1912 cathedral. Wow.

• **Grand Army Plaza** • Flatbush Ave & Plaza St
Site of John H. Duncan's Soldiers' and Sailors'
Memorial Arch.

• **New York Puppet Library** •
Grand Army Plaza [Soliders and Sailors Arch]
347-987-3765
The Memorial Arch at Grand Army Plaza has a
funky theatre at the top. A must-see (Summer
Saturdays only).

• **Park Slope Food Co-op** •
782 Union St [7th Ave]
718-622-0560
These farm-fresh veggies will do for those in
search of their peck of dirt. Rinse.

• **Prospect Park** •
Prospect Park W & Flatbush Ave
718-965-8951
Olmsted & Vaux's true masterpiece.

Coffee

• **Café Grumpy** • 383 7th Ave [12th St]
718-499-4404
Gourmet java comes to strollerland.

• **Cafe Martin** • 355 5th Ave [4th St]
Necessary pit stop in the center 'Slope for java.

• **Café Regular du Nord** •
158 Berkeley Pl [7th Ave]
718-783-0673
Almost more lifestyle than café.

• **Colson Patisserie** • 374 9th St [6th Ave]
718-965-6400
French pastries and fancy lunches.

• **Crop to Cup** • 502 3rd Ave [14th St]
347-599-0053
Good Gowanus spot w/ outdoor space.

• **Elk Cafe** •
154 Prospect Park Southwest [Vanderbilt St]
332-220-7410
Perfect spot for coffee across from Prospect
Park.

• **Hungry Ghost** • 253 Flatbush Ave [6th Ave]
718-483-8666
Perfect coffee and a few fun noshes.

• **Konditori** • 187 5th Ave [Berkeley Pl]
347-384-2028
Cozy/packed mini-chain of Swedish
coffeehouses.

• **Kos Kaffe** • 251 5th Ave [Garfield Pl]
718-768-6868
Bright white space with good salads, too.

• **Lincoln Station** •
409 Lincoln Pl [Washington Ave]
718-399-2211
Coffee, sandwiches, and, most importantly,
fried chicken.

• **Penny House Cafe** •
732 Washington Ave [Prospect Pl]
347-240-7281
Yet another great option for coffee on
Washington.

• **Postmark Café** • 326 6th St [5th Ave]
718-768-2613
Cozy coffee shop w/ chess, too!

• **Root Hill Cafe** • 262 4th Ave [Carroll St]
718-855-3475
A bit of calm on traffic-choked 4th Ave.

• **Sit & Wonder** •
688 Washington Ave [St Marks Ave]
718-622-0299
Good hangover sandwiches and Stumptown
Coffee.

Gourmet cocktails and beers have been sprouting up everywhere at spots like **Union Hall**, or support your local dive at **Freddy's**. Since the untimely demise of Southpaw, **The Bell House** is the place for rock shows and comedy events, but **Barbes** has a fabulous mix of world music jammed into its tiny back room space.

Farmers Markets

- **Bartel-Pritchard Square Greenmarket** •
  Prospect Park W & 15th St
  Wednesday, 8 am–2 pm, year-round. and
  Sunday, 9 am–2 pm, May–Dec.
- **Grand Army Plaza Greenmarket** •
  Flatbush Ave & Eastern Pkwy
  Saturday, 8 am–3 pm, year-round.
- **Park Slope Farmers Market** • 5th Ave & 4th St
  Sunday, 9 am–2 pm, year-round.

Nightlife

- **4th Avenue Pub** • 76 4th Ave [Bergen St]
  718-643-2273
  1. Toss darts. 2. Drink fine draft beer. 3. Repeat.
- **Bar Toto** • 411 11th St [6th Ave]
  718-768-4698
  Great bar food.
- **Barbes** • 376 9th St [6th Ave]
  347-422-0248
  Smart-looking space with eclectic
  entertainment. Recommended.
- **The Bell House** • 149 7th St [3rd Ave]
  718-643-6510
  Huge Gowanus live music venue + front bar;
  stellar.
- **Black Horse Pub** • 568 5th Ave [16th St]
  718-788-1975
  Where to watch footy.
- **Brookvin** • 381 7th Ave [12th St]
  718-768-9463
  Wine. Cheese. Ambience.
- **Buttermilk Bar** • 577 5th Ave [16th St]
  718-788-6297
  A solid more-than dive.
- **Canal Bar** • 270 3rd Ave [President St]
  718-246-0011
  Dive near the Gowanus, but not into it.
- **Commonwealth** • 497 5th Ave [12th St]
  718-768-2040
  So many beers, so little time.
- **Double Windsor** •
  210 Prospect Park West [16th St]
  347-725-3479
  Good food. Great beer.
- **Farrell's** • 215 Prospect Park West [16th St]
  718-788-8779
  No frills neighborhood bar with styrofoam
  cups.

Map 33 Park Slope/Prospect Heights/Windsor Terrace

30
31
32
33
Prosp

- **Freddy's Bar and Backroom** •
627 5th Ave [18th St]
718-768-0131
It lives again! And with great avant-jazz
bookings, too.
- **The Gate** • 321 5th Ave [3rd St]
718-768-4329
Large outdoor area. Twenty beers on tap.
- **Ginger's** • 363 5th Ave [5th St]
Nice and casual for center Slope.
- **littlefield** • 635 Sackett St
Eco-friendly performance space: music, film,
art. Sweet.
- **Lucky 13 Saloon** • 644 Sackett St
718-596-0666
Park Slope's only punk/metal dive bar.
- **Park Slope Ale House** • 356 6th Ave [5th St]
718-788-1756
Good pub grub and beer selection.
- **The Sackett** • 661 Sackett St [4th Ave]
718-622-0437
Hidden on a side street. Cozy spot for a
cocktail.

- **Tooker Alley** •
793 Washington Ave [Lincoln Pl]
347-955-4743
Good cocktail spot.
- **Union Hall** • 702 Union St [5th Ave]
718-638-4400
Quirky spot for indie shows and stuffed birds.
- **Washington Commons** •
748 Washington Ave [Park Pl]
718-230-3666
Rotating beer selection, late happy hour, and a
great outdoor space.
- **Weather Up** • 589 Vanderbilt Ave [Dean St]
Pricey cocktails are justified by very cool
ambience.

Where to begin? There's the Italian at **Al Di La** and Portuguese/Italian at **Convivium Osteria**. Branch out with Colombian at **Bogota** and Ethiopian at **Ghenet**. Then there's the classic diner **Tom's**.

Restaurants

- **7th Avenue Donuts** • 324 7th Ave [9th St]
718-768-3410 • $
Dirt-cheap dinery goodness.
- **al di la Trattoria** • 248 5th Ave [Carroll St]
718-783-4565 • $$$
Chandelier & brick-walled Italian. Super.
- **Alchemy** • 56 5th Ave [Bergen St]
718-636-4385 • $$$
Slick pub grub near Barclays Center. Check it out.
- **Amorina** • 624 Vanderbilt Ave [Prospect Pl]
718-230-3030 • $$$
Watch your perfect pizza get made with sea salt and love.
- **Bogota Latin Bistro** •
141 5th Ave [St Johns Pl]
718-230-3805 • $$$
Stylish South- and Central-American restaurant.
- **Bonnie's Grill** • 278 5th Ave [1st St]
718-369-9527 • $$
Habit-forming contemporary diner.
- **Bricolage** • 162 5th Ave [Degraw St]
718-230-1835 • $$$
Buzzy Vietnamese with delish crispy rolls.

- **Cheryl's Global Soul** •
236 Underhill Ave [Lincoln Pl]
347-529-2855 • $$
Modern, international menu emphasizing comfort.
- **Convivium Osteria** • 68 5th Ave [St Marks Pl]
718-857-1833 • $$$$
Delicious Italian with a Portugese influence. Rustic, warm setting.
- **Cooklyn** • 153 Amity St
917-420-0420 • $$$
Duck spaghetti and octopus on Vanderbilt. Nice one.
- **Cousin John's Café and Bakery** •
70 7th Ave [Lincoln Pl]
718-622-7333 • $
Casual breakfast and lunch.
- **Dinosaur Bar-B-Que** • 604 Union St [4th Ave]
347-429-7030 • $$$
Syracuse BBQ empire.
- **Elora's** • 272 Prospect Park West [17th St]
718-788-6190 • $$
Spanish, Mexican, and margaritas, oh my!

- **Fonda** • 434 7th Ave [14th St]
  718-369-3144 • $$$
  Neighborhood Mexican beloved by all.
- **Four & Twenty Blackbirds** •
  439 3rd Ave [8th St]
  718-499 2917 • $$
  Seasonal pies (and other treats) baked fresh
  daily. Delicious goodness!
- **Geido** • 331 Flatbush Ave [7th Ave]
  718-638-8866 • $
  Get stuffed to the gills.
- **Gen Restaurant** •
  659 Washington Ave [St Marks Ave]
  718-398-3550 • $$$
  Delicious, fresh Japanese cuisine and laid-back
  service.
- **Ghenet Brooklyn** • 348 Douglass St [4th Ave]
  718-230-4475 • $$
  Top NYC Ethiopian, hands-down.
- **Hanco's** • 350 7th Ave [10th St]
  718-499-8081 • $
  Banh mi and bubble tea hotspot.
- **The Islands** • 671 Washington Ave [Lincoln Pl]
  718-398-3575 • $$
  Tasty Caribbean; get the jerk chicken.
- **Java Indonesian Rijsttafel** •
  455 7th Ave [16th St]
  718-832-4583 • $$
  Mom-and-pop Indonesian, natch!
- **Jpan Sushi** • 287 5th Ave [1st St]
  718-788-2880 • $$$
  Excellent, inventive special rolls; weird space.

- **Krupa Grocery** •
  231 Prospect Park West [Windsor Pl]
  718-709-7098 • $$$
  Salt cod croquettes and plenty of alcohol.
- **Littleneck** • 288 3rd Ave [Carroll St]
  718-522-1921 • $$$
  Hip oysters and seafood steps from the
  pastoral Gowanus.
- **Lobo** • 218 Court St
  718-858-7739 • $$
  Guilty pleasure Tex-Mex, not Mexican, plenty
  of tequila.
- **Milk Bar** • 620 Vanderbilt Ave [Prospect Pl]
  718-230-0844 •
  Australian-inflected cafe; unrelated to Chang
  empire.
- **Mitchell's Soul Food** •
  617 Vanderbilt Ave [St Marks Ave]
  718-789-3212 • $
  Seedy, cheap soul food.
- **Ogliastro** • 784 Washington Ave [Sterling Pl]
  718-789-3700 • $$$
  An A-one pizza joint on Washington Ave.
- **Olivier Bistro** • 469 4th Ave [11th St]
  718-768-6600 • $$$
  Steak frites and a good brunch on, yes, 4th
  Ave.
- **Palo Santo** • 652 Union St [4th Ave]
  718-636-6311 • $$$
  South American elegance for date night.

Go to **Bar Chuko** for buzzy izakaya-style Japanese. Also, don't miss the warm and eclectic **Stone Park Cafe** and the burgers at **Bonnie's Grill**.

- **Pino's La Forchetta** • 181 7th Ave [2nd St]
  718-965-4020 • $
  Pizza heavyweight on the Slope.
- **Puerto Viejo** • 564 Grand Ave [Dean St]
  718-398-3758 • $$
  Perfect. Hands-down top NYC Dominican.
  Eat it all.
- **Runner & Stone** • 285 3rd Ave [Carroll St]
  718-576-3360 • $$$
  Coffee, bakery, brunch, and dinner, all good.
- **Scottadito Osteria Toscana** •
  788 Union St [7th Ave]
  718-636-4800 • $$$
  Rustic Tuscan, with wallet-friendly prix fixe
  specials.
- **Shake Shack** • 170 Flatbush Ave [5th Ave]
  347-442-7711 • $$
  Danny Meyer's pitch-perfect burgers, across
  from Barclays Center.
- **Smiling Pizzeria** • 323 7th Ave [9th St]
  718-788-2137 • $
  Good quick happy slices.

- **Song** • 295 5th Ave [2nd St]
  718-965-1108 • $
  Essential, tasty Thai in a pinch.
- **Sotto Voce** • 225 7th Ave [4th St]
  718-369-9322 • $$$
  Italian cuisine with better brunch options.
- **Stone Park Cafe** • 324 5th Ave [3rd St]
  718-369-0082 • $$$$
  Definitely a contender for best Park Slope
  dining.
- **Tom's** • 782 Washington Ave [Sterling Pl]
  718-636-9738 • $$
  Old-school mom-and-pop diner since 1936. A
  cholesterol love affair.
- **The V-Spot** • 156 5th Ave [Degraw St]
  718-928-8778 • $$
  Loads of "meat" options, good for the veggie
  initiate.
- **Wangs** • 671 Union St [4th Ave]
  718-636-6390 • $$
  We are wooed by Wangs' wings.
- **White Tiger** • 601 Vanderbilt Ave [Bergen St]
  718-552-2272 • $$$
  Korean cocktails and small plates. Therefore,
  delicious.
- **Windsor Café** •
  220 Prospect Park West [16th St]
  718-788-9700 • $$
  American diner with something for everyone.

Map 33

Park Slope/Prospect Heights/Windsor Terrace

30
31
32
33
Prosp

🔒 Shopping

- **A Cheng** • 466 Bergen St
  718-783-2826
  Modern classic women's clothing.
- **Beacon's Closet** • 92 5th Ave [Warren St]
  718-230-1630
  Rad resale with lots of gems.
- **Big Nose Full Body** • 389 7th Ave [11th St]
  718-369-4030
  Interesting, diverse rotating stock of wine.
- **Bitter & Esters** •
  700 Washington Ave [St Mark's Ave]
  917-596-7261
  Homebrew kits and supplies in Prospect
  Heights.
- **Bklyn Larder** • 228 Flatbush Ave [Bergen St]
  718-783-1250
  Take home a taste of Franny's every night.
- **Blue Sky Bakery** • 53 5th Ave [St Marks Ave]
  718-783-4123
  Moist muffins full of fresh fruit.

- **Brooklyn Museum** •
  200 Eastern Pkwy [Washington Ave]
  718-638-5000
  Usual art-related offerings plus fun Brooklyn-
  made items.
- **Brooklyn Superhero Supply Co.** •
  372 5th Ave [5th St]
  718-499-9884
  Capes, treasure maps, and bottled special
  powers. Also, McSweeney's publications.
- **Community Book Store** •
  143 7th Ave [Garfield Pl]
  718-783-3075
  General books.
- **Dixon's Bicycle Shop** • 792 Union St [7th Ave]
  718-636-0067
  Classic, friendly, family-owned bike shop.
- **Fermented Grapes Wines & Spirits** •
  651 Vanderbilt Ave [Prospect Pl]
  718-230-3216
  Diverse, affordable selection of wines & spirits
  in Prospect Heights.
- **Fifth Avenue Record & Tape Center** •
  439 5th Ave [9th St]
  929-295-0566
  Unassuming locale for surprising finds.

For food (and beer), try **Bklyn Larder**, **Russo's**, and **United Meat**. **Beacon's Closet** is still a clothing destination, **Dixon's** is a classic bike shop, and get your capes and lasers at **Brooklyn Superhero Supply**.

- **Gureje** • 886 Pacific St [Underhill Ave]
718-541-4307
West African flavored clothing, with a music club in the back!
- **Housing Works Thrift Shop** •
266 5th Ave [Carroll St]
718-636-2271
Used books, shabby-chic home decor, and vintage designer ware.
- **JackRabbit Sports** • 151 7th Ave [Garfield Pl]
917-780-4446
Mecca for runners, swimmers, and cyclists.
- **Prospect Wine Shop** • 322 7th Ave [8th St]
718-768-1232
Well-edited and gets the job done.

- **Ride Brooklyn** • 468 Bergen St [5th Ave]
718-857-7433
Friendly and helpful bike store.
- **Russo's Fresh Mozzarella & Pasta** •
312 5th Ave
718-788-6699
Homemade pasta and sauce. Yum.
- **Slope Cellars** • 436 7th Ave [15th St]
718-369-7307
Helpful staff and wine club loyalty card.
- **Sterling Grapes & Grains** •
115 5th Ave [Sterling Pl]
718-789-9521
Known around the 'hood for good prices.
- **Terrace Books** •
242 Prospect Park W [Prospect Ave]
718-788-3475
Used & new.
- **Trailer Park** • 77 Sterling Pl [6th Ave]
718-623-2170
Unique and handcrafted furnishings.
- **United Meat Market** •
219 Prospect Park West [16th St]
718-768-7231
Butchered sheep flesh never tasted so good.
- **Unnameable Books** •
615 Vanderbilt Ave [St Marks Ave]
718-789-1534
General new and used.

Map 34 · Hoboken

Ⓝ

1

2

to Pier 78
38th St

Viaduct

14th St
13th St
12th St
11th St
10th St
9th St
8th St
7th St
6th St
5th St
4th St
3rd St
2nd St
1st St

Palisade Ave
S Wing Viaduct
Paterson Plank Rd
Paterson St

Monroe St
Madison St
Jefferson St
Adams St
Grand St
Clinton St
Willow Ave
Park Ave
Garden St
Bloomfield St
Washington St
Hudson St

Hoboken
Historical
Museum

Hoboken North
Ferries

Elysian
Park

Castle Point Ter

Sinatra Dr

Hudson
River

HOBOKEN

JFK
Stadium

Columbus
Park

Willow
Terrace

Frank Sinatra's
Childhood House
Location

Church
Square
Park

Stevens
Institute of
Technology

River St

Stevens
Park

Harrison St
Jackson St
Monroe St
Madison St
Jefferson St
Adams St
Grand St
Clinton St

Court St
Hudson St
River St
Sinatra Dr

Newark St

To Pier 78
38th St

Pier A
Park

Hoboken
Terminal

PAGE
300

Hoboken
South
Ferries

To World
Financial
Center

Hudson Pl

To Pier 11
Wall St

Observer Hwy

Paterson St
Newark Ave
Manila Ave
Luis M Marin Blvd

Hoboken

Hoboken - PATH,
NJ Transit, Light Rail

PAGE
312

35

PATH

1/4 mile

.25 km

Map 35 · **Jersey City**

N

1

17th St

18th St

2

New Jersey Tpke

Hoboken Ave

Coles St

Jersey Ave

Erie St

16th St

15th St

Grove St

34

14th St

13th St

Provost St

Hudson-Bergen Light Rail

Washington Blvd

North Blvd

Holland Tunnel

78

11th St

10th St

Newport Pkwy

Newport

Newport Ferries

River Dr

A

City Park

Pavonia Ave

Hamilton Pl

McWilliams Pl

Hamilton Park

9th St

Pavonia Ave

8th St

Luis Munoz Marin Blvd

Court St

Newport Center Mall

Mall Dr

Newport

Pavonia/Newport

Pavonia Ave

Division St

Brunswick St

Monmouth St

Coles St

Jersey Ave

7th St

6th St

5th St

Erie St

4th St

Manila Ave

Thomas Gangemi Dr

PATH

PAGE 300

Harborside Ferries

Mary Benson Park

Newark Ave

3rd St

2nd St

1st St

3rd St

2nd St

1st St

Metro Dr

Harsimus Cove

Harborside

Brunswick St

Maxwell St

Bay St

Provost St

Warren St

Powerhouse

Washington St

Harborside Shopping Complex

PATH

Christopher Columbus Dr

Wayne St

Mercer St

Morgan St

Steuben St

Grove Street

Christopher Columbus Dr

Montgomery St

Monmouth St

Varick St

York St

Bright St

Van Vorst Park

Grove St

City Hall

Washington St

PAGE 312

Exchange Place

B

Colden St

Barrow St

Montgomery St

Exchange Pl

Colgate Clock

Grand St

Canal St

Canal St

York St

Van Vorst St

Grand St

Sussex St

Washington St

Greene St

Hudson St

Colgate Ferries

Jersey Ave

Hudson-Bergen Light Rail

Jersey Ave

Marin Blvd

Morris St

Essex St

PAGE 300

Essex St

Liberty Harbor Ferries

Warren St

Dudley St

Hudson River

| 1/4 mile | | .25 km |

The Bronx

Westchester

Woodlawn

Van Cortlandt
Golf Course

Wave Hill

Van Cortlandt
Park

Riverdale

Marble
Hill

Henry
Hudson
Bridge

University
Heights
Bridge

Washington
Bridge

Hamilton
Bridge

Macombs
Dam Bridge

145 St
Bridge

Madison Ave
Bridge

3rd Ave
Bridge

Willis Ave
Bridge

RFK
Bridge

MANHATTAN

Hudson
River

Woodlawn
Cemetery

Jerome Ave

Mosholu
Golf Course

Norwood

Harris
Park

Kings-
Bridge
Heights

University
Heights

Morris
Heights

Cross Bronx

Claremont
Park

Claremont
Village

Morrisania

Yankee
Stadium

Mott Haven

Port
Morris

Wakefield
E 233rd St.

Williamsbridge

Gun Hill Rd

New York
Botanical
Garden

Fordham
University

Belmont

Tremont

E Tremont Ave

Crotona
Park

Bronx Zoo

East
Tremont

West
Farms

Sheridan

Bruckner

Bronx
River

Baychester Ave

Seton
Falls
Park

Eastchester

Co-Op
City

Haffen
Park

Baychester

BRONX

Morris
Park

Williams Bridge Rd

Bronx and Pelham Expwy

Parkchester

Cross Bronx Expy

Castle Hill Ave

Castle
Hill

Soundview

Clason
Point

Sound View Park

Hunts Point

Pelham
Bay
Park

Shore Rd

Orchard
Beach

Hunters
Island

Rodman
Neck

Eastchester
Bay

Pelham
Bay
Park

Bruckner Expy

Pelham
Bay

St Raymond's
Cemetery

Ferry
Point
Park

Bronx
Whitestone
Bridge

Throgs
Neck

Flushing
Bay

Riker's
Island

QUEENS

Don't be afraid of the Boogie Down Bronx. Decades of entrenched poverty and poor urban planning once frayed many neighborhoods, but the borough today is no longer the burning wreck your parents warned you about years ago.

Communities

Belmont's Arthur Avenue (3) is still an authentic Little Italy even though many businesses now belong to Albanians. Woodlawn (9) is home to many Irish immigrants and it's got the pubs to prove it. With 15,372 units, towering Co-op City (13) is rightly called a city within the city; it even has its own mall! The Mott Haven (14) and Longwood (15) historic districts boast beautiful homes, but "The Hub" (16) features the grand architecture of the past conveniently filled with the discount shopping of today. For antiques, visit the cobblestone corridor of Bruckner Boulevard (17) at Alexander Avenue. Some of the city's grandest homes sit in the wooded environs of Riverdale (4), while City Island (12) resembles nothing so much as a New England fishing village crossed with a New Jersey suburb.

Culture

The New York Botanical Garden (8) and the Bronx Zoo (10) are justly famous, well worth whatever effort it may take to get there. For a beautiful view of the Hudson and the Palisades beyond, choose the botanical garden and historic estate Wave Hill (5) or the quirky Hall of Fame for Great Americans (2) featuring 98 bronze busts of notable citizens in a grand outdoor colonnade. Explore your inner Goth at historic Woodlawn Cemetery (7) or Poe Cottage (18), the American poet's final home. Bronx Museum focuses on 20th- and 21st-century art by African, Asian, and Latin American artists, and it's completely free (and open late on Fridays).

Sports

New Yankee Stadium (1) is not so new anymore, and Old Yankee Stadium is a distant memory, except for its field, which has been preserved across the street. Get the cheapest ticket you can find and just spend the game walking around the concourses, which have the best views of the field. Van Cortlandt Park (6) offers playgrounds, ballfields, tennis and basketball courts, hiking trails, stables for horseback riding, and one of golf's classic courses, "Vanny."

Nature

The restoration of the Bronx River (19) coincides with the improvement of green spaces throughout the borough. Pelham Bay Park (11) is the city's largest at 2,764 acres, offering many recreational opportunities in addition to the Thomas Pell Wildlife Sanctuary, two nature centers, and immensely popular Orchard Beach.

Food

Belmont:
- Dominick's, 2335 Arthur Ave, 718-733-2807. Famous old-school Italian-American where there are no menus and no set prices.
- Full Moon, 600 East 187th St, 718-584-3451—Wonderful pizza and calzones.
- Roberto's Restaurant, 603 Crescent Ave, 718-733-9503. Classic fare; it's that good.
- Trattoria Zero Otto Nove, 2357 Arthur Ave, 718-220-1027. Best high-end pizza in the borough at Roberto sister restaurant.
- Arthur Avenue Retail Market, 2344 Arthur Ave, 718-220-0346. Get all the right ingredients for home-cooked Italian meals.

City Island:
- Johnny's Reef, 2 City Island Ave, 718-885-2086. Local favorite for fresh, inexpensive seafood.

Riverdale:
- An Beal Bocht, 445 West 238th St, 718-884-7127. Café/bar/coffee shop hangout for the hip, young, and Irish.
- S &S Cheesecake, 222 West 238th St, 718-549-3888. Forget Junior's, this is the city's best.

Concourse Village:
- Eating Tree, 892 Gerard Ave, 718-293-5025. Delicious Jamaican food close to Yankee Stadium.

Kingsbridge:
- El Economico, 5589 Broadway, 718-796-4851. Homestyle Puerto Rican meals.

Bedford Park:
- Com Tam Ninh Kieu, 2641 Jerome Ave, 718-450-3833. Best Vietnamese in the Bronx; order the pho.

Pelham Bay:
Louie & Ernie's, 1300 Crosby Ave, 718-829-6230. Thin-crust casual pizza that rivals best in the borough.

Parkchester:
- Taqueria Tlaxcalli, 2103 Starling Ave, 347-851-3085. Authentic Mexican dishes.

Landmarks

1 Yankee Stadium
2 Hall of Fame for Great Americans
3 Arthur Avenue
4 Riverdale
5 Wave Hill
6 Van Cortlandt Park
7 Woodlawn Cemetery
8 New York Botanical Garden
9 Woodlawn
10 Bronx Zoo
11 Pelham Bay Park
12 City Island
13 Co-op City
14 Mott Haven
15 Longwood
16 The Hub
17 Bruckner Boulevard
18 Poe Cottage
19 Bronx River
20 Bronx Museum of the Arts

Thanks to the Great Mistake of 1898, Brooklyn is no longer its own city, but that little technicality hasn't kept the Borough of Kings down. As Manhattan becomes prohibitively expensive and middle-Americanized, Brooklyn's popularity is at an all-time high. Scores of recent college grads, immigrants, ex-Manhattanites, and even celebrities are calling Brooklyn home, whether in a row of brownstones, a pre-war house, or a brand-new high-rise. Along with the residential boom, Brooklyn has firmly arrived as a cultural and entertainment mecca, and it boasts some of the hottest bars, astounding cultural diversity, and stellar parks. Atlantic Yards is now a reality after much protest, but Brooklyn won't let go of its unique character that easily.

Communities

As the largest borough by population (over 2.5 million!), Brooklyn holds a special place as one of the nation's most remarkable urban areas. As many as one in four people can trace their roots here! In Brooklyn, you can find pretty much any type of community—for better or worse. As gentrification marches deeper into Brooklyn, the borough is changing fast.

The first thing you notice when looking at Brooklyn on a map is the sheer size of it. Yet much of Brooklyn is largely unknown to most New Yorkers. Yes, Brooklyn Heights, Williamsburg, and Park Slope are nice communities that are fun to explore. However, if you've never ventured further out into Brooklyn than the obligatory trip to Coney Island, you're missing some fantastic neighborhoods. For instance, Bay Ridge (4) has beautiful single-family homes along its western edge, a killer view of the Verrazano Bridge, and a host of excellent shops and restaurants. Dyker Heights (6) is composed of almost all single-family homes, many of which go all-out with Christmas light displays during the holiday season. Brighton Beach (8) continues to be a haven for many Russian expatriates. The quiet, tree-lined streets of both Ocean Parkway (10) and Midwood (11) can make one forget all about the hustle and bustle of downtown Brooklyn, or downtown anywhere else for that matter. Finally, Bedford-Stuyvesant (12) has a host of cool public buildings, fun eateries, and beautiful brownstones.

Sports

No, the Dodgers are never coming back. This is still hard for many older Brooklynites to accept and accounts for much of the nostalgia that is still associated with the borough. If you can get beyond the fact that Ebbets Field is now a giant concrete housing complex, then you will enjoy spending a fine summer evening watching the Cyclones at Coney Island (7). But really, Brooklynites need to get over it: The Barclays Center (15) is home to two professional basketball teams, the Brooklyn Nets of the NBA and the WNBA's New York Liberty. Elsewhere, Kensington Stables in Prospect Park (1) provides lessons for wannabe equestrians.

Attractions

Coney Island's (7) redevelopment is well underway but has left untouched the Cyclone, the Wonder Wheel, Nathan's, Totonno's pizza, movies at the Coney Island Museum, the beach, the freaks, and The Warriors. Close by is the Aquarium (13). Nature trails, parked blimps, views of the water, scenic marinas, live events and overnight camping all make historical Floyd Bennett Field (9) a worthwhile trip. For more beautiful views, you can check out Owl's Point Park (3) in Bay Ridge, or the parking lot underneath the Verrazano-Narrows Bridge (5) (located right off the Shore Parkway). The Verrazano might not be New York's most beautiful bridge, but it's hands-down the most awe-inspiring. Both Green-Wood Cemetery (2) and Prospect Park (1) provide enough greenery to keep you happy until you get to Yosemite. Finally, Brooklyn Heights (14) is the most beautiful residential neighborhood in all of New York. Don't believe us? Go stand on the corner of Willow and Orange Streets and find out for yourself.

Food

Here are some restaurants in some of the outlying areas of Brooklyn:

Midwood: **DiFara's Pizzeria**, E 15th St & Ave J, 718-258-1367—Dirty, cheap, and fresh as hell.

Sunset Park: **Langkawi**, 5323 Eighth Ave, 718-633-0808—Good quality Malaysian.

Sheepshead Bay: **Russian Bath of NY**, 1200 Gravesend Neck Rd, 718-332-1676—Delicious Russian food after a schvitz.

Landmarks

1 Prospect Park

2 Green-Wood Cemetery	7 Coney Island	12 Bedford-Stuyvesant
3 Owl's Point Park	8 Brighton Beach	13 New York Aquarium
4 Bay Ridge	9 Floyd Bennett Field	14 Brooklyn Heights
5 Verrazano-Narrows Bridge	10 Ocean Parkway	15 Barclays Center
6 Dyker Heights	10 Midwood	

The most diverse borough in the city, people from all over have been "discovering" Queens for years, making it home to some of the city's best ethnic restaurants and neighborhoods. Flushing's Chinatown is rivaling Manhattan's as the center of New York's Chinese community. Queens also has some of the city's best open spaces with everything from forestland to surfing beaches. And at a time when Brooklyn real estate prices push higher and higher toward Manhattan extremes, Queens is a great alternative for those who are willing to explore a little.

Communities

From the stately Tudor homes of Forest Hills Gardens (28) to the hip-hop beat of Jamaica Avenue (11), Queens has it all. Eastern Queens tends toward suburbia, while the communities along the borough's southern border often include active industrial districts. All things Asian can be found in Flushing (20), the city's largest Chinatown. Sunnyside (21) and Woodside (22) are home to Irish and Mexican immigrants alike, making it easy to find a proper pint and a fabulous taco on the same block. Jackson Heights' (6) 74th Street is Little India, while 82nd Street is packed with South and Central American businesses. Corona (23) blends old-school Italian-American delis with Latino dance clubs. Elmhurst (24) has attracted Asian, Southeast Asian, and South American immigrants to set up shop on its crowded streets. Island Broad Channel (12) feels like a sleepy village, while the Rockaways (13) offer the only surfing beaches in the city.

Culture

Fans of contemporary art have long known P.S.1 (4) is the place to be, especially during its summer weekend WarmUp parties. Then head over to the Sculpture Center (31), to see what new exhibit they've cooked up for us. The Noguchi Museum (3), dedicated to the work of the Japanese-American sculptor, and neighboring Socrates Sculpture Park (2), a waterfront space with changing exhibitions, attract visitors from far beyond the five boroughs. The Fisher Landau Center for Art (25) features a world-class collection of modern art (and is free, to boot). Movie buffs should look for repertory screenings at the Museum of the Moving Image (5). The delightfully kitschy Louis Armstrong House (26) is a must-see for jazz lovers. In Flushing Meadows Corona Park, the New York Hall of Science (8) beckons the geeky kid in all of us with its hands-on exhibits while the Queens Museum of Art's (9) scale model of the entire city will wow even the most jaded New Yorkers.

Sports

In 2009, the Mets inaugurated a brand new place to make memories of exquisite disappointment, Citi Field, just in time for the team's ownership and its corporate sponsor to lose proverbial shirts. The U.S. Open takes place right across the street at the Billie Jean King National Tennis Center (7). Check out girls gone wild when our local ladies, The Queens of Pain, compete in the Gotham Girls Roller Derby league. See the ponies and fritter away your hard-earned cash at the Aqueduct Racetrack (14). Hitch a ride to Rockaway Beach (13) for swimming and surfing or paddle out in a kayak on loan from the Long Island City Community Boathouse (27). Astoria Pool (1) is the city's largest with room for 3,000 swimmers. For bowling, all-night Whitestone Lanes (18) is the place to be.

Nature

Gantry Plaza State Park's (29) spacious piers attract strollers and urban fishermen alike with panoramic views of the Manhattan skyline, and a major park expansion will eventually connect the waterfront from Anable Basin to the north all the way down to Newtown Creek. The Jamaica Bay Wildlife Refuge (15) in Gateway National Recreation Area is internationally known for bird-watching. Queens Botanical Garden is a peaceful refuge with its own bee hives out in Flushing. Fort Tilden is becoming more popular, but it's still one of New York's prettiest, natural, non-commercial beaches. Flushing Meadows Corona Park (30) is designed for active recreation, but Alley Pond Park (16) and Forest Park (17) have wooded trails perfect for wandering.

Food

Entire books have been written on where to eat in Queens, so these are just a handful of suggestions:
Corona: **Leo's Latticini** (a.k.a. Mama's), 46-02 104th St, 718-898-6069—Insanely good Italian sandwiches that pair well with dessert from the **Lemon Ice King**, 52-02 108th St, 718-897-9090—a few blocks away.
Rego Park: **Cheburechnaya**, 92-09 63rd Dr, 718-897-9080—grilled meats are the speciality at this Kosher Uzbek gem.
Sunnyside: **De Mole**, 45-02 48th Ave, 718-392-2161— Fresh, simply prepared Mexican food in bistro setting.
Bayside: **Uncle Jack's**, 39-40 Bell Blvd, 718-229-1100—Mayor Bloomberg's favorite steakhouse serves up fine flesh.
Woodside: **Sripraphai**, 64-13 39th Ave, 718-899-9599—Easily the best Thai food in the city; **La Flor**, 53-02 Roosevelt Ave, 718-426-8023—Fantastic neighborhood café with Mexican-inflected dishes.

Landmarks

247

Staten Island

Staten Island, of thee we sing! Don't let the sight of jabronis with fake tans and gelled hair hold you back from exploring, lest you miss out on heaps of excellent pizza, the wild flower meadows at Mount Loretto, the windows on the past at Historic Richmond Town, the small-town charm of minor league baseball at St. George, and the striking design of the Chinese Scholars' Garden at Snug Harbor. It's high time you pulled your head out of your borough and hitched a ride on the ferry, if only to eat at one of SI's "holy trinity" of pizzerias.

Culture

1 Snug Harbor Cultural Center, 1000 Richmond Ter, 718-425-3504. A former sailors' home transformed to a waterfront arts complex, Snug Harbor's 83 acres include classrooms, studio spaces, performance venues, galleries, three museums, and a truly noteworthy botanical garden. Call to learn about cultural events and exhibits on site.

2 Jacques Marchais Museum, 338 Lighthouse Ave, 718-987-3500. A world-class collection of Buddhist art, courtesy of former New York art collector Edna Coblentz, who had the surprising French pseudonym Jacques Marchais.

3 Historic Richmond Town, 441 Clarke Ave, 718-351-1611. Get back to old-timey times visiting restored homes from the 17th to the 19th centuries, most populated by costumed guides. Great for kids and adults who want to learn how to churn butter/forge metal.

4 Wagner College, 1 Campus Rd, 718-390-3100. Wagner's tranquil hilltop location rewards visitors with beautiful views of the serene surroundings, but its best feature is the planetarium.

5 Staten Island Village Hall, 111 Canal St. Last remaining village hall building in Staten Island, a reminder of the borough's rural past.

6 Alice Austen House, 2 Hylan Blvd, 718-816-4506. Alice Austen was an early twentieth-century amateur photographer, and now she's got a museum and a ferry boat named after her. Go figure. Some of her 8,000 images are on view at her house, which has a great view of lower New York Harbor.

Nature

7 Staten Island Greenbelt, 700 Rockland Ave, 718-351-3450. This 2,800-acre swath of land (comprising several different parks) in the center of the island contains a golf course, a hospital, a scout camp, several graveyards, and plenty of wooded areas that remain relatively undeveloped and can be accessed only by walking trails. A good starting point is High Rock Park. Panoramic views abound.

8 Blue Heron Park, 222 Poillon Ave, 718-967-3542. This quiet, 236-acre park has a fantastic Nature Center and plenty of ponds, wetlands, and streams to explore. Noted for bird-watching, hence the name.

9 Great Kills Park, 212-639-9675. Part of the Gateway National Recreation Area, Great Kills boasts clean beaches, a marina, and a nature preserve.

10 Mount Loretto Unique Area, 20 Kenny Rd, 718-482-4900. Flourishing wetlands, grasslands, and beaches all rolled into one serenely beautiful waterfront park. Mysterious sculptures dot the beach.

11 Conference House Park, 298 Satterlee 718-984-6046.The historic house is worth a look, but watching the sunset from the restored waterfront pavilion is a must. You'll also find NYC's very own "South Pole" on the beach here.

12 Clove Lakes Park, Clove Rd and Victory Blvd, 311. Who needs Central Park? Check out these romantic rowboats on the lake in season.

13 Freshkills Park, off Route 440. Former landfill, now a park. Sorta. They're working on it over the next 30 years. Free tours by appointment.

Other

14 110/120 Longfellow Road. Celebrate one of the greatest American films without having to schlep to Sicily. This address is where the Corleone family held court in The Godfather.

15 Ship Graveyard, at Arthur Kill Rd and Rossville Ave. These ships of the damned make a perfect backdrop for Goth photo shoots.

16 Staten Island Zoo, 614 Broadway, 718-442-3100. Kids will go wild here, near the stunning Clove Lakes Park. Be sure to bring them to the vampire bat feedings.

Food

Tompkinsville:
New Asha, 322 Victory Blvd, 718-420-0649. Great Sri Lankan food on the cheap. Spicy!
Port Richmond:
Denino's, 524 Port Richmond Ave, 718-442-9401. Some of the best pizza in town.
Dongan Hills:
Lee's Tavern, 60 Hancock St, 718-667-9749. Great bar with great pizza—get the fresh mozzarella.
Tottenville:
Egger's Ice Cream Parlor, 1194 Forest Ave, 718-981-2110. Old time ice cream and sweets. Kids love it.
Killmeyer's Old Bavaria Inn, 4254 Arthur Kill Rd, 718-984-1202. Historic German beer garden and eats. JÄ¥!
Castleton Corners
Joe & Pat's, 1758 Victory Blvd, 718-981-0887. Completing SI's "Holy Trinity" of pizza.
St. George:
Pier 76 Italian Restaurant, 76 Bay Street, 718-447-7437, What Joe & Pat begat; walking distance to ferry.

Driving In / Through Staten Island

To visit Staten Island, one must either drive/take a bus/take a cab over the Verrazano Bridge (and its ruinously expensive toll) from Bay Ridge, Brooklyn, or catch the ferry from Lower Manhattan. If you elect to do the latter, you'll find myriad buses departing from the St. George side of the ferry as well as the terminal of the Staten Island Railway, ready to whisk you all the way down to Tottenville and back with one swipe of the Metrocard. To reach New Jersey via Staten Island, take the Verrazano to the Staten Island Expressway (Route 278) to Route 440 to the Outerbridge Crossing, and you're almost halfway to Princeton or the Jersey shore. However…the Staten Island Expressway often gets jammed. There are two scenic, though not really quicker, alternatives: one, take Hylan Boulevard all the way south to almost the southwest tip of Staten Island, and then cut up to the Outerbridge Crossing; two, take Richmond Terrace around the north shore and cross to New Jersey via the Goethals Bridge. Remember, neither is really faster, but at least you'll be moving.

General Information

Battery Park City Authority:
212-417-2000

Battery Park City Parks Conservancy:
212-267-9700 or www.bpca.ny.gov

Overview

Welcome to Battery Park City—a master-planned community reminiscent of Pleasantville. Originally the brainchild of Nelson Rockefeller, this urban experiment transformed a WTC construction landfill into a 92-acre planned enclave on the southwestern tip of Manhattan. As space in Manhattan continues to disappear into the stratosphere (literally, the only way to build is up), the idea of BPC requires a doubletake. It's about making public spaces (about 30% of those 92 acres) work within private entities. Imagine taking Central Park, cutting it up, and saying, "Here, your neighborhood can have a chunk of it, and that street down there, and that street over there, too." Admit it: walking among private, commercial spaces day in and day out is enough to make anyone claustrophobic (thank you, Financial District). In BPC you walk through spacious parks with weird statues and brick pavers all on your way to work, the grocery store, the gym, or the movie theater. BPC will have you asking: "What's outside Battery Park City?"

Those looking for all-night eateries and party spots should pass it up, but if you've got kids this is the place for you. Many NY families—roughly 25,000 people—occupy the 40% of BPC that's dedicated residential space, including a future-forward "green" building, the Solaire. Robert F. Wagner Jr. and Rector are good choices for a picnic; The Esplanade or South Cove to walk along the Hudson; Nelson A. Rockefeller to play Frisbee; North Cove to park your yacht; and Teardrop Park for the kids. People of all ages have welcomed the ever-popular Shake Shack (the cheapest meal in the neighborhood), live music at the World Financial Center, and Manhattan's first green LEED-certified branch library.

Seeing: Amazing sculptures by Bourgeois, Otterness, Puryear, Dine, and Cragg. Inspired architecture: Stuyvesant High School, Siah Armajani's Tribeca Bridge, Kevin Roche's Museum of Jewish Heritage, Caesar Pelli's Winter Garden, and the World Financial Center. If you like things nice, neat, and compartmentalized, this 'hood is for you.

O Landmarks

- **The Irish Hunger Memorial** ·
  Vesey St & North End Ave
- **Mercantile Exchange** ·
  1 North End Ave [Vesey St]
- **Museum of Jewish Heritage** ·
  36 Battery Pl [Little West St]
- **Police Memorial** · Liberty St & South End Ave
- **The Skyscraper Museum** ·
  39 Battery Pl [Little West St]
- **Tom Otterness's The Real World Sculptures** ·
  Rockefeller Park
- **Winter Garden** · 37 Vesey St [Church St]

Movie Theaters

- **Regal Battery Park Stadium 11** ·
  102 North End Ave [Vesey St]

Restaurants

- **Black Seed** · 225 Liberty St [South End Ave]
- **Blue Smoke** · 255 Vesey St [North End Ave]
- **El Vez** · 259 Vesey St [North End Ave]
- **Le District** · 225 Liberty St [South End Ave]
- **Mighty Quinn's** ·
  225 Liberty St [South End Ave]
- **P.J. Clarke's on the Hudson** ·
  250 Vesey St [North End Ave]
- **Shake Shack** · 215 Murray St [North End Ave]

Parks & Places · **Central Park**

General Information

Central Park Conservancy: 212-310-6600
Website: www.centralparknyc.org
                             @CentralParkNYC

Overview

Taking a stroll through Central Park is something that tourists and residents can always agree on. This world-class sanctuary is a huge, peaceful lush oasis in the concrete jungle, and who hasn't skipped therapy once or twice in favor of clearing your mind the old-fashioned way, by taking a long walk in the park? On any given day, you'll see people disco roller skating, playing jazz, juggling, walking their dogs, running, making out, meditating, playing softball, whining through soccer practice, getting married, picnicking, and playing chess.

Designed by Frederick Law Olmsted and Calvert Vaux in the 1850s, Central Park has a diverse mix of attractions. The **Central Park Conservancy** (www.centralparknyc.org) leads walking tours, and you can always hail a horse-drawn carriage or bike taxi for a ride through the park if you want to look like a true tourist.

Practicalities

Central Park is easily accessible by subway, since the A, C, B, D, N, R, Q, 1, 2 and 3 trains all circle the park. Parking along CPW is harder, so try side streets. Unless you're heading to the park for a big concert, a softball game, or Shakespeare in the Park, walking or hanging out (especially alone!) in the park at night is not recommended.

Nature

Central Park is the place to see and be seen, for birds, actually; 230 species can be spotted and The Ramble (27) is a good place to stake out. There are an amazing number of both plant and animal species that inhabit the park, including the creatures housed at the zoo (4 & 8). Some people forage for edible plants throughout the park, perhaps out of curiosity, though officials tend to discourage this practice. A good source of information on all of the park's flora and fauna is NYC schoolteacher Leslie Day's book, *Field Guide to the Natural World of New York City*.

Architecture & Sculpture

Central Park was designed to thrill visitors at every turn. The Bethesda Fountain (11), designed by Emma Stebbins, is one of the main attractions of the park. Don't miss the view of Turtle Pond from Belvedere Castle (16). The Arsenal (5) is a wonderful ivy-clad building that houses the Parks Department headquarters. The original Greensward plan for Central Park is located in the Arsenal's third-floor conference room—if there isn't a meeting going on, you might be able to sneak a peek. Two of the most notable sculptures in the park are Alice in Wonderland (15) and the Obelisk (19). Oh, and one other tiny point of interest… the Metropolitan Museum of Art (24) also happens to be in the park.

Open Spaces

New Yorkers covet space. Since they rarely get it in their apartments, they rely on large open areas such as the Great Lawn (26), and Sheep Meadow (28). The Ramble (27) is stocked with trees and is great for hiking around—just use common sense after dark. When it snows, you can find great sledding on Cedar Hill (30), which is otherwise perfect for picnicking and sunbathing.

Performance

In warmer weather, Central Park is a microcosm of the great cultural attractions New York has to offer. The Delacorte Theater (18) is the home of **Shakespeare in the Park**, a New York tradition begun by famous director Joseph Papp. SummerStage (9) is the city's best outdoor concert venue for all types of music, including killer rock shows. Free opera and classical concerts happen all summer long on the Great Lawn (26). Or just enjoy a sing-along with some dude with an acoustic guitar for as long you can stand it at the Imagine memorial to John Lennon at Strawberry Fields (10).

Sports

Rollerblading and roller skating are still popular, as is jogging, especially around the reservoir (1.57 mi). The Great Lawn (26) boasts well-maintained softball fields. Central Park has 30 tennis courts (if you make a reservation, you can walk right on to the clay court with tennis shoes only—212-280-0206), fishing at Harlem Meer, gondola rides and boat rentals at the Loeb Boathouse (13), model boat rentals at the Conservatory Water (14), chess and checkers at the Chess & Checkers House (25), two ice skating rinks (1 & 22), croquet and lawn bowling just north of Sheep Meadow (28), and basketball courts at the North Meadow Rec Center (20). You will also see volleyball, basketball, skateboarding, bicycling, and many pick-up soccer, Frisbee, football, and kill-the-carrier games to join. During heavy snows, bust out your snowboard, cross-country skis, or homemade sled. Finally, Central Park is where the NYC Marathon ends each year.

Landmarks

1 Wollman Rink
2 Carousel
3 The Dairy
4 Central Park Zoo
5 The Arsenal
6 Tavern on the Green
7 Roller Skating Rink
8 Children's Zoo
9 SummerStage

10 Strawberry Fields
11 Bethesda Fountain
12 Bow Bridge
13 Loeb Boathouse
14 Model Boat Racing
15 Alice in Wonderland
16 Belvedere Castle
17 Shakespeare Gardens
18 Delacorte Theater

19 The Obelisk
20 North Meadow Recreation Center
21 Conservatory Garden
22 Lasker Rink
23 Dana Discovery Center
24 Metropolitan Museum of Art

25 Chess & Checkers House
26 The Great Lawn
27 The Ramble
28 Sheep Meadow
29 The Cliff
30 Cedar Hill
31 The Great Hill

Morningside Park

W 122nd St

Grant | Sarasota

Corpus Christi Church

Bancroft | The Fairholm

School of Social Work

Lenfest

W 121st St

Riverside Church

Union Theological Seminary

Claremont Youth Center

Thorndike | Macy | Grace Dodge

Horace Mann

Thompson | Main | Russell | Whittier

Teachers College

Plimpton (Barnard) | Seth Low

W 120th St

60

Interchurch Center

Milbank

Fiske | Minor | Latham Playhouse

Pupin | Schapiro CEPSR | S W Mudd

Hellen Goodhart Altschul | Millicent McIntosh Center

Marcellus Hartley Dodge Physical Fitness Center

Computer Science

419

W 119th St

Elliott Hall (Barnard)

Chandler

Lower Level: University Hall & Gymnasium

Sherman Fairchild Center | Engineering Terrace

Butler Hall

Lehman

Havemeyer

Uris

Schermerhorn

423

W 118th St

Barnard College

Barnard

Mathematics

Computer Center

Avery | Fayerweather

International Affairs | Heyman Center East Campus

Casa Italiana

Earl

Low Memorial Library

St Paul's Chapel

Sulzberger

Hewitt | Barnard Student Store | Helen Reid

Lewisohn

Visitors Center

Buell

Greene Annex | Faculty House

Greene Hall | Wien | President's House

Alma Mater

Brooks

Claremont

Dodge

Maison Francaise

Philosophy

Kent | Ped Bridge

W 116th St

116th Street Columbia University

College Walk

W 116th St

Casa Hispanica

Journalism

Hamilton

King's Crown | Green Nurser School

Woodbridge | Schapiro

Furnald

MAP 18

Hartley

W & J Warren | Deutsches Haus | WC Warren

W 115th St

Watson

Kraft Center

Lion's Court

Wallach

Woman's Hospital | Eli White | Notre Dame Church

St Hilda's & St Hugh's School

Broadway Presbyterian Church

Lerner Hall (Bookstore)

Butler Library

Carman

Harkness Theatre

John Jay

W 114th St

River | 616 | 614 | 606

Hogan

540

Ruggles

St Luke's Hospital

Broadway | Watt

W 113th St

McVickar

McBain | 552 | 514

Amstrong | 535

W 112th St

General Information

NFT Map:	18
Morningside Heights:	2960 Broadway & 116th St
Medical Center:	601 W 168th St
Phone:	212-854-1754
Website:	www.columbia.edu or @Columbia
Students Enrolled:	29,250 (2013)
Endowment:	$8.2 billion (2013)

Overview

Yearning for those carefree days spent debating nihilism in the quad and wearing pajamas in public? Look no further than a quick trip to the Ivy League haven of Columbia University.

Unlike the other collegiate institutions that pepper Manhattan's real estate, Columbia actually has a campus. The main campus, located in Morningside Heights, spans six blocks between Broadway and Amsterdam Avenues. Most of the undergraduate classes are held here, along with several of the graduate schools. Other graduate schools, including the Law School and School of International and Public Affairs, are close by on Amsterdam Avenue. The main libraries, Miller Theater, and St. Paul's Chapel are also located on the Morningside Heights campus. You can even get your intramural fix on a few fields for Frisbee-throwing and pick-up soccer games.

Founded in 1754 as King's College, Columbia University is one of the country's most prestigious academic institutions. The university is well known for its core curriculum, a program of requirements that gives students an introduction to the most influential works in literature, philosophy, science, and other disciplines. It also prepares them for the rigors of those pesky dinner parties.

After residing in two different downtown locations, Columbia moved to its present campus (designed by McKim, Mead, and White) in 1897. Low Library remains the focal point of the campus as does the Alma Mater statue in front—a landmark that continues to inspire student superstitions (find the hidden owl and you might be the next valedictorian) thanks to a thwarted plot to blow it up by the radical Weather Underground in the '60s. Students line the stairs in front of the library on sunny days, eating lunch and chatting with classmates. Columbia even has its own spooky network of underground tunnels (third largest in the world) that date back to the old Morningside mental asylum and were utilized by students and police during the 1968 strike.

Town/gown relations in Morningside Heights are quite controversial. While Columbia students show local businesses the money, the university continues to relentlessly buy up property and expand into the community, to the chagrin of many New Yorkers city-wide. The most famous of these struggles came in response to Columbia's plans to build a gymnasium in Morningside Park. Contentious proposals, approved in 2009, for a 17-acre expansion into Manhattanville (the area north of 125th Street) by 2030 still cause tension and fear of evictions, and the debate between the university and old-time residents continues.

Columbia's medical school is the second oldest in the nation, and the world's first academic medical center. The school is affiliated with the Columbia-Presbyterian Medical Center in Washington Heights and encompasses the graduate schools of medicine, dentistry, nursing, and public health. Columbia is the only Ivy League university with a journalism school, which was founded at the bequest of Joseph Pulitzer in 1912. (The prize is still administered there.) The school is also affiliated with Barnard College, Jewish Theological Seminary, Teachers College, and Union Theological Seminary.

Numerous movies have been filmed on or around the campus including *Ghostbusters*, *Hannah and Her Sisters*, and various iterations of *Spiderman*.

Notable alums and faculty include artists James Cagney, Art Garfunkel, Georgia O'Keeffe, Rodgers and Hammerstein, Paul Robeson, and Twyla Tharp; critic Lionel Trilling; baseball player Lou Gehrig; and writers Isaac Asimov, Joseph Heller, Carson McCullers, Eudora Welty, Zora Neale Hurston, and Herman Wouk. Business alumni include Warren Buffet, Alfred Knopf, Joseph Pulitzer, and Milton Friedman, while government officials Madeline Albright, Dwight Eisenhower, Alexander Hamilton, Robert Moses, Franklin Delano Roosevelt, and Teddy Roosevelt all graced the university's classrooms. In the field of law, Benjamin Cardozo, Ruth Bader Ginsburg, Charles Evans Hughes, and John Jay called Columbia home, and Stephen Jay Gould, Margaret Mead, and Benjamin Spock make the list of notable science alumni.

Tuition

Undergraduate tuition is approximately $68,000 per year plus room, board, books, illegal substances, therapy for your inferiority/superiority complex, etc. We suggest: Shacking up with your Aunt Agatha on the Upper West Side for the duration.

Sports

The Columbia Marching Band plays "Roar, Lion, Roar" after every touchdown, but their instruments remain tragically roarless most of the time. The Lions almost set the record for straight losses by a major college football team when they dropped 44 consecutive games between 1983 and 1988. Success has continued to elude the team. The hapless program even inspired a podcast on the local NPR affiliate. The Lions play their mostly Ivy League opponents at Lawrence A. Wien Stadium (Baker Field), located way up at the top of Manhattan.

Columbia excels in other sports including crew, fencing, golf, tennis, and sailing (silver spoon not included). The university is represented by 29 men's and women's teams in the NCAA Division I. It also has the oldest wrestling team in the country.

Culture on Campus

The ire evoked by its controversial immigration speech, when students stormed the stage, pales when compared to Columbia's 2007 invitation to Iranian president Mahmoud Ahmadinejad to participate in a debate. Good or bad, it created much hype and put the campus in the spotlight for a day or two. Columbia does, however, feature plenty of other less volatile stable. Film, music, theater, lectures, readings, and talks. Venues include: the Macy Gallery at the Teacher's College, which exhibits works by a variety of artists, including faculty and children's artwork; the fabulous Miller Theatre at 2960 Broadway, which primarily features musical performances and lectures; the student-run Postcrypt Art Gallery in the basement of St. Paul's Chapel; the Theatre of the Riverside Church for theatrical performances from their top-rated graduate program; and the Wallach Art Gallery on the 8th floor of Schermerhorn Hall, featuring art and architecture exhibits. Check the website for a calendar of events.

Phone Numbers

Morningside Campus: 212-854-4400
Medical Center: 877-426-5637
Visitors Center: 212-854-4900
Office of Communications and Public Affairs: 212-854-5573
Office of Alumni and Development: 212-851-7800
Public Safety: 212-854-2797, 212-854-5555 (emergency)
Library Information: 212-854-7309

Overview

East River Park is a thin slice of land sandwiched between the FDR Drive and the East River, and running from Montgomery Street up to 12th Street. Built in the late 1930s as part of the FDR Drive, the park's sporting facilities are some of the best Manhattan has to offer. The East River Esplanade welcomes runners, rollerbladers, dog-walkers, and those who just want to enjoy up-close views of the Williamsburg Bridge and across to Brooklyn. Long-term plans call for waterfront parkland from The Battery to Harlem, and in fact East River Park is part of an overall plan to someday create one continuous green stretch from Maine to Florida, known as the **East Coast Greenway**.

Attractions

The park comes alive in the summer and on weekends, when hundreds of families barbecue in the areas between the athletic fields, blaring music and eating to their hearts' content. Others take leisurely strolls or jogs along the East River Esplanade, which offers dramatic views of the river and Brooklyn. Many have turned the park's unused areas into unofficial dog runs, places for pick-up games of ultimate Frisbee or soccer, and sunbathing areas. And aside from bathing beauties, you'll even find fishermen waiting patiently for striped bass (not that we have to tell you, but nothing caught in the East River should be eaten—while the water quality has improved dramatically, it's still full of pollutants).

Sports

The sports facilities at East River Park have undergone heavy reconstruction. The park now includes facilities for football, softball, basketball, soccer, tennis, and even cricket. Thankfully, many of the fields have been resurfaced with a resilient synthetic turf—a smart move given the amount of use the park gets by all the different sports leagues.

Parks & Places • East River Park

Facilities

There are three bathroom facilities located in the park—one at the tennis courts, one at the soccer/track field, and one up in the northern part of the park by the playground. The reconstruction has provided East River Park with new benches, game tables, seal sprinklers for the kids, and new water fountains. Aside from the occasional guy with a cart full of cold drinks, there are no food or drink options close by. Your best bet is to arrive at the park with any supplies you might need—if that's too difficult, try a bodega on Avenue D.

Esoterica

Built in 1941, the Corlears Hook Pavilion was the original home of Joseph Papp's Shakespeare in the Park. However, it closed in 1973, and has never quite returned to its glory days. Plans for the fancy $3.5 million amphitheater/restaurant that was to replace the sad-looking, abandoned, graffiti-covered Corlears Hook Pavilion band shell have been canned.

A less ambitious reconstruction took place in 2001, however, and with new seating, a renovated band shell, and a good scrubbing, the facility is currently open for use.

How to Get There

Two FDR Drive exits will get you very close to East River Park—the Houston Street exit and the Grand Street exit. Technically, cars are not allowed in the park. There is some parking available at the extreme south end of the park by Jackson Street off the access road, but it's hard to get to and poorly marked. Plan to find street parking just west of the FDR and cross over on a footbridge.

If you are taking the subway, you'd better have your hiking boots on—the fact that the closest subways (the J, M, Z, F at Delancey/Essex St and the L at First Ave) are so far away (at least four avenue blocks) is one of the reasons East River Park has stayed mainly a neighborhood park. Fortunately, if you're into buses, the M22, M21, M14 and M8 and get you pretty close. Regardless of the bus or subway lines, you will have to cross one of the five pedestrian bridges that traverse the FDR Drive, unless you approach via the East River Esplanade.

General Information

NFT Map: 9
Address: 350 Fifth Ave (& 34th St)
Phone: 212-736-3100
Website: www.esbnyc.com
                        @EmpireStateBldg
Observatory Hours: Open daily 365 days a year
                        10 am–9 pm. Last elevators
                        go up at 9:15 pm
Observatory Admission: $44 for adults, $38 for kids,
$42 for seniors, $84 if you want to be a show-off
and cut in front of everyone to the front of the line
(we're not lying with this one, folks…our society is
indeed morally bankrupt).

Overview

There may not be a gorilla climbing it, but if you
don't already know the "World's Most Famous Office
Building," the jig is up, Mac. Put down the NFT and
back away sloowly. You're not a true Manhattanite;
you're not even a well-researched tourist. So, folks,
how did the giant end up perching on our block?
In 1930, at the hands of raw men compounding
raw material day after day, four-and-a-half stories
were erected per week. Those ravaged from the
Depression and eager to put their minds to work
built the 1,500-foot structure in just 14 months, way

ahead of schedule. We used to make stuff in this
country. Quickly.

A year later, it served as an ambassador to visiting
dignitaries like Queen Elizabeth and, years later,
your Aunt Elizabeth. These days it is one of New York
City's (and the world's) most famous landmarks.
Movies have been shot there. Big shots work there.
Wherever you are in Manhattan (and sometimes
Brooklyn or Queens), it's there to orient you. And
you can take plenty of snapshots from the reason-
you-go-there observation deck on the 86th floor. No
trick questions asked. Some New Yorkers think it's
hip to have never been to the Empire State Building.
These people are nuts. Whether you choose to go
during the day or at night, it's a totally different but
amazing experience either way.

The Lights

As far away as downtown and all the way uptown,
the lights of the Empire State Building soar above
the clouds, signifying an international holiday and/
or an interminable disease. On the 86th floor, a man
with binoculars and a direct line to the lighting
engineers waits. His raison d'être? Close-flying flocks
of birds. One phone call, and the lights go out, lest
the poor suckers smash their beaks and plunge to
their death from the mesmerizing lights. True story.

Parks & Places • Empire State Building

Lighting Schedule (for updates/changes, check www.esbnyc.com)

- January • Martin Luther King, Jr. Day
- January • March of Dimes
- January–February • Lunar New Year
- February 14 • Valentine's Day
- February • President's Day
- February • Westminster Kennel Club
- February • Swisspeaks Festival for Switzerland
- February • World Cup Archery Championship
- March 17 • St. Patrick's Day
- March • Greek Independence Day
- March • Equal Parents Day/Children's Rights
- March • Wales/St. David's Day
- March • Oscar Week in NYC
- March • Colon Cancer Awareness
- March • Red Cross Month
- March–April • Spring/Easter Week
- April • Earth Day
- April • Child Abuse Prevention
- April • National Osteoporosis Society
- April • Rain Forest Day
- April • Israel Independence Day
- April • Dutch Queen's Day
- April • Tartan Day
- May • Muscular Dystrophy
- May • Armed Forces Day
- May • Memorial Day
- May • Police Memorial Day
- May • Fire Department Memorial Day
- May • Haitian Culture Awareness
- June 14 • Flag Day
- June • Portugal Day
- June • NYC Triathlon
- June • Stonewall Anniversary/Gay Pride
- July 4 • Independence Day
- July • Bahamas Independence Day
- July • Bastille Day
- July • Peru Independence
- July • Columbia Heritage & Independence
- August • US Open

- August • Jamaica Independence Day
- August • India Independence Day
- August • Pakistan Independence Day
- September • Mexico Independence Day
- September • Labor Day
- September • Brazil Independence Day
- September • Pulaski Day
- September • Race for the Cure
- September • Switzerland admitted to the UN
- September • Qatar Independence
- September • Fleet Week/Support our Servicemen and Servicewomen/Memorial for 9/11
- September • Feast of San Gennaro
- October • Breast Cancer Awareness
- October • German Reunification Day
- October • Columbus Day
- October 24 • United Nations Day
- October • Big Apple Circus
- October • Pennant/World Series win for the Yankees
- October • Pennant/World Series win for the Mets
- October • NY Knicks Opening Day
- October–November • Autumn
- October • Walk to End Domestic Violence
- November • NYC Marathon
- November • Veterans' Day
- November • Alzheimer's Awareness
- December • First night of Hanukkah
- December • "Day Without Art/Night Without Lights"/AIDS Awareness
- December–January 7 (with interruptions) • Holiday Season

259

Ramp Access

7 34th Street

W 34th St

W 33rd St

A C E 34th Street Penn Station

West Side Rail Yards

W 31st St

J A Farley Post Office

Penn Statio MSG

W 30th St

Hudson River Park

W 29th St

W 28th St

Chelsea Park

Penn

W 27th St

Station

W 26th St

South

W 25th St

Houses

MAP 8

W 24th St

Eleventh Ave

Tenth Ave

Ninth Ave

Eighth Ave

W 23rd St

C E 23rd Street

Chelsea Waterside Park

W 22nd St

Gallery District

CHELSEA

W 21st St

Hudson River

W 20th St

Chelsea Piers

W 19th St

Chelsea Grasslands

W 18th St

W 17th St

10th Avenue Square

W 16th St

Chelsea Market

Chelsea Market Public Art

W 15th St

Diller - Von Furstenberg Sundeck & Water Feature

MEATPACKING DISTRICT

8th Avenu

W 14th St

A C E 14th Street

L

Washington Grasslands

W 13th St

Gansevoort Woodland

Little W 12th St

Gansevoort Plaza

MAP 5

9A

WEST VILLAGE

Stairs

Elevator

The High Line

General Information

NFT Maps: 5 & 8
Website: www.thehighline.org or @highlinenyc

Overview

Built on top of a disused portion of elevated freight train tracks, The High Line is at once both an escape from the chaos of the city's streets and a celebration of Manhattan's West Side, especially its architecture. The first section between Gansevoort Street and West 20th Street opened in 2009 and was an instant success, proving that open space could be hip and stylish, and causing the city tax assessor's heart to race at the thought of all the surrounding property that suddenly deserved a second look. Section 2, which opened in June 2011, doubled the length of the park up to 30th Street. Section 3, completed in 2014, follows the elevated track to its end at 34th Street.

The rail line was built in the 1930s as part of the West Side Improvement project that eliminated dangerous at-grade railroad crossings and alleviated terrible traffic along Manhattan's West Side. The same project expanded Riverside Park on the Upper West Side. As trucking became more efficient, train traffic on the rail line slowed. By 1980 the entire line shut down and quickly fell into disrepair. Many wanted to demolish the line, which was prohibitively expensive, but a grassroots group, Friends of the High Line, slowly built support that became a groundswell, thanks in part to a mayoral administration that didn't mind investing in high-end development. The final cost of sections 1 and 2 was $152.3 million, including $112 million from the city, $20 million from the federal government and nearly $50 million in privately raised funds.

The High Line is open from 7 am to 10 pm daily (7 pm during winter and 11 pm during summer). The entire thing is wheelchair accessible although there are limited access points along the way. Dogs and bicycles are strictly prohibited, though there are bike racks at street level at various access points. Closest subway access is the A, C, and E along Eighth Avenue or the 1 along Seventh Avenue. The M11, M14, M23 and M34 buses also travel toward the park.

The park has several environmentally friendly touches. The flora planted along the High Line is representative of the region's native ecology. Half of the plants are native to North America and 30% are native to the Northeast, making the park a natural home to birds and butterflies. The park also absorbs and uses rainwater that would otherwise be finding its way into gutters. Although the philosophy is low impact, the High Line has had a decidedly high impact on the surrounding neighborhood. In addition to providing an aesthetically pleasing path from the Meatpacking District north into the heart of Chelsea's art galleries, the High Line has attracted people and businesses to a part of the city that was perhaps better known for its untz-untz dance clubs and Scores. The High Line has been a catalyst for both architectural and cultural development in the area, including The Whitney's new home in the Meatpacking District.

Take a quick survey of the architecture by simply looking up; **The Standard**, which straddles the High Line just south of 14th Street, sports a posh restaurant as well as a beer garden, directly underneath the High Line. Two other stunning architectural gems visible from the High Line (looking west) are Frank Gehry's first commercial office building in New York, Barry Diller's **IAC Building**, and Jean Nouvel's **100 Eleventh Avenue** condo building right across the street. The IAC is one of the most wonderfully luminescent buildings in all of New York, and Nouvel's facade of hundreds of differently sized panes of glass became an instant classic. Of course, the work on the High Line itself, by architects Diller Scofidio + Renfro and landscape architects James Corner Field Operations, is simply amazing. The 10th Avenue Square area, with amphitheater-style seating and a living-room-window view of the northbound traffic of Tenth Avenue, is a favorite as well as a perfect place for a picnic (hit up the nearby Chelsea Market food vendors).

While weekend days during summer on the High Line is already a madhouse, we recommend an early-morning or evening stroll during spring and fall. The cityscape views at night are stunning; early morning is quiet and generally cool, until the sun moves above the skyscrapers to the east of the park. Really, there is no bad time to visit the High Line. The views will be great no matter what time of day it is.

Great food options abound nearby, including hip **Cookshop (Map 8)** and warm Italian **Bottino (Map 8)**. Want cheaper fare? Hit greasy spoon **Hector's (Map 5)** or wait for one of the gourmet trucks to pull up around the corner from the Gansevoort stairs, or go DIY by buying food at **Chelsea Market (Map 8)**. On the High Line itself, look out for stands selling artisanal popsicles, ice cream, tacos and coffee.

At night, you can hang around to rock out at The Standard's **Biergarten (Map 5)**, or better yet, walk the streets of the West 20s in search of gallery openings (read: free wine and cheese). No matter how you slice it, a visit to the High Line will only make you happier. We promise.

General Information

Hudson River
Park Trust: 212-627-2020
                www.hudsonriverpark.org
Twitter: @HudsonRiverPark

Overview

It's up for debate whether Hudson River Park is a beacon for downtown joggers or a Bermuda triangle that pilots should fly away from. In a matter of months, this western stretch of green torpedoed into infamy when two planes and a helicopter crash-landed off the banks of the park. Most famously, the U.S. Airways "Miracle on the Hudson" skidded to a safe water landing in early 2009. Seven months later, a helicopter and a small plane collided in nearly the same spot and killed nine people.

Of course, we'd rather talk about the park's safer aerial acrobatics, like the trapezes and half-pipes that define this 550-acre, $330 million park development along the south and southwest coastline of Manhattan, stretching from Battery Place to West 59th Street.

As part of the New York State Significant Coastal Fish and Wildlife Habitat, 400 acres of the total 550 thrive as estuarine sanctuary. This means the 70 fish species (there are fish in the Hudson?) and 30 bird species on the waterfront won't go belly up or beak down with all the marine preservation. Thanks to this effort, you'll be able to enjoy the winter flounder, white perch, owls, hawks, and songbirds for generations to come. (That's fantastic! Bob, tell them what else they've won...) What downtown, nature-loving, organic-eating savers of the planet have won is in what they've lost. As a mandate, office buildings, hotels, casino gambling boats, and manufacturing plants are prohibited from the HRP, as are residences (sorry, no water-front property next to your yacht) and jet skis (better to leave them in the Caymans). Check out the *Intrepid* aircraft carrier/sea-air-space museum, especially during Fleet Week each year (usually the week of Memorial Day, in May). You'll get to see teeming Navy personnel and much more modern vessels, some of which absolutely dwarf the *Intrepid* itself. A sight not to be missed.

Art

HRP takes its culture cue from the surrounding downtown art scene of TriBeCa, SoHo, and Chelsea. Perhaps you saw one of Merce Cunningham Dance Company's final performances before they shut down. Or maybe you were waiting in line to see *Ashes and Snow*, Gregory Colbert's rendition of the interactions between animals and humans took form in the temporary Nomadic Museum on Pier 54. Or maybe you checked out Malcolm Cochran's *Private Passage* on Clinton Cove (55th–57th St). Similar to your late-night antics, you peered into a gigantic wine bottle. There, from portholes carved on the sides, you could see the interior of the stateroom of the Queen Mary. Or, hearkening back to an early time, the *Shadow of the Lusitania*. Justen Ladda recreated the shadow of the famous ship on the south side of Pier 54 (also home to reconstructed historic ships, not just their shadows), its original docking place, with glass and planters. Jutting out where Pier 49 used to sit is one of the park's more somber exhibits, the New York City AIDS memorial. Dedicated on World AIDS Day in 2008 after 14 years of fundraising and planning, the 42-foot-long memorial is both a striking accomplishment and a sober nod to those whose lives have been lost to the disease. A more permanent piece in HRP: *Salinity Gradient* in TriBeCa. Paver stones spanning 2000 feet take the shape of Hudson marine creatures. Striped bass included. Not impressed? HRP Trust hired different designers for each segment of the five-mile park, with only the esplanade and waterfront railing as universal pieces. Check out the landscape design of each segment.

Attractions

Season-specific events are held year-round at HRP. During the summer, experience fight-night basics on Pier 84 for Rumble on the River with live blood splattering with each KO. Sundays in the summer host MoonDances on Pier 84 with free dance lessons before live New York bands play. Wednesday and Fridays in the summer boast River Flicks on Pier 54 and Pier 84 with throwback films like *The Goonies*. Pier of Fear is mainly a Halloween party for the kiddies, but if you're still down with dressing up as the Scream guy, hey, no one will stop you. An estuarium (dedicated to the science of the river) and a TriBeCa dog run, among other projects, are next on the list of improvements for HRP.

Sports

Think of sports in terms of piers. You already know about ritzy Chelsea Piers, but soon enough "Pier 40" or "Pier 63" will also become vernacular to sports freaks. And there are far less expensive piers beyond CP. Most crucial to athletic-minded souls, a five-mile running/biking/blading path that threads through the piers. It's a miniature divided highway—smooth, simple, and super crowded during peak times (early evening and weekends). You'll find sunbathing lawns throughout (the most sport some will ever do). Pier 40: three and a half ball fields. Area south of Houston: three tennis courts. Mini-golf. Batting cages. Skateboard park. Beach volleyball. Trapeze lessons. Pier 40, CP, Pier 63, Pier 96: free kayaking. Those are the highlights; for more that's up your particular sports alley, check out the website.

How to Get There

Hmmm. How to most efficiently make your way through all the concrete to the shoreline? The 1 and A, C, E between Chambers and 59th Streets will get you the closest. Go west 'til you hit water. You're there.

LEVEL ONE

Special Events Hall

Exhibition Halls

| 1E | 1D | 1C | 1B | 1A |

LEVEL THREE

| 3E | 3D | 3B | 3A |

LEVEL TWO

South Concourse

North Concourse

North Pavilion

LEVEL FOUR

River Pavilion

Galleria

4E Terrace Lounge

General Information

NFT Map:	8
Address:	655 W 34th St
Website:	www.javitscenter.com
	@javitscenter
Phone Number:	212-216-2000

Overview

This massive 2.1 million square-foot glass-and-steel behemoth of a convention hall next to the Hudson River was officially built to house big trade shows, conventions and expositions, but clearly its true purpose is to annoy anyone who has to go there. Located between 34th and 38th Streets, the James Ingo Freed design has been sitting in the middle of nowhere since 1986. Although it generates well over $1 billion of business for New York, dissatisfaction with the convention center has brewed for a number of years, with complaints ranging from the aesthetic (big ugly box) to the practical (lack of space). Various plans have been proposed over the years to expand the center up or over the adjoining west side rail yards, and overhaul the building's facade. The Javits even got dragged into the Jets stadium fiasco, but seems to have emerged with some concrete progress towards a revamping: in late-2006, ground was broken on an expansion that would more than double the size of the Center. The election of a new governor, Eliot Spitzer, and subsequent resignation of said governor due to prostitution allegations resulted in a re-evaluation of the plans. When discovered that most of the $1.6 billion budget would go towards fixing—not expanding—the project would be essentially nixed. Meanwhile, somewhere along the way someone even got the idea to demolish Javits completely, replacing it with a larger version out at the Aqueduct Racetrack near JFK in Queens. In the meantime, a less-ambitious and somewhat less-expensive $465 million renovation added 110,000 square feet of space to the north, connected via level two, and various environmentally friendly features.

What is most important to know about the Javits, and most other convention centers in the world, is that they are essentially soulless, dehumanizing spaces with crappy bathrooms, horrific food, nowhere to sit, and filled (generally) with absolutely slimy, soulless, moronic sales and marketing people; it just depends on which industry is in town that moment as to what exact breed you're getting. Even the presence of cool sports cars (i.e. the Auto Show each Easter week) can't overcome a feeling, after spending even two hours in this convention center, of an absolute black nihilism. Surely someone's come up with something better? Perhaps all trade shows should simply be outdoors in Southern California in the spring—at least, that's our vote. Wait, was that out loud?

All that said, the extension of the 7 train to 11th Avenue and 34th Street should help make the 'ol glass eyesore seem a little more connected to civilization (or at least the rest of Midtown). And plans are in place for the nearby High Line to terminate at Javits' southern edge at West 34th Street. Easier to get to and a more pleasant overall experience—all this in spite of itself (sounds about right).

The main exhibition halls are on the first and third levels. Levels one and three also have ATMs. Go to level two for coffee, newsstands, and transportation. The lounges are on the fourth level.

Food

The food at the Javits Center is, of course, rapaciously expensive, and, if you're exhibiting, usually sold out by mid-afternoon. There are food courts on levels one and three that serve typical food court fare: pizza, deli sandwiches, juices & smoothies, and the requisite mall-style Asian and panini fare. As an alternative, look for people handing out Chinese food menus and have them deliver to your booth. (And yes, they take credit cards. And yes, it's bad Chinese food.)

How to Get There— Mass Transit

Until the extension of 7 train, there was no direct subway access to the center. The next closest subway stop is 34th Street/Penn Station, a good four – to five-block hike away. The M42 and M34 buses travel crosstown on 42nd Street and 34th Street, respectively, connecting with subway stops along the way. Both bus routes drop you off right outside the center.

There are also numerous shuttle buses that run to various participating hotels and other locales free of charge for convention goers. Schedules and routes vary for each convention, so ask at the information desk on the first floor.

From New Jersey, the NY Waterway operates ferries from Weehawken that ships you across the Hudson River to 39th Street and Twelfth Avenue in under 10 minutes, dropping you just one block from the Javits Center. The ferries leave every 15–30 minutes during peak hours. Call 1-800-53-FERRY or go to www.nywaterway.com for a schedule and more information.

General Information

NFT Map: 14
Website: www.lincolncenter.org
@LincolnCenter
General Info: 212-875-5456
Guided Tours: 646-385-0242
CenterCharge: 212-721-6500

Venues

Alice Tully Hall: 212-721-6500
Avery Fisher Hall: 212-875-5656
David H. Koch
Theater: 212-496-0600
Walter Reade
Theater: 212-875-5601

Organizations

The Chamber Music Society: 212-875-5788
Film Society of Lincoln Center: 212-875-5610
Jazz at Lincoln Center: 212-258-9800
The Julliard School: 212-799-5000
Lincoln Center Theater: 212-501-3100
The Metropolitan Opera House: 212-362-6000
New York City Ballet: 212-496-0600
New York Philharmonic: 212-875-5656
New York Public Library for the
Performing Arts: 917-275-6975

Overview

Lincoln Center is the largest performing arts center in the world, which means it's a beloved icon, but it's also guilty of some cultural Disneyfication. It sets the gold standard, but it also needs to make money, which it does by presenting the same venerable artists performing the same standard works, geared toward an aging, wealthy, elitist audience. However, that shouldn't stop you from seeing the Met Opera, hearing the New York Philharmonic, and taking a photo by the fountain at least once in your life. Go ahead, wear jeans to the ballet, in the name of the people!

In 2012 LC completed a massive $1.2 billion renovation, which included a much-needed facelift (inside and out) for Alice Tully Hall and the addition of a lawn-covered café, among other worthy attractions. Don't miss out on discount tickets at the new Atrium, one small step toward lowering LC's snob factor. (But not for long, as LC now hosts Mercedes-Benz Fashion Week.) Jazz at Lincoln Center, opened in 2004, benefits from having Wynton Marsalis as its artistic director; the trumpet god has done wonders for promoting jazz education. That said, JALC embodies the same disparity as the rest of LC: it's an esteemed heavyweight in the jazz world, but it caters to the 1%, despite jazz having been conceived as accessible music for regular folks like you and me.

Who Lives Where

A mecca of tulle, tin, and strings, Lincoln Center houses companies upon troupes upon societies. Matching the performing group to the building means you won't end up watching *Swan Lake* when you should be listening to Mozart. The most confusing part about Lincoln Center is that "Lincoln Center Theater" is actually two theaters—the Vivian Beaumont and the Mitzi E. Newhouse theaters. Jazz at Lincoln Center moved into the Frederick P. Rose Hall in the Time Warner Center.

American Ballet Theater—Metropolitan Opera House
Chamber Music Society—Alice Tully Hall
Film Society of Lincoln Center—Walter Reade Theater
Jazz at Lincoln Center—Frederick P. Rose Hall
Julliard Orchestra & Symphony—Alice Tully Hall
Metropolitan Opera Company—Metropolitan Opera
House
Lincoln Center Theater—Vivian Beaumont Theater and
Mitzi E. Newhouse Theater
Mostly Mozart Festival—Avery Fisher Hall
New York City Ballet—David H. Koch Theater
New York Philharmonic—Avery Fisher Hall
School of American Ballet—Samuel B. and David Rose
Building

Columbus Circle

The crazy-making subterranean Whole Foods in the Time Warner Center is probably the reason most trek over to Columbus Circle, but don't miss the intriguing Museum of Arts and Design, which opened up on the south side of the circle in 2008 following an expansive and controversial renovation of 2 Columbus Circle. Check out its sublime permanent collection, excellent temporary exhibits, and cool design shop. As for the Time Warner Center, the shops therein cohere into something resembling a mall, a Manhattan rarity, though one with a great view of Central Park. Elsewhere there is the Mandarin Oriental Hotel, featuring 18,000-count sheets on which your out-of-town guests will not sleep unless they own a small kingdom. Ditto for eating at Thomas Keller's Per Se ($390-plus per person, not including wine), though his Bouchon Bakery is more within reach. See also the uptown outpost of TriBeCa's cool Landmarc restaurant. The Trump International Hotel and Tower rises up across the street, next to the riff on the Unisphere; Nougatine, of Jean-Georges fame, is its premier lunch spot…ahh…the other reason you go to Columbus Circle.

How to Get There

Lincoln Center is right off Broadway and only a few blocks north of Columbus Circle, which makes getting there easy. The closest subway is the 66th Street 1 stop, which has an exit right on the edge of the center. It's also an easy walk from the trains that roll into Columbus Circle. If you prefer above-ground transportation, the M5, M7, M10, M11, M20, M66, and M104 bus lines all stop within one block of Lincoln Center. There is also a parking lot underneath the complex.

W 16th St

E 16th St

1

3 2

Union Sq W

Union Sq E

PAGE 284

Union Square

W 15th St

E 15th St

N R Q W
4 5 6 L

F M L

L

14th Street **W14th St**

Union Sq. E 14th St 3rd Ave

6
7

5 4

8

W 13th St

E 13th St

9

10 11
12
13

W 12th St

E 12th St

14

15

16

W 11th St

E 11th St

17

W 10th St

E 10th St

MAP 5

Ave of the Americas

Fifth Ave

University Pl

MAP 6

W 9th St

E 9th St

R W

18

W 8th St

E 8th St

8th Street

Astor Place

Broadway

Fourth Ave

Third Ave

6

Astor Place

MacDougal Aly

Washington Sq W

Washington Mews

Washington Sq N

Waverly Pl

F M B D
A C E

Washington Square

Washington Sq E

Washington P

W. 4th St.

Washington Sq S

W 4th St

W 3rd St

Minetta St

MacDougal St

Sullivan St

Thompson St

LaGuardia Pl

Bleecker St

Mercer St

Bowery
St

W Houston St

F M B D

E Houston St

1. 31 Union Sq. W.
   Residence Hall
2. Albert and Vera List Academic Center
   6 E. 16th St.
3. 8 E. 16th St./ 79 Fifth Ave.
4. 25 E. 13th St.
5. 65 Fifth Ave.
6. 80 Fifth Ave.
7. Fanton Hall/Welcome Center
   72 Fifth Ave.
8. Arnold Hall
   55 W. 13th St.
9. 118 W. 13th St.
   Residence Hall
10. 2 W. 13th St.
11. 70 Fifth Ave.
12. 68 Fifth Ave.
13. Shelia C. Johnson Design Center
    66 Fifth Ave.
14. Loeb Hall
    135 E. 12th St.
15. Alvin Johnson/
    J.M. Kaplan Building
    66 W. 12th St.
16. Eugene Lang College
    65 W. 11th St.
17. 64 W. 11th St.
18. 5 W. 8th St.
    Marlton House

General Information

NFT Maps: 5 & 6
Welcome Center: 72 Fifth Ave (at 13th St)
Phone: 212-229-5600
Website: www.newschool.edu
                   @TheNewSchool
Enrollment: 10,340 (2012)
Endowment: $205 million (2012)

Overview

The New School, formerly The New School for Social Research, is a legendary progressive university located in and around Greenwich Village, housing seven major divisions, a world-renowned think tank and the backdrop for Project Runway. Founded in 1919 as a refuge for intellectual nonconformists (including historian Charles Beard, philosopher John Dewey, and several former Columbia professors), The New School credits its philosophy to the fusing of American Intellectual rigor and European critical thought.

The university annually enrolls 10,000 students within seven undergraduate and graduate divisions, including Parsons The New School for Design, The New School for Public Engagement, Eugene Lang College The New School for Liberal Arts, Mannes College The New School for Music, The New School for Drama, The New School for Social Research, and The New School for Jazz and Contemporary Music.

The current New School for Social Research, formerly the Graduate Faculty of Political and Social Science, formerly the University in Exile was a division founded as a haven for dismissed teachers from totalitarian regimes in Europe. Original members included psychologist Erich Fromm and political philosopher Leo Strauss. Quite a lineage with which more recent graduates as Sufjan Stevens and Marc Jacobs have to contend.

Tuition

Tuition for undergraduates can exceed $55,000 per year plus at least $17,000 to share an apartment with two or three other students. Yes, that's a lot of money per month to share a living space for the school year (not the full calendar year). See website for detailed division-by-division tuition information.

Culture on Campus

Parsons is always showcasing something or other, from student shows to MoMA-presented conferences to fine arts lectures. The John L. Tischman Auditorium is the egg-shaped art deco venue for the masses. The quad courtyard, between buildings on 12th and 13th Streets, is the closest thing to a college campus. Otherwise, there's the city.

Transportation

All the subways that Union Square has to offer: N, Q, R, 4, 5, 6, and the L. See also the F and M trains along Sixth Avenue.

General Phone Numbers

Admission and Financial
Aid Information . . . . 212-229-5150 or 800-292-3040
Alumni Relations: 212-229-5662
Campus Security: 212-229-7001

Academic Phone Numbers

Parsons The New School for Design 212-229-8900
Eugene Lang College The New School
   for Liberal Arts 212-229-5100
The New School for Social Research 212-229-5600
The New School for Public Engagement . . . 212-229-5630
Mannes College The New School
   for Music 212-229-5150
The New School for Drama 212-229-5859
The New School for Jazz and
   Contemporary Music 212-229-5150

1. Carlyle Court
2. Coral Towers
3. Thirteenth St Residence Hall
4. 145 Fourth Avenue
5. University Hall
6. Palladium Hall
7. 113 University Place
8. 838 Broadway
9. 7 E 12th Street
10. Casa Italiana Zerilli-Marimò
11. Founder's Hall
12. Third Avenue North Residence Hall
13. Rubin Residence Hall
14. Bronfman Center
15. Brittany Residence Hall
16. Lillian Vernon Creative Writers House

17. Alumni Hall
18. Barney Building
19. 13 University Place
20. Cantor Film Center
21. 10 Astor Place
22. Deutches Haus
23. Glucksman Ireland House
24. Institute of French Studies/ La Maison Française
25. Weinstein Residence Hall
26. Straus Institute
27. 19 Washington Sq. North
28. One-Half Fifth Avenue
29. 1-6 Washington Square North
    - School of Social Work
    - Graduate School of Arts and Science
30. Rufus D Smith Hall
31. Seventh Street Residence
32. 111, 113A Second Avenue

33. Silver Center Block
    - Silver Center for Arts and Science
    - Waverly Building
    - Brown Building
    - Grey Art Gallery
34. Kimball Block
    - Kimball Hall
    - Torch Club
    - Copy Central
    - 285 Mercer Street

35. Broadway Block
    - 715 Broadway
    - 719 Broadway
    - 721 Broadway
    - 1 Washington Place
    - 3 Washington Place
    - 5 Washington Place
36. NYU Health Center, College of Nursing
37. 411 Lafayette Street

38. 48 Cooper Square
39. Hayden Residence Hall
40. Education Block
    - Pless Hall
    - Pless Annex
    - NYU Bookstore
    - East Building
    - Faye's @ the Square
41. Student Services Block
    - 25 West Fourth Street
    - Public Safety
    - 242 Greene Street
    - 14A Washington Place
    - 19 West Fourth Street
    - 8 Washington Place
    - 10 Washington Place
42. Meyer Block
    - Meyer Hall
    - Psychology Building
43. Provincetown Playhouse
    - Wolf Hall
    - Vanderbilt Hall
44. Judson Block
    - Kevorkian Center
    - Skirball Department
    - King Juan Carlos I Center
    - Furman Hall

45. 58 Washington Square South
47. Kimmel Center for University Life
    - Skirball Center for the Performing Arts
48. Bobst Library
49. Schwartz Plaza
50. Shimkin Hall
    - Gould Welcome Center
51. Kaufman Management Center
52. Tisch Hall
53. Courant Institute
54. Silk Building
55. Housing
56. D'Agostino Hall
57. 561 La Guardia Place
58. Mercer Street Residence

59. 530 La Guardia Place
60. Mail Services
61. Off Campus Housing
62. 665 Broadway
63. Second Street Residence Hall
64. University Plaza
65. Silver Towers
66. Coles Sports and Recreation Center
67. 194, 196 Mercer Street
68. Puck Building
    - Wagner Graduate School of Public Service

PAGE 284

Union Square

W 13th St
E 13th St
W 12th St
E 12th St
W 11th St
E 11th St
W 10th St
E 10th St
W 9th St
E 9th St
W 8th St
8th Street
E 8th St
MacDougal Aly
Washington Sq N
Washington Square
W 4th Street
Waverly Pl
Washington Pl
W 4th St
Washington Sq S
Gould Plaza
W 3rd St
Washington Square Village
Bleecker St
Broadway-Lafayette Street
Prince Street

Fifth Ave
University Pl
Washington Sq E
Fourth Ave
Broadway
Astor Pl
Astor Place
Cooper Square
E 7th St
E 6th St
E 5th St
E 4th St
E 3rd St
E 2nd St
E 1st St
Bleecker Street
2nd Avenue
Bowery
Lafayette St
Great Jones St
Bond St
James Aly
Shinbone Aly
Jersey St
Crosby St
Mulberry St

E 14th St
14th Street-Union Square
3rd Avenue
E 13th St
E 12th St
E 11th St
E 10th St
Stuyvesant St
Second Ave
Third Ave
T Shevchenko Pl

Union Sq W
Union Sq E
Thompson St
LaGuardia Pl
Mercer St

MAP 6

General Information

NFT Map: 6
Phone: 212-998-1212
Website: www.nyu.edu or @nyuniversity
Enrollment: 44,599 (2013)
Endowment: $3.1 billion (2013)

Overview

Founded in 1831, one of the nation's largest private universities sprawls throughout Manhattan, though its most recognizable buildings border Washington Square. Total enrollment hovers around 45,000, about half of whom are undergrads, many of whom will flood the city with their artistic product upon graduation, as if there wasn't enough competition for young artists here.

The expansion of NYU during recent years has not been welcomed by local residents. Some Village folks blame NYU's sprawl for higher rents and diminished neighborhood character. On the other hand, the students are a great boon to area businesses, the Washington Square campus is one of the city's largest private employers (this in a sector that enjoyed great growth even despite the country's recent economic downturn), and—to the ostensible point of many of the university's detractors—many historical buildings, such as the row houses on Washington Square, are owned and kept in good condition by the university.

NYU comprises 14 colleges, schools, and divisions, including the well-regarded Stern School of Business, the School of Law, and the Tisch School of Arts. It also has a school of Continuing and Professional Studies, with offerings in publishing, real estate, and just about every other city-centric industry you could imagine. Oh, and somehow they have a Chick-fil-A.

Tuition

If you squint, tuition for undergraduates runs around $60,000, plus $24,000 for room and board. Presented without comment.

Sports

NYU isn't big on athletics. They don't have a football team—where would they play anyway? It does have a number of other sports teams, however, and its fencing teams are highly competitive, with a long list of Olympians. The school competes in Division III and its mascot is the Bobcat, although all of their teams are nicknamed the Violets. The reason for this is explainable but by no means awe-inspiring. "Violets" comes from the cute purple flowers that grew in Washington Square Park. Preferring a more robust identity, in the early 1980s the school turned to the Bobcat, inspired by—no kidding—its novel new computerized Bobst Library Catalog system dubbed "BobCat." Somewhere Albert Gallatin was all like, "SMH," but it stuck and here we are today...

Culture on Campus

The Grey Art Gallery usually has something cool (www. nyu.edu/greyart), and the Skirball Center for the Performing Arts hosts live performances (nyuskirball. org). Still, NYU doesn't host nearly as many events as decent liberal arts schools in the middle of nowhere. But then again, why would they? NYU is in Greenwich Village, surrounded by some of the world's best rock and jazz clubs, and on the same island as 700+ art galleries, thousands of restaurants, and tons of revival and new cinema. This is both the blessing and the curse of NYU—no true "campus," but situated in the middle of the greatest cultural square mileage in the world.

Transportation

NYU runs its own campus transportation service for students, faculty, staff, and alumni with school ID cards. They run 7 am to 12 midnight weekdays and 10 am to 12 midnight weekends. During fall and spring session, free overnight Safe Ride Van Service is available to and from NYU facilities. NYU also has its own bike share program. Unlike Citibike, it's free and users can have bikes for the entire day.

General Phone Numbers

Gould Welcome Center 212-998-4550
Office of Financial Aid 212-998-4444
University Development and
   Alumni Relations 212-998-6912
Bobst Library Information 212-998-2500
Main Bookstore 212-998-4667

Bronx Kill

Bronx Shore Fields

Bronx

PAGE 242

RFK Bridge

10

RFK Bridge

Parks 5 Boro Complex 9

Golf Center 1

Discus Theater

Picnic Area

Sunken Meadows Fields

Randall's Island

Tennis Center 8

FDNY Fire Academy 7

2 Icahn Stadium

Harlem River Event Area

Paladino Ave

E 120th St

E 119th St

E 118th St

MAP 20

Manhattan

E 116th St

Pleasant Ave

E 114th St

FDR Dr

278

Island Rd

Nature Center

East River

Harlem River

Roosevelt Dr

Manhattan Psychiatric Center

6 Wards Island Treatment Plant

Wards Island

Central Fields

Kantor Fields

Children's Playground

Hell Gate Bridge

3

5

Sunken Garden Fields

Picnic Area

Hell Gate Fields

MAP 26

E 103 St Footbridge

4

East River Fields

Wards Meadow Fields

RFK Bridge

Queens

Hell Gate

General Information

Randall's Island Park Alliance: 212-830-7722

Website: www.randallsisland.org or @randallsisland

Overview

If landfills, minimal food options, and a treacherous mix of the Harlem and East Rivers called "Hell Gate" don't entice you over the RFK Bridge, you probably have good instincts. But put Randall's & Wards Islands' sullied past aside, and its 480 acres of open space just across the bridge will surprise you, not only its abundant recreational facilities but also the large concerts, art fairs and various festivals that set up shop each summer.

The islands, which were actually once two separate features since connected by landfill, were once home to hospitals and various social outreach facilities. In the 1930s the site began to transition to its current use as a public park and recreational hub. Over the years the island's Downing Stadium hosted concerts starring the likes of Duke Ellington and Jimi Hendrix. Jesse Owens competed there in Olympic trials, and Soccer great Pele played there with the Cosmos in the 1970s.

As with many of the city's ambitious 1930s-era projects, by the 1980s Randall's Island fell into disrepair, but since 1999 it has undergone a huge overhaul, and now it again boasts some of the city's top recreational amenities. The Randall's Island Park Alliance public-private conservancy now operates the greenspace and keeps progress humming. The foundation kicked off the park's renovation by replacing Downing Stadium with the state-of-the-art Icahn Track & Field Stadium, opened in 2005. Since then, they've restored dozens of ballfields, marshes, and wetlands, and built new waterfront bike and pedestrian paths. Some ideas have not come to pass: in 2007, local activists put the kibosh on a grand plan to build a fancy suburban-style water park.

No matter what, we hope future plans bring in more food facilities. Currently, the only culinary options are a smattering of food trucks near the Icahn Stadium and the golf center's snack bar. One suggestion: make a Whole Foods/Fairway/Zabar pit stop before enjoying a chill weekend afternoon in the park.

How to Get There

By Car: Take the RFK Bridge, exit left to Randall's Island. While you do have to pay the MTA's hefty toll to get on the island, rest assured that it's free to leave!

By Subway/Bus: From Manhattan: take the 4, 5, 6 train to 125th Street, then transfer on the corner of 125th Street and Lexington Avenue for the M35 bus to Randall's Island. There's a bus about every 15-20 minutes during the day.

By Foot: A pedestrian footbridge at 103rd Street was built by Robert Moses in the '50s to provide Harlem residents access to the recreational facilities of the parks after then-City Council President Newbold Morris criticized the lack of facilities in Harlem. The bridge is open to pedestrians and cyclists 24/7.

Facilities

1 **Randall's Island Golf Center**; 212-427-5689; The golf center on Randall's Island features a year-round driving range with heated stalls along with grass tees and an area to practice your short game (complete with sand bunkers). See also their 36 holes of mini-golf, nine batting cages, snack bar, and beer garden. Shuttle service is available weekends year-round and weekdays in season ($12 round trip).

2 **Icahn Track & Field Stadium**; Named for financier Carl Icahn (who contributed $10 million for naming rights), the 5,000-seat stadium is the only state-of-the-art outdoor track and field venue in New York City with a 400-meter running track and a regulation-size soccer field.

3 **Supportive Employment Center**

4 **Charles H. Gay Shelter Care Center for Men**

5 **Odyssey House Drug Rehab Center/Mabon Building**

6 **DEP Water Pollution Control Plant**

7 **Fire Department Training Center**; the NYC Fire Academy is located on 27 acres of landfill on the east side of Randall's Island. In an effort to keep the city's bravest in shape, the academy utilizes 68 acres of parkland for physical fitness programs. The ultra-cool training facility includes 11 Universal Studios-like buildings for simulations training, a 200,000 gallon water supply tank, gasoline and diesel fuel pumps, and a 300-car parking lot. In addition, the New York Transit Authority installed tracks and subway cars for learning and developing techniques to battle subway fires and other emergencies. They're clearly missing an opportunity here…

8 **Sportime Tennis Center**; 212-427-6150; 20 year-round courts, including courts heated for winter use, a training facility and café.

9 **Robert Moses Building**; perhaps a few urban planning students have made a pilgrimage here, the one-time home of Moses' power-consolidating Triborough Bridge and Tunnel Authority.

10 **NYPD**; they launch cool-looking police boats from here.

General Information

Website: riversideparknyc.org
Phone: 212-870-3070

Overview

Riverside Park, stretching from 59th Street to 155th Street along the Hudson River on Manhattan's West Side, is the place where Upper West Siders go to find a little bit of rest and respite in the one of the most crowded neighborhoods in the country. The park also serves as a vital link between Upper Manhattan and Midtown for bicyclists and joggers along the water's edge, and there are ample recreational opportunities all along the way. Oh, and the views to the west across the Hudson from the vistas above are just magnificent.

The park developed in stages. The initial plans, from 72nd to 125th Streets, were conceived in the 1870s by Frederick Law Olmsted, co-designer of Central and Prospect Parks. Those designs were implemented piecemeal into the early part of the 20th century; the garden pathways and vistas along Riverside Drive are part of the original Olmsted plans. In the 1930s the Parks Department under the leadership of so-called master builder Robert Moses undertook a massive expansion of the park when the Henry Hudson Parkway was built along the waterfront and recreational facilities were added, along with the 79th Street Marina and Rotunda. In 1980, the park was designated an official scenic landmark by the City Landmarks Commission; it is one of only a handful of scenic landmarks in the city. The new millennium saw further expansion south of 72nd Street to 59th Street.

Sights & Sounds

The thin path between the Henry Hudson Parkway and the water's edge between 100th and 125th Streets is home to dozens of cherry trees, gifts of the Japanese government from 1909, and from the same batch as were planted in D.C.'s Tidal Basin. In spring the pink flowers are stunning. Speaking of trees, the American Elms along Riverside Drive are a relatively rare living example of a species that has been nearly decimated by disease over the years. Many films and television shows are shot in Riverside Park, but head to the garden at 91st Street to see where Tom Hanks finally met Meg Ryan in *You've Got Mail*. The Soldiers' and Sailors' Monument at 89th Street is the site of the city's annual Memorial Day commemoration. At 122nd Street is the punchline to the old Groucho Marx joke: technically, no one is buried in Grant's Tomb, as the 18th President and his wife lay in rest in two sarcophagi above ground. And if you thought you had a good deal on rent, check out the lucky few who get to dock their houseboats at the 79th Street Boat Basin. But will Zabar's deliver?

Recreation

In the early part of the 20th century park systems across the country began focusing less on passive recreation in favor of active recreation. Part of the Westside Improvement Project that covered the train tracks and built the Henry Hudson Parkway also added recreation facilities on the land below bluffs. Today Riverside Park has ballfields, basketball, tennis, volleyball and handball courts, and even kayak launches. It's safe to say that Olmsted probably never expected dog runs dotting his park.

Practicalities

Take the 1, 2, 3 train to any stop between Columbus Circle and 157th and it's just a short walk west to Riverside Park. The M72 bus gets you closest to Riverside Park South and the M5 bus runs up and down Riverside Drive, right at the edge of the park.

STREET LEVEL

W 51st St

Brooks Brothers

Body Shop

Radio City Gift Shop

Berlitz Language School

Fire Zone Store & Museum

Del Fresco Grille

RA Newsstand

○ **Radio City Music Hall**

Anthropologie

Wells Fargo

Bill's Bar and Burger

Façonnable

Equinox

○ **Atlas Sculpture**

Brasserie Ruhlmann

Banana Republic

W 50th St

New West

Papyrus

Aenigues

Pylones

Erwin Pearl

Galerie Saint Gil

Delfino

Louis Martin Jewelers

Godiva Chocolatier

Top of the Rock

J. Crew

MAP 12

Sixth Ave (Avenue of the Americas)

The Studio

NBC Studios Elevators

Rainbow Room & Grill

○ **30 Rockefeller Plaza**

ROCKEFELLER PLAZA

Christmas Tree

○ Ice Rink

Allen Edmonds

Magnolia

Studio Optix

Onassis

Rain

Botticelli

Tumi

La Maison Du Chocolat

NBC Studios/ NBC Experience Store

Coach

Lago

Botticelli Men

Cole Haan

Bose

Teuscher Chocolates

Longchamp

L'Occitane

Tous

Anne Fontaine

Metropolitan Museum of Art Store

Michael Kors

W 49th St

Loft

Christie's

ALDO

RA Newsstand

Today Show Studio

First Republic Bank

Cosi Sandwich Shop

Central Parking

Christie's

Mendy's

Nintendo

Bouchon Bakery

Morrell Wine Bar & Restaurant

Morrell & Company Wine Store

Minamoto Kitchoan

Free People

Ann Taylor

Aritzia

Citibank

Dean & Deluca

W 48th St

CONCOURSE LEVEL

First Republic ATM

Liberty Deli

Subway

Dunkin' Donuts

Jamba Juice

Splendid Dry Cleaners

GNC

Just Salad

Manchu WOK

Top of the Rock

Lemny's

Tri Tip Grill

Harry's Italian Pizza Parlor

Cucina & Co

Rock Center Café

Starbucks

Hallmark

Posman Books

Its Easy

Top of the Rock Shop

Aunt Annie's

Yummy Sushi

Jacques Torres

Starbucks

Ice Rink

Ice Skate House

United States Postal Service

Dahlia

Au Bon Pain

RA Newsstand

Eddie's Shoe Repair

Frattoo Hair Salon Coloring

AT&T

Pret A Manger

Hale & Hearty

Value Drugs

Potbelly

Crabtree & Evelyn

Gamestop

Brookstone

Swarovski

Sea Grill

Blue Bottle Coffee

Witchcraft

Gary's Top Shoe

General Information

NFT Map: 12
Phone: 212-588-8601
Website: www.rockefellercenter.com
                @rockcenternyc
Rink Phone: 212-771-7200
Rink Website: www.therinkatrockcenter.com
NBC Tour
  Phone: 212-664-3700
Top of
  the Rock: www.topoftherocknyc.com

Overview

Perhaps you've been blinded five streets away by 25,000 Swarovski crystals. Or maybe you've glimpsed a gargantuan King Kong of a tree shooting seventy feet in the air and wondered how on earth such vegetation could grow in concrete. Regardless, you fall for antics, arrive in bewilderment at Rockefeller Center, and stay for the ice skating rink, services at St. Patrick's, and the Rockettes at Radio City Music Hall. When there's not a huge pine tree to distract you, you'll note that Rockefeller Center occupies three square blocks with a slew of retail, dining, and office facilities. Midtown corporate just ain't the same without its magic.

The massive Rockefeller Center complex was begun at the height of the Great Depression and reflects the Art Deco architecture of the era. It opened in 1933 and it's notable that most of the iconic Rockefeller Center attractions actually date back to those early years: the tree tradition began in 1931, the Rainbow Room opened for business in 1934, the wintertime rink first welcomed skaters in 1936, and Radio City Music Hall and its Rockettes date back to the early days. NBC has been headquartered at 30 Rockefeller Plaza (i.e., "30 Rock") since the very beginning; when you go, you'll recognize the Today Show exterior immediately, and *Saturday Night Live*, *The Tonight Show Starring Jimmy Fallon* and *Late Night with Seth Meyers* all take place in the NBC studios on the lower floors of the 30 Rock. NBC offers tours of its facilities; call or visit online for more information.

The Top of the Rock Observation Deck has jaw-dropping, 360-degree views of the skyline from atop 30 Rock. In some ways it's a better view than that from the Empire State Building, if only because it features a great view of the Empire State Building. Top of the Rock is open daily 8 am–12 am (last elevator 11 pm). Tickets are timed entry and cost $42. Guided tours of Rockefeller Center are offered daily throughout the day and combined Top of the Rock/tour tickets are available.

Where to Eat

How hungry are you? Rock Center isn't a prime dining destination, but you won't starve if you find yourself in the area. For cheaper fare, try places down in the Concourse. You'll pay for the view if you eat overlooking the skating rink. For coffee, there is an outpost of Blue Bottle on the Concourse level. The Magnolia Bakery on 49th and Sixth is one of two architectural holdouts that refused to sell to the Rockefellers. Many restaurants in Rockefeller Center are open on Saturdays, but aside from the "nice" restaurants, only a few open their doors on Sundays.

Where to Shop

Much of the Rockefeller Center roster could be at a mall nearly anywhere, but there are some fun standouts in the crowd. **FDNY Fire Zone** (50 Rockefeller Plaza) features both interactive fire safety exhibits and official FDNY merch. **La Maison Du Chocolat** (30 Rockefeller Plaza) sells high-end French chocolate and boffo hot chocolate. **Teuscher Chocolates** (620 Fifth Ave) are Swiss chocolates in the truest sense: they're flown in from Switzerland.

The Rink

To practice your double loop: The rink opens Columbus Day weekend and closes in April to make way for the Rink Bar. Skating hours are 9 am–12 am daily. Rates vary by day and time. Season passes are available. If it all seems a little pricey, keep in mind that only 150 skaters are allowed on the rink at one time, making for a more intimate experience. And that setting, duh.

Overview

Once upon a time, Roosevelt Island was much like the rest of New York—populated by criminals, the sick, and the mentally ill. The difference was that they were the residents of the island's various mental institutions, hospitals, and jails, but these days this slender tract of land between Manhattan and Queens has become prime real estate for families and UN officials.

The 147-acre island, formerly known as "Welfare Island" because of its population of outcasts and the poor, was renamed for Franklin D. Roosevelt in 1973, when the island began changing its image. The first residential housing complex opened in 1975. Some of the old "monuments" remain, including the Smallpox Hospital and the Blackwell House (one of the oldest farmhouses in the city), while the Octagon Building, formerly a 19th-century mental hospital known for its deplorable conditions, has been turned into luxury condos (so yes, you're still in New York). Four Freedoms Park, which dusts off a decades-old design by the architect Louis I. Kahn, is a focal point for the southern tip of the island; the putting green-length grass and severe white granite isn't exactly welcoming, but you certainly can't beat that view of Midtown East.

The island's northern tip is a popular destination for fishermen with iron gullets. It's also the home of a lighthouse designed by James Renwick, Jr., of St. Patrick's Cathedral fame. The two rehab/convalescent hospitals on the island don't offer emergency services, so if you're in need of medical attention right away, you're out of luck. The island's main drag, Main Street (where did they come up with the name?), resembles a cement-block college campus circa 1968. Just south, closer to the tram, is a more recent stretch of development that fetches top dollar. Two of these buildings are residences for Memorial Sloan-Kettering Cancer Center and Rockefeller and Cornell University employees.

Perhaps the best way to experience the island is to spend a little while on the local shuttle bus that runs the length of the island. You'll see a wonderful mix of folks, some crazy characters, and have a chance to grill the friendly bus drivers about all things Roosevelt Island. Trust us.

How to Get There

Roosevelt Island can be reached by the train, but it's much more fun to take the tram. Plus, your out-of-town friends will love that this is the tram Tobey Maguire saved as Spiderman in the first movie. You can board it with a Metrocard (including an unlimited!) at 60th Street and Second Avenue in Manhattan—look for the big hulking mass drifting through the sky. It takes 4 minutes to cross and runs every 15 minutes (every 7 minutes during rush hour) 6 am–2 am, Sunday through Thursday, and 'til 3:30 am on Fridays and Saturdays. To get there by car, take the Queensboro-Ed Koch Bridge and follow signs for the 21st Street-North exit. Go north on 21st Street and make a left on 36th Avenue. Go west on 36th Avenue and cross over the red Roosevelt Island Bridge. There is limited reliable street parking on Roosevelt Island; hit the Motorgate Plaza garage at the end of the bridge at Main Street instead.

O Landmarks

- **Blackwell House** · 500 Main St [River Rd]
- **Blackwell's Lighthouse** ·
  North tip of Roosevelt Island
- **Chapel of the Good Shepherd** ·
  543 Main St [West Rd]
- **Four Freedoms Park** ·
  1 FDR Four Freedoms Park
- **Smallpox Hospital** ·
  South tip of Roosevelt Island
- **Tramway** · 346 Main St [West Rd]

General Information

NFT Maps: 1 & 3
Phone: 212-732-8257
Website: theseaport.nyc
              @TheSeaport

Overview

For years New York's modus operandi has been something along the lines of build, tear down, build bigger, tear down again, and build even bigger until it's the biggest, bestest, most badass thing in the Western Hemisphere. Or something like that. Which is what makes the South Street Seaport such an odd and endearing spot in Lower Manhattan. The old-tymey tyme historic ships and intact nineteenth-century buildings take you back to New York's mercantile/shipping past. If you squint, you just might make out Walt Whitman ducking a roving band of Dead Rabbits. Or something like that. Or maybe those are just a few preteens goofing while their folks settle up at the TKTS booth. Same-same.

Indeed, time was you could be forgiven if you assumed South Street Seaport was just a mall and a cobblestoned pedestrian mallful of chain stores. After Superstorm Sandy, however, the area has undergone quite a physical and spiritual change. Today the Seaport has been rebranded as a spot for container ship pop-ups, artisanal vendors from Brooklyn and a space for live events. Even the bad old mall is scheduled for a major renovation.

Part of the impetus for change has come from the Howard Hughes Corporation, which has plans to shake up what had become a sleepy and, honestly, somewhat stale part of Lower Manhattan. The museum and its picturesque tall ships had been struggling financially for years, the bland shops along Schermerhorn Row amounted to a lesser Faneuil Hall Marketplace, and the less said about that strange Pier 17 mall the better. It remains to be seen whether the plans for a giant tower and multi-screen mixed-use fantasia survive first contact, but the ball is definitely rolling. The restored Tin Building, formerly home to the Fulton Fish Market, reopened in 2022 as a 53,000-square-foot marketplace, with a dozen-plus restaurants and bars of all kinds, overseen by renowned chef and restaurateur Jean-Georges Vongerichten.

The South Street Historic District is at a crossroads, and time will tell whether the development that happens creates something smart and vital or just replicates the same sort of tourist crapola à la Pier 17 mall. Here's hoping for the former—the infrastructure is just too cool, and the stakes are too high to let this fantastic resource wither.

General Information

NFT Map: 12
Website: www.timessquarenyc.org
@TimesSquareNYC
Transit: Take the 1, 2, 3, 7, N, Q, R, and S trains to get to the center of everything at the 42nd Street/
Times Square stop, under Broadway and Seventh Avenue. The A, C, and E trains stop at 42nd
Street along Eighth Avenue.

Overview

Let's get real: the hand-wringing about whether the "old" "gritty" Times Square was somehow better than the "new" "sanitized" "Disneyfied" Times Square is so three decades ago. Times Square is what it is, and the truth is that if you spend any amount of time in Midtown, or if you've ever go to a theatrical presentation, or if you—god forbid!—happen to happen upon one of the most iconic cityscapes on the planet, then you just might find yourself here. And when that occurs, you can either be a dead-ender about it and spar with Elmo about how Show World was so much better than M&M's World or you can accept the fact that, duh, healthy cities evolve. That said, no one's debating the idea that those Hard Gump Planet Fieri ShrimpZone theme restaurants are and always will be patently absurd. Granted. And of course you dislike Times Square—of *course* you do, we get it. But now that you *are* here, let's talk about how to make the most of it.

For starters, now that Broadway between 42nd Street and 47th Street is permanently closed to traffic, Times Square is a lot less of a headache to walk through. There is now ample space to gawk at the underwear ads above. The street preachers have lost their narrow sidewalk gauntlet. Some days you can even walk from one end to the other without once ever having to consider whether you like comedy. The "pilot" project that began in 2009 was made permanent, or permanent enough, by the end of Bloomberg's tenure in 2013.

On the north end of the Times Square district in Duffy Square is the giant red TKTS booth, a sort of ziggurat of cheap Broadway tickets. Climb to the top—don't worry, unlike nearly everything else in the immediate vicinity, it's free—take the customary selfie and admire the view. Come on, admit it: it's pretty neat up there. And now you know what the view is like from the Olive Garden.

Sights

Times Square was known as Longacre Square until 1904, when *The New York Times* moved to the building now known as One Times Square, which is also known as the place where the ball drops each New Year's Eve. The paper has since moved twice—first to 229 West 43rd Street and then in 2007 to a new Renzo Piano-designed 52-story skyscraper on the southeast corner of 42nd Street and Eighth Avenue, just across from the Port Authority Bus Terminal. The Times Building also houses a hip **MUJI** store for all your Japanese design needs. As for the Port Authority, it's not a bad option if you're feeling nostalgic for the gritty days though even it, too, falls into the Latter-Day Lion King camp: the dumpy old bowling alley has been rebranded as **Frames**, with bottle service (!) and the **Port Authority Greenmarket** (!!) is a year-round operation. Or, just embrace the suck, and go for broke at the **View Lounge**, which, for nothing, features a 360-degree rotating bar at the top of the Marriott. Gripe all you want about the overpriced drinks, but you can't beat the view.

Restaurants & Nightlife

Far be it from us to speculate about what compels people to travel all the way to New York, with its tens of thousands of restaurants, some of which being actually very good, only to spend several meals' worth of calories (and a not inconsequential wad of cash) at one of the chains in Times Square. Which is to say, those places exist, but that's not all there is. Cases in point: **Virgil's Real BBQ** (152 W 44th St) serves up quite good grub, although they rush you out like you're in Chinatown; **Marseille** (630 Ninth Ave, off the map) is another French standby that is a good pre-theater option; and there's a branch of Danny Meyer's **Shake Shack** over on Eighth Avenue and 44th St. After dinner, the **Iridium Jazz Club** (1650 Broadway, off the map) showcases top-notch jazz acts; guitar god Les Paul jammed here every Monday before dying of pneumonia in 2009 at age 94. For a drink, the bar at the **Paramount Hotel** (235 W 46th St) is cool (merci, Monsieur Starck), though (of course) not cheap. Our recommendation: head a few blocks north to the **Russian Vodka Room** (265 W 52nd St, off the map) for a singular experience. You won't remember it, but you'll have fun doing it. And finally, for people who say the old Times Square is gone forever, stop in for a shot, a beer, and some boxing nostalgia at **Jimmy's Corner** (140 W 44th St).

General Information

NFT Maps: 6, 9, & 10

Overview

Want to find the real pulse of Manhattan? Head straight to Union Square where thousands of people surge through here everyday to hang out on the steps, shop at the excellent farmers market, protest whatever's wrong with our country this week, and watch the city roll on by. Part of the charm is that there's no real attraction here. There's a park with some benches, a few statues, a dog run, the aforementioned market, and that's about it. After 9/11 New Yorkers congregated under the George Washington monument to console each other and remember the perished. Since that fateful day, Union Square has become the de facto living room of Downtown. Between New School and NYU kids rushing to class, crazy street entertainers, lost tourists, and people just trying to get to work, this place is always jumping. Historical note: The first ever Labor Day celebration took place here, so next time you're sitting in the park enjoying your lunch from the Whole Foods salad bar, give thanks that the legal days of working 14-hour shifts are behind us. Or so they say.

Shopping

Over the years, the area around Union Square gradually filled with the kind of chains that you can find across the country, but if you look very carefully, you'll find a couple of good shopping options in these parts. High on the list is **The Strand** (828 Broadway), the iconic bookstore that keeps on truckin' (thank goodness) with discounted books and literary readings, and don't forget **Alabaster Bookshop** (122 4th Ave) just around the corner. There's also **Forbidden Planet** (840 Broadway), a comic book nerd's heaven. For the sports nuts **Paragon Sporting Goods** (867 Broadway) is the place to get any kind of racquet, ball, or bat you can think of. If you must choose a big name, the **Barnes & Noble** (33 E 17th) at the north end of the park has an amazing magazine selection and of course an incredible selection of NFTs. But the main draw is the **Union Square Greenmarket**—one of the original NYC greenmarkets dating back to 1976, this is one the best spots in the city to stock up on produce, cheese, baked goods, meat, and flowers. Fantastic.

Restaurants

For a true splurge make reservations at **Union Square Café**. Established in 1985, this is restaurateur extraordinaire Danny Meyer's first restaurant, not only has it stayed strong and fresh over the years but many New York chefs have spent time in the kitchen there. Or do what it seems most everyone in the universe seems to be doing and make a trip to the **Whole Foods**' (4 Union Sq E) hot and cold food bars. In the warmer months you can sit in the park, but on colder days walk up to the second floor cafeteria and enjoy an amazing panoramic view. For dessert, try the hot chocolate by **Max Brenner Chocolate by the Bald Man** (841 Broadway).

Nightlife

Ready for a stiff drink? **Old Town Bar** (45 E 18th St) is the prime choice. It has character, cheapish cocktails, and the crowd isn't totally ridiculous (yeah, it's that tough of a neighborhood to find a decent bar). Just west of Union Square is **Park Bar** (15 E 15th St), a perfect place to meet up for an after work blind date—it's small enough to force conversation with your new friend. Or try **Lillie's** (13 E 17th St) just up the block if you have a Irish-Victorian bar décor fetish. You'll know what we're talking about the second you walk in. And for live music, the **Irving Plaza** (17 Irving Pl) is a staple on the New York scene.

Just Plain Weird

See that giant smoking magic wand clocky thingy on the facade on south side of the square? It's actually got a name—**The Metronome**. Installed in 1999, artists Andrew Ginzel and Kristen Jones created something that's supposed to inspire reflection on the pace of time in the city…or something like that. Unfortunately, every time we glance up at it, we feel even more on edge than we already are. The strip of numbers is a sort of clock: the left-hand side counts the hours in the day wile the right-hand side subtracts the hours left—the two numbers crash in the middle. On the right side is a moon with the current phase. Somewhere in the middle at the top is a hand, a riff on George Washington's directly across the street.

Just Off The Map

The post-work rush at **Trader Joe's** (142 E 14th St) is a special kind of torture that we will gladly submit to in order to save a few bucks on Wasabi-Ginger Almonds and Organic Fair Trade Italian Coffee. And those dryer chairs seem to be in good working order over at **Beauty Bar** (231 E 14th St), which features smart cocktails in a repurposed hair salon.

Nations Cafe

Germany

873

General D MacArthur Plaza

FDR Dr

E 48th Street

First Ave

352

Japan Society

Trump Tower

Memorial to the Fallen

E 47th Street

Dag Hammarskjold Plaza

Peace Garden

Venezuela

E 46th Street

Peace Statue

Turkey

Inst. of Int'l Education

Korea

East River

Promenade

E 45th Street

Visitors Entrance

Visitors Plaza

2nd UN Plaza

Uganda

US State Dept

Kuwait

Italy

General Assembly

Rose Garden

MAP 13

E 44th Street

United Nations Plaza

Egypt

International Women's Center

Malaysia

Conference Building

E 43rd Street

Japanese Peace Bell Garden

FDR Dr

Tudor Park

Secretariat Building

Ford Foundation

Tudor City Pl

Fountain

Dag Hammarskjold Library

E 42nd Street

Robert Moses Playground

Queens Midtown Tunnel

Tudor Hotel

To Queens

E 41st Street

495

General Information

NFT Map:	13
Address:	First Ave b/w 42nd & 48th Sts
Phone:	212-963-1234
Website:	www.un.org
Visitor Information:	un.org/visit
Guided Tour Hours:	Monday–Friday 9 am–5 pm
Guided Tour Admission:	$26 for adults, $18 for seniors, $18 for students, and $15 for children ages 5–12. Children under 5 not admitted.

Overview

The United Nations Headquarters building, that giant domino teetering on the bank of the East River, opened its doors in 1951. It's here that the 193 member countries of the United Nations meet to fulfill the UN's mandate of maintaining international peace, developing friendly relations among nations, promoting development and human rights, and getting all the free parking they want. The UN is divided into bodies: the General Assembly, the Security Council, the Economic and Social Council, the Trusteeship Council, the Secretariat, and the International Court of Justice (located in the Hague). Specialized agencies like the World Health Organization (located in Geneva) and the UN Children's Fund (UNICEF) (located in New York) are part of the UN family.

The United Nations was founded at the end of World War II by world powers intending to create a body that would prevent war by fostering an ideal of collective security. New York was chosen to be home base when John D. Rockefeller Jr. donated $8.5 million to purchase the 18 acres the complex occupies. The UN is responsible for a lot of good—its staff and agencies have been awarded nine Nobel Peace Prizes over the years. However, the difficult truth is that the United Nations hasn't completely lived up to the ideals of its 1945 charter. Scandals involving abuses by UN troops in Haiti and other countries have certainly not boosted the UN's reputation recently.

That said, this place is definitely worth a tour. After all, the people in this building do change the world, for better or worse. The UN Headquarters complex is an international zone complete with its own security force, fire department, and post office (which issues UN stamps). It consists of four buildings: the Secretariat building (the 39-story tower), the General Assembly building, the Conference building, and the Dag Hammarskjöld Library. Once you clear what feels like airport security, you'll find yourself in the Visitor Centre where there are shops, a coffee shop, and a scattering of topical small exhibits that come and go. The guided tour is your ticket out into important rooms like the Security Council Chambers and the impressive and inspiring General Assembly Hall. Sometimes tour groups are allowed to briefly sit in on meetings, but don't expect to spy the Secretary General roaming the halls. Take a stroll through the Peace Bell Garden (off limits to the public, but it can be seen from the inside during the guided tour). The bell, a gift from Japan in 1954, was cast from coins collected by children from 60 different countries. A bronze statue by Henry Moore, *Reclining Figure: Hand*, is located north of the Secretariat Building. The UN grounds are especially impressive when the 500 prize-winning rose bushes and 140 flowering cherry trees are in bloom.

N

← Barclay St

Washington St

Greenwich St

Vesey Park

West Broadway

7 WTC

Vesey St

West St

Tower 1:
1 World Trade Center

Performing
Arts Complex

Tower 2

St Pa
Church

Fulton St

Fulton St

Wedge of
Light Plaza

WTC Memorial
North Pool

PATH Terminal

PATH
Plaza

Memorial
Museum

Greenwich St

Tower 3

Dey St

Church St

Cortla

9A

World
Financial
Center

MAP
1

WTC Memorial
South Pool

Tower 4

Liberty St

St Nicholas
Church

Liberty Park

Cedar St

Washington St

Cedar St

Tower 5

Albany St

General Information

NFT Map: 1
Website: www.wtc.com
                    @WTCProgress
National September 11 Memorial
  & Museum: www.911memorial.org
                    @Sept11Memorial
One World
  Observatory: oneworldobservatory.com
                    @OneWorldNYC

Overview

After years of delay, the neighborhood's ongoing rehabilitation now continues apace. One World Trade Center opened in 2014. The National September 11th Memorial opened in 2011 and its accompanying museum opened in 2014. Further afield, Chambers, Fulton, Hudson, and other downtown streets have been structurally improved, downtown parks have been revitalized, and various initiatives have welcomed thousands of new residents to Lower Manhattan.

It remains to be seen how many of WTC's five planned towers will be built, and to what height they will rise. The various claims are complex, and it's unclear how much office space is actually needed downtown—tenants are already heavily subsidized and it's difficult to believe that Port Authority tolls won't eventually have to be applied toward either the development or upkeep of the site, no matter how much the PA denies this to be the case. Also unknown is how the site will function as both a place of mourning and a humming civic space. In short, this is not your typical public project.

Transit has been restored to pre-September 11th order, with all subway lines resuming service to the area, along with PATH service to a new PATH station designed by architect Santiago Calatrava. Even though the end result was pared back somewhat from the original design, the whole thing still cost a cool $3.8 billion.

One World Trade Center, the epic 104-story, 1,776-foot skyscraper whose exact height is no accident, is the tallest building in the Western Hemisphere. Its footprint matches the footprints of the Twin Towers at 200 by 200 feet. The building itself is the same height as the original WTC 1 and 2 and the spire rises to 1,776 feet (remember the early "Freedom Tower" label), something that caused Chicago boosters much consternation when the spire was deemed an architectural feature part of the building and not just an antenna, and thus higher than the Sears/Willis Tower. The building has 2.6 million square feet of office space, restaurants, an observation deck, and broadcasting facilities for the Metropolitan Television Alliance. Suffice it to say, it was built with security and safety at the fore—some even argue the exclusion of aesthetics. One World Observatory, the observation deck is open 10 am–7 pm (until midnight during summer and holidays). More than just an amazing view, the three levels include interactive exhibits, galleries, and dining. Admission is $36; buy tickets in advance online.

The National September 11 Memorial & Museum opened in 2011 and 2014 respectively. The memorial, Michael Arad's *Reflecting Absence* marks the footprints of the Twin Towers with massive waterfalls flowing down into the ground. The museum, designed by Norwegian firm Snohetta, focuses on not only on the events September 11, 2001 but also the original World Trade Center, the first terrorist attack in 1993, the rescue and recovery effort after 9/11, tributes large and small to those who perished and an extensive oral history project. One wall of Foundation Hall is the exposed "slurry wall," part of the original WTC retaining wall that held back the Hudson River. Indeed, the museum is an engineering feat, sited 70 feet underground, and with a price tag to match—the museum and memorial combined are said to cost in excess of $1 billion. Admission to the museum is $33 and it is open Weds–Mon 9 am–7 pm.

Transit • **JFK Airport**

Station D
Jamaica Station **E** **J** **Z**
LIRR

Terminal 7

Terminal 5

To JFK Expy

Terminal 8

Terminal 4

Control Tower

Station C
Federal Circle
Rental Cars

To Van Wyck Expy

Terminal 1

Station B
Lefferts Blvd
Long-Term Parking A, B

Station A
Howard Beach **A**
Long-Term Parking C

Terminal 2

■ AirTrain Stations for service to LIRR, NYC Subway
...... AirTrain Route
...... AirTrain Inter-Terminal Connection

Airline/Terminal	*Airline/Terminal*	*Airline/Terminal*	*Airline/Terminal*
Aer Lingus: 5	Avianca: 4	Icelandair: 7	Qantas: 7
Aeroflot: 1	British Airways: 7	Interjet: 1	Qatar: 8
Aerolineas Argentinas: 7	Caribbean: 4	Japan Airlines: 1	Royal Air Maroc: 1
Aero Mexico: 1	Cathay Pacific: 7	JetBlue: 5 (some	Royal Jordanian: 8
Air Berlin: 8	Cayman Airways: 1	international flights	Saudi Arabian Airlines: 1
Air Canada: 7	China Airlines: 4	arrive at Terminal 4)	Singapore: 4
Air China: 1	China Eastern: 1	KLM: 4	South African: 4
Air Europa: 4	Copa Airlines: 4	Korean Air: 1	Sun Country: 4
Air France: 1	Czech Airlines: 4	Kuwait Airways: 4	Swiss: 4
Air India: 4	Delta: 3	Lan Chile: 8	TAM: 8
Air Jamaica: 4	Delta International: 4	Lan Ecuador: 8	TAME: 1
AirPlus Comet: 1	Egyptair: 4	Lan Peru: 8	Transaero Airlines: 4
Air Tahiti Nui: 4	El Al: 4	LOT: 1	Turkish: 1
Alitalia: 1	Emirates: 4	Lufthansa: 1	United Airlines: 7
Allegro (seasonal): 4	Etihad: 4	Meridiana Fly: 1	US Airways: 8
American: 8	EVA Airways: 1	Miami Air (charter): 4	Uzbekistan: 1
American Eagle: 8	Finnair: 8	North American: 4	Virgin America: 4
ANA: 7	Fly Jamaica Airways: 1	Norwegian Air Shuttle: 1	Virgin Atlantic: 4
Asiana: 4	Hawaiian Airlines: 5	Open Skies: 7	XL Airways: 4
Austrian Airlines: 1	Iberia: 7	Pakistan: 4	

General Information

Address:	JFK Expy Jamaica, NY 11430
Phone:	718-244-4444
Lost & Found:	201-346-4100 or www.panynj.lostandfoundsite.com
Website:	www.jfkairport.com
AirTrain:	www.jfkairport.com/to-from-airport/air-train
AirTrain Phone:	877-535-2478
Ground Transportation:	800-AIR-RIDE (247-7433)
Long Island Rail Road:	www.mta.info/lirr
Port Authority Police:	718-244-4335
Twitter:	@JFKAirport

Overview

Ah, JFK. It's long been a nemesis to Manhattanites due to the fact that it's the farthest of the three airports from the city. Nonetheless, more than 49 million people go through JFK every year. A $9.5 billion expansion and modernization program is transforming the airport, with JetBlue taking about $900 million of that for its gigantic, 26-gate, new HQ.

JetBlue's Terminal 5 rises just behind the landmark TWA building, which you should check out if you have time to kill after getting up an hour earlier. Its bubblicious curves make this 1960s gem a glam spaceship aptly prepared to handle any swanky NY soiree. Top that, Newark.

Rental Cars (On-Airport)

The rental car offices are all located along the Van Wyck Expressway near the entrance to the airport. Just follow the signs.

Avis: 718-244-5400
Budget: 718-656-1890 or 800-527-0700
Dollar: 866-434-2226
Enterprise: 844-648-1609
Hertz: 718-656-7600 or 800-654-3131
National: 844-648-1610

Car Services, Shared Rides & Taxis

All County Express: 800-914-4223
Connecticut Limousine: 203-974-4700
Dial 7 Car & Limo Service: 212-777-7777
Super Saver by Carmel: 212-666-6666

Taxis from the airport to anywhere in Manhattan cost a flat $70 + tolls and tip, while fares to the airport are metered + tolls and tip. The SuperShuttle (800-258-3826) will drop you anywhere in Manhattan, including all hotels, for $40, but be warned it could end up taking a while, depending on where your fellow passengers are going. Nevertheless, it's a good option if you want door-to-door service and have a lot of time to kill, but not a lot of cash.

How to Get There—Driving

You can take the lovely and scenic Belt Parkway straight to JFK, as long as it's not rush hour. The Belt Parkway route is about 30 miles long, even though JFK is only 15 or so miles from Manhattan. You can access the Belt by taking the Hugh L. Cary Tunnel to the Gowanus (the best route) or by taking the Brooklyn, Manhattan, or Williamsburg Bridges to the Brooklyn-Queens Expressway to the Gowanus. If you're sick of stop-and-go highway traffic and prefer using local roads, take Atlantic Avenue in Brooklyn and drive east until you hit Conduit Avenue. Follow this straight to JFK—it's direct and fairly simple. You can get to Atlantic Avenue from any of the three downtown bridges (look at one of our maps first!). From midtown, you can take the Queens-Midtown Tunnel to the Long Island Expressway to the Van Wyck Expressway South (there's never much traffic on the LIE, of course…). From uptown, you can take the Robert F. Kennedy Bridge to the Grand Central Parkway to the Van Wyck Expressway S. Tune into 1630AM for general airport information en route to your next flight. It might save you a headache.

How to Get There—Mass Transit

This is your chance to finish *War and Peace*. A one-seat connection to the airport—any of them—is still a far-off dream, but the AirTrain works fairly well. AirTrain runs 24 hours a day between JFK and two off-site stations, one connecting with the A train at Howard Beach and the other connecting with the E, J, and Z trains at the Sutphin/Archer Ave-Jamaica Station stop. The ride takes around 15–25 minutes, depending on which airport terminal you need.

A one-way ride on the AirTrain is $8.25, so a ride on the subway then hopping the AirTrain will cost $11.15 combined. If you're anywhere near Penn Station or Grand Central and your time is valuable, the LIRR to Jamaica will cost you $11.25 during peak times ($8.25 off-peak and $5 on weekends using a MTA CityTicket). The AirTrain portion of the trip will still cost you an additional $8.25 and round out your travel time to less than an hour.

If you want to give your MetroCard a workout, and ridiculously long bus journeys don't make you completely insane—or if you're just a connoisseur of mass transit—you can also take the E or F train to the Turnpike/Kew Gardens stop and transfer to the Q10 bus. Another option is the 3 train to New Lots Avenue, where you can transfer to the B15 bus to JFK. The easiest and most direct option is to take a NYC Airporter bus (718-777-5111) from either Grand Central Station, Penn Station, or the Port Authority for $16. Since the buses travel on service roads, Friday afternoon is not an advisable time to try them out.

Parking

Daily rates for the Central Terminal Area lots cost $4 for the first half-hour, $8 for up to one hour, $4 for every half-hour after that, up to $33 per 24-hour period. Long-term parking costs $18 for the first 24-hours, then $6 in each 8-hour increment thereafter. The Port Authority website features real-time updates on parking availability, showing what percent of each lot is occupied. Online reservations are available for $5, and EZ-Pass holders can use the tag to pay for parking.

Airline	Terminal
Air Canada:	Terminal B – Concourse A
Air Tran:	Terminal B – Concourse B
American:	Terminal B – Concourse D
American Eagle:	Terminal B – Concourse C
Delta:	Terminals C and D
Delta Connection:	Terminal D
Delta Shuttle:	Terminal A
Frontier:	Terminal B – Concourse B
JetBlue:	Terminal B – Concourses A and B
Southwest:	Terminal B – Concourse B
Spirit:	Terminal B – Concourse B
United:	Terminal B – Concourses A and C
United Express:	Terminal B – Concourses A and C
US Airways:	Terminal C
US Airways Express:	Terminal C
US Airways Shuttle:	Terminal C
WestJet:	Terminal C

General Information

Address:	LaGuardia Airport, Flushing, NY 11371
Phone:	212-435-7000
Lost & Found:	718-505-5839
	lgalostandfound@panynj.gov
Website:	www.laguardiaairport.com
Ground Transportation:	800-AIR-RIDE (247-7433)
Police:	718-533-3900
Twitter:	@NY_NJairports

Overview

The reason to fly from LaGuardia (affectionately known as LGA on your baggage tags) is that it is geographically the closest airport to Manhattan and thus a cheap(er) cab ride when your delayed flight touches down at 1 in the morning. The reason not to fly to and from here is that there is no rail link.

How to Get There—Driving

LaGuardia is mere inches away from Grand Central Parkway, which can be reached from both the Brooklyn-Queens Expressway (BQE) or from the Robert F. Kennedy Bridge. From Lower Manhattan, take the Brooklyn, Manhattan, or Williamsburg Bridges to the BQE to Grand Central Parkway E. From Midtown Manhattan, take FDR Drive to the Robert F. Kennedy Bridge to Grand Central. For a toll-free alternative, take the 59th Street Bridge to 21st Street in Queens. Once you're heading north on 21st Street, you can make a right on Astoria Boulevard and follow it all the way to 94th Street, where you can make a left and drive straight into LaGuardia. This alternate route is good if the FDR and/or the BQE is jammed, although that probably means that the 59th Street Bridge won't be much better.

How to Get There— Mass Transit

Alas, no subway line goes directly to LaGuardia. The closest the subway comes is the 7-E-F-M-R Jackson Heights/Roosevelt Avenue/74th Street stop in Queens where you can transfer to the Q70 limited-stop bus which gets you to LaGuardia in 8-10 minutes. Another option is the M60 bus, which runs across 125th Street and the RFK Bridge to the airport, connecting with the N and Q at Astoria Blvd. The SuperShuttle (800-258-3826) will drop you anywhere in Manhattan, including all hotels, for $20–$30.

How to Get There—Really

Taxis to Manhattan run between $40–$60 depending on your final destination, and there is no flat rate from Manhattan. Alternatively, plan ahead and call a car service to guarantee that you won't spend the morning of your flight fighting for a taxi. Nothing beats door to door service. All County Express: 800-914-4223; Connecticut Limousine: 203-974-4700; Dial 7 Car & Limo Service: 212-777-7777 or 800-777-8888; Super Saver by Carmel: 866-666-6666; ExecuCar: 520-216-5491.

Parking

Daily parking rates at LaGuardia cost $5 for the first half-hour, $5 for every half-hour thereafter, up to $75 per 24-hour period. The Port Authority website features real-time updates on parking availability, showing what percent of each lot is occupied. Online reservations are available for $5, and EZ-Pass holders can use the tag to pay for parking.

Several off-site parking lots serve LaGuardia, including LaGuardia Plaza Hotel (104-04 Ditmars Blvd, 718-457-6300 x295). Each runs its own shuttle from the lots, and they usually charge $14–$25 per day. If all the parking garages onsite are full, follow the "P" signs to the airport exit and park in one of the off-airport locations.

Rental Cars

1 Avis · LGA	718-504-3608
2 Budget · 83-34 23rd Ave	718 639-6400
3 Dollar · 45-01 20th Ave	866-434-2226
4 Enterprise · 9501 Ditmars Blvd	844-648-1612
5 Hertz · LGA;	718-478-5300
6 National · Ditmars Blvd & 95th St	844-727-2707

Transit • Newark Liberty Airport

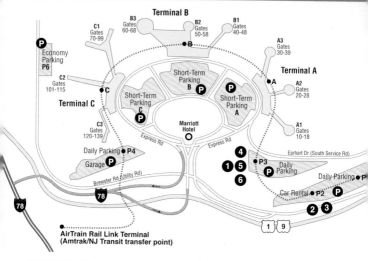

Airline	Terminal
Air Canada	A
Air India	B
Alaska Airlines	A
American	A
American Eagle	A
Avianca	B
British Airways	B
Cathay Pacific	B
Delta	B
El Al	B
Icelandair	B
Jet Airways	B
Jet Blue	A
Lufthansa	B
OpenSkies	B
Porter Airlines	B
SAS	B
Southwest	A
Swiss	B
TAP Portugal	B
United	C (some int'l flights arrive Terminal B)
United Express	A & C
US Airways	A
US Airways Express	A
Virgin America	A
Virgin Atlantic	B

General Information

Address: 10 Toler Pl, Newark, NJ 07114
Phone: 973-961-6000
Lost & Found: ewrlostandfound@panynj.gov
Website: www.newarkairport.com
AirTrain: www.newarkairport.com/to-from-airport/air-train
Ground Transportation: 800-AIR-RIDE (247-7533)
Twitter: @EWRairport

Overview

Newark Airport is easily the nicest of the three major metropolitan airports. The monorail that connects the terminals and the parking lots, the AirTrain link from Penn Station, and the diverse food court (in Terminal C), make the city's preferred point of departure and arrival. There are also plenty of international departures, making it a great second option to the miserable experience of doing JFK.

If your flight gets delayed or you find yourself with time on your hands, check out the d-parture Spa to unwind (Terminal C), or, if you're feeling carnivorous after your screaming match with airline personnel, Gallagher's Steakhouse (Terminal C).

Transit · Newark Liberty Airport

How to Get There—Driving

The route to Newark Airport is easy—just take the Holland Tunnel or the Lincoln Tunnel to the New Jersey Turnpike South. You can use either Exit 14 or Exit 13A. If you want a cheaper and slightly more scenic (from an industrial standpoint) drive, follow signs for the Pulaski Skyway once you exit the Holland Tunnel. It's free, it's one of the coolest bridges in America, and it leads you to the airport just fine. If possible, check a traffic report before leaving Manhattan—sometimes there are viciously long tie-ups, especially at the Holland Tunnel. It's always worth it to see which outbound tunnel has the shortest wait. Tune into 530 AM for information as you arrive or leave the airport.

How to Get There–Mass Transit

If you're allergic to traffic, try taking the AirTrain service to and from the Newark Liberty International Airport station on the main Northeast Corridor line into and out of Penn Station. Both Amtrak long-haul trains and NJ Transit commuter trains serve the stop, which is between Newark and Elizabeth. NJ Transit to Penn Station costs $15.25 one way (price includes the $8.25 AirTrain ticket) and takes about 30 minutes. You can also transfer to PATH trains at Newark Penn Station (confusing, we know) to Lower Manhattan. If you use NJ Transit from Penn Station, choose a train that runs on the Northeast Corridor or North Jersey Coast Line with a scheduled stop for Newark Airport, designated with the "EWR" code. If you use Amtrak, choose a train that runs on the Northeast Corridor Line with a scheduled stop for Newark Airport. The cheapest option is to take the PATH train ($2.75) to Newark Penn Station then switch to NJ Transit bus #62, which hits all the terminals. Why you're skimping on bus fare when you're paying hundreds of dollars to fly is beyond us, however. You can also catch direct buses departing from Port Authority Bus Terminal (with the advantage of a bus-only lane running right out of the station and into the Lincoln Tunnel), Grand Central Terminal, and Penn Station (the New York version—confusing, we know).

How to Get There–Car Services

Car services and ride-share apps are always the simplest option, although they're a bit more expensive for Newark Airport than they are for LaGuardia—expect $50 or more and know you're getting a fair deal for anything under that. Carmel Super Saver (212-666-6666), Dial 7 Car & Limo Service (800-222-9888 or 212-777-7777), and All County Express (800-914-4223) serve all five boroughs. Super Shuttle Manhattan (800-258-3826 or 212-258-3826) and Airlink New York (877-599-8200 or 212-812-9000) serve Manhattan. There are taxis from Newark. Yellow cabs from Manhattan are metered fares with a surcharge of $17.50; all tolls to and from the airport are the responsibility of the passenger.

Parking

Short-term parking directly across from the terminals is $5.25 for the first half-hour and $5.25 for each half-hour increment. There are some off-airport lots; most of them are on the local southbound drag of Route 1 & 9. The Port Authority website features real-time updates on parking availability, showing what percent of each lot is occupied. Online reservations are available for $5, and EZ-Pass holders can use the tag to pay for parking.

Rental Cars

Use free AirTrain link to reach rental car counters. Avis, Enterprise, Hertz, and National are located at Station P3. Alamo, Budget, and Dollar are at Station P2.

Alamo: 844-727-2984
Avis: 973-961-4300
Budget: 973-961-2990
Dollar: 866-434-2226
Hertz: 973-621-0000
National: 844-727-2983
Enterprise: 844-727-2982

Henry Hudson Bridge

The Bronx

George Washington Bridge

Throgs Neck Bridge

Bronx-Whitestone Bridge

La Guardia Airport

Flushing Bay

Manhattan

Hudson River

RFK Bridge

New Jersey

Lincoln Tunnel

Ed Koch Queensboro Bridge

Holland Tunnel

Queens

Queens Midtown Tunnel

Williamsburg Bridge

Manhattan Bridge

Brooklyn Bridge

Hugh L. Carey Tunnel

Brooklyn

Upper New York Bay

Jamaica Bay

Bayonne Bridge

Goethals Bridge

Verrazano-Narrows Bridge

Marine Parkway Gil Hodges Memorial Bridge

Cross Bay Veterans Memorial Bridge

Staten Island

Lower New York Bay

Atlantic Ocean

Outerbridge Crossing

Free Harlem River Crossings

A	Broadway Bridge
B	University Heights Bridge
C	Washington Bridge
D	A Hamilton Bridge
E	Macombs Dam Bridge
F	145th St Bridge
G	Madison Ave Bridge
H	3rd Ave Bridge
I	Willis Ave Bridge

General Information

Port Authority of NY and NJ:	www.panynj.gov or @PANYNJ
DOT:	www.nyc.gov/dot or 311 or @NYC_DOT
MTA:	www.mta.info or @MTA
EZPass:	www.e-zpassny.com
General Information:	www.nycroads.com

Overview

Since NYC is an archipelago, it's no wonder there are so many bridges and four major tunnels. Most of the bridges listed in the chart below are considered landmarks, either for their sheer beauty or because they were the first of their kind at one time. The traffic-jammed Holland Tunnel, finished in 1927, was the first vehicular tunnel connecting New Jersey and New York. King's Bridge, built between Manhattan and the Bronx in 1693, was sadly demolished in 1917. Highbridge, the oldest existing bridge in NYC (completed 1848), is scheduled to reopen to pedestrians in the near future. Brooklyn Bridge, built in 1883, is the city's oldest functioning bridge, still open to vehicles and pedestrians alike, and is considered one of the most beautiful bridges ever built.

The '70s was a decade of neglect for city bridges. Inspections in the '80s and maintenance and refurbishment plans in the '90s/'00s have made the bridges stronger and safer than ever before. On certain holidays when the weather permits, the world's largest free-flying American flag flies from the upper arch of the New Jersey tower on the George Washington Bridge. The Williamsburg Bridge has been completely rebuilt and is almost unrecognizable from its pre-renovation form, especially the pedestrian pathways. The Triborough has been renamed the "RFK" Bridge, and the Queensboro is now officially called Ed Koch Queensboro, to confuse everyone immensely.

		Toll/E-Z Pass Peak/E-Z Pass off-peak	# of lanes	Pedestrians/bicyclists?	# of vehicles/day (in thousands)	Original cost (in millions)	Engineer	Main span	Operated by	Opened to traffic
1	George Washington Bridge	17.63/15.38/13.38 (inbound only)	14	Yes	300	59	Othmar H. Ammann	4,760'	PANYNJ	10/25/31
2	Lincoln Tunnel	17.63/15.38/13.38 (inbound only)	6	No	120	75	Othmar H. Ammann Ole Singstad	8,216'	PANYNJ	12/22/37
3	Holland Tunnel	17.63/15.38/13.38 (inbound only)	4	No	100	54	Clifford Holland/ Ole Singstad	8,558'	PANYNJ	11/13/27
4	Verrazano-Narrows Bridge	11.19/6.94* (westbound only)	12	No	190	320	Othmar H. Ammann	4,260'	MTA	11/21/64
5	Hugh L. Carey Tunnel	11.19/6.94	4	No	60	90	Ole Singstad	9,117'	MTA	5/25/50
6	Brooklyn Bridge	Free	6	Yes	124	15	John Roebling/ Washington Roebling	1,595.5'	DOT	5/24/1883
7	Manhattan Bridge	Free	7	Yes	75	31	Leon Moisseiff	1,470'	DOT	12/31/09
8	Williamsburg Bridge	Free	8	Yes	111	24.2	Leffert L. Buck	1,600'	DOT	12/19/03
9	Queens-Midtown Tunnel	11.19/6.94	4	No	80	52	Ole Singstad	6,414'	MTA	11/15/40
10	Ed Koch Queensboro Bridge	Free	10	Yes	178	18	Gustav Lindenthal	1,182'	DOT	3/30/09
11	Robert F. Kennedy Bridge	11.19/6.94	8/ 6/8	Yes	200	60.3	Othmar H. Ammann	1,380'	MTA	7/11/36
12	Henry Hudson Bridge	8.25/3.18	7	No	75	5	David Steinman	840'	MTA	12/12/36
13	Bronx-Whitestone Bridge	11.19/6.94	6	No	110	20	Othmar H. Ammann	2,300'	MTA	4/29/39
14	Throgs Neck Bridge	11.19/6.94	6	No	100	92	Othmar H. Ammann	1,800'	MTA	1/11/61
15	Cross Bay Veterans Memorial Bridge	5.60/2.60	6	Yes	20	29	n/a	3,000'	MTA	5/28/70
16	Marine Parkway Gil Hodges Memorial Bridge	5.60/2.60	4	Yes	25	12	Madigan and Hyland	540'	MTA	7/3/37
17	Bayonne Bridge	17.63/15.38/13.38	4	Yes	20	13	Othmar H. Ammann	5,780'	PANY/NJ	11/13/31
18	Goethals Bridge	17.63/15.38/13.38	4	No	75	7.2	Othmar H. Ammann	8,600'	PANY/NJ	6/29/28
19	Outerbridge Crossing	17.63/15.38/13.38	4	No	80	9.6	Othmar H. Ammann	750'	PANY/NJ	6/29/28

* $2.75 for Staten Island Residents who are NYCSC E-ZPass account holders.

Commuter Ferry Services

- **ER** East River Ferry
- **NY** NY Waterway
- **SI** Staten Island
- **SS** Sea Streak

16

17

26

Central Park

14

15

QUEENS

MANHATTAN

27

NY Edgewater Landing

11

12

13

NY Port Imperial

ER Hunters Point South/LIC

WEEHAWKEN

28

NY Lincoln Harbor

Pier 78 **NY**
38th St

ER **SS**
34th St/
Midtown

ER India St/
Greenpoint

8

9

10

NY Hoboken North

ER N 6th St/
North
Williamsburg

HOBOKEN

NY Hoboken South

5

6

7

34

ER Schaefer
Landing

NY Newport

29

NY
2
World
Financial
Center

3

4

35

JERSEY CITY

Wall St/Pier 11

ER **NY** **SS**

ER Brooklyn
Bridge
Park

30

31

NY Paulus Hook

SI
Whitehall
Terminal

NY Liberty Harbor

BROOKLYN

32

33

NY Port Liberte

Staten Island
Belford

Atl Highlands
Highlands

Ferries/Boat Tours, Rentals & Charters

Staten Island Ferry: 311; www.siferry.com
This free ferry travels between Battery Park and St. George, Staten Island. On weekdays it leaves every 15–30 minutes 5 am–12:30 am and every hour at other times. On Saturday, it leaves every half-hour 6 am–7 pm and every hour at other times. On Sunday, it leaves every half-hour 9 am–7 pm and every hour at other times.

NY Waterway: 800-53-FERRY; www.nywaterway.com or @ridetheferry
The largest ferry service in NY, NYWaterway offers many commuter routes along the Hudson River to and from New Jersey and points north, and a route to Belford in Monmouth County. Their East River Ferry shuttles folks between Long Island City, Greenpoint, Williamsburg, and Brooklyn Bridge Park to and from 34th Street and Pier 11 in Manhattan.

NY Water Taxi: 212-742-1969; www.nywatertaxi.com or @nywatertaxi
Available mostly for sightseeing, specialty cruises, and charter rides, NY Water Taxi also runs the popular IKEA shuttle to Red Hook.

Sea Streak: 800-BOAT-RIDE (262-8743); www.seastreak.com or @SeaStreakFerry
High-speed catamarans that travel from Atlantic Highlands, NJ to Pier 11/Wall Street in 40 minutes, with connecting service to Midtown at E 35th Street.

Circle Line: 212-563-3200; www.circleline.com or @CircleLine42NYC
Sightseeing Cruises Circle Line offers many sightseeing tours, including their iconic circle around the island of Manhattan that takes it all in over the course of a 2.5 hour journey.

Spirit of New York: 855-647-9714; www.cityexperiences.com/new-york
Offers lunch and dinner cruises. Prices start around $80. Leaves from Chelsea Piers, over toward the Statue of Liberty and up the East River to the Williamsburg Bridge. Make a reservation at least one week in advance, but the earlier the better.

Loeb Boathouse: 212-517-2233; www.centralpark.com/things-to-do/sports/boating
You can rent rowboats from April through November at the Lake in Central Park, open seven days a week, weather permitting. Boat rentals cost $20 for the first hour and $5 for every additional 15 minutes (rentals also require a $20 cash deposit). The boathouse is open 10 am–6 pm. Up to four people per boat. No reservations needed.

Marinas/Passenger Ship Terminal

West 79th St Boat Basin: 212-496-2105; Map 14
This city-operated dock is filled with long-term houseboat residents. It's located at W 79th Street and the Hudson River in Riverside Park.

Dyckman Marina: 212-304-0183; Map 25
Transient dockage on the Hudson River at 348 Dyckman Street

Manhattan Cruise Terminal: 212-641-4400; www.nycruise.com; Map 11
If Love Boat re-runs aren't enough and you decide to go on a cruise yourself, you'll leave from the Manhattan Cruise Terminal. W 55th Street at 12th Avenue. Take the West Side Highway to Piers 88-92.

North Cove Yacht Harbor: 917-677-7680; www.igymarinas.com; Battery Park City
A very, very fancy place to park your yacht in Battery Park City.

Helicopter Services

Helicopter Flight Services: 212-355-0801; www.heliny.com; Map 3, 8
For a minimum of $199, you can hop on a helicopter at the Downtown Manhattan Heliport at Pier 6 on the East River on weekdays or on weekends and spend 15 minutes gazing down on Manhattan. Reservations are recommended, and there's a minimum of two passengers per flight.

Liberty Helicopter Tours: 212-786-5751; www.libertyhelicopter.com or @LibertyHelicop; Map 3, 8
Leaves from the Downtown Manhattan Heliport at Pier 6 on the East River (9 am–6:30 pm). Prices start at $189. Minimum of four passengers per flight.

General Information

E-ZPass Information: www.e-zpassny.com
Radio Station Traffic
Updates: 1010 WINS on the 1s for a five-
                            borough focus and 880 on the 8s
                            for a suburban focus
NYCDOT: www.nyc.gov/dot
                            @NYC_DOT
NYS DMV: 518-486-9786
                            1-800-692-2931
                            dmv.ny.gov
                            @nysdmv
Real-Time NYC
Traffic Cameras: nyctmc.org

Driving in Manhattan

Avoid it. Why drive when you can see the city so well on foot or by bus? (We don't count the subway as seeing the city, but rather as a cultural experience in and of itself.) We know that sometimes you just have to drive in the city, so we've made you a list of essentials.

• Great auto insurance that doesn't care if the guy who hit you doesn't have insurance and doesn't speak any English.
• Thick skin on driver, passengers, and car. Needed for the fender benders and screamed profanity from the cabbies that are ticked anyone but cabbies are on the road.
• Anti-anxiety medication to counteract cardiac arrest-inducing "almost" accidents.
• NFT. But we know you would never leave home without it.
• E-ZPass. Saves time and lives. Maybe not lives, but definitely time and some money.
• New York State license plates. Even pedestrians will curse you out if you represent anywhere other than the Empire State, especially NJ or CT or Texas.
• A tiny car that can fit into a spot slightly larger than a postage stamp or tons of cash for parking garages.
• Patience with pedestrians—they own the streets of New York. Well, co-own them with the cabbies, sanitation trucks, cops, and fire engines.

The following are some tips that we've picked up over the years:

Hudson River Crossings

In the Bridge or Tunnel battle, the Bridge almost always wins. The George Washington Bridge is by far the best Hudson River crossing. It's got more lanes and better access than either tunnel with a fantastic view to boot. If you're going anywhere in the country that's north of central New Jersey, take it. However, inbound traffic on the George can back up for hours in the morning because they don't have enough toll booth operators to handle all those nuts who don't have E-ZPass. The Lincoln Tunnel is decent inbound, but check 1010 AM (WINS) if you have the chance. Avoid the Lincoln like the plague during evening rush hour (starts at about 3:30 pm). If you have to take the Holland Tunnel outbound, try the Broome Street approach, but don't even bother between 5 and 7 pm on weekdays.

East River Crossings

Brooklyn
Pearl Street to the Brooklyn Bridge is the least-known approach. Only the Williamsburg Bridge has direct access (i.e. no traffic lights) to the northbound BQE in Brooklyn, and only the Brooklyn Bridge has direct access to the FDR Drive in Manhattan. Again, listen to the radio if you can, but all three bridges can be disastrous as they seem to be constantly under construction (or, in a fabulous new twist, having one lane closed by the NYPD for some unknown reason). The Williamsburg is by far the best free route into North Brooklyn, but make sure to take the outer roadway to keep your options open in case the BQE is jammed. Your best option to go anywhere else in Brooklyn is usually the Brooklyn-Battery Tunnel, which can be reached from the FDR and the West Side Highway. Fun fact: The water you pass was so dirty in the '50s that it used to catch fire. The tunnel is not free, but if you followed our instructions you've got E-ZPass anyway. The bridges from south to north can be remembered as B-M-W, but they are not as cool as the cars that share the initials.

Queens
There are three options for crossing into Queens by car. The Queens-Midtown Tunnel is usually miserable, since it feeds directly onto the parking lot known as the Long Island Expressway. The 59th Street Bridge (otherwise known as the Ed Koch Queensboro) is the only free crossing to Queens. The best approach to it is First Avenue to 57th Street (after that, follow the signs) or to 59th Street if you want to jump on the outer roadway that saves a ton of time and only precludes easy access to Northern Boulevard. If you're in Queens and want to go downtown in Manhattan, you can take the lower level of the 59th Street Bridge since it will feed directly onto Second Avenue, which of course goes downtown. The Robert F. Kennedy Bridge (née Triborough) is usually the best option (especially if you're going to LaGuardia, Shea, Astoria for Greek, or Flushing for dim sum). The FDR to the RFK is good except for rush hour—then try Third Avenue to 124th Street.

Harlem River Crossings

The RFK will get you to the Bronx in pretty good shape, especially if you are heading east on the Bruckner toward I-95 or the Hutchinson (which will take you to eastern Westchester and Connecticut). To get to Yankee Stadium, take the Willis or the Macomb's Dam (which are both free). When you feel comfortable maneuvering the tight turns approaching the Willis, use it for all travel to Westchester and Connecticut in order to save toll money. The Henry Hudson Bridge will take you up to western Westchester along the Hudson. It wins the fast and pretty prize for its beautiful surroundings. The Cross-Bronx Expressway will take years off your life. Avoid it at all costs.

Manhattan's "Highways"

There are two so-called highways in Manhattan—the Harlem River Drive/FDR Drive/East River Drive (which prohibits commercial vehicles) and the Henry Hudson Parkway/West Side Highway/Joe DiMaggio Highway. The main advantage of the FDR is that it has no traffic lights, while the West Side Highway has lights from Battery Park up through 57th Street. The main disadvantages of the FDR are (1) the potholes and (2) the narrow lanes. If there's been a lot of rain, both highways will flood, so you're out of luck (but the FDR floods first). Although the West Side Highway can fly, we would rather look at Brooklyn and Queens than Jersey, so the FDR wins.

Driving Uptown

The 96th Street transverse across Central Park is usually the best one, although if there's been a lot of rain, it will flood. If you're driving on the west side, Riverside Drive is the best route, followed next by West End Avenue. People drive like morons on Broadway, and Columbus jams up in the mid 60s before Lincoln Center and the mid 40s before the Lincoln Tunnel but it's still the best way to get all the way downtown without changing avenues. Amsterdam is a good uptown route if you can get to it. For the east side, you can take Fifth Avenue downtown to about 65th Street, whereupon you should bail out and cut over to Park Avenue for the rest of the trip. Do NOT drive on Fifth Avenue below 65th Street within a month of Christmas, and check the parade schedules before attempting it on weekends throughout the year. The 96th Street entrance to the FDR screws up First and Third Avenues going north and the 59th Street Bridge screws up Lexington and Second Avenues going downtown. Getting stuck in 59th Street Bridge traffic is one of the most frustrating things in the universe because there is absolutely no way out of it.

Driving in Midtown

Good luck! Sometimes Sixth (northbound) or Seventh (southbound) is best because everyone's trying to get out of Manhattan, jamming up the west side (via the Lincoln Tunnel) and the east side (via the 59th Street Bridge and the Queens-Midtown Tunnel). Friday nights at 9:30 pm can be a breeze, but from 10 pm to midnight, you're screwed as shows let out. The "interior" of the city is the last place to get jammed up—it's surprisingly quiet at 8 am. At 10 am, however, it's a parking lot. Those who plan to drive in Midtown on weekends from about March–October should check parade schedules for Fifth AND Sixth Avenues.

The demarcation of several "THRU Streets" running east-west in Midtown has been with the city permanently since 2004 and when people don't openly flout the no-turn signs, the system works pretty well. See "THRU Streets" section for more information.

Driving in the Village

People get confused walking in the Village, so you can imagine how challenging driving can be in the maze of one ways and short streets. Beware. If you're coming into the Village from the northwest, 14th Street is the safest crosstown route heading east. However, going west, take 13th Street. Houston Street has the great benefit of direct access to FDR Drive, both getting onto it and coming off of it. If you want to get to Houston Street from the Holland Tunnel, take Hudson Street to King Street to the Avenue of the Americas to Houston Street (this is the only efficient way to get to the Village from the Holland Tunnel). First Avenue is good going north and Fifth Avenue is good going south. Washington Street is the only way to make any headway southbound and Hudson Street is the only way to make any headway northbound in the West Village.

Driving Downtown

Don't do it unless you have to. Western TriBeCa is okay and so is the Lower East Side—try not to "turn in" to SoHo, Chinatown, or the Civic Center. Canal Street is a complete mess during the day (avoid it), since on its western end, everyone is trying to get to the Holland Tunnel, and on its eastern end, everyone is mistakenly driving over the Manhattan Bridge (your only other option when heading east on Canal is to turn right on Bowery!). Watch the potholes!

DMV Locations in Manhattan

If you're going to the DMV to get your first NY license (including drivers with other states' licenses), you'll need extensive documentation of your identity. The offices have a long list of accepted documents, but your best bet is a US passport and a Social Security card. If you don't have these things, birth certificates from the US, foreign passports, and various INS documents will be okay under certain conditions. Do not be surprised if you are turned away the first time. This trip requires great amounts of patience. Plan on spending three to six hours here. This is not a lunch-hour errand. That said, there is an online reservation system that takes some of the stress out of the whole endeavor, and do yourself a favor and check online if you might be able to transact business from home.

Greenwich Street Office
11 Greenwich St
New York, NY 10004
(Cross Streets Battery Park Pl & Morris St)
M–F, 7:30 am–5 pm

Harlem Office
159 E 125th St, 3rd Fl
New York, NY 10035
(Lexington and Third)
M–F, 7:30 am–5 pm

Herald Square Office
366 West 31st St
New York, NY 10001
(Between W 33 & W 34th Sts)
Handles out-of-state license exchange.
M–F, 7:30 am–5 pm

Manhattan
License X-Press Office
145 West 30th St
New York, NY 10001
(Between Eighth & Ninth Aves)
Service limited to license and registration renewals and surrendering your license plate. You can't get your snowmobile or boat license here, and they do not do out-of-state exchanges. Oh, and no permit renewals.
M–F, 7:30 am–5 pm

The Pond

PAGE 252

Central Park

Central Park S

Grand Army Plaza

E 61st St

E 60th St

Queensboro Bridge

E 59th St

E 58th St

E 57th St

E 56th St

E 55th St

● Split Phasing

Thru Street

E 54th St

E 53rd St

MAP 12

E 52nd St

E 51st St

MAP 13

E 50th St

Ave of the Americas (Sixth Ave)

Rockefeller Plz

Fifth Ave

Madison Ave

Park Ave

Lexington Ave

Third Ave

Second Ave

First Ave

Rockefeller Center

E 49th St

PAGE 276

E 48th St

E 47th St

E 46th St

Dag Hammarskjold Plaza

Peace Garden

E 45th St

MIDTOWN

Grand Central Station

PAGE 318

Vanderbilt Ave

Depew Pl

Lexington Ave

E 44th St

United Nations Pl

PAGE 286

United Nations

E 43rd St

E 42nd St

E 41st St

Bryant Park

New York Public Library

Tudor City Pl

E 40th St

E 39th St

MURRAY HILL

Midtown Tunnel

E 38th St

Exit St

Entrance St

E 37th St

E 36th St

E 35th St

General Information

NFT Maps: 12 & 13
DOT: 311, www.nyc.gov/dot
                              @NYC_DOT

Overview

In the tradition of "don't block the box" and other traffic solutions (such as randomly arresting political protesters), the city adopted "THRU Streets," in Midtown in 2004. The plan was implemented on some crosstown streets in Midtown in order to reduce travel times, relieve congestion, and provide a safer environment for pedestrians and cyclists. They are still working on cleaning up the exhaust fume issue, for those concerned about said environment. On certain streets, cars are not allowed to make turns between Sixth and Third Avenues (with the exception of Park Avenue). The regulations are in effect between 10 am and 6 pm on weekdays. The affected streets are:

36th & 37th Streets

45th & 46th Streets

49th & 50th Streets

53rd & 54th Streets

60th Street (between Third and Fifth Avenues)

The above streets are easily identifiable by big, purple "THRU Streets" signs. With everything that's going on in midtown Manhattan though, you'd be forgiven for missing a sign (by us, not by the NYPD). If you happen to unwittingly find yourself on a THRU Street and can't escape on Park Avenue, you're going to have to suck it up until you get to Sixth Avenue or Third Avenue, depending on the direction you're heading. If you attempt to turn before the designated avenue, you'll find yourself with an insanely expensive ticket. Of course, if you're trying to drive crosstown, it's in your best interests to take one of these streets.

Both sides of almost every non-THRU Street in this grid have been stuck with "No Standing Except Trucks Loading and Unloading" regulations, supposedly creating up to 150 spaces for truck loading (if you were ever stuck behind a truck in morning rush hour on a THRU Street in 2004, you would rejoice at this news). Additionally, one side of each non-THRU street has been "daylighted" for 80–100 feet in advance of the intersection. We are not exactly sure how they came up with the term "daylighted," but the DOT tells us it allows space for turning vehicles. DOT studies showed that THRU Streets worked— initial studies showed travel times falling by 25% (as people decided to emigrate to New Zealand) and vehicle speeds increasing by an average of 33% (from 4 mph to 5.3 mph). The THRU Streets combined carried 4,854 vehicles per hour (up from 4,187), an average of 74 additional vehicles per hour.

Split Signal Phasing

"Split signal phasing" is just a fancy term for red lights for left- or right-hand turns, allowing pedestrians to cross the street without having to worry about vehicles turning in their path. This is in place at about 40 non-THRU Street intersections in this same grid. Of course, this system assumes that both pedestrians and drivers follow the rules of the road. In spite of the disregard that most New Yorkers display for crossing signals, the number of pedestrian accidents in the eight-month trial period (compared to the eight months prior to implementation) fell from 81 to 74. The number of cycling accidents fell from 30 to 17. Accidents not related to pedestrians or bikes fell from 168 to 102.

Now if the DOT and NYPD could get traffic to flow smoothly onto bridges and into tunnels, they might actually be onto something…

Information

Department of
Transportation (DOT):   311
    www.nyc.gov/dot
    @NYC_DOT
Parking Violations Help Line: 311
Dept of Finance TTY
Hearing-Impaired: 212-504-4115
DOT Alternate Side Parking
Info: www.nyc.gov/dot/asprules
    @NYCASP

Standing, Stopping and Parking Rules

In "No Stopping" areas, you can't wait in your car, drop off passengers, or load/unload.

In "No Standing" areas, you can't wait in your car or load/unload, but you can drop off passengers.

In "No Parking" areas, you can't wait in your car or drop off passengers, but you can load/unload.

NYC also has a "no idling" law, so when you're doing one of the three illegal things mentioned above, shut your car off, so at least you only get one ticket, not two!

Parking Meter Zones

On holidays when street cleaning rules are suspended (see calendar), the "no parking" cleaning regulations for metered parking are also suspended. You can park in these spots but have to pay the meters. Also, metered spots are still subject to rules not suspended on holidays (see below). On MLH (major legal holidays), meter rules are suspended (so no need to feed the meter).

Meters

Instead of old-fashioned individual meters, NYC relies on muni-meters that let you purchase time-stamped slips which you stick in your windshield to show you paid. These machines accept coins, credit cards and payments through the Park NYC app. In the case of a non-functional muni-meter, a one-hour time limit applies. Sundays are free.

Signs

New York City Traffic Rules state that one parking sign per block is sufficient notification. Check the entire block and read all signs carefully before you park. Then read them again.

If there is more than one sign posted for the same area, the more restrictive sign takes effect (of course). If a sign is missing on a block, the remaining posted regulations are the ones in effect.

The Blue Zone

The Blue Zone is a "No Parking" (Mon–Fri, 7 am–7 pm) area in Lower Manhattan. Its perimeter has been designated with blue paint; however, there are no individual "Blue Zone" signs posted. Any other signs posted in that area supersede Blue Zone regulations. Confused yet?

General

• All of NYC was designated a Tow Away Zone under the State's Vehicle & Traffic Law and the NYC Traffic Rules. This means that any vehicle parked or operated illegally, or with missing or expired registration or inspection stickers, may, and probably will, be towed.

• On major legal holidays, stopping, standing, and parking are permitted except in areas where stopping, standing, and parking rules are in effect seven days a week (for example, "No Standing Anytime").

• It is illegal to park in a spot where SCR are in effect, even if the street cleaner has already passed. If you sit in your car, the metermaid will usually let you stay

• Double-parking of passenger vehicles is illegal at all times, including street-cleaning days, regardless of location, purpose, or duration. Everyone, of course, does this anyway. If everyone is double parked on a certain block during street cleaning, the NYPD probably is not ticketing. However, leave your phone number in the window in case the person you blocked in feels vindictive and demand that a cop write you a ticket.

• It is illegal to park within 15 feet of either side of a fire hydrant. The painted curbs at hydrant locations do not indicate where you can park. Isn't New York great? Metermaids will tell you that each cement block on the sidewalk is five feet, so make sure you are three cement blocks from the hydrant (2.5 will not do).

• If you think you're parked legally in Manhattan, you're probably not, so go and read the signs again.

• Cops will now just write you parking tickets and mail them to you if you are parked in a bus stop; so you won't even know it's happening unless you're very alert.

• There is now clearly an all-out effort to harass everyone who is insane enough to drive and/or park during the day in downtown Manhattan. Beware.

Tow Pounds

Bronx

2444 Exterior St

Open Monday–Friday 8 am–8 pm and

Saturday 8 am–3 pm; closed Sunday

718-585-1385 or 718-585-1391

Brooklyn

Brooklyn Navy Yard; 26 Navy St

Monday–Saturday 24 hours; closed Sunday 5 am–7 am

718-237-3300

Queens

31-22 College Point Boulevard, Flushing

Open Monday–Friday 8 am–10 pm and

Saturday 8 am–3 pm; closed Sunday

718-359-6200

Find out if your car was towed (and not stolen or disintegrated) by contacting your local police precinct or online via NYCServ: nycserv.nyc.gov/NYCServWeb/NYCSERVMain.

Once you've discovered that your car has indeed been towed, your next challenge is to find out which borough it's been towed to. This depends on who exactly towed your car—the NYPD, the Marshall, etc. Don't assume that since your car was parked in Manhattan that they will tow it to Manhattan—always call first.

So you've located your car, so now come the particulars: If you own said towed car, you're required to present your license, registration, insurance, and payment of your fine before you can collect the impounded vehicle. If you are not the owner of the car, you can usually get it back with all of the above, if your last name matches the registration (i.e. the car belongs to a relative or spouse); otherwise, you'll need a notarized letter with the owner's signature authorizing you to take the car. The tow fee is $185, plus $20 for each day it's in the pound. If they've put a boot on it instead, it's still $185. You can pay with cash, credit or debit card, certified check or money order. We recommend bringing a wad of cash and a long Russian novel for this experience. The longest waiting times are around noon and the late afternoon hours.

Transit • LIRR

General Information

In New York State:	call 511
All inquiries (24/7)	say "Long Island Rail Road"
From Outside New York State:	877-690-5116
International Callers:	877-690-5116
Schedule Information (24/7)	Say "Schedules"
Fare Information (24/7)	Say "Fares"
Mail & Ride (M-F, 7:30 am-5 pm)	Say "Mail and Ride"
Group Travel and Getaways (M-F, 8 am-4 pm)	Say "Group Travel"
Lost & Found (M-F, 6 am-10 pm)	Say "Lost & Found"
Refunds (M-F, 8 am-4 pm)	Say "More Options"
	then "Ticket Refunds"
Ticket Machine Assistance	Say "More Options"
(M-F, 6:30 am-3:30 pm)	then "Ticket Machines"
Hamptons Reserve Service (May-Sept)	Say "More Options"
	then "Hamptons Reserve"
MTA Police:	212-878-1001
Website:	www.mta.info/lirr
Twitter:	@LIRR

Overview

The Long Island Railroad is the busiest railroad in North America. It has eleven lines with 124 stations stretching from Penn Station in midtown Manhattan, to the eastern tip of Long Island, Montauk Point. Over 80 million people ride the LIRR every year. If you are going anywhere on Long Island and you don't have a car, the LIRR is your best bet. Don't be surprised if the feeling of being in a seedy bar creeps over you during evening rush—those middle-aged business men like their beer en route. Despite a recent movement to ban the sale of alcohol on LIRR station platforms and trains, for now, it's still legal to get your buzz on.

If you're not a regular LIRR user, you might find yourself taking the train to Citi Field for a Mets game (Port Washington Branch), Long Beach for some summer surfing (Long Beach Branch), or to Jamaica to transfer to the AirTrain to JFK (tip—the subway is cheaper). For the truly adventurous, take the LIRR all the way out to the Hamptons beach house you are visiting for the weekend (Hamptons Reserve seating is available during the summer for passengers taking eight or more trips). Bring a book as it is a long ride.

Fares and Schedules

Fares and schedules can be obtained by calling one of the general information lines, depending on your area. They can also be found on the LIRR website. Make sure to buy your ticket before you get on the train at a ticket window or at one of the ticket vending machines in the station. Otherwise it'll cost you an extra $5.75 to $6.50 depending on your destination. As it is a commuter railroad, the LIRR offers weekly and monthly passes, as well as ten-trip packages for on – or off-peak hours. The LIRR's CityTicket

program offers discounted one-way tickets for $5 within the five boroughs during weekends.

Pets on the LIRR

Trained service animals accompanying passengers with disabilities are permitted on LIRR trains. Other small pets are allowed on trains, but they must be confined to closed, ventilated containers.

General Information

In New York State	call 511
All inquiries	say "Metro-North Railroad"
From Connecticut:	877-690-5114
From Outside New York State:	877-690-5116
International Callers:	212-878-7000
Schedule Information (24/7):	Say "Schedules"
Fare Information (24/7):	Say "Fares"
Mail & Ride (M-F, 6:30 am-5 pm):	Say "More Options" then "Mail and Ride"
Group Sales (M-F, 8:30 am-5 pm):	Say "More Options" then "Group Sales"
Lost & Found (M-F, 6 am-10 pm):	Say "More Options" then "Lost & Found"
Ticket Machine Assistance (24/7):	Say "More Options" then "Ticket Machines"
Website:	www.mta.info/mnr
Twitter:	@MetroNorth

Overview

Metro-North is an extremely accessible and efficient railroad with three of its main lines (Hudson, Harlem, and New Haven) originating in Grand Central Station in Manhattan (42nd St & Park Ave). Those three lines east of the Hudson River, along with two lines west of the Hudson River that operate out of Hoboken, NJ (operated by NJ Transit; not shown on map), form the second-largest commuter railroad system in the US. Approximately 250,000 commuters use the tri-state Metro-North service each day for travel between New Jersey, New York, and Connecticut. Metro-North rail lines cover roughly 2,700 square miles of territory. The best thing about Metro-North is that it lands you at Grand Central Station, one of the city's finest pieces of architecture. On weekdays, sneak into the land of platforms via the North Passage, accessible at 47th & 48th Streets. At least for now, it's still legal to have an after work drink on Metro-North. During happy hour (starting somewhere around 3 pm), hit the bar car or buy your booze in advance on the platform at Grand Central. It might make you feel better about being a wage slave. But beware of having too happy of an hour as the bathrooms can be stinky and not all cars have them.

Fares and Schedules

Fare information is available on Metro-North's extraordinarily detailed website (along with in-depth information on each station, full timetables, and excellent maps) or at Grand Central Station. The cost of a ticket to ride varies depending on your destination so you should probably check the website before setting out. Buy advance tickets on MTA's WebTicket site for the cheapest fares. If you wait until you're on the train to pay, it'll cost you an extra $5.75–$6.50. Monthly and weekly rail passes are also available for commuters. Daily commuters save 50% on fares when they purchase a monthly travel pass.

Hours

Train frequency depends on your destination and the time of day that you're traveling. On weekdays, peak-period trains east of the Hudson River run every 20–30 minutes; off-peak trains run every 30–60 minutes; and weekend trains run hourly. Hours of operation are approximately 4 am to 3:40 am. First trains arrive at Grand Central at 5:30 am and the last ones leave at 2 am. Don't miss the last train out as they leave on time and wait for no one.

Bikes on Board

Common sense rules for taking bikes on board include: no bikes on escalators, no riding on the platform, and board the train after other passengers have boarded. Unfortunately there are restrictions on bicycles during peak travel times. Bicycles are not allowed on trains departing from Grand Central Terminal 4 pm–8 pm and connecting trains. In addition, bikes are not allowed on trains leaving from Grand Central between 5:30 am–9 am, 3 pm–3:59 pm, and 8:01–8:15 pm. Bikes are not permitted on trains arriving at Grand Central 5 am–10 am and connecting trains. Bicycles are subject to expanded restrictions around major holidays, including major Jewish holidays, and Fridays before long weekends. No bicycles are allowed on New Year's Eve, New Year's Day, St. Patrick's Day, Mother's Day, Eve of Rosh Hashanah, Eve of Yom Kippur, Eve of Thanksgiving, Thanksgiving Day, Christmas Eve, and Christmas Day. There's a limit of two bikes per carriage, and four bikes per train on weekdays, and eight on the weekends. Unfortunately, the same restrictions are not imposed on passengers with 4 Vera Bradley overnight bags heading off to the country house, but that is another story.

Riders of folding bikes do not have to comply with the above rules, provided that the bike is folded at all times at stations and on trains.

Pets

Only seeing-eye dogs and small pets, if restrained or confined, are allowed aboard the trains.

One-Day Getaways

Metro-North offers "One-Day Getaway" packages on its website. Packages include reduced rail fare and discounted entry to destinations along MNR lines including Bruce Museum, Dia:Beacon, Hudson River Museum/Andrus Planetarium, Maritime Aquarium at Norwalk, Mohegan Sun Casino, New York Botanical Garden, and Wave Hill. Tickets are available at Metro-North ticket offices or full-service ticket vending machines. The MTA website also suggests one-day hiking and biking excursions.

Tonnelle Avenue
Bergenline Avenue
Port Imperial

Tonnelle Ave
JFK Blvd

Lincoln Harbor

WEEHAWKEN

Hudson River

33 St
23 St
14 St
9 St
Christopher St

MANHATTAN

9th St
Congress St

2nd St

Hoboken

HOBOKEN

Holland Tunnel

Pavonia–Newport
Pavonia-Newport

Harborside Financial Center

Pulaski Skwy

139

Journal Sq

Harsimus Cove

WTC

7
To Newark

Harrison

Hackensack River

1
9

Grove St

Exchange Pl
Exchange Pl

Marin Blvd

Essex St

Battery Park

Jersey Ave

Lincoln Park

Communipaw Ave

Liberty State Park

Upper New York Bay

Ellis Island

Governors Island

440

West Side Ave
Martin Luther King Dr
Garfield Ave

Liberty State Park

Liberty Island

JERSEY CITY

Richard St

New Jersey Tpke

78

Danforth Ave

New Jersey Tpke Extension

45th St

Hudson County Park

34th St

22nd St

JFK Blvd

8th St

169

BAYONNE

Newark Bay

Key

PATH
Light Rail

PATH Train

General Information
Phone: 800-234-7284
Police/
Lost & Found: 201-216-6078
Website: www.panynj.gov/path
Twitter: @PATHTrain

Overview

The PATH (Port Authority Trans-Hudson Corp.) is an excellent small rail system that services Newark, Jersey City, Hoboken, and Manhattan. There are a few basic lines that run directly between 33rd Street (Herald Square) in Manhattan & Hoboken, 33rd Street & Jersey City, and Newark & the WTC. Transfers between the lines are available at most stations. The PATH can be quite useful for commuters on the west side of Manhattan when the subway isn't running, say, due to a sick passenger or mysterious police investigation. Additionally, you can catch the PATH to Newark and then either jump in a cheap cab or take New Jersey Transit one stop to Newark Airport.

Check the front or the sides of incoming trains to determine their destination. Don't assume that if a Journal Square train just passed through, the next train is going to Hoboken. Often there will be two Journal Square trains in a row, followed by two Hoboken trains. During the weekend, PATH service can be excruciatingly slow and confusing, and is best only endeavored with a seasoned rider.

Fares

The PATH costs $2.75 one-way. Regular riders can purchase 10-trip, 20-trip, and 40-trip SmartLink cards, which reduce the fare per journey to $2.60. The fare for seniors (65+) is $1.25 per ride. You can also use pay-per-ride MTA MetroCards for easy transition between the PATH and NYC subway.

Hours

The PATH runs 24/7 (although a modified service operates between 11pm–6am, M–F, and 7:30pm–9 am, Sat, Sun, & holidays). Daytime service is pretty consistent, but the night schedule for the PATH is a bit confusing, so make sure to look at the map. You may be waiting underground for up to 35 minutes. During off hours the train runs on the same track through the tunnel. This allows for maintenance to be completed on the unused track.

Hudson-Bergen Light Rail

General Information
Phone: 973-275-5555
Website: www.njtransit.com
Twitter: @NJTRANSIT

Overview

Even though it's called the Hudson-Bergen Light Rail system (HBLR, operated by NJ Transit), it actually only serves Hudson county. Bergen County residents are still waiting for their long promised connection. The HBLR has brought about some exciting changes (a.k.a. "gentrification") in Jersey City, though Bayonne remains (for the moment) totally, well…Bayonne. Currently there are 24 stops in the system, including service to Jersey City, Hoboken, Weehawken, and Union City.

Fares

The Light Rail is $2.25 per trip; reduced fare is $1.10. Ten-trip tickets are $22.50, monthly passes cost $70. Unless you have a monthly pass, you need to validate your ticket before boarding at a Ticket Validating Machine (TVM). Once validated, tickets are only valid for 90 minutes, so don't buy too far in advance. The trains and stations have random fare inspection and the fine for fare evasion is up to $100.

Hours

Light rail service operates between 5 am and 1:30 am. Times are approximate, check the website for exact schedules on each line.

Bikes on Board

Bikes are allowed (no permit or fee required) on board during off-peak times—weekdays from 9:30 am to 4 pm and 7 pm to 6 am, and all day Saturday, Sunday, and NJ state holidays. Bicycles have to be accompanied on the low-floor vestibule section of each rail car.

Pets

Small pets are allowed, as long as they're confined to a carry container. Service animals are permitted at all times.

Transit · NJ Transit

Otisville

Campbell Hall

Middletown

Salisbury Mills - Cornwall

PENNSYLVANIA

Port Jervis Line

Orange

Port Jervis

NEW YORK
NEW JERSEY

Harriman

Tuxedo

Rockland

Sloatsburg

Pascack Valley Line

Suffern   Spring Valley

Nanuet

Sussex

Mahwah
Ramsey Route 17
Ramsey
Allendale
Waldwick
Ho-Ho-Kus

Pearl River
Montvale
Park Ridge
Woodcliff Lake
Hillsdale
Westwood
Emerson
Oradell
River Edge
New Bridge Landing
Anderson St

Main Line & Bergen County Line

Passaic

Ridgewood
Glen Rock-Main Line   Glen Rock-
Hawthorne   Boro Hall
Paterson

Radburn-
Fair Lawn
Broadway-
Fair Lawn
Plauderville

HACKENSACK
Essex St
Teterboro-Williams Ave

Montclair-Boonton Line

Towaco

Lincoln
Park

Warren

Hackettstown

Mt Olive

Netcong

Mount Arlington

Dover

Denville

Mtn View-Wayne
Wayne-Rt. 23
Boonton
Mountain Lakes
Montclair State Univ
Montclair Heights
Mountain Ave
Upper Montclair
Watchung Ave
Walnut St
Bay St

Clifton
Passaic
Delawanna

Garfield

Wood-Ridge
Rutherford

Lake Hopatcong

Mt Tabor

Lyndhurst

Kingsland

Meadowlands
Sports
Complex

Morris and Essex Lines

Morris Plains

Glen Ridge
Bloomfield
Watsessing

Secaucus
Junction

NEW
YORK
CITY

Morristown

Highland Ave
Mountain Station
South Orange

New York
Penn Station

Convent

Essex

Orange

Bridge St

Hoboken

Madison
Chatham

Brick Church
East Orange

Bernardsville

Basking
Ridge

New Providence

Summit

Newark
Broad St

Newark
Penn Station Hudson
Newark Liberty

Gladstone

Lyons

Murray Hill

Short Hills

Roseville
Ave

International Airport

Peapak

Far Hills

Gillette

Millburn

Maplewood

North Elizabeth

High Bridge
Annandale
Lebanon

Stirling

Berkeley Heights

Union

Glen Ridge
Brick

Elizabeth

White House

North Branch

Millington

Chatham
Garwood
Cranford

Linden

Staten
Island

Raritan Valley Line

Somerville

Bound Brook

Fanwood
Westfield
Netherwood
Plainfield

Roselle
Park

Rahway

Avenel

Hunterdon

Raritan
Bridgewater

Dunellen

Woodbridge

Metropark

Metuchen

Perth Amboy

Atlantic Ocean

Somerset

New Brunswick
Jersey Ave

Edison

South Amboy

Middlesex

Aberdeen-Matawan

Hazlet

Northeast Corridor Line

Middletown

Princeton

Red Bank
Little Silver

Princeton Branch

Princeton Junction

Monmouth Park
(seasonal service)

Long Branch

Hamilton

Monmouth

Elberon
Allenhurst
Asbury Park
Bradley Beach
Belmar
Spring Lake
Manasquan

North Jersey Coast Line

NEW JERSEY
PENNSYLVANIA

Trenton

Bucks

Burlington

Ocean

Point Pleasant Beach
Bay Head

● Station
● Under Contruction Station

General Information

Address:	1 Penn Plz E Newark, NJ 07105
Phone:	973-275-5555
Suspicious activity:	888-TIPS-NJT
Lost and Found:	Call main number
Website:	www.njtransit.com
Twitter:	@NJTRANSIT

Overview

With a service area of over 5,000 square miles, NJ Transit (just "NJ," thank you) is one of the largest transit systems in the country. And yet, sandwiched between New York and Philadelphia, and a feeder into both city's transportation systems, you can't blame NJ Transit for feeling a little slighted. And when you think about it, there's a point there: an incredibly large proportion of those urban workforces are utterly dependent on a commuter system that relies on a handful of underground links with Manhattan and a few bridges into Philly. All of which is to say, let's hear it for NJ Transit, for all they do to get us in and out of two major cities day in and day out, as well as moving folks around the Garden State itself.

That said, are the rails prone to power loss and broken switches? Sure. And did someone or something screw pooches when they or it left much of its rolling stock in a flood plain during Superstorm Sandy? Well, yes. And does the Pascack Valley Line seem to just creep along, which can be problematic when you're trying to make a transfer before reaching the Big Apple? Absolutely. And do you wonder who exactly thought it was a good idea to dub Secaucus Junction "Frank R. Lautenberg Station at Secaucus Junction" long before the Senator passed away? No question. But for all that, the trains are usually clean (and immune to the weirdness that seems to plague the LIRR), and there's nothing better than relaxing on one of their brand spanking new Bombardier MultiLevel Coach cars while your boys wait in traffic at one of the three measly Hudson River automobile crossings. And don't forget NJ Transit's convenient and efficient bus lines connecting areas not served by the train lines.

That's right, when you're cruising into the departure lounge at Newark an hour early because your Northeast Corridor line train got you to the airport in just 30 minutes from Midtown, just know who to thank: the good folks at NJ Transit. And when you're settling into your lower-level seat at the Izod Center to check out the latest WWE tour event, remember who took you there—and who you're going home with. That's right: NJ Transit.

Secaucus Junction Station

By way of a history lesson, before the three-level hub with the senatorially laden moniker at Secaucus was built, two major lines crossed but never met, as existential as that sounds. Fourteen years and $450 million later, hundreds of thousands of commuters found relief by being able to connect in Secaucus, without having to travel all the way to Hoboken. That and the super-badass New Jersey Turnpike "Exit 15X" was created from literally nothing. Goya Foods and The Children's Place have their corporate headquarters in Secaucus, and Robert John Burck, otherwise known as Times Square's Naked Cowboy, makes his home in Secaucus. Oh, and if you want to be a huge smartass, know that Secaucus Junction is technically not actually a junction.

For riders, Secaucus Junction is just an 8-minute ride from Penn Station, and connects ten of NJ Transit's 11 rail lines, while offering service to Newark Airport, downtown Newark, Trenton, and the Jersey Shore.

Fares and Schedules

Fares and schedules can be obtained at Hoboken, Newark, Penn Station, on NJ Transit's website, or by calling NJ Transit. If you wait to pay until you're on the train and you board from a station that has an available ticket agent or open ticket machine, you'll pay an extra five bucks for the privilege. NJ Transit also offers discounted monthly, weekly, weekend, and ten-trip tickets for regular commuters. Tickets are valid until used and have no expiration date.

Pets

Only seeing-eye dogs and small pets in carry-on containers are allowed aboard the trains and buses.

Bikes

The short answer is that in general, you can take your bicycle on board a NJ Transit train only during off-peak hours and during all hours on the weekends. The nitty gritty is this: bicycles are permitted on all trains except inbound trains that end in Hoboken, Newark or New York between 6 am and 10 am weekdays, outbound trains that originate in Hoboken, Newark or New York between 4 pm and 7 pm weekdays, and on weekend trains along the Northeast Corridor, North Jersey Coast Line and Morristown Line trains terminating in New York between 9 am and 12 pm and trains originating in New York between 5 pm and 8 pm. If confused, look on the timetables for trains designated by a bicycle symbol. Bikes are not allowed on board most holidays, or the Fridays prior to any holiday weekend; however, a folding frame bicycle can be taken on board at any time. Most NJ Transit buses participate in the "Rack 'n' Roll" program, which allows you to load your bike right on to the front of the bus.

Overview

Phone: 800-USA-RAIL (872-7245)
Website: www.amtrak.com
Twitter: @Amtrak

General Information

Amtrak is our national train system, and while it's not particularly punctual or affordable, it will take you to many major northeastern cities in half a day or less. Spending a few hours on Amtrak also makes you want to move to Europe where France is now running trains at 357 mph (as opposed to 35 mph in the US). We exaggerate. But seriously, if you plan a trip at the last minute and miss the requisite advance on buying airline tickets or want to bring liquids with you on with checking baggage, you might want to shop Amtrak's fares. Bonus: Amtrak allows you to talk on cell phones in most cars and has plugs for laptop computers at your seat.

Amtrak was created by the federal government in 1971. Today, Amtrak services 500+ stations in 46 states (Alaska, Hawaii, South Dakota, and Wyoming sadly do not have the pleasure of being serviced by Amtrak, as much as Joe Biden would like to commit funding toward a trans-Pacific high-speed line). While not being as advanced as the Eurail system, Amtrak does serve over 30 million passengers a year, employs 20,000 people, still has the same decor it did in the early 1970s, and provides "contract-commuter services" for several state and regional rail lines.

Red Caps (station agents) are very helpful, especially for passengers traveling with children and strollers. The only problem is finding an available one!

Amtrak in New York

In New York City, Amtrak runs out of Moynihan Train Hall. Warning: If you hop in a cab to get to Amtrak, specify that you want to be dropped off at Eighth Avenue and 33rd Street in order to avoid LIRR and Madison Square Garden foot traffic. Don't let the cabbie argue with you, especially if you have luggage. He is just trying to make his life easier.

Popular Destinations

Many New Yorkers use Amtrak to get to Boston, Philadelphia, or Washington DC. Of course, these are the New Yorkers who are traveling on an expense account or fear the Chinatown bus service. Amtrak also runs a line up to Montreal and through western New York state (making stops in Buffalo, Rochester, Albany, etc.). Check Amtrak's website for a complete listing of all Amtrak stations.

Going to Boston

Amtrak usually runs about two dozen trains daily to Boston. One-way fares cost approximately $70–$200, and the trip, which ends at South Station in downtown Boston, takes about four-and-a-half hours door-to-door. For over $100 one-way you can ride the high speed Acela ("acceleration" and "excellence" combined into one word, though perhaps "expensive" would have been more appropriate) and complete the journey in three to three-and-a-half hours—if there are not track problems.

Going to Philadelphia

Dozens of Amtrak trains pass through Philadelphia every day. One-way tickets start from about $50–$55 on a regular Amtrak train; if you're really in a hurry, Acela service starts around $100, which will get you there in an hour or so. The cheapest rail option to Philly is actually to take NJ Transit to Trenton and then hook up with Eastern Pennsylvania's excellent SEPTA service—this will take longer, but will cost you approximately $25. Some commuters take this EVERY day. Thank your lucky stars you're probably not one of them.

Going to Washington DC

(Subtitle: *How Much Is Your Time Worth?*)
Amtrak runs dozens of trains daily to DC and the prices vary dramatically. The cheapest trains cost around $85 one-way and take between three and four hours. The Acela service costs at the cheapest $150 one-way, and delivers you to our nation's capital in less than three hours (sometimes). Worth it? Only you can say. Depending on what time of day you travel, you may be better off taking the cheaper train when the Acela will only save you 30 minutes.

A Note About Fares

While the prices quoted above for Boston, Philly, and DC destinations tend to remain fairly consistent, fare rates to other destinations, such as Cleveland, Chicago, etc., can vary depending on how far in advance you book your seat. For "rail sales" and other discounts, check www.amtrak.com. Military IDs will save you a bundle, so use them if you have them. Occasionally (or rarely), Amtrak frequently offers discounts that can be found on their website—hunt around.

Baggage Check (Amtrak Passengers)

A maximum of two items may be checked up to thirty minutes before departure. Two additional bags may be checked for a fee of $20 each (two carry-on items allowed). No electronic equipment, plastic bags, or paper bags may be checked. See the "Baggage Policy" section of their website for details.

General Information

NFT Map:	9
Address:	Seventh Ave & 33rd St
General Information (Amtrak):	800-872-7245
NJ Transit:	Tracks 1–12
Amtrak:	Tracks 5–16
LIRR:	Tracks 13–21
MTA Subway Stops:	1, 2, 3 (Seventh Avenue side) and A, C, E (Eighth Avenue side)
NYCT Bus Lines:	M34, M34A, M20, M7, M4, Q32
Train Lines:	LIRR, Amtrak, NJ Transit
Unofficial Guide to New York Penn Station:	jasongibbs.com/pennstation

Overview

Penn Station, designed by McKim, Mead & White (New York's greatest Beaux-Arts architectural firm), is a treasure, filled with light and…oh wait, that's the one that was torn down. Penn Station is essentially a basement, complete with well-weathered leather chairs, unidentifiable dust particles, and high-cholesterol snack food. Its claim to fame is that it is the busiest Amtrak station in the country. Moynihan Train Hall, an expansion of Penn Station into the Farley Post Office building across Eighth Avenue, finally opened in 2021. The renovation of the Beaux Arts building, also designed by McKim, Mead & White, expanded the LIRR concourse and added a glass-ceilinged central atrium—the first natural light in Penn Station in decades!—and new retail spaces. But not to worry, you can still experience the rat's maze under Madison Square Garden, especially if you're taking NJ Transit.

Penn Station serves Amtrak, the LIRR, and NJ Transit. Amtrak, which is surely the worst national train system of any first-world country, administers the station. How is it that the Europeans have bullet trains and it still takes three or more hours to get from NYC to DC? While we're hoping the new station proposal will come through, will it help the crazed LIRR commuters struggling to squish down stairwells to catch the 6:05 to Ronkonkoma? We can only hope.

The plus side to Penn is that it's easy to get to from just about anywhere in the city via subway or bus. If you are just too ritzy to take the MTA (or you have an abundance of baggage), have your cab driver drop you off anywhere surrounding the station except for Seventh Avenue—it is constantly jammed with tour buses and cabs trying to drop off desperately late passengers.

Temporary Parcel/Baggage Check

The main facility for storing parcels and baggage in Penn Station is at Amtrak Baggage Check (ticketed customers only). The Baggage Check is open from 5:15 am until 10 pm and costs $10 per item for each 24-hour period.

Main Concourse

Tracks 42   35   Tracks 34   11

Vanderbilt Ave

Biltmore Room

Station Master's Office

New York Transit Museum

Exit to MetLife Building

Information

Graybar Passage

Murray's

Grand Central Market

Dishes at Home   Wild Edibles

Lexington Passage

Lexington Ave

Ticketing/ Train Board   Ticketing/ Train Board

Ramp Down   Ramp Down

Vanderbilt Hall

42nd St

Balcony

Vanderbilt Ave

Michael Jordan's Steakhouse

Cipriani Dolci

EXIT

Apple Store

EXIT

The Campbell Apartment

MAP 13

Dining Concourse

Tracks 117   101

Ciao Bella Gelato   West Dining

Information

East Dining

Junior's   Shake Shack

Ramp from Main Concourse Level

Oyster Bar & Restaurant

Transit · **Grand Central Terminal**

General Information

NFT Map:	13
Address:	89 East 42nd St
General Information:	212-340-2583
Website:	www.grandcentralterminal.com
Twitter:	@GrandCentralNYC
Metro-North:	mta.info/mnr or @MetroNorth
MTA Subway Stops:	4, 5, 6, 7, Shuttle to Times Square
MTA Bus Lines:	M1, M2, M3, M4, M5, M101, M102, M103, M42
Newark Airport Express:	www.coachusa.com/airport-transportation

Overview

Grand Central Terminal, designed in the Beaux-Arts style by Warren & Wetmore, is by far the most beautiful of Manhattan's major terminals, and it is considered one of the most stunning terminals in the world. Its convenient location in the heart of Midtown and its refurbishments only add to its appeal.

If you ever find yourself underestimating the importance of the Grand Central renovations (begun in 1996 with continued work and maintenance today), just take a peek at the ceiling toward the Vanderbilt Avenue side—the small patch of black shows how dirty the ceiling was previously (and, believe us, it was really dirty…). In 2013 Grand Central celebrated its 100th anniversary, marked by a comprehensive exhibit in Vanderbilt Hall. The exhibit, worth checking out, survives online at www.gcthistory.com.

As of 2023, the multi-gazillion-dollar East Side Access project was completed, finally connecting the Long Island Rail Road to Grand Central via a new tunnel under 63rd Street, adding an eight-track terminal and concourse below Grand Central. Officially referred to as Grand Central Madison, it's most notable to us for site-specific murals created by Japanese artist Yayoi Kusama and German-American artist Kiki Smith.

Amenities

Diners have any number of choices. As food courts go, the lower level food court isn't half bad. After hitting the raw stuff at Oyster Bar, go right outside its entrance to hear a strange audio anomaly: If you and a friend stand in opposite corners and whisper, you'll be able to hear each other clearly. Alternatively, folks looking to hit the sauce may do so in 1920s grandeur in The Campbell Apartment near the Vanderbilt Avenue entrance, or for a non-edible treat, grab an iPad for your train ride at the shiny Apple Store on the east balcony overlooking the main concourse. One of the more fun spots to shop at in Grand Central is the New York Transit Museum Gallery Annex and Store, a satellite branch of the MTA's excellent Transit Museum in Downtown Brooklyn. The annex features a gallery with changing exhibits and the gift shop has some great gift ideas.

Grand Central Market, located between the east passages of the terminal as you head out toward Lexington Avenue, is a true big-boy market featuring various purveyors of high-quality foodstuffs. Build your own bread-meat-cheese extravaganza here, or take home fresh fish or meat to cook at home later on. Our favorite vendors include Wild Edibles, Dishes at Home and a Midtown branch of the best cheese shop in NYC—Murray's. Market open weekdays 7 am to 9 pm, Saturday 10 am to 7 pm, and Sunday 11 am to 6 pm.

Tours

The Municipal Arts Society runs a 75-minute tour of Grand Central guided by MAS docents. Tours depart daily at 12:30 pm. Tickets cost $25 ($15 reduced) at the tour window on the main concourse. Visit www.mas.org/tours for more information. Grand Central also offers a headset audio tour ($8) daily from 9 am to 6 pm, and an app version of the tour ($4.99) via the website for visitors who want to wander on their own (myorpheo.com/official-grand-central-tour).

General Information

NFT Map:	11
Address:	625 Eighth Ave at 41st St
General Information:	212-502-2200
Website:	www.panynj.gov/bus-terminals/port-authority-bus-terminal.html
Subway:	A, C, E, 42nd St/Port Authority or 1, 2, 3, 7, N, R, Q, S to Times Square
NYCT Bus:	M42, M34A, M20, M11, M104
Newark Airport Express:	www.coachusa.com/airport-transportation

Overview

Devised as a solution to New York City's horrendous bus congestion, the Port Authority Bus Terminal was completed in 1950. The colossal structure consolidated midtown Manhattan's eight, separate, interstate bus stations into one convenient drop-off and pick-up point. Back in the day the Port Authority held the title of "largest bus terminal in the world," but for now we'll have to be content with merely the biggest depot in the United States. The Port Authority is located on the north and south sides of W 41st Street (b/w Eighth Ave & Ninth Ave) in a neighborhood that real estate agents haven't yet graced with an official name. How about Greyhound Gardens?

There are plenty of things to do should you find that you've got some time to kill here. Send a postcard from the post office, donate blood at the blood bank on the main floor, use the refurbished bathrooms, roll a few strikes and enjoy a cocktail at Frames bowling lounge, chug a couple of decent brews at mini-chain Heartland Brewery, or shop the Greenmarket on Thursdays. There are also many souvenir carts, newsstands, and on-the-go restaurants, as well as a statue of beloved bus driver Ralph Kramden located outside of the south wing. The grungiest area of the terminal is the lower bus level, which is dirty and exhaust-filled, best visited just a few minutes before you need to board your bus.

If you can, avoid interstate bus rides from the Port Authority on the busiest travel days of the year. The lines are long, the people are cranky, and some of the larger bus companies hire anyone who shows up with a valid bus operator's license and their very own bus (apparently, easier to obtain than you might think). The odds of having a disastrous trip skyrocket when the driver is unfamiliar with the usual itinerary.

On Easter Sunday, Christmas Eve, or Thanksgiving, one can see all the angst-ridden sons and daughters of suburban New Jersey parents joyfully waiting in cramped, disgusting corridors for that nauseating bus ride back to Leonia or Morristown or Plainfield or wherever. A fascinating sight.

Bus Lines

- Academy (201-420-7000, www.academybus.com): Northeastern US and Florida
- Adirondack Pine Hill New York Trailways (800-858-8555, www.trailwaysny.com): New York State and nearby Canadian destinations
- Coach USA (800-877-1888, www.coachusa.com/community): Morris and Essex Counties (NJ)
- Community Lines (201-309-0006): Hudson County (NJ)
- Greyhound (800-231-2222, www.greyhound.com): US and Canada
- Lakeland (201-366-0600, www.lakelandbus.com): Northern New Jersey
- Martz Trailways (800-233-8604, www.martztrailways.com): New York, New Jersey, Pennsylvania
- Megabus (877-462-6342, www.megabus.com): US and Canada
- NJ TRANSIT (973-275-5555, www.njtransit.com): New Jersey commuter
- Peter Pan (800-343-9999, www.peterpanbus.com): Mid-Atlantic US and New England
- Rockland (Coach USA) (201-263-1254, www.coachusa.com): Rockland County (NY) and Northern New Jersey
- Shortline (Coach USA) (800-631-8405, www.coachusa.com): Upstate NY, Colleges, Orange, Rockland, Sullivan, Bergen and Pike Counties, Woodbury Common Premium Outlets
- Suburban (Coach USA) (800-222-0492, www.coachusa.com): Mercer, Middlesex, and Somerset Counties (NJ)
- Trans-Bridge Lines (610-868-6001, www.transbridgelines.com): Lehigh Valley, PA

General Information

NFT Map: 23
Address: 4211 Broadway at 178th St
Phone: 800-221-9903 or 973-275-5555
Website: www.panynj.gov/bus-terminals/
george-washington-bridge-bus-
station.html
Subway: A to 175th St or 1 or A to 181st St
Buses: M4, M5, M98, M100, Bx3, Bx7,
Bx11, Bx13, Bx35, Bx36

Overview

The George Washington Bridge Bus Station opened in 1963 to consolidate bus operations in the Washington Heights section of Manhattan. Italian architect Pier Luigi Nervi designed the facility and its striking roof consisting of 26 reinforced concrete triangle sections. The design is a great living example of 1960s architecture, and the reinforced concrete material is typical of Nervi's work. This was his first US project, after designing many well-known structures in Italy including the 1960 Olympic Stadium in Rome.

With easy access to the George Washington Bridge, the station connects Upper Manhattan with Northern New Jersey, and is served by several private carriers along with NJ Transit. A passageway connects with the 175th Street station of the A train (open 5 am to 1 am). Sitting directly atop the Trans-Manhattan Expressway (otherwise known as I-95), the views of the George Washington Bridge are pretty spectacular, and worth checking out even if you're not catching the bus to Hackensack.

For years the station's 30,000 square feet of retail space sat underutilized, but change is coming slowly. A $183 million rehabilitation is underway to modernize the facility and expand retail opportunities, including a 120,000-square-foot "MarketPlace" (no room for spaces) that will feature a gym, supermarket and Marshall's department store. Part of us hopes it will never lose its "lived-in" charm, but really, any place with pigeons routinely wandering around indoors can never be too sanitized.

Bus Companies

• New Jersey Transit
(973-275-5555, www.njtransit.com): To 60th St, Bergenfield, Bogota, Cliffside Park, Coytesville, Dumont, Edgewater (including Edgewater Commons Mall), Englewood, Englewood Cliffs, West Englewood, Fair Lawn (including the Radburn section), Fairview, Fort Lee, Glen Rock, Guttenberg, Hackensack (including NJ Bus Transfer), Hoboken, North Hackensack (Riverside Square), Irvington, Jersey City, Kearney, Leonia, Maywood, Newark, North Bergen, Paramus (including the Bergen Mall and Garden State Plaza), Paterson (including Broadway Terminal), Ridgewood, Rochelle Park, Teaneck (including Glenpointe and Holy Name Hospital), Union City, Weehawken, and West New York.

• Rockland Coaches (Coach USA)
(201-263-1254, www.coachusa.com/rockland): To Alpine, Bergenfield, Central Nyack, Closter, Congers, Coytesville, Cresskill, Demarest, Dumont, Emerson, Englewood, Englewood Cliffs, Fort Lee, Grandview, Harrington Park, Haverstraw, Haworth, Hillsdale, Leonia, Linwood Park, Montvale, Nanuet, New City, New Milford, Northvale, Norwood, Nyack, Old Tappan, Oradell, Palisades, Palisades Park, Park Ridge, Pearl River, Piermont, Rivervale, Rockland Lake, Rockleigh, Sparkill, Spring Valley, Stony Point, Tappan, Tenafly, Upper Nyack, Valley Cottage, West Englewood, Westwood, Woodcliff Lake

Overview

High-speed rail is efficient, fast, sleek and…decades away. Which is where low-cost, bare-bones intercity bus travel comes in. No, it's not particularly glamorous, especially when you're fumbling with a vending machine in front of a vending machine at a rest stop along Interstate 91, but it's cheap. Real cheap. Like cheaper than a cab to LaGuardia cheap. Cheaper than a fancy downtown cocktail cheap. Cheaper than an outerborough cocktail cheap. Like $10 cheap. $20 cheap. Even at $30, you're practically saving money sitting quietly on a bus to Boston or DC. No, this is no 300 kilometer-per-hour bullet train. But that *is* a VHS tape of *Look Who's Talking Too*, so what do you want?

There was a moment in time, starting around the late 1990s, when low-cost intercity coach travel was referred to as the "Chinatown Bus." The chartered buses catered to an Asian clientele, traveling between Chinatowns along the Northeast Corridor. The lines had no need for advertising, overhead, or—most importantly—gates at bus stations. Travelers bought tickets on the sidewalk and boarded buses on street corners. They'd play cheesy movies, subtitled in various Chinese dialects. Soon budget travelers began noticing and it wasn't long before the buses revolutionized short-haul travel—the fledgling Acela high-speed train was in an entirely different league, money-wise, and shuttle plane service between Northeastern cities was often not as fast, especially when taking into account post-9/11 security protocols and traffic to and from airports.

The early days of the Chinatown Bus were a hoot. Often trips were perfectly fine. Sometimes they seemed a little too efficient; three hours from Boston is great—except on a Chinatown bus. Other times, odds were high that you experienced at least one problem during the course of your trip including, but not limited to, poor customer service, unmarked bus stops, late departures, less than ideal bus conditions, and loogie-hucking and/or spitting from other passengers. Then there were the cancellations without warning, breakdowns, fires, broken bathrooms, fragrant bathrooms or no bathrooms at all, uncoupled luggage, drop-offs on the side of the road near the highway because bus companies didn't have permission to deliver passengers to central transportation hubs, and (alleged) organized crime links. We exaggerate. But only slightly. And still none of that deterred folks from using the buses. Again, the prices were just too good.

Before long, legacy bus carriers like Greyhound and Trailways began noticing, and rather than trying to beat the Chinatown options, they joined them, creating low-cost carriers like Megabus and BoltBus that mimicked the style and pricing of Chinatown buses. Of course, innovation ruffles feathers, and eventually neighborhoods tired of rolling bags clogging up the sidewalks. Concessions ensued, but for the time being a detente exists; the prices are just too good. The free wi-fi isn't too bad either.

After years of accidents, including a particularly gruesome March 2011 accident along I-95 that killed 15 people, the feds began cracking down on the carriers, shutting down many, including Fung Wah, one of the original lines. Of the organizations that remained, something miraculous happened: prices have stayed relatively low while oversight and regulation have increased. So now at least you can ride with some peace of mind. What were you saying about high-speed what?

Bus Companies

- **Washington Deluxe** (866-BUS-NY-DC, www.washny.com): To Washington multiple times a day; From 36th St & Seventh Ave. Additional departures from Delancey & Allen Sts, and Empire Blvd and Bedford Ave in Crown Heights, Brooklyn to Dupont Circle and Union Station in DC. Schedule varies by day of the week, so it's recommended that you check the website for info. $26-$35 one-way.

- **Flixbus** (212-244-6132, www.flixbus.com): To Washington DC, Baltimore, Rockville, MD, and Richmond, VA; From Allen St/Canal St and 34th St/Seventh Ave.

- **Vamoose** (212-695-6766, www.vamoosebus.com): To Bethesda, MD, Arlington, VA and Lorton, VA; stops at 30th St and Seventh Ave.

- **Megabus** (877-462-6342, us.megabus.com): To destinations across US; departure from 34th St and Eleventh Ave; arrival at 28th St and Seventh Ave.

- **TripperBus** (718-834-9214, www.tripperbus.com): To Bethesda, MD and Arlington, VA; stops at 31st St and Eighth Ave.

General Information

Bike Snob NYC:	www.bikesnobnyc.com
Century Road Club Association (CRCA):	www.crca.net or @crca
Department of City Planning:	www.nyc.gov/site/planning/index.page
Department of Parks & Recreation:	www.nycgovparks.org
Department of Transportation:	www.nyc.gov/html/dot/html/bicyclists/bicyclists.shtml
Five Boro Bicycle Club:	www.5bbc.org or @5BBC
League of American Bicyclists:	www.bikeleague.org or @BikeLeague
New York Bicycle Coalition:	www.nybc.net or @BikeNYBC
NYC Bike Share:	www.citibikenyc.com or @CitibikeNYC
New York Cycle Club:	www.nycc.org or @NYCycleClub
Recycle-A-Bicycle:	www.bike.nyc or @RAB_NYC
Streetsblog NYC:	nyc.streetsblog.org or @StreetsblogNYC
Time's Up! Bicycle Advocacy Group:	www.times-up.org or @nyctimesup
Transportation Alternatives:	www.transalt.org or @transalt

Overview

While not for the faint of heart, biking around Manhattan can be one of the most efficient and exhilarating forms of transportation. The advocacy group Transportation Alternatives estimates that over 200,000 New Yorkers hop on a bike each day. Manhattan is relatively flat, and the fitness and environmental advantages of using people power are incontrovertible. However, there are also some downsides, including, but not limited to: psychotic cab drivers, buses, traffic, pedestrians, pavement with potholes, glass, debris, and poor air quality. For years now biking has enjoyed the support of the city: many new miles of bike lanes have been added, and there has been an effort to create well protected lanes whenever possible including in Times Square, Eighth and Ninth Avenues in Chelsea, and Second and Third Avenues in the East Village. These tend to be the safest places to ride, though they often get blocked by parked or standing cars. Central Park is a great place to ride, as is the Greenway along the Hudson River from Battery Park all the way up to the GWB (it's actually a 32-mile loop around the island). East River Park is another nice destination for recreational riding, as well as skating. The most exciting cycling news in recent years is the launch of the Citi Bike bike share program, designed for quick trips around town.

A word about protecting your investment: bikes have to be locked up on the street and are always at risk of being stolen. Unfortunately, bike racks can be hard to come by in NYC, so you may need to get creative on where to park. Always lock them to immovable objects and don't skimp on a cheap bike lock. With over 40,000 bikes a year stolen in NYC, the extra cost for a top-of-the-line bike lock is worth it.

Now that we've got your attention, let's review some of the various rules and regulations pertaining to biking. First, remember that with great power comes great responsibility: bicyclists not only have all the rights of motor vehicles but they are also subject to all the same basic rules, including obeying all traffic signals, signage and pavement markings. Just as you can't drive a car on the sidewalk, neither are you allowed to ride on the sidewalk. And just as you can't drive a car into a park, remember that bicycle riding is prohibited in parks, except along designated bike paths. Some less-known rules: you can use either side of a one-way roadway; deliverymen must wear apparel with the name of their place of business when riding; when riding, you can't wear more than one earphone; feet must be on pedals; and riders must keep hands on the handlebars, and at least one hand when carrying packages. Also keep in mind the rules of equipment: a white headlight and red taillight are mandatory from dusk to dawn, and both bells and reflectors are required. Here's another thing: hand signals are mandatory. Children bring a whole other set of considerations: children under one year are not allowed on bikes, even in a Baby Bjorn; children ages one through five must wear a helmet and sit in an appropriate carrier. Children five through 13 must wear an approved helmet. Oh, and for Pete's sake, don't be a jerk.

Crossing the Bridges by Bike

Brooklyn Bridge
Separate bicycle and pedestrian lanes run down the center of the bridge, with the bicycle lane on the north side and the pedestrian lane on the south. Cyclists should beware of wayfaring tourists taking photographs. The bridge is quite level and, aside from the tourists and planks, fairly easy to traverse.

Brooklyn Access: Stairs to Cadman Plz E and Prospect St, ramp to Johnson & Adams Sts
Manhattan Access: Park Row and Centre St, across from City Hall Park

Manhattan Bridge
The last of the Brooklyn crossings to be outfitted with decent pedestrian and bike paths, the Manhattan Bridge bike and pedestrian paths are on separate sides of the bridge. The walking path is on the south side, and the bike path is on the north side of the bridge. The major drawback to walking across the Manhattan Bridge is that you have to climb a steep set of stairs on the Brooklyn side (not the best conditions for lugging around a stroller or suitcase). Fortunately, the bike path on the north side of the bridge is ramped on both approaches. However, be careful on Jay Street when accessing the bridge in Brooklyn due to the dangerous, fast-moving traffic.

Brooklyn Access: Jay St & Sands St
Manhattan Access: Bike Lane–Canal St & Forsyth St
Pedestrian Lane–Bowery, just south of Canal St

Williamsburg Bridge
The Williamsburg Bridge has the widest pedestrian/bike path of the three bridges to Brooklyn. The path on the north side, shared by cyclists and pedestrians, is 12 feet wide. The southern path, at eight feet wide, is also shared by bikers and walkers. Now that both sides of the bridge are always open to pedestrians and bikes, this is one of the best ways to get to and from Brooklyn. As a bonus fitness feature, the steep gradient on both the Manhattan and Brooklyn sides of the bridge gives bikers and pedestrians a good workout.

Brooklyn Access: North Entrance–Driggs Ave, right by the Washington Plz
South Entrance–Bedford Ave b/w S 5th & S 6th Sts
Manhattan Access: Delancey St & Clinton St/Suffolk St

George Washington Bridge
Bikers get marginalized by the pedestrians on this crossway to New Jersey. The north walkway is for pedestrians only, and the south side is shared by pedestrians and bikers. Cyclists had to fight to keep their right to even bike on this one walkway, as city officials wanted to institute a "walk your bike across" rule to avoid bicycle/pedestrian accidents during construction. The bikers won the battle but are warned to "exercise extra caution" when passing pedestrians.

Manhattan Access: W 178th St & Fort Washington Ave
New Jersey Access: Hudson Ter in Fort Lee

Robert F. Kennedy Bridge
Biking is officially prohibited on this two-mile span that connects the Bronx, Queens, and Manhattan. Unofficially, people ride between the boroughs and over to Wards Island all the time. The bike path is quite narrow, compared to the paths on other bridges, and the lighting at night is mediocre at best. The tight path sees less pedestrian/cycling traffic than other bridges, which, paired with the insufficient lighting, gives the span a rather ominous feeling after dark. If you're worried about safety, or keen on obeying the laws, the 103rd Street footbridge provides an alternative way to reach Wards Island sans car. This pedestrian pass is open only during the warmer months, and then only during daylight hours.

Bronx Access: 133rd St & Cypress Ave
Manhattan Access: Ramps—124/126th Sts & First Ave Stairs–Second Ave and 124/126 Sts
Queens Access: 26th St & Hoyt Ave (beware of extremely steep stairs).

Ed Koch Queensboro Bridge
The north outer roadway of the Ed Koch Queensboro Bridge is open exclusively to bikers, 24/7, except for the day of the New York Marathon. More than 2,500 cyclists and pedestrians per day traverse the bridge. Bikers complain about safety issues on the Manhattan side of the bridge: With no direct connection from Manhattan onto the bridge's West Side, bikers are forced into an awkward five-block detour to get to Second Avenue, where they can finally access the bridge.

Manhattan Entrance: 60th St, b/w First Ave & Second Ave
Queens Entrance: Queens Plz & Crescent St

Citi Bike Bike Share

The membership-only Citi Bike bike sharing program began in 2013. Designed for short jaunts around town, annual memberships cost $220 and entitle the user to unlimited trips of up to 45 minutes. One-day "Access Passes" for unlimited trips up to 30 minutes are available for $19. Trips exceeding the time limit incur steep overage charges; the program is not intended to function as a bike rental. Bike stations are located all over Manhattan, Brooklyn, the Bronx, and Queens, though they are much sparser in the outer boroughs. The bikes themselves are mostly functional three-speed machines, with easily adjustable seats, bells and LED safety lights, and multiple logos of original sponsor Citibank, which pledged more than $40 million to start the program. For more information visit citibikenyc.com.

Bike Sales and Rentals

Dah Bike Shop · 134 Division St · 212-925-0155 · Map 4
Frank's Bike Shop · 533 Grand St · 212-533-6332 · Map 4
Waterfront Bike Shop · 391 West St · 212-414-2453 · Map 5
Bfold · 224 E 13th St · 212-529-7247 · Map 6
NYC Velo · 64 2nd Ave · 212-253-7771 · Map 6

Recycle-A-Bicycle · 858 Fulton St · 718-858-2972 · Map 1
City Bicycles · 307 W 38th St · 212-563-3373 · Map 8
Enoch's Bike Shop · 480 10th Ave · 212-582-0620 · Map 8
Paragon Sporting Goods · 867 Broadway · 800-961-3030 · Map 9
Liberty Bicycles · 846 9th Ave · 212-757-2418 · Map 11
Conrad's Bike Shop · 25 Tudor City Pl · 212-697-6966 · Map 13
Eddie's Bicycles · 480 Amsterdam Ave · 212-580-2011 · Map 14
Toga Bikes · 110 West End Ave · 212-799-9625 · Map 14
Champion Bicycles · 896 Amsterdam Ave · 212-662-2690 · Map 16
Innovation Bike Shop · 105 W 106th St · 212-678-7130 · Map 16
Heavy Metal Bike Shop · 2016 3rd Ave · 646-952-4390 · Map 20
Junior Bicycle Shop · 1826 Amsterdam Ave · 212-690-6511 · Map 21
Victor's Bike Repair · 4125 Broadway · 212-740-5137 · Map 23
Tread Bike Shop · 250 Dyckman St · 212-544-7055 · Map 25

Bikes and Mass Transit

You can take your bike on trains and some buses—just make sure it's not during rush hour and you are courteous to other passengers. The subway requires you to carry your bike down staircases, use the service gate instead of the turnstile, and board at the very front or back end of the train. To ride the commuter railroads with your bike, you may need to purchase a bike permit. For appropriate contact information, see transportation pages.

Amtrak: Train with baggage car required
LIRR: No permit required
Metro-North: No permit required
New Jersey Transit: No permit required
PATH: No permit required
New York Water Taxi: As space allows; no fee or permit required
NY Waterway: $1.25 surcharge
Staten Island Ferry: Enter at lower level
Bus companies: Call individual companies

If you drive, entering from the south can be a little tricky. It's pretty well signed, so keep your eyes peeled. Basically you exit right at Eleventh Avenue and 22nd Street, turn left onto 24th Street, and then make a left onto the West Side Highway. Enter Chelsea Piers the same way you would if you were approaching from the north. Parking costs $16 for the first hour, $21 for two, $25 for three on up to $60 for eight ($10 for each additional hour thereafter). Street parking in the West 20s is an excellent alternative in the evenings after 6 pm.

Facilities

Chelsea Piers is amazing. There are swimming pools, ice-skating rinks, a bowling alley, spa, restaurants, shops, batting cages—you name it. So, what's the catch? Well, it's gonna cost ya. Like Manhattan rents, only investment bankers can afford this place.

1   **The Golf Club at Chelsea Piers** • 212-336-6400. Aside from potentially long wait times, the 250-yard driving range with 52 heated stalls and automated ball-feed (no buckets or bending over!) is pretty awesome. 55-minute off-peak sessions are $35; peak sessions are $55. If you don't bring your own, club hire is $4/one club, $6/two, $7/three, or $12/ten. Before 6 pm on weekdays, you can whack all the balls you want for $25 between 6:30 and 9 am.

2   **Bowlero** • 212-835-2695 or www.bowlero.com. Schmancy 40-lane bowling alley equipped with video games, bar, and private eight-lane bowling suite.

3   **The Sports Center** • 212-336-6500. A very expensive monster health club with a 10,000-square-foot climbing wall, a quarter-mile track, a swimming pool, and enough fitness equipment for a small army in training. If you have to ask how much the membership is, you can't afford it.

4   **Sky Rink** • 212-336-6100. Two 24/7 ice rinks mainly used for classes, training, and bar mitzvahs.

5   **Pier Sixty & The Lighthouse** • 212-336-6144 or piersixty.com. 10,000-square-foot event space for private gatherings catered by Abigail Kirsch.

6   **The Field House** • 212-336-6500. The Field House is an 80,000-square-foot building with a 23-foot climbing wall, a gymnastics training center, four batting cages, two basketball courts, and two indoor soccer fields.

7   **City Cruises** • 212-727-2789 or www.cityexperiences.com. Ships run out of Chelsea Piers. Dinner cruises start at around $80/person, and if you're having a big function, you can rent the entire boat.

General Information

NFT Map: 8
Address: 23rd Street & Hudson River Park
Phone: 212-336-6666
Website: www.chelseapiers.com
Twitter: @ChelseaPiersNYC

Overview

Opened in 1910 as a popular port for trans-Atlantic ships, Chelsea Piers found itself neglected and deteriorating by the 1960s. In 1992, Roland W. Betts (fraternity brother of George W. Bush) began the plan to renovate and refurbish the piers as a gargantuan 28-acre sports and entertainment center. In 1995, Chelsea Piers re-opened its doors to the public at a final cost of $120 million—all private money. The only help from the state was a very generous 49-year lease. By 1998, Chelsea Piers was the third most popular attraction in New York City, after Times Square.

How to Get There

Unless you live in Chelsea, it's a real pain to get to the Piers. The closest subway is the C or E to 23rd Street and Eighth Avenue, and then it's still a three-avenue block hike there. If you're lucky, you can hop a M23 bus on 23rd Street and expedite the last leg of your journey. L train commuters should get off at the Eighth Avenue stop and take the M14D bus across to the West Side Highway where you'll be dropped off at 18th Street. There are two Citi Bike stations near Chelsea Piers: 22nd Street and 10th Avenue and 18th Street and 11th Avenue.

Unfortunately, but not surprisingly, there are no golf courses on the island of Manhattan. Thankfully, there are two driving ranges where you can at least smack the ball around until you can get to a real course, as well as a golf simulator at Chelsea Piers that lets you play a full round "at" various popular courses (Pebble Beach, St. Andrews, etc.). NYC has a number of private and public courses throughout the outer boroughs and Westchester; however, they don't even come close to satisfying the area's huge demand for courses. **Bally's Golf Links at Ferry Point** in the Bronx is a world-class course with amazing views of the East River, Whitestone Bridge and Manhattan skyline.

Golf Courses

	Borough	Address	Phone	Par	Fee
Mosholu Golf Course	Bronx	3545 Jerome Ave	718-655-0655	18 holes, par 30	$28.75 for adults, $20.50 for seniors, $10 for juniors.
Pelham/Split Rock Golf	Bronx	870 Shore Rd	718-885-1258	18 holes, par 71	Weekend fees $32-$55, weekday fees $30-$45.
Bally's Golf Links at Ferry Point	Bronx	500 Hutchinson River Pkwy	718-414-1555	18 holes	$171 weekdays/$205 weekends (NYC residents)
Van Cortlandt Golf Course	Bronx	Van Cortlandt Pk S & Bailey Ave	718-543-4595	18 holes, par 70	For weekdays–weekends: $21–$23 9 holes early morning; $45–$55 18 holes before noon; $35–$42 18 holes after noon; $30–$32 18 holes at twilight.
Marine Park Golf Club	Brooklyn	2880 Flatbush Ave	718-252-4625	18 holes, par 72	" "
Dyker Beach Golf Course	Brooklyn	1030 86th St Seventh Ave	718-836-9722	18 holes, Par 71	" "
Golf Simulator	New York	Chelsea Piers Golf Club	212-336-6400		" "
LaTourette Golf Course	Staten Island	1001 Richmond Hill Rd	718-351-1889	18 holes, par 72	" "
Silver Lake Golf Course	Staten Island	915 Victory Blvd	718-442-4653	18 holes, par 69	" "
South Shore Golf Course	Staten Island	200 Huguenot Ave	718-984-0101	18 holes, par 72	" "
Clearview Golf Course	Queens	202-12 Willets Point Blvd	718-229-2570	18 holes, par 70	" "
Douglaston Golf Course	Queens	63-20 Marathon Pkwy, Douglaston	718-224-6566	18 holes, par 67	" "
Forest Park Golf Course	Queens	101 Forest Park Dr, Woodhaven	718-296-0999	18 holes, par 70	" "
Kissena Park Golf Course	Queens	164-12 Booth Memorial Ave	718-939-4594	18 holes, Par 64	" "

Driving Ranges

		Address	Phone	Fee
Aviator Sports Center	Brooklyn	3159 Flatbush Ave	718-758-7500	$10 for 60 balls; $13 for 105 balls
Chelsea Piers: Pier 59	Manhattan	Pier 59	212-336-6400	$35–$55 for 55 minute session
Randall's Island Golf	Manhattan	1 Randalls Is Rd	212-860-1899	$12 for 119 balls
Alley Pond Golf Center	Queens	232-01 Northern Blvd	718-225-9187	$16 for large bucket, $11 for small bucket

Sports • **Swimming**

For swimming pools in Manhattan, you pretty much have two options: pay exorbitant gym fees or health club fees in order to use the private swimming facilities, or wait until the summer to share the city's free outdoor pools with openly urinating summer camp attendees. OK, so it's not that bad! Some YMCAs and YWCAs have nice indoor pools, and their fees are reasonable. And several of the same New York public recreation centers that have outdoor pools (and some that do not) have indoor pools for year-round swimming. Though plenty of kids use the pools, there are dedicated adult swim hours in the mornings, at lunch time, and in the evenings (pee-free if you get there early). Just don't forget to follow each pool's admittance ritual, strange as it may seem—the locker room attendants generally rule with an iron fist. And if you can wait the obligatory 30 minutes, there's an authentic local food court near the standout public pool in Red Hook (155 Bay St, Brooklyn).

Then there's the Hudson. Yes, we're serious. There are about eight races in the Hudson each year, and the water quality is tested before each race. New York City also has some great beaches for swimming, including Coney Island, Manhattan Beach, and the Rockaways. If you prefer your swimming area enclosed, check out the pool options in Manhattan.

Pools

	Address	Phone	Type	Fees	Map
92nd Street Y	1395 Lexington Ave	212-415-5500	Indoor	$30/day or $55–$112/month	17
Asphalt Green	555 E 90th St	212-369-8890	Indoor	$35/day; $115/month	17
Asser Levy Recreation Center	E 23rd St & Asser Levy Pl	212-447-2023	Indoor, Outdoor, Outdoor free, Indoor $150/year		10
Athletic and Swim Club	787 7th Ave	212-265-3490	Indoor	Call for fees	12
Chelsea Piers Sports Center	19th St & Hudson River Park	212-336-6000	Indoor	Call for fees	8
Chelsea Recreation Center	430 W 25th St	212-255-3705	Indoor	$150/year for adults, free for children	8
Equinox Sports Club New York	160 Columbus Ave	212-362-6800	Indoor	Call for fees	14
Frederick Douglass	Amsterdam Ave & W 100 St	212-316-3241	Outdoor - Summer months		16
Gertrude Ederle Pool	232 W 60th St	212-397-3159	Indoor	$150/year	11
Harlem YMCA	180 W 135th St	212-912-2100	Indoor	$30/day $62–$75/month	19
Jackie Robinson Pool	85 Bradhurst Ave	212-234-9606	Outdoor - Summer months	Free	21
John Jay	E 77th St & Cherokee Pl	646-522-1538	Outdoor - Summer months	Free	15
Lasker Pool	110th St & Lenox Ave	212-534-7639	Outdoor - Summer months	Free	19
Lenox Hill Neighborhood House	331 E 70th St	212-744-5022	Indoor	Call for fees	15
Manhattan Plaza Health Club	482 W 43rd St	646-590-4411	Indoor - Summer months	$104/month	11
Marcus Garvey Pool	18 Mt Morris Park W	212-410-2818	Outdoor - Summer months	Free	19
New York Sports Club	1637 3rd Ave	212-987-7200	Indoor	$75/month	17
Recreation Center 54 Pool	348 E 54th St	212-754-5411	Indoor	$150/year	13
Riverbank State Park	679 Riverside Dr	212-694-3665	Indoor - Summer months	$2/day	21
Thomas Jefferson Park	2180 1st Ave	212-860-1372	Outdoor - Summer months	Free	20
Tompkins Square Mini Pool	500 E 9th St	212-639-9675	Outdoor - Summer months	Free	7
Tony Dapolito Recreation Center	1 Clarkson St	212-242-5228	Indoor, Outdoor	$150/year	5
Vanderbilt YMCA	224 E 47th St	212-912-2500	Indoor	$30/day or $114/month	13

General Information

Parks Permit Office:	212-360-8131
Website:	www.nycgovparks.org/permits/tennis-permits
Permit Locations:	The Arsenal, 830 Fifth Ave & 64th St
(Manhattan)	Paragon Sporting Goods Store, 867 Broadway & 18th St

Overview

There are more tennis courts on the island of Manhattan than you might think, although getting to them may be a bit more than you bargained for. Most of the public courts in Manhattan are either smack in the middle of Central Park or are on the edges of the city—such as **Hudson River Park (Map 5)**, **East River Park (Map 7)** and **Riverside Park (Map 16)**. These courts in particular can make for some pretty windy playing conditions.

Getting a Permit

The Parks tennis season starts on the first Saturday of April and ends on the Sunday before Thanksgiving. Permits are good for use until the end of the season at all public courts in all boroughs, and are good for one hour of singles or two hours of doubles play. Fees are: Adults (18–61 yrs), $100; Juniors (17 yrs and under), $10; Senior Citizen (62 yrs and over), $20; Single-play tickets $15. Permits can be acquired in person at the Parks Department headquarters Central Park or Paragon Sporting Goods or online via the Parks website or by mail (applications can be found online). Renewals are accepted in person, by mail or via the website, except if originally purchased at Paragon.

Tennis

	Address	Phone	Type/# of Cts./Surface	Map
East River Park	East River Park at Broome St	212-529-7185	12 hardcourts, lessons	4
Manhattan Plaza Racquet Club	450 W 43rd St	212-594-0554	Private, 5 courts, Cushioned Hard	11
Millennium UN Plaza Hotel Gym	2nd Ave & 44th St	212-758-1234	Private, 1 court, Supreme	13
ONE UN New York	1 United Nations Plaza	917-346-2724	Private, 1 hardcourt	13
The River Club	447 E 52nd St	212-751-0100	Private, 2 courts, Clay	13
Town Tennis Club	430 E 56th St	212-752-4059	Private, 2 courts, Clay, Hard	13
Vanderbilt Tennis Club	15 Vanderbilt Ave, 3rd Fl	212-599-6500	Private, 2 courts, Hard	13
Rockefeller University	1230 York Ave	212-327-8000	Schools, 1 court, Hard	15
Sutton East Tennis Club	488 E 60th St	212-751-3452	Private, 8 courts, Clay, Available Oct–April.	15
Central Park Tennis Center	93rd St near West Dr	212-316-0800	Public, Outdoor, 26 Fast-Dry, 4 Hard	16
Riverside Park	Riverside Dr & W 96th St	212-870-3070	Public, Outdoor, 10 courts, Clay	16
PS 146 Ann M Short	421 E 106th St	212-860-5877	Schools, 3 courts, Hard	17
Tower Tennis Courts	1725 York Ave	212-860-2464	Private, 2 courts, Hard	17
PS 125 Ralph Bunche	425 W 123rd St	212-666-6400	Schools, 3 courts, Hard	18
Riverside Park	W 119th St & Riverside Dr	212-978-0277	10 hardcourts, lessons	18
Riverbank State Park	W 145th St & Riverside Dr	212-694-3600	Public, Outdoor, 1 court, Hard	21
Frederick Johnson Playground	W 151st St & Seventh Ave	212-234-9609	Public, Outdoor, 8 courts, Hard	22
Fort Washington Park	Hudson River & 170th St	201-205-6915	Public, Outdoor, 10 courts, Hard	23
Milstein Family Tennis Center	575 W 218th St	212-851-7100	Public, 6 courts, Hard	25
Inwood Hill Park	207th St & Seaman Ave	212-639-9675	Public, Outdoor, 9 courts, Hard	25
Roosevelt Island Racquet Club	281 Main St	212-935-0250	Private, 12 courts, Clay	RI
Sportime at Randall's Island	Randall's Island Park	212-427-6150	Public/Private, 5 indoor hardcourts, 5 indoor/outdoor hardcourts, 10 indoor/outdoor clay courts, lessons	RWI

Billiards Overview

Whether you're looking for a new hobby or need a new atmosphere in which to booze (that isn't your 300 sq. ft. apartment), a good pool-hall is a great way to get the job done. Or perhaps you simply enjoy a hearty game of 8-ball, and it's as simple as that; in any case, an eclectic mix of options dot the island of Manhattan.

	Address	Phone	Map	Fee
Amsterdam Billiards Club	110 E 11th St	212-995-0333	6	$76–$100 per table per hour
Slate Restaurant Bar & Billiards	54 W 21st St	212-989-0096	9	$20 per hour for two players
Society Billiards + Bar	10 E 21st St	212-420-1000	9	$16 per player per hour
Post Billiards Café	154 Post Ave	212-569-1840	25	

Bowling Overview

If you want to go bowling in Manhattan, you have four solid options. Keep in mind that there's just about no way to bowl cheaply, so if you're struggling to keep a positive balance in your bank account, you may want to find another activity or head out to New Jersey.

At **Frames (Map 12)** you can pay per game or per lane. Connected to the Port Authority (remember this in case you have a long wait for a bus), Frames has 30 lanes, a full bar and pub menu, and two game-rooms, with a new dance floor and lounge on the way. You can even make online reservations. At Chelsea Piers, you'll find **Bowlero (Map 8)**. The high-end bowling alley also offers laser tag and a ropes obstacle course. Not cheap but they do feature all-you-can-bowl specials on slow nights.

Finally, for the world's ultimate (hipster) bowling experience, head to **The Gutter (Map 29)** in Brooklyn—the borough's first new bowling alley in over fifty years. It's like a Stroh's ad from the 1980s (except the beer is fancier). It doesn't get any better than bowling on beautiful, old-school lanes and drinking tasty microbrews with your buddies.

But The Gutter now has some serious competition, as sprawling **Brooklyn Bowl (Map 29)** has opened two blocks away. Featuring food by Blue Ribbon and live bands many nights, it's already become another great bowling option—and again, far better than anything in Manhattan.

Manhattan

	Address	Phone	Map	Fees
Bowlero	Pier 60	212-835-2695	8	If you have to ask…
Bowlero	222 W 44th St	212-680-0012	12	If you have to ask…
Frames	550 9th Ave	212-268-6909	12	$60–$75 per lane per hour; $7 shoes

Brooklyn

	Address	Phone		Fees
Brooklyn Bowl	61 Wythe Ave	718-963-3369		$25–$30 per lane per half hour; $5 shoes
The Gutter	200 N 14th St	718-387-3585		$25 per lane per half hour; $3 shoes
Melody Lanes	461 37th St	718-832-2695		$50–$60 per lane per hour; $6 shoes
Bowl 360	1 Bouck Ct	718-336-6700		$7–$15 per game; $8 shoes
FunFest	6161 Strickland Ave	718-763-6800		Call for fees

Queens

	Address	Phone		Fees
Bowlero Queens	69-10 34th Ave	718-651-0440		Varies by time, day, age
Bowl 360	19-45 49th St	718-274-1910		$7–$15 per game; $8 shoes
Bowl 360	98-18 Rockaway Blvd	718-843-5553		$7–$15 per game; $8 shoes
Jib Lanes	67-19 Parsons Blvd	718-591-0600		$6 per game $6 for shoes, $9 per game on the weekends
Whitestone Lanes	30-05 Whitestone Expy	718-353-6300		$25 per person for two games, shoes included

General Information

Address: 620 Atlantic Avenue, Brooklyn NY 11217
Website: barclayscenter.com or @barclayscenter
Nets: www.nba.com/nets or @BrooklynNets
Liberty: liberty.wnba.com
 or @nyliberty
Tickets: 877-77-BKTIX

Overview

Barclays Center, the home of the Brooklyn Nets and New York Liberty, opened in 2012 as part of the controversial $4.9 billion Atlantic Yards redevelopment project that decked over LIRR tracks and focused everyone's attention on controversial eminent domain issues, for a while there at least, until Barbra, Jay-Z, and Deron Williams redirected it again.

The original architectural design was created by Frank Gehry, the king of urban revitalization, but it was horrendously expensive, especially following the 2008 financial collapse, so the firm of Ellerbe Becket took over. The scaled-down plans proved to be horrendously uninspiring, eliciting negative comparisons to an airplane hangar and/or the downtown Indianapolis arena where the NBA's Pacers play (also designed by Ellerbe Becket). In the end, expectations were lowered just enough to make the final product look kind of cool: the brown weathered steel exterior evokes the site's industrial past and pays slight tribute to the brownstone materials in the surrounding neighborhoods. In addition, the height is not overwhelming; the structure almost fits snugly into the Flatbush Avenue streetscape. The triangular public space at the intersection of Flatbush and Atlantic is visually appealing: the new subway entrance features a living planted roof and the arena's exterior structure, along with its oculus sky opening (don't worry, we had to look up what that meant, too) and mesmerizing LED screen is—yikes—almost kind of elegant. As arenas go, it's pretty nice looking. And it's about 59 times more appealing looking than the Atlantic Center Mall, if you want to know the truth.

The Brooklyn Nets began playing at the arena for the 2012–13 season after moving from New Jersey. The WNBA's New York Liberty began playing at Barclays Center for the 2021 season. The arena has hosted college basketball almost since it opened, including the Barclays Center Classic, an early season eight-team tournament. For those who don't dig basketball, the concerts (accommodating 19,000 fans) have been big time: Barbra Streisand, Jay-Z (who owned a small stake in the Nets before becoming a sports agent), Billy Joel, not to mention the MTV Video Music Awards, which were broadcast from Barclays Center.

How to Get There—Driving

Parking is so limited that Barclays Center practically demands that you use public transport, but if you must, you can reserve a spot at the center (should there be any available, being a suiteholder helps), find a nearby garage, or scour for street parking.

How to Get There—Mass Transit

Part of the draw of Barclays Center is its proximity to Brooklyn's largest transportation hub. The 2, 3, 4, 5, B, D, N, Q and R trains all service the arena, and you can also take the to Lafayette Avenue or to Fulton Street. The LIRR stops at Atlantic Terminal, just across the street from the arena. In addition, eleven bus lines stop right outside or nearby.

How to Get Tickets

To avoid exorbitant Ticketmaster charges, the American Express Box Office (yes, even the freakin' box office has naming rights attached to it) is open Monday–Friday 12 pm–6 pm (Saturday 4 pm). Despite being a box office, they will not sell tickets to events on the first day tickets are offered to the public.

333

LOWER
MEZZANINE
UPPER

General Information

Address: 25 Lafayette St Newark, NJ 07102
Website: www.prucenter.com or @PruCenter
NJ Devils: devils.nhl.com or @NHLDevils
Seton Hall: www.shupirates.com or @SHUAthletics
Box Office: 973-757-6600
Ticketmaster: 800-745-3000 or www.ticketmaster.com

Overview

The $380 million Prudential Center (or "The Rock" to the media and fans) opened in downtown Newark in 2007 and immediately became a prime destination for major league sports and top-notch live music. With a capacity of 17,000-plus and all the bells and whistles of the modern sports going experience, the Prudential Center is the full-time home for the NHL's New Jersey Devils and the Big East basketball's Seton Hall Pirates. The Rock is hands down a billion times better than the cold and charmless Izod Center which is sitting in the middle of the Meadowlands all alone and is now used as a television production set.

How to Get There—Driving

Follow NJ Turnpike southbound and take Exit 15W onto I-280 westbound. Turn right on Exit 15A towards Route 21 southbound. Turn right onto Rector Street. Turn left onto Broad Street southbound. Continue on Broad Street to Lafayette Street and make a left. Prudential Center will be on your left hand side. There is lots of parking, but traffic

can still be unpredictable. Always allow more time than you think you'll need. Highways surrounding the arena include 280, 78, NJ Turnpike, 1 & 9, 21, 22, Garden State Parkway, 80 and NJ 3.

How to Get There—Mass Transit

No need to get on a bus anymore at Port Authority, thank goodness, for Devils games. Just take NJ Transit to Broad Street Station, then switch to Newark Light Rail to Newark Penn Station, which is only two blocks west of the Prudential Center. Even easier is taking the PATH train to Newark Penn Station. The arena is only a short walk away. Call or check the website for more details.

How to Get Tickets

The box office is open Monday to Friday from 11 am to 6 pm and is closed Saturday and Sunday, unless there is an event. To purchase tickets without going to the box office, call Ticketmaster at 800-745-3000, or visit their website. Or try StubHub (stubhub.com) the day of the game to find some good deals.

General Information

Address: One MetLife Stadium Dr
                East Rutherford, NJ 07073
Phone: 201-559-1515
Website: www.metlifestadium.com
                or @MLStadium
Giants: www.giants.com or @Giants
Jets: www.newyorkjets.com or @nyjets
Box Office: 201-559-1300
Ticketmaster: www.ticketmaster.com or 800-745-3000

Overview

The $1.6 billion MetLife Stadium is a state-of-the-art facility that hosts 20 NFL games a season—the most of any NFL stadium—as well as the biggest of big name concerts. In February 2014 it became the first cold-weather outdoor stadium to host a Super Bowl (though interestingly it wasn't the coldest temperature ever for a Super Bowl game). The stadium is home to both the New York Jets and New York Giants; the changeover from week to week to give the facility home team touches is fascinating in and of itself. And even the team shop switches from one to another. So that $1.6 billion is put to good use. Did we mention that New Jersey taxpayers are still paying off bonds from the old Giants Stadium, which was demolished in 2010?

How to Get There—Driving

MetLife Stadium is only five miles from the Lincoln Tunnel (closer to Midtown than Citi Field), but leave early if you want to get to the game on time—remember that the Giants and the Jets are a) sold out for every game and b) have tons of fans from both Long Island and the five boroughs. You can take the Lincoln Tunnel to Route 3W to Route 120 N, or you can try either the Holland Tunnel to the New Jersey Turnpike N to Exit 16W, or the George Washington Bridge to the New Jersey Turnpike S to Exit 16W. Accessing the stadium from Exit 16W allows direct access to parking areas. Parking costs $30 for most events except NFL games where all cars must have pre-paid parking permits only.

How to Get There—Mass Transit

On game days NJ Transit now runs trains directly to the stadium (Meadowlands Sports Complex) from Secaucus Junction for events over 50,000. Round-trip tickets are $4.50 and travel time is 10 minutes. Train service begins three hours before the start of a major event or football game. After events, trains will depart frequently from the Meadowlands for up to two hours. Metro-North runs trains directly to Secaucus Junction for selected games.

How to Get Tickets

In general, scalpers and friends are the only options for Jets and the Giants games. Try the resale sites if you're dying to attend a game. The box office is open Monday–Friday 11 am to 5 pm.

335

Sports · **Madison Square Garden**

General Information

NFT Map: 9
Address: 4 Pennsylvania Plz New York, NY 10001
Phone: 212-465-6741
Website: www.msg.com or @TheGarden
Knicks: www.nba.com/knicks or @nyknicks
Rangers: rangers.nhl.com or @NYRangers
Ticketmaster: www.ticketmaster.com or 800-745-3000

Overview

Once resembling the Doge's Palace in Venice (c.1900), the since-relocated Altoid 'tween Seventh and Eighth Avenues atop Penn Station remains one of the legendary venues in sport. Now, for good and ill, "The World's Most Famous Arena" houses the NBA's Knicks (catch Spike Lee and various supermodels courtside), NHL's Rangers, St. John's University's Red Storm, as well as concerts, tennis tournaments, dog shows, political conventions, and, for those of you with 2+ years of graduate school, monster truck rallies and "professional" wrestling. There's also The Theater at Madison Square Garden for more intimate shows. Check out MSG's website for a full calendar of events. A $1 billion (!) renovation completed in 2013 upgraded nearly everything and added two bridges running parallel to the floor that provide a unique view from way, way high above.

How to Get There—Mass Transit

MSG is right above Penn Station, which makes getting there very easy. You can take the A, C, E and 1, 2, 3 lines to 34th Street and Penn Station, or the N, Q, R, B, D and PATH lines to 34th Street and 6th Avenue. The Long Island Rail Road also runs right into Penn Station.

How to Get Tickets

Box Office open Monday–Saturday 10 am–6 pm. Try Ticketmaster or the resale sites for single-game seats for the Knicks and the Rangers. The ubiquitous ticket scalpers surrounding the Garden are a good last resort for when your rich out-of-town friends breeze in to see a game. Tickets for other events are usually available through Ticketmaster. First day of concert ticket sales are via Ticketmaster only.

General Information

Address: 41 Seaver Way
Flushing, NY 11368
Citi Field Box Office: 718-507-TIXX
Website: www.mlb.com/mets/ballpark or @Mets
Mets Clubhouse Shops: 11 W 42nd St & Roosevelt Field
Mall, Garden City, LI

Overview

Shea Stadium, the Mets longtime former home, is all but a very distant memory, except for some rousing Billy Joel concerts toward the end there that they sometimes replay on PBS late at night. And although most find Citi Field appealing enough, its debut coincided with the worldwide economic downturn and a particularly brutal period in the Mets history—connected in more ways than you'd think. The ballpark's corporate sponsorship was questioned and mocked after Citigroup received a government bailout; renaming the stadium "Debits Field" was one of the more inspiring reactions. Then came news that the Mets ownership had been investing with Ponzi pro Bernie Madoff; the team's finances took a, er, real hit, and management began paring its payroll. Thus began a vicious cycle of high ticket prices and mediocre seasons; sort of like the economy itself, come to think of it…

All of that aside—and it's a lot to put aside!—Citi Field is actually a pretty nice ballpark. Fans enter through the Jackie Robinson Rotunda, getting a little lesson on civil rights as they read the inspiring quotes etched in the façade and pose for pictures next to Robert Indiana's sculpture of the number 42. The food options are strong, from Danny Meyer's Shake Shack (beware multi-inning lines) to the Italian sandwiches courtesy Mama's of Corona. Beer options rise above the typical Crud Light—head to the outfield beyond the scoreboard for expanded tap and bottle options.

So much about Citi Field seems to be a response to the old Shea Stadium. Where the old sprawling multi-use facility sometimes seemed cavernous, Citi Field strives for an intimate experience—the only problem is that sightlines are often blocked, even in the high roller seats behind the dugouts. Speaking of which, tickets are expensive—after all, they have to pay for the privately financed $800 million-plus stadium somehow—but the resale market is

robust and the Mets tier ticket prices so that a weeknight game against a lousy team can be a pretty good deal (even if you have no view of the left field corner). Oh, and a bit of advice: steer clear of section 538—yes, the seats are cheap, but that out-of-town scoreboard works hard to block your view from the upper reaches.

How to Get Tickets

You can order Mets tickets by phone through the Mets' box office, on the internet through the Mets' website, or at the Mets Clubhouse Shops (11 West 42nd St, the Manhattan Mall, and Roosevelt Field Mall in Garden City). StubHub (www.stubhub.com) is a good option to scoop up unwanted tickets at reduced prices and there are StubHub kiosks located just outside the entrance to Citi Field.

How to Get There—Driving

Yeah. Good luck trying to make the first pitch on a weekday night. But if you must, take the Robert F. Kennedy Bridge to the Grand Central Parkway; the Midtown Tunnel to the Long Island Expressway to the Grand Central; or the Brooklyn-Queens Expressway to the LIE to the Grand Central. If you want to try and avoid the highways, get yourself over to Astoria Boulevard in Queens, make a right on 108th Street, then a left onto Roosevelt Avenue. Parking is absurdly expensive, but if you're willing to walk 15-20 minutes there is free street parking in the Corona neighborhoods surrounding Citi Field.

How to Get There—Mass Transit

The 7 train runs straight to Citi Field, and the MTA frequently offers special express trains that make limited stops between Citi Field and Times Square, making it by far the easiest way to get to the stadium. The E, F, M and R trains connect with the 7 at 74th Street-Roosevelt Avenue. The other option from Midtown is the Port Washington LIRR from Penn Station, which stops at Citi Field on game days. Seastreak (seastreakusa.com/mets.aspx or 800-BOATRIDE) runs ferries from Highlands, NJ for selected games; see website for details.

General Information

Address: 1 E 161st St, Bronx NY 10451
Telephone: 718-293-4300
Website: www.mlb.com/yankees/ballpark
or @Yankees

Overview

When a city or a team builds a new stadium they usually take the opportunity to come in with something bold and fresh. When the Yankees opened their new stadium in 2009 after 85 years in the old place, it was striking how similar it looked to the old version. And that was by design: after all, as they say, if it ain't broke, spend $1.5 billion to basically replicate it across the street. Architecturally, the exterior and the iconic frieze at the top of the upper decks are just about exactly the same. That said, there are some key changes—the concourses are wide and airy, the concessions are better (the Lobel's Sliced Steak Sandwich Cart is far and away our favorite), that 59-by-101-foot HD LED scoreboard is boffo-redonkulous, and the open-plan lower level allows you to catch a glimpse of the action from the area behind the expensive seats. That's the good. The not so good includes but is not limited to: seats cost more and seem farther away from the field of play, the place doesn't get as loud anymore, there is a stupid wire that runs across your field of vision on the first and third base lines from the upper levels, you have to pay extra to get into the schmancy outfield bar, you can't get into other places without a fancy seat, half the fancy seats go unused so there is all this empty space where all the best seats are, there are major unconscionable blind spots in the bleachers where that schmancy outfield bar juts out—we could go on. One thing that's the same: you still can't bring a bag into the place, which is just asinine if you're coming from work.

If you've never done it, make sure you check out Monument Park at least once. A sort hall of fame for Yankees players, Monument Park sits just beyond the center field wall. The bronze plaques immortalize the great players—and there have been many of them over the years—who made the franchise one of the most successful in all of sports. And then there's the way oversized tribute to George Steinbrenner, the cantankerous owner who rescued the team from irrelevance when he led an ownership group to purchase the floundering team from CBS in 1973 for about $10 million. When Steinbrenner died in 2010, the Yankees were worth $1.6 billion. Situated dead center, Steinbrenner's plaque is about five times the size of any other, including those to Mantle and DiMaggio—both of which dutifully flank The Boss. Monument Park is open until 45 minutes before the start of a game. Follow signs from the main entrance.

Yankee Stadium has hosted several non-baseball events: concerts like Metallica, Jay-Z and Justin Timberlake, European soccer, college football, and several NHL outdoor games. It is also the home of New York City FC (www.nycfc.com or @NYCFC), the city's MLS franchise. The field layout for NYCFC games is slightly odd, with one end of the pitch roughly along the first base foul line and the other end somewhere near the left field wall, meaning that a lot of the seats can seem removed from the action; check the seat map before you buy tickets. And then there's the monumental task of sodding the infield (and removing the picther's mound) for each game. This is no dirt and grass early season Raiders game at Oakland Coliseum, that's for sure. All that aside, soccer in Yankee Stadium is a blast, and (sorry Red Bulls) having a hometown team to root for is a, er, kick.

How to Get There—Driving

Driving to Yankee Stadium from Manhattan isn't as bad as you might think. Your best bet is to take the Willis Avenue Bridge from either First Avenue or FDR Drive and get on the Major Deegan for about one mile until you spot the stadium exit. From the Upper West Side, follow West 155th Street and use the Macombs Dam Bridge to cross over the river to the stadium (thus avoiding crosstown traffic). Parking (in contrast to ticket prices) is cheap, especially at lots a few blocks away from the stadium.

How to Get There—Mass Transit

Getting to the stadium by subway is easy. The 4 and D and the B (on weekdays) all run express to the stadium, and you can easily hook up with those lines at several junctions in Manhattan. A dedicated Metro-North station (Yankees–E 153rd Street) brings folks from Grand Central on the Hudson line in under 15 minutes. Seastreak (seastreakusa.com/yankees.aspx or 800-BOATRIDE) runs ferries from Highlands, NJ for selected games; see website for details.

How to Get Tickets

You can purchase tickets by phone through Ticketmaster, at the box office or the Yankee store, or online through either Ticketmaster or the Yankees website. StubHub is a good option to grab unwanted tickets, especially when the team is underperforming. And of course the illegal scalpers who are all over the damned place.

Beyond the obvious crowd-pleasers, New York City landmarks are super-subjective. One person's favorite cobblestoned alley is some developer's idea of prime real estate. Bits of old New York disappear to differing amounts of fanfare and make room for whatever it is we'll be romanticizing in the future. Ain't that the circle of life? The landmarks discussed are highly idiosyncratic choices, and this list is by no means complete or even logical, but we've selected an array of places, from world famous to little known, all worth visiting.

Coolest Skyscrapers

Most visitors to New York go to the top of the **Empire State Building (Map 9)**, but it's far more familiar to New Yorkers from afar—as a directional guide, or as a tip-off to obscure holidays (orange & white means it's time to celebrate ASPCA Day again!). If it's class you're looking for, the **Chrysler Building (Map 13)** has it in spades. Unfortunately, this means that only the "classiest" are admitted to the top floors. Other midtown highlights include the **Citicorp Center (Map 13)**, a building that breaks out of the boxy tower form, and the **GE Building (Map 12)**, one of the steepest-looking skyscrapers in the city. More neck-craning excitement can be found in the financial district, including the **Woolworth Building (Map 3)**, the **American International Building (Map 1)** at 70 Pine Street (with private spire rooms accessible only to the connected), **40 Wall Street (Map 1)**, the **Bankers Trust Company Building (Map 1)**, and **20 Exchange Place (Map 1)**. For a fine example of blending old, new, and eco-friendly architecture styles, check out the stunning **Hearst Tower (Map 12)**.

Best Bridges

The **Brooklyn Bridge (Map 3)** is undoubtedly the best bridge in New York—aesthetically, historically, and practically; you can walk or bike across on a wooden sidewalk high above the traffic. It's also worth walking across the **George Washington Bridge (Map 23)**, though it takes more time than you'd expect (trust us). The **Henry Hudson Bridge (Map 25)** expresses the tranquility of that part of the island—view it from Inwood Hill Park to see its graceful span over to Spuyten Duyvil.

Great Architecture

The Beaux Arts interior of **Grand Central Terminal (Map 13)** is full of soaring arches and skylights. Head to SoHo to see the **Little Singer Building (Map 6)** and other gorgeous cast-iron structures. You can find intricately carved faces and creatures on the tenement facades of the Lower East Side. **The Flatiron (Map 9)**, once among the tallest buildings in the city, remains one of the most distinctive. The **Lever House (Map 13)** and the **Seagram Building (Map 13)** redefined corporate architecture and are great examples of Modernism. Take the **Ferry to Ellis Island (Map 1)**, devoted solely to the immigrant experience, features domed ceilings and Guastavino tiled arches. **The Guggenheim (Map 17)** is one of New York's most unique and distinctive buildings (apparently there's some art inside, too). The **Cathedral of St. John the Divine (Map 18)** has a very medieval vibe and is the world's largest unfinished cathedral—a much cooler destination than the eternally crowded **St. Patrick's Cathedral (Map 12)**.

Great Public Buildings

Once upon a time, the city felt that public buildings should inspire civic pride through great architecture. Head downtown to view **City Hall (Map 3)** (1812), **Tweed Courthouse (Map 3)** (1881), **Jefferson Market Courthouse (Map 5)** (1877—now a library), the **Municipal Building (Map 3)** (1914), and a host of other courthouses built in the early 20th century. The **Old Police Headquarters (Map 3)**, now a posh condo, would be a more celebrated building if it wasn't located on a little-trafficked block of Centre Street in Little Italy/Chinatown. And what are the chances a firehouse built today would have the same charm as the **Great Jones Firehouse (Map 6)**? If the guys are around outside, they're happy to let you in to look around.

Outdoor Spaces

Central Park obviously. **Madison Square Park (Map 9)** is not as well known as many other central city parks, but it is home to the Shake Shack, where you can grab a burger, a shake, and a bit of peace and quiet on the grass. Newly renovated **Washington Square Park (Map 6)** has re-opened its gates to the NYU students, street performers, tourists, and pot dealers that love to gather there. There's all kinds of interesting folk around **Tompkins Square Park (Map 7)**, which makes it ideal for people watching. In addition to **Union Square (Map 9)** housing a bunch of great statues (Gandhi, Washington, Lincoln), it also hosts an amazing farmers market (Mon, Wed, Fri, and Sat) and is close to great shopping. You can dream all you want about having a picnic at **Gramercy Park (Map 10)**, but until you score a coveted key (or become friends with Julia Roberts), you'll have to admire the greenery from the sidewalk like the rest of us. **Bryant Park (Map 12)** attracts a chi-chi lunch crowd (it's a Wi-Fi hotspot) and hosts movies in the summer. Next door, people lounge on the **New York Public Library (Map 12)** steps and reminisce about their favorite scene from Ghostbusters, no doubt. **Rockefeller Center (Map 12)** tends to get overrun by tourists, but it's still deserving of a visit, especially to view the Art Deco styling. **The Cloisters (Map 24)** and **Inwood Hill Park (Map 25)** are great uptown escapes. Thanks to Stuyvesant Street's diagonal path, **St. Mark's-in-the-Bowery (Map 6)** gets a nice little corner of land in front for a park, which gives a hint of its rural past. Mountainous **Marcus Garvey Park (Map 19)** in Harlem is a good destination on Sundays when the famous drum circle is in full effect.

Lowbrow Landmarks

The **Chinatown Ice Cream Factory (Map 3)** is worth a slog through Chinatown crowds on a hot day. Just around the corner is **Doyers Street (Map 3)**, which retains the slight air of danger from its gang war past. **CBGB's (Map 6)** is gone, but punk spirit survives (somewhat) on the nearby street corner known as **Joey Ramone Place (Map 6)**. If you're in the old-time debauchery, there are tons of classic and historic New York bars including **McSorley's (Map 6)**, **Pete's Tavern (Map 10)**, the **White Horse Tavern (Map 5)**, the **Ear Inn (Map 5)**, and **Old Town Bar (Map 9)**.

Overrated Landmarks

Even the most cynical New Yorker would have to admit that **Times Square (Map 12)** is a unique place, but the truth is that it's no fun to compete in the same scrum as visitors in search of grub at the Bump Wump Shrimp Garden, or whatever it's called. **South Street Seaport (Map 1)** is a marvelous setting in search of an identity. And note the lawyerly language behind **Madison Square Garden's (Map 9)** bold "world's most famous arena" claim—as many a dictator has known firsthand, fame doesn't always equal greatness; aside from a few shining moments, the teams there usually stink, and the architecture is mostly banal. The worst part is that the gorgeous old Penn Station was torn down to make room for it. You can see pictures of the old station when you walk through the new **Penn Station (Map 9)**, which is famous not for its totally drab and depressing environs, but because of the sheer volume of traffic it handles. The **Cross-Bronx Expressway (Map 23)** deserves a mention here just because it's probably the worst highway, like, ever.

Underrated Landmarks

Many of these get overlooked because they are uptown. **Grant's Tomb (Map 18)** was once one of New York's most famous attractions, but these days it's mostly a destination for history buffs. The **City College (Map 21)** campus is quite beautiful, even though a few newer buildings muck things up. Farther north, **Sylvan Terrace (Map 23)** and the **Morris-Jumel Mansion (Map 23)**, a unique block of small row houses and a revolutionary war era house, offer a truer glimpse of old New York than the Seaport or Fraunces Tavern. Memorialized in a beloved children's book, a visit to The **Little Red Lighthouse (Map 23)** will make you feel like you're on the coast of Maine and not actually standing under the George Washington Bridge.

Television

1 NY1 (Time Warner Cable 24-Hour News) www.ny1.com
2 WCBS (CBS) newyork.cbslocal.com
4 WNBC (NBC) www.nbcnewyork.com
5 WNYW (FOX) www.fox5ny.com
7 WABC (ABC) www.abc7ny.com
9 WWOR (My9) www.my9nj.com
11 WPIX (PIX11/CW) pix11.com
12 News12 (Cablevision 24-Hour News) www.news12.com
13 WNET (PBS) www.wnet.org
21 WLIW (PBS Long Island) www.wliw.org
25 WNYE (NYCTV/NYC Media) www.nyc.gov/media
31 WPXN (Ion) iontelevision.com
41 WXTV (Univision) nuevayork.univision.com
47 WNJU (Telemundo) www.telemundo47.com
48 WRNN (RNN) www.rnntv.com
49 WEDW (PBS–Connecticut) www.cpbn.org
55 WLNY (CBS Affiliate)
newyork.cbslocal.com/station/wlny
63 WMBC (Ethnic/Religious) www.wmbctv.com

AM Stations

570 WMCA Religious
620 WSNR Russian
660 WFAN Sports Talk and Giants/Devils/Nets/Yankees
710 WOR Talk/New York Mets
770 WABC Conservative Talk
820 WNYC Public Radio; NPR Affiliate
880 WCBS News
930 WPAT Multi-Cultural (NJ)
970 WNYM Salem Radio Network; Conservative Talk
and College Sports
1010 WINS News
1050 WEPN ESPN Deportes; Spanish Language Sports Talk
and Jets/Mets
1100 WHLI Easy Listening/Standards
1130 WBBR Bloomberg Radio
1160 WVNJ Talk and Brokered Programming
1190 WLIB Gospel
1230 WFAS News/Talk/Iona Basketball
1240 WGBB Mandarin Chinese Language
1280 WADO Spanish Language Talk/Sports/Sports
Broadcasts
1330 WWRV Spanish Language Christian
1380 WKDM Chinese and Spanish Language
Brokered Programming
1430 WNSW Spanish Language Christian
1460 WVOX Variety; Westchester Focus
1480 WZRC Cantonese Chinese Language
1520 WTHE Gospel
1530 WJDM Spanish Language Christian
1560 WQEW Radio Disney
1600 WWRL Spanish Language
1660 WWRU Korean Language

FM Stations

88.1 WCWP College (LIU-Post)
88.3 WBGO Jazz (NJ)
88.7 WRHU College (Hofstra University)
88.9 WSIA College (College of Staten Island)
89.1 WFDU College (Fairleigh Dickinson University)
89.1 WNYU College (NYU)
89.5 WSOU College/Rock (Seton Hall University)
89.9 WKCR College/Jazz (Columbia University)
90.3 WKRB College (Kingsborough Community College)
90.3 WNYE College (City College of New York)
90.3 WHPC College (Nassau Community College)
90.7 WFUV Adult Alternative (Fordham University)
91.1 WFMU Free-form! (NJ)
91.5 WNYE NYC Radio

92.3 WNOW Top 40
92.7 WQBU Spanish Language
93.1 WPAT Spanish Language
93.5 WVIP Caribbean
93.9 WNYC Public Radio; NPR Affiliate
94.7 WNSH Country
95.5 WPLJ Hot Adult Contemporary
96.3 WXNY Spanish Language
96.7 WKLV Contemporary Christian
97.1 WQHT Hot 97; Mainstream Urban
97.9 WSKQ La Mega; Spanish Language
98.3 WKJY Adult Contemporary
98.7 WEPN ESPN New York, Sports Talk and New York Jets
99.5 WBAI Listener Supported Variety
100.3 WHTZ (Z-100) Top 40 Contemporary Hit Radio
100.7 WHUD Adult Contemporary
101.1 WCBS Oldies
101.9 WFAN Sports Talk and Giants/Devils/Nets/Yankees
102.7 WWFS Hot Adult Contemporary
103.5 WKTU Rhythmic Contemporary
103.9 WFAS Adult Contemporary
104.3 WAXQ Classic Rock
105.1 WWPR Power 105.1; Urban Contemporary
105.5 WDHA Rock (NJ)
105.9 WQXR Classical
106.7 WLTW Adult Contemporary
107.1 WXPK Adult Alternative
107.5 WBLS Urban Adult Contemporary

Print Media

AM New York (240 W 35th St, 9th Floor, 212-457-7735, www.amny.
com): Free daily; pick it up at the subway but please dispose of
properly so as to prevent track fires.
Brooklyn Paper (1 Metrotech Ctr, Ste 1001, 212-457-7735,
brooklynpaper.com): Brooklyn's hometown weekly with in-depth
black and kickball coverage.
Daily News (4 New York Plaza, 212-210-2100, www.nydailynews.
com): Daily tabloid; rival of the Post. Good sports.
El Diario (1 Metrotech Ctr, 18th Floor, Brooklyn, 212-807-4600,
www.eldiariony.com): Daily; America's oldest Spanish-language
newspaper.
Newsday (6 Corporate Center Dr, Melville, 800-639-7329, www.
newsday.com): Daily based in Long Island.
New York Magazine (250 Vesey St, 21st Floor, 212-508-0700,
nymag.com): New York City-focused news, arts, culture bi-weekly
with emphasis on cloying trend pieces.
New York Review of Books (207 E 32nd St, 212-757-8070, www.
nybooks.com): Bi-weekly intellectual lit review.
New York Observer (1 Whitehall St, 212-755-2400, observermedia.
com): Weekly that seeks influence by focusing on rich people
problems.
New York Post (800-552-7678, nypost.com): Daily tabloid with
infuriating and irresistible coverage and iconic headlines.
The New York Times (620 Eighth Ave, 800-698-4637, nytimes.com):
Daily; former "Grey Lady," now with Clairol treatments.
The New Yorker (1 World Trade Center, 515-243-3273, www.
newyorker.com): Weekly with intellectualish analysis; often
subscribed, seldom finished.
Staten Island Advance (1441 South Avenue, Suite 603, Staten
Island, 718-816-2804, www.silive.com): Richmond County's
hometown daily; pronounce it "ADD-vance" to sound in-the-
know.
Time Out New York (211 East 43rd St, Suite 1901, 646-432-3000,
www.timeout.com/newyork): Comprehensive weekly guide to
goings-on in the city with crazy-making "Top 5, 10, 15, 20" lists.
The Village Voice (36 Cooper Sq, 212-475-3300, www.villagevoice.
com): Ur alternative weekly trying to rehab from skanky ad
addiction.
Wall Street Journal (1211 Avenue of the Americas,
800-568-7625, www.wsj.com): Financial news with
expanded local coverage.

341

January

Winter Antiques Show: Park Ave Armory at 67th St; Selections from all over the country.
Three Kings Day Parade: El Museo del Barrio; Features a cast of hundreds from all over the city dressed as kings or animals—camels, sheep, and donkeys (early Jan).
New York Boat Show: Jacob Javits Convention Center; Don't go expecting a test drive (early Jan).
Lunar New Year: Chinatown; Features dragons, performers, and parades.
NYC Winter Jazzfest: Greenwich Village; A full weekend of jazz at multiple Village venues.

February

Empire State Building Run-Up: Empire State Building; Run until the 86th floor (0.2 miles) or heart seizure.
Westminster Dog Show: Madison Square Garden; Fancy canines who know more about grooming than most of you deadbeats.
Fashion Week: Lincoln Center; Twice yearly week-long celeb-studded event.

March

The Art Show: Park Ave Armory at 67th St; Art fair organized by Art Dealers Association of America to benefit charity.
St Patrick's Day Parade: Fifth Avenue; Hoochless LIRR holiday, gays need not apply (March 17).
Orchid Show: New York Botanical Garden; Yearly festival with changing themes.
Whitney Biennial: Whitney Museum; Whitney's most important American art, every other year (March–June).
Greek Independence Day Parade: Fifth Avenue; Floats and bands representing area Greek Orthodox churches and Greek federations and organizations (Late March).
The Armory Show: West Side Piers; Brilliant best-of-galleries show.
New Directors/New Films: MoMA/Lincoln Center; Film festival featuring new films by emerging directors.
Pier Antique Show: Pier 94; Look at old things you can't afford.

April

Macy's Flower Show: Broadway and 34th St; Flowers and leather-clad vixens. Okay, just flowers really.
Easter Parade: Fifth Avenue; Starts at 11 am, get there early with your Easter bonnet (Easter Sunday).
New York Antiquarian Book Fair: Park Ave Armory at 67th St; Dealers exhibiting rare books, maps, manuscripts, illuminated manuscripts, and various ephemera.
New York International Auto Show: Jacob Javits Convention Center; Traffic jam.
Tribeca Film Festival: Various Lower Manhattan locations; Festival includes film screenings, panels, lectures, discussion groups, and concerts.
Affordable Art Fair: Midtown; Prices from $100 to no more than $10,000; worth a look if you're buying.
New York City Ballet Spring Season: Lincoln Center; Features new and classical ballet (April–June).

May

Outsider Art Fair: Chelsea; Art in many forms of media from an international set.
The Great Five Boro Bike Tour: The single worst day of the year to use the BQE (first Sunday in May).
Ninth Avenue International Food Festival: Ninth Ave from 42nd to 57th Sts.
Fleet Week: USS Intrepid; Around Memorial Day weekend—Hello, Sailor!
New York AIDS Walk: Central Park; 10K walk whose proceeds go toward finding a cure.
Lower East Side Festival of the Arts: Theater for the New City, 155 First Ave; Celebrating Beatniks and Pop Art (last weekend in May).
Cherry Blossom Festival: Brooklyn Botanic Garden; Flowering trees and Japanese cultural events (late April–early May).
Martin Luther King, Jr/369th Regiment Parade: Fifth Avenue; Celebration of equal rights (third Sunday in May).

June

Puerto Rican Day Parade: Fifth Avenue; Puerto Rican pride (second Sunday in June).
Metropolitan Opera Summer Recital Series: Various locations throughout five boroughs; Free performances through June and July.
Museum Mile Festival: Fifth Avenue; Free admission and block party from 82nd–105th Sts.
NYC Pride: March from Midtown to Christopher St; Commemorates the 1969 Stonewall riots (last Sunday in June).
Blue Note Jazz Festival: Various locations; All kinds of jazz.
Mermaid Parade: Coney Island; Showcase of sea-creatures and freaks/celebration of Coney Island.
Feast of St Anthony of Padua: Little Italy; Patron saint of expectant mothers, Portugal, seekers of lost articles, shipwrecks, Tigua Indians, and travel hostesses, among other things (Saturday before summer solstice).
Central Park SummerStage: Central Park; Free concerts, but get there very, VERY early. (June–August).
Bryant Park Summer Film Festival: Sixth Ave at 42nd St; Free films Monday evenings (June–August).
Midsummer Night Swing: Lincoln Center; Live performances with free dance lessons (June–July).
Big Apple Barbecue Block Party: Madison Sq Park; Endless smoked meats from country's top smokers.
American Crafts Festival: Lincoln Center; Celebrating quilts and such.
Village Voice 4Knots Music Festival: South Street Seaport; Free outdoor show featuring renowned and emerging indie artists.
Howl Festival: Tompkins Square Park; Spirit of Alan Ginsberg lives on in multi-day East Village festival.

July

Macy's Fireworks Display: East River; Independence Day's literal highlight (July 4).
Washington Square Music Festival: W 4th St at LaGuardia Pl; Open-air concert Tuesdays in July.
New York Philharmonic Concerts in the Parks: Various locations throughout five boroughs; Varied programs.
Summergarden: MoMA; Free classical concerts July Sundays in sculpture garden.
Celebrate Brooklyn!: Prospect Park Bandshell; Nine weeks of free outdoor film, music, dance, and theater events (July–August).
Mostly Mozart: Lincoln Center; The name says it all (July–August).
Shakespeare in the Park: Delacorte Theater in Central Park; Every summer two free outsized outside plays with boldface names bring long lunch hour lines for evening shows.
PS1 Warm Up: MoMA PS1, Long Island City; Sweaty DJ-dance-installations every Saturday afternoon (late June–Labor Day).

August

Harlem Week: Harlem; Music and community events last all month long.
Dragon Boat Festival: Flushing-Meadows Park Lake, Queens; Wimpy canoes need not apply.
New York International Fringe Festival: Various locations; 200 companies, 16 days, more than 20 venues, 1,200 performances—and your friends expect you to show up to all of them.
US Open: USTA National Tennis Center, Flushing; Final Grand Slam event of the year (August–September).
Lincoln Center Out of Doors: Lincoln Center; Free outdoor performances throughout the month.

September

Brooklyn Book Festival: Two of Brooklyn's favorite things--books and Brooklyn.
West Indian American Day Carnival: Eastern Parkway from Utica to Grand Army Plaza, Brooklyn; Children's parade on Saturday, adult's parade on Labor Day (Labor Day Weekend).
Richmond County Fair: Historic Richmondtown, Staten Island; Best agricultural competitions (Labor Day).
Fashion Week: Lincoln Center; Twice yearly week-long celeb-studded event.
Feast of San Gennaro: Little Italy; Plenty of greasy street food.
Atlantic Antic: Brooklyn Heights; Multicultural street fair.
DUMBO Art Festival: DUMBO, Brooklyn; Hundreds of artists exhibiting in front of stunning bridge-skyline backdrop.

October

New York Film Festival: Lincoln Center; Features film premieres (early October).
Autumn Crafts Festival: Lincoln Center; Celebrating quilts and such.
Columbus Day Parade: Fifth Avenue; Celebrating the second person to discover America (Columbus Day).
Halloween Parade: West Village; Brings a new meaning to costumed event (October 31).
Halloween Dog Parade: East Village; Cute dogs, terrible puns.
Blessing of the Animals: St John the Divine, Morningside Heights; Where to take your gecko.
Big Apple Circus: Lincoln Center; Step right up (October–January)!
Hispanic Day Parade: Fifth Ave b/w 44th and 86th Sts; A celebration of Latin America's rich heritage (mid-October).
Open House NY: Various locations, all boroughs; Insider access to architecture and design landmarks (early October).
NY Comic Con: Jacob Javits Center; Comic enthusiasts convene at the nerd mecca.

November

New York City Marathon: Verrazano Bridge to Central Park; 26 miles of NYC air (first Sunday of November).
Veteran's Day Parade: Fifth Ave from 26th St to 56th St; Opening service at Eternal Light Memorial in Madison Square Park.
Macy's Thanksgiving Day Parade: Central Park West at 77th St to Macy's in Herald Square; Giant balloons with Santa bringing up the rear.
The Nutcracker Suite: Lincoln Center; Balanchine's ballet is a Christmas tradition (November–December).
Christmas Spectacular: Radio City Music Hall; Rockettes' mesmerizing legs steal show from Santa and little people (November–January).
Origami Christmas Tree: Museum of Natural History; Hopefully not decorated with candles (Nov–Jan).
Pier Antique Show: Pier 94; Look at old things you can't afford.

December

Christmas Tree Lighting Ceremony: Rockefeller Center; Most enchanting spot in the city, if you don't mind sharing it with about a million others.
Menorah Lighting: Fifth Avenue & 59th St; Just the world's biggest menorah, that's what.
John Lennon Anniversary Vigil: Strawberry Fields, Central Park; Every December 8 crowds gather to remember the singer/songwriter on the anniversary of his death.
Holiday Window Displays: Saks Fifth Avenue, Macy's, Lord & Taylor, etc.; A New York tradition.
Alvin Ailey American Dance Theater: New York City Center; Winter season lasts all month long.
Messiah Sing-In: Lincoln Center; For once—just this once—it's OK to sing along. Don't blow it.
New Year's Eve Ball Drop: Times Square; Welcome the new year with a freezing mob (December 31).
New Year's Eve Fireworks: Central Park; Hot cider and food available (December 31).
New Year's Eve Midnight Run: Central Park; Never too soon to start with the resolutions (four miles).

Useful Phone Numbers

Emergencies: 911
General City Information: 311
MTA Hotline 511
City Board of Elections: vote.nyc.ny.us or 212-487-5400
Con Edison: 800-752-6633
Time Warner Cable: 212-358-0900 (Manhattan); 718-358-0900 (Queens/Brooklyn); 718-816-8686 (Staten Island)
Cablevision: 718-860-3514
Verizon: 800-837-4966

Bathrooms

When nature calls, New York can make your life excruciatingly difficult. The city-sponsored public bathroom offerings, including dodgy subway restrooms and the sporadic experimentation with self-cleaning super porta-potties, leave a lot to be desired. Your best bet, especially in an emergency, remains bathrooms in stores and other buildings that are open to the public.

The three most popular bathroom choices for needy New Yorkers (and visitors) are Barnes & Noble, Starbucks, and any kind of fast food chain. Barnes & Noble bathrooms are essentially open to everyone (as long as you're willing to walk past countless shelves of books during your navigation to the restrooms). They're usually clean enough, but sometimes you'll find yourself waiting in line during the evening and weekends. Although Starbucks bathrooms are more prevalent, they tend to be more closely guarded (in some places you have to ask for a key) and not as clean as you'd like. Fast food restrooms are similarly unhygienic, but easy to use inconspicuously without needing to purchase anything.

Public buildings: Libraries, train stations (Grand Central, Penn Station) and shopping areas (e.g., South Street Seaport, World Financial Center, Manhattan Mall, The Shops at Columbus Circle).
Department stores: Macy's, Bloomingdale's, Saks, etc.
Other stores: Old Navy, Trader Joe's, Target, etc.
Supermarkets: Whole Foods is a sure bet; with garden-variety Pathmark, Food Emporium, D'Agostino, Gristedes, Key Food, etc. you'll probably have to ask, because those are usually way in the back among the employee lockers.

Starbucks: In every neighborhood, and usually busy enough that you can simply stride in. Works for us, usually.
Bars: Good option at night when most other places are closed; head straight back; can get raunchy toward closing time.
Parks: Nothing beats a stainless steel "mirror" and a transient bathing in the sink. That said, things aren't always what they used to be—newly renovated parks sometimes have very nice facilities and the public-private Bryant Park bathroom is among the nicest in Midtown (and stocked with fresh flowers, to boot).
Hotels: Midtown hotels are basically public buildings, for all intents and purposes; lobbies are also good for a quick rest.
Times Square Visitors Center: 1560 Broadway.
Subways: At ends of lines, in major transit hubs and some stops between; raunchy, not for the timid.

Websites

boweryboyshistory.com or @BoweryBoys: NYC history.
ny.curbed.com or @CurbedNY: For those who obssess over building permits.
www.eatingintranslation.com or @EIT: One guy eats his away through NYC.
ny.eater.com or @EaterNY: Restaurant gossip galore.
www.forgotten-ny.com or @ForgottenNY: Fascinating look at the relics of New York's past.
www.gothamgazette.com or @GothamGazette: NYC policy and politics website.
www.gothamist.com or @Gothamist: Blog detailing various daily news and goings-on in the city.
newyork.craigslist.org: Classified site that single-handedly put print media out of business.
www.nyc.gov or @nyc311: New York City government resources.
www.nyc-grid.com or @paulsahner: Photo blog of NYC, block by block.
www.nycgo.com or @nycgo: The official NYC tourism site.
www.overheardinnewyork.com: Repository of great overheard snippets.
www.scoutingny.com or @nycscout: The city from point of view of a film scout.
www.vanishingnewyork.blogspot.com or @jeremoss: Chronicling lost or nearly lost old-timey time spots.

New York Timeline — a timeline of significant events in New York history (by no means complete)

1524: Giovanni de Verrazano enters the New York harbor.
1609: Henry Hudson explores what is now called the Hudson River.
1626: The Dutch purchase Manhattan and New Amsterdam is founded.
1647: Peter Stuyvesant becomes Director General of New Amsterdam.
1664: The British capture the colony and rename it "New York."
1754: King's College/Columbia founded.
1776: British drive colonial army from New York and hold it for the duration of the war.
1776: Fire destroys a third of the city.
1789: Washington takes the Oath of Office as the first President of the United States.
1801: Alexander Hamilton founds the New-York Evening Post, still published today as the New York Post.
1811: The Commissioners Plan dictates a grid plan for the streets of New York.
1812: City Hall completed.
1825: Completion of the Erie Canal connects New York City commerce to the Great Lakes.
1835: New York Herald publishes its first edition.
1835: Great Fire destroys 600 buildings and kills 30 New Yorkers.
1854: First Tammany Hall-supported mayor Fernando Woods elected.
1859: Central Park opens.
1863: The Draft Riots terrorize New York for three days.
1868: Prospect Park opens.
1871: Thomas Nast cartoons and New York Times exposes lead to the end of the Tweed Ring.
1880: The population of Manhattan reaches over 1 million.
1883: Brooklyn Bridge opens.
1886: The Statue of Liberty is dedicated, inspires first ticker tape parade.
1888: The Blizzard of '88 incapacitates the city for two weeks.
1892: Ellis Island opens; 16 million immigrants will pass through in the next 32 years.
1897: Steeplechase Park opens, first large amusement park in Coney Island.
1898: The City of Greater New York is founded when the five boroughs are merged.
1904: General Slocum disaster kills 1,021.
1904: The subway opens.
1906: First New Year's celebration in Times Square.
1911: Triangle Shirtwaist Fire kills 146, impels work safety movement.
1920: A TNT-laden horse cart explodes on Wall Street, killing 30; the crime goes unsolved.
1923: The Yankees win their first World Championship.
1929: Stock market crashes, signaling the beginning of the Great Depression.
1929: The Chrysler Building is completed.
1930: The Empire State Building is built, then tallest in the world.
1927: The Holland Tunnel opens, making it the world's longest underwater tunnel.
1931: The George Washington Bridge is completed.
1933: Fiorello LaGuardia elected mayor.
1934: Robert Moses becomes Parks Commissioner.
1939: The city's first airport, LaGuardia, opens.
1950: United Nations opens.
1955: Dodgers win the World Series; they move to LA two years later.
1963: Pennsylvania Station is demolished to the dismay of many; preservation efforts gain steam.
1964: The Verrazano-Narrows Bridge is built, at the time the world's longest suspension bridge.
1965: Malcolm X assassinated in the Audubon Ballroom.
1965: Blackout strands hundreds of thousands during rush hour.
1969: The Stonewall Rebellion marks beginning of the gay rights movement.
1969: The Miracle Mets win the World Series.
1970: Knicks win their first championship.
1970: First New York City Marathon takes place.
1971: World Trade Center opens.
1975: Ford to City: Drop Dead.
1977: Thousands arrested for various mischief during a city-wide blackout.
1981: First NYC AIDS death begins a decade of tragedy.
1977: Ed Koch elected mayor to the first of three terms.
1987: Black Monday—stock market plunges.
1993: Giuliani elected mayor.
1993: A bomb explodes in the parking garage of the World Trade Center, killing 5.
1994: Rangers win the Stanley Cup after a 54-year drought.
2000: NFT publishes its first edition.
2001: The World Trade Center is destroyed in a terrorist attack; New Yorkers vow to rebuild.
2003: Blackout becomes best party in NYC history.
2003: Tokens are no longer accepted in subway turnstiles.
2006: Ground is broken on the WTC memorial.
2007: Construction begins (again) on the Second Avenue subway line.
2009: Bloomberg purchases a third term.
2012: 1 WTC is once again tallest in NYC.
2012: Superstorm Sandy ravages Zone A, altering New Yorkers' relationship with the waterfront.
2014: NYC hosts Super Bowl XLVIII, first outdoor cold-weather city game in history.

General Information • **Practical Info**

Essential New York Songs

"Sidewalks of New York"—Various, written by James Blake and Charles Lawlor, 1894
"Give My Regards to Broadway"—Various, written by George Cohan, 1904
"I'll Take Manhattan"—Various, written by Rodgers and Hart, 1925
"Puttin' on the Ritz"—Various, written by Irving Berlin, 1929
"42nd Street"—Various, written by Al Dubin and Harry Warren, 1932
"Take the A Train"—Duke Ellington, 1940
"Autumn in New York"—Frank Sinatra, 1947
"Spanish Harlem"—Ben E. King, 1961
"Car 54 Where Are You?"—Nat Hiken and John Strauss, 1961
"On Broadway"—Various, written by Weil/Mann/Leiber/Stoller, 1962
"Talkin' New York"—Bob Dylan, 1962
"Up on the Roof"—The Drifters, 1963
"59th Street Bridge Song"—Simon and Garfunkel, 1966
"I'm Waiting for My Man"—Velvet Underground, 1967

"Brooklyn Roads"—Neil Diamond, 1968
"Crosstown Traffic"—Jimi Hendrix, 1969
"Personality Crisis"— The New York Dolls, 1973
"New York State of Mind"—Billy Joel, 1976
"53rd and 3rd"—The Ramones, 1977
"Shattered"—Rolling Stones, 1978
"New York, New York"—Frank Sinatra, 1979
"Life During Wartime"—Talking Heads, 1979
"New York New York"—Grandmaster Flash and the Furious 5, 1984
"No Sleep Til Brooklyn"—Beastie Boys, 1987
"Christmas in Hollis"—Run-D.M.C., 1987
"New York"—U2, 2000
"I've Got New York"—The 6ths, 2000
"New York, New York"—Ryan Adams, 2001
"The Empty Page"—Sonic Youth, 2002
"New York"—Ja Rule f. Fat Joe, Jadakiss, 2004
"Empire State of Mind"—Jay-Z, 2009
"Welcome to New York"—Taylor Swift, 2014

Essential New York Movies

The Crowd (1928)
42nd Street (1933)
King Kong (1933)
Pride of the Yankees (1942)
Arsenic and Old Lace (1944)
Miracle on 34th Street (1947)
On the Town (1949)
On the Waterfront (1954)
The Blackboard Jungle (1955)
An Affair to Remember (1957)
The Apartment (1960)
Breakfast at Tiffany's (1961)
West Side Story (1961)
Barefoot in the Park (1967)
John & Mary (1969)
Midnight Cowboy (1969)
French Connection (1970)
The Out of Towners (1970)
Shaft (1971)
Mean Streets (1973)
Serpico (1973)

Godfather II (1974)
The Taking of Pelham One Two Three (1974)
Dog Day Afternoon (1975)
Taxi Driver (1976)
Saturday Night Fever (1977)
Superman (1978)
Manhattan (1979)
The Warriors (1979)
Fame (1980)
Escape From New York (1981)
Nighthawks (1981)
Ghostbusters (1984)
The Muppets Take Manhattan (1984)
After Hours (1985)
Crocodile Dundee (1986)
Wall Street (1987)
Moonstruck (1987)
Big (1988)
Bright Lights, Big City (1988)
Working Girl (1988)

Do the Right Thing (1989)
Last Exit to Brooklyn (1989)
When Harry Met Sally (1989)
A Bronx Tale (1993)
Kids (1995)
Men in Black (1997)
Bringing Out the Dead (1999)
The Royal Tenenbaums (2001)
Gangs of New York (2002)
Spider-Man (2002)
25th Hour (2003)
The Interpreter (2005)
Inside Man (2006)
The Devil Wears Prada (2006)
American Gangster (2007)
Enchanted (2007)
Sex and the City (2008)
New York I Love You (2009)
Whatever Works (2009)
The Wolf of Wall Street (2013)

Essential New York Books

A Tree Grows in Brooklyn by Betty Smith; coming-of-age story set in the slums of Brooklyn.

The Alienist by Caleb Carr; great portrait of late-19th century New York complete with serial killer, detective, and Teddy Roosevelt.

The Bonfire of the Vanities by Tom Wolfe; money, class, and politics undo a wealthy bond trader.

Bright Lights, Big City by Jay McInerney; 1980s yuppie and the temptations of the city.

Catcher in the Rye by J. D. Salinger; classic portrayal of teenage angst.

The Death and Life of Great American Cities by Jane Jacobs; influential exposition on what matters in making cities work.

The Encyclopedia of New York City by Kenneth T. Jackson, ed.; huge and definitive reference work.

Gotham: A History of New York City to 1898 by Edwin G. Burrows and Mike Wallace; authoritative history of New York.

The Epic of New York City by Edward Robb Ellis; super-readable chapter-by-chapter compendium of hits and highlights of NYC history.

The Fuck-Up by Arthur Nersesian; scraping by in the East Village of the '80s.

Here is New York by E. B. White; reflections on the city.

House of Mirth by Edith Wharton; climbing the social ladder in upper crust, late 19th-century NY.

Knickerbocker's History of New York by Washington Irving; very early (1809) whimsical "history" of NY.

Manchild in the Promised Land by Claude Brown; autobiographical tale of growing up in Harlem.

The Power Broker by Robert Caro; lengthy biography of 20th century municipal titan Robert Moses, you'll never look at the city the same way after reading it.

The Recognitions by William Gaddis; ever thought New Yorkers were phony? They are.

Washington Square by Henry James; love and marriage in upper-middle-class 1880s NY.

The Cricket in Times Square by George Selden; classic children's book.

This Is New York by Miroslav Sasek; charming children's book from 1960; great gift idea.

(347)

The Best of the Best

With all the culture the city has to offer, finding activities to amuse children is easy enough. From fencing classes to the funnest parks, our guide will provide you with great ideas for entertaining your little ones.

Neatest Time-Honored Tradition
There are carousels in all five boroughs; the Central Park Carousel (www.centralparknyc.org) is a vintage carousel featuring Coney Island-style hand-carved horses dating to 1908. Jane's Carousel on the DUMBO waterfront in Brooklyn Bridge Park (www.brooklynbridgepark.org) dates from 1922 and is housed in a striking all-glass pavilion.

Coolest Rainy Day Activity
The Children's Museum of the Arts (103 Charlton St, 212-274-0986 or cmany.org) offers activities for wee ones as young as 10 months, because its never too early to find out whether your child might be the next Picasso. Budding painters can use the open art studio; dramatic ones stage productions in the performing arts gallery; those who must touch everything delight in the creative play stations.

Best Spots for Sledding
Central Park's Pilgrim Hill and Cedar Hill (centralparknyc.org). Kids pray for a snow day for the chance to try out this slick slope. BYO sled or toboggan.

Funnest Park
Pier 51 Play Area (Hudson River Park, Pier 51 at Gansevoort St, www.hudsonriverpark.org) With a beautiful view of the Hudson River, the park features several sprinklers, a winding "'canal,'" and a boat-themed area complete with prow, mast, and captain's wheel.

Best Halloween Costume Shopping
Halloween Adventure (104 Fourth Ave, 212-673-4546) is the city's costume emporium that has every disguise you can possibly imagine, along with wigs, make-up supplies, and magic tricks to complete any child's dress-up fantasy. Open year-round.

Best Place for Sunday Brunch
There are a billion places to take the kids to get pancakes and eggs on Sunday mornings, so why not try something totally different—dim sum in Chinatown! The kids will be entertained as carts of dumplings, pork buns, and unidentified foods constantly roll on by for non-stop eating fun.

Rainy Day Activities

American Museum of Natural History
(Central Park West at 79th St, 212-769-5100 or www.amnh.org) Fantastic for kids of all ages, with something to suit every child's interest. From the larger-than-life dinosaur fossils and the realistic animal dioramas to the out-of-this-world Hayden Planetarium, all attention will be rapt. The hands-on exhibits of the Discovery Room and the IMAX theater are also worth a visit.

Bowlero Lanes
(Chelsea Piers, and Midtown, www.bowlmor.com) Great bowling alley with a retro decor that kids will love. Bumpers are available to cut down on those pesky gutter balls. Children are welcome every day before 5 pm and all day Sunday—a popular birthday spot.

Brooklyn Children's Museum
(145 Brooklyn Ave, 718-735-4400 or brooklynkids.org) The world's first museum for children (opened in 1899) engages kids in educational hands-on activities and exhibits.

Staten Island Children's Museum
(1000 Richmond Ter, 718-273-2060 or sichildrensmuseum.org) Offers plenty of hands-on opportunities for kids to explore everything from pirate ships to the rainforest. There's also an outdoor play space (weather permitting).

Children's Museum of Manhattan
(212 W 83rd St, 212-721-1223 or cmom.org) As soon as you arrive at the museum, sign up for some of the day's activities. While you're waiting, check out the exhibits, which are fun for all ages.

Intrepid Sea, Air & Space Museum
(Pier 86, 46th St & 12th Ave, 212-245-0072 or www.intrepidmuseum.org) Tour the Growler, a real submarine that was once a top-secret missile command center, or take a virtual trip on one of the simulator rides. After you've taken a look at the authentic aircraft on deck—including space shuttle *Enterprise*—visit the museum of the Intrepid to see an extensive model airplane collection and a Cockpit Challenge flight video game for those aspiring pilots.

Little Shop of Crafts
(711 Amsterdam Ave, 212-531-2723 or littleshopny.com) Great space to bead/paint. Stay for hours.

Lower East Side Tenement Museum
(103 Orchard St, 877-975-3786 or www.tenement.org) The museum offers insight into immigrant life in the late 19th and early 20th centuries by taking groups on tours of an historic tenement building on the Lower East Side. One tour called "'Visit the Confino Family'" is led by "'Victoria Confino,'" a young girl dressed in authentic costume who teaches children about the lives of immigrants in the early 1900s. A great place to take your kids if they haven't already been there on a school field trip.

The Metropolitan Museum of Art
(1000 Fifth Ave, 212-535-7710 or www.metmuseum.org) A great museum to explore with audio guides designed specifically for children. From the armor exhibits to the Egyptian Wing, the museum offers art exhibits from all historical periods.

The Noguchi Museum
(9-01 33rd Rd at Vernon Blvd, Long Island City, 718-204-7088 or www.noguchi.org) This museum showcasing the works of Japanese-American artist Isamu Noguchi offers interesting tours and hands-on workshops for toddlers to teens. The fees are minimal, but you must register beforehand.

The Museum of Modern Art
(11 W 53rd St, 212-708-9400 or www.moma.org) Besides the kid-friendly audio guides that help make this renowned museum enjoyable for tykes, MoMA has a lot of exciting weekend family programs that get kids talking about art and film. Lots of fun hands-on programs too. Registration is a must—these programs book up fast.

Outdoor and Educational

Central Park Zoo
(64th St and Fifth Ave, 212-439-6500 or www.centralparkzoo.com) Houses more than 1,400 animals, including some endangered species. Exhibits run the gamut, from the Arctic habitat of penguins to the steamy tropical Rain Forest Pavilion. The Tisch Children's Zoo nearby is more suited for the younger crowd with its smaller, cuddlier animals.

Fort Washington Park
(W 155 St to Dyckman St along the Hudson River, 212-639-9675 or www.nycgovparks.org) The Urban Park Rangers periodically open Jeffrey's Hook Lighthouse to tours. The lighthouse, popularized in the book *The Little Red Lighthouse*, is located at the base of the George Washington Bridge. The lighthouse affords some spectacular views—better than anything they'd see from atop Dad's shoulders.

Historic Richmond Town
(441 Clarke Ave, Staten Island, 718-351-1611 or www.historicrichmondtown.org) A 100-acre complex with over 40 points of interest and a museum that covers three centuries of the history of Staten Island. People dressed in authentic period garb lead demonstrations and tours.

New York Botanical Garden
(Bronx River Parkway at Fordham Road, Bronx, 718-817-8700 or www.nybg.org) 250 acres and 50 different indoor and outdoor gardens and plant exhibits to explore. The Children's Adventure Garden changes each season, and kids can get down and dirty in the Family Garden. Keen young botanists can join the Children's Gardening Program and get their own plot to care for.

Classes

With all of their after-school classes and camps, the children of New York City are some of the most well-rounded (and programmed) in the country. Help them beef up their college applications with some fancy extracurriculars. It's never too early.

92nd Street Y
(1395 Lexington Ave, 212-415-5500 or www.92y.org) The center provides children of all ages with tons of activities, ranging from music lessons and chess to flamenco and yoga. 92nd St is known as ""the Y to beat all Ys.""

Abrons Arts Center
(466 Grand St, 212-598-0400 or www.abronsartscenter.org) A program of the Henry Street Settlement, the Arts Center offers classes and workshops for children of all ages in music, dance, theater, and visual arts.

The Art Farm
(431 E 91st St, 212-410-3117 or www.theartfarms.com) Ecological and animal programs by way of the Hamptons for all ages.

Asphalt Green
(555 E 90th St, 212-369-8890 or www.asphaltgreen.org) Swimming and diving lessons, gymnastics, team sports, and art classes. They've got it all for kids one and up.

Perry School
(155 Bank St, 212-255-1685 or perryschool.com) Enrichment programs for kids 4 months to 13 years.

Church Street School for Music and Art
(41 White St, 212-571-7290 or www.churchstreetschool.org) This community arts center offers a variety of classes in music and art involving several different media, along with private lessons and courses for parents and children.

Dieu Donné
(63 Flushing Ave, 212-226-0573 or dieudonne.org) Workshops in hand papermaking offered for children ages seven and up.

Greenwich House Music School
(46 Barrow St, 212-242-4770 or www.greenwichhouse.org) Group classes and private lessons in music and ballet for children of all ages.

Hamilton Fish Recreation Center
(128 Pitt St, 212-387-7687 or www.nycgovparks.org) The center offers free swimming lessons in two outdoor pools along with free after-school programs with classes like astronomy and photography.

Institute of Culinary Education
(225 Liberty St, 212-847-0700 or recreational.ice.edu) Hands-on cooking classes.

Irish Arts Center
(553 W 51st St, 212-757-3318 or www.irishartscenter.org) Introductory Irish step dancing classes for children five and up.

The Jewish Community Center in Manhattan
(334 Amsterdam Ave, 646-505-4444 or www.jccmanhattan.org) The center offers swimming lessons, team sports, courses in arts and cooking, and summer programs. There's even a rooftop playground.

Kids at Art
(1412 Second Ave, 212-410-9780 or www.kidsatartnyc.com) Art program that focuses on the basics in a non-competitive environment for kids ages 2–11.

Marshall Chess Club
(23 W 10th St, 212-477-3716 or www.marshallchessclub.org) Membership to the club offers access to weekend chess classes, summer camp, and tournaments for children ages five and up.

Tannen's Magic
(45 W 34th St, Ste 608, 212-929-4500 or www.tannens.com) Ask about private and group lessons. Their week-long summer sleep-away camp (www.tannensmagiccamp.com) is also very popular.

The Techno Team
(160 Columbus Ave, 212-501-1425 or thetechnoteam.com) Computer technology classes for children ages 3–12.

Trapeze School
(Locations in Lower Manhattan and Long Island City 212-242-8769 or newyork.trapezeschool.com) Kids ages six and up can learn how to fly through the air with the greatest of ease.

Babysitting/Nanny Services

The Babysitters' Guild
(477 Madison Ave, 6th Floor; 212-682-0227 or babysittersguild.com)

Pinch Sitters (845-323-9690 or www.nypinchsitters.com)

Useful Websites

Mommy Poppins
mommypoppins.com or @mommypoppins

Important Phone Numbers

All Emergencies: 911
Non-Emergencies: 311
NYPD Switchboard: 646-610-5000
Terrorism Hot Line: 888-NYC-SAFE
Sex Crimes Report Line: 212-267-RAPE
Crime Stoppers: 800-577-TIPS
Crime Stoppers (Spanish): 888-57-PISTA
Crime Victims Hotline: 212-577-7777
Cop Shot: 800-COP-SHOT
Missing Persons Case Status: 212-694-7781
Operation Gun Stop: 866-GUN-STOP
Organized Crime Control Bureau: 888-374-DRUG
Civilian Complaint Review Board: 311 or www.nyc.gov/ccrb
Website: www.nyc.gov/nypd
Twitter: @NYPDnews

Precinct

Precinct		Phone	Map
1st Precinct	16 Ericsson Pl	212-334-0611	2
5th Precinct	19 Elizabeth St	212-334-0711	3
7th Precinct	19 Pitt St	212-477-7311	4
6th Precinct	233 W 10th St	212-741-4811	5
9th Precinct	321 E 5th St	212-477-7811	7
Midtown South	357 W 35th St	212-239-9811	8
10th Precinct	230 W 20th St	212-741-8211	9
13th Precinct	230 E 21st St	212-477-7411	10
Mid-Town North	306 W 54th St	212-767-8400	11
17th Precinct	167 E 51st St	212-826-3211	13
20th Precinct	120 W 82nd St	212-580-6411	14
19th Precinct	153 E 67th St	212-452-0600	15
24th Precinct	151 W 100th St	212-678-1811	16
23rd Precinct	162 E 102nd St	212-860-6411	17
26th Precinct	520 W 126th St	212-678-1311	18
28th Precinct	2271 8th Ave	212-678-1611	19
32nd Precinct	250 W 135th St	212-690-6311	19
25th Precinct	120 E 119th St	212-860-6511	20
30th Precinct	451 W 151st St	212-690-8811	21
33rd Precinct	2207 Amsterdam Ave	212-927-3200	23
34th Precinct	4295 Broadway	212-927-9711	24
Central Park Precinct	W 86th St & Transverse Rd	212-570-4820	CP

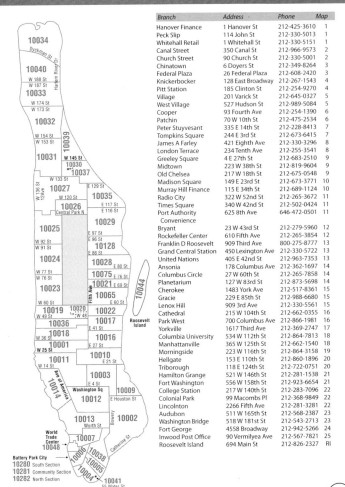

Branch	Address	Phone	Map
Hanover Finance	1 Hanover St	212-425-3610	1
Peck Slip	114 John St	212-330-5013	1
Whitehall Retail	1 Whitehall St	212-330-5151	1
Canal Street	350 Canal St	212-966-9573	2
Church Street	90 Church St	212-330-5001	2
Chinatown	6 Doyers St	212-349-8264	3
Federal Plaza	26 Federal Plaza	212-608-2420	3
Knickerbocker	128 East Broadway	212-267-1543	4
Pitt Station	185 Clinton St	212-254-9270	4
Village	201 Varick St	212-645-0327	5
West Village	527 Hudson St	212-989-5084	5
Cooper	93 Fourth Ave	212-254-1390	6
Patchin	70 W 10th St	212-475-2534	6
Peter Stuyvesant	335 E 14th St	212-228-8413	7
Tompkins Square	244 E 3rd St	212-673-6415	7
James A Farley	421 Eighth Ave	212-330-3296	8
London Terrace	234 Tenth Ave	212-255-3541	8
Greeley Square	4 E 27th St	212-683-2510	9
Midtown	223 W 38th St	212-819-9604	9
Old Chelsea	217 W 18th St	212-675-0548	9
Madison Square	149 E 23rd St	212-673-3771	10
Murray Hill Finance	115 E 34th St	212-689-1124	10
Radio City	322 W 52nd St	212-265-3672	11
Times Square	340 W 42nd St	212-502-0424	11
Port Authority Convenience	625 8th Ave	646-472-0501	11
Bryant	23 W 43rd St	212-279-5960	12
Rockefeller Center	610 Fifth Ave	212-265-3854	12
Franklin D Roosevelt	909 Third Ave	800-275-8777	13
Grand Central Station	450 Lexington Ave	212-330-5722	13
United Nations	405 E 42nd St	212-963-7353	13
Ansonia	178 Columbus Ave	212-362-1697	14
Columbus Circle	27 W 60th St	212-265-7858	14
Planetarium	127 W 83rd St	212-873-5698	14
Cherokee	1483 York Ave	212-517-8361	15
Gracie	229 E 85th St	212-988-6680	15
Lenox Hill	909 3rd Ave	212-330-5561	15
Cathedral	215 W 104th St	212-662-0355	16
Park West	700 Columbus Ave	212-866-1981	16
Yorkville	1617 Third Ave	212-369-2747	17
Columbia University	534 W 112th St	212-864-7813	18
Manhattanville	365 W 125th St	212-662-1540	18
Morningside	223 W 116th St	212-864-3158	19
Hellgate	153 E 110th St	212-860-1896	20
Triborough	118 E 124th St	212-722-0751	20
Hamilton Grange	521 W 146th St	212-281-1538	21
Fort Washington	556 W 158th St	212-923-6654	21
College Station	217 W 140th St	212-283-7096	22
Colonial Park	99 Macombs Pl	212-368-9849	22
Lincolnton	2266 Fifth Ave	212-281-3201	22
Audubon	511 W 165th St	212-568-2387	23
Washington Bridge	518 W 181st St	212-543-2713	23
Fort George	4558 Broadway	212-942-5266	24
Inwood Post Office	90 Vermilyea Ave	212-567-7821	25
Roosevelt Island	694 Main St	212-826-2327	RI

351

If you have to get to a hospital (especially in an emergency), it's best to go to the closest one. However, as a quick reference, the following is a list of the largest hospitals by neighborhood, complete with the name of its corresponding map. But no matter which hospital you drag yourself into, for heaven's sake make sure you have your insurance card.

New York Presbyterian Hospital Lower Manhattan: NYU Downtown Hospital · William & Beekman Sts, just south of the Brooklyn Bridge [Map 3]

East Village: Beth Israel Medical Center · 14th St & Broadway/Union Square · [Map 10]

Murray Hill: Bellevue Hospital Center · First Ave & 27th St [Map 10] ; NYU College of Dentistry · First Ave & 24th St [Map 10]

Hell's Kitchen/Upper West Side: St Luke's Roosevelt Hospital · 10th Ave & 58th St [Map 11]

East Side: NewYork-Presbyterian · York Ave & 68th St [Map 15]; Lenox Hill Hospital · Lexington Ave & 77th St [Map 15]; Mt Sinai Medical Center · Madison Ave & 101st St [Map 17]

Columbia/Morningside Heights: St Luke's Hospital Center · Amsterdam Ave & 114th St [Map 18]

Farther Uptown: Columbia Presbyterian Medical Center · 168th St & Broadway [Map 23]

If you have a condition that isn't immediately threatening, certain hospitals in New York specialize and excel in specific areas of medicine:

Cancer: Memorial Sloan-Kettering

Birthing Center/Labor & Delivery: Mt Sinai West

Digestive Disorders: Mt Sinai

Dentistry: NYU College of Dentistry

Ear, Nose, and Throat: Mt Sinai

Eyes: New York Eye and Ear Infirmary

Geriatrics: Mt Sinai, NewYork-Presbyterian

Heart: NewYork-Presbyterian

Hormonal Disorders: NewYork-Presbyterian

Kidney Disease: NewYork-Presbyterian

Mental Health: Bellevue

Neurology: NewYork-Presbyterian, NYU Medical Center

Orthopedics: Hospital for Special Surgery, NewYork-Presbyterian

Pediatrics: Children's Hospital of NewYork-Presbyterian

Psychiatry: NewYork-Presbyterian, NYU Medical Center

Rheumatology: Hospital for Special Surgery, Hospital for Joint Diseases Orthopedic Institute, NYU Medical Center

Emergency Rooms	Address	Phone	Map
Bellevue Hospital Center	462 First Ave	212-562-4141	10
Harlem Hospital Center	506 Lenox Ave	212-939-1000	22
Lenox Hill Hospital	110 E 77th St	212-434-2000	15
Metropolitan Hospital Center	1901 First Ave	212-423-6262	17
Mount Sinai Beth Israel	16 First Ave	212-420-3900	10
Mount Sinai Medical Center	1468 Madison Ave	212-241-6500	17
Mt Sinai Morningside	419 W 114th St	212-523-4000	18
Mt Sinai West	1000 Tenth Ave	212-523-4000	11
New York Eye and Ear Infirmary	310 E 14th St	212-979-4000	6
New York Presbyterian Hospital Lower Manhattan	170 William St	212-312-5000	1
NewYork-Presbyterian–Weill Cornell Medical Center	525 E 68th St	212-746-5454	15
New York-Presbyterian Hospital Allen Pavilion	5141 Broadway	212-932-4000	25
New-York-Presbyterian Hospital/Columbia University Medical Center	622 W 168th St	212-305-2500	23
North General Hospital	1879 Madison Ave	212-423-4000	20
NYU Langone Medical Center	570 First Ave	212-263-5550	10
NYU Langone Orthopedic Hospital	301 E 17th St	212-598-6000	10
VA NY Harbor Healthcare System - Manhattan Campus	423 E 23rd St	212-686-7500	10

Other Hospitals	Address	Phone	Map
Beth Israel—Phillips Ambulatory Care Center	10 Union Sq E	212-844-8074	10
Coler Goldwater–Coler Campus	900 Main St	212-848-6000	RI
Gouverneur Healthcare Services	227 Madison St	877-692-4692	4
Gracie Square Hospital	420 E 76th St	212-434-5300	15
Hospital for Special Surgery	535 E 70 St	212-606-1000	15
Manhattan Eye, Ear & Throat	210 E 64th St	212-838-9200	15
Memorial Sloan-Kettering Cancer Center	1275 York Ave	212-639-2000	15
Renaissance Health Care Network Diagnostic and Treatment Center	264 W 118th St	212-932-6521	18

General Information · Libraries

Beginner's mistake: Walk into the "main branch" of the New York Public Library at Bryant Park, and ask how to check out books. Trust us; it's happened. Recognizable for its reclining stone lions, *Patience* and *Fortitude*, the famous building is a research library with non-circulating materials that you can peruse only in the iconic reading room. In 2008, the Children's Center, a circulating children's library, moved to this location and now you can check out kids books here, too. If you want to read *War and Peace* or *50 Shades of Da Vinci Pray Love*, it's best to go to your local branch (there are 80 of them spread out through Manhattan, The Bronx and Staten Island). Note: Holds take a very long time to fill, at least a week to a week and a half. If the book you need is only a 20-minute subway ride away, and you need the book now, invest the time and the subway fare.

The main branch of the **New York Public Library (Map 12)** (renamed the Schwarzman Building in 2008, for billionaire donor Stephen A. Schwarzman) is one of Manhattan's architectural treasures. Designed by Carrère and Hastings and opened to the public in 1911, the building was one of the Beaux-Arts firm's most famous commissions. The main branch has several special collections and services, such as the Humanities and Social Sciences Library, the Map Division, Exhibition galleries, and divisions dedicated to various ethnic groups. The main branch contains 88 miles of shelves and has more than 10,000 current periodicals from almost 150 countries. Research libraries require an ACCESS card, which you can apply for at the library and which allows you to request materials in any of the reading rooms. Card sign-up can be slow, so be patient, and it never hurts to bring along multiple kinds of ID, or a piece of mail if you're a new NYC resident.

If it's reference material you're after, there are specialized research libraries to help: The **Schomburg Center for Research in Black Culture (Map 22)** is the nation's foremost source on African-American history. The **Library for the Performing Arts (Map 14)** contains the Theatre and Film and Tape Archive, featuring taped performances of many Broadway shows. There's also the **Andrew Heiskell Braille and Talking Book Library (Map 9)**, designed to be barrier-free. The library contains large collections of special format materials and audio equipment for listening to recorded books and magazines. You can check out the full library system online at www.nypl.org.

Library	Address	Phone	Map
Harry Belafonte 115th Street Library	203 W 115th St	212-666-9393	19
125th St	224 E 125th St	212-534-5050	20
58th St	127 E 58th St	212-759-7358	13
67th St	328 E 67th St	212-734-1717	15
96th Street	112 E 96th St	212-289-0908	17
Aguilar	174 E 110th St	212-534-2930	20
Andrew Heiskell Braille & Talking Book Library	40 W 20th St	212-206-5400	9
Bloomingdale	150 W 100th St	212-222-8030	16
Children's Center	455 5th Ave	212-621-0208	12
Columbus	742 Tenth Ave	212-586-5098	11
Countee Cullen	104 W 136th St	212-491-2070	22
Epiphany	228 E 23rd St	212-679-2645	10
Fort Washington	535 W 179th St	212-927-3533	23
Frick Art Reference Library	10 E 71st St	212-547-0641	15
George Bruce	518 W 125th St	212-662-9727	18
Hamilton Fish Park	415 E Houston St	212-673-2290	7
Hamilton Grange	503 W 145th St	212-926-2147	21
Harlem	9 W 124th St	212-348-5620	19
Hudson Park	66 Leroy St	212-243-6876	5
Inwood	4790 Broadway	212-942-2445	25
Jefferson Market	425 Sixth Ave	212-243-4334	5
Kips Bay	446 Third Ave	212-683-2520	10
Macomb's Bridge	2633 Adam Clayton Powell Jr Blvd	212-281-4900	22
Morningside Heights Library	2900 Broadway	212-864-2530	18
Muhlenberg	209 W 23rd St	212-924-1585	9
Mulberry Street	10 Jersey St	212-966-3424	6
National Archives	201 Varick St	212-401-1620	5
New York Academy of Medicine Library	1216 Fifth Ave	212-822-7200	17
New York Public Library for the Performing Arts	40 Lincoln Center Plz	917-275-6975	14
New York Society Library	53 E 79th St	212-288-6900	15
Ottendorfer	135 Second Ave	212-674-0947	6
Riverside	127 Amsterdam Ave	212-870-1810	14
Roosevelt Island	504 Main St	212-308-6243	RI
Schomburg Center for Research in Black Culture	515 Malcolm X Blvd	212-491-2265	22
Seward Park	192 East Broadway	212-477-6770	4
Stavros Niarchos Foundation Library	455 Fifth Ave	212-340-0863	12
St Agnes	444 Amsterdam Ave	212-621-0619	14
Stephen A. Schwarzman Building	476 Fifth Ave	917-275-6975	12
Terence Cardinal Cooke-Cathedral	560 Lexington Ave	212-752-3824	13
Tompkins Square	331 E 10th St	212-228-4747	7
Washington Heights	1000 St Nicholas Ave	212-923-6054	23
Webster	1465 York Ave	212-288-5049	15
Yorkville	222 E 79th St	212-744-5824	15

Very few places, anywhere, rival New York when it comes to quality gay living. Gay men can get about anything they want, any time of day, with many businesses catering specifically to gay clientele. Bars remain the backbone of the social scene: some, like **Industry (Map 11)**, focus on a chic atmosphere, while **The Phoenix (Map 7)** is a friendly dive bar. You can sing your face off on karaoke nights at **Pieces (Map 5)**, get into trouble at **The Cock (Map 6)**, and dance with the locals at **The Ritz (Map 11)**.

There are more lesbian bars and parties than ever in New York City, so all you have to do is decide what night, which neighborhood and how you'll snag a girl! Although you'll find quality drinks, music, and women at **Henrietta Hudson (Map 5)**, the notorious and intolerable bathroom line might discourage those lesbians who actually have a bladder. Lovergirl (www.lovergirlnyc.com) puts on Saturday night dance parties while **Cubbyhole (Map 5)** promises a homey atmosphere and friendly crowd. In Brooklyn, chill on the patio at **Ginger's (Map 33)**.

Websites

newyork.gaycities.com: New York section of comprehensive LGBT-focused travel site.

www.gayellowpages.com: Gayellow Pages for gay/lesbian-owned and gay/lesbian-friendly businesses in the US and Canada.

Publications

Gay City News: Bi-weekly newspaper for lesbian and gay New Yorkers including current local and national news items. (www.gaycitynews.com or @GayCityNews).

Get Out! Weekly with emphasis on goings on about town (getoutmag.com or @GetOutMag).

Bookshops

Bluestockings: Lesbian/radical bookstore and activist center with regular readings and a fair-trade café. (172 Allen St, 212-777-6028, www.bluestockings.com or @bluestockings).

Health Centers and Support Organizations

Callen-Lorde Community Health Center: Health care and services for the LGBT community (356 W 18th St, 212-271-7200, www.callen-lorde.org or @CallenLorde).

GMHC: Founded in 1981, Gay Men's Health Crisis is dedicated to AIDS awareness and support for those living with HIV (307 W 38th St, 212-367-1000, www.gmhc.org or @GMHC).

The Lesbian, Gay, Bisexual & Transgender Community Center: The largest LGBT multi-service organization on the East Coast. (208 W 13th, 212-620-7310, www.gaycenter.org).

GLBT National Help Center: Switchboard for referrals, advice, and counseling (888-843-4564, www.glnh.org or @glbtNatlHelpCtr).

Identity House: Offers LGBTQ peer counseling services, short-term therapy and/or referrals, groups, and workshops (208 W 13th St, 212-243-8181, www.identityhouse.org).

Lambda Legal: Legal foundation securing civil rights for the entire LGBT population (120 Wall St, 19th Flr, 212 809-8585, www.lambdalegal.org, @LambdaLegal).

National Gay & Lesbian Task Force: National organization building LGBT political power and de-marginalizing LGBT issues. (80 Maiden Ln, Ste 1504, 212-604-9830, www.thetaskforce.org or @TheTaskForce).

New York City Anti-Violence Project: 24-hour crisis support line for violence against LGTBH communities (212-714-1141, www.avp.org or @antiviolence).

PFLAG: Parents, Families, and Friends of Lesbians and Gays working together to raise awareness of LGBT youth and adults (130 E 25th St, Ste M1, 646-240-4288, www.pflagnyc.org or @pflagnyc).

Immigration Equality: Advocates for changing US policy on immigration of permanent partners (40 Exchange Pl, Ste 1300, 212-714-2904, immigrationequality.org or @IEquality).

GLAAD (Gay and Lesbian Alliance Against Defamation): The are the folks who go to bat for you in the media. (104 W 29th St, 4th Flr, 212-629-3322, www.glaad.org or @glaad).

OUTdancing @ Stepping Out Studios: The first LGBT partner dance program in the US. (37 W 26th St, 9th Flr, 646-742-9400, www.steppingoutstudios.com).

LGBT Connections Night at Leo Bar: Each third Friday of the month, Asia Society partners with various LGBT professional organizations; free exhibition tours included (725 Park Ave, 212-327-9352, www.asiasociety.org).

Positive Alliance: Organizes weekly Friday social mixer and party for HIV+ gay men, their friends and supporters at The Ritz (369 W 46th St, 2nd Flr); also provides regular email newsletter with links to resources and news updates (@PozAlliance).

Annual Events

Pride Week: Usually the last full week in June (212-807-7433, www.nycpride.org or @NYCPride).

NewFest: NY's Premier LGBT Film Festival: Showcase of international gay and lesbian films, July (646-290-8136, newfest.org or @NewFestNYC).

General Information · **Dog Runs**

It's good to be a dog in New York. NYC's pooches are among the world's most pampered: they celebrate birthdays, don expensive sweaters, and prance down Fifth Avenue in weather-appropriate gear. Even for those of us who can't afford to dress our pups in Burberry raincoats, there are ways to spoil our canine companions. NYC is full of dog runs—both formal and informal—scattered throughout the city's parks and neighborhood community spaces. Good thing too, as the fine for having a dog off-leash can run upward of $100, and park officials are vigilant. While the city takes no active role in the management of the dog runs, it provides space to the community groups who do. These community groups are always eager for help (volunteer time or financial contributions) and many post volunteer information on park bulletin boards. It can take many years and several thousand dollars to build a dog run in New York. NYC boasts dozens of dog runs, but that doesn't seem like very many when you consider that there are more than a million pooches in the five boroughs. Each dog run is different. It's good to know, for example, that Riverside Park at 87th Street has a fountain and hose to keep dogs cool in the summer. Formal runs are probably the safest bet for pets, as most are enclosed and maintained. For safety reasons, choke or pronged collars are forbidden, and identification and rabies tags should remain on the flat collar. Most runs prohibit dogs in heat, aggressive dogs, and dogs without up-to-date shots. For more information about dog runs in city parks, see www.nycgovparks.org/facilities/dogareas

There are no dog runs in Central Park, but before 9 am the park is full of people walking their dogs off-leash. While this is a strict no-no the rest of the day (and punishable by hefty fines), park officials tolerate the practice as long as dogs maintain a low profile, and are leashed immediately at 9 am. Check out www.centralparknyc.org for more info and check in with Central Park Paws, an initiative of the Central Park Conservancy to connect with dog owners about responsible ways to enjoy the park.

While there are too many dog runs to create a complete list, these are some of the best-established ones.

Fish Bridge Park (Dover and Pearl Sts, Map 3): Concrete-surfaced run; features water hose, wading pool, and lock box with newspapers.
Coleman Oval Park (Pike & Monroe Sts, Map 4): Under the Manhattan Bridge.
West Village D.O.G. Run (Little W 12th St between Washington St and 10th Ave, www.wvdog.org, Map 5): Features benches, water hose, and drink bowl; membership required.
Washington Square Park (MacDougal St at W 4th St, Map 6): Located in the southwest corner of the park, this is a large, gravel-surfaced run with many spectators; popular and gets very crowded, but is well-maintained nonetheless.
Mercer-Houston Dog Run (Mercer St at Houston St, mercerhoustondogrun.org, Map 6): Private run with a membership; benefits include running water and a plastic wading pool for your dog to splash in.
Union Square (Broadway at 15th St, Map 6): Crushed stone surface.
Tompkins Square Park (Avenue B at 10th St, www.tompkinssquaredogrun.com, Map 7): NYC's first dog run opened in 1990; this community-centered run offers lots of shade, benches, and running water—but be aware: toys, frisbees, balls, and dogs in heat are prohibited.
Chelsea Waterside Park (11th Ave at 22nd St, Map 8)
Madison Square Park (Madison Ave at 25th St, Map 10): Medium-sized run with gravel surface and plenty of trees.
DeWitt Clinton Park (11th Ave at 52nd & 54th Sts, Map 11): Two small concrete-surfaced runs.
Astro's Hell's Kitchen Neighborhood Dog Run (W 39th St at 10th Ave, astrosdogrun.org, Map 11): A private dog run featuring chairs, umbrellas, fenced garden, and woodchip surface.
East River Esplanade (East River at 63rd St, Map 13): Concrete dog run by the river.
Peter Detmold Park (Beekman Pl at 51st St, Map 13): Large well-maintained run with cement and dirt surfaces and many trees.
Robert Moses Park (First Ave at 42nd St, Map 13): Concrete surface.
Theodore Roosevelt Park (Central Park W at W 81st St, Map 14): Gravel surface.
Riverside Park (Riverside Dr at 72nd St, Map 14)
Carl Schurz Park (East End Ave at 85th-86th Sts, Map 15, 17): Medium-sized enclosed run with pebbled surface and separate space for small dogs; this run has benches and shady trees, and running water is available in the bathrooms.
Riverside Park (Riverside Dr at 87th St, Map 16): Medium-sized run with gravel surface.
Riverside Park (Riverside Dr at 105th-106th Sts, Map 16): Medium-sized run with gravel surface.
Morningside Park (Morningside Ave b/w 114th & 119th Sts, Map 18).
Thomas Jefferson Park (E 112th St at First Ave, Map 20): Wood chip surface.
J. Hood Wright Park (Haven Ave at W 173rd St, Map 23): An enclosed dirt-surfaced run.
Fort Tryon Park/Sir William's Dog Run (Margaret Corbin Dr, Washington Heights, Map 24).
Inwood Hill Dog Run (Dyckman St and Payson Ave, Map 25): Gravel surface.
Kowsky Plaza Dog Run (Gateway Plaza, Battery Park City): Located near the marina, this area has small hills for your dog to run on, as well as a small fountain and bathing pool.
Battery Park City (Along River Ter between Park Pl W and Murray St): Concrete-surfaced run with a view of the river.

If you're reading this you're probably not a tourist, and if you're not a tourist you probably don't need a hotel. However, chances are good that at some point your obnoxious friend or relative from out of state will suddenly come a-knockin', bearing news of their long-awaited arrival to the big city. "So I thought I'd stay at your place," they will suggest casually, displaying their complete ignorance of the number of square feet in an average New York apartment—and simultaneously realizing your greatest fear of playing host to someone you greatly dislike. Or there's the possibility that your place is infested with mice, bed bugs, or pigeons and you need to escape, pronto. Or maybe you're just looking for a romantic (or slightly less than romantic) getaway without leaving the city. Whatever the case, be assured that there is a seemingly endless array of possibilities to suit all your overnight desires and needs.

Obviously, your options run from dirt cheap (well, by New York standards) to disgustingly, offensively expensive. For those with tons of extra cash, either call us or check out some of the elite luxury chains—The **Ritz Carlton**, The **Four Seasons** (Map 12) at E 57th St, **The W at Union Square (Map 10)** and **Times Square (Map 12)**, **Le Parker Meridien (Map 12)**, **The Peninsula (Map 12)**, **The St. Regis(Map 12)**, and The **Mandarin-Oriental (Map 11)**.

Those hotels that are more unique to Manhattan include: The **Lowell (Map 15)**, a fortress of pretentiousness nestled beside Central Park, which successfully captures the feel of a snobby, high-class gentleman's club. For a similar feeling, only with a heavy dose of Renaissance Italy and a design dating back to 1882, check into The **New York Palace (Map 12)**. If you prefer more modern surroundings, the swank-tastic **Bryant Park Hotel (Map 12)** (once the landmark Radiator building before it was transformed) is a favorite amongst entertainment and fashion industry folks. Similarly, The **Regency (Map 15)**, nicknamed "Hollywood East" in the 1960s, is a must for all celeb-stalkers hangers-on alike. Meanwhile, The **Algonquin (Map 12)** offers complimentary delivery of the New Yorker, as if to suggest that they cater to a more literary crowd (maybe in the 1920s, but whether or not that's the case today is up for debate). If you're feeling fabulous, there's **The Muse Hotel (Map 12)**, located in the heart of Times Square, mere steps away from the bright lights of Broadway. If you're more comfortable with the old-money folks (or if you're a nostalgic member of the nouveau-riche), check out the apartment-size rooms at **The Carlyle (Map 15)**. Then there's **The Shoreham (Map 12)**, which offers complimentary champagne at the front desk (so it's definitely worth a shot to pose as a guest) in addition to a fantastically retro bar, that looks like it's straight out of *A Clockwork Orange*. Last but certainly not least, one can always stay at the world-famous **Waldorf Astoria (Map 13)**, where unrivaled service and a lavish renovation more than justify the cost of staying (at least for the 1% and those who edging close to that elite coterie).

There are additional high-end options downtown, perfect for nights of drunken bar-hopping or cool European friends with deep but chic pockets. The sexier of these hotels include: **The Hotel Gansevoort (Map 5)**, a sleek tower of luxury, located steps away from the Meatpacking District—New York's very own version of Miami Beach! Nearby, you'll find **The Maritime Hotel (Map 8)**, which does a great impression of a cruise ship, replete with porthole-shaped windows and La Bottega, an Italian restaurant with a massive outdoor patio that feels like the deck of a Carnival liner. In trendy SoHo, you'll find **The Mercer Hotel (Map 6)**, **Sixty Soho (Map 6)**, and **The SoHo Grand (Map 2)** (there's also its sister, **The Roxy Hotel (Map 2)**, farther south)—which vary ever-so-slightly in degrees of coolness, depending on your demands. A little ways north, next to Gramercy Park, you'll find **The Inn at Irving Place (Map 10)**—things are a tad less modern at this upscale bed and breakfast (it consists of two restored 19th-century townhouses), but the Cibar Lounge, the rock and fashion royalty, and the lack of any visible signage outside are sure to validate your inner yearning to hip. Speaking of which, there are a few new boutique hotels on the Bowery to make all your rock star dreams come true. **The Bowery Hotel (Map 6)** was the first to make its mark on this former stretch of skid row. The Lobby Bar is worth checking out even if you can't afford a room. Up the street the semi-sleek **The Standard, East Village (Map 6)** is competing for models and I-Bankers expense accounts. Check out how they squeezed the fancy hotel in between two existing tenement buildings. And not too far away is the super fancy **Crosby Street Hotel (Map 6)**, another of those cool hotels we'll never be able to afford. One thing we can afford is a stroll down the High Line to crane our necks at the exhibitionists who often can be spotted cavorting in the floor-to-ceiling windows of **The Standard (Map 5)** which, er, straddles the airborne park. Guests are reminded by staff that their rooms will be highly visible and they should be careful, which of course prompts many to be careful to show off as much as they can for onlookers.

But speaking of money and thrills we can't afford, let's get real—most of us can't begin to afford such luxuries as those outlined above. We live in a city where pay is kinda flat (or at least flatter than expenses), there's a rent affordability crisis unlike anything in NYC history, and the only reason you really need a hotel is because as much as you might love Aunt Edna from Des Moines and want to spend time with her during her fortnight in the city, you don't want to step on her as she sleeps on the floor of your studio apartment when you stumble home after last call. For these real-world occasions, rest assured there are a few hotels in the city where real people can actually afford to stay. Some of these include **The Evelyn (Map 9)**, **The Hotel at Times Square (Map 12)**, and **The Chelsea Savoy (Map 9)**—all solid, safe choices.

More mid-range options include: **Hotel AKA NoMad (Map 9)**, **Comfort Inn (Map 9)**, **Clarion Hotel (Map 10)**, and **The New Yorker Hotel (Map 8)**. Whatever you do, never book your family, friends, or self into a hotel that you don't know or haven't scouted, no matter how appealing the cost—if it seems too good to be true, it may well be. Some of the lowest-priced "hotels" in town appear on some leading hotel booking sites, and they can be really scary. Some are in unsavory neighborhoods, or are in old buildings and barely qualify as hotels. You may arrive and find that someone's suitcases are already in your room, or that there's no heat or hot water, or that the room feels more like a homeless shelter than a hotel. (Yup, this actually happens. Even to seasoned New Yorkers like us, when we get too enamored of a would-be bargain.) And let's not mention the bedbug threat. Suffice it to say, always always always go with a brand you trust, or check it out beforehand in person or online. That's the only way to be sure you or your out-of-town visitors won't end up with the most unwelcome kind of New York story.

No matter what range of hotel you are looking to book, and for whatever reason, note that rates are generally highest during the holiday season and the summer, and lowest during the off season. Other specific events, like Fashion Week or the UN General Assembly, can cause the price of hotel rooms to increase markedly. Regardless of time of year, sometimes you'll get a better deal if you book well in advance, and sometimes you can score an awesome find by booking at the very last minute on a site like **Hotwire. com**. And sometimes you're just out of luck—rates are ballpark and they are subject to change up until you have the reservation. If you find yourself in a bind and you need to get a room for yourself or someone else, also try some of the other aggregator sites: **Hotels.com**, **Priceline**, **Hotwire**, **Travelocity**, **Kayak**, **Expedia**, or even individual company websites. You can also call a hotel directly to ask if they have any specials. Be aware that not all hotels have a star rating and sometimes those that do aren't accurate. The quoted rates will give you an idea of the quality being offered. The bottom line is, like most things in New York, while you have plenty of options, few of them are cheap—but with serendipity and creativity, you may be the lucky one who gets the bargain.

Hotel	Address	Phone	Rate $	Map
Soho Grand Hotel	310 W Broadway	212-390-5147	$$$$$	2
The Roxy Hotel	2 6th Ave	212-519-6600	$$$$$	2
Hotel Gansevoort	18 9th Ave	212-206-6700	$$$$$	5
The Standard	848 Washington St	212-645-4646	$$$$$	5
The Bowery Hotel	335 Bowery	212-505-9100	$$$$	6
The Mercer	147 Mercer St	212-966-6060	$$$$$	6
Sixty SoHo	60 Thompson St	212-431-0400	$$$$	6
New Yorker Hotel	481 8th Ave	212-971-0101	$$$$	8
The Maritime Hotel	363 W 16th St	212-242-4300	$$$$	8
Hotel AKA NoMad	131 Madison Ave	212-448-7000	$$$$	9
Chelsea Savoy Hotel	204 W 23rd St	212-929-9353	$$	9
The Evelyn	7 E 27th St	212-545-8000	$	9
Inn at Irving Place	56 Irving Pl	212-533-4600	$$$$	10
Clarion Hotel Park Avenue	429 Park Ave S	212-532-4860	$$$	10
The Court	130 E 39th St	212-685-1100	$$$$$	10
The Tuscany	120 E 39th St	347-795-0385	$$$$$	10
W New York Union Square	201 Park Ave S	212-253-9119	$$$$$	10
Mandarin Oriental New York	80 Columbus Cir	212-805-8800	$$$$$	11
W New York Times Square	1567 Broadway	212-930-7400	$$$$$	12
Four Seasons Hotel	57 E 57th St	212-758-5700	$$$$$	12
New York Palace Hotel	455 Madison Ave	212-888-7000	$$$$$	12
Thompson Central Park	119 W 56th St	212-245-5000	$$$$$	12
Algonquin Hotel	59 W 44th St	212-840-6800	$$$$	12
Shoreham Hotel	33 W 55th St	212-632-9070	$$$$	12
The Peninsula New York	700 5th Ave	212-956-2888	$$$$$	12
St Regis	2 E 55th St	212-753-4500	$$$$$	12
The Hotel at Times Square	59 W 46th St	212-719-2300	$$$	12
The Muse	130 W 46th St	212-485-2400	$$$$$	12
Ritz Carlton Central Park	50 Central Park S	212-308-9100	$$$$$	12
Waldorf Astoria	301 Park Ave	212-355-3000	$$$$$	13
Carlyle Hotel	35 E 76th St	212-744-1600	$$$$$	15
Lowell Hotel	28 E 63rd St	212-838-1400	$$$$$	15
Regency Hotel	540 Park Ave	212-759-4100	$$$$$	15

Sure, eating out in New York can be a competitive sport, sometimes a contact sport. However, once you're equipped with enough information about New York's 25,000 restaurant choices, the rewards are limitless, and we can confirm that this is one of the best damn towns on Earth to eat in. Certainly you could take advantage of the city's gourmet grocery stores and make fabulous meals at home, but compare your Citarella grocery bill to the check at Westville and you'll be eating out more often. But not to worry, we can always help you find the perfect place. Whether you're looking for a restaurant with a rare 28 from *Zagat*, or you refuse to let that D health rating get between you and good food (re: Kosher delis and Chinatown basements), you'll never have to settle.

Eating Old

Since New York City is a perpetual culinary hotspot featuring tons of celebrity chefs (and *Top Chef* contestants who packed their knives and went), it's easy to get wrapped up in trendy food that looks more like a Rorschach test than dinner. Some experimental restaurants are remarkably on the cutting edge, but when you're not in the mood for aerated olive-chocolate foie gras (Wylie Dufresne, we're looking at you), you can rely on the Big Apple's longstanding heavyweights. Slurp fresh-shucked oysters and enjoy amazing desserts under the vaulted, tiled ceiling at Grand Central Station's **Oyster Bar (circa 1913, Map 13)**; sample more oysters and one of the best burgers in existence at the venerable Midtown watering hole **P.J. Clarke's (circa 1884, Map 13)**; order the sturgeon scrambled with eggs, onions, and a bialy on the side at **Barney Greengrass (circa 1908, Map 16)**; feast like olde world royalty at **The Russian Tea Room (circa 1927, Map 12)**; or expand your culinary horizons with calf's spleen and cheese on a roll at **Ferdinando's Focacceria (circa 1904, Map 32)**.

Eating Cheap

New York has always had options for us broke folks, and the economic collapse (still hanging on, isn't it?) didn't hurt those options either. At **Shake Shack (Map 9, 11, 14, 17, 30, 33, Battery Park City)**, you can still grab a Shack Burger for under $5 or a Shack Stack (twice the goods) for under $10. Ethnic food has always been a great friend to eaters on a budget. For brilliant Middle Eastern go to **Hummus Place (Map 7)** or **Taïm (Map 5)** for some of the best falafel on the planet. For Mexican check out the taquería at The Corner a.k.a. **La Esquina (Map 6)** or head out to Bushwick's factory-restaurant **Tortillería Los Hermanos** for a cheap breakfast that even celebs appreciate, **La Bonbonniere (Map 5)** can't be beat. And many of us can't survive a day without the staples of NYC Jewish eats: bagels and knishes. For bagels, go with perennial winner **Ess-a-Bagel (Map 10, 13)** or try our favorites: **Kossar's Bialys (Map 4)**, **Absolute Bagels (Map 16)**, or the original **Tal Bagels (Map 13, 16, 17)**. For knishes, nothing beats the **Yonah Schimmel Knish Bakery (Map 6)**. Since the NFT office began in Chinatown and we're always broke (free advice: don't go into publishing), we are certified experts on eating cheap in this part of town. At **Deluxe Green Bo (Map 3)**.

Eating Hip

Eating hip usually involves the food of the moment (kale chips and artisanal popsicles), beautiful people (who couldn't possibly eat another bite of that amuse-bouche), and some kind of exclusivity (unpublished phone numbers and hidden entrances). Although, with this little hiccup in our economic stability, even the hippest places have had to let the dirty, burger-eating plebeians through their doors. That being said, the ultimate in cool dining is, of course, **Rao's (Map 20)**—or so we hear. But unless you're the Mayor, the Governor, or Woody Allen, you probably won't be getting a reservation anytime soon. If you can find the unmarked basement door of **Bobo (Map 5)**, you'll really impress your date. Head east to try the always crowded, no-reservations eatery **Freemans (Map 6)**, which hides itself at the end of an alleyway; don't miss the pork chops. For fans of Japanese izakayas, nothing is quite as fun as an evening at **En Brasserie (Map 5)**. Its gourmet menu brilliantly fuses homemade miso with duck, cod, tofu, and anything else you can think of. And the low lighting will make anyone look good. David Chang's restaurant mini-empire is still on people's radars, so try **Momofuku Noodle Bar (Map 6)**.

Eating Late

Some say New York never sleeps, and some (ahem, Madrid) insist that it does, but like any big city it depends on the neighborhood, so let us help you locate some options. **Veselka (Map 6)** is the place for late-night Ukrainian soul food. You'll find cabbies chowing down past 3 am at **Big Arc Chicken (Map 7)** or **99 Cents Fresh Pizza (Map 11, 13)**. **French Roast (Map 5, 14)** serves good croque-monsieurs 24 hours, and that dessert you declined earlier in the evening. If you're near Chinatown at 3 a.m, let the wonton soup and barbecue duck at **Great NY Noodletown (Map 3)** soak up all that beer. And, of course, **Blue Ribbon (Map 6)** is still one of the best places to eat after midnight.

Eating Pizza

We don't care what Chicago says; we do pizza best! The coal oven spots top most lists: **Grimaldi's (Map 30)**, **Lombardi's (Map 6)**, **Luzzo's (Map 7)**, **John's Pizzeria (Map 5)**, and the original **Patsy's (Map 20)** in East Harlem. The coal oven enjoys extra cachet because it's illegal now, except in the aforementioned eateries where they were already in operation. However, the regular brick oven joints, such as **Keste (Map 5)** and **Lucali (Map 32)** are no slouches. Trying to find something edible near Wall Street? Check out **Adrienne's (Map 1)** delicious rectangle pies on Stone Street, or walk up to TriBeCa for a luscious Brussels-sprout-bacon-caramelized-onion pie at **Saluggi's (Map 2)**. For a classic Village scene complete with live jazz, check out **Arturo's (Map 6)** on Houston Street. The outer boroughs seriously represent here: **Louie & Ernie's** in The Bronx, **Tufino** in Queens **(Map 26)**, **Denino's** on Staten Island, and, of course, **Roberta's** and **Di Fara** in Brooklyn. Pizza by the slice practically deserves its own category, but the highlights include **Patsy's (Map 20**, definitely the best slice in the city), **Artichoke Basille's Pizza (Map 6**, get the grandma slice), and **Joe's (Map 5**, classic NY Style).

Eating Ethnic

Spin a globe, blindly stick your finger onto a spot, and chances are you can find that cuisine on offer in New York. And an outstanding offering it will be. To wit:

Argentine: **Buenos Aires (Map 7)**
Australian: **The Thirsty Koala (Map 26)**
Chinese: **Szechuan Gourmet (Map 9)**
Cuban: **Café Habana (Map 6)**
Dominican: **El Malecon (Map 16)** and **El Castillo de Jagua (Map 4)**
Egyptian: **Kabab Café (Map 26)**
Ethiopian: **Ghenet (Map 33)**
German: **Heidelberg (Map 15)**
Greek: **Periyali (Map 9)** and **Pylos (Map 7)**
Indian: **Indian Tandoor Oven (Map 15)**
Italian: **Babbo (Map 6)**, **Sfoglia (Map 17)**, **Al Di La (Map 33)**, and countless others
Japanese: **Nobu (Map 1)**, **Takahachi (Map 7)**, **Ki Sushi (Map 32)** and about 40 others
Jewish: **B &H Dairy (Map 6)**
Malaysian: **New Malaysia (Map 3)**
Mexican: **Alma (Map 32)** and **Mexico 2000 (Map 29)**
Pakistani: **Haandi (Map 10)**
Polish: **Christina's (Map 28)**
Russian: **The Russian Vodka Room (Map 12)** and **Russian Samovar (Map 12)**
Scandinavian: **Aquavit (Map 13)**
Southern American: **Sylvia's (Map 19)** and **Cheryl's Global Soul (Map 33)**
Spanish: **Socarrat (Map 9)** and **Tia Pol (Map 8)**
Sri Lankan: **Sigiri (Map 7)**
Thai: **Sripraphai** (Queens)
Turkish: **Turkish Kitchen (Map 10)**

Eating Meat

New York is home to arguably the world's best steakhouse, **Peter Luger (Map 29)**, but it's competitive at the top, and clawing at Luger's heels are: **Mark Joseph Steakhouse (Map 1)** and classics like **Sparks (Map 13)**, **Palm (Map 13)**, **Smith & Wollensky (Map 13)** and the **Strip House (Map 6)**. For the Brazilian-style "all you can eat meat fest," **Churrascaria Plataforma (Map 11)** does the trick. As for hamburgers, the rankings provide material for eternal debate: **Corner Bistro (Map 5, 26)**, **J.G. Melon (Map 15)** and **Bonnie's Grill (Map 33)**, to name a few. Elsewhere, **Royale (Map 7)** compliments the perfect patty with stellar fixins for a song. Texans and Missourians alike can agree that New York has some damn good BBQ, even if we sometimes recruit our BBQ talent from down South: **Hill Country (Map 9)**, **Dinosaur Bar-B-Que (Map 18)** and **Blue Smoke (Map 2, Battery Park City)** in Manhattan, and **Fette Sau (Map 29)**.

Eating Veggie

You could live your whole life here, never eat a shred of meat, and feast like a king every day (and probably live longer). Try the quality Indian fare at **Pongal (Map 10)**, and, for high-end eats, **Franchia (Map 10)** and **Dirt Candy (Map 7)**. For a delicious macrobiotic meal including dessert, **Souen (Map 5, 6)** has yet to disappoint. For adventurous veggie heads, nothing beats **HanGawi (Map 9)**, consistently voted one of the best vegetarian and Korean restaurants in the city.

Eating Your Wallet

While we technically use the same currency as the rest of the country, it's actually worth about half as much here as elsewhere. Even the most frugal among us have spent 100 New York dollars on a night out and thought we got off easy—the damage can easily exceed $200 per person at a Michelin-starred restaurant. No doubt you're dying to try Eric Ripert's this and Daniel Boulud's that, but treat this like open bar at your holiday office party: Know your limit (financially, emotionally, morally), and try not to do anything you'll regret in the morning. If you can keep your food down after witnessing triple digits on your share of the tab, start on the slippery slope to gastronomically induced bankruptcy at the following restaurants, which rarely disappoint: **Babbo (Map 6)**, **Per Se (Map 11)**, **Gramercy Tavern (Map 9)**, **Le Bernardin (Map 12)**, **Union Square Cafe (Map 9)**, **Craft (Map 9)**, and **Aquavit (Map 13)**. And remember to manage your expectations: unless you fall in love with your server, the experience will probably not change your life. Although **Per Se (Map 11)** comes pretty damn close.

Our Favorite Restaurants

Consensus on this subject is always difficult, but with a group of New Yorkers opinionated enough to produce the NFT, we have to at least try and duke it out. We've historically granted the accolade to **Blue Ribbon (Map 6)**: it's open 'til 4 a.m., it's where the chefs of other restaurants go, it's got fondue, beef marrow, fried chicken, great liquor, a great vibe and great service. And it will always have that special place in our hearts and stomachs, but we also have to give a shout out to a few others: **Alma (Map 32)**, an out-of-the-way rooftop Mexican restaurant with stunning views and equally good tamales, mole, margaritas, and ambiance; **Sigiri (Map 7)**, a spicy Sri Lankan gem that's BYOB to boot; **Babbo (Map 6)**, because it's Babbo (call at least one month ahead); **Arturo's (Map 6)**, a classic, old-school pizza joint with live jazz, Greenwich Village locals and amazing coal-fired pizza.

Arts & Entertainment • **Nightlife**

If you ever get bored in New York City, you have only yourself to blame. When it comes to nightlife in particular, the only difficulty you'll have is in choosing amongst the seemingly infinite options for entertainment. You can just head out with your NFT and see where you end up, because many bars and venues open early and close late (can you say 4am?!). If you need a little more guidance, New York's top weeklies—*The Village Voice* and *Time Out New York*—offer tons of listings and round-ups of goings on about town, as do websites such as **Flavorpill** (www.flavorpill.com), **Brooklyn Vegan** (www. brooklynvegan.com), and **Oh My Rockness** (www. ohmyrockness.com). A favorite for usually cheap and off-beat picks is **The Skint** (www.theskint.com). For those of you who require more than your typical night out, **NonsenseNYC** (www.nonsensenyc.com) is an e-mail newsletter with a ton of dance parties, interactive art shows, guerrilla theater and other unusual events. Just a quick word of caution: don't forget to pace yourselves.

Dive Bars

There is no shortage of dumps in this city, so we've done our best to single out the darkest and the dirtiest. The oldest on our list is, of course, **McSorely's Old Ale House (Map 6)**, which has been in operation 1854, and looks it's straight out of *Gangs of New York*. Best experienced during the day and avoided like the plague on evenings and weekends, it's worth checking out the place where Abe Lincoln drank and soaking in all that old-school barroom atmosphere. A popular choice among our staff is the oh-so-derelict **Milano's (Map 6)**. Tucked away on swiftly gentrifying Houston Street, it's been a boozy refuge since 1880. Other downtown favorites include **Nancy Whiskey (Map 2)**, **Puffy's Tavern (Map 2)**, **Blue & Gold (Map 6)** and **Mona's (Map 7)**. In Midtown, **Jimmy's Corner (Map 12)** is the ultimate escape from Times Square tourist swarms, and the classic **Subway Inn (Map 15)** over on the east side. Uptown, we like **Reif's Tavern (Map 17)**, **Dublin House (Map 14)**, and **1020 Bar (Map 18)**. On the other side of the East River, check out **Turkey's Nest (Map 29)** and the Red Hook classic **Sunny's (Map 32)**. Finally, we offer drunken shout outs to true dives that are gone but never forgotten: Mars Bar, Max Fish, Holiday Cocktail Lounge, Milady's and so many more. If you're new to the city, Google them and see all the grime and grit you missed out on…

Great Beer Selections

It's a marvelous time to be a beer geek in New York City. The number of watering holes with mind-boggling craft beer lists grows every year, so we'll do your liver a favor and suggest a few of the best. If you're braving a bar crawl in Greenwich Village, heavily trodden **Peculier Pub (Map 6)** and **Blind Tiger Ale House (Map 5)** offer large and diverse selections, and **Vol de Nuit (Map 5)** has a huge list of Belgian beers. Going several steps further with the Trappist schtick, the East Village's **Burp Castle (Map 6)** has a fine array of Belgians, but use your inside voice or you'll be soundly shushed. Nearby **d.b.a. (Map 7)** is our neighborhood favorite where beer is concerned, and **Top Hops (Map 4)** offers a great selection of bottles and drafts, as well as a standing bar area, and **Randolph Beer (Map 3)** shines with—surprise, surprise—a great brew list. Chelsea has **Pony Bar (Map 11)** and **Valhalla (Map 8)** to get your hops fix. Our Uptown favorite is **Earl's Beer & Cheese (Map 17)**, which has a small space but excellent beer list.

If you're seeking good beer in Brooklyn, make Williamsburg your first stop. In fact, just head to cozy, Belgian-focused **Spuyten Duyvil (Map 29)**, which has over 100 bottles and a rotating cask ale. From there, **Barcade (Map 29)** achieves an awesome synergy between its classic '80s arcade games and stellar beer list—our only complaint is that we can't drink and play Dig Dug at the same time. If you're a real beer nerd, you must go sipping at **Torst (Map 28)**, a sleek Danish-inspired taproom with incredible beers on draft. In Carroll Gardens, **Bar Great Harry (Map 32)** is not only a great hangout, but it also has tons of find beers to sample.

Outdoor Spaces

Outdoor space is a precious commodity in NYC, so couple it with booze and you've got the perfect destination for cooped-up city dwellers when the weather turns warm. Actually, you can find New Yorkers stubbornly holding court at outdoor venues in all sorts of weather short of electrical storms and sub-freezing temperatures, and they'll only retreat from these conditions when chased indoors by the staff. Although entry to many of the finest outdoor drinking dens requires supermodel looks or celebrity status, or at the very least a staggering tolerance for douchebags, there are plenty of options for the mere mortals among us. For a little fancier but still accessible night out in the open air, try **Bookmarks (Map 12)**, the rooftop bar in the Library Hotel. For drinks with a view, check out **Berry Park (Map 29)** in Williamsburg, which looks out across the river toward Manhattan.

Our favorite places to enjoy a drink outside are in the many back patios that turn the darkest, funkiest watering holes into *bona fide* oases, no matter how small and concrete-laden they may be. Beer lovers congregate in the backyards at **d.b.a. (Map 7)** in the East Village and **Spuyten Duyvil (Map 29)** in Williamsburg, and the aptly named **Gowanus Yacht Club (Map 32)** remains our Carroll Gardens favorite. More outdoor drinking can be had at **Sweet & Vicious (Map 6)** for frozen margaritas in the Lower East Side, **The Heights Bar & Grill (Map 18)** in Morningside Heights, **The Gate (Map 33)** in Park Slope, and **Union Pool (Map 29)** in Williamsburg. Speaking of beer gardens, there's a seeming resurgence of these all-but-disappeared drinking venues, once popular with the central European immigrant set. Predictably packed results can be found at **La Birreria (Map 9)** or **Spritzenhaus (Map 29)**. But if you can only visit one, make it the 100-year-old **Bohemian Hall & Beer Garden (Map 26)** in Astoria. Snag a picnic table in the massive outdoor area with a gang of friends, and knock back frosty pitchers of pilsner just like they did in the old days (polka dancing optional).

Best Jukebox

Personal taste factors heavily in this category of course, but here is a condensed list of NFT picks. For Manhattan: **Ace Bar (Map 7)** (indie rock/punk), **7B (Horseshoe Bar) (Map 7)** (rock all the way), **Rudy's Bar & Grill (Map 11)** (blues), **Welcome to the Johnsons (Map 4)** (indie rock/punk). For Brooklyn: **Boat Bar (Map 32)** (Carroll Gardens—indie rock), the **Brooklyn Social Club (Map 32)** (Carroll Gardens—country/soul) and **The Levee (Map 29)** (Williamsburg—good all around).

DJs and Dancing

New York's old cabaret laws make it tough to find free dance spots, but they do exist (albeit often with the velvet rope scenario that may deter the impatient). On the weekends, entry into the swankier clubs doesn't come without paying your dues in long lines and pricey cover charges. That's not our style. You'll find us dancing and hanging out at **Le Poisson Rouge (Map 6)**. In and around Williamsburg, we suggest checking out a few frames at **Brooklyn Bowl (Map 29)**, which has frequent late-night DJ sets by the likes of Questlove.

Fancy Cocktails

In recent years mixology has practically become a religion in New York, and its temples of worship are conveniently clustered in the East Village. For starters, head to **Death & Company (Map 7)**, tell the knowledgeable servers what you like in a drink, and prepare to be converted. If wait lists aren't your thing (and there often is one) **The Summit Bar (Map 7)**, and bitters-focused **Amor y Amargo (Map 7)** are solid options nearby. **Mayamezcal (Map 6)**, located among 6th Street's Indian restaurants is practically a crash course in all things tequila and mezcal. If hardly-secret speakeasies are your thing, **PDT (Map 7)** is accessible through a telephone booth in deep-fried-dog haven **Crif Dogs** (reservations recommended). In the West Village, **Employees Only (Map 5)** is located behind psychic's shop. And speaking of the West Village, be sure to check out **Little Branch (Map 5)** for live jazz and some of the strongest mixed drinks we've ever had the pleasure of meeting. **The Dead Rabbit (Map 1)** has brought a mixologist den to Wall Street in a historic building from the 1800's. In Midtown, the classy **The Campbell Apartment (Map 13)**, tucked inside Grand Central Terminal, is a must — especially if someone else is paying. **The Penrose (Map 15)** adds a touch of cocktail class to the Upper East Side. And for the blazer/cocktail dress set, there are your opulent hotel bars, such as **King Cole Bar (Map 12)** inside the St. Regis Hotel or **Bemelmans Bar (Map 15)** inside the Carlye Hotel. We're banking on our beverages to ease the pain of that tab.

Considering all the options in Manhattan, it's probably no surprise that Brooklyn has many bars offering just-as-high caliber cocktails, minus some of the crowds. Don't believe us? Head to **Dram (Map 29)**, **Hotel Delmano (Map 29)**, or **Maison Premiere (Map 29)**, or venture a little further east to **Ba'sik (Map 29)** or **The Richardson (Map 29)**. **Clover Club (Map 32)** is our favorite for mixed drinks in Cobble Hill.

If you find yourself in Long Island City, Queens be sure to check out **Dutch Kills (Map 27)** and marvel at that custom-crafted ice that won't water down your drink no matter how slowly you savor it.

Wine Bars

Terroir (Map 2) has some funky wines and a friendly atmosphere despite the self-described "elitist wine bar" label. If it's date night, cozy up in the West Village at **Vin Sur Vingt (Map 5)** for a glass of Bordeaux. Go rustic-chic in at **Black Mountain Wine House (Map 32)** with a working fireplace and country lodge experience. In Brooklyn of course.

Music—Overview

New York caters to a wide array of tastes in everything, and music is no exception. From the indie rock venues of Brooklyn to the history-steeped jazz clubs in Greenwich Village to amateur night at the Apollo, your musical thirst can be quenched in every possible way.

Jazz, Folk, and Country

There are plenty of places to see jazz in the city, starting off with classic joints such as the **Village Vanguard (Map 5)** and **Birdland (Map 11)**. There's also the "Jazz at Lincoln Center" complex in the Time Warner Center on Columbus Circle which has three rooms: the 1,000-plus-seat, designed-for-jazz Rose Theater, the Allen Room, an amphitheater with a great view of the park, and the nightclub-esque Dizzy's Club Coca Cola. For a smaller (and cheaper) jazz experience, try **Jazz Gallery (Map 9)** or **Arthur's Tavern (Map 5)** which always has a no cover charge policy. **The Nuyorican Poets Café (Map 7)** has frequent jazz performances. In Brooklyn, one of your best bets is the small back room at Park Slope's **Barbes (Map 33)**. If you've never done it, do it—it's a truly great and unpredictable band that even surly Mr. Mingus (might) have been proud of. For folk & country, try **Parkside Lounge (Map 7)** or **Jalopy (Map 32)**.

Arts & Entertainment • **Nightlife**

Rock and Pop

In case you've just moved back to NYC from, say, ten years in Mumbai, the rock scene is now firmly entrenched in Brooklyn. However, Manhattan's **Bowery Ballroom (Map 6)** remains the top live venue, with excellent sound and a good layout. **Irving Plaza (Map 10)**, **Terminal 5 (Map 11)**, and **Hammerstein Ballroom (Map 8)** aren't our favorites, but are worthwhile for the occasional top-notch acts. The best remaining small club in Manhattan is **Mercury Lounge (Map 7)**, which gets great bands right before they're ready to move up to Bowery Ballroom. As far as the rest of the Lower East Side, it helps if you like your clubs to be punky basements or former bodegas (**Arlene Grocery, Map 4**).

When it comes to new talent, it's really the clubs in Brooklyn that shine. If you know your way around Bowery Ballroom, you'll feel right at home at Brooklyn's premiere venue, **Music Hall of Williamsburg (Map 29)**. Then there's **Pete's Candy Store (Map 29)**, **Brooklyn Bowl (Map 29)**…basically, the rocking never stops in Map 29. In Greenpoint, check out the **Warsaw (Map 28)** in the Polish National Home. We also love the **The Bell House (Map 33)** in Gowanus, **Brooklyn Masonic Temple (Map 31)** in Fort Greene and **Union Hall (Map 33)** in Park Slope.

Experimental

A number of venues in New York provide a place for experimental music to get exposure. **Experimental Intermedia (Map 3)** is fully dedicated to showcasing the avant-garde. **The Kitchen (Map 8)** features experimental music in addition to film, dance, and other art forms. **Le Poisson Rouge (Map 6)** has brought an exciting mix of different sounds back to the heart of Greenwich Village, and is one of our favorite spots. In Brooklyn, the experimental scene is cranking away, especially at **Issue Project Room**'s **(Map 30)** space in Downtown Brooklyn and **Jalopy (Map 32)** in Carroll Gardens.

Everything Else

A few places run the gamut of musical genres; folksy artists one night, hot Latin tango the next, and a slew of comedy, spoken word, and other acts. **Joe's Pub (Map 6)** presents an excellent variety of popular styles and often hosts celebrated international musicians. Keep an eye on **BAMcafé (Map 31)** for a variety of great performers. For cabaret or piano bar, try **Don't Tell Mama (Map 11)**, **Duplex (Map 5)**, or **Brandy's (Map 15)**. For a more plush experience, try the **Café Carlyle (Map 15)**. If you're seeking some R &B or soul, check out the **Apollo Theater (Map 19)**, though they mostly play "oldies" acts. The Apollo's Amateur Night on Wednesday is your chance to see some up-and-comers. **The Pyramid Club (Map 7)** has open mic MC'ing nights. **Barbes (Map 33)** in Park Slope hosts a wide palette of "world music" (for lack of a better term), including Latin American, European, and traditional US styles, plus more experimental fare. For more sounds of the south, **SOB's (Map 5)** has live South American music and dancing and should definitely be experienced at least once. **Nublu (Map 7)** is always reliable for a fun and sweaty night, especially on Wednesdays when they feature Brazilian bands and DJs. For African music, check out **Barbes (Map 33)** on Wednesday nights with the Mandingo Ambassadors. And oh yeah—then there's all that classical music stuff, at places like **Carnegie Hall (Map 12)** and **Lincoln Center (Map 14)**—maybe you've heard of them?

For a price, you can buy anything here: a live octopus, a bag of Icelandic moss, a vintage accordion, a rolling ladder, a slap bracelet, a 3D printer, a Ferrari, a dozen cronut holes, that thing you jam into an orange to suck the juice out, *anything you want*. Even print books! While we occasionally lament the presence of chain stores, we'll challenge anyone to find a better city for shopping.

Clothing & Accessories

The Upper East Side is a classic destination for high fashion. Madison Avenue is the main artery in the 50s, 60s, and 70s, rounded out by Fifth Avenue and 57th Street. In this neighborhood you'll find **Chanel (Map 12)**, **Burberry (Map 12)**, **Tiffany & Co (Map 12)**, and other names of that ilk. For department stores, start with the original **Bloomingdale's (Map 15)**, which is close to these titans: **Saks Fifth Avenue (Map 12)**, **Barneys (Map 15)**, and **Bergdorf Goodman (Map 12)** if money's no object. We assume it *is* an object, so check out their intricate window displays for free; they're especially good around the holidays.

That being said, there are some bargains on the Upper East Side, too. **Housing Works Thrift Shop (Map 15)** typically has a great selection, and proceeds serve those affected by AIDS and homelessness. If you can deal with the crush of midtown tourists, look for sales at **Macy's (Map 9)**.

These days, "vintage clothing" can mean "cute throwback" or "real period costume." Our favorites overall: **Tokio 7 (Map 6)** in the East Village, **INA (Map 6)** in NoHo, **Edith Machinist (Map 4)** on the Lower East Side, **Monk Vintage (Map 29)** in Williamsburg, and for the especially fashion-forward, **Brooklyn Consignment (Map 32)** in Boerum Hill. Devotees should attend the next Manhattan Vintage Clothing Show, where over 90 dealers sell their finery from the last century.

SoHo looks more and more like an outdoor mall, but it's still a great place to shop because of the variety and uber-high concentration. Beyond **Uniqlo (Map 6)** and **H &M (Map 6)**, there are countless huge names like **Marc Jacobs (Map 6)** and **Balenciaga (Map 6)**.

The West Village (and the Meatpacking District therein) is the spot for small, high-end boutiques. You can check out chic designs at **Stella McCartney (Map 5)**, **Alexander McQueen (Map 5)**, and department store **Jeffrey (Map 5)**.

Flea Markets & Bazaars

For a classic, grungy, sprawling flea market, try **The Annex Markets (Map 11)** on 39th Street between Ninth and Tenth Avenues. The more fashionable **Brooklyn Flea (Map 31)** dominates Fort Greene, Williamsburg, and Park Slope on the weekends with hundreds of hip vendors offering all things handcrafted: wood furniture, picture frames, sock monkeys, gold leaf necklaces, those rings made out of typewriter keys, you get the idea. **Artists & Fleas (Map 8, 29)** has a similar artsy feel in Williamsburg and inside Chelsea Market.

Sports & Outdoors

Paragon Sporting Goods (Map 9) by Union Square isn't cheap, but it's a landmark and it's been there since 1908. **City Sports (Map 1, 12)** offers a broad range of affordable sports clothing, shoes, and athletic equipment.

Furniture

Done with IKEA and curb shopping on trash night? Get your credit card(s) ready for the stuff you can't afford at **West Elm (Map 30)**, **Room & Board (Map 6)**, and **BoConcept (Map 6)**. Have even more money to spend? Check out **Ligne Roset (Map 10)** and the Meatpacking District's brilliant **Vitra (Map 5)**. Regular folks seeking solid pieces should look no further than the quality wood furniture at **Gothic Cabinet Craft (Map 28)** or **Scott Jordan Furniture (Map 5)**.

Housewares & Home Design

You'll lose hours of your life eyeing the exotic furnishings in **ABC Carpet & Home (Map 9)** just off Union Square. For those with shallower pockets, there's **Gracious Home (Map 8, 14, 15)** and any of **Muji's** four Manhattan locations **(Map 3, 8, 9, 12)**. For paint, window dressings, and other home improvement supplies, try **Janovic (Map 11, 16)** or **Crest Hardware** in Williamsburg. Prepare for sensory overload if you take on the 35 showrooms at the **A &D Building (Map 13)**. Showrooms are open to the public, unlike at some smaller designshops nearby, which require business cards upon entry.

The adorable dinnerware at **Fishs Eddy (Map 9)** is a great alternative to mega-chains like Pottery Barn. **Zabar's (Map 14)** often-ignored second floor is a longtime favorite among the city's cooks. Downtown, small but sublime **Global Table (Map 6)** has excellent, reasonably priced housewares.

Food

Three revered emporiums make the Upper West Side a culinary heaven: **Fairway (Map 14, 15)**, **Citarella (Map 5, 14, 15)**, and **Zabar's (Map 14)**. The much more affordable **Trader Joe's (Map 6, 9, 32)** is steadily multiplying, but the lines, *the lines*. **Essex Street Market (Map 4)** on the Lower East Side is a beloved institution filled with amazing meat, fish, produce, and cheese. **Grand Central Market (Map 13)** is equally good, located right in the eponymous station. **Chelsea Market (Map 8)**, housed in a National Biscuit Company factory complex, has excellent restaurants, bakeries, and food vendors (spoiler: it's not really a market).

For farm-to-table, the biggest player is the **Union Square Greenmarket (Map 9)**, which operates year-round on Mondays, Wednesdays, Fridays, and Saturdays, packed with talented chefs. The **Grand Army Plaza Greenmarket (Map 33)** in Brooklyn is also excellent and less claustrophobic than Union Square.

And now, imported foods. When it comes to Italian, Arthur Avenue in the Bronx is famed for its bakeries, butchers, and grocers, and don't forget Graham Avenue in East Williamsburg. The more centrally located **Di Palo Fine Foods (Map 3)** has regional Italian goodies and acclaimed fresh ricotta. Friendly **Despana (Map 3)** will satisfy all your Spanish desires, including $100-a-pound jamon iberico. **Sahadi's (Map 32)** has an impressive range of Middle Eastern specialties, and make time to visit their neighbors on Atlantic Avenue. For Indian and pan-Asian spices, teas, and groceries, try **Kalustyan's (Map 10)**. **New York Mart (Map 3)** is a solid one-stop for Chinese goods, and not just dehydrated scallops!

Cheese mongers? Among the best are **Murray's (Map 5)** in the West Village and **Bedford Cheese Shop (Map 29)** in Williamsburg. They don't give out free samples and the line is always long, but it's one of the cheapest options in Manhattan by far. Then you'll need bread to go with your cheese, of course. Our favorites are **Sullivan Street Bakery (Map 11)**, **Grandaisy Bakery (Map 2, 14)**, and **Amy's Bread (Map 8, 11)**. For prosciutto to accompany the bread and cheese, hit **Faicco's Pork Store (Map 5)**, or **Emily's Pork Store (Map 29)**.

Coffee is absolutely everywhere, so maybe there's no point in trying to pick a favorite, but we do enjoy the beans at **Porto Rico (Map 4, 5, 6)**, or **Colombe (Map 2, 6)** for an excellent step up. Tea drinkers (yes, there are many in this coffee-fueled town!) should consult the knowledgeable staff at **McNulty (Map 5)**, or connoisseurs can head to the exquisite **Bellocq (Map 28)**. For something bigger, **Astor Wines & Spirits (Map 6)** is always reliable and affordable, but **BQE Wine & Liquors** can be even cheaper **(Map 29)**.

Art Supplies

You can't put a bird on it 'til you stock up on paint! Check out **Blick Art Materials (Map 6)**, convenient to both NYU and Cooper Union. **SoHo Art Materials (Map 2)** on Wooster Street is a small, traditional shop that sells super premium paints and brushes for fine artists. As for Williamsburg, **Artist & Craftsman (Map 29)** is a good bet for supplies.

Books

These beloved shops and their adorable cats are disappearing faster than anything else in the city, but thank goodness **The Strand (Map 6)** is still here with 18 miles of new and used books, and those tantalizing $2 carts outside. Right down the street is the smaller **Alabaster Bookshop (Map 6)**, then **Spoonbill & Sugartown (Map 29)** in Williamsburg is full of art and design books, and **Unnameable Books (Map 33)** in Prospect Heights is fun for browsing. **Idlewild (Map 9, 29, 32)** is mecca for travel guides and travel literature. The gift shop at the **Lower East Side Tenement Museum (Map 4)** is a great place to start digging into NYC history, as is **Freebird Books (Map 32)** above Red Hook.

Music Equipment & Instruments

Unfortunately, 48th Street is no longer Music Row, but **Roberto's Winds (Map 12)** still chugs along over on 46th. Our favorites for gigging rock bands include **Matt Umanov Guitars (Map 5)** for guitars and amps, **Rogue Music (Map 9)** for keyboards. Go see the jumble of world instruments hanging from the ceiling at **Music Inn (Map 6)**, which is among the last of a dying breed. Classical violinists and other civilized types should visit **Strings and Other Things (Map 14)**.

Music for Listening

CDs and cassettes are scarce these days, but vinyl is still supremely cool. We always love avant-garde **Downtown Music (Map 3)**. Or head to one of North Brooklyn's many options, like **Earwax (Map 29)** or **Academy Annex (Map 29)**.

Electronics

B&H (Map 8) is the top destination for professionals and amateurs when it comes to photography, audio, and video, plus they have a decent selection of computers. Note that the hectic megastore is run by Orthodox Jews who strictly observe the Sabbath and holidays, so always check the hours online before heading over. For photographic equipment especially, remember the holy trinity of **B&H**, **Adorama (Map 9)**, and **K&M Camera (Map 3)**. B &H is the mothership, Adorama's great if you're nearby, and K&M is the only one open on Saturdays. Remember to flash that student ID if you've got it, as some art stores offer a discount. Audiophiles are wonderfully served by **Stereo Exchange (Map 6)** and the jaw-dropping **Sound by Singer (Map 9)**.

Weird & Bizarre

First on the list is **Brooklyn Superhero Supply (Map 33)**, where your anti-gravity elixir and gold lame sidekick cape are waiting. **Evolution (Map 6)** is mandatory for those with a dark side; think macabre biological jewelry, preserved scorpions, and bat skeletons. Equally bewitching is **Enchantments (Map 7)**, your incense-filled emporium for motherwort, frankincense tears, and all things wicca. Scribes and pen nerds, report to City Hall's **Fountain Pen Hospital (Map 3)**. If you need authentic NYC memorabilia, whether it's a lucky NYPD horseshoe or a real tax cab medallion, go directly to the **New York City Store (Map 3)**. Full disclosure, that medallion isn't actually usable—those can sell for over a million bucks.

Shopping Districts

In the age of internet shopping, these districts are fading out, so see them while you can. The Garment District (25th to 40th Streets, Fifth to Ninth Avenues) has fabrics, buttons, zippers, ribbons, sequins, and doo-dads of all sorts. The Diamond District (47th Street between Fifth and Sixth Avenues) is the world's largest market for the precious stone. The Flower District (28th Street between 6th and 7th Avenues) is right above the Perfume District (Broadway in the 20s and 30s). Bowery below Houston is chock full of restaurant supply stores, and Bowery below Delancey is the Lighting District.

Overview

If you want to see cutting-edge art, go to New York City's galleries. There are more than 500 galleries in the city, with artwork created in every conceivable medium (and of varying quality) on display. SoHo, Chelsea, DUMBO, and Williamsburg are the hot spots for gallery goers, but there are also many famous (and often more traditional) galleries and auction houses uptown, including **Christie's (Map 12)** and **Sotheby's (Map 15)**. With so much to choose from, there's almost always something that's at least *provocative*, if not actually *good*.

The scene at the upscale galleries is sometimes intimidating, especially if you look like you are on a budget. If you aren't interested in buying, they aren't interested in you being there. Some bigger galleries require appointments. Cut your teeth at smaller galleries; they aren't as scary. Also, put your name on the mailing lists. You'll get invites to openings so crowded that no one will try to pressure you into buying (and there's free wine). **The Armory Show** (www.thearmoryshow.com), an annual show of new art, is also a great way to see what the galleries have to offer without intimidation.

SoHo Area

It wasn't so long ago that there were hundreds of art galleries in SoHo. Now it has practically become an outdoor mall. However, there are still some permanent artworks in gallery spaces, such as Walter De Maria's excellent **The Broken Kilometer (Map 6)** (a Dia-sponsored space at 393 West Broadway), and his sublime **New York Earth Room (Map 6)**. A short jaunt down to TriBeCa will land you in LaMonte Young's awesome aural experience Dream House at the **MELA Foundation (Map 2)**. **Artists Space (Map 2)**, one of the first alternative art galleries in New York, is also in TriBeCa. The **HERE Arts Center (Map 5)** showcases a wide range of work and usually offers an exhibit or performance that warrants a visit. On the Lower East Side check out **Canada (Map 3)** for fun openings and **Envoy Gallery (Map 6)** for cutting edge photography and celebrity sightings.

Chelsea

The commercialization of SoHo has helped make Chelsea the center of the city's gallery scene. Our recommendation is to hit at least two streets—W 24th Street between Tenth and Eleventh Avenues, and W 22nd Street between Tenth and Eleventh Avenues. W 24th Street is anchored by the almost-always-brilliant **Gagosian Gallery (Map 8)** and also includes the **Luhring Augustine (Map 8)**, **Barbara Gladstone (Map 8)**, **Marianne Boesky (Map 8)**, and **Matthew Marks (Map 8)** galleries. W 22nd favorites include and **Julie Saul (Map 8)**, **Leslie Tonkonow (Map 8)**, and **Yancey Richardson (Map 8)** galleries. Also, check out the famous "artist's" bookstore **Printed Matter (Map 8)**.

Other recommendations are the **Starrett-Lehigh Building (Map 8)**, not only for the art but also for the great pillars, windows, and converted freight elevators, and **Pace Wildenstein (Map 8)**, which consistently features exciting artists.

Brooklyn

While the concentration of galleries in Brooklyn is nowhere near the same as in Chelsea, added together, there are well over a hundred in the borough now, with the three biggest areas being in DUMBO, Williamsburg, and Bushwick. Look for great events like Bushwick Open Studios and the DUMBO Arts Festival to get yourself oriented to Brooklyn's ever-growing art scene.

Arts & Entertainment • **Bookstores**

The New York City book scene has taken a sharp decline in terms of diversity in recent years, with many excellent bookshops—including Coliseum Books, A Different Light, Academy, A Photographer's Place, Rizzoli SoHo, Tower Books, Brentano's, Spring Street Books, and Shortwave—all going the way of the dodo. The remaining independent stores are now the last outposts before everything interesting or alternative disappears altogether. And some of NYC's richest cultural neighborhoods—such as the East Village and the Lower East Side—don't have enough bookstores to even come close to properly serving their populations. So we thought we'd take this opportunity to list some of our favorite remaining shops…

General New/Used

The **Strand** (Map 6) on Broadway, the largest and arguably most popular independent bookstore in town, boasts staggering range and depth in its offerings (and often the best prices around to boot). Whether you're interested in art tomes, rare first editions, foreign language texts, non-fiction works, or the latest bestseller, it's impossible to be disappointed. In SoHo, **McNally Jackson** (Map 6) might just be our favorite bookstore after The Strand, but **Argosy Book Store** (Map 13) on 59th Street is still a top destination for antiquarian books. Uptown, **Book Culture** (Map 18) serves the Columbia area well. With four locations around the city, the punchy **Shakespeare & Company** (Maps 6, 10, 15) is a local chain that somehow manages to maintain an aura of independence. In the West Village, **Three Lives and Co.** (Map 5) should be your destination. The **Barnes & Noble** (Map 9) in Union Square is their signature store and has a great feel. The **Housing Works Used Book Café** (Map 6) has a vintage coffeehouse feel and is one of our favorite bookstores—all of the profits go to help homeless New Yorkers living with HIV/AIDS.

Several neighborhoods in Brooklyn have great bookstores with lots of local (and well-known!) author readings, such as **Spoonbill & Sugartown** (Map 29) in Williamsburg, **Word** (Map 28) in Greenpoint, and **Greenlight Bookstore** (Map 31) in Fort Greene. DUMBO's **powerHouse Arena** (Map 30) is a great destination for art books. In Queens, **Astoria Bookshop** (Map 26) is a welcoming, uncluttered space with good children's and NYC sections.

Small/Used

Fortunately there are still a lot of used bookstores tucked away all over the city. **Mercer Street Books** (Map 6) serves NYU and **East Village Books** (Map 7) takes care of the East Village, while on the Upper East Side **Corner Bookstore** (Map 17) keeps it old-school. In Brooklyn, check out **Unnameable Books** (Map 33) for hyper-local poetry.

Travel

The city has some excellent travel book outlets, including the wonderful **Idlewild Books** (Map 9, 29, 32), which curates its collection by country where guidebooks, fiction, and travel writing all happily commingle for a unique way of browsing. So if you can't afford to travel, a trip here is the next best thing.

Art

Printed Matter (Map 8) houses one of the best collections of artists' books in the world and is highly recommended. The **New Museum Store** (Map 6) also offers a brilliant selection of both artists' and art books. If you aren't on a budget and have a new coffee table to fill, try **Ursus** (Map 15). For handsome photography collections, check out **Dashwood Books** (Map 6) on super sleek Bond Street.

NYC/Government

The **City Store** (Map 3) in the Municipal Building is small but carries a solid selection (and is still the only store we've seen that sells old taxicab medallions). The **Civil Service Bookstore** (Map 3) has all the study guides you'll need when you want to change careers and start driving a bus. The **United Nations Bookshop** (Map 13) has a great range of international and governmental titles. The **New York Transit Museum Gallery Annex & Store** (Map 13) at Grand Central also has an excellent range of books on NYC.

Specialty

Books of Wonder (Map 9) in Chelsea has long been a downtown haven for children's books. For mysteries, **The Mysterious Bookshop** (Map 2) slakes the need for the whodunit. **Bluestockings** (Map 4) is the epicenter for radical and feminist literature. Professional and amateur chefs turn to **Bonnie Slotnick** (Map 5) and **Kitchen Arts and Letters** (Map 17).

Readings

Anyone can *read* great authors, but New Yorkers have ample opportunities to meet them as well. The four-story **Barnes & Noble** (Map 9) in Union Square regularly hosts major writers. **Housing Works Used Book Café** (Map 6) also draws some big names. And **McNally Jackson** (Map 6) in Nolita is another spot known for hosting great author events. Nearly all bookstores present readings, even if irregularly; check a store's Web page for listings. Even bars have taken a literary turn for the better: **KGB Bar** (Map 6) features literary, poetry, and nonfiction readings each week. In Brooklyn, **Pete's Candy Store** (Map 29) and its weekly reading series are a good bet for your weekly dose of literature.

Multiplexes abound in NYC, though of course you should brace yourself for far steeper ticket and concession prices than in the rest of the country (with the possible exception of LA). Dinner and a movie turns out to be a rather exorbitant affair, but hey, we don't live in the Big Apple because it's cheap. And whether you're looking for the latest box office hit, or a classic from the French New Wave, there's a theater to meet your needs.

If you're after a first-run Hollywood blockbuster, we highly recommend the **AMC Loews Kips Bay (Map 10)** in Murray Hill. It has spacious theaters with large screens, big sound, comfortable seats, plenty of aisle room, and most importantly, fewer people! The **AMC Loews Village (Map 6)** is gargantuan, too, but movies there sell out hours or days in advance on the weekends. An IMAX theater and a cheesy '30s movie palace decorating theme make **AMC Loews Lincoln Square (Map 14)** a great place to catch a huge film, and its ideal location offers loads of after-movie options. Another great choice is the **Regal Battery Park (Battery Park City)**, but it's starting to get just as crowded as the Union Square location.

Don't get us wrong—the Angelika still presents great movies, but the tiny screens and constant subway rumble can sometimes make you wish you'd waited for the DVD. The **IFC Center (Map 5)** always shows great indie flicks. If you're looking for revivals, check the listings at the **Film Forum (Map 5)**, **BAM Rose Cinemas (Map 31)**, and the **MoMA (Map 12)**. Regular attendance at those three venues can provide an excellent education in cinema history. For the truly adventurous, there's **Anthology Film Archives (Map 6)**, which plays a repertory of forgotten classics, obscure international hits, and experimental American shorts. Finally, up in Harlem the tiny but terrific **Maysles Cinema (Map 19)** shows truly brilliant indie movies focusing on New York City. This may be the most unique movie going experience in Manhattan.

The most decadent and enjoyable movie experiences can be found at the theaters that feel the most "New York." Sadly, the Beekman Theatre immortalized in Woody Allen's Annie Hall was demolished in 2005 to make room for a new ward for Sloan-Kettering (it's hard to argue with a cancer hospital, but film buffs can't help but wish they'd found another space for their expansion).

Seeing a movie in Brooklyn a significantly better experience these days. Check out indie/blockbuster mashup **Cobble Hill Cinemas (Map 32)**, **BAM Rose Cinemas (Map 31)**, and food/drink **Nitehawk Cinema** in Williamsburg **(Map 29)**. In Astoria, talk back to the screen at the **UA Kaufman Astoria (Map 26)**, and talk back to an actual director at a screening at the **Museum of the Moving Image (Map 26)**.

Oh, and don't forget to purchase tickets in advance for crowded showtimes (opening weekends, holidays, or pretty much any night when you're trying to see a popular film). Both **Moviefone** (www.moviefone.com) and **Fandango** (www.fandango.com) work.

Manhattan

	Address	Phone	Map	
92nd Street Y	1395 Lexington Ave	212-415-5500	17	Community hub for film, theater, and interesting lectures.
AMC Empire 25	234 W 42nd St	212-398-2597	12	Buy tickets ahead. It's Times Square.
AMC Loews 19th Street East 6	890 Broadway	212-260-8173	9	Standard multiplex.
AMC Loews 34th Street 14	312 W 34th St	212-244-4556	8	The biggest and most comfortable of the Midtown multiplexes.
AMC Loews 84th Street 6	2310 Broadway	212-721-6023	14	Take the subway to Lincoln Square instead.
AMC Loews Kips Bay 15	570 2nd Ave	212-447-0638	10	This multiplex is starting to show its age.
AMC Loews Lincoln Square 13	1998 Broadway	212-336-5020	14	Classy Upper West Side multiplex with IMAX.
AMC Loews Orpheum 7	1538 Third Ave	212-876-2111	17	The Upper East Side's premier multiplex.
AMC Loews Village 7	66 Third Ave	212-982-2116	6	Good-sized multiplex that keeps Union Square crowds in check.
AMC Magic Johnson Harlem 9	2309 Frederick Douglass Blvd	212-665-6923	19	Owned by Magic. Best choice for Upper Manhattan.
American Museum of Natural History IMAX	200 Central Park West	212-769-5100	14	Rest your tired legs and learn something.
Angelika	18 W Houston St	212-995-2570	6	Higher profile indies play here first.
Anthology Film Archives	32 Second Ave	212-505-5181	6	Quirky retrospectives, revivals, and other rarities.
Asia Society	725 Park Ave	212-288-6400	15	Special country-themed programs every month.
Bryant Park Summer Film Festival (outdoors)	Bryant Park, b/w 40th & 42nd Sts	212-768-4242	12	Groovy classics outdoors in sweltering summer heat.

	Address	Phone	Map	
City Cinemas 1, 2, & 3	1001 Third Ave	212-753-6022	15	Ideal cure for Bloomingdale's hangover.
Czech Center New York	321 E 73rd St	646-422-3399	15	Czech premieres and special events.
Film Forum	209 W Houston St	212-727-8110	5	Best place to pick up a film geek.
French Institute Alliance Francaise	22 E 60th St	212-355-6100	15	Frog-centric activities include movies, plays, talks and exhibits.
Guggenheim Museum	1071 Fifth Ave	212-423-3500	17	Special screenings in conjunction with current exhibitions.
IFC Center	323 Sixth Ave	212-924-7771	5	Great midnights, special events, and Manhattan exclusives.
Instituto Cervantes New York	211 E 49th St	212-308-7720	13	Spanish gems, but call to make sure there's subtitles.
Italian Academy	1161 Amsterdam Ave	212-854-2306	18	Fascinating classic film series at Columbia. Feel smart again.
Jewish Community Center in Manhattan	334 Amsterdam Ave	646-505-4444	14	Jewish premieres, previews, and festivals.
Leonard Nimoy Thalia at Symphony Space	2537 Broadway	212-864-5400	16	A different classic movie every week. Good variety.
Maysles Cinema	343 Malcolm X Blvd	646-853-1296	19	Amazing indies and documentaries from local film-makers.
MoMA	11 W 53rd St	212-708-9400	12	Arty programming changes every day.
New York Public Library Jefferson Market Branch	425 6th Ave	212-243-4334	5	Children's films on Tuesdays.
NYU Cantor Film Center	36 E 8th St	212-998-4100	6	Dirt cheap second-run blockbusters on Monday nights.
The Paley Center for Media	25 W 52nd St	212-621-6600	12	Formerly the Museum of Television & Radio.
Regal Battery Park	102 North End Ave	844-462-7342	BPC	Beautiful downtown multiplex. Getting too crowded.
Regal E-Walk	247 W 42nd St	844-462-7342	12	Across the street from the Empire, but not nearly as nice.
Regal Union Square	850 Broadway	844-462-7342	6	Extremely crowded but fairly comfortable.
Village East Cinema	181 2nd Ave	212-529-6998	6	Half the theaters are gorgeous, half are dank pits.
Walter Reade Theater	165 W 65th St	212-875-5601	14	Amazing festivals and rare screenings.
Whitney Museum of American Art	99 Gansevoort St	212-570-3600	5	Artist retrospectives and lectures.

Brooklyn

	Address	Phone	Map	
BAM Rose Cinemas	30 Lafayette Ave	718-636-4100	31	Great seating and mix of first run + revivals.
Cobble Hill Cinemas	265 Court St	718-596-4995	32	Great indie destination, though theaters are small.
Nitehawk Cinema	136 Metropolitan Ave	646-963-9288	29	Dinner, cocktails and craft beer while you watch indie flicks.
Nitehawk Prospect Park	188 Prospect Park W	646-963-9295	33	Nice mix of stuff right across from Propsect Park.
Rooftop Films	various locations	718-417-7362	n/a	Summer rooftop series—check website for locations!

Queens

	Address	Phone	Map	
Museum of the Moving Image	36-01 35th Ave	718-777-6800	26	Excellent alternative to blockbuster crap.
UA Kaufman Astoria & RPX	35-30 38th St	844-462-7342	26	Standard blockbuster destination.

Arts & Entertainment · **Museums**

Make a resolution: Go to at least one museum in New York City every month. There are over 100 museums in the five boroughs, from the **Metropolitan Museum of Art (Map 15)** to the **Dyckman Farmhouse Museum (Map 25)**, an 18th-century relic in upper Manhattan. Many of these museums have special programs and lectures that are open to the public, as well as children's events and summer festivals. When you've found your favorite museums, look into membership. Benefits include free admission, guest passes, party invites, and a discount at the gift shop.

The famous Museum Mile comprises nine world-class museums along Fifth Avenue between 82nd Street and 105th Street, including the **Met (Map 15)**, and Frank Lloyd Wright's architectural masterpiece, the **Guggenheim (Map 17)**. **El Museo del Barrio (Map 17)**, devoted to early Latin American art, **The Museum of the City of New York (Map 17)**, the **Cooper-Hewitt National Design Museum (Map 17)** (housed in the Andrew Carnegie's Mansion), and the **Jewish Museum (Map 17)** are also along the mile.

See medieval European art at **The Cloisters (Map 25)** (also a famous picnic spot), exhibitions of up and coming African-American artists at the **Studio Museum in Harlem (Map 19)**, and **PS1 (Map 27)** for contemporary art. Take the kids to the **Brooklyn Children's Museum** or the **Children's Museum of Manhattan (Map 14)**. The **Lower East Side Tenement Museum (Map 4)** and the **Ellis Island Immigration Museum (Map 1)** will take you back to your roots, and the treasures of the Orient are on display at the **Asia Society (Map 15)**. Couch potatoes can meet their maker at the **The Paley Center for Media (Map 12)**, which features a massive collection of tens of thousands of television and radio programs and advertisements for your viewing pleasure. The **Brooklyn Museum (Map 33)** supplements its wide-ranging permanent collection with edgy exhibitions, performances, and other special events.

Just about every museum in the city is worth a visit. Other favorites include the **New Museum of Contemporary Art (Map 6)** (in its spiffy building on The Bowery), the **New-York Historical Society (Map 14)** (which focuses its exhibits on the birth of the city), the **New York Transit Museum (Map 30)**, the **Morgan Library (Map 9)** (with copies of Gutenberg's Bible on display), the **Museum of the Moving Image (Map 26)**, **The Museum of Sex (Map 9)**, and the **Queens Museum of Art** (check out the panorama of New York City). The **National September 11 Memorial Museum (Map 1)** aims to tell the definitive story of that day, relating the huge implications thereof, at the very spot it happened. The **Whitney Museum of American Art (Map 5)** showcases contemporary American artists and features the celebrated Biennial in even-numbered years. Finally, the **Museum of Arts and Design (Map 12)**, on the southern edge of Columbus Circle, is a bold redesign of Edward Durrell Stone's quirky masterpiece for Huntington Hartford; the excellent permanent collection and diverting exhibitions, plus working artists-in-residence and a small lovely museum store, make the Museum a must-see.

Manhattan

	Address	Phone	Map
American Academy of Arts & Letters	633 W 155th St	212-368-5900	21
American Folk Art Museum	2 Lincoln Square	212-595-9533	12
American Institute of Graphic Arts	185 Madison Ave	212-922-1206	9
American Irish Historical Society	991 5th Ave	212-288-2263	15
American Museum of Natural History	Central Park W at 79th St	212-769-5100	15
American Numismatic Society	75 Varick St	212-571-4470	2
Anthology Film Archives	32 Second Ave	212-505-5181	6
Arsenal Gallery	E 64th St & 5th Ave	212-360-8163	15
Asia Society & Museum	725 Park Ave	212-288-6400	15
Asian American Arts Centre	111 Norfolk St	212-233-2154	4
Children's Museum of Manhattan	212 W 83rd St	212-721-1223	14
Children's Museum of the Arts	103 Charlton St	212-274-0986	3
China Institute	100 Washington St	212-744-8181	15
The Cloisters	99 Margaret Corbin Dr	212-923-3700	24
Cooper-Hewitt National Design Museum	2 E 91st St	212-849-8400	17
Czech Center	321 E 73rd St	646-422-3399	15
Dyckman Farmhouse Museum	4881 Broadway	212-304-9422	25
El Museo del Barrio	1230 Fifth Ave	212-831-7272	17

Arts & Entertainment • **Museums**

Ellis Island Immigration Museum	Ellis Island, via ferry at Battery Park	832-960-0009	1
Fraunces Tavern Museum	54 Pearl St	212-425-1778	1
Frick Collection	1 E 70th St	212-288-0700	15
Gracie Mansion	East End Ave at 88th St	212-570-4751	17
Grant's Tomb	W 122nd St & Riverside Dr	646-670-7251	18
Grey Art Gallery	100 Washington Sq E	212-998-6780	6
Guggenheim Museum	1071 Fifth Ave	212-423-3500	17
Hayden Planetarium	Central Park West & W 79th St	212-769-5100	14
Hispanic Society Museum	613 W 155th St	212-926-2234	21
International Center of Photography (ICP)	79 Essex St	212-857-0000	12
Intrepid Sea, Air and Space Museum	12th Ave W 46th St	212-245-0072	11
Japan Society	333 E 47th St	212-832-1155	13
The Jewish Museum	1109 5th Ave	212-423-3200	17
Madame Tussauds NY	234 W 42nd St	212-512-9600	12
The Merchant's House Museum	29 E 4th St	212-777-1089	6
Metropolitan Museum of Art	1000 Fifth Ave	212-535-7710	15
Morgan Library	225 Madison Ave	212-685-0008	9
Morris-Jumel Mansion	65 Jumel Ter	212-923-8008	23
Mount Vernon Hotel Museum and Garden	421 E 61st St	212-838-6878	15
Municipal Art Society	488 Madison Ave	212-935-3960	12
Museum at Eldridge Street	12 Eldridge St	212-219-0302	3
Museum at the Fashion Institute of Technology	Seventh Ave & 27th St	212-217-4558	9
Museum of Arts & Design	2 Columbus Circle	212-299-7777	12
Museum of Chinese in America	215 Centre St	212-619-4785	3
Museum of the City of New York	1220 5th Ave	212-534-1672	17
Museum of Comic and Cartoon Art	128 E 63rd St	212-838-2560	15
Museum of Jewish Heritage	36 Battery Pl	646-437-4202	BPC
Museum of Modern Art (MoMA)	11 W 53rd St	212-708-9400	12
Museum of Sex	233 Fifth Ave	212-689-6337	9
National Academy Museum	1083 Fifth Ave	212-369-4880	17
National Museum of the American Indian	1 Bowling Green	212-514-3700	1
National Museum of Mathematics	11 E 26th St	212-542-0566	9
Neue Galerie	1048 Fifth Ave	212-628-6200	17
New Museum	235 Bowery	212-219-1222	6
New York City Fire Museum	278 Spring St	212-691-1303	5
New York Public Library for the Performing Arts	40 Lincoln Center Plaza	917-275-6975	14
New York Transit Museum Gallery Annex & Store	Grand Central Terminal, Main Concourse	212-878-0106	13
New-York Historical Society	170 Central Park W	212-873-3400	14
Nicholas Roerich Museum	319 W 107th St	212-864-7752	16
The Paley Center for Media	25 W 52nd St	212-621-6600	12
Rose Museum	154 W 57th St	973-622-4704	12
Rubin Museum of Art	150 W 17th St	212-620-5000	9
Scandinavia House	58 Park Ave	212-779-3587	10
Skyscraper Museum	39 Battery Pl	212-968-1961	BPC
Society of Illustrators	128 E 63rd St	212-838-2560	15
South Street Seaport Museum	12 Fulton St	212-748-8600	1
Statue of Liberty Museum	Liberty Island, via ferry at Battery Park	212-363-3200	1
Studio Museum in Harlem	144 W 125th St	212-864-4500	19
Tenement Museum	103 Orchard St	877-975-3786	4
Ukrainian Museum	222 E 6th St	212-228-0110	6
Whitney Museum of American Art	99 Gansevoort St	212-570-3600	5
Yeshiva University Museum	15 W 16th St	212-294-8330	9

Brooklyn

	Address	Phone	Map
Brooklyn Children's Museum	145 Brooklyn Ave	718-735-4400	n/a
Brooklyn Historical Society	128 Pierrepont St	718-222-4111	30
Brooklyn Museum	200 Eastern Pkwy	718-638-5000	n/a
City Reliquary	370 Metropolitan Ave	718-782-4842	29
Coney Island Museum	1208 Surf Ave	718-372-5159	n/a
Harbor Defense Museum	230 Sheridan Loop	718-630-4349	n/a
Morbid Anatomy Museum	254 36th St	347-799-1017	29
Museum of Contemporary African Diasporan Arts	80 Hanson Pl	718-230-0492	33
New York Aquarium	Surf Ave & W 8th St	718-265-3474	n/a
New York Transit Museum	99 Schermerhorn St	718-694-1600	30
The Old Stone House	336 3rd St	718-768-3195	33
Toy Museum of NY	157 Montague St	718-243-0820	30
Waterfront Museum	290 Conover St	718-624-4719	32
Weeksville Heritage Center	158 Buffalo Ave	718-756-5250	n/a
Wyckoff Farmhouse Museum	5816 Clarendon Rd	718-629-5400	n/a

Queens

	Address	Phone	Map
Bowne House	37-01 Bowne St	718-359 0528	n/a
Godwin-Ternbach Museum	65-30 Kissena Blvd	718-997-4747	n/a
King Manor Museum	Jamaica Ave & 153rd St	718-206-0545	n/a
Kingsland Homestead	Weeping Beech Park, 143-35 37th Ave	718-939-0647	n/a
Louis Armstrong House Museum	34-56 107th St	718-478-8274	n/a
MoMa PS1	22-25 Jackson Ave	718-784-2084	27
Museum of the Moving Image	36-01 35th Ave	718-777-6800	26
New York Hall of Science	47-01 111th St	718-699-0005	n/a
The Noguchi Museum	9-01 33rd Rd	718-204-7088	27
Queens County Farm Museum	73-50 Little Neck Pkwy	718-347-3276	n/a
Queens Museum of Art	Flushing Meadows-Corona Park	718-592-9700	n/a
Socrates Sculpture Park	32-01 Vernon Blvd	718-956-1819	26
Voelker Orth Museum	149-19 38th Ave	718-359-6227	n/a

The Bronx

	Address	Phone	Map
Bronx County Historical Society	3309 Bainbridge Ave	718-881-8900	n/a
Bronx Museum of the Arts	1040 Grand Concourse	718-681-6000	n/a

Staten Island

	Address	Phone	Map
Alice Austen House	2 Hylan Blvd	718-816-4506	n/a
Staten Island Museum	1000 Richmond Terrace	718-727-1135	n/a

Metropolitan Museum of Art

SECOND FLOOR

Modern Art

The American Wing

European Paintings

Musical Instruments

Nineteenth Century European Paintings and Sculptures

Drawings, Prints, and Photographs

Japanese Art

Cypriot Art

Central Asian Art

Islamic Art

Ancient Near Eastern Art

Asian Art

Korean Art

Chinese Art

Great Hall Balcony

Southeast Asian Art

Modern Art

The American Wing

Robert Lehman Collection

The American Wing

Modern Art

European Sculpture and Decorative Arts

Medieval Art

Arms and Armor

Arts of Africa, Oceania, and the Americas

Thomas J Watson Library

Shop

Grace Rainey Rogers Auditorium

Temple of Dendur The Sackler Wing

Greek and Roman Art

The Great Hall

Egyptian Art

FIRST FLOOR

MAP 15

Costume Institute

Uris Center for Education

GROUND FLOOR

General Information

NFT Map: 15
Address: 1000 Fifth Ave at 82nd St
Phone: 212-535-7710
Website: www.metmuseum.org
@metmuseum
Hours: Sun–Tues: 10 am–5 pm;
Thurs: 10 am–5 pm;
Fri–Sat: 10 am–9 pm
closed Thanksgiving Day,
December 25, January 1,
and first Monday in May.
Admission: $30 for adults, $22 for seniors, $17 for
students, and free for children under
12. Pay what you wish for NY state
residents and tri-state area students.

Overview

The Metropolitan Museum of Art is touted as the largest and most comprehensive museum in the Western hemisphere. Established by a group of American businessmen, artists, and thinkers back in 1870, the museum was created to preserve and stimulate appreciation for some of the greatest works of art in history.

In the first few years of its existence, the museum moved from its original location at 681 Fifth Avenue to the Douglas Mansion at 128 W 14th Street, and then finally to its current Central Park location in 1880.

Calvert Vaux and Jacob Wrey Mould designed the museum's Gothic Revival red-brick facade, which was later remodeled in 1926 into the grand, white-columned front entrance that you see today. Part of the original facade was left intact and can still be seen from the Robert Lehman Wing looking toward the European Sculpture and Decorative Arts galleries.

The Met's annual attendance reaches over 4 million visitors who flock to see the more than 2 million works of art housed in the museum's permanent collection. You could visit the museum many times and not see more than a small portion of the permanent collection. The vast paintings anthology had a modest beginning in 1870 with a small donation of 174 European paintings and has now swelled to include works spanning 5,000 years of world culture, from the prehistoric to the present and from every corner of the globe.

The Met is broken down into a series of smaller museums within each building. For instance, the American Wing contains the most complete accumulation of American paintings, sculpture, and decorative arts, including period rooms offering a look at domestic life throughout the nation's history. The Egyptian collection is the finest in the world outside of Cairo, and the Islamic art exhibition remains unparalleled, as does the mass of 2,500 European paintings and Impressionist

and Post-Impressionist works. The permanent gallery of Islamic art underwent renovations in 2008, following the 10-15 year renovation of the Greek & Roman collection. The redesigned galleries display works that have been in storage for decades, assuring even the most frequent visitor something fresh to check out including the museum's newly restored, world-famous, non-gas-guzzling Etruscan chariot.

Other major collections include the arms and armor, Asian art, costumes, European sculpture and decorative arts, medieval and Renaissance art, musical instruments, drawings, prints, ancient antiquities from around the world, photography, and modern art. Add to this the many special exhibits and performances the Met offers throughout the year, and you have a world-class museum with Central Park as its backyard.

This is a massive museum and seating can be difficult to find during busy weekends. When you need a break from all of the culture, sit down for a snack in the American Wing Café or lunch in the cafeteria. Do a triple-dollar-sign splurge and eat in the Members Dining Room overlooking the park. In the summer climb up to the Roof Garden Café for a glass of wine and the most beautiful view of Central Park that your lack of money can buy.

The Greatest Hits

You can, of course, spend countless hours at the Met. Pick any style of art and chances are you will find a piece here. But if you're rushed for time, check out the sublime space that houses the Temple of Dendur in the Sackler Wing, the elegant Frank Lloyd Wright Room in the American Wing, the fabulous Tiffany Glass and Tiffany Mosaics, also in the American Wing, the choir screen in the Medieval Sculpture Hall, the Caravaggios and Goyas in the Renaissance Rooms, the Picassos and Pollocks in Modern Art, and that huge canoe in Arts of Africa and Oceania. For a moment of tranquility, visit the beautiful Chinese Garden Court in the Asian galleries. When it's open, we highly recommend the Roof Garden, which has killer views of Central Park as a side dish to cocktails and conversation. When it's not, check out seasonal specials like the Christmas "Angel" Tree and Neapolitan Baroque Crèche, an annual favorite set up in front of the medieval choir screen.

How to Get There—Mass Transit

Subway
Take the 4, 5, 6 to the 86th Street stop and walk three blocks west to Fifth Avenue and four blocks south to 82nd Street.

Bus
Take the bus along Fifth Avenue (from uptown locations) to 82nd Street or along Madison Avenue (from downtown locations) to 83rd Street.

Museum of Natural History

FIRST FLOOR

Ross Hall of Meteorites
Hall of Minerals
Columbus Avenue
Weston Pavilion
Human Origins
Kaufmann Theater
Linder Theater
Cafe 77
Northwest Coast Indians
Lefrak Imax Theater
Parking Garage
Special Exhibition Gallery 77
Discovery Room
West 77 Street
Exit
Milstein Hall of Ocean Life
Hall of New York State Environment
Sm Mammals
The Museum Shop
North American Mammals
Rose Gallery
Rose Center for Earth and Space
81St Entrance
North American Forests
Hall of Biodiversity
Theodore Roosevelt Memorial Hall
Gottesman Hall of PLanet Earth
Central Park West

SECOND FLOOR

South American Peoples
Mexico and Central America
People Center
White Natural Science Center
Entrance
Birds of the World
African Peoples
Akeley Gallery
Arthur Ross Terrace
Ro Ce fo Ear an Spa
Stout Hall of Asian Peoples
Akeley Hall of African Mammals
Cosmic Pathway
Big Bang
The Museum Shop
Scales of the Universe
Asian Mammals
Theodore Roosevelt Rotunda
The Butterfly Conservatory
Main Entrance

THIRD FLOOR

Margaret Mead Hall of Pacific Peoples
Plains Indians
Eastern Woodlands Indians
Primates
Chapman Memorial Hall of North American Birds
NYS Mammals
NYC Birds
Akeley Hall of African Mammals
Hayden Planetarium Space Theater
Special Exhibition Gallery 3
Reptiles and Amphibians
Rose Center

FOURTH FLOOR

Research Library
Wallach Orientation Center
Vertebrate Origins
Saurischian Dinosaurs
Milstein Hall of Advanced Mammals
Special Exhibition Gallery 4
Primative Mammals
Ornithischian Dinosaurs
Wallace Wing of Mammals & Their Extinct Relatives

MAP 14

General Information

NFT Map: 14
Address: 200 Central Park West
Phone: 212-769-5100
Website: www.amnh.org
             @AMNH
Hours: 10:00 am–5:30 pm;
             closed Thanksgiving Day
             & December 25.
Admission: $28 for adults, $22 for seniors and
             students, $16 for children. Pay what
             you wish for tri-state area residents.
             Special exhibitions, IMAX movies,
             and the space show are extra;
             packages are available. Free to
             members.

Overview

Admit it. You secretly TiVo the Discovery Channel and the History Channel. You've even watched one—if not several—episodes of Star Trek. Something about African beetles, famous dead guys, and the unknown universe strokes your inner Einstein. Focus your microscope on this one, smarty-pants: the American Museum of Natural History, a paradise for geeks and aspiring geeks alike, not to mention good old nature lovers. And don't worry, your TV-watching secrets are safe with us.

Decades before anyone knew what an atom was, and when relativity was just a twinkle in Einstein's eye, Albert Smith Bickmore established the AMNH. Completed in 1869, the museum held its first exhibition in the Central Park Arsenal a few years later, garnering enough respect to acquire space along classy Central Park West. Architects Calvert Vaux and J. Wrey Mould designed the new, posh building on limited Benjamins and opened it to the public in 1877. Key additions followed: The Hayden Planetarium in 1935, the Theodore Roosevelt Memorial Hall and Rotunda in 1936, and the Rose Center for Earth and Space in 2000.

As Saturday morning museum-going ritual dictates, it's going to be painfully crowded. On those days, you dodge out-of-towners, eyes wide, mouths gaping. It's much the same on weekdays with rowdy school kids on field trips. How to avoid the Excedrin-necessitating atmosphere? Two words: permanent collection. The amazing series of wildlife dioramas even inspired an entire Hollywood movie (albeit not a great one, by adult standards). Don't expect to see any PETA supporters in these halls though.

When you can go at off hours, or if you feel you can brave the crowds, make a point of checking out the fascinating and often provocative special exhibits.

The Greatest Hits

Five floors of star-lovin', mammal-gazin', bird-watchin', fossil-fuelin' science await. Rain forest fever? Check out the Hall of Biodiversity. Didn't understand why that movie was called The Squid and The Whale? See the giant squid get his dimly lit comeuppance in the Milstein Hall of Ocean Life. Celebrity astrophysicist Neil deGrasse Tyson is the voice behind the Dark Universe space show. For more instant thrills, check out the gigantic meteorites at the Arthur Ross Hall of Meteorites, or the five-story-tall dinosaur display in the Theodore Roosevelt Rotunda; it's the largest freestanding beast in the world. The AMNH also produces spectacular IMAX features, a great alternative to the museum's amazing but creepy taxidermy. The Hall of Gems houses the Star of India, the largest star sapphire in the world. Finally, for recreation of The Birds variety with less evil, visit The Butterfly Conservatory. Tropical butterflies flit all around you from, you guessed it, all over the world. It's enough to put TiVo on pause.

How to Get There—Mass Transit

Subway
Take the B or C to the 81st Street stop. Or take the 1 to 79th Street and walk two blocks east.

Bus
The M7, M10 and M11 all stop within a block of the museum. Take the M79 across Central Park if you are coming from the East Side.

General Information

NFT Map: 12
Address: 11 W 53rd St
Phone: 212-708-9400
Website: www.moma.org
@MuseumModernArt
Hours: 10:30 am–5:30 pm (Sat until 7 pm); closed Thanksgiving and December 25
Admission: $30 for adults, $20 for seniors, $15 for students; free to members and children 16 and under accompanied by an adult

Overview

The Museum of Modern Art opened in 1929, back when impressionism and surrealism were truly modern art. Originally in the Heckscher Building at 730 Fifth Avenue, MoMA moved to its current address on West 53rd Street in 1932. What started out as a townhouse eventually expanded into an enormous space, with new buildings and additions in 1939 (by Phillip L. Goodwin and Edward Durell Stone), 1953 (including a sculpture garden by Phillip Johnson), 1964 (another Johnson garden), and 1984 (by Cesar Pelli). During the summer of 2002, the museum closed its Manhattan location and moved temporarily to Sunnyside, Queens (MoMA's affiliate, MoMAPS1 remains a proud Queens institution). After a major expansion and renovation by Yoshio Taniguchi, MoMA reopened in September 2004.

After being re-Manhattanized, MoMA made waves when it became the first museum to break the $20 barrier—which sadly became all too common in the years since. If crowds on a typical Saturday afternoon are any indication, hefty entry fees are not keeping patrons away. Frequent flyers take note: If you plan to visit more than three times in a year, the yearly membership is the way to go. Plus, members get a 10% discount at MoMA stores, free tickets to all film screenings, and besides which, you're free to pop in whenever you want to see your favorite Picasso (or just use the restroom). For the best deal, visit the museum from 4–8 pm on Fridays when there's free admission—the crowds aren't as bad as you might think.

What to See

The fourth and fifth floors are where the big names reside—Johns, Pollock, Warhol (fourth floor), Braque, Cezanne, Dali, Duchamp, Ernst, Hopper, Kandinsky, Klee, Matisse, Miro, Monet, Picasso, Rosseau, Seurat, Van Gogh, and Wyeth (fifth floor). More recent works can be found in the contemporary gallery on the second floor. Special exhibitions are featured on the third and sixth floors. The surrealist collection is outstanding, but we've always suspected that MoMA has only a tiny fraction of its pop art on display. Well, you can't have everything…

Moving downstairs to the third floor, it's clear that the photography collection is, as always, one of the centerpieces of the museum and is highly recommended (although the Gursky pieces are actually dotted throughout the building). The architecture and design gallery showcases a range of cool consumer items, from chairs to cars to the first Mac computers, and is one of the most popular destinations in the museum.

Breakdown of the Space

Floor One: Lobby, Sculpture Garden, Museum Store, Restaurant

Floor Two: Contemporary Galleries, Media Gallery, Prints and Illustrated Books, Café

Floor Three: Architecture and Design, Drawing, Photography, Special Exhibitions

Floor Four: Painting and Sculpture II

Floor Five: Painting and Sculpture I, Café

Floor Six: Special Exhibitions

There are two theater levels below the first floor.

Amenities

Backpacks and large purses are not allowed in gallery spaces, and the free coat check can become messy when the check-in and check-out lines become intertwined. Leave large items (including laptops) at home. Bathrooms and water fountains are on all floors. We don't think that there are enough of them, and the bathrooms themselves are way too small to handle the crowds.

There are three places to get food in the museum, which has been elevated from the usual captive-audience fare by Danny Meyer's excellent Union Square Hospitality Group. Café 2, located on the second floor, offers a wide selection of small plates, sandwiches and panini, as well as above-average coffee drinks, beer and wine. Terrace 5 is a full-service establishment overlooking the beautiful sculpture garden serving a la carte entrees and desserts, along with wine, cocktails, coffee, and tea. Both cafés open half an hour after the museum opens its doors and close half an hour before the museum closes.

The ultimate museum dining experience, The Modern (www.themodernnyc.com) boasts three *New York Times* stars and one Michelin star. It has two main rooms—the Dining Room overlooking the sculpture garden, and a more casual Bar Room. An outdoor terrace is also made available when the weather permits. The Modern serves French and New American food and hubba-hubba tasting menus. The Modern is open beyond museum hours, with the Dining Room serving dinner until 10:30 pm Monday-Saturday. The Bar Room is open continuously 11:30 am–10:30 pm daily (9:30 pm Sundays). There's a separate street entrance to allow diners access to The Modern after the museum closes.

So long as there are adventurous artists putting on plays in abandoned storefronts and opportunistic real estate developers knocking down beautiful old theaters to put up hotels, the New York theater scene will always be adding a few venues here and deleting a few venues there. What remains constant is that on any given night there are at least dozens, and more often hundreds, of live theater performances to be seen. And the best ones are not always the most expensive.

Broadway (i.e., theaters in the Times Square vicinity that hold at least 500 people) still has the reputation of being the place to see American theater at its finest, but the peculiar fact of the matter is that there is more much money to be gained by appealing to the infrequent theater goer than there is by trying to please the connoisseur. As a result, shows that are looked down on, if not despised, by many lovers of the theater wind up selling out for years (*Mamma Mia*, anyone?), while more ambitious, artistically admired plays and musicals struggle to find an audience. Check out theater chat boards like BroadwayWorld.com and TalkinBroadway.com to see what the people who see everything have to say.

Nobody gets famous doing live theater anymore, so if you've never heard of the actor whose name is twinkling in lights chances are that person has the stage experience and acting chops to keep you enthralled for two and a half hours, unlike the big name celebrities who make their acting debuts in starring roles they're only sometimes somewhat prepared for. Of course, there are also the big-time actors with extensive stage credits who come back to Broadway regularly after becoming famous; you've got to admire anyone who willingly dives back into the grind of eight performances a week.

Many great performers work Off-Broadway (Manhattan theaters seating 100–499 people) where the writing and directing are actually more important than spectacle and scores made up of classic pop songs. Off-Off Broadway (fewer than 100 seats) is a terrific grab bag of both beginners and seasoned pros doing material that is often unlikely to draw in masses. And tickets are pretty cheap, too.

TheaterMania.com keeps an extensive list of just about every show in New York, with direct links to the websites that sell tickets. Many shows offer a limited number of inexpensive standing room and/or same-day rush tickets. A detailed directory of such offers can be found at TalkinBroadway.com.

Thousands of same-day tickets for Broadway and Off-Broadway shows are sold for 20%–50% off at the TKTS booths in Times Square (long lines), at the South Street Seaport (shorter lines), and Downtown Brooklyn (which sells tickets to matinee performances a day in advance). They take cash, traveler's checks, and credit cards. Check for hours and to see what's been recently available at www.tdf.org. Don't expect to get a bargain for the top-selling hits, but most shows use this booth at some time or another. You can also download discount coupons at Playbill.com that you can use to get seats in advance.

The dirty little secret of New York theatre is that free tickets for high-quality shows are abundantly available through organizations that specialize in "dressing the house" for productions that depend more on word of mouth than expensive advertising costs. By paying a yearly membership fee to TheaterExtras.com or Play-By-Play.com, you can check your computer 24-hours a day to find free tickets (there's a small per-ticket service charge) for a dozen or so Off-, Off-Off-, and sometimes Broadway shows available at the last minute. That dinky little play in some church basement that you went to on a whim might wind up being the next great American classic.

Keep an eye out for shows by these lesser-known companies:

The award-winning Classical Theatre of Harlem (www.cthnyc.org) has earned a reputation for mounting exciting, edgy revivals of classics from Shakespeare and Brecht, as well as solid productions

from more recent greats such as August Wilson and Melvin Van Peebles. A multicultural company that frequently casts against racial type, they draw a youthful audience with imaginative interpretations.

The Mint Theatre Company (Map 11) (www.minttheater.org) specializes in reviving Broadway plays from the past they call "worthy, but neglected." In their tiny space you'll see interesting comedies and dramas from the likes of A. A. Milne, Edith Wharton, and Thomas Wolfe played traditionally with sets and costumes that really make you feel like you're watching a production from over 50 years ago.

Musicals Tonight! does the same kind of thing with forgotten musicals, only presenting them in low budgeted, but highly energized, staged readings. Nowadays most musicals revived on Broadway are revised and updated to the point where they lose their authenticity. But if you're in the mood to see what an Irving Berlin ragtime show from 1915 was really like, or if you want to see a Cole Porter tuner from the '30s with all of the dated topical references that confused audiences even back then, Musicals Tonight! serves up the past as it really was written. And check for their special concerts where Broadway understudies sing songs from the roles they are currently covering. Shows take place at the Lion Theatre (Map 11).

Broadway insiders know that Monday nights, when most shows are dark, is often the hottest night of the week for entertainment. That's when performers use their night off to partake in benefits and special events. Consistently among the best are shows from Scott Siegel's Broadway By The Year series at Town Hall (Map 12) (www.the townhall.org). Each one-night concert is packed with theater and cabaret stars singing hits and obscurities introduced on Broadway in one selected year. Siegel also produces Broadway Unplugged at Town Hall, a concert of theater performers singing showtunes without amplification. The atmosphere is like a sports event, with the audience wildly cheering each naturally voiced solo.

Horse Trade (www.horsetrade.info) produces a crazy assortment of readings, workshops, burlesque performances, and full-out productions in the East Village at venues like The Kraine Theater (Map 6). The multi-arts center HERE (Map 5) (www.here.org) not only houses two small theaters, but it also has an amazing gallery space and a cozy cafe/bar—perfect for pre – or post-show drinks. Located in a former school on First Avenue and 9th Street in the East Village, P.S. 122 (Map 7) (www.performancespacenewyork.org) is a not-for-profit arts center serving New York City's dance and performance community. Shows rotate through on a regular basis, so check the website for the latest schedule. The outdoor Delacorte Theater (Map 15) in Central Park hosts performances only during the summer months. Tickets to the ridiculously popular and free Shakespeare in the Park performances are given away at 1 pm at the Delacorte and also at the Public Theater (Map 6) on the day of each performance. Hopefully, you enjoy camping because people line up for days in their tents and sleeping bags just to secure a ticket!

Just on the other side of the Manhattan Bridge in Brooklyn is the world famous Brooklyn Academy of Music (Map 31). A thriving urban arts center, BAM brings domestic and international performing arts and film to Brooklyn. The center is home to multiple venues of various sizes, including the Harvey Lichtenstein Theater (Map 31), Howard Gilman Opera House (Map 31), the Bam Rose Cinemas (Map 31), and the BAMcafe (Map 31), a restaurant and live music venue. Our favorite season is the Next Wave, an annual three-month celebration of cutting-edge dance, theater, music, and opera. As an alternative to BAM, St. Ann's Warehouse (Map 30) in DUMBO also produces exciting cutting-edge work.

Street Index

Street Index

Street Index

Address Locator

Streets	Riverside	West End	Broadway	Amsterdam	Columbus	C.P.W.	Central Park
110-116	370-440		2800-2950	995-1120			
102-110	290-370	850-920	2675-2800	856-995	850-1021	419-500	
96-102	240-290	737-850	2554-2675	733-856	740-850	360-419	
90-96	180-240	620-737	2440-2554	620-733	621-740	300-360	
84-90	120-180	500-619	2321-2439	500-619	501-620	241-295	
78-84	60-120	380-499	2201-2320	380-499	381-500	239-241	
72-78	1-60	262-379	2081-2200	261-379	261-380	121-239	
66-72		122-261	1961-2079	140-260	141-260	65-115	
58-66		2-121	1791-1960	1-139	2-140	0-65	

Streets	12th Ave.	11th Ave.	Broadway	10th Ave.	9th Ave.	8th Ave.	7th Ave.	6th Ave.
52-58	710-850	741-854	1674-1791	772-889	782-907	870-992	798-921	1301-1419
46-52	600-710	625-740	1551-1673	654-770	662-781	735-869	701-797	1180-1297
40-46	480-600	503-624	1440-1550	538-653	432-662	620-734	560-701	1061-1178
34-40	360-480	405-502	Macy's-1439	430-537	431-432	480-619	442-559	1060-1061
28-34	240-360	282-404	1178-1282	314-429	314-431	362-479	322-442	815-1060
22-28	0-240	162-281	940-1177	210-313	198-313	236-361	210-321	696-814
14-22		26-161	842-940	58-209	44-197	80-235	64-209	5520-695
8-14			748-842	0-58	0-44	0-80	2-64	420-520
Houston-8			610-748					244-402

The address locator below is formatted north-south, from 116th Street to Houston Street. For east-west addresses, simply remember that Fifth Ave. is the dividing line-2 E 54th would be right off of Fifth, while 200 E 54th would be around Third Ave.

5th Ave.	Madison	Park	Lexington	3rd Ave.	2nd Ave.	1st Ave.	York	Streets
1280-1400	1630-1770	1489-1617	1766-1857	1981-2103	2109-2241	2175-2238		110-116
1209-1280	1500-1630	1350-1489	1612-1766	1820-1981	1880-2109	1975-2175		102-110
1148-1209	1379-1500	1236-1350	1486-1612	1709-1820	1854-1880	1855-1975		96-102
1090-1148	1254-1379	1120-1236	1361-1486	1601-1709	1736-1854	1740-1855	1700-end	90-96
1030-1089	1130-1250	1000-1114	1248-1355	1490-1602	1624-1739	1618-1735	1560-1700	84-90
970-1028	1012-1128	878-993	1120-1248	1374-1489	1498-1623	1495-1617	1477-1560	78-84
910-969	896-1006	760-877	1004-1116	1250-1373	1389-1497	1344-1494	1353-1477	72-78
850-907	772-872	640-755	900-993	1130-1249	1260-1363	1222-1343	1212-1353	66-72
755-849	621-771	476-639	722-886	972-1129	1101-1260	1063-1222	1100-1212	58-66

5th Ave.	Madison	Park	Lexington	3rd Ave.	2nd Ave.	1st Ave.	Avenue A	Streets
656-754	500-611	360-475	596-721	856-968	984-1101	945-1063		52-58
562-655	377-488	240-350	476-593	741-855	862-983	827-944		46-52
460-561	284-375	99-240	354-475	622-735	746-860	701-827		40-46
352-459	188-283	5-99	240-353	508-621	622-747	599-701		34-40
250-351	79-184	4-404	120-239	394-507	500-621	478-598		28-34
172-249	1-78	286-403	9-119	282-393	382-499	390-478		22-28
69-170	University	0-285	1-8	126-281	230-381	240-389		14-22
9-69	0-120			59-126	138-230	134-240	129-210	8-14
0-9				1-59	0-138	0-134	0-129	Houston - 8

NOT FOR TOURISTS
PUNCH LIST
NEW YORK CITY

EVENTS

☐ **Brooklyn Book Festival** .... Two of Brooklyn's favorite things: Books and Brooklyn (**mid-September**). .... Downtown Brooklyn .... Brooklyn

☐ **Shakespeare in the Park** .... Free out-sized outside summertime plays with boldface names. .... Delacorte Theater, Central Park .... Manhattan

☐ **Mermaid Parade** .... Slap on your fins and celebrate summer (**late June**). .... Coney Island .... Brooklyn

☐ **NYC Marathon** .... 26 miles of NYC air (**first Sunday of November**). .... Citywide ....Citywide

☐ **Open House New York** .... Insider access to architecture and design landmarks (**early October**). .... Various ....Citywide

SHINY & NEW

☐ **The Whitney** .... Always has something to talk about, now part of the High Line-Industrial Complex. .... 99 Gansevoort St .... Manhattan

☐ **One World Trade Center** .... At 1,776 feet, the tallest building in the Western Hemisphere. ...... Vesey St .... Manhattan

☐ **Ridgewood** .... Queens charm and affordability meets Bushwick. .... Ridgewood ....Queens

☐ **REI (Puck Building)** .... Outdoor gear superstore in the Puck Building. .... 295 Lafayette St .... Manhattan

☐ **Food Halls (list)** .... Food courts go gourmet in the city. Try Gotham West, Hudson Eats, Berg'n, or Eataly. .... Various .... Manhattan/Brooklyn

☐ **Four Freedoms Park** .... Posthumously built Louis Kahn design; FDR memorial and stunning views. .... Roosevelt Island .... Manhattan

☐ **Lincoln Center** .... High culture superblock retrofitted for a human dimension. .... 66th St and Broadway ..... Manhattan

ENDANGERED SPECIES

☐ **Katz's** .... Classic New York pastrami; .... 205 E Houston St .... Manhattan
I'll have what she's having!

☐ **Barbes** .... Smart-looking space with .... 376 9th St .... Brooklyn
eclectic entertainment.

☐ **Sunny's** .... No longer pay-what-you-wish .... 253 Conover St .... Brooklyn
but still cheap and good.

☐ **Crown Heights** .... Officially hot, just this .... Crown Heights .... Brooklyn
side of unafforrdable.

☐ **Di Fara** .... Meticulously crafted .... 1424 Ave J .... Brooklyn
by hand since 1965.

☐ **Anthology Film** .... Jonas Mekas' dream come .... 32 2nd Ave .... Brooklyn
Archives to life–a monument to the
avant-garde in film.

☐ **Economy Candy** .... Floor-to-ceiling candy madness .... 108 Rivington St .... Manhattan

REST IN PEACE

☐ **Pearl Paint** .... Mecca for artists, designers, and ...... 308 Canal St .... Manhattan
people who just like art supplies.

☐ **Pearl River Mart** ...... Chinese housewares and more .... 477 Broadway .... Manhattan
Almost mind-numbing.

☐ **Mars Bar** .... The king of grungy bars sacrificed ... 25 E 1st St .... Manhattan
to the real estate gods.

☐ **wd~50** .... Michelin-starred gastronomical .... 50 Clinton St .... Manhattan
wonderworld sacrificed to the
real estate gods.

☐ **Winnie's** .... The best Chinese gangster .... 104 Bayard St .... Manhattan
karaoke dive in Lower Manhattan.

☐ **Stage Deli** .... Artery-clogging and ridiculously .... 834 Seventh Ave .... Manhattan
expensive but so, so missed.

☐ **Cafe Edison** .... Theater district mainstay for .... 228 W 47th St .... Manhattan
Jewish soul food sacrificed
to the gods of schmancy.

☐ **Williamsburg** .... Real Estate section ink-generating ... Williamsburg .... Brooklyn
hipsturbia. With a Duane Reade.

PUNCH LIST
Continued

CLASSICS

☐ **Cloisters** .... The Met's storehouse of.................. Fort Tryon Park............... Manhattan
medieval art. Great herb
garden, nice views.

☐ **Brooklyn Bridge**........ The granddaddy of them all. .... Lower Manhattan-........... Manhattan
Walking toward Manhattan   Downtown Brooklyn   Brooklyn
at sunset is as good as it gets.

☐ **Recycle-A-Bicycle** .... Non-profit youth organization .... 858 Fulton St .... Brooklyn
refurbishing and selling used bikes.

☐ **West Village** .... Quaint beauty, great restaurants, ... West Village.................... Manhattan
and top-notch/dollar shopping
with faint traces of bohemian past.

☐ **B & H Photo**.............. Where everyone in North .... 420 Ninth Ave .... Manhattan
America buys their cameras
and film. Closed Saturdays.

☐ **Film Forum** .... Best place to pick up a film geek...... 209 W Houston St........... Manhattan

☐ **Coney Island** .... Classic New York summer: .... Coney Island..................... Brooklyn
hot dog, coaster, sideshow, beach.

☐ **Dublin House**............ Great dingy UWS Irish pub. .... 225 W 79th St.................. Manhattan

☐ **Di Palo Fine Foods**.... Delicacies from across Italy. .... 200 Grand St .... Manhattan
Excellent cheese.

☐ **Printed Matter** .... Astounding selection.................... 231 11th Ave .... Manhattan
of artist's books.

☐ **Village Vanguard** ...... Classic NYC jazz venue. .... 178 Seventh Ave So. .... Manhattan
Not to be missed.

HIDDEN GEMS

☐ **Alice Austen**............. Dedicated to the documentary.......... 2 Hylan Blvd .... Staten Island
House   photography and life of Alice Austen.

☐ **Wave Hill**................... The view of the Palisades is .... Independence Ave........... The Bronx
unbeatable.   and W 249th St

☐ **Green-Wood** .... Lots of winding paths and greenery . 500 25th St...................... Brooklyn
Cemetery   good for contemplation.

☐ **Weeksville Center**..... Preserving the history of one of....... 158 Buffalo Ave .... Brooklyn
America's first free black communities.

☐ **Historic** .... Restored buildings from days of .... 441 Clarke Ave .... Staten Island
Richmond Town   yore, most populated by costumed guides.

USED TO BE COOL

- [ ] **Lower East Side** .... Soon the world will be one big .... Lower East Side .... Manhattan
12-story luxury building.

- [ ] **The High Line** .... A revelatory re-purposing; and .... West Village .... Manhattan
then everyone and everything
showed up.

- [ ] **Anything With** .... Do you even realize how many .... Citywide
Cupcakes goddamn calories are in
buttercream frosting?

GASTRONOMIC UNDERGROUND

- [ ] **Do or Dive** .... Definitely Do it. Bizarro small .... 1108 Bedford Ave .... Brooklyn
plates and back garden. Killer.

- [ ] **Jungsik** .... White tablecloth multi-star Korean ... 2 Harrison St .... Manhattan
in former Chanterelle space.

- [ ] **St. Anselm** .... We have no reservations about .... 355 Metropolitan Ave .... Brooklyn
this sizzling steak spot.

- [ ] **M. Wells** .... More boffo dishes from strange .... 43-15 Crescent St .... Queens
Steakhouse animal parts at this hipster
meat palace.

- [ ] **Traif** .... Bacon-wrapped scallops at a .... 229 S 4th St .... Brooklyn
Saturday reception?
Go with your heart.

NEVER BEEN COOL

- [ ] **Javits Center** .... Glass-sheathed behemoth hosting ... 655 W 34th St .... Manhattan
various and sundry cons.

- [ ] **Macy's** .... There's a reason children on .... 151 W 34th St .... Manhattan
Santa's lap start to cry.

- [ ] **Port Authority** .... One day we'll rediscover the .... 625 Eighth Ave .... Manhattan
golden age of bus travel. Until then...

- [ ] **Penn Station** .... Makes commuters scream .... Eighth Ave .... Manhattan
and preservationists cry. and W 32nd St

- [ ] **Times Square** .... Can't there be a middle ground .... Times Square .... Manhattan
between peep shows and
"retail experiences"?

- [ ] **Upper East Side** .... A place everyone's waiting to .... Upper East Side .... Manhattan
move out of. Alive or dead.